SOCIAL PSYCHOLOGY

ROBERT A. BARON
DONN BYRNE

Purdue University

ALLYN AND BACON, INC.
Boston • London • Sydney • Toronto

SOCIAL PSYCHOLOGY

Understanding Human Interaction

SECOND EDITION

Library of Congress Cataloging in Publication Data

Baron, Robert A.
  Social psychology.

  Includes bibliographies and index.
  1. Social psychology. I. Byrne, Donn Erwin, joint author.
HM251.B437 1977   301.1   76-44284
ISBN 0-205-05681-4
Second printing...August 1977

Chapter opening photo credits: page 196 photo by Phil Carver &
Friends; page 302 photo by Anna Kaufman Moon / Stock, Boston;
page 402 photo by Pamela Schuyler / Stock, Boston; page 452 photo by
Rick Smolan / Stock, Boston; page 554 photo by Weston Kemp; page
604 photo by the Port Authority of New York and New Jersey.

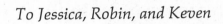

To Jessica, Robin, and Keven

CONTENTS

PREFACE
to the Second Edition

Revising one's work is always a painful process; each slash of the red pencil, after all, consigns hours of hard work to final oblivion. And the larger the revisions made, the more painful the experience. In this sense, at least, constructing this edition of *Social Psychology: Understanding Human Interaction* has been an extraordinarily painful process. Our revisions have been both extensive and general, with the result that much of the effort invested in the first edition has, of necessity, gone by the boards. Indeed, by actual count, more than 80 percent of the writing and associated materials contained in the present volume are new and did not appear in the preceding book.

Since few individuals (not even authors!) wish to suffer unnecessarily, we did not undertake these major alterations lightly. Rather, they grew out of what we interpreted to be compelling grounds for such changes. Basically, our reasons for making these alterations fell into two major categories. First, the need for such revisions was suggested by the extremely rapid pace of change within social psychology. In the few short years since we began work on the first edition, large shifts in interest and emphasis have occurred within the field. Many topics that were just beginning to receive research attention in the early 1970s (for instance, actor-observer differences in attribution, objective self-awareness, group polarization effects, intrinsic motivation, sexism, and learned helplessness) have blossomed into extensive areas of investigation. And others, which were the focus of considerable attention in 1971 and 1972 (such as certain aspects of attitude formation and change), have experienced a reduction in scope and no longer command the central position they once occupied. These and many other shifts within the field

—a number of which are described in Chapter 1—seemed to us to dictate relatively extensive changes in both form and content of our text.

Second and perhaps of even greater importance has been the continued feedback from students and colleagues alike concerning the first edition. This input has taken many forms, including informal comments at parties, letters from interested colleagues, student evaluations and ratings, and formal, extensive reviews. Together, such suggestions and reactions have called our attention to many places in the volume that could be improved and convinced us of the importance of implementing such changes. While the alterations we made in response to such helpful criticism are far too numerous to mention here, several of the most important should be noted.

First, as mentioned above, we have undertaken many substantial changes in content. All chapters contained in the first edition have been thoroughly revised to take account of new trends and developments in the field, and an entirely new chapter on prejudice and discrimination (Chapter 4) has been added. In instituting these changes, we have attempted to reflect the present concerns and findings of social psychology as accurately as possible, and to include materials that would be both comprehensible and appealing to undergraduate readers.

Second, we attempted to eliminate points of confusion called to our attention by students, colleagues, and reviewers. In many cases, these centered around excessively detailed descriptions of the procedures of specific studies. Therefore, we reduced this type of coverage somewhat wherever this seemed appropriate. In other cases, confusion seemed to stem from the discussion of seemingly contradictory research findings. Since such conflicts form a normal part of the scientific process and often seem to spur rapid progress in our knowledge, it would be quite inappropriate to eliminate them from the text. Indeed, such a procedure would smack of sweeping important issues under the rug. What we have done instead is to offer possible resolutions to such disagreements wherever possible.

Third, we have rearranged the chapters so that coverage now moves, in general, from processes centering primarily within one individual (social perception, attitude formation, and change, and the like) through various forms of social interaction (social influence, prosocial behavior, aggression), and finally to more complex group processes. Our decision to re-order the flow of the text in this manner stemmed largely from many colleagues' suggestion that such an arrangement would represent a more logical order than that in the first edition.

Fourth, in an attempt to better convey our own excitement and involvement with social psychology to student readers, we have included three types of special, boxed inserts. The first, labeled *Focus on Research*, describes the methods employed in various lines of research or the findings of studies we feel are of particular interest or importance. The second, *Social Psychology in Action*, outlines simple and safe demonstrations students can perform to gain first-hand experience with the findings and principles described in accompanying portions of the text. Finally, *Capsule Controversy* summarizes recent controversies within social psychology, spotlighting issues about which social psychologists are not yet entirely in agreement. We selected materials for these inserts with special care in the hope that, together, they will help us bridge any vestiges of the communication gap that often intrudes between text authors and their intended audience.

Finally, we have included a number of reader-oriented aids not contained in the first edition. Among these are a glossary for each chapter which simply and briefly defines key terms and phrases, an outline at the opening of each chapter which describes its contents, and an annotated list of suggested readings suitable for examination by undergraduates wishing to go beyond the text in specific areas. Together, these features should make the volume easier to use than was the first edition.

Because these changes have been suggested in large measure by many colleagues, reviewers, and students, we feel they have helped us to improve our text considerably. Of course, once again, only continued feedback will tell us whether we have moved in the right directions. For this reason, we openly invite any and all input which you—our readers and colleagues—may be kind enough to provide.

In preparing this revision, we have been assisted by many individuals who gave generously of their time. Although it would be impossible to name all of them here, we wish to express our special thanks to the following persons for their helpful comments on various parts of the manuscript:

Bill Austin	Robert Hogan	Paul Paulus
Robert S. Baron	Martin Kaplan	Ollie Pocs
Bernice Baxter	Melvin J. Lerner	Harry Reis
Ellen Berscheid	Jerry Leventhal	Zick Rubin
Len Bickman	George Levinger	Barry Schlenker
Tom Cafferty	James Leslie McCary	Carole Smith
Gerald Clore	Stanley Milgram	Mark Snyder
Chris Cozby	Thomas Morarity	Joy Stapp
James H. Geer	William N. Morris	Elaine Walster
Charles L. Gruder	Dave Myers	Bob Wicklund
Dave Hamilton	Ed O'Neal	Mark Zanna

In addition, we wish to express our appreciation to our editor, Frank Ruggirello, and to the staff at Allyn and Bacon (especially Karen Mason, Nancy McJennett, Nancy Murphy, and Jane Richardson) for their outstanding assistance in helping us convert our manuscript into a finished product. And, finally, we thank our wives, Sandra and Lois, for their encouragement and assistance during many different phases of the project. Without their help, understanding, and forebearance, it is unlikely that we could have come even close to meeting the harried schedule we found it necessary to follow.

Robert A. Baron
Donn Byrne

UNDERSTANDING
SOCIAL BEHAVIOR

SOCIAL PSYCHOLOGY: A WORKING DEFINITION
Social Psychology: Science or Art?

SOCIAL PSYCHOLOGY: A CAPSULE MEMOIR
The Roots of Social Psychology in Philosophy and Natural Science
Social Psychology Emerges: The Early Years
Decades of Growth: The 1940's, '50's, and '60's
The 1970's and Beyond: Social Psychology at the Crossroads

**IN QUEST OF UNDERSTANDING: THE NATURE OF SOCIAL
PSYCHOLOGICAL RESEARCH**
The Role of Theory in Social Psychology
The Two Methods of Social Psychological Research
Ethical Issues in Social Research: The Use of Deception
Demand Characteristics: Or, How to Get Positive Results without Really
Trying

USING THIS BOOK: A FUGITIVE PREFACE

1

What makes people fall in—and out—of love?

Why do some persons become leaders while others remain followers?

Is flattery an effective technique for inducing others to do our bidding— or does it often "backfire" and produce more resentment than compliance?

What are the roots of human violence, and how can it be controlled?

Is "playing hard to get" really an effective technique for increasing our appeal to members of the opposite sex?

Can individuals communicate effectively through "body language"?

How do people react when they feel that they have been cheated or shortchanged in their dealings with others?

What are the best means of persuading other persons to accept views similar to our own?

When do individuals offer aid to others, and how do the recipients of such help react to it?

What are the origins of prejudice? How can it be eliminated?

Have you ever wondered about questions such as these? We believe that in all probability you have. Other persons and our relations with them are simply too important a part of our lives for it to be otherwise. In pondering such issues, you have been in very good company. Over the centuries, thoughtful individuals in many different fields (poets, philosophers, novelists) have sought to understand the nature of our interactions with others. Largely as a result of their collective efforts, we now possess a vast body of informal knowledge concerning the nature of social behavior. In many cases, such information appears to be quite accurate and insightful. For example, such statements as "Misery loves company," "Like father, like son; like mother, like daughter," and "Revenge is sweet" do seem to contain a substantial core of truth and remain compelling even today.

In many other instances, though, the information provided by such "wisdom of the ages" is misleading, confusing, or simply wrong. For example, folklore tells us that bonds of affection between individuals are often strengthened by prolonged separation ("Absence makes the heart grow fonder"), while at the same time informing us that they are actually *weakened* by such conditions ("Out of sight, out of mind"). Can it be both ways? Perhaps, but there is no hint in such statements as to how this could be so. In a similar manner, we are instructed that "Birds of a feather flock together" (similarity leads to mutual attraction), while simultaneously being told that "Opposites attract" (*differences* form a basis for mutual liking). We could go on and on, but by now the main point should be obvious: given the existence of such contradictions and inconsistencies, it seems unwise to accept "common sense" or folklore as trustworthy guides to the nature of social behavior.

Unfortunately, our dismissal of common knowledge, no matter how well justified, leaves us in something of a lurch: if such traditional sources of information about social behavior are so often misleading, how can we ever hope to comprehend fully the nature of this complex process? One answer to this puzzle—and a very convincing one, we believe—has been provided in recent years by the rapidly growing field of social psychology. Basically, the solution proposed by social psychologists is as follows: why not apply the methods of science, which have proven so effective in the investigation of many other topics, to the study of social behavior? More concretely, social psychologists have proposed that definitive knowledge concerning human interaction *can* be obtained if we are willing to substitute careful observation and systematic experimentation for the casual inspection and unfounded (though often elegant) speculation which has generally been the rule in the past.

As you can probably guess, this science-oriented approach to the study of human social affairs is relatively new. In fact, as we shall soon see, it is almost wholly a creature of the twentieth century—and primarily the mid-twentieth century at that. Yet despite this fact, social psychologists have already gathered a surprisingly large amount of interesting information about various aspects of social interaction. As a result of their efforts, we will be able to offer at least partial answers to all of the questions raised above, and many, many others, in the pages that follow.

Before plunging directly into social psychology's fascinating but often complex findings, however, it is important to provide you with certain background information about its nature and methods. Thus, we will employ the remainder of this initial chapter for completing three preliminary tasks. First, we will offer a formal definition of social psychology. Second, we will present a brief (and we do mean *brief*) description of its history and development. And third, we will examine the basic methods employed by social psychologists, as well as some of the special problems they encounter, in their systematic investigations of the nature of social behavior.

SOCIAL PSYCHOLOGY: A WORKING DEFINITION

Defining any field that is in the process of rapid growth and development is something of a tricky business. The emergence of new lines of investigation or new theoretical frameworks may quickly render definitions that are suitable today quite obsolete tomorrow. In the case of social psychology, these problems are compounded still further by the great diversity of the field. At first glance, it seems almost impossible to offer a single definition for a discipline in which some researchers are busily investigating the causes of riots, others are examining the basis of first impressions, and still others are studying the effects of erotic stimuli upon various aspects of sexual behavior. Fortunately, though, despite all this diversity, there does seem to be a common thread binding the field together. In general, it appears that social psychologists focus most of their attention upon the manner in which individuals are affected by the persons around them. More formally, then, we will define social psychology as *the scientific field that seeks to investigate the manner in which the behavior, feelings, or thoughts of one individual are influenced or determined by the behavior and/or characteristics of others.* Perhaps some concrete examples will help clarify the meaning of this definition.

That our behavior, feelings, and thoughts are often strongly influenced by the actions of others is readily apparent. For example, imagine your reaction if, while walking down a dark and deserted street, a surly voice called out from the shadows, "Stick 'em up!" There is little doubt that, in this case, strong effects upon your behavior, emotions, and thoughts would be produced. Similarly, consider the reactions you might experience if a member of the opposite sex, to whom you were strongly attracted, looked deep into your eyes and murmured the words, "Darling, I love you." It is not necessary to turn to such dramatic examples to illustrate the impact of other persons' actions upon us, however. Simply recall the last time you agreed to a request from one of your friends or acquaintances, the last time you were influenced to buy a particular product by a commercial you saw on television, a recent occasion on which you were cut off in traffic by another driver, or instances in which you and a date tried to reach a decision about which movie to see or which restaurant to visit. The list could easily continue, but as you can probably see by now, our behavior, feelings, and thoughts are frequently influenced or changed by the actions of the persons around us each day. In view of this fact, it seems quite reasonable to view the investigation of such effects as one of the central tasks of social psychology.

That we are often strongly affected by the characteristics of others as well as by their overt behavior is also quite apparent. For example, consider how your reactions to members of your own sex differ from those toward members of the opposite sex. And recall how differently you often react to highly attractive individuals than to less attractive ones. Similarly, consider the different ways in which you would approach and interact with two of your college instructors, one in her middle twenties and the other in her late sixties. Even these few examples should suffice to call your attention to the fact that our feelings, behavior, and thoughts are often strongly affected by such characteristics of others as their sex, age, physical beauty, and skin color. Indeed our reactions to other persons may be strongly influenced even by such seemingly unimportant characteristics as their style of dress, the sound or tone of their voice, and the ethnic identification of their last names (see Figure 1-1). Given this fact, the investigation of such effects also seems to belong firmly within the scope of social psychology.

In sum, we will define social psychology, throughout the remainder of this text, as the scientific study of the social determinants of behavior. Often, these determinants involve the actions of other persons—what they say or do. Sometimes they involve their real or imagined presence. And, frequently, they

"None of them is it, but I don't like the looks of the one on this end."

FIGURE 1-1. *As shown in this cartoon, we are often strongly affected by the appearance of other persons, as well as by their overt actions.* (*Source:* Drawing by Whitney Darrow, Jr.; © 1975 The New Yorker Magazine, Inc.)

involve the visible characteristics of these individuals—their age, sex, race, appearance, and so on. Regardless of the precise factors involved, however, it is obvious that the persons around us frequently exert profound effects on our feelings, behavior, and thoughts. Indeed, so strong and general do such effects appear to be that, in an important sense, understanding the nature of social interaction may often serve as one important key to understanding the nature of *all* human behavior.

Social Psychology: Science or Art?

Before we proceed to the next of our three preliminary tasks—presenting a brief description of the origins and development of social psychology—we should pause to comment briefly on our suggestion that it be viewed as a scientific field of study. Our past teaching experience suggests that some of you, at least, will take strong exception to this view, objecting that social psychology cannot be a science in the same sense as chemistry, physics, or biology. If you hold such reservations, we must admit that you are not alone. Over the years, many critics outside social psychology, and more recently even some within it (Gergen, 1973), have voiced similar doubts. Although many reasons have been offered in support of the view that social psychology cannot be a "true" science, it is our distinct impression that most, if not all, stem from a basic but widespread misunderstanding regarding the meaning of the term *science* itself (see also Schlenker, 1974).

For some reason, many persons seem to assume that this term refers only to specific fields of study, such as chemistry, physics, or geology, and that only such areas can appropriately be described as scientific in nature. Actually, though, it refers to a general set of methods which are largely independent of any specific topic of study, and can be applied to answering questions of many different types. As we shall soon see in more detail, these general methods largely involve systematic observation and direct experimentation. And philosophers generally agree that to the extent they are employed in any field of study, it may be viewed as scientific in nature (Bergmann, 1966). In short, what is crucial are the approaches taken and the general methods employed, *not* the particular topics under investigation.

Because the fields mentioned above (chemistry, physics, and so on) have existed for several centuries and made great strides, we are most familiar with the use of the scientific method in them. In fact, the image of an astronomer peering through a telescope or a biologist bending over his or her microscope forms part of our basic cultural heritage. But the scientific method can also be employed to study many other topics as well, including fascinating aspects of social behavior.

Of course, when the scientific method is adapted to the study of social interaction, the actual procedures followed and the specific equipment or apparatus employed may differ greatly from that used in other fields. You should not find this either surprising or confusing: scientists always adapt their methods and apparatus to the problem at hand. For example, we would not expect to find an astronomer seeking to study distant galaxies with an electron microscope or a biologist seeking to study cellular growth with a huge reflecting telescope—the very idea of such events is absurd. By the same token, it would be unreasonable to expect social psychologists to use lasers as a means of studying attitudes, test tubes in their investigations of first impressions, or slide rules in their studies of interpersonal attraction. Yet, the fact that they employ different procedures, measuring devices, and apparatus for these tasks does not make their work any less scientific. What *is* crucial is the basic approach taken.

So long as methods based on systematic observation and direct experimentation are strictly followed, the term science, we feel, is quite appropriate.

To make a long story short, we believe that social psychology can reasonably be viewed as scientific in nature because in their work, social psychologists are committed to and rely very heavily upon the scientific method. The topics they seek to study may differ from those in older and more traditional fields of study, but the general methods followed are basically the same.

SOCIAL PSYCHOLOGY: A CAPSULE MEMOIR

As we have already noted, speculation concerning human social behavior is as old as recorded history, and probably preceded even the development of written language. In view of this fact, any attempt on our part to present a complete or comprehensive treatment of the historical roots of social psychology would quickly bog down in discussions of philosophy or literature, and would probably soon exhaust both your interest and patience. The discussion which follows, therefore, touches only briefly on the intellectual roots of social psychology within philosophy and natural science, and concentrates instead upon its emergence and growth during the twentieth century.

The Roots of Social Psychology in Philosophy and Natural Science

Philosophers have long expressed a keen interest in the nature and origins of human social behavior. Indeed, even those two giants of ancient thought, Plato and Aristotle, directed considerable attention to many aspects of social interaction. It appears, however, that philosophical speculation concerning the basis of social behavior reached a peak during the eighteenth and nineteenth centuries—perhaps as a direct result of the major social changes occurring during that period of rapid technological progress and growing industrialization.

Although such speculation took many forms, a considerable portion of these efforts was channeled into the development of what have since come to be termed **simple and sovereign theories** of human social affairs (Allport, 1968). Each theory focused on a single basic principle which its supporters believed to be the root of all social interaction. For example, several noted philosophers whose names you may have encountered elsewhere (Jeremy Bentham, John Stuart Mill, Herbert Spencer) suggested that all social behavior is based upon the desire of human beings to obtain pleasure and avoid pain, a position generally known as *hedonism*. Similarly, others (Nietzsche, Le Dantec) held that all social actions are directed toward the attainment of power—a view usually labeled *egoism*. That all simple and sovereign theories did not adopt such discouraging views of human interaction is suggested by a third position holding that social behavior stems primarily from feelings of love and affection for others (sympathy, as it was often termed). It is a sad footnote to history that supporters of this third view seem to have been greatly outnumbered by proponents of the others.

Today, unitary theories regarding the nature of social behavior are rarely encountered. It is widely recognized that human interaction is far too complex to permit us the luxury of simple explanations. These theories did, though, help to set the stage for the emergence of an independent and science-oriented field of social psychology in two important ways. First, they focused the attention of many scholars on the task of describing and explaining the nature of social interaction in terms more precise than those provided by folklore or "common sense." Second, they implied that social behavior, like other natural events, is both lawful and predictable, rather than random or haphazard. In short, while they were far too simple in orientation to be very useful in explaining the tangled web of human affairs, such unitary theories did help to create conditions favorable to the development of a scientific field of social psychology. In this respect, at least, they served a very useful function.

At the same time that philosophers were directing increased attention to the nature of human social behavior, many of the sciences were undergoing an unprecedented period of growth and progress (see Boring, 1950). The swiftness of these advances led a small number of individuals to propose that similar rapid strides might be made with respect to the understanding of human behavior by extending the methods of science to this complex topic. As this idea began to take root, the science of psychology gradually emerged and was firmly established by the closing decades of the nineteenth century. From there, it was only a relatively small step to the suggestion that similar methods be applied to the study of social behavior, and proposals for just such developments were soon heard. In short, the notion of a scientific social psychology was an idea whose time had finally come, and within a few short decades, the field was off to a healthy and vigorous start.

Social Psychology Emerges: The Early Years

Because no one arose to loudly proclaim the founding of social psychology, it is difficult to choose a single date for the formal launching of our field. Since the existence of textbooks in a particular field is often a sign that it has become accepted as a reasonable field of study, the publication of the first books bearing the title *Social Psychology* may be taken as a convenient marker. The first two books meeting this criterion were published in 1908 by William McDougall, a psychologist, and E. A. Ross, a sociologist. Although Ross's book was concerned with topics closer in scope to those of modern social psychology (crowd behavior, social influence), McDougall's volume exerted a much greater impact upon the field. Apparently, the time was ripe for the emergence of an independent social psychology, but not for the appearance of one resembling its modern form.

Basically, McDougall adopted an instinct approach to the study of social behavior. That is, he held that social behavior is largely determined by a group of innate (i.e., inborn) tendencies. Some of the major instincts suggested by McDougall, along with the emotional states he believed they induced, are listed in Table 1-1.

TABLE 1-1. *Some of the major instincts suggested by McDougall, along with the emotional states he believed they induced. (Source: Based on a list proposed by McDougall, 1908.)*

Instinct	Associated Emotional State
Flight	Fear
Repulsion	Disgust
Curiosity	Wonder
Pugnacity	Anger
Self-abasement	Subjection
Self-assertion	Elation
Parental	Tenderness

McDougall's suggestions regarding the central role of instincts in human social interaction received a mixed reception from his colleagues. Although John Dewey stated in his presidential address to the American Psychological Association in 1917 that the science of psychology must be based largely on the principle of instincts, others quickly denounced this suggestion (see Dunlap, 1919). Indeed, as the idea of instinctive patterns of behavior fell out of favor in psychology as a whole, criticism of McDougall's views became so intense that he eventually retreated from his early suggestions. Although there were many reasons for the rejection of instincts as an explanation for human social behavior, one of the most important centered around the apparent circularity of such a suggestion. That is, the common *occurrence* of some form of behavior was often taken by instinct theorists as an indication of the *existence* of an instinct for such behavior. Then, in what can only be described as a dazzling display of mental gymnastics, the presumed instinct was used as an "explanation" for the occurrence of the behavior in question. For example, an instinct theorist might begin by observing that human beings often aggress against others. This observation would then serve as the basis for the suggestion that they possess an aggressive instinct. And finally, the supposed existence of such an instinct might be used to "explain" the high frequency of interpersonal aggression (see Figure 1-2). Interestingly, the notion of instincts—or at least *some* innate determinants of behavior—has recently made something of a comeback in psychology (Mason and Lott, 1976). To date, though, no prominent social psychologist has seriously suggested that complex forms of social behavior stem largely from such innate tendencies.

In the years following publication of McDougall's book, social psychologists did more than simply argue about the existence and role of instincts in social behavior. In fact, they began to conduct actual investigations concerned with such behavior. As a result, when Floyd H. Allport published his influential text

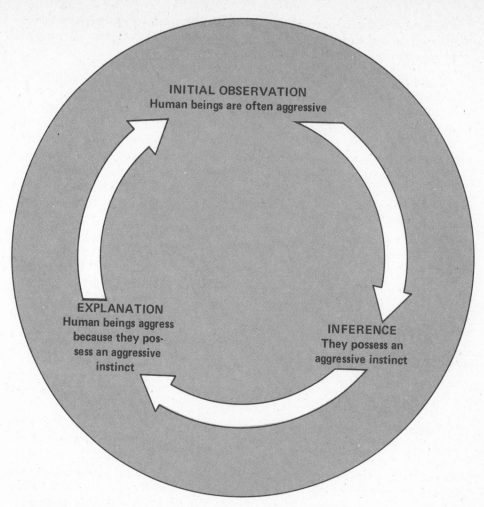

FIGURE 1-2. *Largely because they often fell victim to the type of circular reasoning shown above, attempts to explain social behavior in terms of instincts were soon abandoned during social psychology's early years.*

entitled *Social Psychology* in 1924, he was able to include reports of research concerned with such topics as the ability of individuals to "read" the facial expressions of others, the impact of an audience upon performance, and conformity.

Allport's text is also of interest because it argued strongly, at a point in time when such argument was needed, that social psychology should focus primarily on the social determinants of individual behavior—*not* on groups or social institutions. In his own words (1924, p. 4):

There is no psychology of groups which is not essentially and entirely a psychology of individuals. Social psychology . . . is a part of the psychology of the individual, *whose behavior it studies in relation to that sector of the environment comprised by his fellows . . . Psychology in all its branches is a science of the individual. To extend its principles to larger units is to destroy their meaning.*

If you find some of Allport's comments reminiscent of our own suggestions regarding the nature of social psychology, don't be too surprised. Writing in the early 1920's, he defined the field as that branch of psychology concerned with the study of social influences on individual behavior—a proposal remarkably similar to the one we offered on page 4. The fact that Allport was able to offer such a definition more than fifty years ago suggests that, although social psychology has suffered a number of problems and growing pains over the passing years, it managed to resolve its own personal identity crisis at quite an early point. (For a discussion of some of the problems faced by social psychology in recent years, see Elms, 1975.)

As you can probably guess by the publication date of Allport's text, social psychology became fully established as an independent field of study during the 1920's and 1930's. These decades were marked by the important early work of Muzafer Sherif and Kurt Lewin, two major pioneers in the history of our field. Sherif (1935) began the investigation of *social norms*—generalized rules of conduct which tell us how we should or ought to behave and which exert a surprisingly powerful influence on our actions. Lewin and his colleagues (Lewin, Lippitt, and White, 1939) began the systematic study of leadership and related processes. By the end of the 1930's, therefore, social psychology was clearly a going concern. New and interesting topics were continually being brought under investigation, and systematic methods for studying these topics were rapidly being developed.

Dates are always somewhat abstract, so in order to make the ones mentioned so far a bit more meaningful, we have summarized some of the significant events occurring around the world during this period (1908–1939) in Figure 1-3. As you can see, social psychology arrived on the scene at about the same time that Admiral Peary became the first person to reach the North Pole; it grew during the "roaring twenties"; and it was already delving into many interesting aspects of social behavior as the double disaster of painful depression and growing political tyranny struck the world in the dark and gloomy 1930's.

Decades of Growth: The 1940's, '50's, and '60's

As you might well anticipate, social psychology was strongly affected, during the 1940's, by the tragic events of World War II. During this decade, social psychologists turned increasing attention to such topics as prejudice, persuasion, and propaganda. To a large extent, their interest in these topics stemmed from concern over the manner in which the Nazis had been able, within a few short years, to turn a modern, culturally advanced nation such as Germany into a living nightmare in which millions were murdered solely on the basis of their religious beliefs or ethnic backgrounds. Indeed, at the end of the decade one group of social scientists (Adorno et al., 1950) published an account of a major research

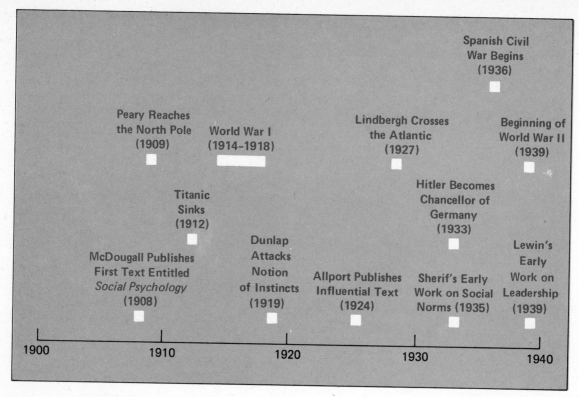

FIGURE 1-3. *Social psychology's first thirty years. As shown above, the years during which social psychology emerged and took root as an independent field were marked by many other important events.*

project designed to identify those personality characteristics which might dispose individuals toward the acceptance of fascism or similar political views. Through this and related research, social psychologists attempted to come to grips with one of the major tragedies of recent history.

During the 1950's, the scope of social psychological research widened to include a number of new topics. One important theme, especially in the early years of the decade, was the influence of groups and group membership on individual behavior (see Steiner, 1974). A second important theme concerned the relationship between various personality traits or characteristics (for example, the *need for achievement* or the *need for social approval*) and social behavior. For example, many studies were conducted to determine whether individuals high in a particular trait or characteristic would be more or less susceptible to social influence than individuals lower in such a trait. Perhaps the major event of the decade, however, was the formulation of the theory of *cognitive dissonance* by Leon Festinger (Festinger, 1957). Basically, he proposed that human beings dislike inconsistency and will strive to reduce it whenever it occurs. In particular, they find inconsistency between specific attitudes or between attitudes and behavior highly unpleasant, and seek to eliminate it in many different ways. Although this suggestion may not strike you as particularly surprising, it actually leads to many intriguing predictions regarding the effects of making a decision, the results of having suffered to obtain some goal only to find that it is useless, or the effects of arguing against one's own views. Festinger's proposals captured the interest and attention of many prominent social psychologists, and research on cognitive dissonance remained a major theme within the field for many years. (We will discuss this topic in some detail in Chapter 3.)

In an important sense, the turbulent decade of the 1960's may be viewed as the period during which social psychology finally came into its own. While research on cognitive dissonance continued at a furious pace, many new areas of investigation either opened or underwent rapid expansion during this time. So numerous were these new lines of research that we could not possibly hope to list them all here. Among the topics receiving greatly increased attention, though, were the following: *aggression and violence* (what are the causes of human violence? what steps can be taken to prevent or control such actions?); *attraction and love* (what are the bases of attraction between individuals?); *altruism and helping* (when will individuals offer assistance to others and when will they refuse?); *social exchange* (what conditions foster cooperation as opposed to competition? how do we react when we feel that we have been treated unfairly by others?); *imitation and modeling* (what are the effects on our feelings, behavior, and thoughts of exposure to the actions of others?); *group decision making* (how do groups make decisions, and do these differ in any manner from those of individuals?); and *person perception* (how do we form impressions of others? how do we go about determining their motives, intentions, and characteristics?). As you can probably tell from even this partial list, by the end of the 1960's social psychologists had broadened the scope of their investigations to include almost every conceivable aspect of social behavior.

The 1970's and Beyond: Social Psychology at the Crossroads

After the period of rapid change and growth experienced in the 1960's, you might expect that social psychology would take something of a "breather" in the 1970's. Actually, nothing could be further from the truth. Instead, the field has been even more active and more subject to the currents of change than ever before. First, many of the lines of research begun in the 1960's have continued and actually expanded in scope. In an important sense, you should not find this very surprising; it would be quite unrealistic to expect that a full understanding of such complex forms of behavior as aggression, helping, and love could be obtained in only a few short years. Rather, a great deal of hard work lies ahead before such knowledge can be acquired.

Second, several new topics—all of which are represented in this book—have come to the fore. First, social psychologists have turned their attention to the important effects of *environmental factors,* such as heat, noise, and crowding, upon social behavior. As a result, they have made an important contribution to the growing, interdisciplinary field of environmental psychology. Second, *attribution*—the process through which we infer the motives, intentions, and characteristics of other persons from their behavior—has become a major theme of social psychological research. Many investigations have been conducted both to determine the nature of this process itself, and to examine the influence of attributions, once formed, on our interactions with others. Third, there has been growing interest in the topic of *nonverbal communication,* the manner in which we communicate with others through the language of gazes and gestures. And finally, increasing attention has been directed to the systematic study of *sexual behavior*—a topic of some sensitivity even in the 1970's.

Over and above these important developments, two major trends which cut across the entire field and so exert a more general impact upon it have also made their appearance. First, there has been a growing concern on the part of many social psychologists with the social relevance of their research. That is, many have come to feel that their investigations should provide a practical "payoff" for society, preferably by contributing to the solution of serious social problems. Largely as a result of this belief, increasing attention has been directed to the problems faced by various minority groups, especially blacks, and to the topics of sex discrimination and sex differences. In order to reflect the growing concern with these and related issues, we have added a new chapter on prejudice and discrimination to our text (see Chapter 4).

Second, there has been an increasing tendency on the part of social psychologists to conduct their studies in real-life settings, as well as in the controlled environment of the research laboratory. Since we will consider the advantages—and some of the problems—associated with this approach in a later section (see pp. 28–29), we will not comment further on it at this time. For the present, we merely wish to call your attention to the fact that the growing popularity of field research seems to stem from the desire of many social psychologists to investigate social behavior under the kinds of conditions and in the types of settings where it normally occurs.

Together, these trends toward social relevance and field research have led to important changes and reorganizations within social psychology. Large as these have been, however, some experts believe that they represent only a beginning—the tip of the iceberg, so to speak—and that our field is actually poised on the brink of even greater alterations (McGuire, 1973). Since the shape of the "new" social psychology some believe will soon emerge is as yet unclear, we will not venture any firm predictions concerning its general nature at this time. One prediction we *are* willing to make, however, is that whatever its final form, this new "brand" of social psychology will prove to be even more sophisticated and better suited to the task of furthering human welfare than its present vigorous parent.

In our discussion up to this point, we have noted that social psychology seeks to investigate virtually every imaginable aspect of human interaction, from attraction and liking on the one hand, to aggression and violence on the other. Until now, however, we have left the crucial question or precisely *how* social psychologists attempt to carry out this difficult task largely unanswered. In this final section, therefore, we will turn to the nature of social psychological research. In order to acquaint you with the complexities of conducting systematic investigations of social behavior, we will consider four distinct but interrelated topics. First, we will comment on *the nature of theory* in social psychology, paying special attention to its important role in the generation of testable hypotheses concerning social behavior. Second, we will consider the two major methods used by social psychologists in their research, the **correlational** and **experimental approaches.** Here field, as well as laboratory, research will be considered. Third, we will examine some of the unsettling and complex *ethical issues* raised by research on social behavior, especially those stemming from the use of a technique known as deception. And finally, we will examine the nature of one major pitfall of social research, which can sometimes invalidate the findings of otherwise carefully conducted experiments—**demand characteristics.**

The Role of Theory in Social Psychology

It has often been suggested that science has three interrelated goals: *prediction, control,* and *understanding* (see Hendrick and Jones, 1972). Prediction refers to the ability to forecast the course of future events; control to the ability to shape the course of these events; and understanding to the ability to explain their occurrence. In many fields of science, prediction and control have often preceded the attainment of full and comprehensive understanding. For example, early chemists were able to produce a large number of reactions in their laboratories long before they had any accurate notion of the manner in which such reactions took place. Similarly, physicians have long been able to cure—or at least treat—many diseases whose causes remain something of a mystery even today.

Despite the practical benefits often yielded by prediction and control, however, the attainment of understanding is still central in any branch of science. Without such understanding, the scientist is in the same position as an individual who learns to drive an automobile without acquiring any knowledge about what is going on under the hood. As long as the car continues to function normally, everything is fine. But if it will not start, or begins making strange noises, or veers from side to side while on the road, the individual in question is completely at a loss, and must seek the assistance of others who do, in fact, possess some knowledge of the workings of the unreliable vehicle.

In a similar manner, the scientist who can only predict and control the phenomena in which he is interested will also be confused in the face of unexpected events. Indeed, in the absence of understanding, he or she can only speculate about the possible causes of such occurrences. For this reason, it is usually considered very important, in all branches of science, that a thorough understanding of the topics under study be acquired. And such understanding in science is usually assumed to lie in the development of adequate and comprehensive **theories.**

Basically, theories may be viewed as consisting of two essential parts: a set of basic concepts, and a number of statements concerning the relationships among these concepts which are assumed to be true. For example, a theory in physics might consist of the terms pressure *(p)*, volume *(V)*, and temperature *(T)*, along with a number of statements concerning the relationships between such statements. Similarly, a theory in social psychology might consist of such terms as intervention in an emergency, the psychological costs of helping, and the psychological costs of not helping, along with several statements regarding the presumed relationships among *these* concepts (Piliavin and Piliavin, 1976). In an advanced and highly sophisticated field such as physics, the statements relating various concepts of the theory to each other would probably take mathematical form (for example, the famous equation $E = mc^2$), while in social psychology, which is still a relatively new arrival among the sciences, they would often appear as simple verbal statements (for example: "The probability that bystanders will intervene during an emergency is a function of the psychological costs incurred by helping and the psychological costs incurred by not helping"). It is important to note, however, that in both fields the essential nature of theory is precisely the same.

Once a theory has been formulated, it is possible, employing the basic laws of logic, to generate new propositions relating to its basic concepts from the original ones. For example, consider the statement presented above, "The probability that bystanders will intervene during an emergency is a function of the psychological costs incurred by helping and the psychological costs incurred by not helping." On the basis of this assertion, it is possible to derive the following new proposition: "The greater the psychological costs of helping, and the lower the psychological costs of not helping, the less likely are bystanders to intervene during an emergency." Although such propositions—which are known as **hypotheses**—are derived in a direct and straightforward manner from the theories to which they relate, they are *not* assumed to be true. Rather, it is one of the major purposes of research in any field to subject them to direct, empirical test. This is very much the case in social psychology, and at many points throughout this book, we will have reason to consider experiments specifically designed to assess the validity of hypotheses derived from formal theories. It is important to note that if a theory does *not* lead to the formulation of testable hypotheses, it is essentially useless from a scientific point of view. This is the case because there is simply no way to acquire information regarding its accuracy—it must be accepted or rejected solely on the basis of faith (see Figure 1-4).

FIGURE 1-4. *A theory that does not lead to testable hypotheses can never be directly evaluated and is, therefore, essentially useless. (Source: B.C. by permission of Johnny Hart and Field Enterprises, Inc.)*

You should not assume from our comments so far, however, that *all* social psychological research is of this type. As noted by McGuire (1973), interesting hypotheses may actually stem from many different sources. For example, they may be suggested by conflicting findings in earlier studies, or by the occurrence of puzzling real-life events. An example of the latter source is provided by recent research on bystander intervention in emergencies, a topic to which we have already referred. Here, a chilling incident in which a number of individuals failed to offer aid to a young woman who was being brutally murdered right outside their windows led several researchers (Darley and Latané, 1968; Latané and Rodin, 1969) to hypothesize that, contrary to what common sense might suggest, the greater the number of witnesses to an emergency, the lower the victim's chances of obtaining help. As we shall see in Chapter 8, subsequent research actually tended to confirm this surprising suggestion. Still another source of interesting hypotheses for social research is the intuition, past experience, or informal observation of individual investigators. Research stemming from such sources may also be of great value, particularly in cases where theories relating to interesting aspects of social behavior have not as yet been formulated. And in a field as new and active as social psychology, it is our impression that such instances are far from rare. In sum, you should not be surprised to find that many of the experiments we discuss throughout this text were designed to test hypotheses derived from sources other than formal, comprehensive theories. At the present time, this is often the rule, rather than the exception, in social psychology.

Regardless of the source of their hypotheses, social psychologists tend to go about testing the accuracy of these suggestions in much the same way. Because we feel that understanding the methods they employ will help you to both grasp and interpret many of the findings discussed in later chapters, they will now be considered in some detail.

Social psychologists generally adopt one of two major methods of investigation in their research: the correlational or experimental approaches. Although both methods can and have been employed to gain useful and interesting information concerning social behavior, there are important differences between them which should not be overlooked. Thus, we will treat them separately in the discussion which follows.

Systematic Observation: The Correlational Method of Research. In investigations employing the correlational method, researchers attempt to determine whether two or more *variables* (factors of interest which can take different values ranging, for example, from low to high) are related through careful observation. That is, they simply make systematic observations of the variables in question in order to determine whether any relationship between them can be uncovered. Depending on the factors under study, this may involve direct observations of the behavior of many persons, careful study of their responses to questionnaires, or even examination of public or government records of various kinds. Regardless of the precise methods followed, however, the underlying approach remains the same: systematic observations of the variables of interest are conducted in order to determine whether they are related in any manner.

Such relationships, should they be uncovered, can take any one of several different forms. First, increments in one factor can be shown to be associated with increments in the other. In such cases, a *positive correlation* is said to exist between the variables of interest. For example, a social psychologist may observe that the intensity of romantic feelings reported by young couples increases as the degree of parental attempts to interfere with their relationship increases (the so-called "Romeo and Juliet" effect, see pp. 231–232).

On the other hand, increments in one variable may be related to decrements in the other. Here, a *negative correlation* is said to exist between the two factors. For example, it might be observed that the poorer the economic conditions in a given location, the greater the incidence of certain types of crime. The essential point to note is that when employing the correlational method, the investigator makes no attempt to change or alter the variables in which he or she is interested. Instead, he merely observes and records the existence of any relationships between them. Perhaps a specific example of the use of the correlational method of research will help clarify these points. For this purpose, we will consider a study conducted by Leonard Eron (1963).

In his research, Eron was primarily concerned with the possible existence of a relationship between the exposure of young children to violent television shows and their level of aggression toward peers. In order to examine this possibility, he gathered information on the aggressive behavior and TV viewing habits of 875 third-grade children. Information concerning the children's aggressive behavior was obtained by means of ratings by their classmates, while data regarding their viewing habits were gathered by questioning their parents. When the relationship between these two variables was then examined by appropriate statistical procedures, Eron found that there was indeed a link between them: in the case of boys, at least, the greater the children's preferences for (and presumably exposure to) violent shows, the greater their level of aggression in the classroom (see Figure 1-5). Interestingly, when a follow-up investigation was conducted, fully ten years later, evidence of this positive relationship still persisted. That is, the greater subjects' preference for violent TV shows as third graders, the more aggressive was their behavior reported to be by their classmates in high school (Lefkowitz et al., 1972).

As you probably realize by now, the correlational method of research can be employed to study many interesting topics. Moreover, it offers several important advantages. For example, it can often be used to collect large amounts of

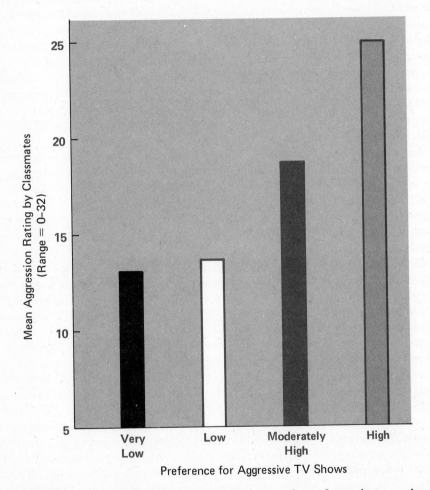

FIGURE 1-5. *The relationship between preference for violent television shows and aggression among third-grade boys. The greater the subjects' liking for such shows, the more aggressive were they rated as being by their classmates. (Source: Based on data from Eron, 1963.)*

data very quickly and efficiently. Similarly, it can be readily employed to study social behavior in natural settings—something, as we noted above, social psychologists are increasingly eager to accomplish. Unfortunately, though, the correlational approach suffers from one major disadvantage which greatly weakens its appeal: the findings it provides are usually somewhat ambiguous with respect to cause-and-effect relationships.

More specifically, the fact that two variables are found to be related in a correlational study tells us nothing about either (1) the existence of a direct causal link between them, or (2) the direction of such a relationship should it actually exist. With respect to the first of these points, assume that in a correlational study a psychologist finds evidence for a strong negative relationship between two factors: the number of years of education completed by male subjects and the amount of hair remaining on their heads. One possible interpretation of these results is that there is a direct causal link between education and baldness—that is, learning somehow causes hair loss—while another is that both factors are closely related to a third, *age,* and tend to increase as this variable rises. In this particular instance, the second explanation is far more convincing than the first, and there can be little doubt that it is correct. But in other cases, the fact that an apparently close relationship between two variables is actually underlain by a third is much harder to recognize, and the temptation to assume that the first causes the second is strong.

For example, it has recently been reported that there is a positive relationship between temperature and the incidence of collective violence such as riots, so that the hotter the weather, the more frequent the occurrence of such events. Does this mean that uncomfortable heat causes aggression? Such a conclusion is certainly more reasonable than the assumption that education causes hair loss, but it may also be false, and for much the same reason. That is, it may actually be the case that more riots occur on hot than cool days because more people are out on the streets on such days, and so are present to get involved in any budding disturbance. In short, it may be this factor—the number of people out on the street—and not high temperatures themselves which accounts for the occurrence of "long, hot summers." (A summary of these suggestions is presented in Figure 1-6). The moral contained in both examples we have presented is simple, but important: the existence of a correlation between two factors is *not* a definite indication of a causal relationship between them, and should be interpreted as such only in the presence of additional supporting evidence.

Second, even if it is the case that the relationship between two factors is a direct one and is not produced by some additional variable, it is still impossible to determine the direction of this bond from a correlation between them. For example, recall that in his investigation on the effects of televised violence, Eron (1963) uncovered a positive relationship between children's preference for violent television shows and their level of aggression against their classmates. Because his investigation employed the correlational method of research, these findings may indicate that (1) exposure to televised violence leads to heightened levels of aggression on the part of young children, or (2) the more aggressive an individual is, the more likely he or she is to prefer (and watch) violent television shows.

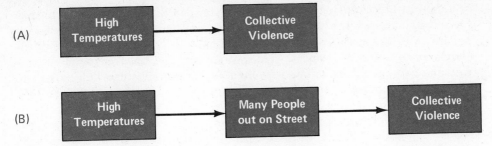

(A)

High Temperatures → Collective Violence

(B)

High Temperatures → Many People out on Street → Collective Violence

FIGURE 1-6. *Recent evidence suggests that high temperatures are associated with an increase in the incidence of collective violence in major cities. This may mean that uncomfortable heat is a direct cause of such behavior (A). It may also mean that such conditions drive many people out onto the street, and that this factor—a large number of potential participants—is responsible for the increased occurrence of riots, looting, etc. (B). On the basis of correlation evidence, it is impossible to choose between these two possibilities.*

Clearly, the first of these possibilities is far more interesting and provocative than the second. However, both are quite reasonable, and it is impossible to choose between them on the basis of correlational evidence alone. (Before concluding this discussion, we should note that in recent years, more sophisticated correlational techniques which *do* seem to provide firmer grounds for establishing cause-and-effect relationships have been developed. However, even these techniques suffer from a degree of ambiguity in this respect. Thus, although they tend to counteract the disadvantages described above, they by no means eliminate them completely.)

The Experimental Method of Research. Because of the problems outlined above, many social psychologists prefer to employ the experimental rather than the correlational method in their research. Although students often assume that there is something very mystifying or complex about this approach, it is, in its basic logic, remarkably simple and straightforward. Essentially, an investigator employing the experimental method attempts to determine whether a given factor or variable influences some form of social behavior by (1) systematically varying its presence or strength, and (2) observing whether such variations have any effects on the behavior under study. The factor systematically varied by the experimenter is usually termed the **independent variable,** while the behavior being studied is termed the **dependent variable.** In a typical experiment, then, subjects are randomly assigned to various groups corresponding to different levels of the independent variable (i.e., low, moderate, high), and their behavior is measured or observed to determine whether it is in fact affected by such variations. If this proves to be the case and if—very importantly—two other conditions have also been met, it can be concluded that the independent variable is indeed one of the determinants of the behavior under study.

The first of the two conditions to which we referred above is the random assignment of subjects to the various experimental groups. This is important for the simple reason that if subjects are *not* assigned to each group in this manner, it may later prove impossible to determine whether differences in their behavior stem from the effects of the independent variable or simply from important differences between the subjects in the various groups. For example, imagine that we conducted a study to compare the levels of sexual arousal induced by two different types of erotic stimuli. Further, imagine that we showed the first type of stimuli to a group of happily married couples, and the second to a group of single individuals, most of whom were not romantically involved at the time. If we then found that subjects exposed to the second type of stimuli demonstrated greater arousal than those exposed to the first, could we conclude that one type is indeed more arousing than the other? Actually, we could not, and for a very important reason: it is quite impossible to tell whether the higher levels of arousal shown by subjects in the second group stemmed from the fact that the stimuli they saw were actually more arousing, or simply from the fact that they have enjoyed fewer recent sexual experiences, and so would be more highly aroused by virtually *any* erotic stimulus. In order to avoid such ambiguity in the interpretation of results, it is necessary to ensure that subjects are randomly assigned to the various groups in an experiment.

The second condition to which we referred above involves the elimination, insofar as possible, of the effects of all factors other than the independent variable that might also influence the behavior in question. In practical terms, this usually means that all other factors of this type—or at least as many as possible—are held constant across experimental groups. This is important because if such factors are allowed to vary in a systematic manner, it is impossible to determine whether differences in the behavior of subjects in the various experimental groups stem from the effects of the independent variable, or from the effects of these other, extraneous factors. For example, imagine that we conducted an experiment concerned with the effects of eye contact upon first impressions, because we have reason to believe that the greater the amount of eye contact between strangers, the more favorable their impressions of each other will be. Further, suppose that in this study, one group of subjects is exposed to a stranger working in our employ who purposely engages them in a great deal of eye contact (he constantly looks them in the eye), while a second group is exposed to the same individual under conditions where he purposely avoids such eye contact. Because we do not conduct our experiment very carefully, however, we also allow the stranger to act in a very friendly manner when meeting individuals in the first, high eye-contact group, but in a very unfriendly manner when meeting persons in the second, low eye-contact group. If our results now show that subjects in the first group report a more favorable impression of the stranger than those in the second, what can we conclude? Actually, very little, because in this case, it is impossible to determine whether their favorable impressions stemmed from the higher level of eye contact they experienced, or simply from the stranger's friendlier behavior. In order to avoid such confusion, it is necessary to hold all factors other than the independent variable constant when conducting experimental research.

In sum, the results of an experiment are usually only informative when both of these conditions—random assignment of subjects to groups and adequate control of factors other than the independent variable—have been met. Fortunately, social psychologists are quite sophisticated about such matters and rarely overlook them in their research. Thus, as a general rule, you can assume that all the research discussed in this text has met these requirements and does provide useful information on the topics under study.

Admittedly, our discussion up to this point has been a bit abstract. Perhaps, therefore, it is best to turn to a specific example through which we can illustrate both the logic of the experimental method in actual operations and the differences between this approach and the correlational method. For this purpose, let us consider an experiment conducted by Liebert and Baron (1972).

These investigators were concerned with the same general topic as Eron (1963) in the study described above. That is, they wished to examine the relationship between exposure to violent television programs and the level of aggression later demonstrated by young viewers. In contrast to Eron, however, Liebert and Baron decided to employ the experimental method in their research. Thus, instead of simply observing subjects' TV viewing habits and aggressive behavior and noting the existence of any relationship between these factors, they *systematically varied* the amount of aggression contained in the programs witnessed by subjects in order to determine whether such variations would be reflected in their subsequent willingness to harm another child. Basically, then, their investigation proceeded as follows. When they arrived for their appointments, subjects participating in the study (young boys and girls) were randomly assigned to one of two different groups: an *aggressive program* condition, in which they viewed excerpts from an actual TV show containing a considerable amount of interpersonal violence, or a *nonaggressive program* condition, in which they viewed excerpts from an exciting but nonviolent track race. Immediately after witnessing one of these two programs, subjects in both groups were provided with an apparent opportunity to harm another child: they could push a special red button which supposedly burned this individual's hand. (In reality, of course, there was no victim, and no child was ever harmed in any way during the experiment.)

The results of the experiment indicated that, as expected by the investigators, children exposed to the aggressive program did in fact demonstrate higher levels of aggression than those exposed to the nonaggressive program; that is, they pushed the red button more often and for a longer period of time than those who saw only the track race. (See Figure 1-7.) Because subjects were randomly assigned to the two experimental groups, and because other factors which might have affected their behavior (for example, the experimenter's comments, the location of the study, etc.) were held constant, these findings are not subject to the serious kinds of confusion described above. Thus, they were interpreted by Liebert and Baron as suggesting that exposure to televised violence may produce at least a short-term increase in the level of aggression demonstrated by young children. (We will return to a fuller discussion of this issue in Chapter 7, pp.

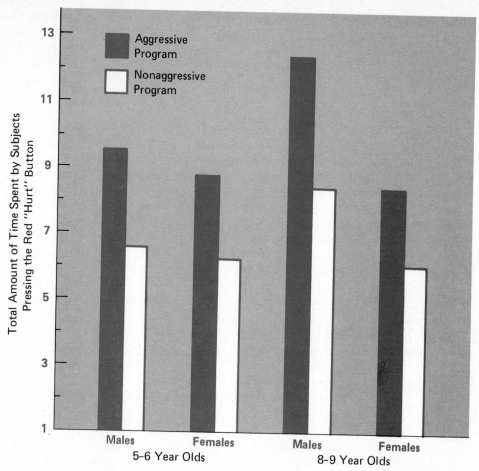

FIGURE 1-7. *The results of the Liebert and Baron (1972) experiment. Boys and girls in two different age groups demonstrated higher levels of aggression after viewing a violent television program than after viewing an equally exciting but nonviolent show. (Source: Based on data from Liebert and Baron, 1972.)*

317–323). Please note once again that in contrast to the correlational procedures employed by Eron (1963), Liebert and Baron sought to examine the possibility of a link between exposure to televised violence and aggressive behavior by systematically varying the former (the *independent variable* in their study), and then observing the effects of such variations upon the latter (the *dependent variable* in their experiment).

Field Research in Social Psychology: Experimentation Outside the Laboratory. You may recall that in our discussion of recent trends in social psychology we mentioned the increasing popularity of **field research.** In the past few years, there has been a growing tendency on the part of social psychologists to conduct their experiments in the real world beyond the confines of the research laboratory. The advantages offered by such a shift are obvious. First, by conducting their experiments in naturalistic settings, social psychologists are able to observe the behavior of a more diverse sample of subjects than is usually possible in the laboratory. That is, by choosing the locations of their experiments carefully, they can investigate the behavior of individuals from virtually every walk of life and every socioeconomic level. Second, by moving their studies to the open field, researchers gain the opportunity to observe various forms of social behavior under the conditions where they normally occur. As you might suspect, the knowledge that they are participating in an experiment may often alter the behavior of subjects taking part in laboratory studies. In many field experiments, such problems do not arise because participants are not even aware that an investigation is in progress. As a result, their reactions may often be far more indicative of their normal patterns of behavior than those observed in the laboratory. And finally, by conducting their experiments in the open field, researchers are often able to obtain more realistic measures of the behaviors they wish to study. Given the existence of these advantages, it is little wonder that the volume of field research has shown a sharp rise in recent years.

Such procedures are by no means an unmixed blessing, however. Along with these gains come a number of serious problems. First, it is often far more difficult to manipulate independent variables systematically in real world settings than in the laboratory. Extraneous and unpredictable events frequently arise and play havoc with completion of even the most carefully planned studies. Second, conducting field research raises important ethical issues. Perhaps the most serious of these centers around the question of whether it is ethical—or even legal—to expose passersby to experimental manipulations without their prior knowledge or consent. Since we will shortly return to a general discussion of ethical issues in social research, no attempt will be made to deal with such questions here. We do wish to point out in advance, though, that there are no simple or easy answers.

Despite these disadvantages, many social psychologists believe that, on balance, the benefits of field research far outweigh the drawbacks. As a result, they have recently conducted many ingenious experiments in such varied and unlikely settings as busy restaurants (McGee and Snyder, 1975), bustling supermarkets (Harris, 1974), crowded beaches (Moriarty, 1975), and even New York City subway trains (Piliavin and Piliavin, 1975). As a specific example of such field experimentation, we will consider a study by Leyens et al. (1975).

This investigation was concerned with the same general topic as our earlier examples of systematic observation and laboratory experimentation—the effects of witnessed violence on subsequent aggression. In order to study this issue in a field experiment, Leyens et al. (1975) began by observing both the aggressive and nonaggressive behaviors of a large number of boys living at a private school in Belgium. As you might expect, the boys' behavior was observed in such a manner that their normal activities were neither changed nor interrupted. After one week of such observation, subjects were divided into two groups on the basis of the particular housing units in which they lived, and were then exposed to

In recent years, social psychologists have conducted a growing number of experiments in natural settings. Busy markets, bustling restaurants, and even crowded subway cars have served as locations for systematic research.

either five violent or five nonviolent movies. These films were shown one each day, in the evening, for five consecutive days, and varied greatly in the amount of aggression they contained. (For example, among the highly aggressive films were *Bonnie and Clyde* and *The Dirty Dozen*.) Observation of the boys' activities was also continued on days when the films were shown in order to obtain evidence on the major question of interest: would exposure to the violent movies lead to an increase in their level of aggression? The answer was a qualified "yes": subjects exposed to the highly violent movies did show an increase in some, but not all forms of aggression. Subjects exposed to the nonviolent films, of course, failed to demonstrate any similar changes in behavior (see Figure 1-8).

While similar results have been obtained in many laboratory studies, the advantages provided by this field experiment should be obvious. First, subjects were exposed to several whole movies over a period of several days, rather than simply a single, brief segment from a film or TV show. Second, they watched these films in a relaxed and natural setting, rather than as part of a formal experiment. And third, the measures of aggression obtained—subjects' actual attacks against others or their property—were highly realistic. (Compare these measures with the button-pushing task employed by Liebert and Baron.) It is largely because of advantages such as these that field research is often so appealing to social psychologists.

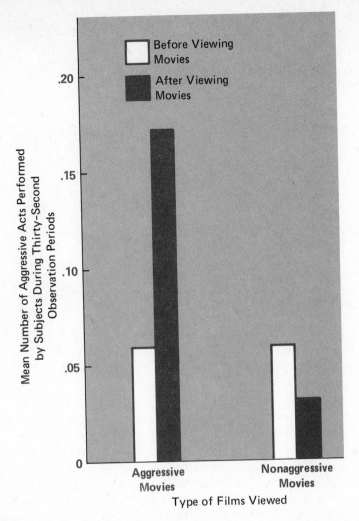

FIGURE 1-8. *The findings of the field experiment conducted by Leyens et al. (1975). Consistent with the results of previous laboratory studies, exposure to several violent movies led to an increase in subjects' level of aggression. In contrast, exposure to several nonviolent films failed to produce similar changes in subjects' behavior. (Source: Based on data from Leyens et al., 1975.)*

At this point, we should insert a word of caution: please don't jump to the conclusion, on the basis of our comments up to this point, that field research is always or even usually more effective than laboratory experimentation. As we noted above, both practical and ethical problems often make it difficult, if not impossible, to conduct appropriate field studies. Similarly, it is often difficult to test complex hypotheses, especially ones stemming from formal theories, in field settings—the precise manipulation of independent variables required for such tasks simply cannot be obtained In sum, there is no single "best" method for conducting social psychological research. In many, if not most cases, the particular method we choose depends quite heavily on the topics selected for study.

Ethical Issues in Social Research: The Use of Deception

In their use of the correlational and experimental methods of research, social psychologists do not differ from investigators in many other fields. In fact, these same basic procedures are employed in one form or another by virtually all scientists. There is one research technique, however, which, if not unique to social psychology, is at least most closely identified with it—experimental **deception.** Because this procedure is employed in many of the experiments we will discuss throughout this text, and because it has recently become the focus of rather severe criticism (Schultz, 1969), it seems worthy of our careful attention.

Basically, the use of deception in social psychological research involves an attempt to conceal the true purposes of an experiment from the subjects participating in it. This may be accomplished by the omission of crucial information, the provision of false or misleading instructions, convincing subjects that they are assistants or accomplices of the experimenter when they are not, or disguising the fact that an experiment is being conducted. The use of such procedures stems from the widely held belief that if subjects know the true purpose of an experiment, their behavior will be different from what it would otherwise be, and any findings obtained will be invalid. For example, imagine that in an experiment concerned with the topic of social influence, subjects are informed that the purpose of the study is to determine how readily they can be swayed by the judgments or opinions of others. Under such conditions, they may actually lean over backwards to "prove" that they are independent souls, not readily influenced by the persons around them. Or suppose that in an experiment concerned with helping behavior, participants are told that the purpose of the study is that of learning how quickly they will help a person in distress. In this case, most individuals will probably rush to provide assistance as rapidly as possible in order to demonstrate that they are just as kind and compassionate as the next person. In these and many other cases, temporary deception regarding the purposes of social research does in fact seem necessary: without it, the chances of obtaining meaningful results are slim indeed.

Unfortunately, although deception often seems to be a valuable tool for research, its use raises serious ethical issues. In particular, the possibility exists that deception—no matter how temporary—may actually result in harmful psychological or even physical consequences to subjects (Kelman, 1967). Although in almost all cases the deceptions employed by socal psychologists appear to have little likelihood of producing negative effects, there have been some experiments in which the possibility of harmful consequences cannot be ruled out. For example, in one controversial study, Bramel (1962) provided male college students with false information indicating that they were sexually aroused by pictures of partially nude young men. This suggestion—that they harbored hidden homosexual impulses—may have been extremely unsettling to at least some of the subjects in the study. Similarly, in a series of famous experiments, Milgram (1963, 1965b, 1974) placed subjects in a situation where they were ordered by a stern and authoritative experimenter to deliver electric shocks of increasing intensity to a helpless and protesting victim (see pp. 289–294). Although some individuals refused to obey, most followed the experimenter's commands and soon found themselves delivering what they believed to be 450-volt shocks to the victim! In reality, of course, this seemingly unfortunate person was a confederate working in the employ of the experimenter, and never received any shocks during the study. But the subjects, being totally ignorant of this important fact, often experienced extreme conflict and distress over the experimenter's demands that they harm another person who had done nothing to deserve such harsh treatment. Indeed, some became so upset that they experienced reactions akin to full-blown anxiety attacks.

As a final example, consider a recent study by West, Gunn, and Chernicky (1975) in which the experimenter attempted to induce subjects to participate in an illegal burglary similar in nature to the well-known Watergate incident. In some conditions—for example, when they were offered complete immunity from future prosecution—many individuals agreed. Imagine, then, how these participants may have felt when they later realized that they had consented to engaging in actions which had been strongly condemned by the courts, the mass media, and overwhelming public opinion, and which they themselves had probably also denounced. The very real possibility that they experienced such negative reactions as lowered self-esteem, severe embarrassment, or intense guilt raises serious questions about the ethical nature of this experiment.

Of course, all these researchers (Bramel; Milgram; West and his colleagues) provided subjects in their studies with a full explanation of the deceptions employed at the end of the session—a procedure known as **debriefing** (see below). However, as noted by Kelman (1967), it is possible that even after hearing these explanations, some individuals continued to harbor negative feelings about themselves or their behavior as a result of their participation in the research.

At this point, we should pause to emphasize very strongly that the studies mentioned above represent extreme instances of the use of deception, and were specifically chosen to illustrate the possible harmful effects that may result from such procedures. In actual practice, deception usually takes a much less unsettling form. For example, subjects may be informed that the lights on a panel in front of them represent the answers of several other subjects to a series of simple questions, when in fact they are controlled by the experimenter, or that a written communication with which they are presented comes from some authoritative source when in fact it was specifically prepared for the experiment. In such instances, it is hard to imagine how the deceptions employed can exert any harmful effect upon subjects; indeed, they seem much more likely to slightly bore or mildly amuse them than to induce any lasting negative changes in their self-image or emotional well-being. Yet, the fact that deception is usually quite harmless does not guarantee that it is *always* inoffensive. In fact, the examples presented above suggest that it may sometimes be otherwise.

Because of the serious ethical issues involved in the use of deception, some critics (Ring, 1967; Schultz, 1969) have recommended that it be replaced with an entirely different technique known as **role playing.** Briefly, this procedure involves the strategy of providing subjects with complete information concerning the purposes and methods of an experiment, and then asking them to play the role of a naive subject who has *not* been supplied with such knowledge. According to supporters of these procedures, subjects are readily able to adopt such a role, and the behavior they then demonstrate closely approximates that which they would have shown had deception actually been employed. In short, role playing has been recommended as a way of enjoying all the benefits provided by deception, without exposure to any of its risks.

Unfortunately, there seem to be strong grounds for questioning the usefulness of this solution. First, as noted by Freedman (1969) and others, the information yielded by role playing represents subjects' *guesses* about the manner in which they would behave if they were in a particular situation (that is, if they had *not* been provided with full information about the methods and purposes of the experiment), rather than information about the manner in which they would *actually* behave in that situation. This would pose no serious difficulty if human beings were always capable of making accurate predictions regarding their own behavior. As you probably know from your own experience, however, this is not always the case. As a result, data gathered from role-playing subjects are always open to question on these grounds.

Second, a growing body of research suggests that the behavior of role-playing and deceived subjects often differs in important respects (Darroch and Steiner, 1970; Willis and Willis, 1970). For example, in a recent experiment conducted by Holmes and Bennett (1974), one group of subjects was informed that they would soon receive painful electric shocks, while another was asked to behave *as if* they were going to receive these unpleasant stimuli (that is, they were asked to role play). In reality, neither group ever received any shocks, but the subjects who had been deceived showed much higher levels of physiological arousal (higher pulse rate, respiration, etc.) than those in the role-playing condition. Thus, contrary to what supporters of role playing have contended, role-playing subjects were *not* able to simulate the reactions of the other participants. In view of such findings, it does not seem reasonable to accept role playing as a fully adequate substitute for experimental deception (Miller, 1972).

Continued Use of Deception: Informed Consent and Debriefing. The possible dangers involved in the use of deception, coupled with the apparent failure of role playing to provide a useful substitute for such procedures, seems to leave social psychologists facing something of a dilemma: should they continue to employ deception in their research, knowng that it possesses at least the potential for harm to subjects? Or should they abandon this technique as inappropriate for use in their investigations? This is a complex problem, and has often served as the basis for heated debate. It is our impression, though, that the present consensus in social psychology points to the following conclusion:

continued use of deception is permissible, but *only* if certain safeguards and procedures are adopted. Briefly, these are as follows.

First, deception should by employed only when no other means of conducting the research in question exists. It should never be adopted as a matter of course or simply because it is the easiest route to follow. Rather, it is appropriate only under conditions where all other possibilities have been carefully considered and found to be unsuitable.

Second, whenever researchers consider using deception in their experiments, they must carefully weigh the potential benefits and contributions of their studies against any possibilities of harm to participants. That is, they must try to determine whether the new knowledge and any potential benefits to society that may be obtained outweigh the psychological costs to subjects. Needless to say, such decisions are largely value judgments, and will be strongly influenced by each researcher's personal views. When any doubt arises, however, experimenters have a firm responsibility to seek the opinions of other persons concerning the cost/benefit ratio of their studies before proceeding.

Third, subjects should be informed about any threatening, frightening, or upsetting features of the study prior to their participation in it. This is the important principle of **informed consent**, which requires that participants learn about any possible risks they will face *before* agreeing to serve in an experiment. In actual practice, this usually means that subjects are provided with a brief description of the general procedures to be followed, and are then asked to sign a special form indicating that they have agreed to participate of their own free will. It is not considered essential that they learn all the details of the study at this time—if they did, many projects could not be conducted. What is essential, though, is that they be informed about any unpleasant aspects of the study, and be given the opportunity to withdraw without penalty if they so desire.

Fourth, and equally important, once the study is completed, subjects must be provided with a full and thorough debriefing. This should involve several points. First, and most obvious, all deceptions must be explained and the true purpose of the experiment revealed. Second, the need for deception must be clarified, and the experimenter's distress at having found it necessary to make use of such procedures should be noted. The contribution of the study both to scientific knowledge and to society should also be discussed, and any further questions on the part of participants honestly answered. The major purpose of the debriefing, of course, is that of ensuring that any negative reactions experienced by subjects during the study are entirely eliminated before their departure.

In most cases, the steps outlined above are sufficient to accomplish this goal. In others, however, it may be necessary to schedule further meetings with particular individuals who appear to remain anxious, upset, or depressed in any manner (Cook, 1975). Fortunately, there is growing evidence that debriefing is usually quite effective in counteracting any negative feelings induce during an experiment. For example, in a study we have already mentioned before, Holmes and Bennett (1974) found that a thorough debriefing was effective in completely eliminating the physiological arousal and feelings of anxiety experienced by subjects who had been informed that they would soon receive severe electric shocks. Additional studies in which subjects have been contacted weeks or even months after their participation in social psychological research have yielded similar results (Clark and Word, 1974; Zimbardo, 1974). Thus, it does appear that debriefing goes a long way toward eliminating any negative reactions stemming from the use of experimental deception.

By way of conclusion, we should note that, in recent years, psychologists in general, and social psychologists in particular, have become increasingly concerned with the ethical issues raised by their research. Indeed, the American Psychological Association (1973) has recently issued a set of guidelines similar to the ones described above to be followed by all researchers in studies of human behavior. It is our impression that at present the overwhelming majority of social psychologists follow these principles in their research. Thus, they generally do everything in their power to assure the safety and well-being of the individuals particiating in their experiments. Under these conditions, we believe, the continued use of temporary deception is permissible. We also feel, however, that even when these guidelines are strictly followed, the byword for concerned social researchers must always remain *caution.*

At the conclusion of any social psychological experiment—but especially in cases where deception has been employed—subjects must be provided with a thorough debriefing.

Suppose that one day, you participate as a subject in the following experiment. The investigator begins by informing you that the purpose of the study is that of determining the effects of stress upon problem-solving ability. In order to study this topic, another individual will attempt to formulate a solution to a particular problem, knowing that you will then evaluate his work. Stress will be introduced into the situation by the fact that you will indicate your evaluation of this work by means of electric shocks. If you evaluate the solution very positively, you will deliver only one shock to the problem solver; if you evaluate it somewhat more negatively, you will give him two shocks; and so on up to seven. After presenting these instructions, the experimenter conducts you to another room where the apparatus for delivering the shocks is located. As you enter, you notice that lying on the table next to this equipment are a revolver and a twelve-gauge shotgun. The experimenter then remarks, in a very casual manner, "Don't pay any attention to these. They're just left over from another study." After she leaves and you wait for the other subject's problem solution, your eyes keep returning to the two weapons. Why, you wonder, are they present on the table? You don't really believe that they are unconnected with the study, and after a few minutes' thought, you hit upon one possible solution. "Aha!" you say to yourself, "They must be here because the experimenter thinks they'll make me deliver more shocks." You are very pleased with having outguessed the researcher and discovered the purpose of her study. But now you are left facing a bit of a dilemma: what should you do about your new information? Three possibilities cross your mind.

First, you can help the experimenter confirm her hypothesis by actually delivering a large number of shocks to the other person. Second, you can do the opposite and deliver a small number of shocks, thus demonstrating that you are too smart to be fooled by such transparent procedures. Third, you can behave in whatever manner you think will present you to the experimenter in the most favorable light. For example, you might choose to deliver the precise number of shocks you feel the problem solution deserves, and so demonstrate that you are a totally fair individual, unaffected in your judgments by irrelevant conditions or events. Although it is difficult to predict which of these possibilities you as an individual would select, several recent studies point to the conclusion that most subjects participating in psychological research choose the third when they discover the hypothesis under study (Rosnow et al., 1973; Sigall, Aronson, and Van Hoose, 1970).

Regardless of which strategy they follow, however, the end result is much the same: to the extent that subjects are able to determine the hypothesis under study, the findings of the experiment may be rendered totally invalid. This is because, in such cases, the results obtained stem from the subjects' perceptions of the purposes of the experiment and the role they believe they are expected to play in it, rather than from the effects of the independent variables being

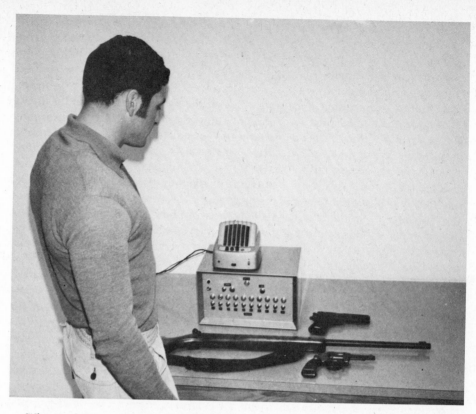

When subjects succeed in guessing the hypothesis under investigation in an experiment, meaningful results usually cannot be obtained. As a result, social psychologists must always guard against the influence of demand characteristics— cues which communicate their hypotheses to subjects. If you were a participant in a study where a revolver and a shotgun were placed next to equipment used to deliver electric shocks to another person, do you think you would guess the experimenter's hypothesis?

investigated. Psychologists generally refer to any cues which tip the experimenter's hand in this manner as *demand characteristics,* and unless they are controlled, the results of even highly ingenious studies may be quite meaningless (Orne, 1962). For example, in the study mentioned above—which was actually conducted in slightly modified form by Berkowitz and LePage (1967)—subjects delivered a greater number of shocks to the problem solver (who was actually an accomplice of the experimenter) when the weapons were present than when they were absent. Berkowitz and LePage interpreted these findings as suggesting that the presence of weapons may sometimes facilitate aggression. As noted by several subsequent investigators, however, it is difficult to tell whether this was due to the effects of the weapons themselves, or merely to subjects' desires to help the experimenter confirm his obvious predictions (Buss, Booker, and Buss, 1972; Page and Scheidt, 1971).

In the "weapons" study described above, the cues revealing the experimenter's hypothesis to subjects were quite obvious. You should not jump to the conclusion that such noticeable hints are necessary for participants to guess the purpose of an experiment. In fact, such cues can be far more subtle in nature and still produce similar results. For example, demand characteristics can stem from vague rumors concerning the nature and purpose of the experiment heard by subjects before participating in it. Or they can be provided by the experimenter himself in the form of subtle changes in emphasis during the reading of instructions, fleeting glances at crucial points during the study, or even alterations in his or her posture (Chaikin, Sigler, and Derlega, 1974; Jones and Cooper, 1971). The task of controlling such influences, then, is more difficult than might at first be imagined.

Fortunately, there are several means for eliminating or drastically lessening their impact. First, experimenters can do everything in their power to conceal the true purposes of their investigations from subjects. Since we have already devoted considerable attention to the nature of such deception, and the ethical problems it raises, we will not return to it here. We do wish to note, however, that the potentially damaging impact of demand characteristics on the interpretation of experimental findings provides one of the strongest arguments for the continued use of such procedures. Second, studies can be conducted in such a manner that the persons collecting the data are not familiar with the hypotheses under investigation. For example, a social psychologist can hire special assistants and train them to conduct his or her research, but refrain from informing these persons about the hypotheses under study. Since they do not know the predictions themselves, it is impossible for them to communicate such information to subjects. Third, experiments can be automated to as great a degree as possible. Instructions can be tape-recorded, data collected by automatic equipment, and so on. In this way, subtle cues communicated by experimenters themselves regarding their expectations or hypotheses can be largely eliminated. And, finally, researchers can turn to disguised experiments, in which subjects do not even know that they are participating in a study until it is over, or to field research. Together, such procedures can go a long way toward eliminating the potentially disruptive effects of demand characteristics.

As you might well guess, social psychologists are quite familiar with the potential dangers of demand characteristics, and take many precautions to guard against them. As a result, it is our impression that they now present much less of a problem in social psychological research than was once true in the past. Indeed, you can be confident that the many studies we discuss in other chapters of this text are generally as free from such influences as humanly possible.

USING THIS BOOK: A FUGITIVE PREFACE

Before concluding, we feel that it may be useful to comment briefly on several features of this text. Such information could, of course, have been included in the preface. Since it is our impression that fewer and fewer people read prefaces these days, however, we decided to increase the chances that you would encounter these comments by locating them here.

First, we wish to call your attention to the general organization of the text. Basically, our plan has been to move from topics centering around reactions occurring largely within single individuals, to behaviors and processes involving interaction between two or more persons. As a result, we begin with consideration of such topics as social perception, attitudes, prejudice, and interpersonal attraction, and only then turn to such forms of overt social behavior as aggression, social influence, and altruism. Our reason for adopting this strategy is quite simple: we feel that understanding the processes of of person perception, attitude formation and change, and so on is often essential to understanding the nature of complex forms of social interaction.

Second, we wish to mention several specific features of our text designed to make it easier and more convenient for you to use. First, each chapter is preceded by an outline of the major topics it covers, and followed by a summary which reviews most of the important points made. Second, key terms or concepts are printed in **boldface** and defined in the glossary following each chapter. Third, all figures, tables, and graphs are as simple to read as we could make them, and are explained as fully as possible in the accompanying captions. And fourth, a brief list of suggested readings—most of them quite nontechnical in nature—follows each chapter.

Finally, we have made use of three distinct types of inserts, or "boxes," which should be explained. The first is labeled *Focus on Research* and usually appears at the end of a major section within a chapter. Inserts of this type contain either descriptions of special research techniques or recent experiments which we view as particularly interesting or important. Their main purpose is to provide you with a general "feel" for what is currently going on at the frontiers of social psychological research.

The second type of insert is labeled *Social Psychology in Action,* and is included because of our belief that one effective demonstration is often worth at least a thousand words. Inserts of this kind describe simple experiments or observations you can perform to demonstrate important principles described in the text. All are safe, and consistent with the most rigorous ethical principles, and should provide you with first-hand evidence regarding many of the findings we discuss.

Finally, the third type is labeled *Capsule Controversy,* and summarizes recent disputes in social psychology. This last type of insert is included for two reasons. First, we wish to avoid conveying the impression that social psychology is very much a cut-and-dried affair. Complex forms of social behavior are open to many different interpretations, and often social psychologists have disagreed quite strongly about such issues. Thus, omitting mention of these controversies might leave you with a false impression of tranquility and consensus, when in fact quite the opposite has often been true. Second, it is our impression that major advances have often stemmed from just such disagreements, and that, as a result, it is worthwhile to call them to your attention.

The remaining chapters of this book deal with a number of distinct topics currently of major interest to social psychologists. Each is concerned with a wide range of issues and many contrasting forms of social behavior. Together, we feel that they provide a broad introduction to our current understanding of the nature of human interaction.

SUMMARY

Social psychology is at once both a very ancient and a very modern field of study. Speculation concerning the nature of human social interaction has gone on without interruption since the days of antiquity. However, it is only during the twentieth century that scientific investigation of this fascinating topic has begun. Today, social psychologists generally view their task as that of examining the manner in which the behavior, feelings, and thoughts of one individual are influenced by the behavior and/or characteristics of others. As a result, they seek to investigate virtually every imaginable aspect of human social behavior.

In conducting their research, social psychologists generally adopt one of two major approaches known, respectively, as the correlational and experimental methods. The first is characterized by the observation of existing relationships between variables, while the second is distinguished by attempts to examine such relationships by systematically varying one factor, and observing the effects of such variations upon the other. Both approaches offer important advantages, but most social psychologists tend to favor the experimental method because of its greater ability to deal with questions of cause and effect. In recent years, there has been a growing tendency on the part of social psychologists to conduct their experiments in the field as well as the laboratory. Such procedures offer the advantages of a more diverse sample of subjects, and the opportunity to study social behavior in natural settings. However, they are also more susceptible to the impact of uncontrolled, extraneous events.

In many cases, social psychologists employ the technique of *deception* in their research. This involves attempts to conceal the true nature of an experiment from participants. The use of deception is based on the belief that if subjects know the true purpose of an experiment, their behavior will be altered in undetermined ways, so that valid results cannot be obtained. The use of deception raises important ethical issues, but most social psychologists now believe that it is permissible, provided such precautions as the use of *informed consent* and a thorough *debriefing* of subjects at the conclusion of the study are adopted.

When subjects discover the hypothesis under study in an experiment, valid or meaningful results cannot usually be obtained. Thus, cues serving to communicate the hypothesis to research participants—*demand characteristics*, as they are usually termed—must be carefully eliminated from social psychological research. Fortunately, several techniques for accomplishing this goal have been developed, and demand characteristics now appear to be far less of a potential problem than was once the case.

GLOSSARY

Correlational method of research. An approach in which researchers attempt to determine whether two or more variables are related through careful observation of each.

Debriefing. Procedures following the end of an experiment whereby participants are informed of all deceptions employed, the true purposes of the study, and its possible contributions both to scientific knowledge and society. One major purpose of the debriefing is that of eliminating any negative reactions experienced by subjects during the study.

Deception. A procedure in which the true purposes of an experiment are withheld or concealed from subjects. The use of deception stems from the widely held belief that if subjects know the true goal of an experiment, their behavior will be altered from what it would normally be and no valid results can be obtained.

Demand characteristics. Any cues serving to communicate the hypothesis under investigation in an experiment to the subjects participating in it.

Dependent variable. The form of behavior (anything from direct acts toward others through expressions of social attitudes) under investigation in a social psychological experiment. The dependent variable is generally expected to change with alterations in the presence or strength of the independent variable.

Experimental method of research. An approach in which researchers attempt to determine whether a given factor influences some form of social behavior by (1) systematically varying its presence or strength, and (2) determining whether such variations have any effects on the behavior under study.

Field research. Research conducted in natural settings outside the laboratory. Field research has become increasingly popular in social psychology within recent years.

Hypothesis. A testable proposition, sometimes derived from a formal theory, but often suggested by other sources (e.g., conflicting findings in earlier research, observations of real-life events).

Independent variable. The factor systematically varied in an experiment. In social psychological research, the independent variable is generally some aspect of the social environment (the behavior or characteristics of others).

Informed consent. The principle that subjects be informed of any possible risks they will face in an experiment *before* agreeing to participate in it.

Role playing. A proposed alternative to deception in which subjects are provided with complete information concerning the purposes and methods of an experiment, and then asked to play the role of a naive participant who has not been supplied with such knowledge.

Simple and sovereign theories. Philosophical theories proposed mainly during the nineteenth century, which suggested that social behavior is based primarily on a single basic principle (e.g., the desire to obtain pleasure and avoid pain).

Theory. A systematic attempt to explain the occurrence of some natural phenomenon, consisting of (1) a set of basic concepts, and (2) a number of statements regarding the relationships between these concepts. In social psychology, theories are usually attempts to explain the occurrence of some important form of social behavior.

SUGGESTED READINGS FOR CHAPTER 1

Cook, S. W. A comment on the ethical issues involved in West, Gunn, and Chernicky's "Ubiquitous Watergate: An Attributional Analysis." *Journal of Personality and Social Psychology,* 1975, *32,* 66–68. A brief but insightful statement concerning several of the complex problems—and responsibilities—facing social scientists who wish to conduct research on human social behavior.

Gergen, K. J. Social psychology as history. *Journal of Personality and Social Psychology,* 1973, *26,* 309–320. A controversial article taking the position that because the phenomena it studies are subject to constant change over time, social psychology cannot be a science in quite the same sense as such fields as chemistry or physics. (If you choose to read this paper, be sure to see the reply by Schlenker listed below.)

Hendrick, C., and Jones, R. A. *The nature of theory and research in social psychology.* New York: Academic Press, 1972. A full-length treatment of the nature of theory in social psychology, and the various methods of research employed by social psychologists in their attempts to understand various aspects of human social behavior.

Schlenker, B. R. Social psychology and science. *Journal of Personality and Social Psychology,* 1974, *29,* 1–15. A spirited defense of the view that, in principle, social psychology can be just as rigorous and scientific in nature as older and more established disciplines such as chemistry, biology, or physics.

SOCIAL PERCEPTION: KNOWING OTHERS AND OURSELVES

NONVERBAL COMMUNICATION: THE LANGUAGE OF GAZES AND GESTURES

Unmasking the Face: Recognizing the Emotions of Others

Gazes and Stares: Eye Contact as a Clue to Others' Feelings

Body Language: Every Little Movement Has a Meaning of Its Own

ATTRIBUTION: INFERRING THE TRAITS AND MOTIVES OF OTHERS

From Acts to Dispositions: Knowing Others through Their Behavior

Attributions of Causality: Inferring the Causes of Behavior

Attributions of Sincerity: How to Recognize an Honest Person When You See One

Self-attribution: Knowing and Understanding Ourselves

PUTTING IT ALL TOGETHER: FORMING IMPRESSIONS OF OTHERS

Cognitive Algebra in Impression Formation: Do We Average or Add?

2

Usually, you make it a practice to refuse blind dates. This is because you have had so many unpleasant experiences in such situations that you decided long ago to avoid them at all costs. For once, though, you have been persuaded to make an exception to your rule. One of your friends has described a young man she knows in such glowing terms that you feel it may be worth one last try. At this very moment, the bell to your apartment rings, and your date arrives. As soon as you open the door, you realize that your friend did not exaggerate: the young man standing outside is indeed one of the best looking you have ever seen. As he enters, though, you notice a strange inconsistency in his style of dress. Above the waist, he looks as though he has just stepped out of a magazine ad for fashionable men's clothing (he is wearing a shirt, tie, and expensive-looking sport coat); below the waist he looks like a fugitive from skid row (he is wearing incredibly filthy jeans and old, ripped tennis shoes).

Since he greets you with a warm smile, though, you shrug off this unusual costume, and quickly agree to his suggestion that you dine at a locally popular (and quite expensive) restaurant. As he ushers you to his car, you notice that it is a sleek sports model, built for speed and fast maneuvers. Yet, much to your surprise, he drives at such a slow and torturous pace that you are soon followed by a long line of honking cars, each of which attempts to pass you on every straight piece of road. During dinner, your date acts in a very friendly and charming manner. He gazes into your eyes a great deal, leans over the table whenever you speak, and gives every sign of liking you very much. Yet, at the same time, he treats the waiter in a very hostile and rude manner. He rejects the wine he has ordered as unfit to drink, and sends several dishes back to the kitchen with loud complaints and demands for better service. In view of these actions, you are quite surprised when he leaves an extremely large tip on the table as you depart. You can't help wondering whether he has left such a large amount in order to impress you, to make amends for his harsh treatment of the waiter, or simply because he always shows such generosity.

As you walk out of the restaurant, your date suggests going to a movie, and offers two possible choices: a sugar-coated Walt Disney production, or a kinky, off-beat film known for its brutal violence. These suggestions take you by surprise, for you wonder how he can find both films appealing. During the movie (you opt for Walt Disney) he continues to act in a very friendly manner, holding your hand and complimenting your appearance. Yet, when he takes you home, he *refuses to come in for a cup of coffee, and instead of kissing you good night, shakes your hand in a cold and formal manner. As he leaves, he murmurs that he had a very enjoyable time, and will call you again soon—but frowns at precisely the same moment he is making these statements. After he departs, you sit in your apartment in a state of mild confusion, pondering many questions about your date. Is he really a warm and friendly person, as his actions toward you during most of the evening suggest, or a cold and hostile one as his treatment of the waiter and cool parting indicate? Why did he drive so slowly? What accounts for his unusual taste in films? Did he really like you as much as he seemed to, or was it all part of a carefully staged act? And do you yourself like him? So confusing and inconsistent are your thoughts on these and other issues that you sit up late into the night trying to make sense out of your conflicting reactions.*

Fortunately for our peace of mind, most of the individuals we meet provide us with far more consistent information than the person described above. Yet, despite this fact, getting to know and understand them is still a complex and challenging task. Basically, this is the case for two major reasons. First, other persons are—like ourselves—highly complex individuals. In fact, each presents us with something of a unique puzzle: they are all different, and the differences between them occur along an almost limitless number of dimensions. As a result, just when we think we have finally managed to figure out what makes them "tick," they say or do something which throws us into a state of total confusion. Second, for reasons of their own, others often attempt to conceal their true feelings, motives, and characteristics from us. They often say things they don't mean, hide their emotions behind an impassive mask, attempt to alter their physical appearance, and either pretend to possess characteristics they don't really have, or conceal ones they do possess. As a result, looks are often deceiving, and understanding others is a far more complex task than might otherwise be the case (see Figure 2-1).

Despite these formidable obstacles, though, we usually manage to obtain a relatively good understanding of others. Since we can't read their minds and find out about their inner thoughts and feelings directly, it is obvious that we must accomplish this task in a less direct manner. Like amateur detectives, we attempt to piece together an accurate understanding of others on the basis of the external clues they provide—their behavior, physical appearance, mode of dress, manner of speech, facial expressions, and so on. As you can probably guess, there is a great deal of room for error in such judgments, and serious misunderstandings often result when individuals "read" each other incorrectly. Yet, in general, our perceptions of others are remarkably accurate.

In an important sense, our perceptions of other persons set the stage for our later interactions with them. That is, our perceptions of their feelings, motives,

"No, I'm the one from Rhode Island . . . he's from Texas."

FIGURE 2-1. *As shown in this cartoon, looks are often deceiving and lead us to draw false conclusions about others. (Source: Copyright 1968; reprinted by permission of* Saturday Review *and Bill Hoest.)*

intentions, and characteristics strongly affect the way in which we react to and with them.   Indeed, it is hard to imagine any aspect of our social relations which is *not* strongly affected by such perceptions.   Largely for this reason, we have chosen to begin with the process of **social perception.**   In particular, we will focus on three different aspects of this important topic.   First, we will examine the manner in which we attempt to determine the temporary states of others— their present emotions and feelings.   As we shall soon see, **nonverbal cues,** such as facial expressions, body posture, and expressive movements, play an important role in this process.   Second, we will consider the manner in which we seek to infer the more stable characteristics of others—their motives, intentions, and traits—from careful observation of their overt actions.   As we have already noted in Chapter 1, the study of this process (usually known as **attribution**) has recently become one of the dominant themes of social psychological research.   Thus, we will consider it in some detail here.   Finally, we will examine the manner in which information about others, once obtained, is combined into consistent and unified impressions of them (**impression formation**).   As will soon become apparent, it is largely through these processes of nonverbal communication, attribution, and impression formation that we come to know the persons around us, and, to a surprising extent, ourselves as well.

One task we must often seek to accomplish in terms of social perception is that of determining the temporary states of others—their present moods, emotions, and feelings. Accurate knowledge of such states is important for several reasons. First, as you probably know from your own experience, others' behavior is often as strongly affected by temporary fluctuations in their mood or feelings as by their more lasting dispositions. Even the sweetest persons have their irritable days on which they are best avoided, and even cruel and hostile individuals are capable of friendly acts at times when they are in especially high spirits. Second, information regarding others' moods or feelings frequently provides us with some indication of their reactions to us and our behavior. And feedback of this type is often essential for effective interaction with them.

In many cases, we learn about the emotional states or moods of others in a very straightforward manner—they simply tell us how they feel. In other instances, however, they do not provide us with such information, or may actually attempt to conceal it from us. Fortunately, even under these conditions we can usually obtain some indication of their present mood or emotions from careful observation of subtle nonverbal cues. That is, we can tell how they feel by observing their facial expressions, pattern of eye contact with us, and position, movement, and posture of their bodies. Together, this subtle language of gazes and gestures can often tell us much about the emotional reactions or current feelings of the persons around us.

Unmasking the Face: Recognizing the Emotions of Others

The notion that others' emotions are often revealed in their facial expressions is far from new. For example, writing more than two thousand years in the past, the Roman orator Cicero remarked that, "The face is the image of the soul . . . ," and in his famous play *Macbeth,* Shakespeare wrote the lines, "Your face . . . is a book where men may read strange matters." Yet, despite its long history in philosophy and literature, the suggestion that facial expressions provide us with reliable clues to the internal states of others was not the subject of systematic study until well into the twentieth century.

The first question raised by researchers interested in studying facial expressions seemed quite straightforward: what emotions, precisely, are reflected on the face? Despite its apparent simplicity, though, it proved very difficult to answer. Conflicting results were reported for many years, and it is only in fairly recent times that an acceptable resolution has emerged (Woodworth, 1938). At present, it is generally agreed that six different emotions are represented by distinctive facial expressions: happiness, sadness, surprise, fear, anger, and disgust (Ekman and Friesen, 1975; Ekman, Friesen, and Ellsworth, 1972). This does not mean, of course, that we are capable of only six different emotional expressions. Rather, since our emotions can occur in many combinations (for example, anger along with fear), and since they can all vary greatly in terms of intensity, the number of possible variations on these six basic themes is almost limitless.

Two additional questions regarding the nature of facial expressions stemmed from the writings of Charles Darwin (1872), originator of the famous theory of natural selection. Briefly, Darwin held that such expressions represent part of our basic biological inheritance, and as such, are innately determined. This conclusion then led him to formulate two interesting predictions. First, since they are largely inherited, similar facial expressions should be shown by all human beings whenever they experience specific emotions (i.e., we should all smile when happy, frown when sad, and so on). Second, since these facial expressions are presumably universal, they should always be recognized as indicative of particular emotional states (i.e., a smile should always be recognized as a sign of happiness, a scowl as a sign of anger, etc.). Initial attempts to investigate the accuracy of these suggestions yielded largely negative results: if there were universal facial expressions of emotion, early researchers had a great deal of difficulty in finding them (Feleky, 1914). However, evidence gathered within the past few years by Paul Ekman and his associates (Ekman and Friesen, 1975; Ekman, Friesen, and Ellsworth, 1972) now provides impressive support for at least modified versions of both of Darwin's proposals.

Turning first to the suggestion that facial expressions of emotion are themselves universal, Ekman and his colleagues performed a series of studies in which the faces of individuals from widely different cultures were videotaped as they watched stress-inducing films. The results of these investigations were quite clear-cut: despite large cultural differences between them, subjects from different countries generally showed very much the same facial expressions in response to the events on the screen. Even more impressive evidence for the apparent universality of at least some facial expressions was obtained in a later series of investigations conducted with subjects from isolated regions of New Guinea. These individuals, who had previously experienced only limited contact with the members of other cultures, were asked to imagine various emotion-producing events (e.g., your friend has come and you are happy; your child has died), and then asked to show how they would feel in each case. As you can readily see in Figure 2-2, the facial expressions they demonstrated were virtually identical to those we might show ourselves in response to such events.

On the basis of such findings, it seems reasonable to conclude that when experiencing one of the six emotions mentioned above, human beings do generally show a tendency to demonstrate distinctive and universal facial expressions. But please take note: the fact that we possess a *tendency* to demonstrate such expressions in no way implies that we will always do so. Cultural norms often prohibit us from showing our true emotions, even when they are quite intense. For example, it is considered quite rude and inappropriate to smile broadly during a serious meeting or lecture, or to show open signs of anger against others in many situations. In these cases, even strong emotional experiences will often fail to be accompanied by corresponding facial expressions.

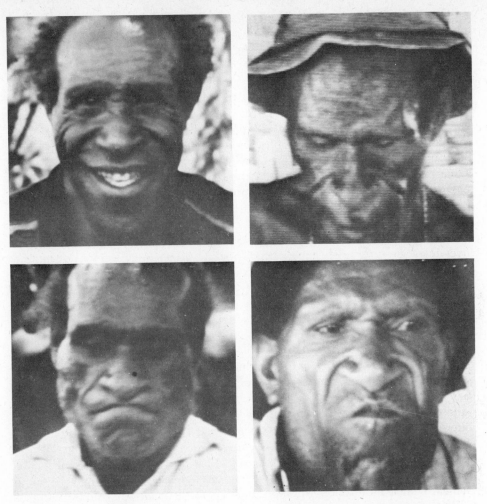

FIGURE 2-2. *When asked to imagine various emotion-producing events, members of isolated groups living in New Guinea demonstrated facial expressions highly similar to those shown by individuals in many other countries. These findings provide evidence for the view that there are at least some universal facial expressions of emotion. (Source: From Ekman and Friesen, 1975, p. 27, by permission of the authors.)*

And large individual differences in emotional expressiveness and style (to which we will soon return) often tend to cloud the picture. As a result, although all human beings do seem to possess tendencies to smile when they are happy, frown when they are sad, and so on, they will not necessarily demonstrate such expressions whenever these feelings are aroused.

If various facial expressions are indeed universal, it seems quite reasonable to expect that they will be readily recognized by individuals in all corners of the earth. That this is actually the case is suggested by additional studies conducted by Ekman and his co-workers. For example, in one investigation a set of photographs depicting the six emotions mentioned above were presented to subjects in several different nations (the U.S., Brazil, Chile, Argentina, Japan), along with instructions to identify the emotion being shown. As you can see in Figure 2-3, subjects' responses generally evidenced a high degree of consensus. That is, a smile was recognized as indicating happiness, a scowl as representing anger, and so on, in all of the countries involved.

Although these findings seem to provide strong evidence for the view that various facial expressions are interpreted and "read" in much the same manner all over the world, they are open to question in one respect. Specifically, it is possible that the subjects in these studies had merely learned to identify such expressions as a result of the indirect contact with each other's cultures provided by television, movies, magazines, and similar sources. In order to determine if this was the case, Ekman and his colleagues conducted several additional studies with the isolated groups from New Guinea mentioned earlier. Since these individuals had previously experienced very little contact with persons from other cultures, it was reasoned that if they, too, recognized various facial expressions, convincing evidence for the universality of such expressions would be obtained. In the studies performed, subjects were read stories involving various emotions, and then asked to point to the photograph which fit each one. As you can see in Figure 2-3, their responses were quite similar to those of individuals from other, less isolated regions.

Taken together, the research conducted by Ekman and others (Izard, 1971) seems to suggest that there is indeed a degree of universality in facial expressions of emotion. Individuals all over the world do tend to show distinctive expressions when experiencing anger, sorrow, joy, and other strong feelings. Further, they readily recognize such expressions when they are shown by others. In sum, it appears that in contrast to the language of spoken words, the language of the face usually requires no interpreter.

Individual Differences in Emotional Expression: Good "Senders" and Bad. As we noted above, there are large individual differences in degree of facial expressiveness. That is, some persons tend to demonstrate more distinct and visible facial expressions than others. In your own experience, you have probably known individuals who show very little facial expression, remaining "poker-faced" most of the time, as well as others whose emotions seem to spill out onto their faces in a very uninhibited manner. Obviously, those in the second category are much easier to "read" than those in the first—they provide us with more external clues to their internal feelings and moods. But what factors account for these large individual differences? Why are some persons much better transmitters of emotional messages than others? A recent series of investigations conducted by Ross Buck and his colleagues sheds some light on this interesting issue (Buck, 1975; Buck, Miller and Caul, 1974).

In these experiments, one group of subjects *(senders)* was given the task of observing a diverse series of slides (e.g., pictures of male and female nudes, pleasant landscapes, etc.) and describing their emotional reactions to each.

Percent Agreement in Judging the Photos

		United States	*Brazil*	*Chile*	*Argentina*	*Japan*	*New Guinea*
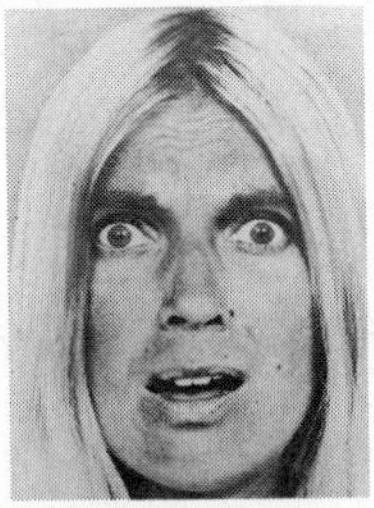	Fear	85%	67%	68%	54%	66%	54%
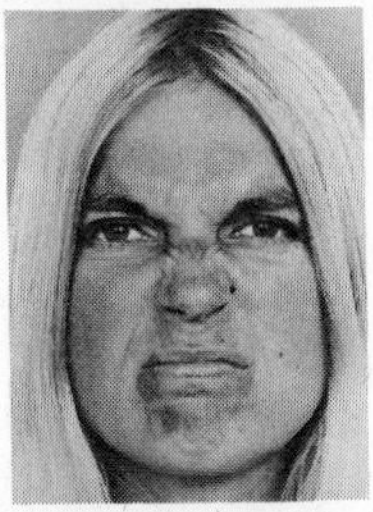	Disgust	92%	97%	92%	92%	90%	44%
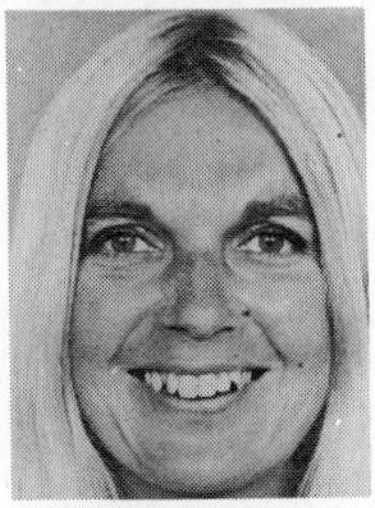	Happiness	97%	95%	95%	98%	100%	82%
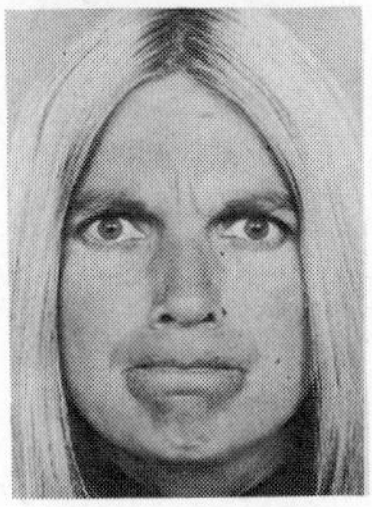	Anger	67%	90%	94%	90%	90%	50%

FIGURE 2-3. *When asked to identify the emotions shown in photos similar to the ones shown above, individuals from several different countries, as well as those from culturally isolated groups living in New Guinea, showed a relatively high degree of consensus. These findings suggest that certain facial expressions are universally recognized as indicative of particular emotional states. (Adapted from Ekman and Friesen, 1975, pp. 25, 27, 62, 76, 97, 112.)*

Their physiological responses (heart rate, skin conductance) were also recorded during this period. Unknown to the senders, a second group of subjects observed their facial expressions by means of a TV camera as they watched the slides. The observers' task was that of guessing what emotion the senders experienced on each occasion. Results indicated that, in general, observers were quite accurate in their performance. That is, they were often successful in identifying the emotions actually reported by the senders. As you might suspect, however, large individual differences existed, so that some senders were much easier for their observers to "read" than others. When these differences were examined more closely, an interesting pattern came to light. It appeared that senders could be divided into two groups on the basis of their degree of expressiveness and their level of physiological arousal. One group—labeled **internalizers** by Buck—evidenced very little facial expressiveness, but a high level of physiological arousal as they watched the slides. Not surprisingly, they were quite difficult for observers to "read." In contrast, a second group—labeled **externalizers**—showed a great deal of facial expressiveness, but low levels of physiological arousal. Not surprisingly, observers had much less difficulty in guessing the emotional reactions of these persons. In short, it appeared that senders fell into two distinct categories: either they seemed to "bottle up" their emotional reactions, showing little in the way of overt facial expressions, but a high level of internal arousal, or they let their emotions appear freely on their faces, while at the same time showing lower levels of internal arousal.

Further comparisons between the two groups by means of personality inventories revealed that internalizers were also significantly lower in self-confidence and extroversion than externalizers. These findings seem to confirm what informal observation and common sense suggest: individuals who are outgoing and self-confident often show their emotions openly and provide us with many clues to their internal state. Those who are inhibited and lacking in such confidence often inhibit external signs of emotion and provide us with fewer clues of this type.

One additional finding of Buck's research we should also mention is that, as has been the case in many other studies, women were found to be much better transmitters of nonverbal cues than men. That is, regardless of their sex, observers were more successful in identifying the emotions experienced by female than male senders. Given the fact that males in our society (and many others) are taught from early childhood on to inhibit outward signs of emotion, this is not very surprising. In a very real sense, they are trained to adopt an inexpressive style. That such differences between men and women stem from the contrasting socialization practices they encounter, rather than from innate factors, is suggested by the fact that similar large differences between the sexes have failed to emerge in studies with young children (Buck, 1975). Apparently, it takes several years for males to learn to inhibit outward signs of emotion. Perhaps these differences between men and women will fade in the coming years as some of the traditional distinctions between male and female roles become more diffuse (see Chapter 4).

Facial Deceit: The Eyes Don't Lie—Or Do They? Given that there are universal facial expressions of emotion, it seems only reasonable to expect that we will usually be quite accurate in reading the faces of the persons around us. In general, this is quite true; both informal observation and the results of several experiments suggest that we *can* usually recognize the emotional states of others quite accurately from their facial expressions (Buck, Miller, and Caul, 1974; Ekman and Friesen, 1975). Yet, there are also many cases in which we make errors in this respect. For example, we may overlook warning signs indicating that we are angering or annoying another person, ignore the fact that they are surprised or upset by our words, or fail to notice that they are in a sad or depressed mood. One reason for such errors has already been discussed: many individuals inhibit their overt facial expressions and so provide us with very little to go by. Another reason for such errors is that often, we simply don't watch the faces of others closely enough to notice the clues they present. This is due partly to the fact that it is impolite to gaze directly at others for long periods of time, and partly because we simply don't want to be burdened with knowledge of their emotional reactions—after all, we might have to do something about them! Perhaps the most important reason for our errors in reading the facial expressions of others, however, lies in the fact that they frequently seek to deceive us.

In many cases, other persons attempt to demonstrate emotions they don't feel, hide ones they are experiencing, or substitute one for another. There are several reasons why they may choose to engage in **facial deceit.** First, they may simply be following cultural rules or norms which indicate that it is inappropriate to demonstrate certain emotions in particular situations. Second, they may be complying with the requirements of a particular vocation. Actors, diplomats, trial attorneys, doctors, politicians, and many others often find it essential, as part of their job, to control their facial expressions. For example, physicians are not supposed to evidence signs of shock or disgust while examining patients. Similarly, diplomats are routinely expected to conceal their own emotions and to demonstrate reactions they don't actually feel while conducting their countries' foreign affairs. Perhaps the most common reason why individuals attempt to control their facial expressions, however, is simply their own selfish needs. That is, it is frequently to their personal benefit to deceive us in this manner. To mention just two examples, a rising young executive may find it necessary to demonstrate positive reactions to her immediate superior even if she finds her repellent; any other course of action might damage her chances for advancement. And a bully attempting to out-bluff an opponent must conceal all signs of fear. With a little thought, you can easily come up with many other instances in which one individual can benefit from deceiving others regarding his or her true emotional states.

Facial deceit can take many different forms, but the three most common are qualifying, modulating, and falsifying. In **qualifying,** individuals add a further expression to one they have just shown as a comment upon it. For example, an angry person may smile as a sign that he or she is not quite as upset as it seems. In **modulating,** individuals adjust their facial expressions so as to show more or less of an emotion than they are really experiencing. For example, a person on the receiving end of a series of flattering comments may pretend to experience less pleasure than he really does. Finally, in **falsifying,** persons either pretend to experience some feeling which they do not have, show no emotion when they are actually aroused, or substitute one reaction for another. This is the most deceitful form of facial control, and can often be used to seriously mislead others about our true emotional states.

As you probably know from your own experience, some individuals acquire great skill at controlling their emotional expressions—and not all of them are on the stage! Confidence artists, petty swindlers, and even successful salesmen and women frequently manage to wring a handsome living from this ability. Indeed, through long years of practice, such persons may become so skilled at controlling their emotional expressions that it is virtually impossible to penetrate their deceit. In most cases, though, subtle clues indicating that another person is attempting to mislead us are present, and can be readily observed if we take the trouble to look for them with care. Basically, such clues stem from three different sources.

First, they may be provided by gaps in the total pattern of reactions shown. When others attempt to control their facial expressions, they generally concentrate on one part of the face or another. Thus, by looking for inconsistencies in the pattern of reactions shown, we can often get some hint that deception is occurring. For example, an individual feigning surprise may raise his brows and open his eyes widely—but forget to let his mouth drop open. Second, such clues to deception may be provided by the timing of the reactions shown. Genuine emotional responses appear on the face very quickly. Thus, if several seconds elapse between a crucial stimulus and another person's facial reaction, there may be grounds for suspecting that the emotion shown is not a genuine one. For example, if there is a long pause between the end of your joke and another person's laughter, you can be fairly certain that the reaction is staged. And finally, deceit may be betrayed by what Ekman and Friesen (1975) term **microexpressions**—very brief reactions lasting for a small fraction of a second which reveal an individual's true emotions. By keeping a careful watch for these three types of subtle clues, we can often succeed in unmasking the face, and so acquire accurate information about the true emotional states of the persons around us.

Gazes and Stares: Eye Contact as a Clue to Others' Feelings

The eyes have frequently been described as "windows to the soul," and in some respects, at least, this appears to be true. A growing body of research suggests that we often *can* learn a great deal about others' internal states from their eyes (Exline, 1971; Mehrabian, 1971). In particular, much is revealed by the amount and pattern of others' eye contact with us. First, we often use such information as a rough indicator of their overall affective state: the more they gaze at us, at least up to a point, the more positive we assume they feel. Indeed, when others avoid our gaze we usually conclude that they feel guilty, are harboring negative thoughts, or are generally depressed (Knapp, 1972).

Second, and perhaps of even greater importance, we use the amount and pattern of others' gazes as evidence of their feelings toward us. A number of experiments indicate that we interpret a high level of eye contact from another as a sign of friendliness and liking. For example, in a study conducted by Kleinke, Meeker, and La Fong (1974), college students watched videotapes of supposedly engaged couples. In one condition the couples (actually confederates of the experimenters) never looked into each other's eyes during their conversation, while in another, they demonstrated a high level of eye contact. When later asked to report their reactions to the couples they viewed, subjects rated those showing a high degree of eye contact as liking each other more, and as having better potential for a successful marriage. That amount of mutual gazing is actually closely related to feelings of liking or love, and not merely preceived in this manner, is suggested by another experiment conducted by Rubin (1970). In this investigation couples who reported being strongly in love did actually gaze into each other's eyes more often and for a longer period of time than couples who were either weakly in love or were strangers.

Since we generally interpret a high level of eye contact from another as an indication of friendliness or liking, it might be expected that, in general, we will both like and prefer individuals who show such behavior. These predictions, too, have been confirmed. Several studies have demonstrated that subjects report more favorable reactions to persons who engage in a great deal of eye contact with them than to persons who show a lower level of gazing (Kleinke, Staneski, and Berger, 1975). Moreover, when given a choice between high and low gazers, they generally choose the former (Stass and Willis, 1967).

Although a high level of eye contact from another person is usually interpreted as a sign of positive feelings on the part of the individual, there is one important exception to this rule—*staring*. When another individual gazes at us in a continuous manner, and maintains such eye contact, regardless of any actions on our part, his or her behavior may be interpreted as a sign of hostility rather than friendship. Research with animals suggests that stares are often used as a threatening gesture, and frequently precede overt attacks (Van Hoof, 1967). Some indication that stares may sometimes have similar negative effects upon human beings is provided by an ingenious series of field studies conducted by Ellsworth, Carlsmith, and Henson (1972).

In these investigations, motorists waiting at a red light were exposed to either stares from another driver, stares from a pedestrian, or no stares from any source. The speed with which they drove off once the light turned green was then recorded in order to determine whether subjects exposed to the stares would seek to escape from these stimuli as quickly as possible. Results offered strong support for this suggestion: drivers who received stares from either another motorist or a pedestrian crossed the intersection significantly faster than drivers who received none (see Table 2-1). Moreover, they evidenced many signs of tension and nervousness during the period when they were receiving the confederate's continuous gaze. For example, they fumbled with their clothing,

TABLE 2-1. *Stares are often interpreted as a sign of hostility on the part of others. Motorists waiting at a red light who received expressionless stares from another driver crossed the intersection significantly faster when the light turned green than motorists who received no stares. Further, these effects occurred regardless of the sex of the person doing the staring, and regardless of the sex of the drivers. Numbers shown represent seconds to cross the intersection. (Adapted from Ellsworth, Carlsmith, and Henson, 1972.)*

STARE				NO STARE			
Male Confederate		*Female Confederate*		*Male Confederate*		*Female Confederate*	
Male Drivers	Female Drivers	Male Drivers	Female Drivers	Male Drivers	Female Drivers	Male Drivers	Female Drivers
5.6	5.8	5.5	5.6	6.3	6.5	6.0	7.0

tuned and retuned their radios, revved up their engines, and glanced repeatedly at the traffic signal. In contrast, drivers who were not the recipients of stares rarely showed such behavior.

Together with the findings of other studies (Ellsworth and Carlsmith, 1973; Ellsworth and Langer, 1976), these results suggest that eye contact can communicate negative as well as positive feelings. In short, it appears that we can often learn as much about another person's feelings toward us from cold and icy stares as from warm and friendly glances.

Body Language: Every Little Movement Has a Meaning of Its Own

Have you ever (1) felt so dejected that your whole body seemed to droop, (2) pounded your fist on a table in anger, or (3) found yourself leaning toward a person you liked as you held a conversation? If so, you will not be surprised to learn that we can often obtain a great deal of information about others' internal states from the position, posture, and movements of their bodies. First, such **body language** can help reveal their current emotional state. On a global level, a large amount of body movement (e.g., fidgeting, continuous shifting of legs and arms) suggests that an individual is emotionally aroused—although it does not in itself indicate which emotion he or she is experiencing (Knapp, 1972). More specific information about a person's feelings is often provided by *gestures*. For example, a clenched fist usually indicates anger, a covering of the eyes shame or embarrassment, and a rubbing together of the hands anticipation or excitement (Knapp, 1972; Krout, 1954).

Together, clues from another person's movements and gestures can often paint a vivid picture of his or her present emotional state. But this is far from the entire story; body language also tells us much more. In particular, it frequently

Gestures often reveal that an individual is experiencing a particular emotion. Can you guess what emotions are being revealed by the gestures shown above?

reveals positive or negative feelings toward us on the part of others. Perhaps one of the clearest clues in this respect is another's bodily orientation. If someone with whom we are conversing faces us directly and leans forward, this is usually a clear sign that he or she likes us. In contrast, if another individual orients his or her body away from us and leans back while we interact, this creates the impression that he or she dislikes us (Mehrabian, 1968a).

Some idea of the many other expressive acts which may reveal another's liking or disliking for us is provided by a recent study conducted by Clore, Wiggins, and Itkin (1975). These researchers first presented a list of over 100 nonverbal behaviors to a group of students, asking them to select the ones which would be interpreted as most positive and most negative. Among the behaviors included in the first category by subjects were: sitting directly facing another person, moving toward him, and nodding one's head in agreement. Included in the second category were: looking at the ceiling, shaking one's head in disagreement, cleaning one's fingernails, or playing with the ends of one's hair. (Your own personal experience probably suggests how behaviors in the first category would give you the distinct impression that another person was interested in and liked you, while those in the second would suggest that he or she was bored with and disliked you.) In a second part of their investigation, Clore, Wiggins, and Itkin had a female actress make two videotapes in which she held a brief conversation with a man she was supposedly meeting for the first time. In one tape she performed the positive actions mentioned above, while in the second, she performed the negative responses. When subjects watched these films, they reported that the woman seemed to like her partner much more in the first version than in the second, and also indicated liking her better in the first film themselves.

In addition to revealing others' liking or disliking for us, body cues can also transmit a somewhat stronger reaction—sexual interest or receptivity. For example, consider the following description of the manner in which a woman who finds a particular man attractive may communicate this information to him (Fast, 1970, p. 88):

A big part of the way she transmits her message is also in stance, posture, or movement. An available woman moves in a studied way . . . the movement of her body, hips, and shoulders telegraphs her availability. She may sit with her legs apart, symbolically open and inviting, or she may affect a gesture in which one hand touches her breast in a near caress. She may stroke her thighs as she talks or walk with a languorous roll to her hips. Some of her movements are studied and conscious, some completely unconscious.

That men, too, can communicate sexual interest or attraction through body language is indicated by the following description of one proverbial "ladies' man" (Fast, 1970, p. 85):

But Mike has more. He has dozens of little gestures, perhaps unconscious ones that send out elaborations of his sexual message. When Mike leans up against a mantel in a room to look around at the women, his hips are thrust forward slightly . . . and his legs are usually apart. There is something in this stance that spells sex.

Of course, such cues are often far more subtle than the ones described above. Given the importance of the message they convey, however, searching carefully for them may well prove worth the effort!

Nonverbal Communication: A Concluding Comment. Although we have described nonverbal cues from others' faces, gazes, and bodies separately, it is obvious that they generally occur together. When we interact with another person we usually receive input from all three sources at once. Sometimes the cues from one source conflict with those from another (Ekman and Friesen, 1974), but generally, they provide a fairly consistent picture. In most cases, then, the information provided by this unspoken language of expressions, gazes, and gestures gets us off to a very good start in our attempt to know the feelings and emotions of the persons around us.

ATTRIBUTION: INFERRING THE TRAITS AND MOTIVES OF OTHERS

Accurate knowledge of others' emotional states and feelings is both useful and important. After all, such information often helps us to interact with them in an effective and appropriate manner. Yet, it is only part of the picture. Knowing how someone feels at the present time may help explain his or her current behavior, but it is usually of little use in predicting how this person will behave tomorrow—or perhaps even ten minutes in the future. Emotions, moods, and feelings generally fluctuate so quickly that they do not provide a lasting basis for understanding or predicting others' behavior. In our attempts to know the persons around us, therefore, we are often concerned with more lasting causes of their actions, such as their stable characteristics, intentions, and motives. The process through which we acquire such knowledge is known as **attribution**, and has recently become one of the dominant themes of social psychological

NONVERBAL CUES AND CONVERSATIONS: KNOWING WHEN IT'S YOUR TURN TO SPEAK

As we have already seen, nonverbal cues from others' facial expressions, gazes, and body movements often provide us with important information regarding their internal states. Such cues also play another, and perhaps less obvious, role in social interaction. Specifically, they often serve as regulators of social behavior, providing for its smooth and orderly flow. Perhaps this function is best illustrated in the realm of conversation. Generally, conversations proceed in an orderly manner, with the participants alternating turns as speaker and listener. Although this might at first seem to be an automatic process, research by Duncan (Duncan, 1972; Duncan and Niederehe, 1974) and others suggests that, in fact, it is heavily dependent upon sets of subtle signals through which participants indicate to each other that they wish to take the floor, are willing to give it up, or are unwilling to yield in this fashion. Careful analysis of actual conversations suggests that listeners frequently signal their desire to take the floor by such cues as (1) shifting their heads away from the speaker, (2) engaging in audible inhalation (taking a deep breath in preparation for speech), and (3) gesticulating (motioning) with their hands. Similarly, speakers often signal their willingness to yield the floor by (1) ending hand gesticulations (returning their hands to a resting position), (2) stretching out the final syllable in their last sentence, or (3) showing a drop in the volume of their voice (a kind of trailing-off effect). Finally, speakers frequently signal their unwillingness to yield to

the listener by beginning hand gesticulation. In short, they indicate that they wish to continue speaking by literally waving the listener off.

You can readily demonstrate the function of such cues for yourself in two ways. First, simply observe several conversations between other persons. While doing so, it is best to remain as inconspicuous as possible. For example, you might pretend to be reading or writing. Pay special attention to the points at which participants shift roles (i.e., the listener becomes the speaker, and vice versa). If you watch carefully, you will almost always notice one or more of the turn-yielding and turn-taking signals mentioned above.

Second, you can demonstrate the importance of these cues in your own conversations. Try getting the floor without giving the appropriate turn-taking signals, and purposely ignore the turn-yielding signals provided by your partner. Our reactions to and use of these cues is normally so automatic that you may have some difficulty in omitting or ignoring them. To the extent you succeed, though, you will probably find that your conversations with others become increasingly choppy and disorganized. You will interrupt each other repeatedly, and the whole interaction will take on a confused and disconnected character. These effects illustrate an important point: while we are usually quite unaware of the presence and operation of many nonverbal cues, they often play a crucial role in the regulation of social behavior.

research. Indeed, it may well be the single topic receiving the greatest amount of attention from social psychologists at the present time. This flood of interest in attribution processes seems to have stemmed from two major sources: increasing recognition of its central role in social perception, and growing awareness of its widespread impact upon virtually all forms of social behavior (Shaver, 1975). For both of these reasons, it is well deserving of our careful and detailed attention.

From Acts to Dispositions: Knowing Others through Their Behavior

In our attempts to know and understand the persons around us, we usually draw on several different sources of information. First, we often pay close attention to their physical appearance, realizing that such factors as their age, style of dress, physical attractiveness, and even skin color can yield important clues regarding their major characteristics. Second, we frequently attempt to acquire such knowledge in an indirect manner, by questioning their friends or acquaintances. Such individuals frequently have access to information of an intimate or personal nature which we could not readily obtain ourselves, and winning their cooperation and assistance may greatly simplify our task. Third, we may attempt to gain increased knowledge of others directly, simply by asking them to confide their hidden thoughts and motives to us. Although most persons are reluctant to engage in such self-disclosure, they do occasionally "let their hair down" and provide us with the information we desire.

Although all of these potential sources of information are important, there is little doubt that the major basis of our knowledge about others is careful observation of their overt actions. That is, we seem to acquire the bulk of our information about other persons by (1) observing their behavior, and then (2) *inferring* their possession of various traits, motives, or intentions (Heider, 1958; Kelley, 1972, 1973). As we noted above, the process by which we infer the stable characteristics of others from their overt actions is known as *attribution,* and it is with this important process that the remainder of the present discussion will be concerned.

At first, it might seem that our task in moving from the overt acts of others to inferences regarding their characteristics or intentions would be a relatively simple one. After all, the behavior of other persons is highly varied, and provides us with a rich source of data upon which to base our attributions. Unfortunately, though, this task is greatly complicated by two important factors.

First, other people often seek to mislead or deceive us. For example, they may say things they don't mean, act in ways inconsistent with their actual beliefs and values, and attempt to disguise their true motives or intentions. In such cases, we can learn nothing about the persons involved except, perhaps, that they are dishonest, deceitful people. Even worse, we may actually be led to form erroneous impressions of them if we do not take care.

Second, and of even greater importance, the actions of others are frequently shaped and determined not by their internal states or dispositions, but rather by external factors beyond their control. For example, students often slog painfully on through dull and tedious assignments not because of any intrinsic interest in such materials, but simply because they are course requirements. Similarly, it is often necessary to be polite to one's in-laws or superiors on the job even if they are strongly disliked; the consequences of acting in any other manner are too painful to permit any choice. In these and many other cases, the behavior of other persons is shaped by various external factors and cannot by employed as a valid basis for inferring their major characteristics. A preliminary step in the attribution process, therefore, is often that of determining whether the actions of others stem primarily from internal or external causes. This is an especially important point, and one to which we will soon return below.

Given these complicating factors, the task of inferring the stable characteristics of others from their overt behavior appears to be a formidable one. Yet, common sense suggests that we are frequently able to perform it quite effectively. Usually, we *can* identify their major dispositions, determine the goals they are seeking, and recognize the motives behind their behavior, despite the complexities already mentioned. Although it is not yet entirely clear how we manage to accomplish this task, a theoretical framework proposed by Jones and Davis (1965) seems to shed considerable light on this question.

According to these investigators, the secret of our success in moving from observations of overt behavior to accurate attributions concerning other persons lies in our tendency to focus on two specific aspects of their behavior. First, Jones and Davis suggest that we pay particular attention to those actions by others for which they could have had one or at most a few distinct reasons. The major advantage offered by this strategy is that it permits us to draw firm conclusions regarding the motives behind their actions. For example, imagine that you learned that one of your casual acquaintances, whom you do not know very well, has accepted a job which (1) requires her to move to one of the most attractive cities in the nation, (2) involves extremely stimulating and interesting work, and (3) pays $35,000 per year. Would this information tell you anything conclusive about this individual? Probably not, for there are so many potential reasons for her having accepted this job (its favorable salary, geographic locale, etc.), that it is impossible to determine which one, if any, was of primary importance. But now imagine that instead, you learn that the same person has accepted a job which (1) requires her to move to a small town in a very unattractive part of the country, (2) involves extremely dull and tedious work, but (3) pays $35,000 per year as a starting salary. Here the situation is entirely different for there is only one apparent reason for her decision: the princely rate of pay. Thus, in this case, you could probably conclude that this person values money more than pleasant geographic surroundings, interesting or fulfilling work, the cultural opportunities available only in larger towns, and so on. By comparing these two examples, you can probably see why we can generally acquire more useful information about others from behavior for which they could have had only one or at most a few distinct reasons than from behavior for which they could have had many (Newtson, 1974).

Second, Jones and Davis suggest that we tend to focus our attention on those actions of others which depart from usual patterns of behavior. That is, we concentrate upon those actions which set them apart from most other persons, and so may reasonably be assumed to reflect their unique motives, characteristics, and goals. Again, the advantages to be gained from such a strategy are easily illustrated. For example, imagine that all you know about another person is that he (1) eats a light breakfast in the morning, (2) drives his car to work, and (3) goes to the movies on the weekend. Would such information provide you with firm grounds for inferring much about his unique personality? Probably not, for all these actions are quite ordinary in nature and would also be demonstrated by many other persons. But imagine that instead, you learn that this person (1) swims nude in the ocean in December, (2) has a ten-foot electric fence around his property, and (3) keeps a pet cobra in his basement. You can probably see at once that such information provides fertile ground for attributing all sorts of interesting characteristics to him (for example, he is a health fanatic, suffers from strange anxieties, but enjoys living dangerously), and that you would find it much more useful to know these facts than those contained in the first set. It is little wonder then, that in our attempts to unravel the mysterious inner workings of other persons, we often focus on those aspects of their behavior which set them apart from typical or average members of their society. Indeed, for this purpose, the more unusual or bizarre their actions, the better!

A third type of behavior not mentioned by Jones and Davis (1965), but which may also be of particular value in our attempts to infer the characteristics of others is suggested by the fact that behavior demonstrated in public is usually far more conventional and conforming than that shown in private. For example, persons who enjoy unusual sexual practices tend to behave much like their more conventional friends and neighbors in public and indulge their exotic tastes only in the privacy of their own homes. Similarly, individuals holding extreme or unpopular political or social views often refrain from voicing them in public, and will discuss them only under relatively private conditions. This disparity between public and private behavior suggests that, in general, actions shown in private are more indicative of individuals' unique characteristics, motives, and beliefs than those demonstrated in the public domain. As a result, it seems reasonable to expect that more can often be learned from careful observation of the former than similar study of the latter.

In sum, it appears that our success in inferring the characteristics, motives, and intentions of others stems, in large measure, from careful attention to certain aspects of their behavior. Like amateur detectives, we tend to focus on those clues most likely to yield the information we are seeking, and go on to construct our "case"—our understanding of others—on this basis.

Attributions of Causality: Inferring the Causes of Behavior

Suppose that you witnessed a scene in which one person securely bound the hands of another, and then beat him over the back with a whip until he passed out from pain. Would you be willing to conclude that the perpetrator of these actions is a cruel and hostile person? In all probability you would, for at first glance such behavior seems to fit the criteria outlined above: there seems to be only one possible motive for its performance (inflicting suffering on the victim), and the actions shown are certainly out of the ordinary. But what if you now learned that the person administering the beating was doing so at gun point, under the threat of instant death for failure to comply? This information would radically alter your judgment, and you would probably no longer be willing to jump to the conclusion that the individual in question is both cruel and sadistic. The reason for this should be obvious, and we have mentioned it before. However, it is so important as to bear repeating: to the extent another's actions are shaped or determined by external causes, they cannot be employed as valid grounds for inferring anything conclusive about his or her unique characteristics. Thus, a preliminary task we must face is **causal attribution**—determining whether others' actions stem primarily from internal or external causes. Perhaps the most thorough and searching analysis of the manner in which we form such judgments of causality has been provided by Harold Kelley (1972, 1973).

Kelley's Theory of Causal Attribution: How We Answer the Question of "Why?" According to Kelley, we are often interested in determining whether the actions of other persons are attributable to (1) internal factors (something about the persons themselves); (2) external factors (something about the stimuli to which they are reacting, or the environment); or (3) transient factors (something about the specific situation or particular moment in time). Continuing with this analysis, Kelley has also proposed that in attempting to reach such decisions, we rely primarily on information concerning three basic factors: (1) *consensus*—the extent to which other persons act in the same manner as the individual in question; (2) *consistency*—the extent to which this person acts in the same manner on other occasions; and (3) *distinctiveness*—the extent to which this person acts in the same manner in other situations or only in this situation. Specifically, Kelley's theory suggests that we are most likely to attribute another's behavior to internal causes under conditions of low consensus, high consistency, and low distinctiveness, but to external causes under conditions of high consensus, high consistency, and high distinctiveness (see Figure 2-4 for a summary of these suggestions). Perhaps a concrete example will help illustrate the nature of these predictions.

First, imagine that you observe another student in one of your classes get into a violent argument with the professor. Further, imagine that (1) no other students in the class argue with the professor in this manner (consensus is low), (2) this student has often had similar run-ins with the professor in the past (consistency is high), and (3) he also gets into arguments with other instructors (distinctiveness is low since he shows the same behavior in other situations). Under these conditions, Kelley's theory predicts that you are most likely to attribute the student's behavior to internal factors (for example, the student's belligerent and quarrelsome nature) rather than to external factors (e.g., a strong provocation from the professor).

But now imagine that, instead, you observe the following pattern of events: (1) a student in your class gets into a violent argument with the professor, and in addition, several other students also get involved in such disagreements (consen-

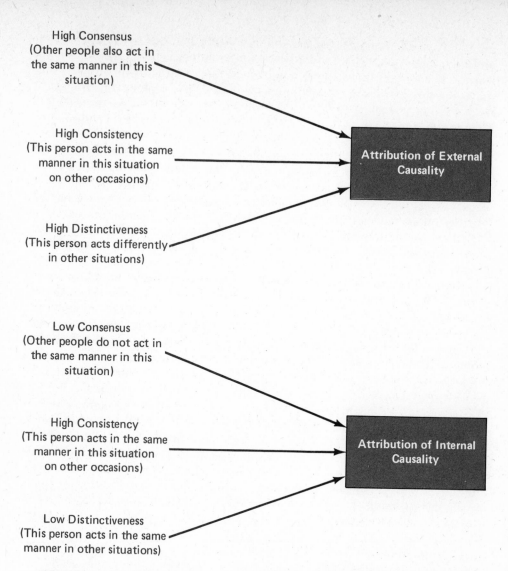

High Consensus
(Other people also act in
the same manner in this
situation)

High Consistency
(This person acts in the same
manner in this situation
on other occasions)

High Distinctiveness
(This person acts differently
in other situations)

**Attribution of External
Causality**

Low Consensus
(Other people do not act in
the same manner in this
situation)

High Consistency
(This person acts in the same
manner in this situation
on other occasions)

Low Distinctiveness
(This person acts in the same
manner in other situations)

**Attribution of Internal
Causality**

FIGURE 2-4. *Kelley's theory of causal attribution. As shown above, the theory predicts that we will usually attribute another person's behavior to external causes under conditions of high consensus, high consistency, and high distinctiveness, but to internal causes under conditions of low consensus, high consistency, and low distinctiveness.*

sus is high); (2) the student in question has often had similar run-ins with the professor in the past (consistency is high); but (3) he does not have similar arguments with any other professor (distinctiveness is high). Under these conditions, Kelley's theory predicts that you would be most likely to attribute the student's behavior to external factors (e.g., strong provocation from the professor) rather than to internal ones (e.g., the student's own argumentative nature).

These simple examples suggest the reasonable nature of Kelley's proposals, and provide informal evidence for their accuracy. More rigorous evidence for the validity of his suggestions has been obtained in several different studies. For example, in one well-known experiment conducted by McArthur (1972), subjects were first presented with brief descriptions of sixteen different responses supposedly performed by other persons (e.g., John laughs at the comedian), along with additional information concerning consensus (do others also laugh at him?), consistency (does John also laugh at this comic on other occasions?), and distinctiveness (does John also laugh at other comedians?). Information relating to each of these factors was then varied systematically to be either high or low. When subjects were then asked to indicate whether they thought each of the actions described was caused by something about the person involved (internal factors), or something about the stimulus to which he or she responded (external factors), their responses were generally in accordance with Kelley's theory. For example, subjects attributed John's behavior to *internal* factors when consistency was high (John has almost always laughed at this comedian in the past), consensus was low (hardly anyone who hears the comedian laughs at him), and distinctiveness was low (John also laughs at almost every other comedian). However, they attributed John's behavior to *external* factors when consistency was high (John has almost always laughed at this comedian in the past), consensus was high (almost everyone who hears the comedian laughs at him) and distinctiveness was high (John does not laugh at other comedians).

Additional support for Kelley's theory has also been obtained from several other studies (e.g., Frieze and Weiner, 1971; Gilmore and Minton, 1974). Indeed, recent findings suggest that we even seem to pay close attention to information regarding consensus, consistency, and distinctiveness in attempting to determine whether a particular horse has won or lost a race because of its own characteristics, or external factors such as the field in which it ran (Karaz and Perlman, 1975)! Together, the findings of such research suggests that in answering the question of "why" about others' behavior, we do in fact rely heavily on the three types of information suggested by Kelley.

Actors versus Observers: A Source of Bias in Causal Attributions. Suppose that while walking along the street one day, you saw another person trip, fall, and land in a very undignified sitting position on the sidewalk. How would you explain this behavior? Although we can't say for sure, there is a very good chance that you would explain it in terms of characteristics of this person. That is, you might conclude that he is quite careless or clumsy, and often trips over his own feet in this manner. In short, you would attribute his actions largely to internal factors. But now suppose that on another occasion precisely the same thing happened to you. Would you be likely to account for your own behavior in the same manner? In all probability, you would not. Instead, you would be more likely to explain it in terms of various situational factors. For example, you might conclude that you tripped because of an irregularity in the sidewalk left there by a careless paving crew, or that you stumbled because your heel got caught in some chewing gum, and so on.

While these incidents are certainly quite trivial in nature themselves, they point to an important fact about causal attributions that should not be overlooked: in general, we tend to perceive our own behavior as occurring largely in response to various situational factors, but that of others whom we observe as stemming primarily from internal dispositions or characteristics (Jones and Nisbett, 1972). Convincing evidence for the existence of this important form of bias in our attributions has been obtained in a number of recent experiments (Arkin and Duval, 1975; Nisbett et al., 1973; Storms, 1973).

For example, in one interesting study, Nisbett et al. (1973) asked male college students to write brief paragraphs explaining why they liked their girlfriends and why they had chosen their college major, plus other paragraphs explaining why their best friend liked *his* girlfriend and had chosen *his* major. When the paragraphs were then scored in terms of the number of situational or dispositional causes mentioned by subjects, large differences emerged between those written about themselves and those written about their friends. In explaining their own choice of girlfriend or college major, participants tended to emphasize external factors (their girl's looks or behavior, the opportunities afforded by the field they had chosen). In explaining their friend's choices, however, they tended to emphasize his personal dispositions (e.g., he needed a particular type of companion, was best suited for a particular field, etc.).

In a second, related study, the same investigators asked subjects to indicate which of a series of paired traits (e.g., quiet-talkative; lenient-firm) were true of themselves and of four other persons: their best friend, their father, a casual acquaintance, and Walter Cronkite. On each item, subjects could also choose a third alternative—"depends on the situation"—and it was predicted that, in general, they would tend to select this option more frequently in describing themselves than in describing others. That is, they would tend to attribute their own actions to situational factors, but those of others to specific traits or dispositions. As you can see in Figure 2-5, these predictions were confirmed: subjects did indeed perceive others as possessing more traits than themselves.

The findings obtained by Nisbett et al. (1973) and many other investigators (e.g., Harvey, Harris, and Barnes, 1975; Storms, 1973) provide strong support for the view that we tend to perceive our own behavior as stemming largely from situational factors, but that of others as primarily the result of internal dispositions or characteristics. While such effects have not been observed in all investigations concerned with possible differences in the attributions of actors and observers (Taylor and Koivumaki, 1976), the weight of existing evidence seems to favor their occurrence. But why, you may be wondering, should this be so? Why should behaving individuals (actors) generally view their own actions as stemming primarily from external factors, while persons who watch their behavior (observers) attribute it mainly to internal dispositions? Two possible answers have been suggested by Jones and Nisbett (1972).

The first of these explanations relates to differences in the focus of attention between actors and observers. Since actors cannot observe their own behavior in a direct manner, they usually focus their attention on situational cues, and so tend to perceive these as the major causes of their actions. In contrast, observers

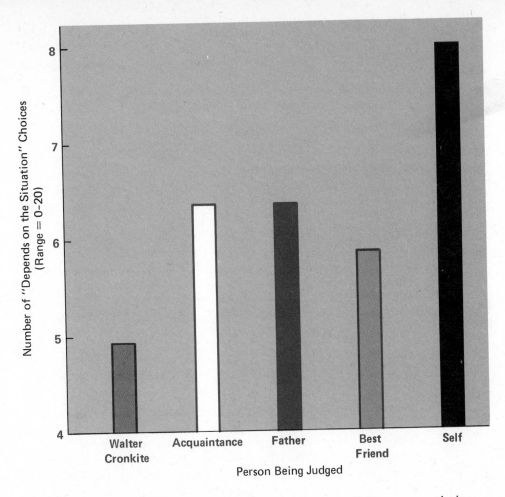

FIGURE 2-5. *Actor-observer differences in attribution. Subjects were asked to indicate which trait in each of twenty trait-pairs best described themselves and four other persons. In each case, they could also choose a third alternative—"depends on the situation." As shown above, they tended to choose this alternative more frequently in describing their own behavior than in describing that of other persons. (Based on data from Nisbett, et al., 1973.)*

tend to concentrate on the actor's behavior. As a result, they often overlook important situational determinants of this person's actions, and emphasize the role of internal traits or characteristics instead.

The second explanation proposed by Jones and Nisbett (1972) concerns the different types of information available to actors and observers. Actors know that they have behaved differently in other situations, and often feel that they would act in a different manner now, too, if conditions were changed. In contrast, observers usually have little information regarding an actor's prior behavior at their disposal (unless, of course, they know her very well). As a result, they often tend to assume that her present behavior is indicative of her past actions, and attribute it to stable dispositions.

Although both explanations seem to make good sense, a growing body of research suggests that it may be the first which is largely responsible for the different causal attributions of actors and observers. Thus, we will concentrate most of our attention on this proposal. Initial evidence supporting the focus-of-attention explanation was obtained in an ingenious experiment by Storms (1973). In this study, two subjects held a brief discussion (actors) while two others watched (observers). Following these procedures, some subjects were shown videotapes in which the discussion was presented to them from the same perspective as before—that is, actors saw a tape of their partner in the conversation, and observers saw a tape of the actor they had been asked to watch. A second group of subjects saw tapes in which the discussion was presented from a different perspective—actors saw a tape of themselves during the conversation, while observers saw a tape of the person with whom the actor they watched had been speaking. Finally, a third group of subjects saw no videotapes at all. The reasoning behind these procedures was as follows: if subjects saw either no videotapes or ones showing the same perspective as they had previously enjoyed, the usual actor-observer difference should be apparent. That is, actors should attribute their behavior primarily to situational causes, while observers should attribute the actors' behavior primarily to internal dispositions. If subjects saw the videotape showing a new perspective, however, this difference should be reversed. This would be the case because actors would now be focusing their attention on their own behavior, whereas observers would be focusing on the actor's environment—the situation in which he had previously behaved.

In order to test these predictions, subjects completed a questionnaire in which they indicated the extent to which they believed the actor's behavior was caused by personal characteristics, and the extent to which they believed it was caused by the situation. (Actors completed these questions about themselves, and observers completed them about the actor they had watched.) As you can see in Figure 2-6, results offered strong support for Storms's predictions: when subjects saw a videotape showing the conversation from the same perspective as before or no videotape at all, actors generally attributed their behavior to situational factors while observers attributed it to internal dispositions. When they saw a videotape in which their perspective was altered, however, this pattern of findings was reversed. In short, conditions which induced actors to focus upon their own behavior and observers to focus upon the situation in which actors behaved markedly changed their pattern of causal attributions. Actors no longer saw their own behavior as stemming primarily from situational causes, and observers no longer viewed the actors' behavior as stemming primarily from internal dispositions.

Further evidence for the importance of focus of attention in determining our causal attributions has been obtained in several additional studies (Arkin and Duval, 1975; Taylor and Fiske, 1975). For example, in the study by Taylor and Fiske (1975), subjects watched two people (actually confederates) hold a conver-

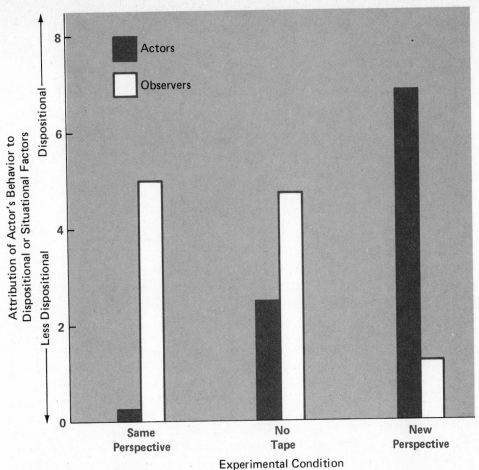

FIGURE 2-6. *Reversing actor-observer differences in attribution. When they viewed tapes which showed a conversation between two persons from the same perspective as before, or saw no tape, actors demonstrated a strong tendency to attribute their behavior to situational factors, while observers attributed it to internal dispositions. When they saw a videotape in which the conversation was shown from a different perspective, however, these findings were reversed: actors now attributed their behavior to dispositions, while observers attributed it to situational factors. (Based on data from Storms, 1973.)*

sation. Six subjects were present during each session, and conditions were arranged so that two sat facing one of the confederates, two sat facing the other, and the two remaining persons sat facing each other (see Figure 2-7). It was reasoned that when later asked to rate the two discussants in terms of the degree to which they had set the tone of the conversation and influenced their partner, subjects would perceive the persons they faced as more causal, or influential. Results offered strong support for these predictions: subjects who faced the first

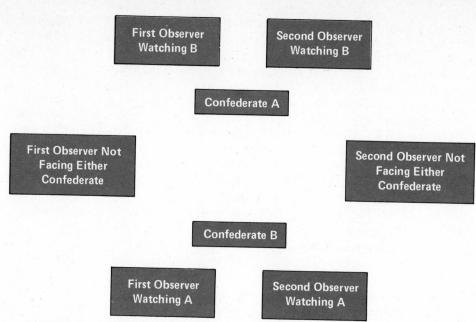

FIGURE 2-7. *Seating arrangements in the Taylor and Fiske (1975) experiment. Two observers sat facing one of the confederates, two sat facing the other confederate, and two sat on the sides, not facing either of these individuals.*

confederate rated him as more causal than the second, subjects who faced the second confederate rated him as more causal than the first, and those who faced each other rated the two confederates about equally.

Together, the findings of the experiments by Storms, Taylor and Fiske, and others seem to suggest that given several possible causes for an event or behavior, the one on which we focus our attention will often be viewed as the most important. To the degree this is indeed the case, it seems reasonable to conclude that causality will usually be seen in those quarters where we happen to search for it hardest.

An Attributional "Error": Blaming Innocent Others. Closely related to our tendency to perceive the causes of others' behavior as largely internal is another attributional bias or "error": our strong tendency to blame innocent victims for the suffering they experience. Since we tend to assume that others' behavior is largely a result of their internal dispositions and traits, it is only one relatively small step to assuming that they must, somehow, be responsible for their own unhappy fates. Thus, we frequently hold them responsible for negative outcomes they could not possibly have caused or foreseen.

One unsettling example of our tendency to blame innocent others is provided by reactions to the victims of forcible rape. Often, these unfortunate women find that many persons—both men and women alike—assume that they must have invited or provoked the attack they suffered in *some* manner, or, at the very least, taken foolish chances (Jones and Aronson, 1973). Thus, they find themselves the recipients of blame and even scorn rather than sympathy and help. Indeed, so strong is the tendency of many persons in our society to blame such innocent victims for their misfortune, that many refrain from reporting the harm they have suffered.

Another type of situation in which our tendency to hold others responsible for events and outcomes beyond their control is seen in reactions to the victims of serious accidents or natural disasters. Often, such persons are blamed for their unhappy fate (Brickman, Ryan, and Wortman, 1975), and the greater the harm they have suffered or the more serious the consequences produced, the greater the responsibility attributed to them (Walster, 1966). In such cases, we seem to assume that since others' behavior is largely a result of their internal dispositions, they must have brought their suffering upon themselves in some manner—through carelessness, unwillingness to heed warnings, and so on.

An additional reason why we frequently blame innocent victims for their plight is that by doing so, we gain a degree of reassurance that we will not suffer their misfortunes ourselves. As long as we view such persons as completely blameless, we are faced with the threatening possibility that the world is unjust, and that similar events may overtake *us* (Lerner, Miller, and Holmes, 1975). If we can somehow hold them responsible for their misfortunes, however, we can avoid this implied threat by assuming that we are different from these careless or foolish persons, and will never act in a manner which will bring similar catastrophes crashing down upon our own heads. In short, we hold them responsible for their own suffering in order to reassure ourselves that we will never share their unpleasant fate (Walster, 1966). Regardless of the precise reasons for our strong tendency to assign responsibility to others for events and outcomes they were probably quite unable to affect, it is clear that in many cases innocent victims receive our criticism and blame rather than our sympathy and compassion.

Attributions of Sincerity: How to Recognize an Honest Person When You See One

Once we have decided, either rightly or wrongly, that another person's actions stem largely from internal factors, we usually go on to employ his or her behavior as a clue to underlying motives, intentions, and characteristics. As you can easily guess, we use others' actions as the basis for making a large number of different attributions. Thus, we could not even begin to consider all of them here. As an example of the process involved, however, let us consider one type of judgment we must make with unsettling frequency during the normal course of social interaction: attributions of sincerity. The basic question here is whether other people mean what they say or are merely using their words as tools to mislead and deceive us. Given the truly remarkable ability of many persons to engage in hypocrisy, flattery, and deceit, there is little doubt that this is one of the most difficult tasks we face in our dealings with others. Yet, often, we *can* separate truth from fiction and honesty from dishonesty. Some hints as to how we accomplish this task are provided by the theoretical framework proposed by Jones and Davis (1965). Specifically, this theory suggests that our ability to make these judgments in an effective manner may stem at least in part from close attention to such factors as (1) the extent to which others' statements depart from popular or widely accepted views, and (2) the number of reasons they have for expressing such opinions. Encouragingly, actual research suggests that both do indeed play an important role in our attributions of sincerity or honesty.

First, in judging the sincerity of various statements by others—particularly statements of opinion—we seem to pay special attention to the degree to which they depart from widely accepted positions or beliefs. That is, the greater the degree of disparity between an individual's own statements and those which would probably be made by most other persons, the greater our confidence that he really means what he says (Eisinger and Mills, 1968; Jones et al., 1971). For example, if we heard an individual issue an impassioned plea for legislation requiring that all dogs and cats wear pants in public, we would probably conclude that it represents an expression of his or her true beliefs; such views are so extreme and rare, that no other interpretation seems possible. Similarly, if we heard one of our friends go into ecstasy over the charms of a member of the opposite sex viewed as unattractive by all of our other acquaintances, we would have little doubt that his or her statements are sincere (although perhaps indicative of an amazing lack of good taste). Our faith in the sincerity of others' statements in such cases seems to stem from our conclusion that if they are willing to "stick their necks out" in this manner—to risk the scorn, derision, and disapproval of others by voicing such unpopular or extreme views—they must in fact hold them with relatively deep conviction.

Second, we seem to pay close attention, in judging the honesty or sincerity of statements made by others, to the extent to which they can profit from our acceptance of their remarks. The more they have to gain from obtaining our trust and confidence, the less we tend to believe that they are indeed sincere. For example, most of us tend to be quite skeptical with respect to the claims of salesmen, for we know that they have a great deal to gain from convincing us that their statements are accurate. On the other hand, we are more willing to believe the statements of individuals such as Ralph Nader, or of organizations such as Consumer's Union, for we perceive that they have nothing to gain from recommending or condemning various products; in fact, we often believe that they probably have our protection and safety at heart.

Extending this argument a bit further, it would be expected that we would be even more likely to accept as sincere statements by others which actually seem to endorse positions *against* their own best interests. For example, we would probably attribute a high degree of sincerity to a physician who urged a crackdown on Medicare payments to doctors, to a lawyer who argued for "no-fault" auto insurance (a reform that would almost certainly reduce legal fees), or to a politician who recommended strict controls over political contributions. In general, we would tend to accept the words of these persons at face value because they have little to gain and much to lose by persuading us to adopt the actions they recommend. That this is actually the case is suggested by several studies in which communicators arguing for positions contrary to their own best interests have in fact been judged as more sincere or honest by subjects than individuals arguing for views favorable to these interests (Walster, Aronson, and Abrahams, 1966). Such findings seem to confirm the informal observation that our degree of trust or confidence in the truthfulness of statements by others is greater when they appear to have no ulterior motives for expressing these views than when they seem to have something to gain from advocating them.

A third factor which seems to influence our attributions of sincerity or honesty to others is the extent to which they express views contrary to our own. In general, we tend to view others who disagree with our own beliefs as less objective, credible, and trustworthy than those who share our views (Aronson, Turner, and Carlsmith, 1963). Moreover, this seems to be especially true in cases where we expect them to be totally objective, and avoid letting their own opinions influence their behavior. It is for this reason that newscasters, reporters, and others who are supposed to convey the news and other facts in a purely objective manner are attacked so bitterly when they drop their impartiality and permit their own views to color their statements. Convincing evidence for the negative effects of such actions on others' credibility or trustworthiness is provided by a recent experiment by Zanna, Chereskin, and Darley (1976).

In this study, subjects who had previously expressed pro-student or pro-police attitudes saw newscasts describing an incident in which a peaceful demonstration erupted into open violence between students and police. In one condition, the newscaster reporting these events blamed the students for initiating the violence, while in another, he blamed the police. After watching the program, subjects were asked to rate the objectivity, credibility, and trustworthiness of the newscaster. Results indicated that as expected, they derogated him on all these dimensions when his statements had been contrary to their own views (see Figure 2-8).

In one respect, at least, these findings appear to have unsettling implications. Specifically, they suggest that when another person expresses views contrary to our own—and especially when we expect him to be quite objective— we do not simply criticize his views on the particular issue involved. Rather, we seem to disparage his trustworthiness or credibility on *all* issues. The message for newscasters, reporters, and other representatives of the mass media contained in such effects is clear: total objectivity may not simply be the correct or appropriate course to follow; it may be the only one that will protect against the total destruction of one's future credibility.

Self-attribution: Knowing and Understanding Ourselves

So far in our discussion of social perception, we have focused on the manner in which we come to know and understand others. Now, however, we will turn to

THE EFFECTS OF LABELING OTHERS: ATTRIBUTION
AND THE VICIOUS CIRCLE

As we have already noted, one of the prime tasks of attribution is that of identifying the major motives and characteristics of others. In many cases, then, the final step in this process involves the assignment of simple labels, representing various traits, to the persons around us. For example, we may label friends or acquaintances as friendly or hostile, stubborn or yielding, cheerful or gloomy, and so on. Often, this is a very useful outcome. When accurate, such labels do in fact provide us with a kind of summary of the unique traits of other persons. Unfortunately, though, such labeling frequently seems to occur within the context of a closed and circular system. Once we have decided—however rightly or wrongly—that another person possesses certain traits, we often seem quite reluctant to alter these judgments. Behaviors inconsistent with our labels are viewed as exceptions to the rule. And actions which would normally be open to multiple interpretations are always viewed as supporting our initial judgments. For example, if we have labeled an individual as relatively dull, his success in intellectual tasks will usually be attributed to luck, or to an especially "good day"; our initial attribution of his relative lack of intelligence will not be altered. Similarly, if we have labeled another person as hostile, friendly overtures on her part will only serve to arouse our suspicions; what, we may wonder, is she really up to?

Perhaps the most dramatic demonstration of the important effects which may stem from assigning such labels to others has been provided by David Rosenhan (1973). In a bold and ingenious field study, Rosenhan and seven of his colleagues (mostly advanced graduate students in clinical psychology) feigned certain symptoms of mental illness in order to gain admission to several mental hospitals. (Specifically, they claimed to hear voices which said "empty," "hollow," and "thud.") Using such a ploy, they were readily diagnosed as schizophrenic, and admitted for treatment to twelve different hospitals.

Once in these institutions, Rosenhan and the other "pseudopatients" dropped all pretense of mental illness, and acted in a completely normal manner. Yet, despite this fact, they found it extremely difficult to convince members of the staff of their sanity. Psychiatrists, nurses, and orderlies continued to view them as seriously disturbed. Indeed, these trained individuals frequently interpreted perfectly normal actions on the part of the false patients as signs of their supposed illness. For example, while in the hospitals, the investigators took detailed notes concerning their experiences and the events occurring around them. While other patients soon noticed this behavior, and concluded from it that Rosenhan and his colleagues were not real inmates, members of the hospital staffs reached a strikingly different conclusion: in many cases they viewed such behavior as a clear sign of their patients' disturbance. Indeed, one nurse even went so far as to describe note taking as a symptom of a disordered, abnormal compulsion! In short, once they had been labeled as mentally ill, all actions on the part of the persons involved were interpreted as consistent with this label. In fact, even when they were finally released, they were described as "recovered schizophrenics" rather than as normal individuals.

Obviously, all the labels we assign to others do not produce such general or potentially harmful effects. Yet, the findings reported by Rosenhan (1973) point to the conclusion that once we have assigned a trait or label to another person, it does tend to stick. And if, as is often the case, it turns out to be false, it may continue to color our perceptions of these persons in a misleading and confusing manner. Given the existence of such effects, it seems important that in our attributions about others, we adopt the following rule: Don't jump to conclusions!

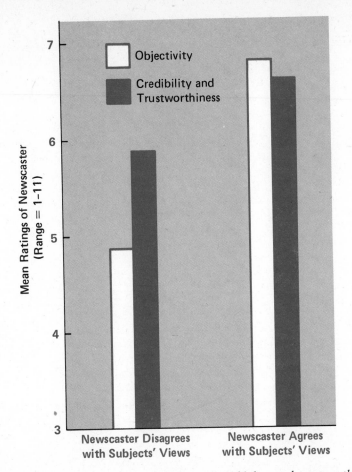

FIGURE 2-8. *Disagreement and attributions of credibility and trustworthiness. When a presumably objective source (a newscaster) expressed views contrary to those held by subjects, they downrated his objectivity, credibility, and trustworthiness. (Based on data from Zanna, Chereskin, and Darley, 1976.)*

a related question of equal importance: how do we come to know and understand *ourselves?* At first glance, this might appear to be a very simple task. After all, unlike the situation we face in attempting to know other persons, *our* internal states and dispositions are always open to direct inspection and study. As a result, it might be expected that obtaining information about ourselves would be relatively easy. To an important degree, this is certainly the case. We do often obtain valuable information about our own internal states and dispositions through a process of introspection in which we ask ourselves such questions as "Do I really want to act this way?", "How do I really feel?", or "What did I mean by that?" But it is also apparent that in our attempts to understand our own intentions, motives, feelings, and traits, we also make extensive use of clues provided by external sources (see Figure 2-9).

First, there is little doubt that we come to possess knowledge of many of our

Attribution: Inferring the Traits and Motives of Others

FIGURE 2-9. *In many cases we seem to employ information about our overt behavior as a basis for inferring our own internal states. (Source: Copyright King Features Syndicate 1975.)*

most important characteristics only through social interaction with others. For example, we learn whether we are attractive or unattractive by listening to others' comments about us, whether we are intelligent or unintelligent by comparing our abilities with theirs, and whether we are charming or boring by observing the frequency with which they seek out or avoid our company. In short, our perceptions of many of our most central characteristics are socially determined and based on information provided by others.

Second, there is growing evidence which points to the conclusion that even our perceptions of many of our own internal states may be strongly influenced by various external factors. Perhaps the most famous illustration of this important fact is provided by the work of Stanley Schachter and his associates (Schachter, 1964; Schachter and Singer, 1962).

In this research, Schachter reasoned that the labels we attach to feelings of heightened physiological arousal will be determined, to an important degree, by various situational factors. That is, we will label such arousal as one emotion or another depending on the situation in which we find ourselves. Thus, if we feel aroused in the presence of an attractive member of the opposite sex, we will probably label our feelings as "sexual excitement"; if we feel aroused after learning of the death of a loved one, we will label these sensations as "sorrow"; and if we feel aroused after receiving a severe insult, we will label them as "anger." In short, we will perceive ourselves as experiencing the emotion which external cues tell us we *should* be feeling.

In order to demonstrate that this is indeed the case, Schachter performed an ingenious experiment (Schachter and Singer, 1962) in which, under the guise of investigating the effects of a vitamin compound known as "Suproxin," college students received injections of epinephrine, a drug which produces heightened physiological arousal. One group (the Epinephrine Informed condition) was then told that as a result of this injection, they would experience such side effects as increased heart rate or a flushing of the face, while a second group (the Epinephrine Ignorant condition) was not provided with similar information. Both groups were then exposed to the actions of a confederate who either behaved in a highly euphoric manner (e.g., he shot crumpled papers at a wastebasket, built and flew paper airplanes, etc.), or demonstrated signs of extreme anger while filling out a questionnaire containing many irritating items (e.g., "With how many men other than your father has your mother had extramarital relationships?"). After witnessing these actions, subjects rated their own present mood on a brief questionnaire. It was anticipated that those in the Epinephrine Ignorant group, who had not been informed about the side effects they would experience, would lack a ready explanation for their heightened arousal, and so would tend to interpret their feelings in a manner consistent with the confederate's actions. That is, they would report feeling happy when he acted euphorically and report feeling angry when he behaved in an angry manner. In contrast, individuals in the Epinephrine Informed group, who had been informed about the side effects of the injection, would attribute their heightened arousal to the drug, and be largely unaffected by the behavior of the confederate.

Results offered support for both predictions. Subjects in the Epinephrine Ignorant group reported feeling happier when they observed the confederate behaving euphorically, and angrier when they observed him demonstrating signs of anger than those in the Epinephrine Informed condition. Together, these findings provided support for Schachter's suggestion that feelings of heightened physiological arousal for which we have no ready explanation will often be interpreted in terms of various external cues, such as the reactions of the persons around us.

Additional evidence for the view that our perceptions of our own internal states can frequently be shaped or determined by external factors has also been provided by a number of other studies. For example, in one investigation, Nisbett and Schachter (1966) gave subjects pills which actually had no effect upon them. However, half were informed that this "drug" would cause them to experience feelings of arousal similar to those produced by strong electric shock, while the others were told that it would produce such symptoms as itching sensations and numbness of the feet. When both groups then received a series of increasingly strong electric shocks, those led to believe that the drug was accounting for at least part of their reactions accepted higher levels of shock before reporting pain than those who could attribute their arousal only to the shock itself. In short, their perception of how much discomfort they were experiencing was influenced by external cues regarding the source of these feelings.

Similarly, in another experiment, Valins (1966) exposed male college students to sounds described as an amplified version of their own heartbeat while they viewed ten slides of attractive *Playboy* nudes. On five of the slides (chosen at random), their heart rate appeared to either sharply increase or sharply decrease, while on the others, it remained unchanged. Later, when asked to rate all ten slides, they described the ones associated with apparent changes in their heart rate as more attractive (see Figure 2-10). Apparently, external cues regarding their level of arousal influenced subjects' perceptions of how much they liked each of the women they saw.

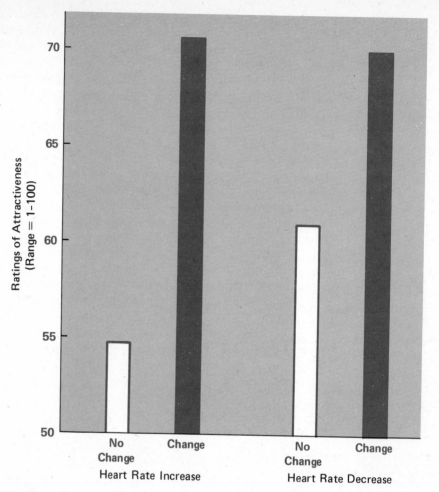

FIGURE 2-10. *The effects of external cues on sexual attraction. Male subjects reported liking pictures of Playboy nudes which produced changes in a sound described to them as their heart beat more than nudes which did not seem to produce such changes. (Based on data from Valins, 1966.)*

We could go on to describe many other investigations, for experimental evidence now suggests that our perceptions of such internal states as anger (Berkowitz, Lepinski, and Angulo, 1969), fear (Ross, Rodin, and Zimbardo, 1969), and pain (Davison and Valins, 1969) can all be strongly affected by external cues or information. By now, however, the main point should be obvious: in determining how we feel, we often pay as much—or even more—attention to external information as to feedback from our own bodies.

On the basis of such evidence, and several studies of his own, Daryl Bem (1972, p.2) has recently proposed a theory of **self-perception** centering around the following basic suggestion: "Individuals come to "know" their own attitudes, emotions, and other internal states partially by inferring them from observations

Chapter 2   Social Perception: Knowing Others and Ourselves

of their own overt behavior and/or the circumstances in which behavior occurs. . . . " According to Bem's theory, therefore, we are not as efficient at perceiving our true internal states as we generally believe. In fact, we must often seek to infer them from our overt actions.

That this is indeed the case is suggested by the occurrence of instances in which we are surprised both by the direction and intensity of our behavior, and find it to be inconsistent with what we had believed to be our present feelings. For example, we may find ourselves eating with a much greater appetite than we had anticipated ("I must have been a lot hungrier than I thought"), or responding to others in an entirely unexpected manner ("I didn't realize I liked/disliked him/her so much"). In these and many other cases, we use our own actions as a basis for inferring how we must *really* feel.

Bem's theory has had an important impact on several areas of research in social psychology. For example, it provides one possible explanation for the fact that when individuals agree to engage in behavior which is inconsistent with their true beliefs for small rewards or payoffs, they often change their attitudes so as to bring them into line with these actions. Since we will return to this topic in some detail in Chapter 3, we will not examine it here. Instead, let us focus on another interesting aspect of Bem's theory—its implications regarding the possible effects of providing individuals with external rewards for engaging in activities they find enjoyable for their own sake.

Self-perception and Intrinsic Motivation: Turning Play into Work. That there are many activities individuals enjoy performing simply for themselves is obvious. Amateur sports, hobbies, and many other forms of behavior all fit under this general heading. In such cases, persons take part in the activities in question primarily because they find them pleasurable in and of themselves, without any hope of external rewards for doing so. What would happen, then, if they were actually provided with extra payoffs for performing such actions? Bem's theory leads to an interesting prediction. Specifically, it suggests that under conditions where individuals are offered external rewards for taking part in intrinsically appealing activities, their interest in these tasks or responses may actually be reduced. This may be the case because, on observing their own behavior and the conditions under which it occurs, such persons conclude that they chose to engage in these activities mainly because of the external rewards provided, and were actually less interested in them than they previously believed. In short, they may shift from explaining their behavior in terms of internal interest ("I engage in this activity because I enjoy it") to accounting for their actions in terms of external rewards ("I engage in this activity in order to obtain various rewards"). The result, of course, is that the behavior in question comes to be seen as a means to various ends rather than as an end in and of itself.

That this may actually be the case is suggested by the findings of several recent experiments. For example, in one of these studies (Lepper, Greene, and Nisbett, 1973), nursery school children who were known to enjoy playing with colorful marking pens (they often chose to play with these toys during free play periods) were provided with an external reward for doing so. One group of children was told in advance that they would receive this reward (a "Good Player

Award") if they agreed to play with the toys when asked to do so by the experimenter, while a second group received the same reward unexpectedly. Subjects in a third, control group were neither told about the rewards nor received them. On the basis of Bem's self-perception theory, it was predicted that subjects who expected to receive the rewards and played with the toys in order to earn them would experience a reduction in their intrinsic interest in these playthings. That is, having played with them in order to earn an external reward, they would perceive their interest in the toys to be lower than had originally been the case. In contrast, subjects who received the rewards unexpectedly, or who received no rewards at all, were not expected to show a similar reduction in intrinsic motivation.

In order to assess the accuracy of these predictions, the toys were placed in the children's classrooms during a free play period, and the amount of time they spent playing with them was observed. As you can see in Figure 2-11, results were as anticipated: subjects who had both expected and earned an external reward for playing with the toys spent a smaller proportion of the time in contact with them than subjects in the other two conditions. In short, being "paid" for engaging in an activity they had previously found appealing in its own right seemed to reduce their **intrinsic motivation** to participate in it.

These results concerning the effects of external rewards on intrinsic motivation have been confirmed in several other studies (Calder and Staw, 1975; Deci, 1975). Moreover, additional findings suggest that such motivation can also be reduced by several other factors which would be predicted to exert such effects by Bem's theory. For example, placing individuals under surveillance while performing a task they initially enjoy seems to sharply reduce their intrinsic interest in it. Apparently, such conditions lead individuals to perceive that they are performing this activity primarily because of external pressures—because someone is checking up on them—rather than as a result of their intrinsic interest in it (Lepper and Greene, 1975).

Taken together, such findings seem to have several important implications. First, they suggest that by offering many forms of extrinsic rewards (e.g., gold stars, high grades, etc.) for "good" performance, teachers may often sharply reduce their students' intrinsic interest in many kinds of learning. Second, they suggest that individuals who initially enjoy their jobs will often have this intrinsic interest eroded by the external rewards they earn. Although it is obviously impossible to eliminate external rewards or surveillance from many situations, it appears that their use should be avoided wherever possible (Lepper and Greene, 1975). Only in this way can we hope to avoid the subtle changes in self-perception which often tend to convert pleasant, enjoyable play into serious, tedious work.

Intrinsic Motivation: Overjustification or Competing Responses? Before concluding our discussion of intrinsic motivation, we should note that the "overjustification" interpretation offered by Lepper and Greene to explain the results of their research has recently been the subject of a heated controversy. In particular, two other investigators—Steven Reiss and Leonard Sushinsky (1975,

1976)—have argued that the findings reported by Lepper, Greene, and others stem not from shifts in self-perception or attribution, but rather from the influence of what they term *competing responses*. While the reasoning behind this alternate interpretation is somewhat complex, it can be summarized as follows.

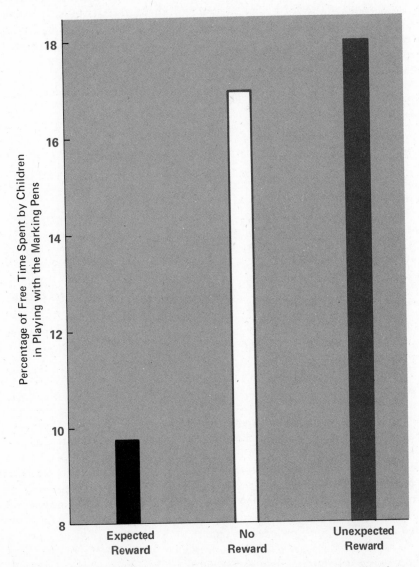

FIGURE 2-11. *Turning play into work. Children who both expected and received an external reward for performing an activity they initially enjoyed (playing with colorful marking pens) later chose to play with these toys less than children who received the external reward unexpectedly, or who received no reward at all. (Based on data from Lepper, Greene, and Nisbett, 1973.)*

OBJECTIVE SELF-AWARENESS: THE EFFECTS OF LOOKING INWARD

In a very real sense, we are each the center of our own private universe. As a result, we often turn our attention inward, attempting to know and understand ourselves more effectively. Together with clues provided by external events (observations of our own behavior or the reaction of others to us), such self-examination often yields the information we seek. But what of the very act of looking inward; does this have any effects in and of itself? According to a theory proposed by Duval and Wicklund (1972; see also Wicklund, 1975), it actually does.

Basically, Duval and Wicklund have suggested that when we shift our attention inward and enter a state they term *objective self awareness,* we experience an initial reaction of self evaluation. That is, we compare what we see with our standards or ideals. In most cases, these researchers feel, the result is a negative discrepancy: we fall short of our ideals. In others—especially immediately after a recent success experience—it may be positive (we actually exceed our own standards). Thus, focusing our attention on ourselves may result in either positive or negative feelings. Wicklund further proposes that such feelings have motivating properties. If they are negative, we seek first to avoid whatever stimuli have caused us to focus attention

on ourselves or, failing this, to distract ourselves from this state of objective self-awareness. If the feelings generated by self-evaluation are positive, in contrast, we may actually seek out stimuli encouraging this state. Finally, Wicklund suggests that in situations where the discrepancy between what we observe about ourselves and our ideals is negative, *and* we cannot escape objective self-awareness, we will attempt to reduce such discrepancies. That is, we may

When we shift our attention inward toward ourselves, we may experience either positive or negative feelings, depending on the extent to which we fall short of—or exceed—our standards and ideals.

When subjects expect a reward for performing some activity, they frequently engage in various responses which compete with the enjoyable performance of that behavior. For example, they may be distracted by the prospect of the reward, and think about it constantly. Similarly, they may feel frustrated over its delay, and engage in hurried, low-quality performance in order to obtain it as soon as possible. Because such reactions reduce subjects' enjoyment of the task at hand, they may ultimately contribute to a reduction in their intrinsic motivation to perform it on future occasions. Thus, according to Reiss and Sushinsky, the finding that children offered a reward for engaging in intrinsically appealing activities later show lessened tendencies to perform them in a free-play situation stems from the impact of such competing responses.

change our behavior, our attitudes, or even our internal standards.

Considerable evidence for the effects proposed by Duval and Wicklund has accumulated in recent years. First, several studies suggest that when we focus attention on ourselves, we do indeed experience the positive or negative self-evaluation they predict (Ickes, Wicklund, and Ferris, 1973). In these studies, subjects have generally been induced to focus their attention inward by hearing their own tape-recorded voices, seeing themselves in a mirror, or viewing televised images of their own faces. Results have suggested that individuals exposed to such conditions do report more extreme evaluations of themselves than subjects not exposed to such treatments. For example, in one study by Ickes, Wicklund, and Ferris (1973), subjects took a bogus test supposedly designed to measure a particular personality trait, and were then given either positive or negative feedback about their scores. Half were then confronted with a mirror, and half were not. Results indicated that among subjects who had received negative feedback about their personalities, exposure to the mirror led to lowered self-esteem; among those supplied with positive feedback, it led to higher self-ratings.

Second, it has been found that under conditions where subjects experience negative self-evaluations, they do actually attempt either to avoid stimuli which cause them to focus their attention on themselves, or to seek distraction. For example, they spend less time in a room with a mirror (Duval, Wicklund, and Fine, 1972), and less time listening to their own tape-recorded voices than subjects experiencing positive self-evaluation (Wicklund, 1975). Finally, under conditions where subjects cannot avoid the stimuli inducing objective self-awareness, they attempt to eliminate any negative discrepancies they notice. For example, in one study (Wicklund and Duval, 1971), subjects wrote a series of essays arguing for positions contrary to their own personal views. Half wrote these essays in the presence of a television camera pointing directly at their faces, while the remainder wrote them in the absence of a camera. As expected, subjects who wrote in the presence of the camera (and who presumably experienced objective self-awareness) changed their attitudes so as to be consistent with their essays to a greater extent than those who wrote without the camera.

Together, the findings of these and many other studies (e.g., Davis and Brock, 1975; Scheier, Fenigstein, and Buss, 1974) provide impressive support for the theory of objective self-awareness. Apparently, focusing our attention on ourselves not only yields the increased self-understanding or self-knowledge we seek; under some conditions, at least, it may also lead to changes in our attitudes, behavior, or even internal standards.

In reply to such criticisms, Lepper and Greene (1976) have noted that the distracting effects of expected reward noted by Reiss and Sushinsky could have exerted little if any effect on the behavior of subjects during the free-play portion of their study, when no further rewards were expected. Similarly, they note that, contrary to the competing-response hypothesis, individuals led to expect external rewards for engaging in intrinsically appealing activities do not always demonstrate reductions in performance, as the competing response hypothesis would suggest (Calder and Staw, 1975; Kruglanski et al., 1975). And finally, they point to the results of several recent studies which offer support for their overjustification hypothesis, and argue against the competing response interpretation (e.g., Ross, Karniol, and Rothstein, 1976).

Not surprisingly, Reiss and Sushinsky (1976) have responded to this reply, and the debate promises to continue. Regardless of the final outcome, however, recent research on intrinsic motivation seems to point to one important, general conclusion: while techniques based on the promise or delivery of external rewards may often prove effective in modifying others' behavior, they may, at the same time, tend to undermine the intrinsic motivation of these persons to engage in various activities. In this sense, at least, they may frequently prove to be something of a mixed blessing.

PUTTING IT ALL TOGETHER: FORMING IMPRESSIONS OF OTHERS

When we meet another person for the first time, we are literally swamped with a flood of new information. We notice her physical appearance, style of dress, and manner of speech. Nonverbal cues provide us with some idea of her emotional state, and conversations with her begin to reveal something about her attitudes and beliefs. Through observation of her actions and the attribution processes described above, we quickly gain some notion of her stable traits and characteristics.

Given this rapidly accumulating wealth of knowledge, our next step in the social perception process is clear: somehow, we must combine all this diverse information into a consistent and unified impression of the individual in question. That we are able to accomplish this task with amazing efficiency is obvious. Even a brief meeting with another person is usually enough to leave us with a distinct first impression of her. But how, precisely, do we go about it? Although we might actually accomplish this task in any one of a large number of ways, only two basic techniques based, respectively, on adding and a special kind of averaging, have been seriously suggested. Thus, it is upon these two basic procedures that our present discussion will focus.

Cognitive Algebra in Impression Formation: Do We Average or Add?

At first glance, it might seem that whether we combine information about others by simply adding it together or through some form of averaging would have little impact on the final impressions we form. Even a casual examination of these methods suggests, however, that this is far from the case. To illustrate this important fact, let us consider a very simple situation in which you, as the perceiver, are presented with only one piece of information about another person: he or she is *sincere*. In view of the fact that sincerity is a highly valued trait (Anderson, 1968b), it is probably safe to conclude that on the basis of this information, you would begin to form a favorable impression of the person involved. Of course, since you have very little evidence to go by, your confidence in this impression would be low. Nevertheless, to the extent it exists, it will probably tend to be fairly favorable in nature.

Now let us assume that you acquire a second piece of information about the same person: he or she is also *friendly*. Certainly this is another favorable characteristic, but what will it do to your developing impression? The answer depends on how you now combine it with the fact that this person is sincere. If you added these two pieces of information together, your impression would become even more favorable; after all, two pieces of favorable information about another person would be expected to produce a more positive impression of him than only one piece. But if, instead, you averaged them together, your impression would probably not change at all, since the average of the two closely approaches the value of each one alone. Perhaps these contrasting predictions of the adding and averaging models are best illustrated by assigning arbitrary numerical values to the two traits, and examining the results which follow when these values are combined in accordance with each. Such procedures have been followed in Table 2-2, and we urge you to examine it carefully before proceeding. (Please note that in Table 2-2 and our discussion so far, we have described only a *simple* averaging model. We will soon return to a slightly more complex version of this approach.)

At this point, a second example may also prove to be of value. Let us assume that, once again, you begin with only one piece of information about another person and that, as before, this information indicates that he is *sincere*. Now, however, let us also assume that you learn that this person is, in addition, *dignified*. This is also a positive characteristic, but there is little doubt that it is

TABLE 2-2. *Numerical comparison of the adding and averaging models of impression formation. The adding model predicts that two pieces of highly positive information about another person will produce a more favorable impression than only one piece. In contrast, the averaging model predicts that if the value of each of the pieces of information combined is equal, similar impressions will be produced in both cases. (Note that in the examples shown above, it is assumed that the higher the number obtained through adding or averaging, the more favorable the impressions produced.)*

ADDING

One Piece of Information	Two Pieces of Information
He is sincere. (+3)	He is sincere. (+3) He is friendly. (+3)
Total Value = (+3)	Total Value = (+6)

AVERAGING

One Piece of Information	Two Pieces of Information
He is sincere. (+3)	He is sincere. (+3) He is friendly. (+3)
Average Value = (+3)	Average Value = $\frac{(+6)}{2}$ = (+3)

not nearly as desirable as the traits of sincerity and friendliness. Although dignity may be highly commendable in supreme court justices, it may not be nearly so positive when it is possessed by our friends. As a result, you are now faced with the task of combining two pieces of information about another person, one of which is highly favorable and the other only moderately so. What would the adding and averaging models predict in this case? If you combined the two traits through addition, it would be expected that your impression would become more favorable, just as before. Since dignity is a less favorable characteristic than friendliness, however, the increase would be smaller than in our preceding example. In contrast, if you combined these two traits through averaging, your impression would actually tend to become *less* favorable, since the value of dignified is lower than that of sincere, and the average of the two must, of course, be lower than that of sincere alone. In this case, therefore, the two methods of combining information would lead to opposite predictions (please refer to Table 2-3).

From these simple examples, you should now be able to see that the manner in which we combine information about others may exert a powerful effect on the final impressions we obtain. But which of these two methods—adding or averaging—do we actually employ? The weight of existing evidence strongly favors averaging—and as we shall soon see, a special type of averaging (Anderson, 1968a, 1974; Kaplan, 1975). As an example of this research, let us consider a study conducted by Anderson (1965).

TABLE 2-3. *A further numerical comparison of the adding and averaging models of impression formation. The adding model predicts that when a moderately favorable piece of information about another person is combined with a highly favorable piece of information about this individual, a more positive overall impression will be produced. In contrast, the averaging model predicts that the favorability of the impressions yielded will actually decrease under such conditions.*

ADDING

One Piece of Information	Two Pieces of Information
He is sincere. (+3)	He is sincere. (+3) He is dignified. (+1)
Total Value = (+3)	Total Value = (+4)

AVERAGING

One Piece of Information	Two Pieces of Information
He is sincere. (+3)	He is sincere. (+3) He is dignified. (+1)
Average Value = (+3)	Average Value = $\dfrac{(+4)}{2}$ = (+2)

In this experiment, subjects were asked to indicate their degree of liking for a stimulus person who was described as possessing two highly favorable traits (e.g., truthful-reasonable), and one who was described as possessing two highly favorable characteristics *and* two moderately favorable ones (e.g., truthful-reasonable-painstaking-persuasive). If subjects combined the information they received about the stimulus person simply by adding it together, it would be expected that they would like the second individual better than the first, since he was described as possessing a greater number of positive characteristics. If they integrated this information through a process of averaging, however, they would be expected to like the first one better, since the average of two highly favorable traits is necessarily higher than the average of two highly favorable *and* two moderately favorable characteristics. The results of the experiment provided clear support for the predictions of the averaging formulation. That is, subjects reported liking the individual described by only two favorable characteristics better than the one described both by two highly favorable and two moderately favorable traits.

The findings of this and many other studies suggest that averaging does in fact provide a more accurate description of the manner in which we combine diverse information about others than adding. But the story does not end there. More recent investigations have gone even further, and now suggest that this process actually involves a special type of averaging, somewhat more complex than the simple formula we have been discussing. Specifically, it now appears that our impressions of others actually represent a **weighted average** of (1) all available information about these persons (each item weighted by its relative importance), and (2) our own initial dispositions to evaluate them in a positive or negative manner (with this factor too, weighted by its relative importance). Since there is now considerable evidence indicating that this more sophisticated formulation is closer to the truth than the simple averaging model, let us examine it in more detail (see Figure 2-12).

A Resolution: The Weighted Average Model. First, when we say that information about others is weighted according to its importance, we simply mean that all input about others does *not* exert an equal impact upon our final impressions. Rather, some has a greater and some a lesser influence. This important point is illustrated in the following simple example.

Suppose that, as the personnel director of a large company, you were attempting to fill an important position. One of the applicants for this job has provided two pieces of information: a letter from his former employer—an individual you both know and trust—and a second letter from one of his close personal friends. The first is largely negative, describing him as unreliable, lazy, and hard to get along with, while the second is highly positive, describing him in glowing and favorable terms. Would you assign equal importance to these two pieces of information in forming your impression of this person? Obviously, you would not; the first would probably influence your judgment to a much greater extent than the second, which you might well perceive as being both

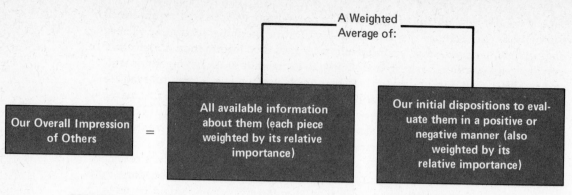

FIGURE 2-12. *Recent evidence suggests that our overall impressions of others represent a weighted average of (1) all available information about them (with each piece weighted by its relative importance), and (2) our initial dispositions to evaluate them in a positive or negative manner (with this factor, too, weighted by its relative importance).*

biased and inaccurate. In short, you would weight each piece of information at your disposal according to the credibility of the source from which it came.

This tendency to weight various pieces of information about others differentially seems to be a basic aspect of the process through which we form impressions of them. And, obviously, the information we weight most heavily has the greatest impact on our final impressions. As you might guess, several factors determine the importance we attach to information about others. First, as suggested by the preceding example, we pay careful attention to the *credibility* of the source from which it originates. Information from reliable or highly credible sources is given greater weight than information from less reliable sources (Rosenbaum and Levin, 1968, 1969). Second, we seem to assign greater importance to the information about others we obtain first (Asch, 1946). Such *primacy effects,* as they are often termed, seem to explain why it is so hard to alter impressions of others once they are formed, and why we often strive so hard to make a good impression on other persons ourselves. Third, we weight incoming information according to its relevance to the judgment being made (Hamilton and Fallot, 1974). For example, in attempting to choose another person for a job, we assign most importance to characteristics which seem relevant to its performance; in choosing a romantic interest, we assign most importance to characteristics related to such intimate relationships, and so on. Finally, we generally seem to assign greater weight or importance to information regarding negative characteristics than to information concerning positive ones (Hamilton and Zanna, 1972). Apparently, we are so concerned about the possibility of unpleasant interactions with others that we assign special importance to any indications that they possess characteristics that might lead to such outcomes.

Although information about others and the weight it is assigned certainly exert a strong influence upon our final impressions of such persons, this is by no means the entire story. In addition, our impressions are influenced by our initial dispositions to evaluate others in a positive or negative manner. These dispositions seem to exist prior to our receipt of any information about other persons, and in a sense reflect tendencies we bring with us to first meetings with them. They can run the entire range from the strong tendency to evaluate everyone favorably (shown in Will Rogers's comment "I never met a man I didn't like") to the opposite tendency to evaluate everyone negatively (demonstrated by Ebenezer Scrooge in Dickens's "A Christmas Carol"). Such extremes are rare, of course, and most persons fall somewhere in the middle.

These dispositions to evaluate others positively or negatively can be readily measured. For example, Kaplan (1976) has devised a simple procedure in which subjects are asked to select the twelve traits which they would be most likely to use in describing other people from a larger list consisting of twelve high-likability, twelve medium-likability, and twelve low-likability traits. The pattern of their choices then reveals their dispositions to evaluate others positively or negatively. Reasearch has shown that such tendencies often exert a strong influence on our impressions of others (Kaplan, 1976). However, as you might expect, their influence varies, so that they have a greater impact under some conditions than others. For example, they seem to play a more important role when we have little information about others at our disposal than when we have a great deal available (Kaplan, 1972). Similarly, they exert more influence when the source of our information about others is viewed as being unreliable than when it is viewed as being reliable (Kaplan, 1971). Regardless of the precise weight they are assigned, such tendencies always seem to exert some effect on our final impressions.

In sum, existing evidence suggests that our overall impressions of others do seem to be the result of a process in which information about them is averaged. However, the form of such averaging is somewhat more complex and involves a greater number of factors than was at first assumed.

SUMMARY

Accurate knowledge of others is essential for effective social relations with them. Yet such information is frequently difficult to obtain. Looks are often deceiving, and others frequently attempt to conceal their true feelings or characteristics from us. As a result, we must often attempt to piece together an accurate understanding of the persons around us from all the clues at our disposal.

In attempting to know the feelings and emotions of other persons, we often make use of subtle *nonverbal cues.* First, we examine their facial expressions, for these often reveal the emotions they are experiencing. Second, we notice the pattern and amount of their eye contact with us. A high level of such contact is usually a sign of positive feelings on the part of others, but may actually be interpreted as a sign of hostility in instances of staring. Finally we examine the posture, position, and movements of their bodies, for these often reveal their level of arousal, present emotions, and even their liking or disliking for us.

In seeking to acquire knowledge of the more stable characteristics of others, we generally begin by observing their overt behavior, and then attempt to infer their traits, motives, and intentions from these. Before we can make such *attributions* with confidence, however, we must first determine whether their actions have stemmed primarily from internal cuases or from external factors beyond their control. Only in the former case can we use others' behavior as a basis for inferring their characteristics. /In general, we seem to perceive others' actions as stemming primarily from internal dispositions, while viewing our own as largely a response to environmental factors. / This attributional bias often leads us to hold other persons responsible for outcomes and events they did not intend to produce, and over which they had little control.

In addition to our desire to know and understand others, we also wish to know and understand ourselves. Although we acquire much important information on this issue through direct introspection, we also learn a great deal from external sources. For example, in many cases we seek to infer our own internal feelings from observation of our own behavior, and even our perceptions of such internal states as anger, fear, and pain seem to be strongly affected by external factors. Focusing our attention on ourselves—a state known as *objective self-awareness*—often results in either positive or negative feelings. Positive feelings occur when we perceive that we have surpassed our ideals or some private standard, while negative feelings result when we perceive that we have fallen short of such standards. When we cannot readily avoid such negative feelings by turning our attention away from ourselves, we may attempt to reduce the discrepancies we observe.

When we meet another person for the first time, we are faced with the complex task of combining a wealth of information about him into a consistent and unified impression. Apparently, we accomplish this task by means of a special type of averaging process. Specifically, our *impressions of others* seem to represent a weighted average of all available information about them, and our own initial tendencies to evaluate other persons in a positive or negative manner.

GLOSSARY

Attribution. The process through which we attempt to infer others' motives, characteristics, and intentions from observation of their overt behavior.

Body language. Cues stemming from the position, posture, and movement of another person's body which provide information regarding his or her emotional states and feelings.

Causal attributions. Judgments on our part concerning the question of whether another person's behavior is caused primarily by internal or external factors.

Externalizers. With respect to facial expressions, individuals who show considerable facial expressiveness, but a relatively low level of physiological arousal in response to emotion-provoking stimuli.

Facial deceit. Refers to several techniques through which individuals attempt to control their facial expressions, and so mislead others with respect to their present emotional state.

Falsifying. A form of facial deceit in which an individual either pretends to be experiencing some feeling he or she doesn't actually have, shows no emotion when he or she is actually aroused, or substitutes signs of one emotional reaction for those of another.

Impression formation. The process through which we combine and integrate diverse information about others into unified impressions of them.

Internalizers. With respect to facial expressions, refers to individuals who show little facial expressiveness, but a relatively high level of physiological arousal in response to emotion-provoking stimuli.

Intrinsic motivation. Motivation to engage in some activity which is based on the rewarding nature of the activity itself; no external rewards are gained through its performance.

Microexpressions. Extremely brief facial expressions lasting a small fraction of a second which reveal an individual's true emotions when he or she is attempting to conceal them.

Modulating. A form of facial deceit in which individuals adjust their facial expressions so as to show more or less of an emotion than they are actually experiencing.

Nonverbal communication. Refers to a process in which others reveal their present feelings or emotional states through their facial expressions, the pattern of their eye contact with us, and the posture and movement of their bodies.

Objective self-awareness. A cognitive state in which attention is focused inward on the self. Objective self-awareness may be encouraged by such stimuli as the sight of one's face in a mirror, the sound of one's own voice on a tape recorder, and so on.

Qualifying. A mild form of facial deceit in which individuals add a further expression to one they have just shown as a comment on it. For example, an individual who has just shown signs of anger may smile as a sign that he or she is not as angry as may have seemed to be the case.

Self-perception theory. The view that we often infer our attitudes, emotions, and other internal states partly from observations of our own behavior and the circumstances under which it occurs.

Social perception. The process through which we come to know and understand the persons around us.

Weighted average model. The view that our impressions of others represent a weighted average of all available information about them and our own dispositions to evaluate other persons in a positive or negative manner.

SUGGESTED READINGS FOR CHAPTER 2

Bem, D. J. Self-perception theory. In L. Berkowitz (Ed.), *Advances in experimental social psychology.* New York: Academic Press, 1972. A comprehensive discussion of the view that, often, we know our own attitudes, emotions, and other internal states partly by inferring them from observations of our own behavior and the circumstances under which it occurs.

Ekman, P., and Friesen, W. V. *Unmasking the face.* Englewood Cliffs, N.J.: Prentice-Hall, 1975. A discussion of facial expressions as a guide to the emotions of others. Research on facial expressions is reviewed, and a large number of photos of faces are included as a means of illustrating the expressions discussed and of helping readers learn to distinguish between genuine emotions and facial deceit.

Greene, D., and Lepper, R. Intrinsic motivation: How to turn play into work. *Psychology Today,* 1974, *8,* 49–52. An interesting discussion of the manner in which providing individuals with external rewards for engaging in activities they enjoy may undermine their intrinsic motivation to engage in such activities.

Kleinke, C. L. *First impressions: The psychology of encountering others.* Englewood Cliffs, N.J.: Prentice-Hall, 1975. A brief (approximately 130 pages) summary of research findings concerning the processes at work when individuals meet for the first time. Among the topics included are the influence of physical attractiveness, eye contact, body language, facial expressions, and personal space.

Shaver, K. G. *An introduction to attribution processes.* Cambridge, Mass.: Winthrop, 1975. An introduction to the processes through which we attempt to infer the traits, motives, and intentions of other persons. An especially interesting chapter on the social consequences of attributions is included.

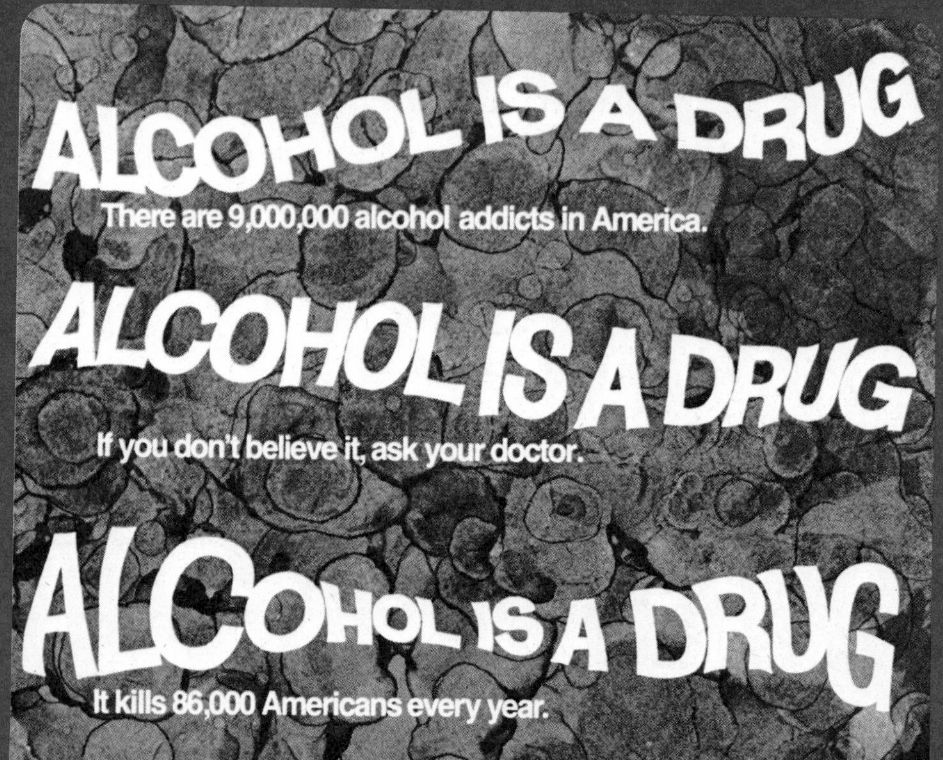

ALCOHOL IS A DRUG

There are 9,000,000 alcohol addicts in America.

ALCOHOL IS A DRUG

If you don't believe it, ask your doctor.

ALCOHOL IS A DRUG

It kills 86,000 Americans every year.

ALCOHOL IS A DRUG

Getting drunk is like a bad trip.

ALCOHOL IS A DRUG

Get the facts. Write: N.I.A.A.A., Box 2045, Rockville, Md. 20852

ATTITUDES: THEIR NATURE, FORMATION, AND CHANGE

3

It is the end of a long day, and after returning to your home, you switch on the TV and sink into your favorite chair. Soon, Walter Cronkite appears on the screen and proceeds to deliver the evening news. The first item he covers shows the President making a speech in which he announces a new hike in oil tariffs designed to boost the price of gasoline another dime per gallon, and so reduce the volume of imports. Remembering the state of your aging, gas-guzzling car, you groan at the thought of this new economic blow to your already overextended budget.

Your unpleasant revery about this problem is quickly interrupted by the next story, a report of serious famine in certain portions of central Africa. The sight of the suffering people shown on the screen is very upsetting, and your sympathy goes out to these unfortunate victims. As you consider their miserable state, you silently vow to make a contribution to the relief fund set up for their assistance which you've noticed on campus. At this point, not too surprisingly, the program is interrupted by a loud commercial for frozen pizza. Since you haven't eaten dinner, and love pizza, you sit up a bit in your chair, and begin making plans for obtaining this delicious food. As you continue watching, though, you notice that the ad is one for a brand you've already tried and disliked, so you stop concentrating on it and let your thoughts wander to the day's past events. You recall meeting an attractive member of the opposite sex, and for a few minutes, you daydream about the possibility of future interactions with this person. As a result of your fantasies, you manage to avoid noticing several other commercials, and before you know it, Walter Cronkite is back on the screen, this time describing a military take-over in some obscure country. Since this is the third such coup of the week, you quickly lose interest, and begin thinking about a party you will attend in a few days. You like most of the people who will be there, and so look forward to it with pleasure. Soon your thoughts are interrupted once again by Walter's kindly face, and he now proceeds to describe some complicated political maneuvering which has taken place on Capitol Hill. Since this type of politics bores you at best, and sometimes makes you physically ill, this is the last straw, and you angrily switch off the set and turn to other things such as getting your dinner (or even reading the next assignment for your social psychology class).

Obviously, the point of this anecdote is not that of providing you with a list of reasons why people either watch or turn off the evening news. Rather, it is presented to call your attention to the important fact that, as thinking, feeling individuals, we all have rich and varied reactions to other people, groups, ideals, and objects—virtually everything and everybody we encounter in the course of our daily lives. Basically, these reactions are of three major types: *affective*—involving feelings of liking or disliking for the objects or persons in question; *cognitive*—involving beliefs about them; and *behavioral*—involving tendencies to act in certain ways toward them. Thus, continuing our example from above, if you like pizza very much, you probably also demonstrate a strong tendency to eat it on many occasions, and may hold such beliefs about it as (1) it is quite nutritious, (2) it is a good value for the money, and (3) it is—alas!—also quite fattening. When such reactions cluster around a single object, and are relatively enduring in nature, they constitute an **attitude.** Thus whenever we use this term in the present chapter (and throughout this text), we will be referring to *relatively enduring organizations of feelings, beliefs, and behavior tendencies toward other persons, groups, ideas, or objects* (see Fishbein and Azjen, 1975; Kiesler and Munson, 1975).

Attitudes have long been of major interest to social psychologists. Indeed, at one time in the not-too-distant past, the study of such reactions dominated the field (Hendrick, 1976). This situation has changed somewhat in recent years as social researchers have extended their attention to an ever-widening range of topics. But even today, the study of attitudes remains one of their central concerns. The reason for this emphasis is apparent: attitudes, as we have defined them, play an important role in virtually every aspect of social life. First, they exert a powerful influence upon the nature of our relations with others. For example, positive attitudes toward particular persons lead us to seek them out, to do things for them, and to imitate their actions, while negative ones lead us to avoid, reject, and possibly even harm them. In a sense, then, many of our reactions to others may be viewed as largely attitudinal in nature. Second, attitudes influence many of our most important decisions. Our choice of political candidates, college, profession, and lifestyle, to mention just a few, are all strongly determined by attitudes, and often stem directly from them. And finally, they determine our position on many crucial social issues, and in this manner indirectly shape the nature of the society in which we live. Perhaps this relationship between individual attitudes and social structure can best be illustrated by means of the following simple question: can you imagine the existence of co-ed dorms, X-rated movies, or no-fault divorce during the 1890's? In all probability, you find the existence of such innovations during that period quite hard to visualize, for you realize that they would have been markedly out of line with the attitudes of most persons toward sex, marriage, and related issues. The fact that such reforms are often taken for granted in the 1970's, however, suggests how shifts in individual attitudes can often be reflected in major social change.

Given the important influence of attitudes on both individuals and society, it is not surprising that they have been the subject of several decades of intensive study. Generally, such investigations have focused on one of two major topics: the manner in which attitudes are formed and the ways in which they can be altered or changed. Both of these issues will be examined in the present chapter, but because the second has been the subject of a much greater volume of research, it will serve as the focus of most of our attention. Obviously, if we wish to study either the formation of attitudes or their change, it is essential that we possess some means of measuring them. Before turning to either of these major topics, therefore, we must first address an important, preliminary question: how can attitudes be measured?

MEASURING ATTITUDES: METHODS FOR GETTING THE INSIDE STORY

When you meet another person for the first time, some things about him are immediately apparent. For example, you can get some rough idea of how attractive he is, his age, height, style of dress, color of eyes, hair, and so on. Others' attitudes, however, are not usually visible in the same direct manner. In most cases, it is impossible to tell a bigot from a liberal, a Democrat from a Republican, or a pacifist from a militarist at first glance. Moreover, most people do not usually go about proclaiming their attitudes on important matters for all to hear. Rather, they usually perfer to keep most of these views very much to themselves, revealing them only to their closest friends or associates. Given these facts, psychologists wishing to study attitudes in a systematic manner have usually found it necessary to employ special techniques for measuring both their presence and strength. Although many of these have been developed over the years, most fall into three major categories which may be described as involving *self-report, behavioral,* or *physiological* measures of attitude.

Self-report Measures: Asking the Right Questions

Perhaps the most direct means of determining others' attitudes is that of simply asking them how they feel about various persons, issues, or groups. We all employ this technique in an informal manner when we ask friends or acquaintances: "What do you think?" It is also used by roving reporters who stop passers-by on busy streets and ask them to express their opinions for the viewing or listening audience. Although such procedures often provide a general idea of others' opinions—and some amusing comments as well—they generally lack the kind of precision needed for serious, scientific study. Unfortunately, when asked to express their views in this open-ended fashion, many persons tend to ramble on and on, getting farther off base with every passing minute. In order to avoid these and other difficulties, psychologists wishing to employ the self-report approach to measuring attitudes usually make use of some type of *attitude questionnaire* or *scale*. Such questionnaires generally consist of several items relating to the issue or object in question, and individuals' attitudes are presumably revealed through their responses to these questions. As you might suspect, the items included in attitude questionnaires can be chosen or constructed in several different ways, and presented in a number of different formats. Although a technical discussion of such procedures is clearly beyond the scope of this chapter, a brief description of several of the most important procedures does seem in order.

Thurstone Scales. One of the first methods for assessing attitudes was developed about fifty years ago by Thurstone and Chave (1929). This procedure of **Thurstone scaling**—which now bears Thurstone's name, but not that of his all-but-forgotten colleague—consists of two major steps. In the first, construction of the attitude scale, one group of individuals (usually known as *judges*) is asked to rate a large number of statements about some attitude object in terms of their degree of favorability to this object. Statements which are highly favorable receive high ratings (11 is usually the ceiling), those which are very unfavorable receive low scores (1 is generally the minimum), and statements of intermediate favorability receive ratings in between these two values. In making these ratings, judges are cautioned to ignore their own attitudes; their task is simply that of indicating how favorable or unfavorable each statement seems to be. Although this might appear to be a difficult or confusing task, it is actually quite simple. For example, regardless of their own views on this matter, most individuals would probably agree that the statement "Money spent on manned space flights is a terrible waste of funds" is highly unfavorable to the attitude object (manned explorations of space), and should receive a low rating of perhaps 1 or 2. On the basis of the judges' ratings, a smaller number of items (usually 25 or fewer) are selected for inclusion in the attitude questionnaire. Many factors

The most direct means of determining others' attitudes is that of simply asking them to express their views. This technique is often used by "roving reporters" who stop pedestrians on the street and ask them for their opinions on various issues.

enter into the final selection process, but, basically, items which represent varying degrees of favorability (ones receiving ratings of 1 through 11), and which receive consistent evaluations from judges, are sought.

Once the attitude scale has been constructed, the second step—administration of this questionnaire to the persons whose attitudes are to be measured—may proceed. These individuals are simply told to indicate whether they agree or disagree with each statement, and a measure or index of their attitudes is then obtained by averaging the scale values of all the items they endorse. For example, in the sample questionnaire shown in Table 3-1, an individual who endorses items 1, 6, and 9 would obtain an attitude score of 8.8 (the average of the scale values for these items), while an individual who endorses items 2, 5, and 8 would receive an attitude score of 2.3 (again, the average of the appropriate scale values). Thus, the second individual would be viewed as having a more negative attitude toward the object in question—politicians—than the first (he might also be viewed as either more realistic or more cynical, depending upon who is doing the viewing!) In short, Thurstone's method for assessing attitudes is based on the very reasonable assumption that the more favorable the statements about an issue, object, person, or group an individual is willing to endorse, the more his or her attitude may be viewed as positive.

Likert Scales: The Method of Summated Ratings. A second technique for measuring attitudes, **Likert scaling,** is based on the fact that individuals are capable of indicating not only whether they agree or disagree with various statements, but also the extent to which they endorse or reject them. For example, consider the following item: "Members of OPEC (the Organization of Oil-producing States) have generally shown little regard for the welfare of other nations." If you were asked to indicate whether your feelings about this statement could best be described by the terms "Strongly Agree," "Agree," "Undecided," "Disagree," or "Strongly Disagree," you would probably have little difficulty in making a choice. Moreover, you could also easily make similar judgments for each of a whole series of statements about the same attitude object (i.e., OPEC). The pattern of your responses would then provide a good indication of your attitude toward this particular organization. If you generally agreed with *unfavorable* statements such as the one above, it would be clear that you held a negative attitude toward this group, while if you generally disagreed with such statements—or agreed with ones which were *favorable* (e.g., "Oil-producing states have the right to charge as much for their petroleum as they wish")—it would be apparent that you held a positive attitude toward this exclusive "club."

When procedures of this type are employed to measure attitudes, responses of "Strongly Agree" to *positive* statements about the attitude object in question are scored as 5, those of "Agree" are scored as 4, and so on through the "Strongly Disagree" category which receives a score of 1. The system is reversed for responses to *negative* statements so that in this case, responses of

TABLE 3-1. *Statements which might be employed in a Thurstone scale designed to measure attitudes toward politicians. An individual's attitude score is based on the average scale value of the statements he or she endorses. The higher this value, the more favorable is this person's attitude toward the object or issue in question. (The scale values for each statement are derived from judges' ratings.)*

Statement	Scale Value
1. Many politicians are basically honest, decent human beings who do the best they can under difficult circumstances.	9.7
2. Only a very special type of evil person is cut out for the role of politician.	2.1
3. Politicians are honest public servants who do the best they can to promote the general welfare.	10.4
4. Politicians vary greatly in their abilities and beliefs.	5.2
5. An individual who becomes a politician must be prepared to compromise most of his or her values on a daily basis.	3.4
6. Although some politicians are self-serving, most take their responsibilities seriously and try to do the best job they can.	7.9
7. In most elections, there is a clear choice between the candidates, since different politicians stand for different points of view.	4.8
8. Politicians are the curse of humanity: if they could be eliminated, most of our problems would vanish along with them.	1.4
9. Today, politicians are the closest thing we have to the great heroes of days gone by.	8.8

"Strongly Disagree" receive a score of 5, those of "Disagree" a score of 4, etc. (This is only logical, since strong disagreement with a negative statement about some issue, object, or group reflects a positive attitude toward it.) An individual's attitude score is then computed simply by adding (summing) the numbers representing his responses; the higher this total, the more positive is his or her attitude assumed to be. For example, an individual who replied "Agree," "Strongly Disagree," "Disagree," "Strongly Agree," and "Agree" to the five statements shown in Table 3-2 would receive a score of 8, a figure indicative of a very negative attitude toward the group in question.

Because they are easy to administer and usually do not require the type of preliminary ratings essential to the Thurstone technique, Likert scales are probably the most popular self-report measure of attitudes in use today. As a result, many of the studies we will describe in later sections of this chapter have made use of these procedures to measure the attitudes of their participants.

The Semantic Differential: Measuring Attitudes through Evaluations. Suppose you were asked to rate an object with which we are sure you are familiar—the "Big Mac"—along the following dimensions: Good-Bad; Weak-Strong; Pleasant-Unpleasant; Worthless-Valuable; Satisfying-Unsatisfying. Further, imagine that you made each rating along seven point scales where 1

TABLE 3-2. *Sample items from a Likert scale designed to measure attitudes toward OPEC (the Organization of Oil-producing States). Persons responding to such attitude questionnaires indicate the extent to which they agree or disagree with each of the items presented. (In this case, respondents might circle the appropriate choice for each item.)*

1. By more than tripling the price of oil, the members of O.P.E.C. have endangered the economy of the entire world.

   Strongly Agree Agree Uncertain Disagree Strongly Disagree

2. The oil-producing nations have a perfect right to charge anything they wish for their oil; no one forces other countries to buy more than they can afford.

   Strongly Agree Agree Uncertain Disagree Strongly Disagree

3. By raising the price of oil sharply, members of O.P.E.C. are merely evening the score with the industrial nations who exploited them for so many years.

   Strongly Agree Agree Uncertain Disagree Strongly Disagree

4. Members of O.P.E.C. have generally shown little regard for the welfare of other nations.

   Strongly Agree Agree Uncertain Disagree Strongly Disagree

5. The actions of O.P.E.C. have probably been more harmful to the poor, developing nations of the world than to the rich, highly developed ones.

   Strongly Agree Agree Uncertain Disagree Strongly Disagree

represented the most unfavorable rating and 7 the most favorable. Do you think that your responses would then reveal anything about your attitudes concerning "Big Macs"? It seems quite reasonable to assume that they would, and that the greater your tendency to rate this fast-food "classic" toward the favorable ends of these dimensions—that is, toward Good, Strong, Pleasant, Valuable, and Satisfying—the more positive your attitude toward it. This basic idea lies at the heart of a third self-report technique for measuring attitudes known as the **semantic differential** (Osgood, Suci, and Tannenbaum, 1957). In this procedure, an individual's attitude score is determined by adding his other ratings (from 1 to 7) along all the dimensions employed; the higher this number, the more favorable the attitude. Because it can be adapted to virtually any object or issue, and seems to tap the affective (feeling) component of attitudes more directly than other procedures, the semantic differential has attained widespread use in attitude research. When using this procedure, however, investigators must take care to avoid the inclusion of dimensions that will seem irrelevant—or even silly—to subjects. (For example, continuing our hamburger illustration, individuals asked to rate the "Big Mac" along such dimensions as "Hostile-Friendly" or "Wild-Tame" might well give up in despair—or break up in amusement—when confronted with this task.) When such potential problems are avoided, the semantic differential can often serve as a useful and effective technique for measuring attitudes toward a wide variety of issues, objects, and groups.

Behavioral Measures: Actions as Clues to Attitudes

Although self-report measures such as the ones described above are by far the most popular means used by social psychologists to assess attitudes, other approaches also exist. Perhaps the most important of these is based upon the fact that it is often possible to learn much about the attitudes of others by observing their behavior. Sometimes, individuals' attitudes are revealed through their actions in a very obvious and dramatic manner. For example, they may join various demonstrations, picket their employers, attend political rallies at which they shout their approval or rejection of various candidates, or donate large sums of money to causes they support. Even when they do not reveal their feelings in such dramatic and obvious ways, however, much can often be learned from careful study of their actions. For example, imagine that you were riding a public bus when a racially mixed couple got on. Although few passengers who disapproved of such crossing of racial barriers would get up and shout angrily at the couple or attempt to eject them from the bus, they might demonstrate their disapproval in other, more subtle ways, such as frowning, changing their seats, or looking studiously the other way. In short, they might reveal their true reactions through such subtle cues as facial expressions, body position or posture, and expressive gestures. Since we have already considered the manner in which others' behavior can be used as a source of information about them in Chapter 2, we will not return to this topic in any detail here. For the present, we merely wish to call your attention to the fact that attitudes can often be revealed through overt actions as well as responses to paper-and-pencil questionnaires.

Physiological Measures: Autonomic Indicators of Attitudes

Suppose that a strong conservationist were presented with the following statement: "Since industry has always done a good job of protecting the environment, special laws to prevent air and water pollution are totally unnecessary." Do you think that this person might show signs of emotional arousal (e.g., raised blood pressure, faster heartbeat, etc.) in response to such a stimulus? The fact that he might suggests still another type of attitude measure, one based on physiological reactions. That is, it seems reasonable to expect that the stronger an individual's views about a given issue, object, or group, the stronger will his or her physiological (emotional) reactions to statements about it be. Several experimenters have examined this suggestion, and while results have not always been simple or clear-cut, positive findings have generally been obtained (Cooper, 1969; Woodmansee, 1970). As expected, the intensity of subjects' attitudes have actually been reflected in their heart rate, blood pressure, or other autonomic

FOCUS ON RESEARCH

THE BOGUS PIPELINE: TELLING IT LIKE IT IS?

When individuals respond to any of the self-report measures of attitude described above, it is assumed that their answers reflect their true attitudes or beliefs. Unfortunately, as you may have already guessed, this is not always the case. Often, subjects wish to conceal their true opinions for reasons of their own. For example, given the present social climate prevailing on most college campuses, few racially bigoted students would be willing to reveal their strong prejudices to prying psychologists. And even on occasions when subjects are not reluctant to reveal their true opinions, they may be led to report false information by their desire to "help" the experimenter obtain the results he or she desires. In view of such problems, it is generally impossible to tell whether subjects' responses to various attitude questionnaires reflect their true attitudes, or merely irrelevant sources of bias.

Until quite recently, no simple or effective means for resolving this dilemma existed. Researchers simply cautioned their subjects to be honest, assured them that their responses would be anonymous, and attempted to remove any clues as to their own expectations or hypotheses. Within the past few years, however, Jones and Sigall (1971) have developed a technique which, they feel, may largely help to overcome such problems. In their procedure, often known as the *bogus pipeline*, subjects are told that they will be hooked up to a machine which—by measuring tiny muscle potentials—can accurately guage their true opinions. (See Figure 3-1.) In reality, of course, the equipment does nothing of the kind; all the feedback it provides is controlled by an assistant of the investigator. To convince subjects that the apparatus really operates in this fashion, however, they are then asked to respond to a few innocuous sample questions. Since their views on these issues are already known (they were obtained some time ago in an entirely different context), the machine appears to provide accurate feedback in every case. Thus, although they are skeptical at first, most subjects soon come to believe that the equipment can in fact monitor their actual attitudes.

Once they are convinced of the effectiveness of the apparatus, subjects are presented with a new set of questions designed to assess their attitudes on some topic of interest to the experimenter. During this period, they receive no feedback from the equipment, but believe that such information is being provided to the investigator. Since their "true" attitudes will be revealed to this person anyway, there is no reason for them to fake their responses, and, presumably, they then report their actual views in each case. Evidence that these procedures do actually reduce attempts at concealment by subjects has been obtained in several experiments (see Allen, 1975). For example, in one study, Jones, Bell, and Aronson (1972) found that white subjects rated blacks as more honest than other Americans on a standard attitude scale, but reversed these ratings when the bogus pipeline was employed. Apparently, the belief that their true opinions would be revealed to the experimenter caused them to drop the pretense of a total lack of prejudice they had adopted on the questionnaire.

Despite such promising results, the bogus pipeline has already been subjected to criticism on several grounds (Cherry, Byrne, and Mitchell, 1976; Ostrom, 1973). First, there is as yet no convincing evidence that it is always more accurate or sensitive than more standard techniques. In fact, in some situations, quite the opposite may be true. Second, in contrast to standard self-report procedures, the pipeline involves a potential-

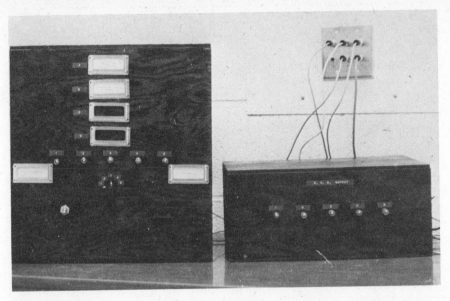

FIGURE 3-1. *Apparatus of the type employed in the "bogus pipeline." Subjects are asked to hold the switch in the center of the larger panel, and to think about their answers to each of a series of attitude items. An electrode is attached to their arms, and they are informed that the apparatus will process information from it to provide an indication of their "true" attitudes. These are then represented by the series of lights on the smaller console. In reality, the lights are controlled by an accomplice in the next room, and simply indicate subjects' previous answers to the same items. Once participants have been convinced that the equipment actually works in the manner described, they are asked to respond to other attitude items. Since they believe that the equipment will reveal their true beliefs in each case, it is assumed that they will make no attempt to "fake" their responses. Thus, an accurate measure of their attitudes can be obtained. (Photo courtesy Dr. Bem P. Allen.)*

ly upsetting and confusing deception. As we noted in Chapter 1, such practices should be avoided unless absolutely essential. Since this is clearly not the case with respect to the bogus pipeline (effective questionnaire techniques already exist), extreme caution should be employed in its use. And finally, the pipeline approach involves many practical problems. For example, because of the equipment needed, responses can usually be obtained from only one subject at a time. As a result, collecting data on the attitudes of large numbers of persons may often prove to be quite difficult.

Even considering these potential drawbacks, it is our view that the bogus pipeline is an intriguing and promising technique. Although it may not provide the direct link to the "soul" suggested by Jones and Sigall (1971), it may indeed sometimes yield a more accurate picture of individuals' attitudes than standard questionnaires. To the extent that this is shown to be the case in future research, the bogus pipeline will represent a valuable addition to existing techniques for the accurate assessment of attitudes.

Individuals' attitudes are often revealed through their overt actions. (Photo: Phil Carver & Friends.)

reactions. And recently, techniques for determining the direction, positive or negative, as well as the strength of subjects' attitudes from such responses, have been developed (Tognacci and Cook, 1975). Such findings suggest that with further refinement, the false claim in the "bogus pipeline" procedures outlined above that the experimenter possesses a machine to directly measure subjects' attitudes may actually be converted to a true one.

Heroes may be born, but bigots are clearly made. No one would seriously suggest, in the 1970's, that children spring from the womb with all the complex attitudes they will later show as adults firmly in place. Rather, there is virtually universal agreement that they acquire these reactions in precisely the same manner that they acquire other forms of behavior—largely through a prolonged period of learning. Three simple but powerful processes seem to play a crucial role in such development: classical conditioning, instrumental conditioning, and observational learning. Although you are probably already familiar with all three from your previous courses in psychology, we will introduce them here in what you will almost certainly find to be quite a new context—as a basis for the development off all social attitudes.

Classical Conditioning: Guilt (or Innocence) by Association

The basic principle of **classical conditioning** is simplicity itself: some neutral stimulus initially incapable of evoking a particular response gradually acquires the ability to do so through repeated pairing with another stimulus which *is* initially capable of eliciting this response. The usual examples of classical conditioning presented in most psychology textbooks involve ringing bells and salivating dogs. For the sake of variety, then, let us use another illustration to refresh your memory about the nature of this process.

Imagine that you buy an electric toaster at a garage sale. When you use it for the first time, you discover that, at odd intervals, it makes a soft popping sound and then, without additional warning, hurls the toast across the room. Since you can't afford another, you continue to use your strange appliance. As you do, though, a gradual change comes over your behavior. At first, you would probably show little reaction to the soft popping sound when it occurs; in fact, you might not even notice it. After being bombarded with pieces of toast on several occasions, however, you might begin to react quite strongly to this previously neutral sound. For example, you may find yourself feeling anxious when it occurs, and may begin engaging in such protective reactions as covering your eyes, ducking your head, or even hiding under the table. These alterations in your behavior are due to a process of classical conditioning in which the initially neutral sound (a conditioned stimulus) has gradually acquired the ability to elicit reactions similar to those produced at first only by the flying pieces of toast (the unconditioned stimulus).

At this point, you may be beginning to wonder how this process can play a role in the development of social attitudes. The answer lies in the fact that it often exerts a strong impact on our feelings of liking or disliking for various objects—the *affective* component of attitudes. Specifically, any attitude object which is repeatedly associated with stimuli capable of evoking positive or negative feelings will itself soon acquire the ability to evoke such reactions. Perhaps the nature of this process—and its role in attitude formation—is best illustrated by means of a specific example.

Consider the case of a child whose parents are strongly prejudiced against Chicanos. On many different occasions, she hears her father and mother describe this group with such words as "dirty," "ugly," and "lazy." At first, the word Chicano is quite neutral, and elicits no strong reaction from the child. After repeated pairings with such negative words, however, it acquires a similar, negative meaning. As a result, the child comes to experience strong negative feelings whenever she hears this word, just as she did initially to the words "dirty," "ugly," and so on. In this simple manner, classical conditioning has planted the seeds for later strong racial or ethnic bigotry.

Direct evidence for the occurrence of such a process has actually been obtained in a number of laboratory studies (e.g., Lohr and Staats, 1973; Zanna, Kiesler, and Pilkonis, 1970). For example, in one of the first of these investigations, Staats and Staats (1958) paired the names of two nationality groups—Dutch and Swedish—with either positive or negative words. On each trial, one of these names was projected onto a screen, and while being shown, the experimenter pronounced either a positive word (e.g., gift, happy, sacred), or a negative word (bitter, ugly, failure). When subjects were later asked to rate both nationalities, the one paired with positive words received more favorable ratings than the one paired with negative words (see Figure 3-2). In short, there was some indication that positive or negative attitudes could be created in the laboratory within the space of a few minutes. Needless to say, the strength of such reactions was quite minimal, but given a much larger number of pairings under a wide variety of circumstances, as might well be the case under actual life conditions, it seems possible that attitudes of considerable intensity might soon be created.

Additional studies by Staats and his colleagues (Lohr and Staats, 1973) have demonstrated that such effects are not restricted to a single language or culture; rather, they appear to be quite general in nature. Moreover, there is also some evidence suggesting that, once formed, attitudes developed through classical conditioning generalize readily. For example, in one study, Zanna, Kiesler, and Pilkonis (1970) found that positive or negative attitudes conditioned to the words "light" and "dark" generalized to the terms "white" and "black." The role of this basic psychological process in the formation of even socially significant attitudes, therefore, should not be overlooked.

Instrumental Conditioning: Reinforcing the "Right" Views

Until they enter their teens, most children seem to share virtually all the attitudes of their parents. They agree with them on almost every issue, adopt their biases and beliefs, and share their likes and dislikes with respect to food, clothing, furniture, and almost every other imaginable topic. In fact, as far as attitudes are concerned, they often seem to be virtual carbon copies of their mothers and

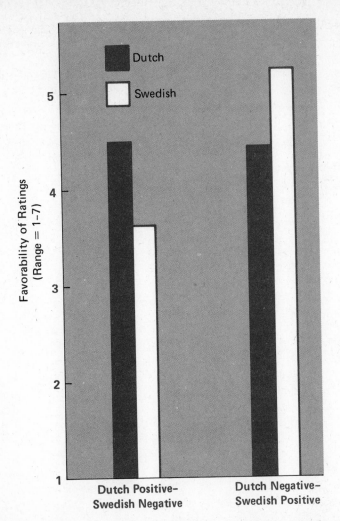

FIGURE 3-2. *Positive and negative attitudes developed through classical conditioning. The names of two nationality groups—"Dutch" and "Swedish"—were paired repeatedly with positive or negative words. When subjects later rated both, the one previously paired with positive words received more favorable evaluations than the one paired with negative words. (Source: Based on data from Staats and Staats, 1958.)*

fathers. Interestingly, this powerful allegiance to parental attitudes is often quite "blind" in the sense that it is totally lacking in cognitive rationale. For example, young children can often be heard heatedly defending their parents' preferences with respect to make of automobile, religious affiliation, or political party without showing the slightest understanding of the grounds on which such choices might be made. In short, full comprehension of parental attitudes does not seem to be required for their strong support; their mere existence often seems to be enough.

Several factors probably play a role in producing this high degree of

Highly prejudiced parents often reward their children for expressing beliefs similar to their own. As a result, these youngsters often come to hold identical bigoted views. (Wide World Photo.)

correspondence between the attitudes of parents and their children, but perhaps the most important involves the process of **instrumental conditioning.** Parents (and later other agents of socialization such as teachers, ministers, girl or boy scout leaders) often go out of their way to reward children for expressing the

Chapter 3   Attitudes: Their Nature, Formation, and Change

"right" views—those held by the adults in question. While the specific form of such rewards may vary greatly, ranging from praise, affection, and approval on the one hand, to open bribes of candy, privileges, or money on the other, the result is usually the same: the children quickly learn to voice only approved attitudes and preferences. Since parents usually spare no effort in this undertaking, wishing to take a strong hand in shaping their children's development, it is not at all surprising that they usually succeed in transmitting most of their attitudes to their offspring. Largely as a result of this process, then, the children of Republicans usually turn out to be Republicans, those of environmentalists show deep concern for the physical world around them, and those of prejudiced racists turn out to be chips off the old bigoted block. Indeed, so powerful and lasting are the effects of this continuing process of instrumental conditioning that, by the time they are adults, most persons hold certain views so strongly that they are all but impervious to change.

Informal evidence concerning the role of instrumental conditioning in attitude formation is confirmed by a large body of research. Many studies have shown that individuals quickly come to express specific points of view when they are rewarded for such behavior. In fact, even such seemingly minimal rewards as hearing the experimenter murmur "good" or "mmm-hmmm" after appropriate attitude statements appear to be effective in this regard (e.g., Insko and Melson, 1969). Additional findings suggest that the acquisition of attitudes through instrumental conditioning is influenced by many of the same factors which affect the development of other responses through this process. For example, Kerpelman and Himmelfarb (1971) found that the more consistently subjects were rewarded for describing a nonexistent group in favorable terms, the more positive was their attitude toward them when later measured by means of a Thurstone-type scale (see Figure 3-3). (Reward involved subjects' learning that their guesses concerning the characteristics of this group were accurate.)

When it is considered that the presentation of such minimal reinforcements as hearing the experimenter say "good" are successful in creating prositive or negative attitudes in brief laboratory sessions, it is hardly surprising that parents, with their long-term control over vastly more important forms of reward, can often shape the attitudes of their offspring to a remarkable degree.

Observational Learning: Attitudes through Example

While instrumental conditioning seems to account for the development of attitudes which parents wish their children to adopt, it cannot explain the ready transmission of views or reactions they hold themselves, but do *not* wish to impart to their offspring. For example, consider the case of a mother who was raised with the belief that the human body is a source of shame and should be concealed at all times. Now, years later, she wishes to teach her children quite a different view—that the human body is actually a thing of beauty, not a source of shame or guilt. Yet try as she may, she finds her own conflicted feelings about nudity being transmitted to her offspring. In cases of this type—which are far

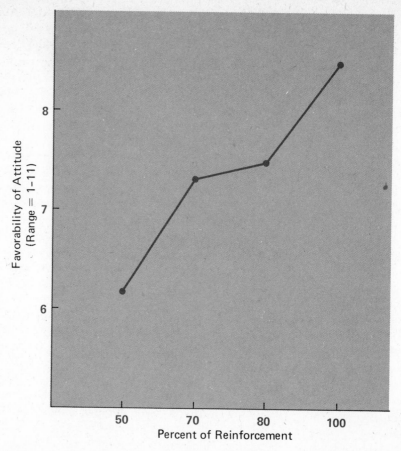

FIGURE 3-3. *The instrumental conditioning of attitudes. The more consistently subjects were rewarded for expressing favorable views toward a hypothetical group, the more positive their attitudes became toward this group. (Source: Based on data from Kerpelman and Himmelfarb, 1971.)*

from uncommon—the process of **observational learning** plays a crucial role. Since we will return to this process in more detail in Chapter 7, we will not attempt to describe it fully here. Basically, though, it centers around the fact that human beings can acquire new responses simply by observing the actions and outcomes of others. Thus, returning to our example, it seems likely that the parent in question managed to transmit her own negative reactions toward nudity to her children through her behavior—by demonstrating signs of shame or anxiety whenever her children were unclothed, by refusing to expose her own body, and so on.

As a result of observational learning, children often acquire attitudes, preferences, and values which their parents make no attempt to reward, and which in some cases they actually try to discourage. Perhaps the most unsettling influence of observational learning on the formation of attitudes is visible in situations where parents verbally state or endorse one attitude, but then demonstrate quite another in their own behavior. For example, a father may urge honesty upon his offspring, but then demonstrate dishonesty and deceit in his overt actions (see Figure 3-4). In such cases, children often seem to pay more attention to deeds than words, and so acquire many attitudes and values their parents would prefer that they avoid (Bryan, Redfield, and Mader, 1971; Rushton, 1975). Given such effects, it appears that parents will be most successful in creating the desired attitudes among their children when they take great care to practice as well as merely preach such views.

Attitude Formation: A Concluding Comment. Although we have discussed the roles of classical conditioning, instrumental conditioning, and observational learning separately, there is little doubt that in many cases they operate together. While attitudes may be acquired through any one of these processes alone, under actual life conditions they probably often function in a complementary manner. For example, consider the development of a strong racial prejudice. Such negative attitudes toward others often begin to take form when children acquire—largely through the process of classical conditioning—negative emotional reactions to the members of groups hated or disliked by their parents. The development of such reactions may then pave the way for observational learning (and later imitation) of their parents' prejudiced behavior. Instrumental conditioning may then begin to play a role, as mothers and fathers reward their offspring with praise and approval for voicing the "right" attitudes—bigoted views similar to their own. Given the fact that the acquisition of attitudes continues for ten, fifteen, or even twenty years, it is far from surprising that once acquired in this manner, many are highly resistant to later change (see Cook, 1970).

CHANGING ATTITUDES: THE POWER OF POSITIVE
PERSUASION

The business of changing attitudes is, in late twentieth century America, a very big one. If you have any doubts that this is so, simply switch on your TV or radio, or flip through the pages of any handy newspaper or magazine. Almost at once, you will find yourself flooded with attempts to change your attitudes on a wide variety of issues. Commercials will cry out at you to buy some particular brand of detergent, cereal, or beer; political candidates will plead for your vote; public service organizations will caution you against smoking, drinking, speeding, or overeating; and ads paid for by private groups of citizens will attempt to persuade you that their views on various issues are the correct ones. In the face of this barrage, you may quickly conclude that someone is trying to alter your attitudes at every turn.

Fortunately, as we noted above, many attitudes are quite resistant to influence attempts, and are left largely untouched by such appeals. Many others, though, are much weaker or only partially formed, and can be readily

FIGURE 3-4. *When parents preach one attitude or value, but then demonstrate another in their overt actions, children often pay more attention to their deeds than to their words. (Source: Reprinted by permission of Newspaper Enterprise Association.)*

swayed by appropriate procedures. Although many different approaches have been employed to alter such attitudes, ranging from threats on the one hand ("I'll make him an offer he can't refuse"), through bribes on the other, most attempts involve one of two major techniques: **persuasive communications,** or the induction of **attitude-discrepant** behavior. While the first is probably more common in daily life, the second is closely related to the theory of **cognitive dissonance,** an intriguing framework which has probably generated more research by social psychologists during the past two decades than any other. In view of their importance, both procedures will be examined in some detail.

Persuasive Communications: Is Seeing (or Hearing) Believing?

Most attempts to modify our attitudes involve persuasive communications— spoken, written, televised, or filmed messages that seek to alter our views through logical arguments, convincing information, and authoritative facts. Of course, in many cases, the arguments contained in such appeals turn out to be far from logical, the information is not very convincing, and the facts are anything but authoritative. Generally, though, such communications attempt to maintain at least a semblance of reason as part of their overall structure.

That all persuasive appeals do not succeed in influencing our attitudes is obvious. Some ad campaigns are successful in selling their products, while others are not; some political candidates win elections while others lose; and some charitable organizations succeed in wringing contributions from potential donors while others do not. As we have noted before, part of the reason for such differences lies in the nature of the attitudes in question: some are simply far more resistant to influence than others. A major portion of such differences, however, stems from various features of the persuasive communications themselves, with some being far more effective than others. Although a number of different factors seems to determine the success of such appeals, the most

Persuasive appeals take many different forms, but their major goal is always the same: altering the attitudes of the people toward whom they are directed. (Photo: Phil Carver & Friends.)

important seem to involve characteristics of (1) *the communicator*—who delivers the message; (2) *the communication*—what are its contents, how is it structured; (3) *the recipients*—who are the people who receive it; and (4) *the context in which it is presented.*

Characteristics of the Communicator: If You Can't Trust the Experts, Who Can You Trust? Do you remember when, as a child, you mailed away the box-tops from various breakfast cereals in order to obtain what the packages promised to be exciting toys? If so, you probably recall your bitter disappointment when, after weeks of endless waiting, you finally received a flimsy and far less fascinating object back through the mail. It is on the basis of such experiences that we begin to learn, quite early in life, that all communicators are *not* equally reliable. Some are to be believed and trusted, while others are to be doubted and mistrusted. For example, in trying to determine whether smoking is harmful to your health, you would probably pay more attention to information provided by the Surgeon General than to paid advertisements by the tobacco industry. Similarly, in deciding whether to purchase a particular product you would probably be more willing to accept statements by your friends regarding its quality or performance than those of a salesman who stands to earn a large commission from the transaction. The effectiveness of persuasive communications in influencing our attitudes, then, is strongly affected by the **credibility** of their source: the more credible (believable) the person delivering them, the greater their success in changing our opinions. (Please note that to a large degree, credibility is located in "the eye of the beholder." For example, Ronald Reagan may well be a high-credibility source to conservative Republicans, but is probably a low-credibility source to liberal Democrats.)

Although our judgments regarding communicators' degree of credibility are influenced by many different factors, three seem to be of greatest importance: their apparent level of *expertise,* their *intentions* or *motives,* and their level of *attractiveness.* The importance of the first of these factors has been examined in a number of different studies (e.g., Aronson, Turner, and Carlsmith, 1963; Hovland and Weiss, 1951). In general, the results of these studies have been consistent in suggesting that communicators high in expertise tend to induce greater degrees of attitude change than those lower in this dimension. More recent evidence suggests that this is the case because a high degree of competence or expertise increases the value or appeal of the communicator's message (Mills and Harvey, 1972). In short, an appeal deliverd by a noted expert on the topic often seems more convincing and reasonable than one delivered by a communicator lacking in expertise.

One interesting question raised—but as yet unanswered—by such research concerns the extent to which communicators can use their expertise in one area to increase the success of their appeals in another. Advertising executives seem to believe that such generalization often occurs, for they frequently hire individuals noted for their competence in one field to endorse products totally unrelated to their achievements. (For example, do you recall the commercials in which Joe Namath extolled the virtues of a particular brand of pantyhose?) Informal observation suggests that communicators may indeed be able to generalize their expertise in one area to others, but the extent to which such effects occur remains an open issue.

The influence of the second factor, a communicator's apparent *motives* or *intentions,* is also readily apparent. For example, imagine that one day you switched on the radio and heard the president of General Motors make an impassioned appeal for tougher measures to control air pollution. After recovering from your initial shock, there is a good chance that you would be greatly affected by this speech; since the individual making it might lose much if his recommendations were accepted, there would be strong grounds for assuming that his motives were of the most admirable type. In contrast, if you heard a similar speech by the president of a company which manufactured devices designed to reduce such pollution you might be influenced to a much smaller degree; this person's communication could readily be attributed to a selfish desire for gain.

More formal evidence for the effect of a communicator's apparent motives upon his or her credibility has been obtained in several laboratory studies (Walster, Aronson, and Abrahams, 1966; Walster and Festinger, 1962). For example, in the investigation by Walster and Festinger, married female students heard a conversation in which two individuals concluded that student husbands should spend more time at home. In one experimental condition, subjects were led to believe that the persons discussing this issue were unaware of their presence, while in a second condition, they were told that these individuals knew they were listening. It was expected that the women would be influenced to a greater degree in the first condition, for in that case, it would appear that the communicators were not attempting to influence them and were being totally candid. Results confirmed these predictions, for when subjects were asked to indicate their own views on this issue, those who thought their presence had been unknown showed greater agreement with the opinions of the two communicators than those who thought it had been known. The findings of this and other experiments suggest that we are usually much more likely to be influenced by appeals from communicators who have little to gain from a shift in our views, or who are not trying to persuade us, than by messages from individuals who stand to profit greatly from shifts in our views, and who are actively attempting to induce such change.

A final characteristic of communicators which seems to exert an important effect upon their ability to alter the attitudes of others is their degree of *attractiveness* to these persons. Other factors being equal, the more a communicator is liked, the greater his or her success in inducing change among members of the audience (Berscheid, 1966; Mills and Harvey, 1972). As we will soon see in Chapter 5, liking for others, including communicators, can be affected by a number of different factors. Among the most important, however, are physical beauty and apparent similarity. In general, communicators who present an attractive physical appearance and who seem highly similar to the recipients of their appeals will be liked more than those of less impressive physical appearance or those who seem quite dissimilar to their audience (Byrne, 1971; Berscheid and Walster, 1974b). Both politicians and advertising executives seem to be well aware of these facts, and use them to maximum advantage in their attempts to alter the attitudes of large numbers of people. For example there has been a growing tendency in recent years, to select political candidates as much on their good looks as their abilities or integrity. And once chosen, candidates often go out of their way to demonstrate that they are basically "just plain folks," quite similar in many ways to the voters they hope to represent. Apparently, a high level of attractiveness increases the ability of communicators to induce attitude change among their audience because of a strong desire on the part of most individuals to be similar to persons they admire (Mills and Harvey, 1972). Since one means of accomplishing this goal is that of adopting their views, acceptance of the communicators' appeal is often enhanced.

Communicator Credibility and the "Sleeper Effect." Before concluding this discussion of communicator characteristics and their impact on persuasion, we should briefly mention a phenomenon often known in social psychology as the **sleeper effect.** Initially, this term referred to the suggestion that the influence of low credibility communicators increases over time, as the audience "sleeps on" the persuasive message delivered by such persons (Hovland, Lumsdaine, and Sheffield, 1949). Soon, however, it came to refer to the somewhat broader proposal that the influence of communicator credibility decreases over time, so that the impact of low-credibility sources rises, and that of high-credibility sources drops. Presumably, this is due to the fact that the content of a message becomes dissociated from its source over time, with the result that *what* has been said comes to exert a more powerful effect than *who* has said it.

Because results consistent with these suggestions were obtained in several early studies, they were widely accepted as established fact in social psychology for more than two decades. Unfortunately, however, their existence has been called into serious question by more recent findings (Gillig and Greenwald, 1974). Indeed, it now appears that while the influence of high-credibility sources may indeed decrease with the passage of time, that of low-credibility sources does not actually increase. In view of such results, it seems that, as Gillig and Greenwald (1974) suggest, it may well be time to lay the sleeper effect itself to a quiet, final rest.

Characteristics of the Communication: It's Not Only Who You Are, But What You Say. Imagine that you are sitting in the audience at a large meeting when a world-famous physicist, known to be one of the greatest living experts on the nature of the universe, is introduced. As a distinguished member of the scientific community and a former Nobel prize winner, his honesty and trustworthiness are unquestioned. Further, as he mounts the podium, you notice that he is an individual of impressive physical appearance—a true spellbinder. The room becomes hushed, and he begins to speak, announcing with great conviction and forcefulness that the moon is made of Swiss cheese. For a moment there is stunned silence, then wild howls of laughter erupt, and the speaker is driven from the stage.

This extreme and admittedly farfetched incident serves to illustrate an important point: the effectiveness of a persuasive appeal depends not only on its source—who delivers it—but also on the message it contains and the manner in which it is presented. Since the specific contents of any persuasive message must vary with the particular issue involved, most research on this topic has focused on either (1) the *form* of such appeals (should **one** or **two-sided arguments** be used? is it better for the communicator to advocate positions highly or moderately discrepant from those held by the audience?) or (2) on the *general nature* of its arguments (are appeals based on fear an effective technique?)

The issue of one versus two-sided arguments centers around the question of whether it is better for a communicator to present only the view he would like his audience to adopt, or both this view and competing positions. Existing evidence suggests that the answer to this question depends on whether the audience is initially favorable or unfavorable to the communicator's views. If they are favorable, it is better to employ the one-sided approach, for in this case, they are disposed to accept the message anyway, and the presence of competing views will only cloud the issue. When they are unfavorable however, the two-sided approach appears to be more effective, probably because the communicator seems more credible and less biased when presenting both sides of the story.

Evidence relating to the size of the discrepancy between the position advocated by the communicator and that held by the audience suggests that, up to a point, greater discrepancies lead to greater attitude change, but that beyond some crucial level, attitude change may actually begin to decrease as the communicator-audience gap continues to widen (e.g., Eagly and Telaak, 1972). Apparently, this sort of "boomerang" effect is due to the fact that beyond some specific point, audience members begin to find the communicator's position unreasonable or extreme, and reject it as being invalid or ridiculous. For example, an individual addressing wealthy members of the American Medical Association might be hooted from the stage if she called for an immediate shift to socialized medicine, but might have some impact (or at least manage to get her message across), if she recommended a moderate increase in existing government programs such as Medicare.

Not too surprisingly, the point at which increasing discrepancy size begins to produce less rather than more attitude change varies with the credibility of the communicator. Highly credible sources can advocate relatively extreme positions with little or no reduction in their persuasive impact, while less credible sources may begin to experience strong "boomerang" effects as the statements they make depart to increasing degrees from the beliefs of their audience. For example, in one well-known study (Aronson, Turner, and Carlsmith, 1963), female college students evaluated two passages of poetry and then received communications concerning these verses from either a high or low credibility source (T. S. Eliot or an undergraduate student at an obscure college, respectively). The discrepancy between their own ratings and those provided by these sources was varied in a systematic manner so as to be small, medium, or large. When subjects later reevaluated the poems, it was found that those exposed to a communication from a high-credibility source showed increasing attitude change as discrepancy size increased, while those exposed to a communication from a low-credibility source actually showed less attitude change when discrepancy size was large than when it was moderate (see Figure 3-5).

Emotional Appeals: Persuasion through Fear. While most attempts to change our attitudes involve the use of persuasive communications, others employ strong **fear-inducing appeals** for this purpose, suggesting that failure to adopt certain positions or recommended actions will lead to truly disastrous results. For example, politicians often suggest that the election of their opponents will lead to corruption and chaos, clergy often state that failure to adopt certain religious beliefs will result in eternal damnation, and public service organizations announce that failure to follow good health or safety practices will lead to injury, illness, or even death.

In view of the frequency with which such fear communications are employed to alter our attitudes, it is important to ask whether they are indeed successful in this respect. A large number of experiments have been concerned with this question, and in general, results have suggested that strong fear messages do indeed tend to induce greater attitude change than weak ones (see Higbee, 1969).

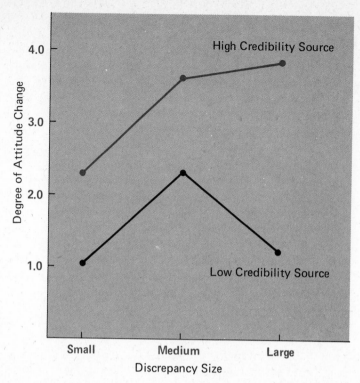

FIGURE 3-5. *The effects of communicator-audience discrepancy size on persuasion. Attitude change increases with increasing discrepancy size for high credibility communicators, but may first increase and then decline in the case of low credibility sources. (Source: Based on data from Aronson, Turner, and Carlsmith, 1963.)*

For example, frightening films showing diseased lungs and actual lung cancer operations have been found to produce greater shifts in smokers' attitudes toward their habit than milder communications depicting smoking machines, charts, and graphs (Leventhal, Watts, and Pagano, 1967). Similarly, unsettling pictures of decayed teeth and diseased gums have been shown to produce greater changes in attitudes toward dental hygiene than less frightening communications based on pictures of plastic models of teeth (Evans et al., 1970). Strong fear appeals are not always successful in changing attitudes, however, and other findings suggest that they are most effective in this regard when recipients are also provided with concrete recommendations for avoiding the negative outcomes shown (Leventhal, 1970; Rogers and Mewborn, 1976).

This fact—that fear appeals seem to function best when followed by clear recommendations—points to one possible explanation for their success. Specifically, it may be the case that acceptance of the recommendations offered produces a sharp reduction in subjects' level of arousal. Since reductions in unpleasant emotional arousal are reinforcing, recipients' tendencies to accept these recommendations may then be strengthened and attitude change en-

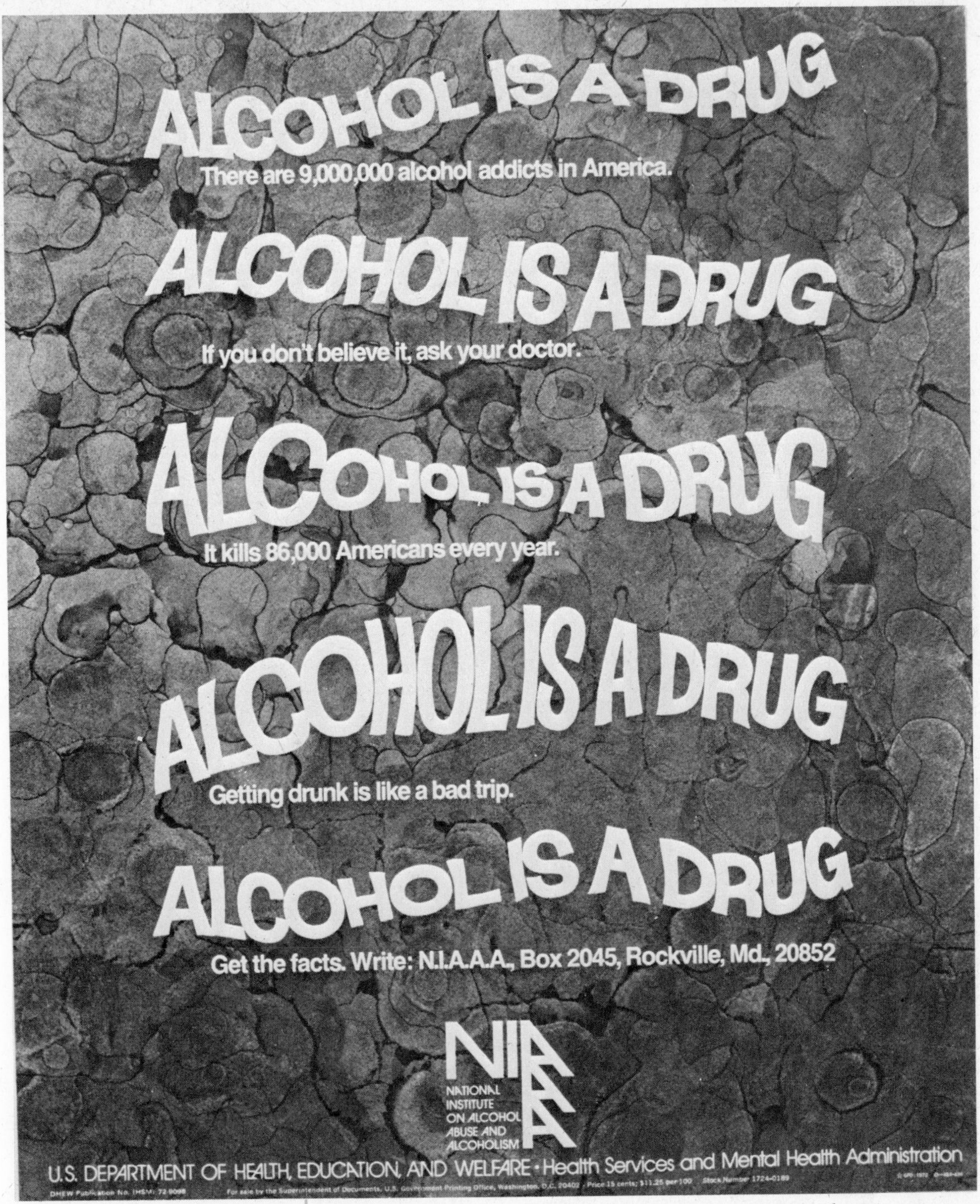

Fear appeals which threaten recipients with highly unpleasant outcomes, such as those shown above, are often quite effective in changing both attitudes and behavior. (Photo: Phil Carver & Friends.)

Changing Attitudes: The Power of Positive Persuasion   **119**

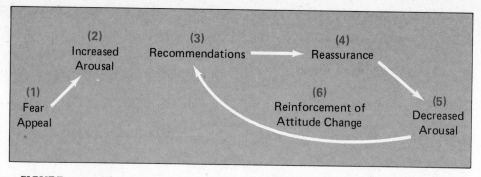

FIGURE 3-6. *The drive-reduction explanation for the success of fear appeals in changing attitudes. According to this view, fear communications (1) lead to increased arousal (2). Recommendations following the fear appeal (3) then lead to reassurance on the part of recipients (4), which serves to reduce their negative arousal (5). These reductions in arousal are reinforcing and strengthen acceptance of the recommendations, thus producing attitude change (6).*

hanced. Moreover, since the reduction of high levels of arousal is more reinforcing than the reduction of lower ones, strong fear appeals would be expected to produce greater degrees of attitude change than weak ones. (A summary of these suggestions is presented in Figure 3-6.)

Evidence for this drive-reduction explanation for the operation of fear appeals has been obtained in several recent experiments (Harris and Jellison, 1971; Giesen and Hendrick, 1974). In the study by Harris and Jellison, female undergraduates listened to a tape-recorded communication concerning the potential hazards resulting from the widespread use of pesticides. This message consisted of two distinct parts, the first containing fear-arousing comments, and the second containing specific recommendations for avoiding the dangers described. As they listened to both portions, subjects received feedback from a physiological recording device which supposedly indicated their level of fear. In reality, however, the information provided by this meter was controlled by the experimenter and varied in a systematic manner across four different groups. In one condition (no arousal), subjects' fear seemed to remain low during the entire communication. In a second (arousal, no reduction), it increased during the fear-inducing part and then remained high even during the recommendations. In a third (arousal-reduction), it rose during the first portion of the communication and then dropped sharply during the second. Finally, in a fourth group (variable arousal), subjects' arousal seemed to be low during the fear-inducing comments, but then actually rose when the recommendations were provided. On the basis of the drive-reduction interpretation described above, it was expected that subjects provided with feedback suggesting that their arousal was reduced by the recommendations would show a greater degree of attitude change than those in the other groups. As can be seen in Figure 3-7, this is precisely what happened; when subjects were later asked to express their attitudes toward the issue discussed by the communication, those in the arousal-reduction group showed the greatest acceptance of his views.

Chapter 3   Attitudes: Their Nature, Formation, and Change

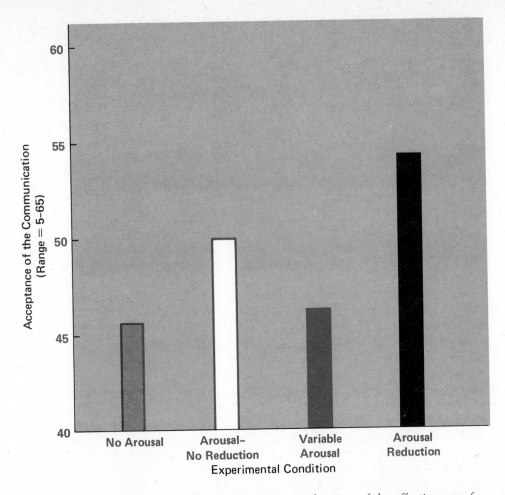

FIGURE 3-7. *Evidence for the drive-reduction explanation of the effectiveness of fear appeals. Subjects led to believe that their level of arousal increased during the fear-induction portion of a communication but then decreased following the recommendations (black bar) showed greater attitude change than those in three other groups. (Source: Based on data from Harris and Jellison, 1971.)*

These findings, and similar results in other studies, suggest that the effectiveness of fear appeals may indeed stem from the relief individuals experience when—by shifting their attitudes—they succeed in reducing their feelings of fear. We should hasten to add, however, that not all findings lend support to this conclusion. Instead, the results of other studies suggest that the arousal of fear itself, even without any reduction of such reactions, may sometimes be sufficient to induce attitude change (Hendrick, Giesen, and Borden, 1975). Apparently, in some cases, individuals who find that they have been made fearful by a persuasive communication reason as follows: "Anything which can frighten me so badly must be very convincing." And then, on the basis of such conclusions, they alter their attitudes accordingly. While it is not yet clear whether fear reduction, or merely fear arousal, plays a dominant role in accounting for the effectiveness of emotion-provoking appeals, there is currently little doubt that frightening one's audience may often prove to be an effective technique of persuasion.

Characteristics of the Recipients: Are Some People Easier to Persuade Than Others? Informal observation suggests that even an extremely convincing persuasive appeal delivered by a highly credible source will fail to change the attitudes of all the persons who receive it, and even a very weak appeal presented by a source low in credibility will succeed in changing the attitudes of *some* listeners. This is the case because, as is true of virtually every other imaginable characteristic, people vary greatly in terms of their susceptibility to persuasion. Some are highly resistant to virtually all forms of influence, others are swayed easily by even weak appeals, and most are somewhere in between these two extremes. Over the years, many attempts have been made to relate various personality characteristics to differences in persuasibility. The findings of these investigations, however, have often been quite inconsistent (see Skolnick and Heslin, 1971b). For example, to mention just one factor which has been the subject of much continuing study, self-esteem has been found—in different experiments—to be positively related, negatively related, or totally unrelated to persuasibility.

Fortunately, a theoretical framework proposed by William McGuire (1969) offers a ready explanation for these contradictory results. According to McGuire, personality factors probably influence the acceptance of persuasive communications in two ways. First, they affect recipients' *reception* or *comprehension* of such messages, and second, they influence their *willingness to yield* to them. Since any given personality characteristic may affect these two processes in different ways, the relationship between such traits and persuasibility may often be quite complex. For example, consider the case of self-esteem. Individuals low in this characteristic are usually lacking in self-confidence or assurance. Thus, it seems reasonable to expect that they will often yield more readily to persuasive appeals from others than persons who are higher in self-esteem. At the same time, however, their low self-confidence may interfere with their reception and understanding of many messages—especially ones they find threatening to their already low self-image. In such cases, they may remain largely uninfluenced by persuasive appeals simply because they are not able to receive or comprehend them.

If this reasoning is correct, it would be expected that the influence of self-esteem upon persuasibility will depend, to an important degree, on the complexity of the communications delivered. When such messages are quite simple, even low self-esteem individuals will understand them. Under these conditions, they would be expected to demonstrate greater attitude change than persons who are high in self-esteem. When the communications employed are complex, however, low self-esteem individuals may fail to grasp their meaning. In such cases, they may demonstrate the same low degree of yielding as persons who are high in this characteristic. These predictions have actually been confirmed by Zellner (1970), who found that individuals moderately low in self-esteem demonstrated more attitude change than persons high in self-esteem when exposed to simple communications but *less* change than such individuals when exposed to complex messages (see Figure 3-8). Additional studies which have attempted to extend McGuire's suggestions to other personality factors (e.g., the need for approval from others) have also yielded positive results (Skolnick and Heslin, 1971a). Thus, at present, it appears that the framework he proposes may be an extremely useful one for understanding the complex links between personality on the one hand, and persuasion on the other.

Characteristics of the Context: Mood and Distraction. Persuasive communications do not occur in a social vacuum. Rather, they are usually part of a broader, ongoing context. For example, the physical setting in which they are delivered may vary from the stages of giant auditoriums, to TV screens in recipients' own homes. Similarly, they may be presented as part of highly formal programs, or in a totally spontaneous and unrehearsed manner. And often, other events which can affect either the ability of the audience to receive the message presented or their willingness to accept its contents are taking place at the same time. In short, it seems likely that many aspects of the context surrounding persuasive appeals will strongly influence their success in producing attitude change. Although a number of different factors might be expected to exert such effects, two have received most attention in recent research: the *current mood of recipients,* and the presence of any factors which *distract their attention.*

Common sense suggests that people are much easier to influence when they are in a good mood than when they are feeling irritable or grouchy. In accordance with this widespread belief, businessmen often attempt to "wine and dine" their potential clients before entering into serious negotiations, and, largely for similar reasons, most seductions are attempted after a good meal, and in the presence of soft lights and pleasant music. Politicians, too, seem to follow this suggestion, frequently providing free refreshments and entertainment at political rallies in order to put potential voters in a good mood before beginning their appeals.

In this particular instance, informal observation seems to be correct, for experiments undertaken to examine the relationship between mood and the acceptance of social influence have generally yielded positive results. For example, it has been found that providing subjects with a light snack during the period when they are exposed to persuasive messages increases their degree of attitude change in the direction advocated (Janis, Kaye, and Kirschner, 1965). Similarly, the presence of pleasant music seems to increase the acceptance of persuasive appeals dealing with serious social issues (e.g., water pollution and the desperate plight of the aged; see Galizio and Hendrick, 1972). Such findings suggest that songs with a "message," which were very popular a few years in the past, may actually have been quite effective in changing several important social attitudes.

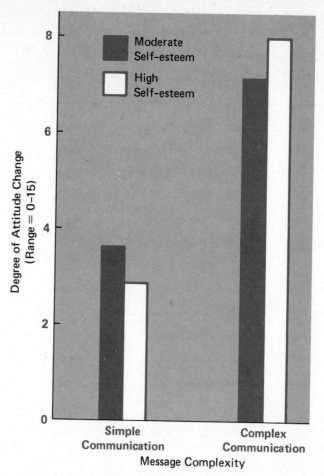

FIGURE 3-8. *The relationship between self-esteem and persuasibility. Individuals of moderate self-esteem demonstrated more attitude change than those high in self-esteem when exposed to simple communications, but less attitude change when exposed to complex messages. (Source: Based on data from Zellner, 1970.)*

Although it is not yet clear why persuasion is enhanced by positive feelings, one possible explanation for the occurrence of such effects may be suggested. Specifically, it may be the case that the positive reactions experienced by recipients generalize to the communications they receive, and so cause them to evaluate these messages in a more favorable manner. Regardless of whether this is shown to be the case in further research, it appears that attempts to "soften up" the targets of persuasion by placing them in a relaxed and pleasant mood may often yield handsome dividends in terms of increased attitude change.

The Effects of Distraction. Suppose that while listening to a persuasive message arguing against your own views, your attention was distracted in some manner (for example, extraneous noises made it hard to concentrate on the

Putting another person in a good mood is often a highly effective first step to persuasion.

speaker's words). Would your tendency to accept this appeal be raised or lowered? At first, you might expect that it would be reduced, since it would be difficult to concentrate on the message and understand its contents. On the other hand, **distraction** might have another effect: it would prevent you from formulating good counterarguments to the speaker's views in your own mind. As a result, you might actually be swayed to a greater extent than would be the case if distraction was absent. Whether distraction increases or reduces persuasion, therefore, may depend on which of these contrasting effects predominates.

Proceeding from this assumption, Regan and Cheng (1973) have argued that the relative importance of these two effects is determined by the nature of the communication delivered. If this message is readily understood but not very convincing, distraction will interfere with its reception to a minimal degree, but still prevent counterarguing. As a result, persuasion will be enhanced. If the communication is complex but convincing, however, the interference with reception or comprehension produced by distraction will be crucial, and attitude change may be sharply reduced. In sum, distraction should increase persuasion in the case of simple messages, but reduce it in the case of complex ones. In order to investigate these suggestions, Regan and Cheng conducted an experiment in which subjects heard either a complex and convincing or a simple but unconvincing communication which argued that brushing one's teeth is *not* an effective method of dental care. While listening to these communications, half were distracted by a tape recording of rock music which was played simultaneously; the remainder heard the messages without such distraction. It was predicted that in the case of the simple communication, distraction would actually increase persuasion, while in the case of the complex appeal, it would have the opposite effect. As can be seen in Figure 3-9, results provided strong support for this hypothesis. These findings and the results of other studies (Keating and Brock, 1974) suggest that distraction is indeed a two-edged sword, increasing persuasion under some conditions, but reducing it under others.

Frequency of Exposure: Familiarity Breeds Content. Members of the advertising profession often seem to operate under the assumption that repetition is an effective prelude to persuasion. Thus, they repeat the same ads or commercials over and over again in the hope that such exposure will induce a

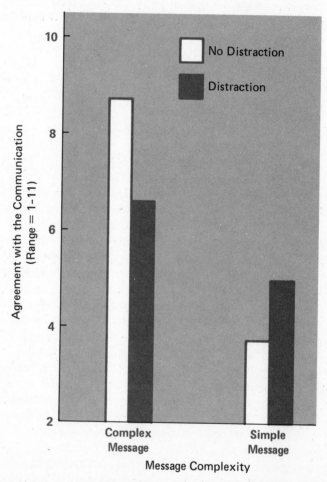

FIGURE 3-9. *The effects of distraction on persuasion. While distraction reduces attitude change in response to complex communications, it actually seems to enhance persuasion in the case of simple appeals. (Source: Based on data from Regan and Cheng, 1973.)*

positive attitude among consumers toward the products in question. Despite the irritation many of us experience as a result of such procedures, a growing body of research suggests that within limits, this belief in the effectiveness of **mere exposure** may be justified. That is, it appears that, up to a point, increasing frequency of exposure may actually enhance our attitudes toward many different stimuli.

The first systematic evidence concerning this relationship was gathered by Robert Zajonc (1968). In a series of integrated studies, he demonstrated that the more frequently various words or stimuli either occur naturally in the world around us, or are presented in the laboratory, the more favorably they are rated by subjects. For example, in one study, he asked participants to indicate which of the words in antonym pairs (e.g., fast-slow, hot-cold) was the more favorable. Results indicated that 82 percent of the time, subjects chose the word that occurred more frequently in actual use. Similarly, when subjects were asked to rate the names of various cities, flowers, trees, fruits, and vegetables, the same relationship between frequency of natural occurrence and liking were obtained: the more often such words appear in common use, the more they were liked. In still other studies, Zajonc systematically varied the frequency with which subjects were exposed to various stimuli such as Chinese characters, specially constructed "Turkish" words (e.g., zabulon, civadra, afworbu), and even photos of other persons. In each case, he found that subjects' reactions to these stimuli became more positive as frequency of exposure increased (see Figure 3-10).

Stimulated by Zajonc's work, many other researchers turned their attention to this topic. Their investigations soon extended his initial findings to many other stimuli. For example, it was reported that the favorability of subjects' reactions toward art reproductions, simple drawings, music, and geometric figures all increased with frequency of exposure (Heingartner and Hall, 1974; Smith and Dorfman, 1975). That such effects also seem to occur in potentially important social settings is indicated by the findings of a recent study by Hamm, Baum, and Nikels (1975), who reported that after viewing photos of several black persons on ten occasions, white subjects reported more favorable reactions to them than they had upon seeing them for the first time.

As might be expected, increasing frequency of exposure does not always lead to more positive reactions. First, it appears that such effects are restricted to relatively complex stimuli; when simple ones are presented over and over again, liking often fails to increase, and may in fact decrease (Saegert and Jellison, 1970; Smith and Dorfman, 1975). Second, increased frequency of exposure does not lead to more favorable reactions when stimuli are presented in a negative context (Suedfeld et al., 1971). And finally, as suggested by our reactions to the thousandth viewing of the same commercial, there may be limits to the relationship; beyond some point, further exposure may lead to less rather than more liking (see Zajonc et al., 1972).

Although several explanations have been offered for the relationship between frequency of exposure and liking, one in terms of *response competition* seems to have received the most attention. According to this interpretation, unfamiliar stimuli tend to elicit many different reactions or response tendencies from us. Since some of these prove to be incompatible with each other (e.g., a

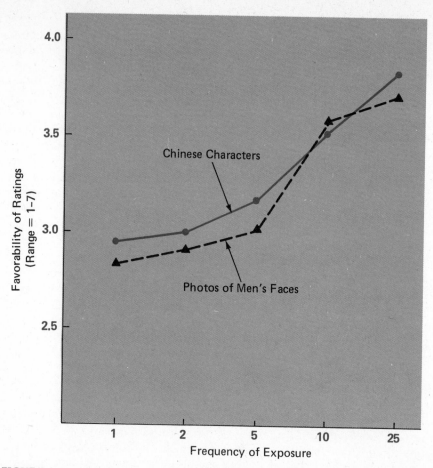

FIGURE 3-10. *The effects of repeated exposure on attitudes. The more frequently various stimuli were presented, the more favorable were subjects' reactions to them. Results for two types of stimuli, Chinese characters, and photos of men's faces, are presented. (Source: Based on data from Zajonc, 1968.)*

tendency to approach and explore the stimulus and a tendency to flee from it), an unpleasant state of tension is induced. With repeated exposure, one of these tendencies usually becomes dominant, and this negative state is reduced. As a result, our reactions to the stimulus become more favorable. While some evidence for this view has been obtained (Harrison, 1968), the issue is far from closed (see Smith and Dorfman, 1975). Thus, at present, the precise mechanisms underlying the effects of repeated exposure have not been clearly established. What does seem certain, however, is the existence of this effect and the fact that it influences our reactions to a wide variety of stimuli in a number of different settings.

Resistance to Persuasion: Reactance and Negative Attitude Change. Judging from the information we have presented so far, you might well expect that when they are exposed to convincing communications from credible communicators, most individuals will in fact be persuaded and alter their attitudes to a considerable degree. Although this is certainly often the case, there are also many instances in which individuals resist even very powerful forms of persuasion. A number of different factors play a role in this ability to withstand influence from others, but one of the most important centers around the process of **psychological reactance** (see Brehm, 1972). If you have ever been in a situation where, because you felt someone was trying to exert undue influence upon you, you leaned over backwards to do the opposite of what he or she wished, you have had first-hand experience with this process. Basically, it refers to the fact that most persons have a strong desire to maintain their freedom of action. As a result, when they feel that this freedom is threatened, as it often is by influence attempts from others, they act so as to maintain or restore it. In the case of persuasion, such actions often take the form of rejection of the communicator's appeals, or even changes in a direction opposite to that which is being advocated—so-called "boomerang" effects.

The occurrence of such reactions has been observed in a number of experiments conducted by Jack Brehm and his associates (e.g., Sensenig and Brehm, 1968; Worchel and Brehm, 1971). In general, the results of these studies suggest that when confronted with influence attempts from others—and especially when such appeals take the form of arbitrary orders or commands—many individuals experience strong reactance, and actually shift in a direction opposite to that which is being advocated. Indeed, so strong is the desire to maintain one's freedom of action that such effects even seem to occur in situations where the views being recommended are quite similar to those which individuals would normally choose themselves. Apparently, many persons find the idea of being influenced by another so objectionable that they would rather adopt a position they do not really support than accept the one being urged on them by a communicator. Such effects are reminiscent of the "negativism" often shown by young children, who consistently choose to do the opposite of what their parents suggest or command. In the case of adults, of course, the decision to reject social influence from others and to move in the opposite direction is far more adaptive and rational. But the same basic principle—a strong desire to maintain or restore one's freedom of action—may play a role in generating both forms of behavior.

More recent experiments have indicated that reactance can be aroused even in the absence of actual influence attempts from others. In particular, it seems to be the case that merely learning that another person intends to exert influence on us is often sufficient to induce strong feelings of this type. For example, in one study conducted by Heller, Pallak, and Picek (1973), male and female college students overheard comments suggesting that another person (actually an accomplice of the experimenter) either wished to influence their views on a particular issue, or had no such intentions. (Subjects in a third, control group learned nothing about this person's intentions one way or the other.) They then received a note from this person which either threatened or did not threaten their freedom of action: in the first case, the note ordered them to write an essay supporting one side of the issue, while in the second it merely suggested that they do so. (Again, subjects in a third group received no message from the accomplice whatsoever.) Following these procedures, subjects indicated their own opinion on the issue. Consistent with the results of previous investigations, individuals whose freedom of action was threatened by the accomplice shifted their attitudes in a direction opposite to the one he recommended. In addition, subjects who learned that this person intended to influence them showed similar, strong "boomerang" effects even when he did not directly threaten their freedom (i.e., even when he transmitted no message to them). Apparently, merely discovering that he intended to exert such pressure was sufficient to arouse strong feelings of reactance whether he followed through on this intention or not (see Figure 3-11).

Findings such as these allow us to conclude this discussion of persuasion on a positive note by suggesting that human beings are actually far more resistant to such pressure than might at first be suspected. Although highly credible communicators uttering convincing appeals under highly favorable circumstances may often produce considerable amounts of change, the strong desire on the part of most persons to maintain their freedom of action frequently reduces the impact of such messages. Reactance, in short, often places severe limits upon the success of various "hard-sell" attempts at persuasion.

Creating Resistance to Persuasion: Inoculation against "Bad Ideas." A second factor which may also play a role in increasing resistance to persuasion has been identified by William McGuire (1961, 1969). Basically, McGuire has argued that exposing individuals to arguments against their views—but which are then refuted—may often serve to "inoculate" them against later persuasive appeals. That is, having heard various arguments against their attitudes invalidated, individuals may be better equipped to withstand later attempts at persuasion. Indeed, according to McGuire, such immunizing treatments may prove to be more effective than ones in which individuals are merely presented with arguments favoring their initial views.

In order to test these proposals, McGuire and Papageorgis (1961) exposed subjects to two contrasting procedures designed to strengthen their resistance to persuasive communications. The first (a *supportive defense*) involved the presentation of several arguments supporting their views on various noncontroversial issues (e.g., the benefits of penicillin). The second (a *refutational defense*) involved the presentation of several weak arguments against subjects' initial views, which were then strongly refuted. A third experimental condition involved the absence of both types of immunization.

Several days later, subjects were exposed to strong attacks against their views. Following these attacks, their attitudes were assessed once again. As predicted by McGuire, the refutational defense was quite effective in protecting participants against later attitude change. Indeed, it proved to be much more successful in this respect than the supportive defense. Together with the results of other research (McGuire, 1969), these findings point to the conclusion that our ability to resist persuasive appeals is often substantially increased by exposure to

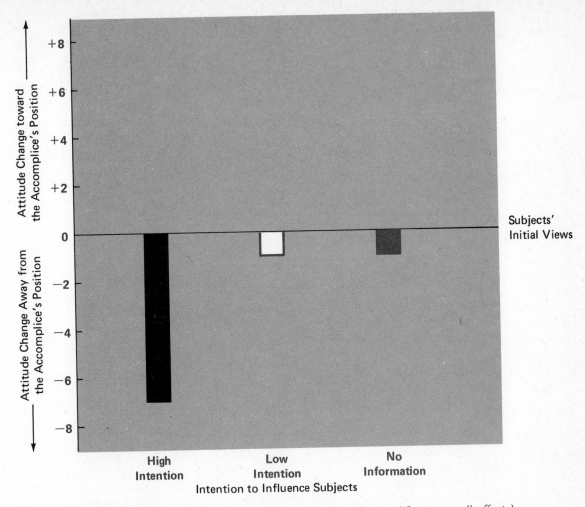

FIGURE 3-11. *Reactance and negative attitude change ("boomerang" effects). Individuals led to believe that another person wished to influence their views (shaded bar) actually shifted their opinions in a direction opposite to that which he advocated. Moreover, this was true even under conditions where he did not overtly attempt to influence them in this manner. (Source: Based on data from Heller, Pallak, and Picek, 1973.)*

conditions in which competing views are presented, but then strongly refuted. In short, previous exposure to "bad ideas" in a weak or readily refuted form may indeed serve to "immunize" us against later attempts at persuasion.

Attitude-discrepant Behavior: Dissonance as a Basis for Change

For a wide variety of reasons, individuals often behave in a manner which is inconsistent with their true attitudes. Legal restraints, social norms, or simple

AN INFORMAL SURVEY OF PERSUASION

In our discussion of persuasive communications, we have examined a large number of factors that seem to influence the success of such appeals in altering the attitudes of recipients. Although we have tried to mention the practical applications of each as it was introduced, perhaps the best way for you to gain an appreciation of their widespread use is by conducting your own informal survey. Since television happens to be where the advertising and political "action" are in the 1970's, this is probably the best place to begin. Given the frequency of commercials and other paid announcements, one evening of viewing will probably suffice. Thus, even if you are a dyed-in-the-wool TV hater, you should be able to conduct your survey without encountering too much discomfort.

Begin by making a list of the factors we have considered (e.g., communicator credibility, one versus two-sided arguments, etc.). Be sure to leave enough space below each heading to record several instances of its use. Then simply go ahead with your survey, recording examples of each factor as they occur in commercials or paid political announcements. Although you may well encounter virtually every variable we have discussed, you may wish to keep a special watch for the following techniques:

1. Commercials which make use of communicator expertise. These may include messages in which sports stars endorse razors, beautiful models recommend cosmetics, and Ph.D's endorse the nutritional benefits of breakfast drinks or cereals.

2. Commercials which make use of communicator attractiveness. Here you will probably find highly attractive models selling everything from ballpoint pens to automobiles.

3. Ads which attempt to benefit from a high degree of communicator sincerity or trustworthiness. These include commercials in which average persons with no obvious axe to grind are shown selecting the brand of beer or coffee being promoted from among several unmarked containers.

4. Emotional appeals: messages by public-service organizations designed to prevent us from speeding, taking illegal drugs, smoking or drinking too much, etc.

5. Frequency of exposure: the use of this factor will probably be so painfully obvious as to require no comment!

After you have completed your informal survey, you may wish to ponder such questions as these: Which of the factors did you encounter most frequently? Which seemed to you to be used most effectively? Finally, do you think that the understanding of these techniques you have gained from this chapter (and your survey) will help you to resist their influence in the future?

good sense dictate that they contradict their own beliefs or preferences. To mention just a few examples, we must often act in a friendly, pleasant manner toward superiors we dislike; to do otherwise would result in highly unpleasant consequences. Similarly, we must obey many rules or laws with which we disagree, and for which we can see no good purpose. And we must often say things we do not really believe in order either to please others, or to avoid hurting their feelings. (Have you ever praised a friend's clothing, hairstyle, or appearance even though you found it quite unattractive?)

In many cases, individuals pass through such situations with their attitudes largely intact; they behave the way they must, and their beliefs remain unaltered.

In many others, however, the performance of such attitude-discrepant behavior seems to result in important internal shifts. Once an individual has said or done something inconsistent with his or her attitudes, some degree of change often follows. The occurrence of such effects is readily visible in the social world around us. For example, liars often come to believe the falsehoods they utter, so that they can no longer tell truth from fiction. And persons who engage in some action they find objectionable often come to view it in a more favorable light once it is completed. (They seem to reason that if they did it, it can't really be that bad after all.) In order to understand why the performance of actions inconsistent with one's own attitudes often results in the modification of these feelings and beliefs, we must turn to the theory of *cognitive dissonance,* one of the most important perspectives ever developed by social psychologists (Festinger, 1957).

The Theory of Cognitive Dissonance: Inconsistency Hurts. Despite the fact that dissonance theory has probably generated more excitement and more research in social psychology than any other framework, the basic ideas it involves are both simple and straightforward. Essentially, the theory begins with the very reasonable assumption that human beings dislike inconsistency. More specifically, they do not like inconsistency between their various attitudes, on the one hand, or inconsistency between their attitudes and behavior, on the other. When such conditions arise, they experience an unpleasant state known as *dissonance.* More formally, dissonance is said to occur whenever one cognitive element—anything an individual knows or believes about himself, the environment, or his behavior—implies the opposite of the other. Put another way, dissonance occurs whenever the opposite of one cognitive element follows from another. Perhaps a specific example will help clarify matters further.

Consider the case of a young woman who believes that she is extremely attractive, but finds that she has no dates. These two cognitive elements—"I'm very attractive," and "I have no dates"—are clearly inconsistent. In fact, the opposite of one does indeed follow from the other ("I have *many* dates" should follow from the cognition "I'm very attractive," or, conversely, "I'm *not* very attractive" should follow from the cognition "I have no dates"). Given this situation, dissonance will result. The magnitude of dissonance in this and any other context depends primarily on the number of dissonant elements involved, and the importance of these to the person. Since, in this case, the cognition "I'm very attractive" is probably an important part of the young woman's self-image, a considerable amount of dissonance would be likely to result.

As you might suspect, dissonance is a highly unpleasant state. Generally, it has been compared to feelings of anxiety, tension, or uneasiness and, like these unpleasant states, seems to exert motivating or arousing effects on behavior (Pallak and Pittman, 1972; Zanna and Cooper, 1974). Since it is an unpleasant form of arousal, individuals usually seek to reduce it, just as they seek to reduce or eliminate other, similar reactions. Fortunately, this can be accomplished in a number of different ways. For example, persons experiencing dissonance can cognitively *reduce the importance of the elements involved.* Returning to the example above, the young woman in question might somehow convince herself that it is not really very important to have many dates. Since the importance of the elements involved would then be reduced, the magnitude of dissonance generated would also drop sharply. Second, individuals experiencing dissonance can *add consonant elements*—ones which are consistent with those generating dissonance—and so help explain away the discrepancy. For example, the young woman in question might say to herself "The reason I have so few dates is that I'm very choosey." Since this cognition fits neatly with the cognition "I'm very attractive" (attractive people are, after all, often quite selective), dissonance would be reduced. Third, and most important in the context of our present discussion of attitude change, individuals can *change one or both of the dissonant elements* so that they are no longer inconsistent. Thus, the woman in our example could either admit that she is not as attractive as she thought, or somehow convince herself that she really *does* have many dates.

When individuals choose to follow the last of these three methods of dissonance reduction, they usually adopt a general strategy employed in many other situations as well: they select the path of least resistance. In our example, the woman involved would probably alter the cognition concerning her degree of beauty. Painful as it may be to admit to herself that she is not quite as attractive as she thought, this is still somewhat easier than convincing herself that she has gone out on many nonexistent dates. In short, when dissonance is intense, something has to "give," and this is usually the cognitive element which is least resistant to change.

The basic ideas of dissonance theory have been applied by social psychologists to many different situations (see Kiesler and Munson, 1975). Since the main purpose of this duscussion is that of examining the effects of attitude-discrepant behavior, however, we will restrict our attention to only two of these interesting applications.

First, dissonance theory has been applied to situations in which people make important decisions. Here, it suggests that any decision with more than trivial consequences will result in a considerable amount of dissonance. /This is the case because by choosing one of two alternatives, the individual has automatically given up all of the positive features of the other./ In sum, the cognition "I chose X" (where X is one of the alternatives) is inconsistent with all other cognitions involving positive features of "Y" (the unchosen alternative). Similarly, the cognition "I chose X" is also inconsistent with all thoughts involving negative features of "X" itself. One way of eliminating such dissonance, of course, is to deny or actually reverse the decision—"X" can be rejected and "Y" chosen instead. Since many decisions are difficult to reverse once made, however, our rule of "least effort" suggests that individuals will generally choose another means of reducing their dissonance in such situations. Specifically, they will seek to eliminate such reactions by magnifying or emphasizing the positive features of the chosen alternative, and magnifying or emphasizing the negative features of the alternative they have rejected. As a result of this process, the two choices—which may have been quite similar in overall appeal prior to the decision—will soon come to be seen as quite far apart on this dimension. You have probably often observed this tendency to overvalue the things you have chosen and undervalue the things you have rejected in your own behavior, and they have also been demonstrated in a number of different experiments (Brehm, 1956). For example, in one ingenious field study conducted by Knox and Inkster (1968), two groups of individuals at a race track were approached and asked to rate their horse's chances of winning. One group was questioned approximately thirty seconds before placing their bets, while the second was approached shortly after plunking down their money. Dissonance theory suggests that those questioned *after* making their decision (i.e., after placing their bets) would express greater confidence that their horse would win than those questioned *before* making their selection, and results actually confirmed these predictions (see Figure 3-12). Thus, having made a choice among several different alternatives (in this case horses), individuals quickly came to view the one they had selected as more attractive than the others. Results such as these suggest that the theory of cognitive dissonance provides a good explanation for our strong tendency to perceive most—if not all—of our decisions as good ones soon after they have been made.

A second class of situations to which dissonance theory seems applicable are those in which strong expectations held by an individual are disconfirmed. For example, suppose that a person has worked long and hard to obtain a particular goal, such as a Ph.D. degree in physics. Presumably, since he has invested a great deal of effort in obtaining this goal, he expects it to be quite worthwhile. But now imagine that such expectations are strongly disconfirmed; after receiving his degree, he finds that he cannot obtain a job. An individual facing such a situation would be expected to experience a tremendous amount of dissonance since the two inconsistent cognitions "I worked long and hard to reach this goal" and "I now find that it is worthless" are both quite important. In order to reduce such unpleasant reactions, he might either convince himself that he did not

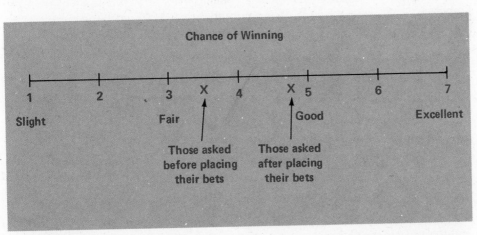

FIGURE 3-12. *Dissonance at the race track. When questioned, individuals who had just placed a bet at the $2 window indicated greater confidence that their horse would win than those who had not yet actually placed their bet. (Source: Based on data from Knox and Inkster, 1968.)*

actually invest much effort in obtaining the goal ("I really didn't work very hard in graduate school"), or come to evaluate it more favorably ("I may be unemployed, but after all, I have still earned the title 'Dr.' and the respect of my relatives.") Since it is usually very difficult for individuals to convince themselves that they did not invest great effort in obtaining such a goal (years of toil cannot be lightly disregarded), they are usually more likely to adopt the second strategy, convincing themselves that the goal for which they labored was indeed worthwhile.

The occurrence of such effects has been demonstrated in several interesting experiments. For example, in the first of these investigations, which is now something of a "classic" in social psychology (Aronson and Mills, 1959), female college students in three groups underwent either a mild initiation, a severe initiation, or no initiation at all in order to gain entry to a group which would presumably be discussing sexual behavior. The *mild* initiation consisted of reading five nonobscene but sex-related words to the male experimenter (e.g., prostitute, virgin, petting), while the *severe* initiation required the women to read twelve obscene, four-letter words and two lurid sexual passages to this individual. After completing these initiations (or, in the case of the control group, after simply being made part of the group), subjects listened to a discussion supposedly carried on by the other members. In reality, what they overheard was a tape-recording of a conversation designed to be as dull, boring, and senseless as possible. After listening to this session, subjects were asked to rate both the discussion and group members on a number of different dimensions such as dull-interesting, and intelligent-unintelligent. On the basis of dissonance theory, it would be expected that those who had undergone the severe initiation would experience a great deal of dissonance; after all, they had suffered through the embarrassing initiation for nothing. Since they could not deny the fact of this initiation (their cheeks might still be burning!) they would be expected to increase their evaluation of the group in order to reduce their unpleasant reactions. In contrast, those in the mild initiation group, who had suffered very little to join the group, would experience a much smaller degree of dissonance, and those in the control group, none at all. Thus, subjects in these conditions should show little or no tendency to overvalue the dull, tedious discussion they heard. As can be seen in Table 3-3, these predictions were clearly supported. Subjects in the severe initiation condition rated the group much more favorably than those in the two remaining groups. Subsequent research has confirmed these findings, and generally pointed to the conclusion that they are indeed due to attempts by subjects to reduce dissonance (Gerard and Mathewson, 1966). Thus, while the possibility that other processes, too, play a role, has not been conclusively eliminated (Alexander and Sagatun, 1973), the theory of cognitive dissonance seems to offer a convincing explanation for the fact that in many cases, we seem to like best those things for which we have expended most effort or endured most suffering.

Attitude-discrepant Behavior: Forced Compliance. Now that we have at least touched on some of the more interesting implications of dissonance theory

TABLE 3-3. *Evidence that suffering often leads to liking. Female students who underwent an embarrassing initiation in order to join a discussion group which proved to be quite dull later reported more favorable reactions both to the group and its members than those who underwent only a mild initiation or none at all. See text for further explanation. (Source: Adapted from Aronson and Mills, 1959.)*

	No Initiation	Mild Initiation	Severe Initiation
Ratings of the Discussion (Range = 0 – 135)	80.2	81.8	97.6
Ratings of the Group Members (Range = 0 – 120)	89.9	89.3	97.7

for other situations, we can return to the main point of the present discussion: providing an explanation for the influence of attitude-discrepant behavior. If you have followed our comments up to this point, you may have already guessed how dissonance can account for such effects. Briefly, the argument goes something like this. Whenever an individual says or does something inconsistent with his or her true beliefs or feelings, dissonance is produced. These negative reactions can then be reduced in one of two ways: (1) the person involved can change his or her attitudes so that they are consistent with the action already taken, or (2) the person can alter his or her cognitions about this behavior. For example, imagine the case of a congressional representative who votes against a bill she actually supports. The dissonance produced by such attitude-discrepant behavior can then be reduced in either of the two general ways mentioned above. She can change the relevant attitudes, and decide that she was actually against the bill from the start, or alter her cognitions concerning her vote. Since behavior often produces important and irreversible consequences (in this case, the representative's vote is entered in the Congressional Record), it is usually easier for individuals to bring their attitudes into line with already completed actions than to deny that these have occurred. Thus, the performance of attitude-discrepant actions often results in corresponding shifts in attitudes for these reasons.

So far, our explanation of the influence of attitude-discrepant behavior is quite straightforward. But up to this point, we have ignored a very important question: *why*, precisely, did the person involved behave in a manner inconsistent with his or her beliefs? In our specific example, why did the congressional representative vote against a bill she supported? This is a crucial question because to the extent that persons acting in an attitude-discrepant manner have good reasons for their behavior, little or no dissonance will be produced. For example, imagine that our congressional representative voted against the bill because in this way, she was able to obtain a promise of future support from the majority leader of her party for another bill which she views as even more important. Under these conditions, she would probably experience little or no dissonance, for there was clear and sufficient justification for her action. In contrast, imagine that she voted against the bill because she had been asked to do so by a casual acquaintance, or because she experienced an unpleasant encounter with its sponsor the day before. Under these circumstances, a considerable amount of dissonance might well be generated because good or compelling reasons for her action are lacking. In short, the better justification an individual has for engaging in attitude-discrepant behavior, the less dissonance he or she will experience as a result of such action and, consequently, the less attitude change which will be produced.

→ This general principle leads to an interesting if unexpected prediction concerning situations in which individuals are offered rewards for engaging in attitude-discrepant behavior. In particular, it suggests that the amount of dissonance generated in such situations—and therefore the degree of attitude change which follows—will be at a maximum when such rewards are just barely sufficient to induce the inconsistent actions. Any smaller, and such behavior will not be induced; any larger, and the increased justification provided will serve to lessen the dissonance experienced. In sum, dissonance theory leads to the somewhat paradoxical prediction that in many cases, less may well produce more: lesser amounts of reward will actually induce greater degrees of change (see Figure 3-13).

The first attempt to test these predictions was carried out by Festinger and Carlsmith (1959) in what has proven to be another social psychological "classic." In this study, subjects were first required to perform extremely dull tasks for an hour (e.g., placing spools on a tray, dumping them out, and repeating this process over and over again) while the experimenter pretended to record their

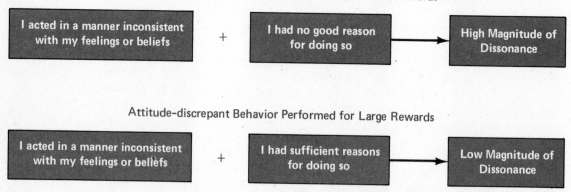

FIGURE 3-13. *Dissonance theory leads to the intriguing suggestion that when individuals choose to engage in attitude-discrepant behavior for relatively small rewards, they will often demonstrate greater amounts of change than when they engage in such actions for relatively large payoffs.*

Chapter 3   Attitudes: Their Nature, Formation, and Change

performance. Following these procedures, they were informed that the purpose of the study was that of examining the effects of expectancies on performance and asked if they would help the investigator study this topic by informing the next scheduled subject that the dull, boring tasks they had performed were actually quite interesting. As an incentive for engaging in such attitude-discrepant behavior, subjects in one group were offered a payment of $1.00, while those in a second were offered a payment of $20.00. (Individuals in a third condition were not asked to lie to the next participant.) Not surprisingly, almost all subjects in the two experimental groups agreed to help the investigator in this manner. After giving their consent, they were conducted to another room where they met with and lied to the next participant (actually an assistant of the experimenters). Following these events, they completed a brief questionnaire on which they indicated their reactions to the experiment, and were then provided with full information concerning its true nature and purpose.

On the basis of dissonance theory, it was predicted that subjects who had been paid only $1.00 for lying to the accomplice would report more favorable reactions to the experiment and tasks than those paid $20.00, because they would have far less justification for having engaged in attitude-discrepant behavior (i.e., for having lied to this person). As can be seen in Figure 3-14, this is precisely what occurred: subjects paid $1.00 for lying actually reported liking both the experiment and tasks to a greater degree than those paid $20.00 for such behavior, or those who had never been asked to mislead the confederate.

Although the results of the Festinger and Carlsmith (1959) study seemed to offer clear support for predictions derived from the theory of cognitive dissonance, they sometimes proved difficult to reproduce. In fact, several follow-up experiments indicated that large rewards for engaging in attitude-discrepant behavior may actually produce greater degrees of change than small ones (e.g., Rosenberg, 1965). Fortunately, more recent investigations have largely resolved these inconsistent findings. In particular, it now appears that the "less leads to more" effect predicted by dissonance theory does indeed occur, but only under certain circumstances.

First, as might be expected, such outcomes are produced only in situations where individuals believe that they had a choice as to whether to perform the attitude-discrepant behavior or not. When they feel that they had such freedom of action, the fact that they chose to behave in a manner inconsistent with their beliefs leads to the occurrence of dissonance, and results similar to those obtained by Festinger and Carlsmith are obtained—small rewards produce greater degrees of change than large ones. When they feel that they had no choice but to behave the way they did, however, no dissonance is produced, and larger rewards often lead to greater shifts in attitude (Linder, Cooper, and Jones, 1967). Second, dissonance effects seem to occur only when individuals feel that important and foreseeable consequences have stemmed from their actions (e.g., Cooper, Zanna, and Goethals, 1974; Hoyt, Henley, and Collins, 1972). If, in contrast, they feel that no effects (or only trivial ones) have been produced, little or no attitude change follows; after all, what difference does it make if one's behavior has been inconsistent with one's attitudes, if the behavior in question produces no effects?   And finally, it seems to be important that individuals feel a sense of personal responsibility both for their chosen course of action and the consequences it might produce; in the absence of such feelings of responsibility, little or no dissonance is generated, and the "less leads to more" effect often fails

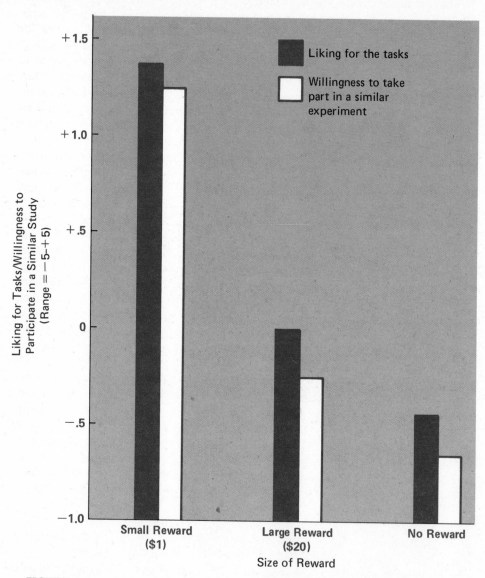

FIGURE 3-14: *Evidence that with respect to attitude change, "less" sometimes leads to "more." Individuals offered $1 for informing another person that dull tasks were actually quite interesting later rated these tasks more favorably than subjects offered $20 for engaging in such attitude-discrepant behavior, or those who never performed such actions. (Source: Based on data from Festinger and Carlsmith, 1959.)*

to occur (e.g., Worchel and Brand, 1972). Perhaps the importance of such factors in determining whether small rewards for engaging in attitude-discrepant behavior lead to greater or lesser amounts or attitude change than large ones is most clearly illustrated in a study by Calder, Ross, and Insko (1973).

In this investigation, which employed procedures quite similar to those of the Festinger and Carlsmith study, subjects were offered either a small or a large reward (0.5 or 2 hours credit toward satisfying a course requirement) for informing another person that dull, tedious tasks were actually quite fascinating. Half the subjects in each group were led to believe that they had a choice as to whether to engage in this attitude-discrepant behavior, and half were led to feel that it was simply a requirement of the study which they had to perform. Finally, within each of these conditions, half of the participants found that their false statements led to important consequences (the confederate indicated that he was convinced the study was interesting, and would skip studying for a quiz in order to take part in it), while half found that their statements had no important effects (the confederate remained totally unconvinced). On the basis of dissonance theory and previous research, it was predicted that small rewards would lead to greater amounts of attitude change than large ones only when (1) subjects believed that they had a choice concerning the performance of the attitude-discrepant behavior, and (2) their actions produced important consequences. As can be seen in Figure 3-15, this was precisely what happened. When later asked to rate the enjoyableness of the tasks they had performed, subjects in the "high choice-important consequences" group reported much more favorable reactions when they had been offered a small reward for lying to the accomplice than when they had been offered a large one. Moreover, consistent with results obtained in previous studies, these findings were reversed under conditions where they believed that they had no choice about uttering these falsehoods (in the "no choice-high consequences" group).

In sum, it appears that "less" does indeed lead to "more," but only under specific circumstances. Since individuals often believe that they enjoy freedom of action (even when they do not), and frequently find that their behavior produces important consequences, it seems likely that the occurrence of such effects is actually quite widespread. As a result, the strategy of offering individuals just barely enough reward to induce them to engage in attitude-discrepant behavior may often be an effective means of changing both their feelings and their beliefs.

Attitudes and Behavior: How Big Is the Gap between Actions and Words?

As we have just seen, research on the effects of attitude-discrepant behavior suggests that in many cases, attitudes can be shaped by overt actions: once we have performed some behavior, we often experience considerable pressure to bring our attitudes into line with what we have said or done. But what about the reverse of this relationship: do attitudes also shape and determine behavior? That they do has always been an implicit assumption of attitude-change

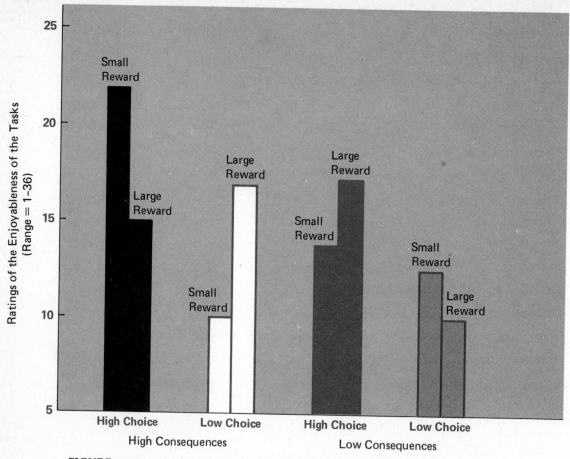

FIGURE 3-15. *Some limitations on the effects of forced compliance. Small rewards for engaging in attitude-discrepant behavior led to significantly greater amounts of change than large ones only under conditions where subjects believed that they had a choice concerning the performance of such actions, and felt that this behavior had produced important consequences (black bars). (Source: Based on data from Calder, Ross, and Insko, 1973.)*

research, for unless attitudes exert a strong effect on overt actions, attempts to change them will usually be of little practical importance. Unfortunately, early research on this topic seemed to suggest that the gap between attitudes and actions—between words and deeds—may sometimes be a considerable one. For example, in one well-known study, LaPiere (1934) toured the country with a young Chinese couple, stopping at more than 250 hotels, motels, and restaurants during a journey of some 10,000 miles. In all that time, he and his companions were refused service only once. However, when LaPiere wrote to the same establishments several months later, asking whether they would agree to serve Chinese patrons, fully 92 percent of those responding indicated that they would refuse. Although this and similar early studies have been criticized on the

DISSONANCE VERSUS SELF-PERCEPTION: DO WE INFER OUR ATTITUDES FROM OUR BEHAVIOR?

*Although dissonance theory seems to provide an adequate explanation for the fact that small rewards for engaging in attitude-discrepant behavior sometimes serve to induce greater amounts of change than large ones, another interpretation of these effects should also be mentioned. This explanation is based on Daryl Bem's (1972) **self-perception** theory—a view we have already encountered in Chapter 2. As you may recall from our previous discussion, Bem's theory centers around the reasonable suggestion that we often infer our attitudes from observations of our own behavior and the conditions under which it occurs. For example, we may conclude that we were hungrier than we thought once we start eating, or that we like or dislike another person because we have treated him in a friendly or hostile manner.*

Applying this general suggestion to studies such as the one conducted by Festinger and Carlsmith (1959), Bem has argued that the reason subjects in the small and large reward groups later report different degrees of liking for the dull, tedious tasks is that they reach different conclusions about the causes of their own behavior. Specifically, those in the large reward group reason as follows: "I said that I liked the tasks I performed, but since $20 is enough money to induce me to lie, I really don't like them." In contrast, those in the small reward group follow this type of logic: "I said I liked the tasks I performed, and since $1 is not enough to induce me to lie, I must really like them." In short, those offered a small reward for engaging in attitude-discrepant behavior later report greater liking for the tasks because they can perceive no other reason for their having described them in a highly favorable manner.

Several experiments have been conducted to determine which of these two explanations is the more accurate. Unfortunately, results have been quite mixed, with some studies offering
support for the self-perception view (e.g., Snyder and Ebbesen, 1972), and others offering support for dissonance (Green, 1974). Despite the inconclusive nature of these findings, two facts seem, at least to us, to give the edge to dissonance. First, Bem's view suggests that when faced with inconsistency between their attitudes and actions, individuals will attempt to infer their true beliefs from the information at their disposal in a totally "cool" and dispassionate manner. That is, they will examine their actions and the circumstances under which they occurred in order to reach a resolution. In contrast, dissonance theory suggests that such inconsistency will result in the arousal of negative emotional reactions. Since several studies have confirmed the fact that cognitive inconsistency is indeed upsetting or arousing (Pallak and Pittman, 1972), it appears that dissonance theory probably provides a more accurate description of the events occurring in such situations than self-perception theory. Second, while there is little doubt that we do often infer our attitudes from our behavior, this is probably more likely to occur in situations where our feelings are not very clear or intense. In most studies on forced compliance, however, the tasks performed by subjects have been so dull and tedious that they probably had very clear, negative feelings about them.*

For these reasons, it appears that dissonance offers a somewhat more adequate interpretation of the effects of attitude-discrepant behavior than self-perception theory. As we have already seen in Chapter 2, however, Bem's suggestions have proven to be of great value in many other contexts (e.g., in explaining various aspects of self-perception, and in relation to intrinsic motivation). Thus, in an important sense, neither dissonance nor self-perception has "won"—the two theories simply seem differentially useful in accounting for various aspects of social behavior.

grounds that the persons who offered service may well have been different individuals from those who responded to the questionnaires (Dillehay, 1973), more recent experiments not subject to such objections also point to a gap between attitudes and behavior (e.g., Wicker, 1971; Wrightsman, 1969). In view of such evidence, it seems safe to conclude that attitudes do not always determine overt actions in a direct and simple manner (see Figure 3-16).

While there are several reasons why this might be so, two seem to be of greatest importance. First, other factors often intrude and prevent individuals from acting in accordance with their true feelings or beliefs. As we noted above, laws, social norms, or the desire to please others sometimes force us to engage in attitude-discrepant behavior. For example, a racial bigot running a restaurant in the 1970's cannot refuse to serve members of the groups he dislikes: legal sanctions simply make such behavior far too costly. Largely as a result of such constraints, attitudes fail to predict overt actions in many situations. Second, shortcomings in existing measurement techniques occasionally lead to the appearance of a gap between attitudes and behavior even when none actually exists. To mention only a few possible sources of such error, individuals may misunderstand the questions asked, or think that they refer to one attitude object when they actually refer to another. In such cases, individuals' responses do not reflect their true feelings or beliefs, and the fact that their replies seem unrelated to their overt actions is far from surprising. For example, consider the statement "Greater protection of the environment is definitely needed." Most persons who indicate agreement with this item are probably endorsing tougher laws to control air and water pollution. A few, however, might be indicating their support for strong protection of owners' rights to do anything they wish on their property! Given such differences of interpretation, we might well find individuals in the first group supporting environmental legislation and those in the second opposing it, despite the fact that they respond similarly on an attitude questionnaire. In such cases, of course, the gap between attitudes and behavior is more apparent than real.

For these and other reasons, attitudes sometimes seem to be greatly out of line with overt actions. This does not mean, however, that such disparity is either common or usual. On the contrary, quite the opposite seems to be true. Individuals generally act in a manner consistent with their beliefs and feelings, and even in situations where attitudes are not directly reflected in overt actions, they exert a strong pressure on the persons involved to behave in specific ways. Moreover, recent investigations suggest that under certain conditions, attitudes can in fact serve as accurate predictors of behavior (Fishbein and Azjen, 1975; Rokeach and Kliejunas, 1972). One of the clearest recent demonstrations of this fact has been provided by Heberlein and Black (1976).

In this study, motorists who had been observed to purchase either lead-free or regular gasoline were mailed questionnaires designed to assess their attitudes toward(1) environmentalism in general, (2) air pollution, (3) lead-free gasoline, or (4) the importance of purchasing such fuel. (Note that the study was conducted in 1973, a time when most cars did *not* require lead-free gasoline.) Subjects' replies to these items were then related to their actual behavior. The

"A final question. Would you put your money where your mouth is?"

FIGURE 3-16. *On some occasions, there is a considerable gap between verbally expressed attitudes and overt behavior. (Source: Drawing by Whitney Darrow, Jr.; © 1975 The New Yorker Magazine, Inc.)*

results of the study were quite straightforward: as the attitude items increased in specificity, their accuracy as predictors of subjects' behavior also rose (see Table 3-4). Such findings suggest that while global attitudes toward complex issues

TABLE 3-4. *Attitude specificity and the prediction of behavior. As shown above, the more specific the attitudes assessed, the greater the accuracy with which subjects' behavior could be predicted. (Based on data from Heberlein and Black, 1976.)*

	Correlation between attitude measure and behavior	Index of the accuracy with which behavior could be predicted (Range = 0.00–1.00)
Attitudes toward environmentalism	+.12	.02
Attitudes toward air pollution	+.21	.04
Attitudes toward lead-free gasoline	+.36	.13
Attitudes toward the purchase of lead-free gasoline	+.59	.35

may fail to serve as accurate predictors of specific behaviors, more focused attitudes relating to specific courses of action may well be successful in this respect.

In a similar vein, Fishbein and Azjen (1975) have conducted a number of studies which point to the conclusion that individuals' later actions can often be quite accurately predicted from knowledge of their *behavioral intentions*—how they plan to behave. Together, the findings obtained by Fishbein, Azjen, Heberlein, Black, and many others suggest that, given appropriate information, the gap between attitudes and behavior can be markedly narrowed. Thus, while changing attitudes does not always guarantee corresponding changes in behavior, it frequently represents a crucial first step in this important direction.

SUMMARY

We are rarely completely neutral to the persons, groups, objects, or ideas around us. Rather, we usually have beliefs about them, feelings toward them, and behavioral tendencies with respect to them. When these three types of reactions cluster around a particular object and are relatively enduring, they may be viewed as constituting an *attitude*.

It is obvious that children are not born with all their complex attitudes in place. Rather, these are formed through a gradual process in which *classical conditioning, instrumental conditioning,* and *observational learning* all play a role. Acting together over a period of many years, these result in the development of many attitudes which are highly resistant to later change.

Attempts to alter attitudes often involve persuasive communications. While many factors influence the success of such appeals, the most important seem to involve: (1) *characteristics of the communicator* (e.g., his or her expertise, sincerity, or attractiveness); (2) *characteristics of the communication* (e.g., the presence of emotional appeals, one-sided versus two-sided arguments); (3) *characteristics of the recipients* (their self-esteem, need for social approval, etc.); and (4) *characteristics of the context* (e.g., recipients' current mood, the presence of distraction). Recent evidence suggests that attitudes toward many different stimuli are also influenced by their frequency of exposure: the more often they are encountered, the more they are liked.

A second major technique for altering attitudes involves the induction of *attitude-discrepant behavior*. Whenever individuals either say or do something inconsistent with their true beliefs or feelings, a negative emotional state known as *cognitive dissonance* is induced. In order to eliminate such reactions, the persons involved then often alter their attitudes so as to bring them into line with their overt actions. Interestingly, when individuals choose to engage in attitude-discrepant behavior to obtain relatively small rewards, they often show greater degrees of change than when they are induced to perform such actions by the promise of large rewards. This is the case because large rewards provide them with a good reason for having engaged in attitude-discrepant behavior, and so reduce the amount of dissonance they experience. As a result, maximum change is often produced under conditions where individuals are provided with rewards just barely sufficient to induce them to engage in attitude-discrepant behavior.

Because of the influence of many factors which prevent individuals from acting in a manner consistent with their true feelings and beliefs, attitudes sometimes seem unrelated to behavior. Such instances are the exception rather than the rule, however, and individuals usually behave in a manner consistent with their attitudes. As a result, alterations in such reactions often serve as an important first step to changing behavior.

GLOSSARY

Attitudes. Relatively enduring organizations of feelings, beliefs, and behavior tendencies toward other persons, groups, ideas, or objects.

Attitude-discrepant behavior. Actions that are inconsistent with an individual's true feelings or beliefs. The performance of such behavior often leads to changes in the attitudes involved.

Bogus pipeline. A technique for measuring attitudes in which subjects are led to believe that their true reactions will be revealed by a device which records their physiological reactions.

Classical conditioning. A basic learning process in which stimuli initially incapable of eliciting various reactions acquire the capacity to do so through repeated pairing with stimuli capable of evoking such responses. Classical conditioning has been found to play an important role in the development of many attitudes.

Cognitive dissonance. An unpleasant emotional state, somewhat akin to anxiety, tension, or unease, which is induced whenever individuals experience inconsistency between their attitudes, or between their attitudes and their behavior.

Communicator credibility. Refers to the extent to which a given communicator is viewed as being a believable or reliable source of information. Judgments concerning this characteristic seem to depend largely on the communicator's apparent expertise, sincerity, and attractiveness.

Distraction. In the case of persuasive communications, any factor which prevents individuals from concentrating on the message being delivered. Distraction seems to increase attitude change under some conditions, but to reduce it under others.

Fear appeals. Persuasive communications containing fear-arousing materials. Most fear appeals suggest that highly unpleasant consequences will result if individuals do not alter their attitudes in the recommended directions.

Forced compliance. Refers to situations in which individuals are somehow induced to say or do something inconsistent with their own attitudes.

Instrumental conditioning. A basic learning process in which particular responses are followed by the presentation of reinforcement, and thus strengthened. Both informal observation and a large body of research suggest that instrumental conditioning plays an important role in the development of many attitudes.

Likert scaling. A technique for measuring attitudes in which individuals indicate the extent to which they agree or disagree with various statements.

Mere exposure effect. Refers to the fact that liking for various stimuli is increased by repeated exposure to them.

Observational learning. A basic learning process in which individuals acquire new responses not previously at their disposal merely by observing the actions and outcomes of others. This process seems to play an important role in the transmission of various attitudes from parents to their children.

One-sided argument. Persuasive communications in which only one side of an issue is presented to recipients.

Persuasive communications. Written, spoken, filmed, or televised messages designed to alter the attitudes of persons to whom they are directed.

Reactance. An unpleasant emotional state aroused by threats to one's freedom of action. Individuals experiencing reactance often seek to restore their lost sense of freedom.

Self-perception. The view that we often infer our attitudes from observation of our own actions. For example, we often conclude that we are hungrier than we thought once we start eating, or that we either like or dislike another person because we treat him in a friendly or harsh manner.

Semantic differential. A technique for measuring attitudes in which individuals rate the attitude object along several different dimensions labeled, at either end, with opposing adjectives (e.g., good-bad; pleasant-unpleasant, etc.).

Sleeper effect. Refers to the suggestion that the impact of low-credibility communicators increases over time, as the source and content of a persuasive appeal become dissociated. Recent investigations have cast doubt on the existence of such an effect.

Thurstone scaling. A technique for measuring attitudes consisting of two major parts. In the first, a large number of statements concerning the attitude object are scaled in terms of their favorability toward this object by a group of judges. In the second, a smaller number of these statements are administered to persons whose attitudes are to be measured.

Two-sided argument. Persuasive communications in which both sides of an issue are presented to recipients.

SUGGESTED READINGS FOR CHAPTER 3

Bem, D. J. *Beliefs, attitudes, and human affairs.* Belmont, Calif.: Brooks/Cole Publishing Co., 1970. A well-written, often witty discussion of the origins of attitudes and beliefs. The chapters on cognitive consistency and the effects of behavior on attitudes are especially interesting.

Brehm, J. W. *Responses to loss of freedom: A theory of psychological reactance.* Morristown, N.J.: General Learning Press, 1972. An intriguing discussion of the complex effects which may occur when individuals feel that their freedom has been threatened or reduced by others.

Himmelfarb, S., and Eagly, A. H. *Readings in attitude change.* New York: Wiley, 1974. A carefully selected collection of readings concerned with the topic of attitude change. Many interesting articles are included, and several of the topics considered in this chapter are examined (e.g., attitude change as a result of mere exposure, persuasive communications, and attitude-discrepant behavior). The concluding paper, written by the editors, examines current trends in attitude theory and research.

Suedfeld, P. *Attitude change: The competing views.* Chicago: Aldine-Atherton, 1971. A collection of articles concerned with the general topic of attitude change. Several competing theoretical views regarding this important process are described.

Triandis, H. C. *Attitude and attitude change.* New York: Wiley, 1971. A well-organized, comprehensive discussion of attitudes and attitude change. The separate chapters on attitude measurement and theory are particularly useful.

Zimbardo, P. G., and Ebbesen, E. G. *Influencing attitudes and changing behavior*, 2nd editon. Reading, Mass.: Addison-Wesley, 1977. A well-written, relatively non-technical discussion of the nature of attitudes, and methods for changing them. Attempts by the authors to relate research findings to many "real life" events (e.g., Patty Hearst's actions following her kidnapping) are of special interest.

PREJUDICE AND DISCRIMINATION

4

It's a cold, starless night, and after attending a late meeting, you find yourself waiting for a bus on a totally deserted corner. After a few minutes, another person approaches, and as he draws closer, you can see that it is a young black man. Despite his neat appearance, and the fact that he smiles at you as he nears the corner, you begin to feel uneasy. Stories of assaults by blacks against whites pass through your mind, and you begin to imagine all sorts of unpleasant events. As the minutes pass and no bus appears, you grow increasingly tense. In fact, you begin considering walking to another corner, where you can wait out of sight of your unwanted companion. Just as you are about to leave, however, a fancy limousine pulls up to the curb. A well-dressed man inside rolls down the window and leaning out, remarks: "Hello Dr. Wilson. Would you like a lift?" The stranger answers immediately: "Yes, thanks Bill, I sure would. My car's in the shop, and it's pretty cold out here tonight." Then, turning to you, he adds: "Would you like a lift too, Miss? This is Judge Phillips, and I'm sure he'd be glad to help you too. It's certainly no evening for a young lady to be out alone." As you mumble your agreement, you feel your ears beginning to burn in embarrassment. Why, you wonder, should you have judged this pleasant and obviously polished young man in such a negative manner? Why did you so readily assume the worst about him when you had absolutely no grounds for jumping to such conclusions?

It's a bright Wednesday morning, and you are on your way to a job interview. The position for which you are applying is at the top of your list, and you would like to land it very badly. It's with a company known for their policy of rapid advancement, involves exactly the kind of work you'd like to do, and offers a very high starting salary. For days you've been preparing for your meeting with the Personnel Director, and are as ready as you'll ever be. Yet, you can't help feeling nervous as you walk to your interview. Just ahead, you see a sign on the wall reading "Office of the Personnel Director." You knock on the door, and a voice from within answers "Come in." You enter, and find an attractive woman in her early thirties standing in front of a file cabinet apparently searching for some papers. You hesitate for a moment, and then approach. "Hello," you remark, "I'm looking for the Personnel Director. Are you his secretary?" Immediately, the woman begins to scowl, and fixes you with an icy stare. "No," she answers, "I'm not his secretary; I'm the Personnel Director. Come with me, please." Your knees turn to water as the realization of your blunder begins to sink in. For days you've worried about beginning with a good first impression, *and now, for no apparent reason, you've started by putting your foot squarely into your mouth. As you follow the Director into her plush office, you find yourself wondering what possessed you to leap to the conclusion that the Director must be a man. Why, you wonder, did you ignore the possibility that this prestigious position could be filled by a woman?*

While these incidents involve sharply contrasting events, they both serve to underscore an important and timely fact: in many cases, we tend to jump to conclusions about others—to prejudge them in many important ways. And, often, such prejudgments prove to be quite negative in nature. Thus, in the first incident described above, the young woman involved experienced negative and fearful reactions to a stranger not because of any actions on his part, but simply because he was black. And in the second, the hopeful job applicant leaped to the conclusion that the woman he encountered in the Personnel Director's office must be "only" a secretary, despite the absence of any firm grounds for forming this judgment. In both cases, of course, the persons involved were quite embarrassed upon learning of their mistakes. Yet, these errors still occurred, and influenced both their feelings toward and interactions with the other individuals in question.

This strong tendency to prejudge others on the basis of their racial, ethnic, or even sexual identity lies at the heart of the two processes on which we will focus in the present chapter: *prejudice* and *discrimination*. As you know quite well if you ever watch the evening news or leaf through your local newspaper,

Public demonstrations such as the one shown above have often been employed as a means for combating prejudice and producing desired social change. (Photo: Phil Carver & Friends.)

these processes have been, and continue to represent, major problems for society. As such, they have commanded considerable attention from social psychologists, and served as the subject of much systematic study. In the present chapter, then, we will attempt to summarize a portion of the information gathered about these topics in recent years. In broad outline, our discussion will proceed as follows.

First, we will offer definitions of both prejudice and discrimination, attempting to distinguish between these two closely related, yet distinct processes. Next, we will examine contrasting theoretical approaches to these topics— different perspectives for understanding their origins and occurrence. Third, we will consider possible means for combating their impact, ways of lessening or eliminating their negative effects on social behavior. And finally, we will turn special attention to prejudice and discrimination toward women, a topic of much current concern in social psychology. Our main goal, of course, is that of acquainting you with the findings of recent research regarding both prejudice and discrimination. Hopefully, though, increased understanding of these processes may provide you with another benefit as well: increased ability to counteract the negative influence of both on your own feelings, beliefs, and behavior.

PREJUDICE AND DISCRIMINATION: DEFINITIONS AND MEASUREMENT

As you probably already know, the terms prejudice and discrimination are often used interchangeably in everyday speech. Before proceeding further, therefore, we should distinguish between them. Generally speaking, **prejudice** is used by social psychologists to refer to negative attitudes, and **discrimination** to negative behavior, directed against the members of specific racial, ethnic, or religious groups. To assist us further in defining the targets of such negative attitudes and behavior, we should go one step further, and also distinguish between racial groups, ethnic groups, and the more general term, **minority group**. Ashmore (1970, p. 250) provides a useful analysis of these terms:

> *Racial groups* are distinguishable solely in terms of genetically determined biological criteria such as skin color and hair texture. *Ethnic groups* are distinguishable primarily in terms of cultural or learned factors (examples: religion and language). . . . It's hard to define a *minority group* since a group's numerical smallness is not enough to enable it to qualify as a minority. . . . The key point about a minority group is that it is in a subordinate position with regard to status and power.

Please try to remember, then, that when we use the term *minority group* in the pages which follow, we will not necessarily be referring to racial, ethnic, or religious groups which are greatly outnumbered in a purely numerical sense. Rather, we will be referring to groups which are lacking in—or have actively been deprived of—power and status. It is in this sense, of course, that women have often been viewed as a stereotyped "psychological" minority (Myrdal, 1944;

Weisstein, 1971). Although they actually constitute a clear majority of the world's population, they have generally been so deprived of economic and political power, that many social psychologists feel they should be viewed as the victims of strong prejudice and discrimination.

Prejudice: Defining the Beast

The term prejudice has come to have many meanings in everyday use:

1. A judgment or opinion formed beforehand without thoughtful examination of the pertinent facts, issues, or arguments; especially an unfavorable, irrational opinion.
2. The act or state of holding preconceived irrational opinions.
3. Hatred of or dislike for a particular group, race, religion, etc.

Despite all of these meanings, social psychologists have generally come to some agreement about a useful definition of prejudice for purposes of research. Basically, by this term they mean an attitude (usually negative) toward the members of some specific group (racial, ethnic, religious, etc.) which causes the person holding it to evaluate others negatively, solely on the basis of their identification with that group. Thus, to say that an individual is prejudiced against the members of some group indicates that he or she tends to evaluate such persons in a negative manner not on the basis of their individual characteristics or behavior, but simply because they belong to or can be identified with that group. In a sense, therefore, prejudice represents a kind of blanket rejection or condemnation—a strong tendency to dislike others and evaluate them negatively, which is independent of their unique characteristics or behavior.

Historically, prejudice has formed a part of the vast literature in social psychology concerned with attitudes (see Chapter 3). As such, we can view it as an attitude having three components—*cognitive* (beliefs, thoughts, etc.), *affective* (feelings, emotions, etc.), and *conative* (behavioral tendencies)—and examine each of these parts separately. (As you probably recall, we have already considered these three components of attitudes in Chapter 3, but perhaps they bear repeating in the present context.)

The *cognitive* component of an attitude refers to the perceptions, beliefs, and expectations that an individual holds with regard to a particular person, object, or event. In the case of prejudice, such beliefs and expectations often involve **stereotypes**—clusters of preconceived notions regarding various groups. Unfortunately, such stereotypes often include strong tendencies to overgeneralize about individuals solely on the basis of their membership in particular racial, ethnic, or religious groups, and an unwillingness to consider new information which might lead to alterations or revisions in one's opinions. In short, all members of a particular group are perceived in very much the same manner, regardless of their unique traits and characteristics. We shall have more to say about stereotypes shortly.

The *affective* component of an attitude refers to our emotional feelings or reactions toward people and events. This aspect of prejudice, then, refers primarily to negative emotional states and strong feelings of dislike toward the members of particular ethnic, racial, or religious groups. As we noted in Chapter 3, such feelings may be acquired before the development of consistent beliefs about such persons, and can often serve as the initial foundation on which full-scale prejudices are later erected.

The *behavioral* component of an attitude refers to behavior tendencies or action orientations with respect to some person, object, or group. Thus, from this perspective, prejudice is reflected in an individual's verbal support for discriminatory practices. We should note here that a prejudiced person might well advocate discrimination against minority group members, yet refrain from engaging in overt actions against them. This important point—to which we will return on several occasions in the course of our discussion—leads us to the distinction between prejudice and discrimination.

Discrimination: Defining the Next Beast

Social psychologists have long been aware of the fact that an individual's feelings toward various groups may not always be reflected in his or her actions toward them (Allport, 1954). In fact, as we noted in Chapter 3, there is growing evidence that the relationship often proceeds in the opposite direction. For example, an individual might observe that she usually acts in an unfriendly or hostile manner toward blacks, and from this *infer* that she must dislike them (Bem, 1972).

Regardless of the direction of the link between attitudes and behavior, the gap which often develops between them has led many social psychologists to distinguish clearly between *prejudice*—negative attitudes toward the members of some social group—and *discrimination*—actual harmful, negative behaviors directed toward them. We will follow this distinction throughout the present discussion, and urge you to keep it clearly in mind while reading further.

As you probably already know, racism, sexism, and other forms of prejudice have often found expression in a wide variety of actions. Over the years, and across nations, these have ranged from such relatively mild forms as avoidance or failure to provide assistance, to more damaging actions such as exclusion from employment and denial of residential or educational facilities. And in extreme cases, they have involved open physical hostility, or even attempts at total extermination. In short, while strong prejudice generally lies behind such actions, it is the overt discriminatory practices themselves which exert harmful effects on the unfortunate objects of bigotry and hatred.

Reverse Discrimination and Tokenism: When Leaning over Backward Hurts. While discrimination often takes the open and direct forms mentioned above, it is also frequently much more subtle in nature. As an example of such disguised prejudicial reactions, let us consider the related topics of **reverse discrimination** and **tokenism** (Dutton and Lake, 1973; Dutton and Lennox, 1974).

Over the years, discrimination has taken many different forms, ranging from avoidance and exclusion on the one hand, to open physical violence on the other. (Photo: Donald Wright Patterson, Jr.; Stock, Boston.)

Basically, reverse discrimination refers to cases in which individuals seem to lean over backward to avoid appearing prejudiced. That is, they respond more favorably to members of various minority groups than they do to members of their own group (see Allen, 1976). At first glance, such reactions seem to be potentially beneficial ones—after all, minority group members may find themselves treated in a more positive manner than members of the majority. Unfortunately, though, it appears that, in many cases, reverse discrimination takes on strong tokenistic overtones. That is, such reactions seem to occur in relatively trivial situations, and do not generalize to more significant ones. Thus, an individual may lean over backward to act in a positive, friendly manner toward minority group members when the effort involved in such actions is minimal, but may then use his or her token actions as a rationale for prejudiced behavior in more important settings. "Don't bother me," such persons may argue, "Haven't I done enough for (blacks, Chicanos, etc.) already?" Evidence for the occurrence of such reactions has actually been obtained in several recent experiments (Dutton and Lake, 1973; Dutton and Lennox, 1974).

For example, in one of these studies (Dutton and Lennox, 1974), white subjects who had previously described themselves as being low in prejudice viewed a series of slides showing interracial couples and black and white children playing together. While watching these slides, they received false physiological feedback indicating that they actually harbored repressed feelings of prejudice and hatred toward blacks. Following this part of the experiment, subjects went to collect payment for their participation in the study from a secretary whose office was located in another part of the building. During this trip, they were approached and panhandled by a black or white confederate. It was predicted that in order to restore their unprejudiced self-image, subjects approached by the black confederate would be more likely to part with some money than those approached by the white confederate. As you can see in Table 4-1, this was actually the case; more subjects gave money to the black than to the white panhandler, and the amount they donated to the former person was larger than that donated to the latter.

Of even greater interest than this, however, was a second major question: would subjects' willingness to behave in an unprejudiced manner in more important situations now be reduced by their tokenistic behavior (i.e., their small contributions to the black panhandler)? In order to examine this possibility they were asked, two days later, to complete a form committing themselves to various activities on behalf of a fictitious group supposedly working to promote interracial tolerance on campus. The activities they could agree to perform ranged from relatively trivial in nature (e.g., posting notices announcing an impending "Brotherhood Week") to quite substantial (e.g., agreeing to work in a booth in the student center for ten hours). It was predicted that subjects who had previously been approached by the black panhandler would now show lower willingness to contribute their time and effort than subjects approached by the white panhandler, or those not approached by any confederate. As shown in Figure 4-1, these predictions were strongly confirmed. In short, it appeared that having engaged in relatively trivial, tokenistic pro-black actions, subjects were less willing to commit themselves to more significant interracial projects. It is through such effects that reverse discrimination, and the tokenistic actions it often involves, can, in the long run, often turn out to be more harmful than beneficial to the members of ethnic or racial minorities.

The Relationship between Prejudice and Discrimination: Another Gap between Words and Deeds

As we have already noted attitudes are not always reflected in instances of overt behavior. Often, situational constraints prevent us from behaving in a manner consistent with our private feelings or beliefs. As you might suspect, a substantial gap of this type frequently exists between prejudice and discrimination. In many cases, persons holding strong, negative attitudes toward the members of various racial, religious, or ethnic groups find it impossible to translate these prejudiced reactions into overt behavior—the costs for doing so are simply too high. For example, the owner of a restaurant may find it quite impossible to refuse service to blacks, Chicanos, Jews, or any other group he or she happens to dislike; such actions will result in costly legal suits, and may even force the closing of his or her business. Similarly, the owner of an apartment house cannot reject potential tenants solely on the basis of racial, ethnic, or religious background—such actions are expressly forbidden by the law of the

TABLE 4-1. *Reverse discrimination and helping.* *After receiving false information suggesting that they harbored hidden feelings of prejudice, white subjects were more willing to donate money to a black than to a white panhandler.* *(Based on data from Dutton and Lennox, 1974.)*

	Race of Panhandler	
	Black	White
Percent of Subjects Making a Donation	84	54
Average Size of Donation	68.2	35.6

land. In these and many other cases, bigoted persons must refrain from acting on their prejudiced beliefs, no matter how unpleasant they find this task to be.

Of course, as is always the case, there are numerous exceptions to the rule. Thus, newspapers, magazines, and the evening news are often filled with reports of individuals for whom prejudice is such a central or important trait that they seek to engage in overt discriminatory practices, regardless of the consequences. It is such persons who close their businesses, sell their property, or attack school buses in the streets rather than tolerate the presence of the group they hate or dislike. Fortunately, with the passage of stronger and stronger legislation outlawing discriminatory practices, the prevalence of such individuals seems to have decreased. The frequency with which minority group members must resort to legal action in order to gain fair and equal treatment, however, suggests that extreme bigots are not yet a vanishing species in American society or elsewhere in the world.

Racial and Ethnic Minorities: The Measurement of Prejudice

Historically, the measurement of prejudice has included attempts to define cognitive, affective, and behavioral dimensions of prejudicial attitudes. We will now examine the most widely used techniques in each of these areas.

The Measurement of Prejudiced Beliefs: Stereotyping Then . . . and Now. The assessment of stereotypes of various minority groups was begun several decades ago by Katz and Braly (1933), in a study of Princeton undergraduates. In this classic investigation, students were presented with a list of eighty-four traits (e.g., aggressive, imaginative, persistent, etc.) and asked to indicate which were most characteristic of several racial and ethnic groups (blacks, Chinese, Jews, etc.). Not too surprisingly, Katz and Braly found strong agreement on the perceived characteristics of these groups.

Since this early study, a number of additional investigations have also

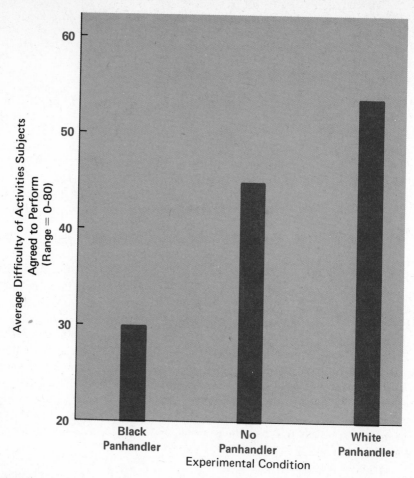

FIGURE 4-1. *The long-term effects of tokenism. After making a small donation to a black panhandler, white subjects were less willing to commit themselves to more significant pro-black actions. (Based on data from Dutton and Lennox, 1974.)*

examined the existence of such stereotypes. Somewhat surprisingly, these studies suggest that preconceived notions about the members of various groups have persisted up until the present. Thus, although Gilbert (1951) found a weakening of stereotypes among a second generation of Princeton students at the time of the Korean War, a more recent investigation (Karlins, Coffman, and Walters, 1969) found evidence for their continued existence in the late 1960's—a time when concern about social reform and racial equality was very high. While the traits assigned by subjects to various groups were somewhat different than in earlier investigations, the degree of consensus regarding which traits were characteristic of which groups was as high, in some categories, as in the original study conducted in 1933 (see Table 4-2). Thus, while stereotypes seem to have shifted a bit in terms of content, they continue to exist even during the presumably enlightened 1970's.

TABLE 4-2. *Stereotypes then and now. The numbers shown represent the percent of students who assigned specific traits to various minority groups at three different times. As you can see, while the stereotypes represented seemed to change over time, they by no means disappeared. (Adapted from Karlins, Coffman, and Walters, 1969.)*

| Minority Group | Trait | Percent Checking Trait | | |
		1933	1951	1967
Jews	shrewd	79	47	30
	mercenary	49	28	15
	ambitious	21	28	48
Blacks	superstitious	84	41	13
	lazy	75	31	26
	musical	26	33	47

The Measurement of Prejudiced Feelings. Stereotypes, as we have already noted, represent only one aspect of prejudiced attitudes. Thus, social psychologists have also attempted to learn more about the affective (feeling) component of such reactions. Generally, this has been accomplished through the use of various types of *attitude scales.* Since we have already described the nature of such measuring devices in Chapter 3, we will not return to this topic here. However, we should note that when used to investigate prejudice, attitude scales generally contain items designed to assess the strength of subjects' positive or negative feelings toward various racial or ethnic groups.

The Measurement of Discriminatory Tendencies. Attempts to measure behavioral tendencies or orientation toward minority groups have often involved the use of **social-distance** scales. These scales are designed to assess the degree of closeness or intimacy to which individuals are willing to admit members of various racial or ethnic minorities. Basically, social-distance scales list a number of relationships, and the subjects' task is simply that of indicating whether they would be willing to admit a particular minority group to that degree of social closeness or intimacy. One social-distance scale is shown in Table 4-3, and, as you can see, the intimacy of the relationships included increases as we proceed through the items presented.

While social-distance scales were initially devised as a means for measuring one aspect of prejudiced attitudes (the behavioral component of such reactions), the concept of social distance has recently proven useful in resolving a much debated issue in social psychological research: the question of whether race or similarity of beliefs exerts a greater influence on interpersonal relations.

Race versus Beliefs: A Question of Priorities. The race-versus-belief controversy began when Milton Rokeach (1960), a noted investigator in the area of prejudice, argued that positive or negative reactions between individuals are determined more by perceived similarity in beliefs than by racial background. In

FOCUS ON RESEARCH

BEAUTY OR RACE? PHYSICAL ATTRACTIVENESS AND SKIN COLOR AS DETERMINANTS OF DATING CHOICE

As we have just seen, under conditions where intimate contacts are expected, race seems to be a more potent determinant of liking between individuals than belief simularity. Thus, if presented with a choice between a roommate of their own race who does not share their views on many issues, or a roommate of another race who does, existing research evidence suggests that most persons would choose the former. Just because racial identity seems to outweigh belief similarity, however, does not mean that it will necessarily outweigh other factors as well. For example, what would happen, you might wonder, if race were pitted against physical attractiveness? That is, presented with a choice between a potential date with an unattractive member of their own race or a highly attractive member of a different race, how would most persons react? Would race still predominate in determining subjects' choices? Unfortunately, a recent series of investigations conducted by Allen (1976) suggest that it would.

In these studies, male and female subjects (white college students) were asked to rate a number of different persons in terms of their desirability as a date. Some of these individuals were of the same race as themselves, and some were black. In addition, within each of these groups, some had previously been rated by a panel of undergraduate judges as being quite attractive, and others as being quite unattractive. The major question of interest, of course, was whether subjects' ratings would be more strongly affected by the race or physical attractiveness of these potential dating partners.

Discouragingly, results pointed to the conclusion that while both factors had an effect, the influence of race was somewhat stronger. When subjects rated white dating partners, beauty had the anticipated effect: attractive individuals were rated more favorably than unattractive ones. When they rated black individuals, however, physical attractiveness failed to produce similar outcomes. Instead, both attractive and unattractive persons received similar, low ratings. While this pattern of findings was obtained both for male and female subjects, there was some indication that males were somewhat less influenced by race, and somewhat more influenced by attractiveness than females. Taken as a whole, however, the results of Allen's (1976) research suggest that even in the supposedly enlightened 1970's, restrictions against intimate contacts between the races are so strong that skin color outweighs even physical attractiveness as a determinant of liking and dating choice.

short, Rokeach proposed that our feelings toward others are determined more by the extent to which they share our views than by their membership in a particular race. These suggestions were soon confirmed by several studies, which reported that feelings of liking are indeed influenced to a greater degree by similarity in beliefs about important topics than by racial identity (Hendrick, Bixenstine, and Hawkins, 1971; Rokeach, Smith, and Evans, 1960).

In sharp contrast to these findings, however, other studies reported that race was indeed an important determinant of interpersonal attraction, and actually outweighed belief similarity in this respect (Triandis, 1961; Triandis, Loh, and

TABLE 4-3. *An example of a social-distance scale. Individuals completing the scale indicate those relationships to which they would admit members of various racial or ethnic groups.*

Type of relationship to which I would admit minority groups:	Racial or Ethnic Group			
	Blacks	Chinese	Chicanos	etc. . . .
As visitors only to my country				
To live in my country				
To citizenship in my country				
To employment in my occupation				
To my street as neighbors				
To my club as personal friends				
To close kinship by marriage				

Levin, 1966). Fortunately, a resolution of this controversy based largely on the concept of social distance has now been obtained. Briefly, it appears that in the case of relatively nonintimate contacts or relations, beliefs may indeed be dominant in determining the level of attraction between individuals. That is, we tend to like others who share our beliefs more than those who do not, regardless of their race (Goldstein and Davis, 1972). However, when intimate relationships are involved, just the opposite may be true, and race seems to play a more important role in determining attraction than beliefs (Stein, Hardyck, and Smith, 1965).

This latter fact has been demonstrated in several different studies (Rokeach, 1968; Rokeach and Mezei, 1966). For example, in one investigation (Silverman, 1974), white students were asked to evaluate eight possible roommates who varied in both racial background and attitudinal similarity to themselves. Some students were led to believe that their choices would actually determine who they would be living with during their first year in college, while others were led to believe that their choices would have no bearing on their actual roommates. Consistent with the suggestions outlined above, results indicated that subjects who believed that their choices would have real consequences were strongly influenced by race, while those who did not expect their choices to affect their actual roommate were not appreciably influenced by this factor (see Figure 4-2). Such findings suggest that the resolution of the race-versus-belief controversy is as follows: when the contacts anticipated with other persons are relatively nonintimate, their similarity to us in terms of attitudes or beliefs outweighs their race as a determinant of our liking for them. However, when close, intimate contacts or relationships are expected, race may turn out to be more important than attitudes or beliefs.

THEORETICAL APPROACHES TO PREJUDICE: THE ORIGINS OF HATE

Where does prejudice come from? Why do individuals so frequently hold strong negative attitudes toward the members of ethnic or racial groups other than their

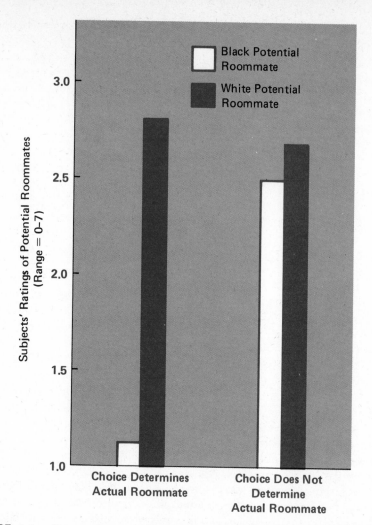

FIGURE 4-2. *Race and social distance. Subjects' ratings of potential college roommates were influenced by this person's race only when they thought their choices would actually determine the person with whom they would live. (Based on data from Silverman, 1974.)*

own? And why do they come to view these persons as somehow inferior to themselves, and thus appropriate objects for mistreatment or exploitation? Given their important practical and theoretical implications, questions such as these have long been of interest to psychologists and other social scientists. Over the years, many possible answers concerning the nature and origins of prejudice have been suggested. Within social psychology, however, three major approaches, which view prejudice largely as the result of (1) intergroup conflict, (2) personality dynamics, or (3) social-learning experiences, have received most attention. It is upon these suggestions, then, that we will now focus.

One approach to the origins of prejudice suggests that it arises primarily out of intergroup conflict. That is, the minority group attempts to improve its status and power in the face of strong majority opposition, and prejudice is then viewed as the result of the competitive and often hostile interactions which follow.

A series of well-known field studies conducted by Sherif and his associates (Sherif, 1966; Sherif et al., 1961) provide support for the view that negative intergroup contact can frequently lead to strong intergroup prejudice. In these studies, eleven and twelve-year-old boys attending special summer camps were divided into two groups and assigned serarate sleeping quarters. During the next week, the groups took part in many enjoyable activities (e.g., boating, camping out). As a result, the boys' feelings of attachment to them increased, and each soon took on a strong, individual identity. Indeed, both groups were soon assigned special names by their members—the Bull Dogs and Red Devils.

Once the groups had attained these strong feelings of cohesiveness and solidarity, a second phase of the study was begun. During this portion, the groups were brought into competitive conflict with one another through a series of contests, sports events, and similar activities. In each case, conditions were arranged so that only one of the groups could obtain an attractive prize, and once obtained, the prize was always shared among all group members.

At first, the effects of such competition were not apparent—the groups continued to enjoy friendly relations. Gradually, however, the situation changed and they came to view each other in a negative fashion. For example, when asked to describe their own group, the boys used mostly positive adjectives (e.g., brave, tough, friendly). When describing the opposing team, however, they used mainly negative terms (e.g., sneaky, smart aleck, etc.). These negative feelings quickly spilled over to their behavior. The two groups began by calling each other names, moved to creating problems for one another (e.g., one group made a mess at breakfast so that the other's task of cleaning up would be more difficult), and eventually took part in open fights. Thus, competitive contacts between the groups did seem to produce strong, negative feelings between them.

In a final stage of the experiment, attempts were made to reduce these negative feelings of hostility. While a number of procedures were attempted, only one proved effective: arranging conditions so that the groups were required to work together to achieve various goals or overcome a common threat (for example, joining forces to pull a disabled truck, competing against a group of outsiders). Taken as a whole, the findings of this research have often been viewed as demonstrating the powerful influence of group conflict and competition on the development of prejudice.

Personality Structure and Dynamics: Individual Differences and Prejudice

A second approach to the origins of prejudice focuses on personality structure and dynamics. Within this general framework, prejudice is viewed as stemming primarily from specific traits or characteristics of individuals which predispose them toward such negative reactions. Thus, supporters of this theoretical approach focus mainly on isolating the traits of highly prejudiced (and perhaps unprejudiced) individuals, rather than on specifying situational conditions likely to encourage the development of prejudice.

Perhaps the most extensive view of prejudice as an outgrowth of total personality structure was offered some years ago by Adorno et al. (1950). These authors contended that prejudice is often related to a much broader, antidemocratic character structure which they termed the *authoritarian personality*. Briefly, high-authoritarian individuals were thought to be reared by harsh, punitive parents who created in their offspring a pattern of submissive obedience to authority, and punitive rejection of groups other than their own. Largely as a result of such characteristics, high-authoritarian individuals were held to view the world in rigid black-and-white categories: either you are a member of their own group and are for them, or you are a member of some other, rejected group and must be against them. These intriguing suggestions were soon examined in a large number of experiments, conducted over a period of more than two decades (see Mischel, 1976). While the findings of these investigations have not always been consistent, most have confirmed the existence of a link between the traits described by Adorno et al., and prejudice. Thus, strong, negative reactions to groups other than one's own does seem to be related to certain personality characteristics (Cherry and Byrne, 1976).

The Many Faces of Prejudice: Contrasting Patterns of Bigotry. While research on authoritarianism and related traits has continued, recent attempts to examine the possible role of personality factors in the development of prejudice have often concentrated on consistent differences in the ways in which individuals think and feel about, as well as behave toward, minority group members. Such research has pointed to the conclusion that, at least with respect to racial bigotry, several distinct groups of prejudiced individuals can be clearly distinguished (Gaertner, 1976; Jones, 1972; Kovel, 1971).

First, there is what has been termed the *dominative racist*—the individual who acts directly out of bigoted, prejudiced beliefs. This is the type of person who throws rocks at school buses bringing black (or white) children to his neighborhood, or who commits acts of vandalism against the home of a black family who has recently moved into his or her neighborhood. Such individuals represent the open flame of race hatred, or other forms of prejudice, and are willing to use force to keep minority group members in their "place."

Second, there is the *ambivalent* prejudiced person. Such individuals may express negative feelings toward minority group members but, at the same time, sympathy for their plight. They do not generally view themselves as bigots, often claiming that they would be glad to have blacks, Chicanos, Jews, etc., for neighbors, if only they would learn to live "decently," like other people (Gaertner, 1976). Such persons are the ones who wonder what the new black family in their neighborhood did to encourage the destruction of their home by an angry mob.

FIGURE 4-3. *Unlike the character shown above, many persons do not recognize their negative feelings toward various groups as prejudice. (Source: B.C. by permission of Johnny Hart and Field Enterprises, Inc.)*

Third, there is the *aversive racist.* These are persons who view themselves as liberal, unprejudiced, and favorably disposed toward programs designed to aid minority group members. They will act in a friendly, polite manner when contacts with minority group members occur, but will attempt to avoid such interactions whenever possible. In short, such persons harbor negative attitudes and reactions to the members of other groups, but deny quite strongly that this is the case. Indeed, they will often carry out prominority actions in order to add luster to their liberal self-image, and to convince others that they are entirely unbigoted. (At this point, you may notice a degree of similarity between aversive racists and the subjects in the research on reverse discrimination by Dutton we described previously. Recall that these individuals viewed themselves as entirely unprejudiced. Yet, this liberal self-image did not prevent them from using tokenistic behavior as an excuse for refusing to engage in other, prominority actions.)

Finally, we may turn to the *nonracist*—the truly unprejudiced person. Surprisingly, social psychologists have had relatively little to say about such individuals. It seems quite reasonable, though, to view them as persons whose actions are in keeping with the norms of rationality, justice, and human-heartedness (Harding, et al. 1969). In short, these are the persons who genuinely believe—and behave—as though others' racial, religious, or ethnic heritage is not appropriate grounds for reacting to them in positive or negative ways. Only their actual behavior as individuals is judged to be important.

Social-learning Mechanisms: Prejudice as an Acquired Response

The final approach to prejudice we will consider focuses on the learned aspects of this phenomenon. Basically, it suggests that children acquire negative attitudes toward racial and ethnic minorities during the process of **socialization.** As we have already noted in Chapter 3, the primary agents of this process are undoubtedly parents, but the influence of peers, teachers, and the mass media

Theoretical Approaches to Prejudice: The Origins of Hate   **167**

cannot be overlooked. That is, children can be exposed to prejudiced beliefs, statements of negative feelings about minority group members, and open discriminatory behavior on the part of many persons around them. In some cases, simple exposure to such beliefs or actions seems to be sufficient, and prejudice is transmitted through the process of **observational learning** (please refer to Chapter 7 for more detailed coverage of this topic). In many others, children are directly rewarded by their parents, peers, teachers, and others for holding and expressing the "appropriate" prejudicial attitudes.

Once such negative reactions have been transmitted, they seem to pass through several stages of development and refinement. Harding and his colleagues (1969) have divided the development of racial and/or ethnic prejudice into three major phases: *awareness, orientation,* and *attitudes.* Awareness of one's ethnic background or racial differences can be established as early as the tender age of three or four, and this awareness gradually increases (Clark and Clark, 1947; Goodman, 1952). Continuing from the point of awareness to approximately eight years of age, children often acquire general, negative orientations toward racial or ethnic minorities, which are reflected in the phrases and terms used to describe such groups. Their conceptual grasp of the labels might not be fully formed, but their verbal fluency in repeating such phrases is often quite impressive. Finally, from the grade school years on, children begin to integrate their beliefs, feelings, and behavioral orientations toward ethnic or racial minorities. As a result, full-blown prejudiced attitudes emerge.

In a process paralleling the majority child's developing prejudice, minority children may develop a negative attitude toward themselves or their group identity. Several studies have provided evidence for this possibility. For example, in one early investigation (Clark and Clark, 1947), many black children were found to prefer to play with a white doll rather than a black doll. Moreover, the children described the white doll as nicer, looking better, and looking more like themselves. These findings were replicated in other studies, and were often taken as evidence for the view that black children frequently reject their own black identity. However, growing doubt has been cast upon such conclusions in recent years.

First, it has been argued that subjects' reported preferences in such studies may have been strongly influenced by the race of the experimenters (Porter, 1971). That is, subjects may have chosen the white dolls in order to be friendly to the white investigators. Second, their choices may well have been affected by actual differences in the attractiveness of the dolls. That is, given the type of toys on the market when many early studies were conducted, the white dolls may actually have been more attractive in terms of characteristics other than skin color. Third, more recent studies employing other methods have reported high self-esteem among black children (McCarthy and Yancey, 1973), and no tendency to reject their own racial identity. And finally, in a recent investigation conducted by Hraba and Grant (1970), black children showed a marked preference for *black* rather than white dolls. Since the procedures of this study were as similar as possible to those of the famous investigation by Clark and Clark (1947), it is clear that a major shift in the preferences of black children occurred during the intervening decades (see Figure 4-4). In short, the increased racial and ethnic pride shown by blacks and many other groups during the 1960's seems to have largely counteracted any previously existing tendencies toward self-rejection.

Before concluding this discussion of prejudice as a learned form of behavior, we should consider the potentially important role played by the mass media in this process. Until quite recently, television, magazines, movies, and other forms of public entertainment generally showed minority group members only in highly negative settings. That is, they were usually depicted as holding menial jobs, living in substandard homes, speaking with an almost imcomprehensible

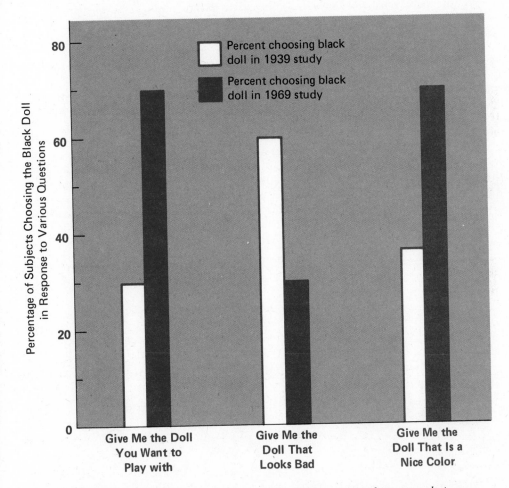

FIGURE 4-4. *At one time in the past, black children seemed to reject their own racial identity, preferring white dolls to black ones, and perceiving white dolls in more favorable terms than black ones. More recent findings, however, suggest that this preference has now been reversed, and that blacks prefer dolls similar in racial identity to themselves. (Based on data from Hraba and Grant, 1970.)*

FOCUS ON RESEARCH

ARCHIE BUNKER: THE LOVABLE BIGOT?

One of the most important constants in the lives of both children and adults is the television set. For many of us, the portrayal of various racial and ethnic groups in this medium may play a strong role in shaping and maintaining our prejudicial attitudes. Such effects have recently been investigated in a provocative study conducted by Vidmar and Rokeach (1974).

In the past few years, a controversy has emerged over the question of whether the hero of the popular television show "All in the Family"—Archie Bunker—is helping to overcome the prejudice of white viewers or, in fact, helping to make them worse. This controversy has had advocates on both sides. For example, the author Laura Z. Hobson argues that "making light of racial and ethnic slurs condones and encourages bigotry." In contrast, the show's producer, Norman Lear, argues that humor is an effective weapon against prejudice. By getting bigotry out into the open, he contends, we can talk about it and perhaps, by laughing at it, release some

of the tension which it creates for us. Blacks, too, have spoken out in favor of both sides of this issue. For example, in a controversial article, Sander (1972) charged that the show appeals to racism and may, in fact, be teaching racial slurs. The NAACP, in contrast, gave its "Image Award" for 1972 to "All in the Family" in recognition of its contribution to improved race relations.

What, then, are the social psychological data bearing on this controversy? Vidmar and Rokeach (1974) questioned American and Canadian viewers about their reactions to the show and to its major characters. Using the concepts of *selective perception* and *selective exposure*, they were able to shed some light on this issue. The first process suggests that bigots who watch the show "see what they want to see, and hear what they want to hear" (Nillson, 1971). That is, according to this process, prejudiced viewers will identify with different characters and will interpret the outcome of various episodes differently than nonprejudiced viewers. The second process,

accent, and so on. Given repeated exposure to such materials, it is not at all surprising that many children soon acquired the idea that the members of such groups must generally be quite inferior—after all, why else would they always be shown in such demeaning circumstances (Ashmore, 1970)? Fortunately, this situation has altered greatly in recent years, and at the present time, blacks, Chicanos, and the members of many other racial and ethnic groups are being portrayed in TV commercials and programs in higher status roles and circumstances. Hopefully, such changes will help to eliminate preconceived notions concerning the "nature" of various racial, ethnic, or religious groups, and so pave the way for a sharp reduction in prejudice toward them.

ATTEMPTS TO CHANGE PREJUDICE AND DISCRIMINATION: SLAYING THE BEAST

As you might suspect, social psychologists have examined a variety of techniques for reducing prejudice and discrimination. However, we will focus here on only selective exposure, suggests that bigots and nonbigots do not watch the show to the same extent. Specifically, it suggests that bigots watch "All in the Family" more because they can identify with Archie and so obtain support for their prejudiced views.

In order to investigate these possibilities, two samples of subjects (American adolescents and Canadian adults) were divided into prejudiced and nonprejudiced groups on the basis of their responses to six questions concerning negative attitudes toward different minorities (e.g., do you think Blacks are as intelligent as whites?). The reactions of both groups to "All in the Family" were then compared. Results were quite intriguing.

First, with respect to the selective-perception hypothesis, it was found that high and low-prejudice subjects did not differ in their ratings of how funny or enjoyable the program is. However, prejudiced Americans and Canadians liked and admired Archie more than Mike (the ideological liberal) and perceived Archie as winning at the end of the program. Prejudiced American adolescents also indicated that their values would be similar to Archie's in twenty years. Thus, there was some indication that the two groups did see what they each wanted to see in the show.

With respect to the selective-exposure hypothesis, the study found that frequent U.S. viewers (persons who watched every week or every other week) scored higher on the measure of prejudice. Since prejudiced viewers did not watch more television overall than nonprejudiced viewers, there was some indication that "All in the Family" has greater appeal for highly bigoted persons than for less prejudiced individuals.

Together, the pattern of findings obtained by Vidmar and Rokeach suggest that "All in the Family"—and perhaps similar shows as well—may be serving to increase rather than reduce prejudice for some viewers. We should hasten to add, of course, that such conclusions are only tentative in nature, and should not be viewed as final or certain. However, given the vast audiences who regularly tune their sets to this and other popular television shows, even the possibility of such effects is quite unsettling.

two major approaches: *socialization* by parents and teachers, and *intergroup* contact. Put simply, the former focuses on preventing prejudice from developing while the latter focuses on the elimination of prejudices that have already taken shape.

Socialization: Nipping Prejudice in the Bud

Earlier, we suggested that authoritarian child-rearing techniques, namely, harsh discipline and overobedience to authority, were closely related to the development of prejudice, at least in the case of some individuals. It follows, then, that reducing authoritarianism in child-rearing practices might be one effective means of preventing the occurrence of prejudice. For obvious reasons, there have been very few attempts by psychologists to intervene in parent-child relations. However, the recent increase in parent-effectiveness training workshops may provide a starting point for at least examining ways in which parents can effectively prevent the acquisition of prejudicial attitudes by their offspring. Further, guidelines for parents of children who are victimized by racism and seek to combat its effects have recently become available (Comer and Poussaint, 1975). Some especially interesting leads in this respect are provided by Harrison-Ross and Wyden (1973).

In a book entitled *The Black Child: A Parent's Guide to Raising Happy and Healthy Children,* these authors offer many examples of how interracial encounters can be turned into preventive lessons for the white child, and can spare the black child from a demeaning self-evaluation. For example, what does a white parent do when his or her child sees a black child and asks "Why does that child have such a dirty face?" Derogation and avoidance of the issue are, of course, possibilities. On the other hand, the parent can confront the situation directly. For example, a concerned parent might say something like "That little child isn't dirty. You're all mixed up just because his skin is brown. There are lots of people in the world with brown skins. Did you know that there are more people in the world with dark skins than with light ones?" Through such reactions, parents can help their children avoid the joint pitfalls of prejudice and bigotry.

Teachers can also play an important role in this respect. One dramatic illustration of this fact is provided by an informal study conducted by an Iowa school teacher, and represented in the documentary film *The Eye of the Storm.* In an attempt to help her all-white class of third graders understand the negative impact of prejudice and discrimination, the teacher (Mrs. Jane Elliot), divided her students into two groups on the basis of eye color. That is, special brown-eyed and blue-eyed groups were established. On the first day, the brown-eyed group was assigned an inferior status in the classroom. Brown-eyed children were ridiculed by the teacher and the blue-eyed students, and were made to wear special collars. Further, they were denied classroom privileges afforded the blue-eyed students. This treatment was continued for several days, and then reversed, so that blue-eyed students now became the victims. As you can guess, the experience of being the victim of discrimination was quite demoralizing for the children, and even lowered their performance on standard classroom tasks (see photograph). The purpose of this exercise, of course, was that of providing the children with direct evidence of the evils of discrimination and in this way, perhaps, reducing their tendency to engage in such negative practices themselves.

A more rigorous experimental study, based on the procedures followed in *The Eye of the Storm* has recently been conducted by Weiner and Wright (1973). On the first day of this study, children in one third-grade class (the experimental group) were randomly assigned by their teacher to be Orange or Green people. Colored armbands were used to identify the group to which each child belonged, and initially, Orange people were assigned a superior position (e.g., they were described as smarter, cleaner, etc., than Green people, and received many special privileges). On the second day, however, conditions were reversed, and Green people were designated as being superior. (In contrast, children in a second, control class were not exposed to these procedures.)

On the third day of the study, and again two weeks later, the members of

In a recent classroom demonstration (The Eye of the Storm), *children were made the victims of discrimination on the basis of eye color. It was hoped that after experiencing the negative effects of such treatment first-hand, they would be less likely to engage in such practices themselves.*

both classes were asked whether they would like to attend a picnic with some black children from a nearby school. The results of the experiment were quite straightforward: on both occasions, a much higher proportion of children in the experimental class than in the control class (96 percent versus 62 percent) indicated a desire to attend. Thus, it appeared that having experienced the evils of prejudice and discrimination first-hand, children became less willing to adopt such practices in their own relations with others.

Unfortunately, as you can probably guess, the impact of teachers on their students is not always so beneficial as was the case in the experiment by Weiner and Wright (1973), or in *The Eye of the Storm.* Often, negative rather than positive effects are produced. This is not to say that teachers set out to make their pupils more prejudiced, or to convince the members of minority groups that they are somehow inferior. On the contrary, most teachers *do* wish to combat prejudice and avoid actions which might negatively affect the self-image of minority group children. Unfortunately, though, such good intentions are often counteracted by subtle cues which communicate the fact that they *expect* certain children to do better than others. Thus, a white, liberal-minded teacher who, despite the best of motives, still expects black children to do more poorly than whites, may quickly transmit these expectations to his or her class, and so shape the behavior of the children involved until they fit these expectations. Such unsettling effects have been demonstrated in a large number of studies (see Rosenthal and Jacobson, 1968).

For example, in one interesting experiment (Rubovits and Maehr, 1973), white female undergraduates enrolled in a teacher-training course were asked to prepare a lesson for four seventh and eighth grade students, two of whom were white and two black. Just before meeting with the students, the teachers received information indicating that two of the students in the group (one white and one black) were "gifted" and had high IQ's, while the others (again, one white and one black) were "nongifted," and possessed average intelligence. In reality, all the children were about equal in ability, and these labels were assigned in a completely arbitrary manner. The teachers were then observed during a forty-minute period, while they interacted with the four students.

Results indicated that, as expected, both the pupils' race and information regarding their supposed intelligence exerted strong effects on the teachers' behavior. First, children described as "gifted" were generally called upon more often and given greater attention than those described as "nongifted." (As we shall soon see, however, this was primarily true in the case of white students). Second, black children were treated in a less positive fashion than whites. They were ignored more, praised less, and criticized on a greater number of occasions. Finally, and perhaps most unsettling of all, the teachers reacted differently to the label "gifted" when it was applied to black or to white children. While white students described in this manner were called upon more frequently than white children described as "non-gifted," just the opposite was true for blacks. Supposedly gifted children received less attention than nongifted ones (see Figure 4-5). While these findings are difficult to interpret, one possible explanation for their occurrence may be suggested. Perhaps the white student teachers found the disconfirmation of their expectancies regarding the supposed inferiority of black students so disturbing that they chose to largely ignore the source of such inconsistency! Needless to say, this suggestion is quite speculative in nature, and must be examined in future research. At present, however, the findings of the study by Rubovits and Maehr and other investigations as well, do point to one firm conclusion: both children's racial identity and teachers' preconceived notions regarding their ability may strongly affect the manner in which they are treated in the classroom. And, unfortunately, such differential treatment may then have the effect of confirming the expectations they reflect. Given the potentially damaging influence of such unintentional—but powerful— teacher-expectancy effects, educators must always be on guard to protect against the possibility of harming children they would actually strongly prefer to help.

Intergroup Contact: Is Knowing a First Step to Accepting?

A second major technique for counteracting the negative impact of prejudice involves direct contact between minority and majority group members. Basically, this approach assumes that, after getting to know one another as individuals, members of both groups will find it more difficult to maintain stereotyped beliefs about and negative attitudes toward each other (Amir, 1969; Ashmore, 1970; Pettigrew, 1969). As we saw in Chapter 3, a considerable body of evidence lends support to the view that repeated contact between individuals

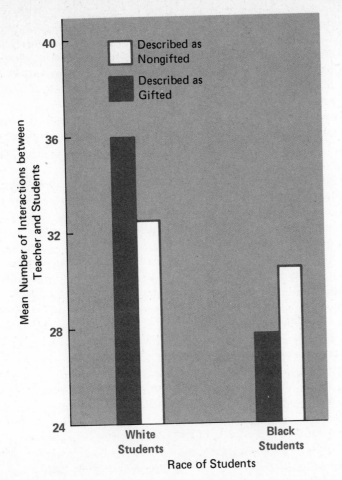

FIGURE 4-5. *Students' race and apparent intellectual ability as determinants of their treatment in the classroom. As shown above, teachers generally directed more attention to white pupils when they were described as "gifted" than when they were described as "nongifted." However, precisely the opposite was true in the case of blacks. (Adapted from Rubovits and Maehr, 1973.)*

may in fact often lead to increased attraction between them. However, additional findings suggest that prejudice will usually be reduced by such procedures only under certain specific conditions.

First, it seems essential that contact occur under conditions of equal social and economic *status.* If, instead, the members of the two groups differ in these respects, communication will be difficult, and mistrust and suspicion may actually increase rather than drop. Second, it is crucial that the two groups be approximately equal in *social power* (Taylor, 1974). That is, each must have equal capacity to influence the outcomes of the other. When this is not the case, and one group has much greater power than the other, the less powerful individuals may feel that they are being patronized, with the result that prejudice will not be lessened. And finally, it seems beneficial for the two groups to meet under conditions where they share *common goals*. As indicated by Sherif's research (discussed previously) such conditions seem to reduce intergroup hostility, and encourage the development of friendships and positive feelings. Thus, they can often facilitate the reduction of prejudice through intergroup contact (Ashmore, 1970).

When these conditions are fulfilled, contact between the members of different racial or ethnic groups does often lead to reductions in prejudice. The occurrence of such beneficial effects is demonstrated very clearly in a recent study conducted by Eaton and Clore (1975).

In this investigation, black and white children attended a week-long summer camp involving intimate contact between them (they lived together in tents with black and white counselors, ate their meals together, etc.). Since the children were of comparable social and economic backgrounds and participated in many activities involving shared goals, conditions were optimal for reduced prejudice stemming from intergroup contact. In order to assess the occurrence of such effects, Eaton and Clore employed a relatively indirect measure—subjects' tendencies to imitate the actions of a racially different model. It was expected that the greater the degree of contact between campers of the two races, the more willing they would be to imitate the actions of members of the other group. This hypothesis was tested in an ingenious and amusing way. Subjects took part in an "initiation" ceremony in which one adult, dressed as an Indian chief, ordered another who was either black or white, to perform certain behaviors (e.g., painting a "magic square"). After observing the models' actions, subjects were provided with an opportunity to imitate them. One group took part in this initiation after only one day of intergroup contact, while another performed it after five days of such contact. Consistent with the view that this type of experience would reduce subjects' prejudice, those in the second, high-contact group did show a greater tendency to imitate the different-race model than those in the first, low-contact group.

The results of this and other investigations dealing with the effects of intergroup contact seem to have important implications with respect to recent attempts at desegregation. Specifically, they suggest that such actions as school busing, open-housing laws, and affirmative-action employment practices will lead to reduced prejudice only when the persons brought into contact through such procedures are roughly equal in status and power, and share common goals. When such conditions are not met, increased contact between the members of different racial or ethnic groups will often fail to reduce negative feelings of mistrust and hostility. Indeed, as recent incidents suggest all too clearly, they may actually serve to fan rather than quench the flames of racial hatred.

WOMEN AS A MINORITY GROUP

Earlier in this chapter, we noted that women have often been viewed as a "psychological" if not numerical minority by virtue of their exclusion from

ARE YOU A CLOSET SEXIST?

A father and his son were driving along the highway when the father suddenly lost control of the car and crashed into a telephone pole. The father was killed instantly and his son was badly injured. The boy was rushed to the local hospital where it was found that he was suffering from serious internal injuries. A prominent surgeon was immediately summoned. When the surgeon arrived and went to the operating room to examine the boy, a loud gasp was heard. "I can't operate on this boy," the surgeon said, "He is my son."

Can you solve this riddle? The father is dead; how could the boy be the surgeon's son?

The answer, of course, is quite straightforward: the surgeon is a woman and also the boy's mother. If you were unable to provide it, though, don't be too upset. In a recent study (Goldberg, 1974), only 3 out of 26 males

and 4 out of 24 females who had not heard the story before were able to answer correctly. Not too surprisingly, when this riddle is modified slightly so that the surgeon is described as bursting into tears and becoming hysterical upon seeing the boy, many more subjects are able to solve it correctly (Gorkin, 1972). Apparently, these extra clues, which are consistent with widely held stereotypes concerning women, are sufficient to suggest the correct answer.

This riddle, and many others like it, point to two important facts about our views concerning women. First, our inability to solve them derives, in part, from the stereotyped expectancies we hold for females, regardless of their individual skills, occupation, or training. And second, such stereotyping of women is not restricted to a few "chauvinistic male pigs"; rather, it is shared by many men and women alike.

economic and political power. This parallel between women and the members of ethnic and racial minorities is most apparent in two respects. First, women—like the members of such groups—have often been the victims of widespread stereotyping. All are assumed to share certain characteristics, and in many cases, these are quite negative in nature (does the phrase "woman driver" ring a bell?). Second, women, like the members of racial or ethnic minorities, have often suffered from overt discriminatory practices with respect to employment and education. That is, they have been barred from many types of jobs and several forms of training because it was held that they were simply not suited to such endeavors (O'Leary, 1974). Fortunately, **sexism** has been sharply reduced in recent years. Yet, it continues to linger on in many settings (Beale, 1970; Hacker, 1974).

Perhaps the most important difference distinguishing racial and ethnic minorities from women as a "psychological" minority relates to the concept of social distance, which we considered earlier. Whereas racial and ethnic minorities have traditionally been "separate and unequal"—held at arm's distance by the dominant, majority group—women have been "together but unequal." That is, they have been readily accepted into the most intimate relationships, while being rejected at lower levels of intimacy. In short, the attitude held by many men toward women has been something like the following: "I wouldn't mind marrying (or living with) one, but I certainly wouldn't want one for my business partner, teammate, etc."

Prejudice against Women: A Not-So-Subtle Put-down

So far, we have noted that women are often the victims of widespread stereotyping, but have not yet described the nature of such beliefs. Some of these assumptions regarding the characteristics of women—as well as those concerning men—are summarized in Table 4-4, and you may find it interesting to examine them at this point. As you will see, the traits generally assigned to women form a cluster which might be described as involving warmth and expressiveness, while those assigned to men generally seem to involve aspects of competence, aggressiveness, and achievement.

Unfortunately, as Table 4-4 suggests, men and women are not merely preceived as being different; in addition, they are also viewed as being quite unequal. The set of traits attributed to women are generally less valued or desirable than those assigned to men. Further, and consistent with this picture of a negative stereotype regarding women, activities which are perceived as essentially "masculine" in nature are often viewed more favorably than those which are seen as essentially "feminine." This latter fact is illustrated quite vividly by a recent experiment conducted by Touhey (1974b).

In this investigation, male and female subjects were provided with descriptions of five traditionally male occupations (e.g., architect, professor, lawyer, physician, scientist) which indicated either that (1) the percentage of women in these fields was increasing rapidly, so that they would soon form a majority of the persons in it, or (2) the percentage of women was relatively stable and would not increase in the years ahead. Subjects in both groups were then asked to rate

TABLE 4-4. *Some stereotyped beliefs about the characteristics of men and women. As you can see, women are generally assumed to possess such traits as gentleness, tenderness, and emotional expressiveness, while men are assumed to show such characteristics as aggressiveness, competence, and achievement-orientation. (Adapted from Broverman et al., 1972.)*

Beliefs about Women	Beliefs about Men
Very gentle	Very rough
Very aware of feelings of others	Not at all aware of feelings of others
Very quiet	Very loud
Very strong need for security	Very little need for security
Easily express tender feelings	Do not express tender feelings easily
Enjoy art and literature	Do not enjoy art and literature
Very passive	Very aggressive
Not aggressive	Very active
Not ambitious	Very ambitious
Almost never act as leaders	Almost always act as leaders

the prestige of each occupation. As you can see in Figure 4-6, those who anticipated female majorities rated the occupations lower than those who expected continued male domination. In short, the prestige or desirability of each field decreased when it was viewed as one which would be increasingly dominated by women.

Male and Female Stereotypes: Myth or Reality? One important question which often arises in relation to stereotypes of both men and women is whether such views are based, at least to some degree, on reality. Specifically, is it true that women differ sharply from men in many of the ways popular wisdom

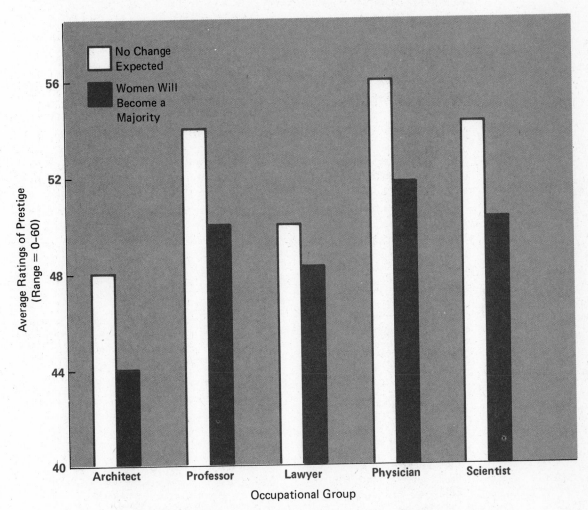

FIGURE 4-6. *As shown above, the prestige of various occupational fields was sharply reduced when subjects were led to believe that women would soon constitute a majority of the persons working in them. (Based on data from Touhey, 1974b.)*

suggests? At present, the investigation of differences between the sexes is an active field of research in social psychology, and the total picture is far from clear (Deaux, 1976a; Maccoby and Jacklin, 1974; Tavris, 1973). What does seem to be emerging, however, is increasing evidence for the conclusion that common sense tends to overstate the case. While men and women do indeed differ in several respects, such differences have often been exaggerated, and other differences between the sexes suggested by informal observation have failed to emerge in more systematic investigations (see Table 4-5). In short, as often seems to be the case with respect to stereotypes, there may be a grain of truth hidden inside widespread beliefs relating to the behavior of men and women. However, in this case, the grain may be far smaller than has often been suggested.

Discriminatory Practices against Women: Keeping Females in Their Place

As we noted earlier, women are not only the victims of persistent and often erroneous stereotypes; often, they have been confronted with actual discrimination as well. Such practices have occurred most frequently with respect to employment, where at one time in the past, many occupations were all but closed to female applicants. And even when they succeeded in obtaining jobs in such all-male preserves, women frequently found themselves passed over for promotions, raises, and other benefits (O'Leary, 1974). As a result of such practices, women presently constitute a far smaller proportion of the individuals working in

TABLE 4-5. *Just how different are the two sexes? As shown below, many of the differences suggested by common sense do not hold up under close, experimental scrutiny. (Based on information from Maccoby and Jacklin, 1974.)*

Differences Generally Shown to Be True	Differences in Doubt	Differences Shown to Be False
Males are generally more aggressive	Girls are more timid and anxious (?)	Girls are more sociable
Girls have greater verbal ability	Boys are more active (?)	Girls are more suggestible
Boys excel in visual-spatial ability	Boys are more competitive (?)	Girls have lower self-esteem
Boys excel in mathematical ability	Boys are more dominant (?)	Girls lack motivation to achieve
	Females are more passive (?)	Boys are more "analytic" in cognitive style
		Girls are more affected by heredity, boys by environment

professional and technical fields than their numbers in the general population would suggest, and a far greater proportion of persons working in various "dead end," low-status jobs (Bem and Bem, 1970).

While many women have been subjected to the negative impact of such discrimination, perhaps those who have suffered most in this respect are the individuals who choose to step outside traditional roles and pursue success and achievement in "masculine" endeavors—a group often referred to as *competent* women. Because a great deal of recent research has focused on the kinds of discrimination faced by such persons, we will now consider this topic in some detail.

Sex Bias in the Treatment of Competent Women. One major type of discrimination frequently encountered by competent women centers around evaluations of their accomplishments. Often, such individuals find that their efforts are downgraded relative to those of men, and that they receive less praise and smaller financial rewards for similar performances. Evidence for the occurrence of such effects has been obtained in many different studies. For example, in one well-known investigation (Goldberg, 1968), college women were asked to rate a series of manuscripts attributed either to male or female authors, and dealing with either traditionally masculine (law) or traditionally feminine (dietetics) fields. Results indicated that regardless of the topics of the manuscripts, they received lower ratings when attributed to female than to male authors.

Similar findings have also been obtained in several later studies (Etaugh and Rose, 1975; Mischel, 1974). Together, the results of these investigations point to the general conclusion that the achievements of competent women are frequently devalued relative to those of men. Further evidence also suggests that such reactions are especially likely to occur under certain conditions. First, as you might well guess, the accomplishments of women in traditionally masculine fields are more likely to be devalued by men and women holding conventional sex-role beliefs than by those holding more liberal views (Spence, Helmreich, and Stapp, 1975). Second, such devaluation is more likely to occur among men when they anticipate actual interactions with competent women than when they do not (Hagen and Kahn, 1977). Apparently, when men feel that they will not have to meet and deal with a successful, competent woman, they are willing to evaluate her and her accomplishments favorably. However, when they believe that they will have to meet her in a face-to-face encounter, they feel more threatened and reject her quite strongly. Finally, such devaluation seems to occur most strongly under conditions where competent women openly adopt competitive orientations, and reject traditional female roles and behavior. This latter fact is clearly illustrated by the results of an experiment by Shaffer and Wegley (1974).

In this investigation, male and female subjects read descriptions of a competent woman—a highly successful female student viewed as having great potential for a successful career in her chosen field by her college instructors. Two characteristics of this fictitious individual—her degree of success orientation and her preference for masculine or feminine sex roles—were varied systematically. Thus, she either appeared to be strongly oriented toward success or not oriented in this direction, and either seemed to prefer traditional feminine roles, or competitive, masculine ones. It was predicted that subjects would tend to reject and devalue her most strongly when she was both success oriented and preferred masculine sex roles, and as you can see in Figure 4-7, this was actually the case. In short, both men and women seemed to be highly threatened by this aggressive, achievement-oriented female, and devalued her strongly when she showed such a pattern.

The findings of this and many other investigations seem to paint a rather bleak picture for success-oriented, competent women. In many cases, their strivings for achievement, coupled with rejection of stereotyped "feminine"

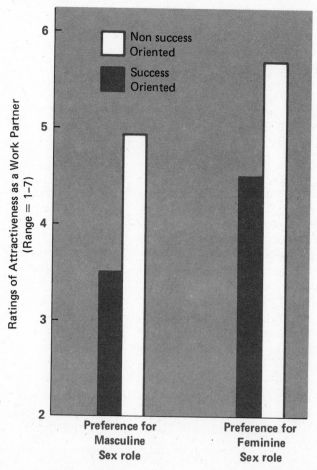

FIGURE 4-7. *Evaluations of competent women. Women who demonstrate strong success orientation and a rejection of traditional feminine sex roles are rejected both by men and other women. (Based on data from Shaffer and Wegley, 1974.)*

characteristics such as passivity and a lack of ambition, are quite threatening to the persons around them—both men and women—and may result in their strong rejection. It is for this reason that many successful women learn to "soft-pedal" their strivings and accomplishments, concealing their competence behind a mask of helpless femininity (see Figure 4-8). Perhaps as sexual stereotypes continue to weaken in the years ahead, such tactics will become less and less essential, and competent women will be able to take as much open pride in their accomplishments as men.

Explanations for Women's Competence: Is Luck a Sex-linked Trait?
Another—and perhaps more subtle—form of bias which serves to undermine the position of competent women is the attribution of their success to luck or temporary effort rather than to superior ability. That is, if a man and a woman attain the same level of performance, the woman's achievements are often attributed to transient factors such as luck, while the man's are attributed to more

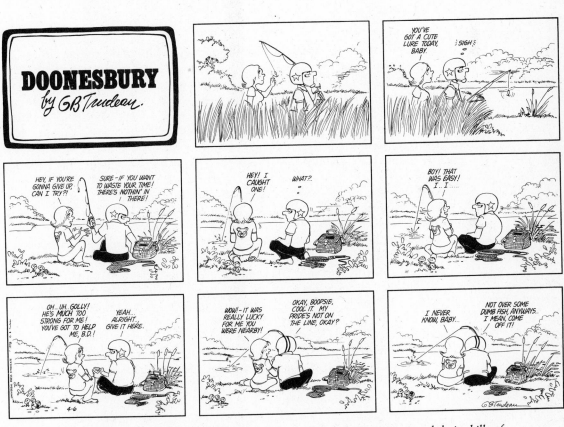

FIGURE 4-8. *Often, competent women find that they must conceal their skills of accomplishments behind a mask of helpless femininity in order to avoid threatening the egos of the men around them.* (*Source: Copyright, 1975, G. B. Tradeau/ Distributed by Universal Press Syndicate.*)

lasting factors such as ability. The result, of course, is that various accomplishments by females are viewed as being somehow less important or deserving than those by males—after all, they were simply "lucky!" Evidence for the occurrence of this type of antifemale bias has been obtained in several different studies (Deaux and Emswiller, 1974; Feldman-Summers and Kiesler, 1974).

For example, in the study by Deaux and Emswiller (1974), male and female subjects listened to tape recordings which indicated that a man or woman had succeeded either at a traditionally masculine task (identifying wrenches, screwdrivers, etc.) or at a traditionally feminine task (identifying various cooking utensils). When subjects were then asked to indicate whether the success of these individuals was due to ability or luck, an interesting pattern of findings emerged: both men and women attributed the male's success on the masculine task to ability, but that of the female to luck, while in the case of the feminine task, the success of both persons was attributed largely to ability. Thus, overall, both men and women showed a tendency to attribute successful performance by a male to lasting factors of ability, and that of a female to more temporary conditions (see Figure 4-9).

The Self-fulfilling Prophecy: Do Women Fear Success? In our discussion of racial or ethnic prejudice, we called attention to the fact that expectations often have a nasty habit of causing their own confirmation. For example, as we noted earlier, a white, middle-class teacher who expects black or Chicano children to perform more poorly than whites may communicate such expectations to her pupils, and so adversely influence their self-esteem and actual achievement. Not surprisingly, similar effects seem to occur in the case of women. A number of investigations (see Deaux, 1976a) suggest that, as a result of the negative stereotypes so prevalent in our culture, women often tend to express lower expectations regarding success than men, and more frequently attribute their accomplishments to luck and other temporary factors. Perhaps even more unsettling, there is also some indication that, as a result of stereotypes regarding traditional sexual roles, many women learn to equate success or achievement with a loss of femininity. That is, they may come to believe that the attainment of excellence in intellectual or occupational pursuits will somehow make them less of a woman, and bring about such unpleasant consequences as social rejection or disapproval. As a result of such feelings, it has been suggested, women may often develop an actual **fear of success,** and so seek to avoid competition or advancement (Horner, 1970).

Initial evidence for the existence of such anxieties was obtained by Matina Horner (1970, 1972). In these investigations, male and female subjects were presented with the following brief statement, and asked to write stories based on it: "After first-term finals (Anne/John) finds (herself/himself) at the top of (her/his) medical class." For females, the character was named Anne while for males, he was named John. Systematic analysis of the stories written by subjects indicated that women expressed ambivalence or conflict over Anne's success far more frequently than men did over John's achievements. Indeed,

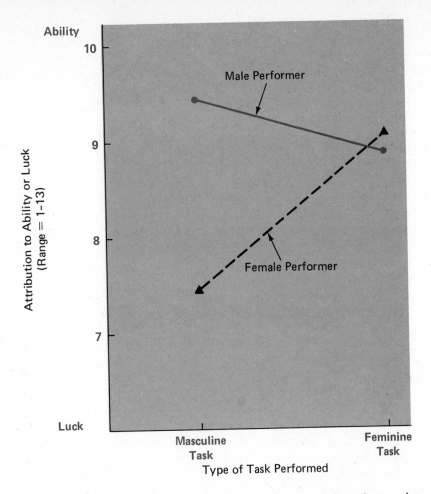

FIGURE 4-9. *Explaining male and female success. As shown above, when a woman succeeds on a traditionally masculine task, her performance is often attributed to luck or chance. When a man succeeds on traditionally feminine tasks, however, his performance may still frequently be attributed to high ability. (Adapted from Deaux and Emswiller, 1974.)*

while fewer than 10 percent of the stories written by men contained any hint of a fear of success, fully 65 percent of those produced by women demonstrated the presence of this theme. Fortunately, more recent experiments have reported a sharp reduction in the incidence of such themes among female undergraduates (Spence, 1974). And it now appears that men as well as women often share such fear of success (Zuckerman and Wheeler, 1975). The possibility that traditional stereotypes regarding feminine characteristics may be causing at least *some* women to actively avoid success and achievement, however, is unsettling enough to demand further, close attention.

Do women fear success? Although this question is a far from resolved, some social scientists believe that, as a result of traditional sexual roles, they do.

ACQUIRING SEXUAL IDENTITY: SEX TYPING AND SEX-ROLE STEREOTYPING

From the moment they hear a nurse or physician proclaim the magic words "It's a girl!" or "It's a boy!" parents begin to both treat and to think about their male and female children in markedly different ways. It is little wonder, then, that, within a few short years, toddlers have established a strong sexual identity. By the time they are two, many seem to have a relatively clear idea of their gender firmly in mind. For example, they will choose sex-appropriate toys in a free-play environment (Fagot and Patterson, 1969), and show considerable agreement about which toys are suitable for the members of each sex (Hartley and Hardesty, 1964; Schell and Silber, 1968). And by the time they are three, they will even actively avoid toys they consider inappropriate for their sex (Hartup and Zook, 1960; Hartup, Moore, and Sager, 1963). While several different perspectives have been offered to explain the rapid manner in which such **sex typing** occurs, two have received the greatest amount of attention: the *social-learning* and *cognitive* approaches.

Social Learning: "I Want to Be Just Like Mommy/Daddy"

The **social-learning view** begins with the suggestion that toddlers have a strong tendency to imitate the actions of others (see Chapter 7 for additional information on this topic). Further, the more similar they are to a given social model, the more likely they are to match his or her behavior. Since little boys are physically more similar to their fathers and little girls are more similar to their mothers, they tend to emulate the parent of their own sex to a greater degree (Mischel, 1966). As a result, boys come to act increasingly like their fathers, and girls increasingly like their mothers. In addition, of course, parents often help this process along by offering rewards (smiles, verbal praise, etc.) on occasions when their children imitate the "appropriate" model, and criticism when they match the "inappropriate one" (Grusec and Brinker, 1972). For example, a little boy may be praised for helping his father in the shop, while a little girl is flattered for helping her mother in the kitchen. As children become increasingly similar to their same-sex parent in terms of behavior, they show a growing awareness of sexual identity. Thus, as the process nears completion, they may be heard to remark "I'm a boy like daddy," or "I'm a girl like mommy."

The social-learning view suggests that children acquire clear sexual identities by imitating their same-sex parent.

Cognitive Development: Doing the "Right" Things

In contrast to the social learning view, which sees the emergence of a clear sexual identity as one of the final steps in an ongoing imitative process, cognitive theory suggests that the process of sex typing actually starts with such recognition. Presumably, toddlers begin by identifying themselves as a boy or a girl—with the help of their parents, of course—and then proceed to adopt those behaviors which they perceive as being appropriate to their gender. As suggested by Kohlberg (1966), it is as if the child begins by saying to himself or herself: "I am a girl (boy); therefore, I want to do girl (boy) things"—and then goes on to do them!

Although cognitive theory provdes an intriguing explanation for the growth of sexual identity, it is weakened by the fact that young children who declare emphatically that they are a boy or a girl often lack full understanding of the meaning of such statements. For example, they continue to believe that it is possible for a person to change his or her sex, and become upset if a teasing adult threatens to reverse their gender. In view of this fact, it appears that, at present, the social-learning position provides a more adequate explanation for rapid sex typing.

Sex-role Stereotyping: Learning about the Relative Status of Men and Women

In addition to acquiring a firm sexual identity and knowledge of the kinds of behavior viewed as "appropriate" for males and females, children quickly learn a great deal about the relative status of men and women. Indeed, by the time they are five, they have often acquired a remarkable knowledge of the **sex-role stereotypes** present in their society (Williams, Bennett, and Best, 1975). Unfortunately, as we have pointed out before, these stereotypes generally give a decided edge to men, assigning many more valued or desirable traits to males than to females. Thus, by the time they enter school, most children have already begun to conclude that it is males who occupy the favored position in our society.

While parents play a major role in transmitting such sex-role stereotypes, the mass media are also very important in this respect. Turning first to the impact of television, the results of a recent investigation by Sternglanz and Serbin (1974) are very informative. These researchers set out to analyze the content of the most popular shows for children in order to determine whether any differences existed in the treatment of male and female characters. Unfortunately, they soon found that a number of these shows could not even be studied in this manner: they simply failed to contain any female "regulars." And even among the remaining programs ("Pebbles and Bamm Bamm," "Archie's TV Funnies," etc.) males outnumbered females by a ratio of 2 to 1.

With respect to the specific behaviors shown by male and female characters,

Sternglanz and Serbin found several striking differences. For example, males were much more likely to be shown aggressing against others, making plans and carrying them out, or seeking help and information from others in order to complete some project. In addition, they were generally more active than females, and were more frequently rewarded for their behavior. In contrast, females were more frequently shown as following directions from others (usually males!) and receiving punishment for high levels of activity. Finally, their actions generally had less effect on the environment than those of males.

Taken together, these findings suggest that popular television shows are indeed teaching young viewers a great deal about the contrasting roles—and value—of women and men. In particular, they seem to be informing youngsters that males are active, planful leaders, while females are passive, inactive followers. Of course, not all television shows fit this description. For example, programs such as "Sesame Street" or "The Electric Company" make consistent attempts to show equal numbers of male and female characters, and to demonstrate that many characteristics are not the sole property of one sex or the other. And several popular television shows ("Maude," "Rhoda," "The Bionic Woman") now depict women in more active and central roles. In general, though, commercial television seems to operate as an essentially conservative force with respect to sex-role stereotypes.

If the current situation with respect to television shows is somewhat discouraging, it is even more disappointing in the area of children's books. First, the ratio of male to female characters is even greater, fully 11 to 1 in one recent survey (Weitzman et al., 1972). Further, adherence to traditional sexual stereotypes seems to be even stronger than on television. Girls are portrayed as passive when they do appear, while boys are active and engage in more exciting and adventurous activities. Girls remain at home and carry out traditionally feminine chores such as helping in the kitchen, while boys are shown outdoors, in a much wider range of settings. Motherhood is generally presented as a full-time job, and fathers are rarely, if ever, seen helping with the duties of child care. And when women are presented as having careers, they are almost always the traditionally feminine ones (secretary, stewardess, nurse, etc.). Again, the past few years have brought some changes in this dismal picture. For example, at least one major publisher has recently directed its authors to stop using occupational terms ending in "man," such as fireman or mailman, and to replace these with more neutral terms unrelated to sex, such as fire fighter and mail carrier. And an increasing number of school texts and other books for children do make some attempt to avoid communicating the notion that women are somehow doomed to a lower status than men. At present, though, it is probably safe to say that, on the whole, children's literature—as well as children's television programming—generally tends to support traditional sex-role stereotypes. Given continued exposure to such materials, it is far from surprising that when asked what they wish to be when they grow up, many little girls still reply "a nurse," "a Mommy," or "a teacher," while many little boys reply "a doctor," "a scientist," or "an astronaut."

COUNTERACTING PREJUDICE AND DISCRIMINATION AGAINST WOMEN

Although the problems faced by women have not been similar in all respects to those confronted by the members of racial or ethnic minorities, there seems little doubt that they, too, have often been the victims of prejudice and discrimination. In many cases, these negative forces have been cloaked in the velvet glove of love, physical attraction, and male protectiveness; yet, their impact has frequently been negative nonetheless. In view of this fact, it seems only reasonable for us to conclude by examining some means for counteracting the influence of these forces. Since overt discrimination against women, at least in the areas of employment and education, is currently on the wane, we will focus instead on two possible techniques for counteracting the internal barriers which have frequently prevented them from assuming a fully equal position in society: *exposure to appropriate role models,* and *training for a degree of androgyny.*

The first of these techniques simply involves exposing females (especially young girls) to concrete instances of women who have excelled in nontraditional activities. For example, women who have attained success in such fields as law, medicine, or science might be presented. The purpose of such procedures, of course, is merely that of demonstrating that women, like men, have the option of pursuing virtually any career or life goals they desire. We should hasten to add that this by no means implies any disparagement of the traditional feminine roles of mother, homemaker, and so on. On the contrary, such roles continue to offer fulfilling and satisfying lives to millions of women, and should *not* be maligned. All that is sought is the goal of calling women's attention to the fact that other options exist, and may readily be followed without any necessary loss of femininity. Recent investigations suggest that exposure to role models of success and achievement can be highly effective in overcoming women's reluctance to enter fields previously considered the sole province of men, and may also sharply reduce their anxieties concerning such activities (Cherry, 1975; Wolf, 1973). Thus, it seems possible that the simple technique of presenting women in the roles of physician as well as nurse, business executive as well as secretary, and scientist as well as lab technician, may go a long way toward overcoming the internal forces that have often prevented them from obtaining a fully equal position in society.

The second technique—training for a degree of androgyny—brings us to a somewhat more sensitive area. Basically, it suggests that a softening or blurring of our currently sharp sex-role distinctions might be of benefit to both sexes. For example, women might well profit from a greater degree of decisiveness and assertiveness, while men might benefit from greater tendencies toward gentleness and expressiveness (Bem, 1972, 1975). At the present time, members of both genders feel strong restraints against borrowing any of the behavior patterns of the other and, often, this leads to a great deal of internal conflict and frustration. Women feel compelled to refrain from competitiveness and assertiveness, even when they would like to behave in these ways, while men feel that any gentleness or open expression of emotions on their part will be viewed as a sign of weakness, and so refrain from such actions. It seems reasonable to propose that a loosening of such artificial distinctions might help women to overcome both internal and external restraints that have often prevented them from attaining success or achievement, and at the same time assist men in overcoming the rigid "macho" cult which so often forces them to be tough when they would rather be more yielding.

Together, these procedures may help to counteract the negative stereotypes and subtle forms of discrimination which have often placed women in the paradoxical position of being a psychological minority while constituting a numerical majority. The result, it is hoped, will not be a worsening in the position of men, or a new era in the battle of the sexes; rather, it will be a richer, more open, and more just relationship between men and women than has ever existed before.

SUMMARY

Prejudice is generally defined, in social psychology, as a negative attitude toward the members of some racial, ethnic, or religious group. As an attitude, it is

Rigidly defined sex roles which pressure men to be "tough" and women to be passive or gentle, regardless of their personal inclinations, may well exact a heavy psychological toll from both sexes. (Photo: Phil Carver & Friends.)

viewed as consisting of three distinct but closely related parts: negative, stereotyped beliefs about minority group members, negative, hostile feelings about them, and tendencies to behave in harmful ways toward such persons. When such tendencies are put into actual practice, *discrimination*—negative actions toward the members of various groups—results.

In some cases, individuals lean over backward to act in a friendly, positive manner toward minority group members. Unfortunately, such *reverse discrimination* often occurs in relatively unimportant (tokenistic) situations, and is then used by the individuals involved as an excuse for bigoted actions in other, more important settings.

One continuing controversy regarding the nature of prejudice has involved the question of whether racial identity or similarity in beliefs is more important as a determinant of liking between individuals. Recent findings suggest that beliefs may be more important when relatively nonintimate contacts are involved, while racial identity becomes dominant in situations involving more intimate relationships.

Prejudice has been viewed as stemming from several different sources. One approach suggests that it arises out of intergroup conflict, a second that it stems from the personality structure of prejudiced individuals, and a third that it represents a learned or acquired reaction. Attempts to reduce or eliminate prejudice have often centered on alterations in child-rearing practices which might operate to "nip prejudice in the bud," before it develops, and increased contact between different ethnic or racial groups. This latter strategy seems to be successful only when such contact occurs under conditions of equal status and power.

While women constitute a majority in terms of sheer numbers, their exclusion from political and economic power has often been viewed as qualifying them for the status of a "psychological" minority. As is the case with ethnic or racial minorities, women are often the subject of negative stereotypes. Further, they have frequently been the victims of actual discrimination with respect to employment or educational opportunities. While all women have suffered from such practices, *competent women*—those who attempt to excel in areas outside traditional sexual roles—have often experienced the most negative outcomes. Such women are frequently rejected by men and other members of their own sex, especially when they demonstrate strong success orientations, and a rejection of traditional feminine roles.

Sexual identity is acquired early in life, probably through a process of social learning in which children imitate their same-sex parents. *Sex-role stereotypes* regarding the "appropriate" behavior or characteristics of men and women are learned at the same time. Television and children's literature seem to play an important role in this respect, and generally tend to support traditional views concerning the roles and relative value of men and women.

Various techniques for overcoming the negative impact of prejudice against women have been suggested. Among the ones which may prove most useful, however, are exposure of women to female models of success and achievement, and a degree of blurring in currently existing sexual roles, so that both men and women feel less restrained against demonstrating characteristics traditionally reserved for the opposite gender.

GLOSSARY

Authoritarianism. A personality "syndrome" assumed to involve such characteristics as blind submission to authority and strong rejection of members of groups different from one's own. Authoritarianism is often believed to play an important role in racial or ethnic prejudice.

Discrimination. Negative behavior directed toward the members of some disliked group. Discrimination is generally viewed as arising out of prejudice.

Fear of success. Refers to the supposed anxiety on the part of some women that success or achievement in traditionally male-dominated spheres of activity will lead to a loss of femininity.

Minority group. Any social group which is in a subordinate position with respect to status and power to some other, dominant group.

Observational learning. Refers to the process whereby individuals acquire new responses not previously at their disposal merely through exposure to the actions of others.

Prejudice. A negative attitude toward the members of some disliked racial, ethnic, or religious group. As an attitude, prejudice involves negative beliefs about such persons, hostile feelings toward them, and tendencies to treat them in a negative manner.

Reverse discrimination. Refers to instances in which individuals "lean over backward" to react more favorably to the members of a minority group than to members of their own group.

Sexism. Refers to discriminatory behavior directed toward women.

Sex typing. The process through which children acquire a clear sexual identity and knowledge of the behaviors considered appropriate for their gender.

Sex-role stereotyping. Refers to the process through which children acquire information regarding the supposed characteristics of the two sexes, as well as their relative position or value in society.

Social distance. Refers to the degree of intimacy individuals are willing to permit between themselves and the members of various minority groups.

Socialization. The complex process through which children acquire the many attitudes, behaviors, beliefs, and skills required to function as an adult member of their society.

Social-learning theory of sexual identity. The view that children acquire sexual (gender) identity through a process in which they match their behavior to that of their same-sex parent.

Stereotype. A cluster of beliefs—usually lacking a rational basis—regarding the members of some group.

Tokenism. Refers to instances in which individuals direct some trivial positive action toward members of racial, religious, or ethnic groups, often as a means of demonstrating that they are not actually prejudiced against such persons.

Deaux, K. *The behavior of women and men.* Belmont, Calif.: Brooks/Cole, 1976. A highly readable survey of the most recent literature on sex differences in social behavior. Covers differences in achievement behavior, aggression, altruism, and several other topics.

Guthrie, R. V. *Even the rat was white.* New York: Harper & Row, 1976. An interesting historical analysis of psychology from a black perspective. The implications of the intelligence-testing movement for blacks and other minority groups are considered, and an excellent section on the history of psychology in black colleges and the work of early black psychologists is included.

Jones, J. M. *Prejudice and racism.* Reading, Mass.: Addison-Wesley, 1972. A relatively brief but informative discussion of the causes, effects, and reduction of prejudice and racism.

Jones, R. L. *Black psychology.* New York: Harper & Row, 1972. An excellent book of readings on the issues of concern to black psychologists. Covers psychological assessment, counseling, racism, and education as they affect black lives.

Maccoby, E. E., and Jacklin, C. N. *The psychology of sex differences.* Stanford, Calif.: Stanford University Press, 1974. Provides an extensive bibliography plus a very thorough survey of sex differences in cognitive functioning and social behavior. Chapters on the role of modeling and socialization of boys and girls are also included.

Roszak, B., and Roszak, T. *Masculine/feminine.* New York: Harper & Row, 1969. An edited book of readings on the history of Western thinking about women. Provides much information concerning the roots of prejudice and discrimination against females.

ATTRACTION AND LOVE

THEORETICAL APPROACHES TO ATTRACTION
Cognitive Theory: Boy Like Tarzan, Tarzan Like Jane, So Boy Like Jane
Reinforcement Theory: What You Feel Is What You Like

INTERPERSONAL DETERMINANTS OF ATTRACTION
Attitude Similarity: Do Birds of a Feather Flock Together?
Physical Attractiveness: Judging Books by Their Looks
Personal Evaluations: If You Like Me, I Like You

SITUATIONAL INFLUENCES ON ATTRACTION
Propinquity: Sidewalks, Hallways, and Seating Assignments
Emotional Arousal: Feeling Good and Feeling Bad

DEVELOPING A RELATIONSHIP: THE ACQUAINTANCE PROCESS
From Zero Contact to Awareness
Surface Contact: Getting to Know You
Mutuality: From Friendship to Love

CONSEQUENTS OF ATTRACTION: INTERPERSONAL DECISIONS, OVERT BEHAVIOR, AND PERFORMANCE
Interpersonal Decisions: If I Like You, You Must Be a Good Person
Overt Behavior and Attraction: Close to You
Attraction and Performance: Friends Make a Difference

INCREASING INTERPERSONAL HARMONY

5

Have you ever watched your pet dog encounter something new in his environment, for example another dog who is a newcomer to the neighborhood? First, he is very much alert to the novel stimulus and approaches it warily to get a good look and to sniff. On the basis of whatever information he is able to obtain, he may approach the other dog wagging his tail, or he may back away uttering a warning growl or two. In effect, such behavior permits the animal to investigate any new aspect of his surroundings in order to evaluate it as good or bad, as something pleasant or unpleasant; this evaluation then leads him to approach whatever appears to be positive and to avoid whatever appears to be negative. Novelist Jack London wrote about this form of animal behavior in 1906 in the book, *White Fang:*

> With the simpler creatures, good and bad are things simply understood. The good stands for all things that bring easement and satisfaction and surcease from pain. Therefore, the good is liked. The bad stands for all things that are fraught with discomfort, menace, and hurt, and is hated accordingly.

This tendency to evaluate and then to approach or avoid apparently has had survival value in the evolution of our species because we human beings display similar tendencies in our everyday lives. In a more primitive time, life itself probably depended on making wise decisions about what was good and bad in the environment, what was beneficial or dangerous. Those individuals who were not inclined to make such decisions, or who made them unwisely, did not last long. Those who made frequent and wise evaluations lived long enough to become our ancestors.

Our concerns today do not ordinarily revolve around tigers in the jungle or quicksand in the swamp, but rather with our current surroundings. When you go to a movie or hear a new rock group for the first time, what sort of comment are you most likely to make? You probably evaluate the experience. It seems to be important to say that the movie was great and that the rock group stinks, or vice versa. Studies of language usage indicate that most of our communications involve just such evaluations and that our conversations are primarily concerned with our likes and dislikes. Among the most crucial aspects of our world, both in prehistoric times and today, are other human beings. Other people provide most of our pleasures—companionship, security, love, sexual gratification, and admiration, for example. They can also provide us with unpleasantness and danger—hate, ridicule, rejection, pain, and even death. It is not surprising, then, that our tendency to evaluate is often directed at our fellow human beings, and we decide as quickly as possible whom we like and dislike, who is a friend or an enemy, who it is we love or hate. Try to describe your most recent date, your roommate, or your social psychology instructor. Your response is very likely to contain positive or negative evaluations, either generally or in quite specific terms. In effect, you are indicating your **attraction** toward the other person. *Interpersonal attraction is the evaluation of another person in a positive or negative way.* There are, of course, degrees of attraction, and we can differentiate among those whom we hate and those we mildly dislike, those we consider casual friends and those toward whom we feel love. Attraction is often defined as an attitude toward other people (Berscheid, 1976), and much of the work on attitude formation and change that was described in Chapter 3 could be applied to attraction as well.

Looking at attraction from another perspective, not only are we evaluating others, they are also evaluating us. Even though we frequently express both likes and dislikes, with respect to ourselves we ordinarily want very much to be liked rather than disliked. Further, most of us desire to form close personal relationships with at least a few friends. Ideally, most of us want at some point to establish a relatively permanent love relationship with someone. When we consider the possible interpersonal disasters that can be encountered—including loneliness, rejection, unhappy love affairs, broken marriages—it is clear that the study of interpersonal attraction deals with the search for crucially important knowledge about a central aspect of our lives. As we will show in the present chapter, social psychologists are interested in identifying the variables that influence our interpersonal likes and dislikes and in determining the effects of these interpersonal attitudes on many aspects of our behavior. Six aspects of attraction research will be discussed.

First, we will look at two major *theoretical approaches to attraction;* the cognitive model and the reinforcement model will be described and compared. Second, some of the major *interpersonal determinants of attraction* will be examined, and we will describe the effects of such variables as attitude similarity, physical attractiveness, and the communication of personal evaluations. Third, we shall examine *situational influences on attraction* and show the extent to which our likes and dislikes are influenced by such factors as physical proximity and any variables which affect our mood states. Fourth, the operation of all such variables will be shown as we describe how two individuals go about *developing a relationship* from initial contacts all the way to the most positive interpersonal relationship—love. Fifth, the *consequents of attraction* will be shown with respect to its influence on our judgments and on our overt behavior. Finally, it will be suggested that there are ways of *increasing interpersonal harmony* and helping even very dissimilar individuals to tolerate and sometimes to like one another.

THEORETICAL APPROACHES TO ATTRACTION

The two most common ways in which theorists have tried to explain attraction involve formulations based on *cognitions* and formulations based on *reinforcement.* These theories are not necessarily competing in a contest to determine which is correct and which is incorrect; instead, they are alternative ways of describing interpersonal behavior and alternative strategies for conducting research on that behavior. **Cognitive theories** tend to emphasize what goes on in our thought processes when we struggle to make consistent sense out of the world and the people in it. Though there is not sufficient space to describe *all* of the cognitive theories of attraction, it should be noted that both *integration theory* (discussed in Chapter 2 in relation to person perception) and *dissonance theory* (discussed in Chapter 3 in relation to attitude change) have been extensively employed as explanations of interpersonal attraction. **Reinforcement theories** tend to stress our feelings, their effects on our sometimes irrational judgments, and the way in which attraction responses are learned. The distinction between cognitive and reinforcement theories is a useful way to classify different research approaches, but most theorists are not as narrow-minded and zealous as such descriptions sometimes make them appear. That is, cognitive theorists realize that people respond to emotions and that they learn; similarly, reinforcement theorists realize that people have ideas and that they try to understand what is going on around them. Different theoretical emphases primarily serve to guide us toward specific kinds of research and toward specific ways of interpreting a given set of findings.

Cognitive Theory:
Boy Like Tarzan, Tarzan Like Jane, So Boy Like Jane

In the cognitive approach to attraction, the primary focus has been on the way in which an individual organizes his conceptions of the relationships among himself, another person, and whatever they happen to be communicating about (for example, an object, an idea, another person, or anything else). The theories of Fritz Heider (1958) and Theodore Newcomb (1971) attempt to describe how we think about these Person-Other-Object (P-O-X) relationships and how we strive to be consistent in our pattern of likes and dislikes. The Tarzan example in the heading above was jokingly suggested by Walter Mischel as an example of a familiar P-O-X relationship. If Boy (P) likes Tarzan (O), and if Tarzan likes Jane (X), a consistent and **balanced** relationship follows if Boy also likes Jane. With that happy triangle in mind, we will turn to a more general description of a cognitive theory of attraction.

Newcomb's Balance Theory. To the cognitive theorist, the basic unit in interpersonal relationships is the *cognition*—by which is meant " . . . any knowledge, opinion, or belief about the environment, about oneself, or about one's behavior that a person might hold" (Berscheid and Walster, 1969, p. 14). According to theorists such as Newcomb, what is important about these cognitions is the way in which they are organized. It is proposed that there is a basic tendency for P to organize his cognitions about O and X in a way that is naturally "harmonious," "symmetrical," or "balanced." That is, certain relationships are experienced as more satisfying than others. A state of positive balance occurs when P likes O and they agree in evaluating X. If Boy likes Tarzan and they both like Jane, the relationship is balanced. If Boy likes Tarzan and they both dislike the dreaded flying tarantula, that relationship is also balanced. Balance, then, refers to a satisfying interpersonal relationship between two individuals who hold similar views. In a classic field study, Newcomb (1961) recruited a group of male college students to live rent-free in a co-op housing unit for one semester. He observed the way in which these strangers became acquainted and gradually formed friendships. It appeared that one of the most important factors for each friendship was how the two individuals felt about the other people who lived in the residence. In effect, friendships were formed in part on the basis of agreement about who were the good guys and who were the bad guys. As the semester progressed and the students became better acquainted, the number of balanced relationships steadily increased.

The most unsatisfying relationships are those that are **imbalanced.** Imbalance occurs when P likes O, but they disagree about X. If you have a good friend and the two of you suddenly discover that you disagree about the morality of legalized abortions, uncomfortable feelings are aroused. Once P finds himself in an imbalanced relationship, Newcomb would say that he is motivated to do something to alter the situation. The goal is to alter the P-O-X relationship in a way that will restore balance. For example, if P can persuade O to change his mind about X, the imbalance no longer exists. Numerous studies show that a common response to someone who disagrees is increased communication with that individual in an effort to change his attitudes. One of our first responses whenever we find that a friend disagrees with us about something is to try to convince him that his ideas are wrong. (If only he will listen closely to my arguments, surely he will be as sensible as I am—then, we'll happily agree.) A second way to restore balance is for P to change his own attitude about X. When someone we like and respect expresses an opinion different from our own, we sometimes stop and evaluate our position. This is the kind of process that advertisers hope will operate when a popular movie star or athlete announces that a particular brand of coffee is delicious or that a particular political candidate is an inspired statesman. The third way to change an imbalanced relationship into a balanced one is for P to misperceive O's attitude about X. From the viewpoint of cognitive theory, it doesn't matter whether P and O actually disagree about X so long as they think they agree. For example, husbands and wives often believe that they agree about various issues more than is actually the case, and the happier the marriage the greater this perceived agreement (Levinger and Breedlove, 1966). Through misperception, spouses can change a potentially upsetting situation of imbalance into an emotionally satisfying situation of balance simply by assuming incorrectly that agreement exists.

There is a fourth way to resolve an imbalanced relationship, but instead of restoring balance it brings about another type of relationship—**nonbalance.** Nonbalance occurs whenever the relationship between P and O is negative, regardless of whether they agree or disagree about X. Unlike a balanced state which is emotionally pleasant or an imbalanced state which is emotionally unpleasant, nonbalance is accompanied by feelings of indifference. If you and a friend have a generally good relationship but discover too many major areas of disagreement, you become unhappy and dissatisfied and at first work hard to

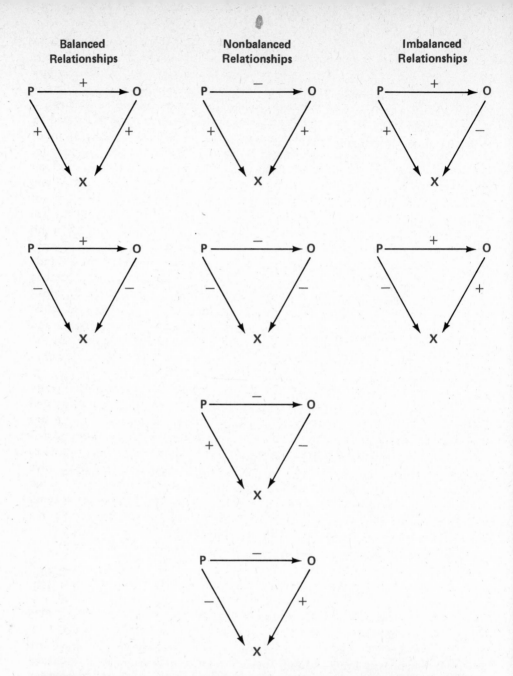

FIGURE 5-1. *Newcomb's conceptualization of relationships among a person (P), a second individual (O), and an object of communication (X) with respect to states of balance. The + and − signs refer, respectively, to positive and negative evaluations. Balanced relationships are emotionally pleasant, and nonbalanced relationships are characterized by feelings of indifference. Imbalanced relationships are sufficiently unpleasant that the individual is motivated to alter the relationship in order to restore balance or at least to achieve nonbalance.*

restore balance. If neither of you alters your views and if the disagreements are too obvious to allow you to misperceive each other's position, the relationship is likely to dissolve, and unhappiness will change to indifference. When unhappy lovers break up or quarreling friends decide to go their separate ways, there is often a feeling of relief. Indifference seems to be preferable to unhappiness.

The three types of relationship specified by Newcomb are illustrated in Figure 5-1. Research suggests that most people are at least partially aware of these different interactions and how they operate (Wellens and Thistlewaite, 1971). For example, if you were told that John loves to watch football on television and that Harry feels that all sports are a waste of time, how do you think John feels about Harry? With no additional information, the best guess, of course, is that John is not exactly wild about Harry. When subjects are presented with parts of a P-O-X relationship such as this, they tend to fill in the missing part in a way that corresponds with the predictions of balance theory, and they even remember balanced relationships better than the other kinds (Picek, Sherman, and Shiffrin, 1975). Other research indicates that Newcomb is correct about the feelings that are associated with each type of relationship— balanced situations are perceived as positive, imbalanced ones as negative, while nonbalanced relationships arouse indifferent feelings (Price, Harburg, and Newcomb, 1966). Also, as would be predicted, imbalanced relationships are the least stable, because individuals are motivated to change them into balanced or at least nonbalanced ones (Miller and Geller, 1972).

It may be seen, then, that **balance theory** provides a way to describe many aspects of interpersonal attraction, specifies the different emotions associated with each degree of balance, and predicts the various behaviors that are motivated by unsatisfactory cognitive interrelationships. The general emphasis is on the person and his or her perception of the world—cognitive theory tries to tell us "what goes on inside the head." Next we will describe an alternative theoretical approach to attraction that shifts the focus to stimulus events in the person's surroundings that elicit positive and negative feelings and to the manner in which an individual learns to associate these feelings with other people—in a way, reinforcement theory tries to tell us about our "gut reactions."

Reinforcement Theory: What You Feel Is What You Like

Reinforcement theories of attraction have their historical roots in learning theory, and they treat interpersonal likes and dislikes simply as learned responses. Most often, cognitive theory deals with the situation in which two people already have a relationship and are communicating about something. Reinforcement theory goes back a step and asks how the relationship between P and O began in the first place. The rationale for this approach has been presented by the husband and wife team of Albert and Bernice Lott (1974) and by one of the present authors and his colleagues (Clore, 1975; Clore and Byrne, 1974; Griffitt, 1974). We will now describe the way in which attraction is conceptualized as being based on emotions and on learning.

The Byrne-Clore Reinforcement-affect Model. In a theory first outlined in 1970, Byrne and Clore proposed that our evaluations of anything, including other people, are based on whatever positive or negative feelings we are experiencing at the time. To take an obvious example, if a stranger were to walk up to you on the street and give you a swift kick in the shins, negative feelings would be aroused. If you were asked to evaluate the experience, you would say that you didn't like getting kicked and didn't like the person who kicked you. It may be less obvious, but your negative feelings would also be likely to extend to any innocent bystander who happened to be there, to the street where the kicking took place, and to anything else that was associated with the unpleasant interaction. In an analogous way, if on the following day another passing stranger gave you a year's supply of free movie passes, your feelings would be positive and you would probably express liking toward your surroundings.

Few people would argue that getting kicked has more negative effects than getting free tickets to the movies. Reinforcement theory goes an important step further, however, and it is proposed that our interpersonal likes and dislikes are primarily based on just such feelings and their association with other individuals. The basic principles of the **reinforcement-affect model** can be summarized as follows:

1. Most stimuli to which we are exposed can be identified as either rewarding or punishing. We tend to approach rewarding stimuli such as ice cream or praise or free tickets to the movie; we learn to behave in such a way as to obtain these rewards. We try to avoid coming in contact with punishing stimuli such as electric shock or criticism or a kick in the shins; we learn to behave in such a way as to keep our punishments at a minimum.
2. Rewarding stimuli arouse positive feelings while punishing stimuli arouse negative feelings. These feelings, or affective responses, are believed to fall along a continuum from extremely positive to extremely negative.
3. The evaluation of any given stimulus as good or bad, enjoyable or unenjoyable, depends on whether it arouses positive or negative feelings. The strength of the aroused affect is reflected in how positively or negatively we express our evaluations. The result is that we can order our likes and dislikes along a rough scale. For example, you may like chocolate ice cream better than vanilla, you probably like both of them better than turnip soup, and you dislike having your dentist drill a hole in one of your teeth more than you dislike turnips.
4. Through the process of simple conditioning, any neutral stimulus that is associated with a reward or with a punishment will acquire the capacity to arouse positive or negative feelings, respectively, and therefore will be liked or disliked as a consequence. If the neutral stimulus is a person, he or she will be liked if associated with rewards and disliked if associated with punishments. The relationships among reinforcement, affect, and evaluation of associated stimuli are shown in Figure 5-2.

What Happens When Our Feelings Are Mixed? It is seldom that anyone (or anything) is associated exclusively with rewards or exclusively with punishments. Most of the people we know are associated with both. Reinforcement-affect theorists suggest that we regularly combine our positive and negative

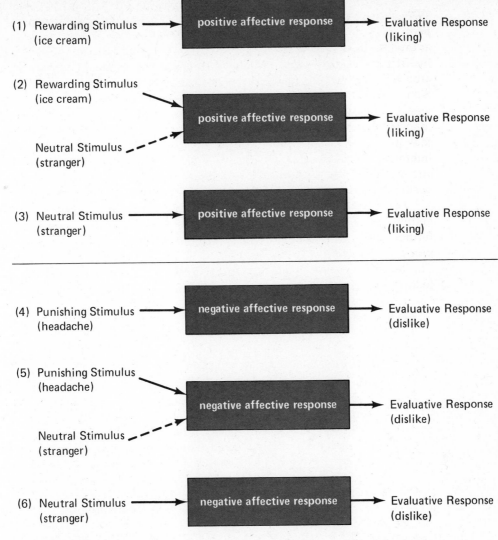

FIGURE 5-2. *According to the reinforcement-affect model, evaluative responses such as attraction are learned through conditioning of affective responses to previously neutral stimuli through a simple process of association with rewards and punishments. If the neutral stimulus is a person, he or she is liked if associated with rewards (1, 2, 3) and disliked if associated with punishments (4, 5, 6).*

affective responses into some sort of average response that falls along a positive-negative evaluation dimension.

Let's assume that we can classify various stimuli with respect to whether they are rewarding (+) or punishing (−) and also with respect to their strength (or "weight") and see how this might influence your attraction toward someone. We will indicate the weighting factor by the number of plus and minus marks in each parenthesis. One morning, you wake up with a moderately painful headache (−−) which continues to bother you as you go to a class that you find fairly dull (−). After class, you meet someone of the opposite sex you had not noticed before. The stranger's association with the headache and the boring lecture causes you to respond somewhat negatively to the individual. Then, you notice that your new acquaintance is really very attractive in appearance (+++), wears a button supporting one of your favorite political candidates (++), and has a class notebook that is your favorite color (+). Under these conditions, the six units of positive reinforcement will be strong enough to outweigh the three units of punishment. Thus, your net feelings and your evaluation of that person should be positive, perhaps positive enough that you make an approach response by starting a conversation. According to reinforcement theory, attraction increases as the proportion of positive units increases. In this instance, the number of positive units (6), when it is divided by the total number of units (9), yields a proportion of .67. Anyone associated with a lower proportion of rewards than your classmate would be liked less, and anyone associated with a higher proportion would be liked more.

This way of conceptualizing attraction has led to research that is designed to determine precisely how rewards and punishments elicit affect, become associated with particular people, and how we are able to combine our positive and negative responses into a single evaluation.

INTERPERSONAL DETERMINANTS OF ATTRACTION

In trying to identify the interpersonal variables that determine attraction, both cognitive theorists and reinforcement theorists have tended to rely initially on common-sense extensions of everyday observations. For example, think of your best friend of either sex. Why do you like him or her? Perhaps you have a lot in common in terms of your attitudes and values. Perhaps you were first attracted by the way he or she looks. Perhaps you got to know one another when you were assigned neighboring seats in one of your classes. Attraction research first began by determining the extent to which just such variables as these influence our likes and dislikes.

Attitude Similarity:
Do Birds of a Feather Flock Together?

There is one basic fact on which both types of theorist can easily agree. People tend to like those who agree with them and to dislike those who disagree. Suppose that two people meet and one remarks that the President of the United States is a brilliant leader whose policies are the salvation of this country; the other indicates that he is convinced that the President is an even bigger fool than he thought during the election campaign and that his policies are leading us to disaster. Do you believe that this is the beginning of a beautiful friendship? Probably you don't think so, and neither would those who have conducted research in the area. In fact, people have known about the effects of agreement and disagreement on friendship formation at least since Aristotle wrote an essay on that topic in the fourth century B.C. Psychological research in the first half of the twentieth century confirmed this ancient observation by means of numerous correlational field studies of acquaintances, friends, and married couples—those who liked each other were found to have similar attitudes about most topics. When the similarity-attraction phenomenon was brought into the experimental laboratory, the goal was to establish a cause and effect relationship between the variables, to identify the precise form of the relationship, and to explain it.

As Similarity Increases, Attraction Increases: The Linear Relationship. As was pointed out in Chapter 1, a correlation between two variables such as similarity and attraction cannot tell us anything about cause and effect. It could be that friends have similar attitudes because agreement led them to like one another in the first place, or because a close friendship leads people to reach agreement on various issues, or because some other variable (for example, having the same religious affiliation) is responsible for both the friendship and the similar attitudes. In the first experimental studies in the laboratory, however, whenever attitude similarity was manipulated as an independent variable, there was an obvious effect on the dependent variable of attraction (Schachter, 1951). It was thus established that similar attitudes elicited liking while dissimilar attitudes elicited feelings of dislike.

The details of the relationship were still unknown, however. Consider a situation in which you and an acquaintance find that you agree about four issues and disagree about none, whereas you and another acquaintance agree about eight issues and disagree about four. Which individual would you like better? You have more agreements with the second person than with the first, but you also have more disagreements. The question to be answered by research is whether you are likely to respond to the absolute number of agreements or to the relative number of agreements and disagreements. An experiment by Byrne and Nelson (1965) was designed to answer that question by systematically varying both the number of similar attitudes expressed by a stranger and also the proportion of topics on which there was similarity. It was found that subjects respond only to the proportion of similar attitudes and that they are unaffected by the number of such attitudes. In the example suggested earlier in this paragraph, you should like the acquaintance who agrees on four issues and disagrees on none (1.00 similar) better than the acquaintance who agrees on eight issues and disagrees on four (.67 similar) because the proportion of similar attitudes is higher in the first instance.

A further step in specifying this relationship was taken by plotting the attraction responses of hundreds of subjects who had been exposed to what were described as the attitudes of a stranger. Each subject read the attitude scale of someone they did not know; then they indicated how much they liked or disliked the individual and how much they would enjoy or not enjoy working with such a person. These two questions are part of the **Interpersonal Judgment Scale** and have been used in many experiments to measure attraction; the lowest score is two, which indicates an extremely negative reaction, and the highest score is fourteen, which indicates an extremely positive reaction. As shown in Figure 5-3, these attraction responses are influenced by the proportion of similar attitudes in a very consistent way—as the proportion of similar attitudes increases, attraction toward the person who expressed the attitudes increases in a linear fashion. This straight-line function has been verified numerous times and, in fact, it is so consistent that a descriptive formula can be written which allows us to predict the way in which future subjects can be expected to respond (Schönemann, Byrne, and Bell, 1977). This formula ($Y = 5.44X + 6.62$) simply means that the best prediction of an attraction response (Y) may be obtained by multiplying the proportion of similar attitudes (X) by 5.44 and then adding 6.62. Subsequent research has shown, by the way, that this relationship between similarity and attraction is true not only of college students who are the usual experimental subjects, but also for elementary school children, high school dropouts, and senior citizens; in addition, cross-cultural studies indicate that those in countries as diverse as India, Mexico, and Japan respond in much the same way (Byrne, 1971).

In summary, then, a relationship commonly observed over the centuries was first verified in field studies. Then, experimental research went on to establish a

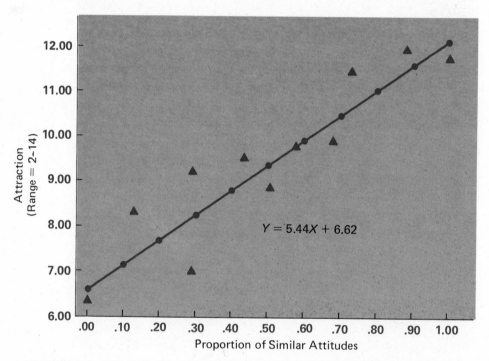

FIGURE 5-3. *Attraction toward a stranger is a positive linear function of proportion of similar attitudes. Attraction as measured by the Interpersonal Judgment Scale can be predicted by multiplying the proportion of similar attitudes by 5.44 and adding 6.62. (From Byrne and Nelson, 1965, p. 661. Copyright 1965 by the American Psychological Association. Reprinted by permission.)*

Chapter 5   Attraction and Love

causal relationship, to determine that the proportion of similar attitudes is the crucial stimulus variable, and to discover that the effects of attitude similarity on attraction can be described by means of a simple mathematical formula.

Similarity and Attraction in the Real World. Even though it has now been shown in hundreds of experiments that attitude similarity determines attraction, this does not mean that you should conclude that it is possible to make instant predictions of any and all relationships on the basis of attitudes. In generalizing from laboratory findings to real-world interactions, even experienced social psychologists sometimes overlook that point. An example may help to explain why it is necessary to be very cautious in making such generalizations.

Now that you know about the laboratory studies of attitude similarity and attraction, you could conduct such an experiment and predict its outcome with some degree of accuracy. If a subject is shown the attitude responses of a stranger who agrees with her on ten out of twelve topics, you would predict that she would like this other person. You could even say that on the Interpersonal Judgment Scale, she is expected to give a response of about 11.14 ($Y = 5.44 \times$ .83 + 6.62). After the experiment, while drinking coffee in the student union, you happen to learn that Mary and Susan agree on ten out of twelve topics. So, you introduce them and they become good friends. Right? Wrong, or, at least, not necessarily. There are several reasons why this is so.

First, outside of a controlled experimental situation, knowledge of similarity on a small number of topics would not always predict liking because the two individuals may disagree about hundreds of other topics. Unless you know how Susan and Mary feel about every issue that arises in their conversations, the similarity-attraction formula would not be of any help in making predictions.

Second, the many additional determinants of attraction besides attitude similarity may or may not be positive for Mary and Susan. The reinforcement-affect model suggests that any reinforcing event leads to greater attraction (for example, they may enjoy playing tennis together) and any punishing event leads to negative interpersonal feelings (for example, Mary may be sarcastic in making fun of Susan's southern accent). Their attraction, then, will depend on the total effect of all such interactions, not on just twelve attitudes.

The third reason for caution in generalizing to the real world is that most such studies deal with similarity between a subject and a stranger who is from his or her same basic group. Thus, college students respond to other college students, fourth graders respond to other fourth graders, job corps trainees respond to other job corps trainees, and so forth. When the other person is from a very different group, attitude similarity may have a much weaker effect. For example, college students and senior citizens respond to one another in part on the basis of differences in their ages (Griffitt, Nelson, and Littlepage, 1972). In addition, it has been argued that similarity to someone in an "undesirable" category (such as psychiatric patients or drug addicts) actually has a negative effect (Lerner and Agar, 1972). We seem to feel that similarity in this instance means that "it could happen to us," and so it is actually more pleasant to feel that we are unlike such individuals. There is also a reverse version of this situation.

FOCUS ON RESEARCH

TEN DAYS IN A FALL-OUT SHELTER

Considering all of the differences between the laboratory and the real world, it is not at all surprising that the relationship between attitude similarity and attraction is often obscured in nonlaboratory studies (Levinger, 1972; Wright and Crawford, 1971). In order to establish the power of the attitudinal variable under very realistic conditions, Griffitt and Veitch (1974) utilized an unusual research setting.

To determine the effects of a limited diet on individuals confined to a fall-out shelter, 13 male volunteers who did not know one another were paid to spend ten days in a small (12' by 24'), simulated fall-out shelter that was both hot (86°) and humid (80%). Their diet was limited to 1.25 quarts of water each day plus a few crackers and sugar candies. One toilet was available behind a cloth partition. Under these very unpleasant conditions, is it possible that similarity of attitudes would have any effect on interpersonal attraction?

Before they were confined in the shelter, the subjects filled out a 44-item attitude scale. At various times during the 10-day period, subjects were asked to indicate the individuals they would most like to keep with them in the shelter and those they would most like to have leave the experiment. Thus, it was possible to determine whether attitudes (measured before the individuals first met) would predict who would like one another and who would reject one another.

The results are shown in Figure 5-4. It was found that the first two choices of a stranger to remain in the shelter were of individuals with the highest proportion of similar attitudes, and the first two choices of a stranger to be kicked out were of individuals with the lowest proportion of similar attitudes. The relationship was not a perfect one, and it was not as strong as in the laboratory studies. Even though these individuals were freely interacting for over a week under highly unpleasant circumstances, the effect of attitudes on attraction could nevertheless be observed.

Why should similarity have been related to attraction in this situation when it was suggested earlier that agreement on a few topics is not necessarily a predictor of liking in real-life settings? One possibility is that, in the Griffitt and Veitch study, the subjects were confined within a limited space with little to do—they may have talked about the attitude scale they filled out in order to pass the time. Such conversations would serve to emphasize their similarities and differences.

How do you feel when someone just like yourself is more successful than you are? Nadler, Jazwinski, and Lau (1975) hypothesized that similarity in this instance would be more threatening than dissimilarity because it makes one's own failure much more difficult to rationalize. A male subject interacted with a similar or a dissimilar male confederate. Afterward a female confederate was asked to choose just one of them to work with her. When an attitudinally similar confederate was chosen, this made the subjects feel unhappy, uncreative, and angry, but the choice of a dissimilar other did not have these negative effects.

A fourth limitation on overgeneralizing about similarity effects has been pointed out in a series of studies by Fromkin (1971, 1972). He proposes that each individual has a need to be unique, to be somebody special who has an identity.

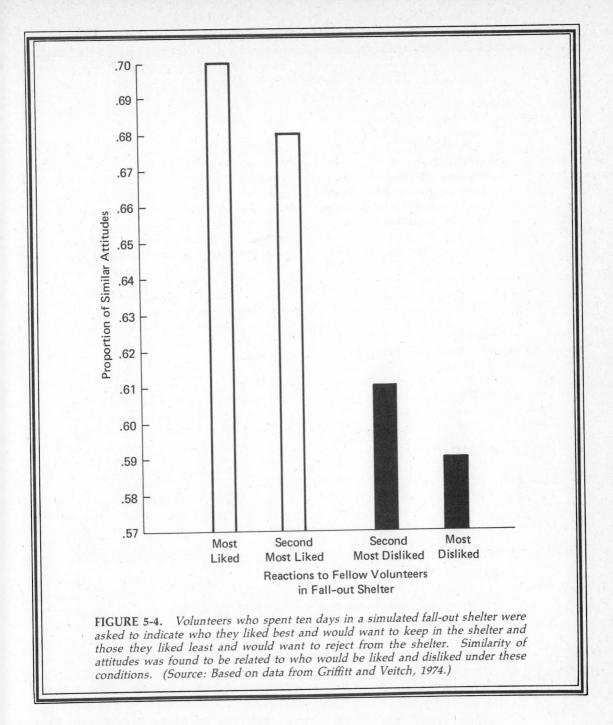

FIGURE 5-4. *Volunteers who spent ten days in a simulated fall-out shelter were asked to indicate who they liked best and would want to keep in the shelter and those they liked least and would want to reject from the shelter. Similarity of attitudes was found to be related to who would be liked and disliked under these conditions. (Source: Based on data from Griffitt and Veitch, 1974.)*

In fact, when we find ourselves just an anonymous clog who has a number rather than a name, it tends to be upsetting. When experimenters increase such feelings by informing subjects that their opinions are just like those of thousands of other college students, subsequent reactions to a stranger with similar attitudes is not very positive. In that situation, similarity is only a reminder that the individual is ordinary and undistinctive.

Finally, it should be noted that not all individuals respond the same way to attitude similarity-dissimilarity. At least two personality characteristics have been shown to yield important differences. Those who evaluate themselves extremely negatively do not seem to react very strongly to the similarity or dissimilarity of others' attitudes (Goldman and Olczak, 1976; Leonard, 1975). And, individuals who are extremely anxious about social situations are much more negative toward those who disagree with them than individuals who are socially relaxed (Gouaux, Lamberth, and Friedrich, 1972; Smith, 1970).

The limitations pointed out here should not be taken to mean that laboratory findings are irrelevant to the real world. They are extremely relevant. The difference is simply that more variables are operating in the complexity of the real world than in the deliberately more simple laboratory setting. Once all of the variables in the real-life situation are identified, they can be expected to operate just as they do in the laboratory.

Physical Attractiveness: Judging Books by Their Looks

An important, and often misleading, determinant of the way we respond to strangers is their appearance. Each of us seems to have acquired a set of very strong preferences with respect to the way that our fellow human beings should look. We respond with positive and negative feelings on the basis of facial features, weight, height, hair color and length, and numerous other aspects of the anatomy from bow legs to mustaches. It is assumed that those who look a particular way will behave so as to match our stereotypes (Hochberg and Galper, 1974). Before two individuals have had an opportunity to talk and to find out anything about one another, they can form very favorable or very unfavorable first impressions simply on the basis of some aspect of physical attractiveness. You might not be surprised to learn that interpersonal attraction is strongly influenced by such variables.

Beauty Seems to Be in the Eyes of Many Beholders. The standards of physical attractiveness vary from culture to culture and from one time period to another. When we see pictures of the "beautiful people" from another time or place, we tend to laugh more often than to feel awestruck. The cartoon in Figure 5-5 depicts the way in which the notion of beauty may be limited to a specific group. Nevertheless, within a particular culture at a particular time, there is fairly good agreement as to just who should be classified as beautiful women or handsome men (Berscheid and Walster, 1974a). Not only do we agree concerning attractiveness, but our culture places great value on this superficial attribute. The advertising industry spends much time and effort trying to convince us that

"Mother, am I pretty?"

FIGURE 5-5. *In any culture, the tendency to stress physical attractiveness leads individuals to feel concern about how they "measure up" in this respect. The fact that there are different criteria as to what constitutes beauty and handsomeness in different cultures and different historical times means that physical attractiveness is a relative concept and one defined by the group. (Source: Drawing by Hoff; © 1972 The New Yorker Magazine, Inc.)*

we can attract and hold onto a potential mate only if we are very appealing physically. The message is that if we spend vast amounts of money on products that give us suitably attractive hair, complexion, teeth, skin color, posture, weight, bustline, odor, and whatever, we will each become a much sought-after sex object. Considering the profits that result from this continual hard-sell, the advertisers have probably succeeded in convincing us very well. It would be difficult to argue that it is reasonable or fair to judge other people on the basis of looks. Nevertheless, that appears to be exactly what many people do.

Most studies of this variable deal with responses to members of the opposite sex. For example, in one well-known experiment, male and female freshmen were randomly paired as dates at a computer dance. The experimenters (Walster et al., 1966) had observers rate the physical attractiveness of each student at the time he or she purchased a ticket for the dance. Halfway through the evening, questionnaires were administered asking students to indicate their attraction toward their dates and whether future interactions were desired. For both sexes, it was found that the more physically attractive the date, the more he or she was liked and seen as a good prospect for future dates. Such variables as intelligence, grade point average, and personality characteristics were found to be irrelevant in predicting who would like whom—everyone simply liked the most attractive dates. Subsequent studies of the dating process have confirmed this general finding that physical appearance is one of the most powerful determinants of attraction toward those of the opposite sex (Curran and Lippold, 1975).

Although it is obvious that only a minority of the population can possibly fall into the category of "extremely attractive," it is also obvious that the rest of us are nevertheless able to have dates and get married. If almost everyone prefers attractive others, how are alternative choices made? The **matching hypothesis** states that people tend to pair off on the basis of appearance—that is, people who are similar in their degree of physical attractiveness select each other. In the computer-dating studies, there is no possibility of rejection, so most individuals aspire to the most attractive partner possible. When, however, potential computer dates get a chance to meet first and then decide whether to say yes or no, individuals tend to choose prospective dates who are like themselves in attractiveness (Berscheid et al., 1971). The possibility of rejection seems to lead many individuals to "lower their aspirations" and settle for a less attractive partner. You may think that such reactions only influence first impressions among freshmen, but Murstein (1972) has shown that the matching phenomenon holds even with respect to marriage. It appears that we tend to judge others in part on the basis of physical attractiveness from the time we are in elementary school (Maruyama and Miller, 1975), through casual dates, courtship, and marriage.

What Is Attractiveness and What Do We Think It Means? Most people find it fairly hard to verbalize exactly what they mean by attractiveness—they just know it when they see it. Some characteristics have been identified as having a generally negative effect on our judgments. For example, most individuals respond to excess weight as an unattractive physical characteristic (Lerner and Gellert, 1969). Also, a few specific positive features have been noted; tall males are seen as attractive (Berkowitz, Nebel, and Reitman, 1971). In responding to females, the average male reacts most positively to someone with medium sized legs, medium to small buttocks, and larger than average breasts (Wiggins, Wiggins, and Conger, 1968). In responding to males, on the other hand, females (at least, traditional ones) are most positive to someone with thin legs, a medium-wide upper trunk, and a medium-thin lower trunk—"the Robert Redford tapered V-look" (Lavrakas, 1975). Mostly, however, it seems that we respond to our total impression of face, body, and even the presence of such expressive behaviors as smiling (Holstein, Goldstein, and Bem, 1971) and whether or not the person spends much time gazing in our direction (Kleinke, Staneski, and Berger, 1975).

What is the explanation for our response to the attractiveness of others? One possibility is suggested by balance theory. If we have been taught that attractiveness is good, we would assume that good-looking individuals agree with us on most attitudinal issues in order to achieve balance. Schoedel, Frederickson, and Knight (1975) found that students and also an older sample of apartment house residents do, in fact, assume that very attractive strangers hold attitudes similar to their own. Reinforcement theory would suggest that, through association, we have learned that attractiveness connotes many types of positive qualities and hence is a positive cue for us because we have seen this fact portrayed over and over again in movies, television, and pictorial advertising. It has been found that when subjects are shown pictures of physically attractive strangers, they assume that these individuals have socially desirable personality characteristics, are successful in their professions, and have good marriages—"what is beautiful is good" (Dion, Berscheid, and Walster, 1972). Again, the positive response to attractiveness is not limited to young people. Attractive middle-aged adults were judged by subjects of various ages to have a higher occupational status, to be more socially outgoing, to be more pleasant, and to be higher in self-esteem than unattractive ones (Adams and Huston, 1975). Some of the stereotypes about attractive individuals are true, incidentally. Probably because of the positive responses they receive from others, attractive children are high in self-esteem (Maruyama and Miller, 1975) and attractive college students have more dating experience, less anxiety about dates, and more sexual experience than unattractive ones (Curran and Lippold, 1975). It should be added, in fairness, that some not so positive assumptions are also made about attractive individuals; they are sometimes perceived as vain, egotistical, and likely to engage in extramarital intercourse (Dermer and Thiel, 1975). Similarly, in many situations, attractiveness is usually a positive attribute but it occasionally has bad connotations. For example, a physically attractive defendant accused of cheating on an exam or committing a burglary is better liked, is seen as less guilty, and is given less severe punishment (Efran, 1974). When the misbehavior is related to attractiveness, however, as in the case of swindling, the attractive defendant actually is treated more harshly (Sigall and Ostrove, 1975).

Finally, it is comforting to know that there are some individual differences with respect to specific physical characteristics that are viewed as attractive and unattractive. One such characteristic that elicits very different responses from different viewers is hair length in males. Currently, male styles range all the way from above the ears to below the shoulders. How do females respond to these differences? Peterson and Curran (1976) sought an answer to this question by preparing videotape recordings of three different undergraduate males, each of whom wore short, medium, and long wigs in different tapes. Each of a large number of female students looked at tapes depicting the three hair lengths (with a different male as the stimulus person representing each hair length) and indicated how much she liked the three individuals. When these preferences were examined, it became clear that some females liked short-haired males and some liked those with long hair. More important, these differing preferences were expressed by females who were themselves different in many respects, as can be seen in Table 5-1. With this physical characteristic, at least, attraction is influenced by an interaction between physical appearance and the personal characteristics of the individual responding to that appearance. Peterson and Curran suggested that male hair length has come to be associated with liberal and conservative ideology and that liberal and conservative females are simply responding to males on the basis of assumed similarity in political and social views. Once again, it is possible that assumptions of attitude similarity are involved in judgments of physical attractiveness.

TABLE 5-1. *Female college students who prefer long-haired males are relatively liberal in a number of respects, while females who prefer short-haired males are relatively conservative. Presumably, females are responding to hair length as an indication of the male's liberalism or conservatism. (Source: Based on data from Peterson and Curran, 1976.)*

Characteristics of Female Students Who Prefer Long-haired Males	Characteristics of Female Students Who Prefer Short-haired Males
Use wide variety of drugs.	Have not experimented with drugs.
Are sexually experienced.	
Have dated more men.	Have dated fewer men.
Read liberal magazines.	Do not read liberal magazines.
Are assertive and happy-go-lucky.	Are humble, conscientious, and conservative.
Attend church infrequently.	Attend church regularly.

Personal Evaluations: If You Like Me, I Like You

One of the most powerful variables influencing our attraction toward another person is the way that person feels about us. When someone tells you that you are bright or amusing or interesting or attractive or likable, those statements are pleasant to hear even if you happen to be dumb, dull, boring, ugly, and dislikable. We all enjoy hearing positive things about ourselves and can't stand hearing negative things. Even if success is a familiar experience (as with a student who always writes good term papers), the individual tends to agonize about the quality of his most recent effort and to jump for joy when he is told that it is good. Similarly, even if failure is familiar and well deserved, it is no less unpleasant to be told that you did a bad job. Such interpersonal rewards and punishments influence our feelings and thus our attraction toward the persons responsible for them.

Research has consistently shown that individuals like those who evaluate them positively and dislike those who evaluate them negatively. In the reinforcement formula, described earlier, each personal evaluation receives a weight equivalent to three attitude statements because evaluations have that much more effect on attraction than attitudes. Thus, the fact that two people disagree about presidential candidates, marijuana laws, and abortion can be overcome if each indicates admiration of the other's intelligence. The joint effects of personal evaluations and attitude similarity were shown in a study by Byrne and Rhamey (1965). In an attraction experiment, subjects examined a stranger's attitudes on twelve topics and discovered that this other person agreed with them on none of the issues, a third of them, two-thirds, or on all twelve. In addition, each subject was told that the other person had examined his attitudes and then rated him on a series of characteristics. These "ratings" were actually prepared by the experimenters and were either all very positive or all very negative. The effects of these two variables (attitude similarity and personal evaluations) on attraction are shown in Figure 5-6; both influenced attraction, and the strongest effects were those created by the personal evaluations.

An indirect type of evaluation can be assumed when an individual is ignored by others. How have you felt in such situations? Geller et al. (1974) proposed that an ignored person feels less liked and even begins to feel less positive toward himself. They arranged a group discussion among three female undergraduates, two of whom were confederates of the experimenters. In half the groups, the confederates were taught to ignore the subject by glancing at her only briefly, responding only minimally and without interest to what she said, and by changing the topic whenever the subject said anything. The ignored subjects spoke much less than those in the control groups and afterwards described themselves in negative and unhappy terms—alone, withdrawn, shy, dull, anxious, bored, unhappy, and uninteresting. In interviews afterward, the

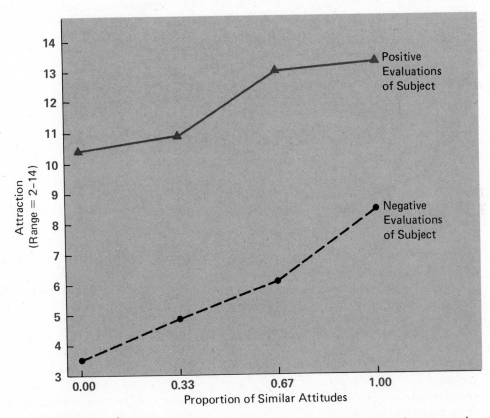

FIGURE 5-6. *Attraction can be influenced by both personal evaluations and proportion of similar attitudes. A positive stranger is liked much better than a negative one, and attraction increases as attitude similarity increases under both conditions. (Source: Based on data from Byrne and Rhamey, 1965.)*

subjects described their experience by saying such things as "when they spoke, they didn't look at me. Their questions were not directed to me. I spoke three times, yet they passed me over. . . . I wanted to get up and leave." It seems that being ignored is a very unpleasant emotional experience.

Evaluations have also been studied in combination with physical attractiveness. Sigall and Aronson (1969) proposed that positive evaluations given by someone who is attractive should be more rewarding than when they are given by someone who is unattractive. In effect, such evaluations are "worth more" when they come from an attractive person than from an unattractive one. The subjects were male undergraduates who were being tested and evaluated by a female assistant. The assistant was an attractive brunette who either appeared as herself or was made to appear unattractive. The latter transformation was accomplished by leaving off all makeup and wearing a frizzy blond wig. The evaluations were prearranged to be either positive or negative, no matter how well the subject actually did. Later in the experiment, subjects filled out a form which included a question about how well they liked the assistant. As shown in Figure 5-7, the positive evaluations from an attractive girl had a much greater effect on attraction than the same evaluations given by an unattractive girl.

SITUATIONAL INFLUENCES ON ATTRACTION

We have just seen that various things an individual says and various aspects of physical appearance determine whether he or she is liked or disliked. Some determinants of attraction have nothing to do with the person's characteristics but, rather, with certain aspects of the situation. We will examine two such determinants: physical proximity and emotional arousal.

Propinquity:
Sidewalks, Hallways, and Seating Assignments

It is an obvious but nevertheless important fact that the probability of any two individuals becoming friends is determined in part by the structural details of their environment—details that control their physical proximity or **propinquity.** In early research on this variable, Festinger, Schachter, and Back (1950) described two different types or propinquity. First, there is the actual physical distance between individuals as determined by the location of their respective houses, dormitory rooms, classroom seats, and so forth. Second, there is the functional distance between them, which determines the probability that they will have random contacts. For example, two pairs of dormitory rooms may be equally close but if the doorways of one pair are side-by-side, those who live in such rooms are more likely to bump into one another (figuratively) than if the doorways are around the corner from one another. The functional distance is closer in the first instance. In a similar way, in a classroom you are more likely to have face-to-face contact with someone who sits beside you than with

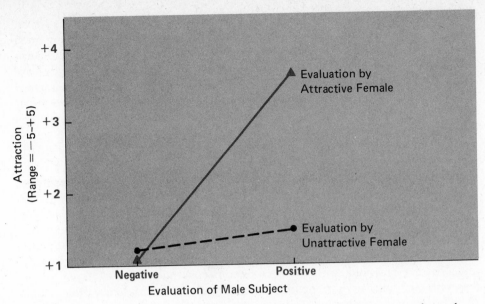

FIGURE 5-7. *Personal evaluations by a member of the opposite sex have the greatest effect on attraction when the evaluator is physically attractive. (Source: Based on data from Sigall and Aronson, 1969.)*

someone who sits directly behind you, even though the seats may be equal in physical distance. We will now show how these effects are surprisingly strong in determining the relationships that people actually form with one another.

Propinquity and Attraction. In studies conducted in a variety of natural settings, the powerful effects of propinquity have been demonstrated countless times. It has been found that friendships develop as a function of the physical distance between apartments in married student housing units (Caplow and Forman, 1950). In a similar setting, functional distance is found to influence friendships also—individuals having an apartment on the ground floor which is located by a stairway are the only ones likely to become friends with second-floor residents (Festinger, Schachter, and Back, 1950). In a city housing project with elderly residents, most friendships are between those living on the same floor (Nahemow and Lawton, 1975). In a suburban housing development, friendships are most likely to occur between neighbors in adjacent houses, especially if their driveways are close together (Whyte, 1956). In the classroom, two students are most likely to become acquainted if they are assigned to adjacent seats (Byrne and Buehler, 1955). Because so many seating assignments are made on an alphabetical basis, it is perhaps not surprising to find that friendships occur more often among those whose last names start with the same or "nearby" letters than among those whose names are farther away in the alphabet. In a group of Maryland State Police trainees, almost half of the friendship choices were of someone adjacent to the chooser in alphabetical order (Segal, 1974).

At first glance, many of these findings appear to be simply a demonstration of the obvious. That is, people get to know other people who live nearby or who sit next to them—so what? On reflection, however, it is a bit surprising to learn that the various personal determinants of attraction can be overwhelmed by such seemingly nonpsychological variables as the location of stairs and driveways. Not only is attraction influenced by the physical aspects of the environment, such accidental factors play a large role in determining a major share of our friendships and even how many friends we have. For example, a lifelong friendship can be determined by random dormitory room assignments, and a marriage can be the end result of an instructor's arbitrary seating chart. The number of one's friendships is also affected in that someone in a centrally located apartment, room, or classroom seat is likely to have more friends than someone in an end location. It's not just that those who are popular are the center of attention, those in the actual center become more popular.

At the practical level, these findings raise the possibility of manipulating the environment deliberately in order to increase the frequency with which people form positive relationships. In a classroom experiment, for example, it was found that the number of friendships formed by each student during the semester could be increased simply by shifting everyone's assigned seat every seven weeks (Byrne, 1961). In a similar fashion, the decision to assign apartments in public housing projects without respect to race has been found to lead to more positive relationships between blacks and whites (Deutsch and Collins, 1951). Not only are such policy decisions important with respect to interpersonal relationships, but even architectural decisions are crucial. Apartments, dormitories, and neighborhoods could be designed so as to foster propinquity effects and therefore to foster positive interpersonal interactions.

Why Should Propinquity Lead to Liking? If you pass a neighbor on the way to the garbage can once or twice each week, why should that be the basis for the two of you becoming acquainted? Festinger and his associates (1950) proposed a common-sense explanation of such findings by describing the typical way in which strangers interact. For example, if two apartments are located in such a way that the occupants use the same hallway to reach the garbage area, these individuals are likely to come into contact on a random basis several times a month. These unplanned contacts lead to mutual recognition—the other person becomes a familiar face. At this point, people tend to nod, to say hello, and eventually to engage in brief exchanges of idle chitchat about the weather, the Superbowl, or whatever. From these humble beginnings, friendships and even romances can grow.

There is still the question of why the repeated contacts should lead to friendly nods and to conversation. Why don't people continue to pass silently in the hallway or to sit beside one another in silence in the classroom? A possible explanation is provided by the work of Zajonc (1968), who proposes that repeated exposure to any stimulus results in an increasingly positive evaluation of that stimulus. When you first encounter a new work of art or a new song or your mother's new hairstyle, you may be indifferent or even slightly negative in your evaluation. With repeated exposure, however, you are most likely to become gradually more positive. In other words, you develop a favorable *attitude* as is discussed in Chapter 3. This is one reason that advertisements repeat the names of products and of political candidates over and over—it is found that the consumers come to recognize and like what is being sold (Grush and McKeough, 1975). Zajonc quoted a newspaper story in which a student at Oregon State came to class each day wearing a large black bag that covered everything but his bare feet. The other students were originally hostile to this very unusual member of the class; over the weeks this feeling decreased and was replaced by curiosity and then friendship. People seem to be wary of anything too new and different, but they are comfortable with whatever becomes familiar. It appears that anything unfamiliar leaves us with feelings of uncertainty; repeated exposure reduces the uncertainty and results in more *positive affect* (Smith and Dorfman, 1975; Stang, 1975). In fact, it has been suggested that one explanation of the attitude-similarity effect is that we prefer whatever is familiar, including familiar attitudes (Brickman, Meyer, and Fredd, 1975). In experimental work, repeated exposure has been found to increase positive responses to such stimuli as Turkish words (Zajonc and Rajecki, 1969), Japanese ideographs (Moreland and Zajonc, 1976), public figures (Harrison, 1969), and photographs of strangers (Wilson and Nakajo, 1965). This effect is most likely to occur, however, if the initial reaction to the stimulus is not a strongly negative one (Suedfeld et al., 1971). The more one is exposed to an extremely negative stimulus, the greater the *dislike* (Grush, 1976).

Is it possible to demonstrate the exposure effect experimentally as a determinant of interpersonal attraction? Saegert, Swap, and Zajonc (1973) told a group of female undergraduates that they were participating in an experiment having to do with the sense of taste. They were to enter a series of booths, two at a time, to sample and rate various flavored liquids. The real purpose of the experiment was to test the exposure effect by arranging for different numbers of interactions to occur among subjects. The schedule was carefully arranged so that a given subject was in a booth with another subject either zero times, once, twice, five, or ten times. When the series of taste tests was completed, the students filled out a questionnaire which included an indication of attraction toward the others in the experiment. As may be seen in Figure 5-8, the more contacts an individual had had with someone else during the brief experiment, the more she was liked. Other experiments show that even those with dissimilar attitudes are liked more as frequency of exposure increases (Brockner and Swap, 1976). It appears that this process of familiarity leading to liking is just the sort of thing that occurs when we interact with others in our daily lives.

Emotional Arousal: Feeling Good and Feeling Bad

From the point of view of the reinforcement-affect model, emotional responses are the crucial element in determining attraction. That is, the *reason* that

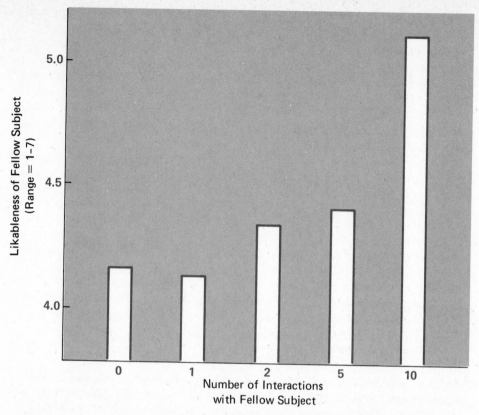

FIGURE 5-8. *In an experiment testing the effects of mere exposure on attraction, subjects had a series of brief interactions with strangers that ranged from no contact at all to ten meetings. It was found that the more frequently they interacted, the more positively the other person was rated. (Source: Based on data from Saegert, Swap, and Zajonc, 1973.)*

The reason that variables such as attitude similarity, physical attractiveness, or propinquity have an effect on liking is that they influence the affective state of the individual. If so, it also follows that any environmental conditions that have a direct influence on emotions should influence attraction toward anyone who happens to be around at the time. For example, if you unexpectedly receive an "A" on a midterm exam, you should feel not only elated but also relatively positive toward anyone you encounter (as long as that emotional state lasts). Or, if you discover that someone has stolen your stereo, you might be depressed and angry; in addition, you should have relatively negative responses toward those you encounter. This proposed relationship suggests that we are not always entirely reasonable in our interpersonal responses, but there is considerable evidence to support such a conclusion.

Affect and Attraction. One of the experiments testing this general idea was conducted by Gouaux (1971), using emotion-arousing movies to manipulate the feelings (affect) of his subjects. Female undergraduates saw either a funny film which was designed to make them feel elated (*Good Old Corn* was the name of this slapstick comedy) or a sad film which was designed to make them feel depressed (a documentary about the life and death of John F. Kennedy). Mood measures indicated that most subjects who saw the funny film were elated, most who saw the sad film were depressed, and some were unaffected. Just after the films were over, the subjects participated in what they believed to be a totally different experiment involving attitude similarity. As usual in such studies, the subjects responded to a stranger whose attitudes were at one of several levels of similarity with respect to their own. Their attraction responses toward the stranger revealed the influence of both types of variables. Attitude similarity again had an effect, of course, but the effects of emotions were also quite clear. At every level of similarity, the elated subjects liked the stranger most while the depressed subjects liked the stranger least, as may be seen in Figure 5-9. It appears that most individuals are inclined to evaluate another person in part on the basis of their own general emotional state, even though that person is not in the least responsible for how the individual feels.

Not only is attraction influenced by an individual's affective state, but people also respond positively to the affect of others. That is, we tend to like someone who is elated better than someone who is emotionally neutral or depressed (Bell, 1976). Perhaps happy people make us feel good and hence we like them.

Our positive and negative feelings are affected by a great many things ranging from the unpleasantness of a sore toe to the joy of a brisk shower. As we will describe in Chapter 13, emotions, and therefore attraction, are even influenced by room temperature and humidity (Griffitt and Veitch, 1971). In the age of transistor radios, there is another aspect of our surroundings which hits most of us several times a day—the news broadcasts and spot announcements that bombard us regularly. Veitch and Griffitt (in press) proposed that good news should make us feel good and bad news make us feel bad; if so, attraction toward others should vary as a function of what we hear about world and local events. CBS reporter Charles Kuralt (1972) has also suggested that the bad news that gets dumped on us each day is part of the reason for the current discontent of Americans. He says, "I find it helpful to my peace of mind to sometimes turn off the radio and turn off the TV and throw away all those magazines and go contemplate the sun going down" (p. 21). Veitch and Griffitt tested the effects of news broadcasts on interpersonal reactions by bringing subjects to an "office" where they had to wait while the experimenter left, supposedly to make a phone call. A "radio" seemed to be playing, but actually it was a cassette recorder which played either a good news or a bad news tape during the five minutes the subject waited. (See Table 5-2 for the news stories.) After the music portion of the program began, the experimenter returned and conducted an attitude-attraction experiment in which a stranger was either relatively similar or dissimilar to the subject. It was found that the brief news broadcast did have the expected effects on the subjects' emotions and also the expected effects on attraction. After hearing the good news, subjects felt positively and liked the stranger they were asked to rate. After hearing the bad news, subjects felt

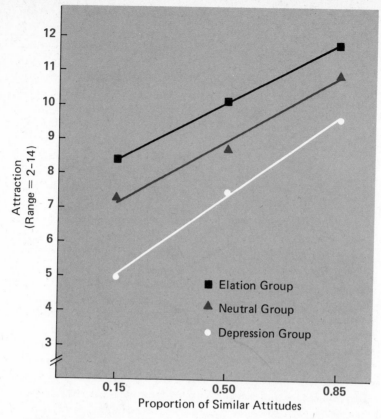

FIGURE 5-9. *Attraction toward a stranger as a function of mood manipulation and attitude similarity. At each level of attitude similarity, attraction is more positive when the subjects have been made to feel elated, and more negative when they have been made to feel depressed. (Source: From Gouaux, 1971, p. 40. Copyright 1971 by the American Psychological Association. Reprinted by permission.)*

negatively and disliked the stranger. A song popular in 1973 told us to "Turn the Radio On," but Charles Kuralt may be right in proposing that we might sometimes benefit from turning it off. Another solution, suggested by Veitch and Griffitt is that the negative emotional effects of bad news could presumably be overcome if there were a concerted attempt to report an equal quantity of good news on each program.

DEVELOPING A RELATIONSHIP: THE ACQUAINTANCE PROCESS

In describing the research on interpersonal attraction, we may have given you the impression that a miscellaneous list of variables has been investigated and that all this has very little to do with *real* interpersonal attraction. Some social

TABLE 5-2. *Contents of good news and bad news radio broadcasts. In a successful attempt to show that the content of news broadcasts influences the emotions of listeners and then their attraction toward others, Veitch and Griffitt created a series of four news stories that were either positive or negative in content. When these were broadcast, they had the expected effects on both affect and interpersonal attraction. (Source: Veitch and Griffitt, Good News—Bad News: Affective and Interpersonal Effects. Journal of Applied Social Psychology, 1976, 6. Reprinted by permission of Scripta Publishing Co., 1511 K St., NW, Washington, D.C. 20005.)*

	Good News	*Bad News*
1.	There is a new breakthrough in the treatment of cancer.	A presumed cancer breakthrough was found to have painful and fatal side effects.
2.	A federal grant was approved to fund new health facilities at a local orphanage.	A federal grant application to fund health facilities at a local orphanage was not approved.
3.	It was forecast that local food prices would decrease substantially.	It was forecast that local food prices would increase substantially.
4.	All campus parking lots will now be open to faculty and students alike, on a first-come, first-served basis.	New student parking lots will be built at some distance from the campus, and students will have to walk a long way to reach their classes.

psychologists would agree with that conclusion, and they argue that most studies of attraction, whether based on balance theory or on reinforcement theory, really only deal with first impressions. The **interaction theorists** feel that it is preferable to examine actual relationships that people form in everyday life and to study these over a long period of time (Levinger, 1974; Murstein, 1971, 1974; Wright, 1969). Most often, these investigators have been interested in the way in which relationships develop and change in a series of interactions, usually in the sequence from casual dating to love, courtship, and marriage.

Rather than argue about what is the best way to study attraction, we take the position that all types of investigations are valuable, and that the findings of relatively simple laboratory and field studies may fruitfully be applied to the study of relationships in the real world. Studies of actual relationships, in turn, lead us to modify our theories and to conduct new experimental research to test the modified ideas. As an example of the interaction between research findings and a real-world relationship, we will take the descriptive framework developed by Levinger (1974) and apply it to a specific type of sequence—the way in which two individuals of the opposite sex might meet and fall in love.

From Zero Contact to Awareness

Let's imagine that two students, Kathy and Paul, attend the same college but do not know one another. The first two circles in Figure 5-10 show this level of **zero contact.** It is obvious that for them to become acquainted they must somehow

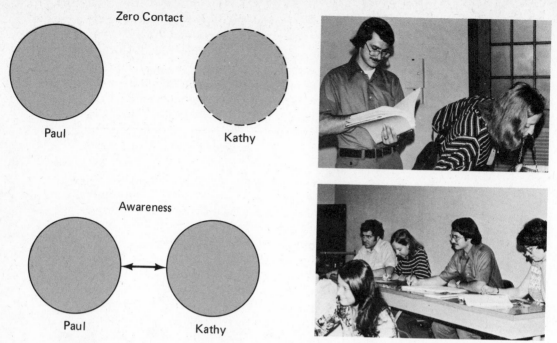

FIGURE 5-10. *In Levinger's (1974) theoretical system, relationships progress through a series of levels. Here, the first level is that of zero contact in which two individuals are not even aware of one another. The second level is that of awareness in which the individuals gain some impression of one another, but they have not yet interacted. (Source: Drawings based on Levinger and Snoek, 1972, p. 5.)*

come to be aware of one another as suggested by the next two circles in the figure. How does this step occur? There are instances when complete strangers meet as the result of deliberate effort. That is, a mutual friend may make introductions, a roommate may arrange a blind date for you with his cousin from Omaha, and two individuals may fill out questionnaires provided by a computer dating organization and be given one another's name. Much more often, however, people meet by accident, and we have already described the way in which propinquity factors bring people together and how frequent exposure leads to liking. If, for example, Kathy and Paul were assigned to adjacent seats in a classroom, they would necessarily become aware of one another and they would be very likely to become acquainted in a matter of weeks.

This initial level of **awareness**, before two people actually interact, is very much dependent on visible characteristics. We have described the power of physical attractiveness, especially in the way in which males and females respond to one another. In one study of individuals who were brought together for a thirty minute Coke date, physical attractiveness was strongly related to judgments as to whether the other person was desirable as a future date, as a potential spouse, and as a sexual partner (Byrne, Ervin, and Lamberth, 1970). Both males and females respond to this variable, so for the relationship between Kathy and

Paul to develop, each would probably have to find the other at least acceptably attractive. Otherwise, they may do no more than politely nod "hello" when they get to class each day. There are also cultural norms with respect to appropriate male-female matches. For example, most people in our culture feel uncomfortable in a relationship unless the male is slightly taller than the female. Therefore, for no very good reason, any future relationship between Paul and Kathy would be very limited if she happened to be two inches taller than he is. Finally, as we have seen earlier, there are individual differences among members of each sex in the stress placed on variables like breast size and beardedness. Our two college students would be more likely to become friends if they meshed properly with respect to the preferences of each in conjunction with the appearance of the other. There are also behavioral characteristics that can be offensive to a great many people and hence turn them off; for example, those who smoke cigarettes incessantly and without regard for the comfort of others evoke negative responses even among fellow smokers (Bleda, 1976).

There is an additional determinant of friendship formation which has not been mentioned yet—**need for affiliation.** Individuals differ in the extent to which they are motivated to form close interpersonal relationships and in the value they place on making new friends (Shipley and Veroff, 1952). Even among engaged couples, males and females who are high in the need for affiliation rate their partners more positively than do those low in this need (Centers, 1971). It has also been found that individuals who are well adjusted and who are high in self-esteem are more motivated to form close interpersonal relationships than those who are maladjusted (Scott and Peterson, 1975; Ueda and Taniguchi, 1974). Besides this personality trait, affiliation need fluctuates over time as a function of how well it is being satisfied. That is, if Kathy were currently in love with someone else and if Paul were currently dating several other girls, the two of them would not be strongly motivated to form a new relationship. If both were currently without a love interest, however, the chance meeting in the classroom would be much more likely to be pursued by each of them.

Surface Contact: Getting to Know You

At this point, if all of the preliminary influences on attraction are positive, the two individuals in our example may begin interacting in terms of **surface contact,** as shown in Figure 5-11. As was discussed before, much of their initial conversations will probably involve a series of attitudinal comparisons as they make remarks to one another about a current movie, an upcoming musical concert, the instructor of the course, political candidates, pizza, religion, and anything else that is currently of concern to them. One of the authors once mentioned to a female classmate that, as a child, he used to read what was written on the cereal boxes while he ate breakfast. The student was overjoyed to find that they shared this childhood habit, because she thought she was unusual for having done the same thing. Perhaps *both* individuals were unusual, but it was nevertheless pleasant for them to discover even this trivial similarity. Just as

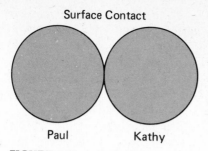

Surface Contact

Paul   Kathy

FIGURE 5-11.   *At the level of surface contact, two individuals begin to interact in a relatively shallow way and to exchange casual remarks. Questions are asked and answered as they begin to discover details about one another's attitudes and interests. (Source: Drawing based on Levinger and Snoek, 1972, p. 5.)*

in the similarity experiments, Kathy and Paul might be expected informally to compare their own attitudes and values and beliefs with those of the other person to find out how well they match.   Such conversations also serve to establish whether the two people have any interests in common.   Do they both play tennis or chess?   Do they both like to attend horror movies or go swimming?   Again, there is a tendency to determine the extent to which there is some degree of similarity or compatibility.   We also know that an individual's emotional state influences evaluative judgments.   For this reason, two individuals might be expected to have a more positive interaction if the classroom atmosphere were a pleasant one, if the room temperature were at a comfortable level, etc.

   In the course of their exchanges, many aspects of each participant are continually being revealed and evaluated.   Is the person entertaining, witty, hostile, conceited, shy, and so forth?   With respect to such characteristics, sometimes similarity is sought and sometimes just the opposite (Grush, Clore, and Costin, 1975).   What is important is reinforecment (Lombardo, Steigleder, and Feinberg, 1975).   For example, an individual who is fond of hostile, cynical wisecracks is often attracted to a similar individual with whom such remarks can be exchanged.   On the other hand, the outgoing, talkative, "life of the party" is often attracted to someone who can act as a quiet, but appreciative, audience.   This complementarity effect (or "opposites attract") holds whenever dissimilar characteristics provide mutual reinforcement.   It is also found that people who brag and announce positive things about themselves ("I have been accepted by a number of excellent graduate schools") are frequently disliked, but an extremely negative reaction to such self-praise is greatest among those who are low in self-esteem (Izzett, 1976).   With respect to all such variables, the process of learning about one another can cause a relationship to become closer and to progress or, as in the cartoon in Figure 5-12, to terminate.

Mutuality: From Friendship to Love

Just Good Friends.   If all the signs are still positive, the next step for Kathy and Paul is friendship **(mutuality).**   As shown in Figure 5-13, they have

"It's been a wonderful evening, Ed. Don't spoil it by asking for another date."

FIGURE 5-12. *When two people interact as acquaintances or as casual dates, they are engaged in a learning process with respect to one another. Very often, what is learned is that there is no reason to continue to interact. (Source: Copyright © 1974 by permission of Saturday Review and Jerry Marcus.)*

discovered that they have something in common and they slowly begin to think of themselves as "we." They meet outside the classroom to have refreshments, to talk, to study together, and to have dates. The success of these early dates depends on a number of factors, and one of the more interesting is the match between the two individuals with respect to their roles as siblings in their own families. If the male had a younger sister and the female an older brother, for example, the dating relationship would be a replay of the childhood experiences with a member of the opposite sex, a complementary relationship. An example of a completely noncomplementary relationship would be if the male had only a younger brother and the female only a younger sister. As part of a computer dating experiment, Mendelsohn et al. (1974) studied such possible pairings and found that the greater the complementarity, the more satisfied the individuals were with the date and the more subsequent dates they had. It was suggested that the social skills important for a date are first learned and practiced with one's siblings. A somewhat different, but related, finding is that later-born children are more popular with their classmates than early-born children—presumably because the later-borns have to learn how to get along with their older siblings (Miller and Maruyama, 1976).

The relatively shallow conversations and interactions that lead up to an initial date begin to be replaced by deeper and more honest exchanges. In an

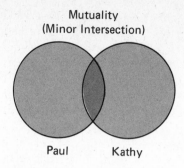

Mutuality
(Minor Intersection)

Paul   Kathy

FIGURE 5-13. *When two individuals discover that they have something in common, they are at the mutuality level in Levinger's (1974) schema. Here we see a "minor intersection" in which there is only a modest degree of overlap between two people. (Source: Drawing based on Levinger and Snoek, 1972, p. 5.)*

atmosphere of trust, two individuals begin to feel close enough to disclose things about themselves—their fears and embarrassments, their fantasies about the future. In general, people are most attracted to those who match them in *how much* is disclosed and who are similar in *what* is disclosed (Daher and Banikiotes, 1976). Such mutual openness suggests strongly that those involved like each other very much, and some of the self-disclosure involves personal evaluations of the other's attractiveness, honesty, interestingness, intelligence, wit, or whatever. We have seen that when these evaluations are positive, the one who receives them is strongly attracted to the one who gives them.

An idea frequently expressed in fictional accounts of such interactions suggests that an individual can create great interest in the other person by "playing hard to get." Walster et al. (1973) conducted a series of studies to verify that and they failed to do so. It was found instead that what we like is a member of the opposite sex who is hard for others to get but who readily accepts us. The notion of standing in line while a potential date decides among numerous other partners is apparently not what really turns most of us on. Even though we like to be favored from the beginning, when we see hard-to-get happen to others it seems fine. Subjects who watched a videotape of a male and female interacting felt that the male was more attracted to his partner when she was first cold to him and then switched to warm than when she was consistently warm throughout the interaction (Clore, Wiggins, and Itkin, 1975). Such a finding fits in with what Aronson and Linder (1965) call "gain-loss" theory; that is, changes in how others feel are especially important in determining attraction.

A very common question that males and females ask themselves as the relationship deepens in this stage is, "Am I in love?" In undergraduate classes dealing with attraction or sexual relationships, students often want to know how to determine whether they are in love. They sometimes ask, "What *is* love?" Though poets and novelists and playwrights have dealt with that topic for centuries, psychologists tended to ignore it entirely until very recently (Rubin, 1973). What insights have we gained from this new line of research?

Love, Love—Hooray for Love! What would make Kathy and Paul decide that they love one another? **Love** seems to involve both what we have been taught about the phenomenon and the presence of very intense feelings. Because heterosexual love is not a universal concept, it appears that early learning experiences in our culture must be responsible for planting the idea in our heads. If we must learn to experience love, it is not surprising that there are individual differences in the frequency with which love is felt and in the strength of such feelings. For example, females are more likely to report being in love than males, and personality variables such as internal-external control (belief that one's behavior is influenced by oneself or by outside variables) and self-esteem are related to the likelihood of love—externals and those low in self-esteem report more love experiences (Dion and Dion, 1973, 1975). Udry (1971) suggests that love involves numerous myths that begin with our fairy tales. Cinderella, Sleeping Beauty, Snow White, the Frog Prince, and all the rest fall madly in love with an astonishingly attractive person of the opposite sex, undergo trials and tribulations, finally marry, and then ride off together on a white horse to find eternal happiness. After a childhood filled with such stories followed by the slightly more realistic depictions of love in movies, on television, and in books, most of us are primed and ready to hear bells ring and birds sing by the time we reach adolescence.

When the conditions are right, therefore, we find ourselves feeling **passionate love** for another person. As with other emotional states, there must be arousal *and* a reason to give that arousal a particular label. According to Berscheid and Walster (1974b), this type of love involves a combination of strong interpersonal attraction plus sexual attraction. They suggest that it is most likely to occur when individuals who are attracted to one another are in a situation in which there is some kind of strong physiological arousal. The arousal may be sexual desire, the excitement generated by a basketball game, or even anxiety and fear. For example, Dutton and Aron (1974) found that when males were interviewed by a female on a frightening suspension bridge high above a canyon, they gave evidence of being sexually aroused (as indicated by the content of a story they wrote) and half of them were sufficiently attracted to the experimenter to telephone her afterward. Such responses did not occur on a solid, safe low bridge nor when the interviewer was male. Thus, fear arousal on the bridge plus the presence of a member of the opposite sex may have been interpreted by the subjects as a passionate emotional response—love at first sight. Similarly, when males in a laboratory expected to receive an electric shock, they were more attracted to a female confederate and expressed a greater desire to kiss her and ask her for a date than was true for control-group males who were not expecting a shock. In summary, there is some evidence that passionate love is a combination of expectancies about love, attraction, emotional arousal, and the appropriate external cues.

When two individuals decide that they are, in fact, in love, what happens next? The feeling of closeness and mutuality increases, as depicted in Figure 5-14. The two people want to be together, to talk, to touch, and individuals who are deeply in love actually do spend an unusual amount of time looking into each

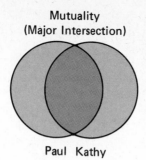

Mutuality
(Major Intersection)

Paul Kathy

FIGURE 5-14. *As mutuality moves further to a "major intersection," the overlap between individuals becomes greater, and they increasingly think of themselves as "we." They want to be together, to talk, and to touch. These intense feelings and the accompanying behavior clearly fit our culture's expectations about love. (Source: Drawing based on Levinger and Snoek, 1972, p. 5.)*

other's eyes (Rubin, 1970). Our Kathy and Paul would be expected to hold hands, kiss, to think about each other when apart, and to desire to be together as much as possible. Rubin developed a test, the love scale, to try to measure the intensity of these feelings. The test contains items with which our couple would agree, such as "I would do almost anything for Kathy." Or, "If I could never be with Paul, I would feel miserable."

The course of true love may never run smooth, but what specific factors might influence these feelings? Driscoll, Davis, and Lipetz (1972) investigated the **Romeo and Juliet effect** and found that when parents try to interfere with a love affair, *reactance* is aroused and the two lovers often feel even closer to one another and more in love. If Kathy's mother disapproved of Paul, for example, and criticized him or tried to keep the two separated, the results would very possibly be the opposite of what she intended. That theme is also a major element in the longest continuous running play in American theater history, *The Fantastiks*.

Also, it is becoming increasingly true in our culture that love for many people means that it is appropriate to engage in sexual intercourse. The vast change in sexual attitudes and behaviors over the past several decades has not involved random and promiscuous sexual activities, but it has meant that more and more couples engage in premarital sex in the context of a loving, committed relationship (Hunt, 1974). Though many chauvinistic males may falsely use the word "love" simply as a tactic to obtain sex (Mosher, 1971), it is also true that sexual closeness can have a positive effect on feelings of love. That is, love may lead to sex, and sex in turn may intensify the loving relationship.

Happily Ever After? Despite many changes in our society, the ideal still held by most people is that of a happy, lifelong marriage characterized by perpetual love (Shope, 1975). Levinger (1974) has indicated that some would see the perfect relationship as a complete blending of two individuals into one, as shown in Figure 5-15. He notes that this is a fantasy, something that is not

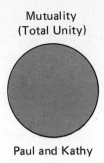

Mutuality
(Total Unity)

Paul and Kathy

FIGURE 5-15. *The final step of the mutuality level is "total unity," a fantastic extreme in which two individuals become one. Though it is impossible, two happily married individuals can become almost a unit with similar desires, concerns, and behaviors. (Source: Drawing based on Levinger and Snoek, 1972, p. 5.)*

really attainable. In fact, he says that only the Internal Revenue Service *really* believes in the fiction of total unity, when a couple fills out a joint tax return.

As we all know, people can fall out of love, remain locked in unhappy marriages, or seek divorce. One of the problems is that situations change and people change—it takes effort and commitment by two people to maintain a positive relationship over time whether as lovers or as loving spouses. In addition, to the extent that passionate love is based on strong emotional arousal, such emotions cannot last indefinitely: you eventually get off the "suspension bridge" and calm down. The meaning of love among dating couples seems to change over time. Rubin (1974) has found that, although the early stages of love may be characterized by blind passion, in a successful relationship the two individuals progress toward deep feelings of attachment, concern about the other person's welfare, and respect for the other's abilities and personal qualities. It is hard to make an exciting movie about concern and respect, but that seems to be the realistic endpoint of a successful love affair.

CONSEQUENTS OF ATTRACTION: INTERPERSONAL DECISIONS, OVERT BEHAVIOR, AND PERFORMANCE

When we strongly like or dislike other individuals, more is involved than simply attraction. Our interpersonal feelings have been found to influence the supposedly objective judgments we make about others, our overt actions, and even the way in which we perform simple and complex tasks.

Interpersonal Decisions: If I Like You, You Must Be a Good Person

It appears that many of our opinions and judgments about other people are based not only on rational, intellectual considerations, but also on our feelings. First, there is an affective response along a pleasant-unpleasant dimension, and, as we

SHOULD PSYCHOLOGISTS STUDY LOVE?

It was mentioned earlier that research on the phenomenon of love is a relatively recent venture for social psychologists. Previous reluctance to conduct investigations related to this topic was in part based on the notion that love is elusive and subjective and in part on the idea that it might not seem quite respectable in the scientific community to carry out experiments dealing with something called "passionate love." Once research was underway, however, it became obvious that the emotions and the behaviors involved in love are as open to research as those involved in such standard areas of interest as fear, aggression, friendship, and altruism. As we have seen, social psychologists have already produced interesting new theories, measuring devices, and data which are helping us to understand a very important aspect of human behavior.

Some are critical of this new development, however, and "love research" has come under attack. The battle began when Senator William Proxmire (a Democrat from the state of Wisconsin) was examining the budgets of various federal agencies and discovered that the National Science Foundation had awarded a research grant to a psychologist who was studying why people fall in love. In March of 1975, Proxmire issued a statement which said that the grant to Professor Ellen Berscheid at the University of Minnesota was his choice "for the biggest waste of the taxpayer's money for the month of March." He went on to say, "I believe that 200 million Americans want to leave some things in life a mystery, and right at the top of things we don't want to know is why a man falls in love with a woman and vice versa." Soon afterward, he discovered that a similar project was underway by Elaine Walster at the University of Wisconsin, and her work, too, was equally criticized. This high-level blast at psychological research was quickly relayed by the news media, and the issues raised by the senator were quickly taken up by editorial writers, columnists, and concerned citizens. Some agreed with the senator, and some provided strong support for the social psychologists.

There were two basic points made by Senator Proxmire, and you might consider how you personally would respond to each. First is the belief that some aspects of human behavior should not be studied, that ignorance is occasionally preferable to knowledge. Second is the assertion that taxpayers should not be asked to provide financial support for certain kinds of research. How do you feel about each point? If you agree with both, how would you decide which aspects of behavior should not be studied or at least not funded? For a sampling of how others responded to this controversy, examine the accompanying quotations in Table 5-3 taken from various publications.

In Support of Proxmire's Argument	In Opposition to Proxmire's Argument
In a second news release after the controversy was underway: "I think it is time the National Science Foundation put a stop to this federal version of 'The Love Machine' and rearrange its research priorities to address our scientific, not our erotic curiosity." William Proxmire U. S. Senator, Wisconsin	"It's not a question of only why they fall in love, but it's a question of why relationships, marriages included, continue or flounder. I would say that has some pretty important consequences in our society." Roland Radloff Program Director for Social Psychology National Science Foundation

"It's a waste of money, because we already know why people fall in love. If 'science' were not a sacred cow which destroys a sense of humor in its followers, we would all shudder and laugh at the ponderous nonsense which this 'scientific study' will bring forth."
> Right Reverend Richard S. Emrich
> Columnist

"Heavenly days, just clue me in on who OKd such a grant for such a stupid reason . . . and you can be sure they'll never receive any of my votes."
> Mrs. A. B., Franklin Park, Ill.
> In letter to *Chicago Daily News*

"The value of such 'research' is highly suspect. Sloppy methodology, amorphous results and patchwork theories are par for the social psych course. Concrete results, if any, are usually pitifully meager. There's no reason to believe that this case is any different."
> Editorial
> Wisconsin *Badger Herald*

"By a ratio of 3 to 1, *Daily News* readers who responded to a recent series of articles on the subject agree with Sen. William Proxmire in his opposition to federal funding of a love-research project."
> Article
> Chicago *Daily News*

After chipping in 50 cents each to buy Proxmire a year's subscription to *Scientific American*: "Let us remark finally that if the title and text prove too abstruse, all articles in the journal can be effectively understood by looking at the pictures and diagrams."
> A group of distinguished scientists
> University of Chicago

"God knows marriage causes so much human misery. Why are we so willing to spend billions on any research that advances our technology and yet are so miserly about examining our emotional lives? We leave our children the tools to annihilate the human race and incredibly little knowledge of themselves."
> Mrs. L. V., Whiting, Ind.
> In letter to *Chicago Daily News*

"With more and more marriages lasting about as long as a cake of Oscar Mayer ice at a Fourth of July picnic, somebody ought to be trying to get at the roots of the alienation. Proxmire ought to have been broadminded enough to understand that instead of playing for snickers and guffaws."
> Editorial
> *Madison Capital Times*

"If the sociologists and psychologists can get even a suggestion of the answer to our patterns of romantic love, marriage, disillusion, divorce—and the children left behind—it could be the best investment of federal money since Jefferson made the Louisiana Purchase."
> James Reston
> Columnist, *New York Times*

TABLE 5-3. *Selected samples of published statements concerning Senator William Proxmire's criticism of "love research."*

have seen, these feelings lead us to conclude that we like or dislike whomever or whatever is associated with them. A second process then begins to operate. It is seemingly difficult for most of us simply to say, for example, that Joe makes us feel good and Mary makes us feel bad and that consequently we like him and dislike her. Rather, there is a tendency to attempt to justify these attraction responses by attributing various positive characteristics to Joe and various negative characteristics to Mary. At that point, instead of having to admit the emotional basis of our reactions, we can give "more rational" reasons for our likes and dislikes.

This general process has been shown in several of the attitude-similarity studies. Why should you dislike someone just because he or she disagrees with you about politics or religion or science fiction? How do you justify such a response to yourself? Your dislike seems much more reasonable if you are also able to conclude that the person is stupid or uninformed or evil or maladjusted. In experiments, when subjects are asked to evaluate a stranger with whom they agree, that person is rated as intelligent, well informed, moral, and well adjusted; a disagreeing stranger is negatively evaluated on each of these characteristics (Griffitt, 1974). We will now show how such attraction-based judgments have a pervasive effect on the way many interpersonal decisions are made.

Political Decisions: Charisma Means "I Like You." Perhaps the most rational of the decisions influenced by attraction are those having to do with political candidates. Our initial political choices seem to be based on the views of parents, and an offspring is likely to reflect the political attitudes of the parent toward whom he or she feels most positively (Cundy, 1975). In an experiment to determine the relationship between liking and voting, the attitudes of a large group of Stanford undergraduates were measured, and they were later presented with what were supposed to be excerpts from the speeches of two congressional candidates (Byrne, Bond, and Diamond, 1969). It was found, as you might expect, that the relative similarity of attitudes between a subject and each candidate was an excellent predictor of voting decisions. There would seem to be no great harm if our political choices were based on attitude similarity (unless perhaps a candidate deliberately misrepresented his attitudes in order to get elected). The problem becomes more serious when other determinants of attraction also influence voting. For example, Efran and Patterson (1974) found that physically attractive candidates in a Canadian federal election received almost three times as many votes as did unattractive candidates. It has also been found that the taller of the two candidates running for president of the United States has most often won the election. Despite the obvious irrelevancy of such factors in predicting performance in office, these variables influence voters, and, as a result, makeup men, stylists, photographers, and film editors do their best to enhance the appearance of most candidates.

The relationship between reactions to physical appearance and decision making can also involve an intervening step in which attitudes are attributed on the basis of such variables as hairstyle and type of clothing. In this instance, the inferences may well be incorrect, and it is possible to alter aspects of one's appearance in order to influence the decisions of others. In a field experiment during the Vietnam War, Suedfeld, Bochner, and Matas (1971) sent two female experimenters to a peace demonstration in Washington to solicit signatures for an antiwar petition. Each experimenter had the same petition, and presumably most of those attending the demonstration were in favor of its contents. One girl was dressed as a "hippie" and resembled most of the demonstrators, while the other wore "straight" attire and was thus different in appearance from the average demonstrator. The petition was signed by eighty percent of those asked by the hippie girl versus only sixty-five percent of those asked by the straight girl. It seems there was some distrust of the political motives of the individual who looked straight and hence a greater reluctance to sign her petition.

Among a different group of people, the two styles of clothing would be expected to have just the opposite effect. For example, Darley and Cooper (1972) suggested that the success of Senator Eugene McCarthy's 1968 New Hampshire primary campaign was in part due to the efforts of his collegiate campaign workers to change their hair and clothing styles to conform to the prevailing code of the middle-aged voters—the "Clean for Gene" strategy. To demonstrate this phenomenon experimentally, male students from Princeton went into a shopping center either dressed in conventional sportswear with their hair cut short or dressed in dungarees and old army jackets with long hair and beards. They attempted to hand out an innocuous leaflet that advocated free speech and standing up for one's beliefs. More shoppers accepted the leaflet from the straight students than from the "freaky" ones. Also, they were less likely to throw the leaflet away if it had been given to them by a straight student.

It is generally assumed in such studies that a person's appearance leads others to make inferences about his attitudes; so, their responses are based on the attitude-attraction effect. Darley and Cooper (1972) tested this assumption. Tables were set up in a shopping center supposedly to provide support for two bogus political candidates. One of the tables was manned by workers who were conventional in appearance and the other by workers styled as hippies. Pollsters interviewed the shoppers to ask about their impressions of the two nonexistent candidates. Simply on the basis of the appearance of the "campaign workers," the two candidates were assumed to be different with respect to liberal-conservative beliefs and in their views on marijuana, Nixon's Asian policies, the use of police on campus, and the expulsion of students who disrupt universities.

What happens when a candidate's spokesman does not "look right"? McPeek and Gross (1975) investigated the situation in which the attitudes suggested by physical appearance did not match the attitudes actually expressed by a campaign speaker. During the 1972 Nixon-McGovern campaign, undergraduates witnessed a speaker who was either young and "freaky" looking or old and "straight" looking. Each speaker expressed a preference for McGovern and for Nixon for different subject groups. When appearance and candidate choice did not match, subjects seemed to explain it on the basis of occupation. The straight speaker who supported McGovern was guessed to be a liberal college professor or in a similar occupation; the freaky speaker who supported Nixon was guessed to be a blue-collar worker. It has also been found that if the issue is sufficiently important, individuals may ignore the appearance of the other person entirely (Bryant, 1975).

Other Interpersonal Decisions. A good deal of research evidence indicates that attraction plays a major role in most of our interpersonal decisions, even though it may be totally irrelevant to the matter at hand. This seems to be generally true whether the decision involves hiring an employee, evaluating a loan applicant, or judging the guilt of a defendant in a courtroom. The extent of this influence can best be seen by examining Table 5-4. In each of the findings summarized there, liking and disliking were created by the experimenter, usually by means of an attitude-similarity manipulation. Then, the subjects were asked to make some sort of judgment or evaluation concerning the liked or disliked individual, a judgment that, objectively at least, should be unrelated to attraction. As you can see, a wide variety of judgments tend to be influenced by interpersonal feelings. When making judgments yourself, it might help to keep such findings in mind as you try to be as objective as possible. When judgments are

TABLE 5-4. *Interpersonal attraction has been found to influence many of the decisions individuals make about one another. The findings outlined here represent a sample of the kinds of situations in which judgments have been found to be more positive toward someone who is liked than toward someone who is disliked.*

Type of Interpersonal Decision	Effect of Being Liked	Experimenters
Choosing a group member with whom to work.	More likely to be selected even if others are more appropriate.	Castore and DeNinno (1976)
Hiring a research assistant.	More likely to be hired and to be recommended for larger salary.	Griffitt and Jackson (1970)
Evaluating husband and wife who wish to adopt a baby.	More likely to be judged as suitable adoptive parents.	Aves and Byrne (1976)
Approving application for a bank loan.	More likely to have loan approved.	Sung (1975)
Judging a defendant in a trial.	More likely to be judged innocent or, if guilty, to receive lighter sentence.	Griffitt and Jackson (1973)
Believing a witness who testifies in a trial.	More likely to be perceived as telling the truth.	Garcia and Griffitt (1976)
Deciding qualifications of psychological counselors.	More likely to be perceived as sympathetic, understanding, and effective.	Good and Good (1972)
Evaluating performance on a learning task.	More likely to be rated as having done well.	Smith, Meadow, and Sisk (1970)
Giving rewards and punishments to a trainee on a performance task.	Less likely to be punished for making mistakes.	Banks (1976)

being made about you, you might do well to remember that it is probably going to be to your advantage to be liked rather than disliked. It is not necessarily what you know, or even who you know, but who knows and likes you.

Overt Behavior and Attraction: Close to You

Not only does attraction influence what we say about others and our evaluative judgments about them, it also affects what we do when we are together. It was indicated earlier that the physical distance between two people can influence their attraction. The reverse is also true; attraction influences how closely two people will approach one another. With two individuals of the opposite sex, the relationship between attraction and closeness is very clear. The more positive their feelings, the closer together a male and female will stand in a dating situation (Byrne, Ervin, and Lamberth, 1970). Also, when there are several empty seats available, individuals will select a seat close to an opposite-sex individual they like, and a more distant seat will be chosen when the person is disliked (Allgeier and Byrne, 1973). Also, once two individuals have selected an appropriate distance to stand or sit, posture is related to interpersonal feelings— we tend to lean toward someone we like and away from someone we dislike (Mehrabian, 1968b).

The fact that people attempt to get physically close to a liked member of the opposite sex may not be startling news to you, but what would you predict about two people of the same sex? Here, the situation becomes more complicated. It seems that there are sex differences, at least in our culture, with respect to what is appropriate for males and females. Sommer (1969) observed the seating arrangements of individuals interacting in small discussion groups. He noted that females sit side-by-side whereas males tend to choose seats that are face-to-face with another person. Casual observation at parties is consistent with that. Two females are likely to sit beside one another on a couch, and a male and female may also sit next to each other, but it is rare for two males to choose such a seating arrangement. In two experiments conducted by Byrne, Baskett, and Hodges (1971), the effect of attraction on seating choice was studied in two different physical settings as shown in Figure 5-16. In each experiment, subjects learned the attitudes of two same-sex confederates (one was always similar and thus liked, the other always dissimilar and thus disliked). The confederates were seated in a nearby room, and the subject later was asked to join them. Empty seats were available in the second room, and the question was where subjects would choose to sit in relation to the liked and disliked confederates. The first experiment involved side-by-side seating, and in this instance females sat closer to a liked female than to a disliked one; males sat equally close to a liked and to a disliked male. The second experiment involved face-to-face seating, and males overwhelmingly chose to sit across from a liked male; here, females showed no seating preferences. It seems that the physical distance individuals place between themselves and others depends on attraction, on the physical details of the setting, and on the sex of those involved.

Because the physical distance we place between ourselves and others is often not a conscious decision, such behavior may sometimes serve as a more sensitive measure of attraction than what we say. Earlier in the chapter, a study was described in which a male subject experienced negative affect when a female chose a similar male in preference to him. Nevertheless, he did not indicate dislike for the lucky rival—such a response is not really socially acceptable. In a follow-up experiment, a measure of physical distance was obtained when the subject sat at a table where the successful male was already seated (Jazwinski, Nadler, and Lau, 1976). As shown in Figure 5-17, subjects sat equally close to the male confederate in every condition but one. When a similar male had been chosen by the female, the subject sat the greatest distance away from the other male even though he said that he liked him. It should not be assumed, however, that physical measures are *always* superior to verbal indications of attraction (Latta, 1976).

Another aspect of behavior that is affected by attraction is visual. The more one person likes another, the more time is spent in looking at that person as they interact (Efran, 1969). In addition, when someone gazes at us, at least in a friendly interaction, we are likely to interpret that behavior positively (Kleinke, Staneski, and Pipp, 1975). There are sex differences, however, in that a direct gaze is perceived as more pleasant and intimate by females than by males (Ellsworth and Ross, 1975).

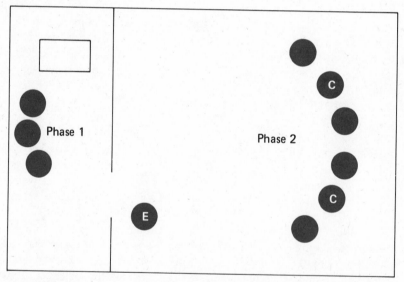

FIGURE 5-16. *In the study of side-by-side seating (panel above), subjects discussed attitudes with two confederates in phase 1 and later joined them and sat in one of two empty chairs. Females chose to sit beside a liked female. In the study of face-to-face seating (at right), subjects watched two confederates express opinions on closed-circuit television in phase 1 and later joined them and sat in one of the empty chairs. Males chose to sit across from a liked male. (From Byrne, Baskett, and Hodges, 1971, pp. 141 and 145. Reprinted by permission of Scripta Publishing Co., 1511 K Street, N.W., Washington, D. C. 20005.)*

In most of our activities we find ourselves in the company of others—at school, at work, and in recreational settings. To what extent are we responsive to these other individuals, and does it matter whether we like or dislike them? When similar individuals are together in groups, they feel that the atmosphere is pleasant and more relaxed, they communicate better, and they even laugh more at jokes (Wolosin, 1975). We will take one familiar situation, the classroom, and explore the role of attraction in that setting. Specifically, we will examine whether a student's behavior is influenced by his or her feelings toward classmates.

There are a number of reasons for suspecting that an ideal educational environment is one in which the interpersonal relationships are positive. In general, most of us simply prefer a pleasant environment to an unpleasant one. There are, however, two practical reasons for suggesting that school should be made as positive as possible. First, in addition to learning whatever content is being taught, students also acquire evaluative responses toward the whole process on the basis of the affect that is aroused. The reinforcement-affect model indicates that to the extent that education involves interpersonal competition, negative evaluations, punishment, and rigid regimentation, the learning process itself should acquire a negative value. It is not surprising that the eager

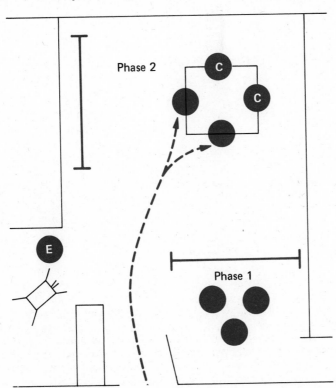

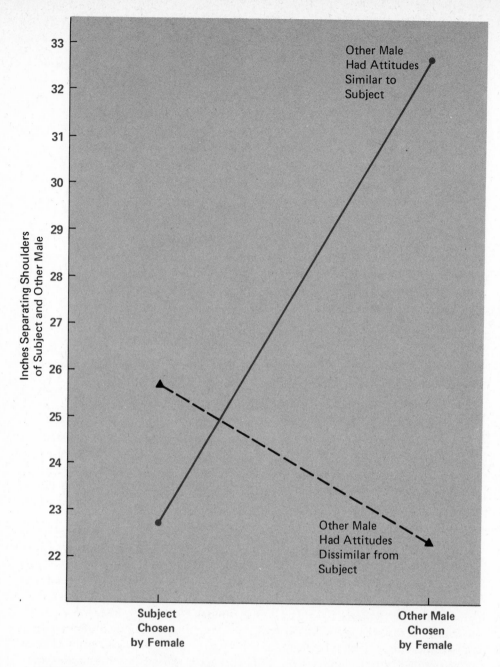

FIGURE 5-17. *When a male subject finds that a female has chosen to work with another male in preference to himself, he expresses more negative affect when that male is similar to himself than when he is dissimilar. Though he does not verbally indicate dislike for the similar successful rival, a measure of physical proximity indicates that he places himself at a greater distance from such an individual. (Source: Based on data from Jazwinski, Nadler, and Lau, 1976.)*

The physical distance between two opposite-sex individuals is a good indication of their mutual attraction. (Photo: Phil Carver & Friends.)

kindergarten student too often loses his or her natural curiosity and desire to learn. Wonder and awe are frequently replaced by a prevailing desire for recess periods and vacations and "no more school, no more books—no more teacher's dirty looks." Positive emotions in the classroom, in contrast, should result in positive evaluations of the educational process. Second, it has been proposed that a positive interpersonal atmosphere in education actually results in better performance (Lott, 1969). In other words, not only are students happier when learning in an atmosphere of friendship, they also learn more!

Evidence supporting the idea that interpersonal attraction enhances learning has been provided by a few scattered studies. Lott and Lott (1966) found that children did better in learning Spanish when they worked with liked classmates than with disliked ones. Similarly, pairs of college students who believed that they held similar attitudes performed better on a simple mechanical task than pairs who believed they held dissimilar attitudes (Nelson and Meadow, 1971). In order to test the general proposition about learning and attraction in a controlled setting, Krivonos, Byrne, and Friedrich (1976) placed pairs of male college students in a situation in which the partner's supposed attitudes were manipulated to create either mutual liking or mutual dislike. Then, each pair was given material to read followed by a particular type of intellectual task. Some were asked to recall details of what they had read, some had to synthesize the material with other material in their textbook, and still others had to evaluate the reading on the basis of specific criteria. The predicted positive effect of liking on performance may be seen in Figure 5-18.   On each of the three very different kinds of tasks, subjects paired with a liked partner did better than subjects paired

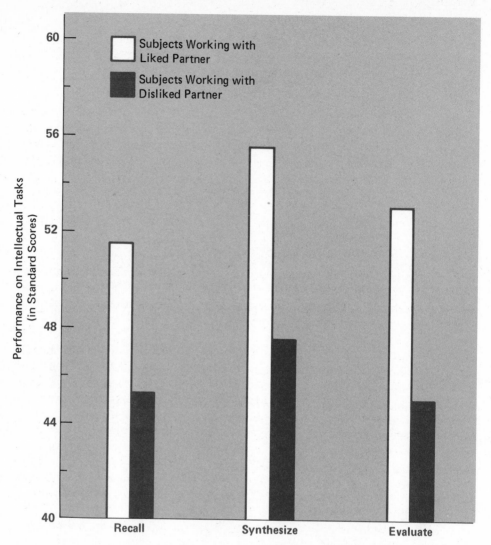

FIGURE 5-18.   *The effect of interpersonal attraction on intellectual performance was shown in an experiment with undergraduate male students.   They worked in pairs and were made to like or dislike one another on the basis of false attitudinal information.   On the basis of material they read, they were asked to carry out one of three types of intellectual tasks.   In each instance, those working with a liked partner outperformed those working with a disliked partner.   (Source: Based on data from Krivonos, Byrne, and Friedrich, 1976.)*

with a disliked partner. On the basis of such findings, it appears possible that positive and negative interpersonal relationships may be a critical element in school performance.

INCREASING INTERPERSONAL HARMONY

Embedded in research on the determinants and the effects of attraction is an underlying assumption that it is good to like and be liked, bad to dislike and be disliked. It seems reasonable to believe that efforts to increase liking among people would be a beneficial undertaking. It may be unduly optimistic to think it possible to create an interpersonal climate in which there is universal good will, but any step in that direction seems preferable to a climate too often characterized by hate, suspicion, and prejudice.

One solution, of course, is to try to bring compatible people together—those whose appearance, attitudes, and abilities are similar—and to separate such homogeneous groups from those who are dissimilar. While such efforts probably would be helpful in some respects, the kind of world suggested by that type of segregation seems less than perfect. A quite different approach is to find ways of overcoming or counteracting the negative effects of such variables as physical unattractiveness and attitude dissimilarity. One problem with attitudes, for example, is that they are frequently stated in an extremely dogmatic manner. In *Penthouse* magazine, a reader wrote in to defend premarital chastity and noted, "I'm all for seeing more virgins reach their wedding day. I think all other views are impractical, irresponsible and ignorant." The tone of that statement is such that any kind of disagreement could only lead to anger and dislike. It has been found that attitude dissimilarity need not lead to strong negative feelings (Hodges and Byrne, 1972). The individual defending virginity, for example, could be taught to express the same viewpoint in an open-minded way—"I'm all for seeing more virgins reach their wedding day. I know that others hold quite different views, and I respect their right to do so." Given this gentler style, disagreement would be more likely to lead to an interesting discussion than to name calling. Research on the effects of wording one's views in this way indicates that the general level of attraction might increase if we could learn to present our beliefs and attitudes less dogmatically.

There is another way in which people are brought to tolerate and even like those who ordinarily would be disliked. It has been noted many times that in certain unusual situations even very dissimilar strangers will interact in the friendliest of ways. For example, in stressful circumstances such as a power failure that paralyzes a city, an oil spill that blackens a beach, or in a natural disaster such as an earthquake, people often come together to cooperate and help one another in an unexpectedly positive fashion. In part this seems to be because both human beings (Schachter, 1959) and other mammals (Latané and Glass, 1968) tend naturally to affiliate with one another when under stress, and because the presence of others actually serves as an anxiety reducer (Wrightsman, 1960). That is, in the words of the old saying, misery loves company. There are other, very different situations which have the same positive effects, however. The spirit of togetherness that is caused by stress can be seen in very pleasant encounters such as among spectators at a football game, those at a rock festival or a Mardi Gras carnival, or among party-goers playing charades. It has been hypothesized that what these diverse situations have in common is that people are emotionally aroused, the emotion is shared by others, and the situation requires them to engage in behavior that is not characteristic of their everyday lives (Byrne et al., 1975). To test that hypothesis, a series of experiments was conducted in which a subject was with a liked or disliked stranger (created by manipulating attitude similarity) and then placed in a situation involving the three factors suggested above. For example, some subjects had an anxiety-evoking experience in which two people were videotaped while trying to communicate certain words nonverbally. There was thus a shared unpleasant emotion while engaging in unusual behavior. Others had a pleasant unusual experience in which two people had to pass a "laughing bag" (a gadget that emits hearty laughter when it is picked up) back and forth to evaluate it. In each instance, when attraction was measured afterward, the dissimilar stranger was liked as well as the similar one. In control groups in which only two of the three hypothesized factors were present, the dissimilar stranger was still disliked at the end of the experiment. It was suggested that communities might work to create situations in which such variables operate to bring people together. It is possible that the general level of friendliness experienced at Halloween, at amusement parks such as Disney World, and among the cast members of a college play is not an accident and that analogous events could be deliberately utilized to foster attraction.

Finally, another interesting way to increase tolerance has been demonstrated by Clore and Jeffery (1972). They cited many real-life instances in which role playing has been used as a way to let one group of individuals know how those in very different circumstances might feel. Los Angeles police have spent the night locked up in jail, a white writer disguised himself as a black and traveled through the South, and, as you may recall in Chapter 4, a school teacher segregated her students by eye color and had them play the roles of superior and inferior racial groups. A similar technique was used by these experimenters to increase attraction toward a female graduate student who was in a wheelchair. Some subjects had to role play her situation by sitting in a wheelchair and making their way to the Student Union and back. Compared to control subjects who simply watched such a wheelchair trip or who just walked to the Union, the role players were most attracted to the handicapped assistant. The effect was a lasting one in that follow-up studies some months later indicated that the experimental subjects were most willing to help show a disabled prospective student around the campus and to spend money on facilities for the handicapped. Clore and Jeffery proposed that this means of increasing tolerance and empathy could be applied in the educational system by having individuals try out many different role experiences. If we could each learn to experience the world as others do, it might be considerably harder to dislike them.

SUMMARY

We each tend to evaluate all aspects of our environment, including other human beings, along a like-dislike dimension. Interpersonal attraction is the evaluation of another person in a positive or negative way.

The two most common ways in which theorists have tried to explain attraction involve formulations based on cognitions and formulations based on reinforcement. In cognitive theory, the primary focus is on the way an individual organizes his cognitions involving the relationships among himself, another person, and the object of their communication. Newcomb proposes that there is a basic tendency to organize these cognitions in a way that is balanced and satisfying. Imbalanced relationships are unsatisfying, and the individual is motivated to try to attain or restore balance. Nonbalance involves negative interpersonal relationships and a feeling of indifference. With the reinforcement-affect model, Byrne and Clore propose that all evaluations are based on whatever positive or negative feelings are being experienced. Such feelings become associated with external stimuli through the process of classical conditioning. When feelings involve a mixture of positive and negative emotions, individuals respond to their combined average value.

The interpersonal determinants of attraction include attitude similarity, and it is found that attraction toward another person is a positive linear function of the proportion of similar attitudes expressed by that person. In real-world interactions, of course, other variables are also involved. Physical attractiveness is one such variable, and both males and females seem to be strongly influenced by the appearance of others. One of the most powerful determinants of attraction is the personal evaluations another person makes of us—we like those who evaluate us positively and dislike those who evaluate us negatively.

Among the situational determinants of attraction is propinquity, or the physical distance between people in their environmental settings. Presumably, propinquity leads to attraction because repeated exposure to most stimulus objects results in a more favorable evaluation of that object. If emotional responses are crucial mediators of attraction, it follows that anything which makes people feel good will enhance attraction, while negative emotions will have the opposite effect.

Interaction theorists such as Levinger deal with the development of a relationship among ongoing real-life couples. The first step is going from zero contact to awareness, and often propinquity variables determine this event. Variables such as physical appearance and individual differences in need for affiliation determine the outcome of this stage. At the level of surface contact, people interact and discover the attitudes and values of one another. If all is positive, the relationship proceeds to mutuality as the individuals become friends and slowly begin to think of themselves as "we." If one has learned to expect to fall in love and if there is strong attraction and sexual desire, two individuals are likely to experience passionate love. Whether this relationship matures into one of mutual caring and respect or whether it dissolves in disillusionment depends on many factors related to the individuals and their interactions.

When we like or dislike other people we tend to let these feelings influence our other judgments about them. Thus, attraction has been found to influence such interpersonal decisions as voting for a political candidate, hiring an employee, judging the guilt of a defendant in a trial, and many others. Attraction also leads us to move toward those we like and away from those we dislike, though males and females differ in their pattern of approaching liked members of their own sex. Finally, attraction has been found to influence intellectual performance, in that individuals working with someone they like do better than those working with a disliked other.

Most social psychologists would agree that efforts to increase liking among people would be a beneficial undertaking. Though segregating individuals into homogeneous subgroups would be one possible technique to reach such a goal, other possibilities seem preferable. It has been found that tolerance for a dissimilar other can be greatly increased if the dissimilar attitudes are expressed in an open-minded rather than a dogmatic fashion, if circumstances cause individuals to share strong emotions and to behave in uncharacteristic ways, and if one has the opportunity to play the role of disliked others and thus share their experiences.

GLOSSARY

Affect. Emotions or feelings.

Attraction. The evaluation of another person in a positive or negative way.

Awareness. In Levinger's schema, the level of relationship in which at least one of the individuals is aware of the other.

Balance. In Newbomb's theory, the pleasant state that exists when two people like each other and agree about the object of their communication.

Balance theory. Newcomb's cognitive theory of interpersonal attraction.

Cognitive theory. A theory that stresses thought processes and the interrelationships among one's cognitions.

Imbalance. In Newcomb's theory, the unpleasant state that exists when two people like each other and disagree about the object of their communication.

Interaction theory. An attraction theory that emphasizes the factors involved in the interactions between two people in an ongoing relationship.

Interpersonal Judgment Scale. An instrument which measures interpersonal attraction in terms of ratings of likability and desirability as a work partner.

Linear relationship. The straight-line function describing the relationship between proportion of similar attitudes and attraction.

Love. An intense emotional state involving strong feelings of attraction, sexual desire, and concern about the other person's welfare.

Matching hypothesis. The idea that males and females of approximately equal physical attractiveness will select one another as partners.

Mutuality. In Levinger's schema, the deepest level of relationships in which two people find they have something in common. This level of relationship can vary from a minor overlap of interest to a theoretical total overlap.

Need for affiliation. The motive to be with other people, make friends, and establish close interpersonal relationships.

Nonbalance. In Newcomb's theory, the indifferent state that exists when two people dislike each other.

Passionate love. A combination of strong interpersonal attraction plus sexual attraction.

Propinquity. Proximity or nearness. As propinquity increases, usually because of environmental factors, two people are more likely to become acquainted.

Reinforcement-affect model. The theory of Byrne and Clore which proposes that all evaluations are based on positive and negative emotions which become associated with people and other stimulus objects.

Reinforcement theory. A theory which stresses the process of learning.

Romeo and Juliet effect. The finding that parental interference in a love affair causes the two individuals to feel even closer.

Surface contact. In Levinger's schema, the level at which two people first begin to interact.

Zero contact. In Levinger's schema, the period before two people meet and are as yet unaware of one another.

SUGGESTED READINGS FOR CHAPTER 5

Clore, G. L. *Interpersonal attraction: An overview.* Morristown, N.J.: General Learning Press, 1975. A brief and lucid description of the major current trends in attraction research and theorizing.

Duck, S. W. (Ed.). *Theory and practice in interpersonal attraction.* London: Academic Press, 1976. A group of original chapters describing current theoretical approaches to interpersonal attraction and their application to specific problems.

Huston, T. L. (Ed.). *Foundations of interpersonal attraction.* New York: Academic Press, 1974. A collection of original chapters written by the major investigators in this field of research. This volume contains the most complete coverage of the diverse aspects of work on attraction and love.

Murstein, B. I. (Ed.). *Theories of attraction and love.* New York: Springer, 1971. A brief collection of original chapters by representatives of the primary theoretical approaches to interpersonal relationships.

Rubin, Z. *Liking and loving: An invitation to social psychology.* New York: Holt, Rinehart and Winston, 1973. An informal and very readable introduction to the social psychological approach to attraction and love.

SOCIAL INFLUENCE: CONFORMITY, COMPLIANCE, AND OBEDIENCE

6

When you interact with other people, many of the things you say or do represent attempts to influence their behavior—you may want to convince someone to stop studying so that the two of you can go to a movie. In a similar way, others are regularly trying to influence your behavior—a friend may ask you to give him a ride into town. Sometimes **social influence** is indirect and not at all obvious; for example, most students attending college for the first time *conform* to the appearance and to the activities of those already there. At other times the influence is relatively direct and obvious; for example, when someone asks to borrow your biology notes, he hopes that you will *comply* with the request. Social influence at its strongest comes in the form of orders; a policeman who tells you to move your bicycle away from the building's entrance assumes that you will *obey.* The factors determining the effectiveness of each type of social influence will be described in the present chapter.

In every group, there are generally accepted rules or **social norms** that characterize how those in the group ordinarily behave. In a classroom you sit quietly (more or less) when the instructor is talking. At a football game you feel free to stand up from time to time and even to shout normally objectionable expletives on occasion. At a crowded party you are likely to stand up or sit on the floor, talk periodically, and say things that are pleasant and, whenever possible, amusing. When things are flowing smoothly and everyone is follow-ing the unspoken rules, the norms are generally not noticeable to those who are behaving in the expected way. Most of us simply assume that we are doing what we want to in each situation, and our behavior seems to be "natural." When we act according to our group's norms, interpersonal behavior is relatively simple and predictable. We usually know what to do and how to act, and we are comfortable in our interactions with others. If the norms are violated, there is sudden confusion and discomfort as we face an unpredictable social situation. If you were to shout "Up your nose, Prof!" at your next class meeting or were to sit silently taking notes at your next party, you would see instantly how others feel when norms are broken. Let's consider another example of such non-normative behavior and try to imagine what the consequences might be.

You and a date are having a special dinner at one of the nicer, more expensive restaurants in town. At other tables, couples are talking, drinking, eating, interacting with waiters, and listening to the music of a small combo playing in the adjoining lounge. You, the others in the restaurant, the employees, and the entertainers are all engaging in the appropriate, expected behavior for that particular situation. Then, another couple enters and is escorted to the table next to yours. Both the man and the woman are totally nude except for the presence of graphic four-letter suggestions neatly printed on their backs. The man sets a badly stained paper sack on the table, knocking the silverware and glasses to the floor. They each grab a dripping hunk of raw liver from the bag and begin chewing lustily. The man shouts for a magnum of champagne which he drinks from the bottle after neatly cracking off the top on the edge of the table. The two somewhat unusual individuals then throw the empty sack on the floor, the woman begins to dig wax from her ear, and the man walks over to a potted palm to urinate. Shortly afterward, they start to leave the restaurant, belching loudly as they pass the other tables. When the cashier requests that they pay for the champagne, they begin beating her about the head and face while shouting obscenities. Just in time, a policeman runs in the door, politely reminds them of their constitutional rights, and then orders them up against the wall. Instead, they dash out the door and disappear into the night.

Would such behavior be at all upsetting to you? Would you do what they did? The nude diners violated a series of norms which most of us would find very difficult to break, and those who witness such behavior tend to react with surprise, outrage, and even fright. Though there is a range of freedom permitted by society, we know that we are expected to wear clothes in public, leave our brown bag lunches at home when we dine out, avoid expressing certain words to strangers in a public place, respect the property of others, eat with silverware, cook our meat, drink champagne from a glass, eliminate bodily wastes in private, pay for what we order, and refrain from physically attacking cashiers. Society hangs together in part because most of us tend to follow such formal and informal rules. We normally conform to social pressure with respect to what we do and how we look, we comply with reasonable requests, and we obey the law. That is, we respond to social influence in many respects, and we normally expect others to do the same thing. Social influence is generally so powerful that we seldom if ever come in contact with anyone as deviant as our imaginary nude couple. What precisely constitutes this type of influence?

Social influence occurs whenever our behavior, feelings, or attitudes are altered by what others say or do. Such influence can be open or hidden, conscious or unconscious, formal or informal. The effect, however, is to enforce the rules of the game and to maintain the established *social norms*—those behaviors that define what is appropriate and acceptable within each group.

In a large, complex society such as ours, however, there are many groups with somewhat different norms. There are some norms which almost all of us follow, but substantial numbers of people can be found who are different from ourselves in clothing and hairstyles, in sexual orientation, in beliefs about drugs, in respect for the law, in political behavior, and in many other ways besides. One outcome of such diversity is strong pressure to get others to behave and believe and feel as we do. In the novel, *Brave New World,* Aldous Huxley (1932) presented a society of the future in which each class of citizens is taught to share a single norm with respect to work, entertainment, drugs, and sex. In that environment, there was no necessity for social influence except on the part of those in ultimate control who programmed everyone from the time of conception. In our world, however, there are no officially established controllers and consequently there is intense frustration if we are not successful in bringing social influence to bear. Some individuals may embrace the philosophy of "doing your own thing," but most people really want you to "do *their* own thing." The intensity of the feelings aroused by those who march to the sound of different norms is suggested by the following letter to the *Indianapolis Star* from a pastor who expresses concern about variations in the appearance of others:

> When you see one young man who wears clean, neat clothes with a tie and has closely cropped hair and is clean shaven and then you look at another young man with a scraggly beard, long hair, pants with ragged edges and maybe an old sweat shirt, you can certainly arrive at one quick decision. There's a world of difference in those two young men. If you were an employer, there isn't any doubt as to which you would hire even if their abilities were the same. Even if their clothes were the same, the young man with the normal, standard haircut would have an immense advantage over the one with the hippie style uncut hair. And this could be so for several reasons. First, real men, like soldiers and working men throughout history, have kept their hair cut short. The Bible indicates (I Corinthians 11:14–15) that even nature teaches that it is a shame for a man to have long hair, because long hair is the glory of women. Don't be fooled for a minute by the sissy effeminate and false pictures of Jesus. He was a rugged carpenter and outdoorsman. . . .
>
> —Robert Lee Shotts

In the present chapter, we will discuss three major types of social influence. **Conformity** involves the way in which we are influenced by others in that their behavior establishes an expectation as to the social norms of the group; there is the general unspoken assumption that behavior like that of others is more acceptable than behavior which is different. **Compliance** involves a response to direct attempts to influence someone by means of requests that he or she behave in a particular way. Approval for compliance and disapproval for noncompliance are much more explicit than in the case of conformity. Finally, studies of **obedience** deal with the effects of direct commands; approval for obedience and disapproval for disobedience are very explicit. Each type of social influence will be considered with respect to the variables that determine the extent to which behavior is actually affected, theoretical explanations of each process, and individual differences in response to attempts to influence behavior.

CONFORMITY

In many situations, especially ones that are somewhat ambiguous, the most common response is to let our behavior match that of others—to conform. Have you ever been in a clothing store, been undecided and uncertain about whether to buy something unusual, and then selected the same type of apparel that your companions wear? When several other individuals are doing or saying the same thing, there is a very strong tendency to follow their example and to do as they do. It is as though there were an unwritten law against acting in a way that is deviant from the group.

Each of us tends to conform to the prevailing norms of a particular group with which we identify. When individuals from quite different groups come in contact with one another, there sometimes are negative feelings and problems in communicating.

Early Research on Conformity:
The Power of the Group

Sherif and the Autokinetic Phenomenon. After social norms are established and operating, we can only speculate about the origins of the diverse customs and practices that have developed. Even when we happen to see a new phenomenon introduced into the culture, it is difficult to perceive just how each new pattern of behavior develops. For example, people tend to sit quietly in their seats to watch television, movies, plays, and symphony orchestras—how did it happen that very different normative behavior developed for those attending rock concerts? To take a different example, no one ever passes a cigarette around after taking a puff (except to a dying buddy in old war movies), but such sharing is expected of those smoking grass—why? It is obvious that definite interpersonal norms develop, but we are unable to reconstruct the process.

A method to study the development of such norms was first devised by Muzafer Sherif, utilizing a perceptual illusion. When a person is placed in a completely dark room and is exposed to a single, stationary point of light, he or she cannot determine precisely where the light is located in space. There are no cues to size or distance. The typical subject in such a situation perceives the light as moving about, even though it is actually not moving at all. This perceived activity is called *autokinetic* movement.

Sherif (1937) decided that the **autokinetic phenomenon** might provide a useful technique to observe the creation of a social norm and the operation of social influence. Previous research had indicated that an individual who is exposed to the light on a series of trials will gradually settle on a particular range within which it is seen as moving. Also, different subjects develop different specific ranges. When several individuals are placed in this setting, and each person is asked to report about what the light is doing, the group establishes its own range, and each individual tends to report that the light moves within that range. When the same individuals later are in the experimental room alone, they continue to respond to the norm established by the group. Faced with this ambiguous situation, each person's perceptions clearly are influenced by what others say they perceive.

In a series of investigations, this type of social influence was manipulated in various ways. For example, it was found that the experimenter or a confederate could control the extent of perceived movement by making specific suggestions to the subject about the pattern of movement supposedly seen. The experimenter might say that the light seemed to him to move in a wide arc, and then the subject would be very likely to report seeing just such an arc. Those taking part in these experiments were usually not aware of the way their responses could be influenced by others, and they sometimes became angry when informed about what actually happened. Such studies are still being conducted (Pollis, Montgomery, and Smith, 1975), and they continue to provide knowledge about the way in which norms are established and how they can easily be influenced in a given direction.

On the basis of such research, it appears that in an unfamiliar social setting an individual or, even more so, a group of individuals would be able to direct the development of some type of normative behavior simply by engaging in it. It seems likely that the crucial variables would include the prestige of the norm setters within the total group, the ambiguity of the situation, and the degree to which the normative behavior itself was within an acceptable range. It is interesting to note that males who violate norms tend to have more influence over the behavior of others than females who violate norms (Wahrman and Pugh, 1974). Both males and females who act in a nonconforming way tend to be disliked, but individuals nevertheless let themselves be influenced by what the male does. You might try to remember just how and when you decided to buy the type of clothes you now have on, to style your hair in the way you do, or to interact with the opposite sex as you do. Can you identify any social influences that affected your present behavior?

Weick and Gilfillan (1971) devised a way to study norms that did not use the autokinetic phenomenon. The idea was to create a normative tradition in a laboratory setting and then to determine what happens to that norm across "generations." In the first stage, the experimenters instructed three-man groups with respect to a target game. One "culture" (six different groups) was given an arbitrary and relatively easy strategy for playing the game. A second "culture" (six additional groups) was given another, more difficult strategy. Thus, two different normative behaviors were established. When the game was over in each group, one of the three subjects was excused, and a new one took his place. The new subject was not given instructions about the strategy but had to pick it up from his experienced teammates as the game progressed, much as a child learns the norms of the culture. This process of substituting a new member after each game was continued for eleven "generations" and the game-playing behavior was observed. The group with the easy strategy passed it along through eleven generations. Even though members of the later groups had never been instructed in that strategy, the norm persisted. Those with the difficult strategy, on the other hand, abandoned it by the fourth generation and developed a variety of easier methods across the successive generations. This procedure provides an intriguing way to study the manner in which some normative traditions persist while others tend to "fall by the wayside."

Asch and Group Pressure. You are with a group of friends in the student union and someone happens to mention an exam he took that asked about the vice-presidential candidates in the 1968 election. After some discussion, the group decides that the right answer was Sargent Shriver and Sprio Agnew. You remember that Humphrey's running mate was Ed Muskie, but five people have just agreed otherwise. What do you do? Do you argue with them and try to convince them you are right? Do you politely acquiesce to the group decision even though you privately keep your own opinion? Do you change your mind and decide that maybe they are correct after all?

In a series of experiments begun in the early 1950's, Solomon Asch (1951) studied the way in which an individual reacts when confronted by a group that unanimously and incorrectly agrees on a particular judgment. He chose to have the judgment involve a factual matter, and the situation was arranged so that each person's judgments were stated publicly. Asch (1956, p. 2) pointed out the importance of the problem as follows, "Granting the great power of groups, may we simply conclude that they can induce persons to shift their decisions and convictions in almost any desired direction, that they can prompt us to call true what we yesterday deemed false, that they can make us invest the identical action with the aura of rightness or with the stigma of grotesqueness and malice?" Unfortunately, within limits, the answer to his question seems to be "yes."

Asch's initial experiment illustrates the general pattern that has since been adopted frequently in the study of conformity. A group of seven to nine students gathered in a classroom to take part in what was described as a study of visual discrimination. Their task was to match the length of a standard line with one of three comparison lines; eighteen such comparisons were made. In each instance, one comparison line was the same length as the standard, while two were different, as shown in the sample in Figure 6-1. Actually, these experimental groups contained only one real subject. All the others were confederates who had been instructed by the experimenter to give an agreed upon incorrect response on twelve of the trials and a correct response on the other six. As shown in Figure 6-2, the seating arrangement was such that all but one of the confederates were asked to respond before it was the real subject's turn. The confederates did not act surprised or angry when the subject disagreed with them; instead, they just continued to give their incorrect judgments impersonally and unemotionally. There was also a control group which made the same perceptual judgments but without confederates present giving the wrong answers.

The results indicated the powerful effect of an incorrect majority on the responses of an individual. In the control group, 95 percent did not make any errors in matching the lines. In the experimental group, 76 percent made at least one error by going along with the group. Interestingly, most subjects were aware of the discrepancy between themselves and the group. Many said that they felt puzzled and tried to explain to themselves what might be happening. "I thought they were measuring width after a while." "Thought there was some trick to it—optical illusion." After several trials had been run, they began to have doubts about themselves with respect to eyesight, judgment, understanding of the instructions, or even their mental functioning. Surprisingly, those subjects who did not conform also expressed doubts about themselves, but such individuals eventually decided that the group must have a problem rather than themselves. "Gee, I feel like Columbus—I feel the others were wrong. I wondered how they could possibly see something different from what I saw."

In another experiment, Asch (1956) asked subjects to make their judgments privately by writing down their answers rather than publicly stating each one. Under these conditions, much less conformity occurred. Thus, when speaking of conformity, it is useful to make a distinction between *public compliance* and *private acceptance* (Kiesler and Kiesler, 1969). Public compliance refers to a skeptical person who simply behaves like those in the group in order not to be conspicuous, while private acceptance refers to the person who actually changes and becomes like those in the group.

The social influence exerted by a group on an individual has been characterized by Deutsch and Gerard (1955) as consisting of two components. They suggest that there is **normative social influence** which induces us to conform to the positive expectations of others. In addition, there is **informational social influence** which induces us to conform because we are seeking evidence about reality. Subjects in the Sherif and Asch experiments are probably responding primarily to informational social influence in that they want to carry out the task correctly and are seeking cues from others as to what should be done. In many

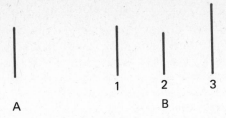

FIGURE 6-1. *In the perceptual-judgment task devised by Solomon Asch, the subjects were asked to decide which of the comparison lines (B) was the same length as the standard line (A). How would you respond if six fellow students said that comparison line 2 was the correct answer?*

social situations, conformity is more likely to involve normative social influence in that we usually are striving to be liked and to do what others expect of us. Much of the time, we are probably affected by both types of social influence.

The Crutchfield Apparatus. One feature of the Asch procedure makes it somewhat inconvenient to use in research—every time a subject participates in a conformity experiment, a small troupe of confederates must be present to play their parts. Besides the time and effort involved, there is the very real possibility of differences in the quality of their performance from subject to subject and from experiment to experiment. It would obviously be preferable if the conformity task did not depend on the consistent acting skills of confederates.

A few years after Asch's first experiment was published, Richard Crutchfield designed what is now called the **Crutchfield apparatus** in which five subjects

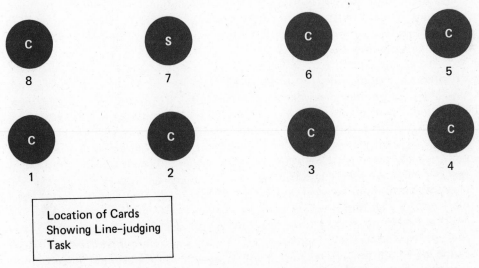

Location of Cards
Showing Line-judging
Task

FIGURE 6-2. *Seating arrangement of the confederates (C) and the subject (S) in the Asch conformity experiment. Numbers refer to the order in which each individual responded on each trial of the perceptual-judgment task.*

could participate simultaneously and in which conformity pressures could be created without having to use any confederates. Five subjects sit side by side, separated by partitions, each individual facing an electrical panel. They are informed that the responses of each person are displayed on all five panels. Actually, the information that is presented is controlled entirely by the experimenter. The judgments that each subject is asked to make can involve almost anything, from length of lines to attitudes and opinions. The order of responding varies, but it is arranged that every subject is the last to respond on one-fifth of the trials; at that time he or she receives false information about how the other four people responded, thus creating the conditions for conformity pressures.

Using this apparatus, Crutchfield (1955) found that substantial proportions of those taking part in such an experiment responded so as to conform to what seemed to be the majority opinion on almost all types of judgment. For example, when they were asked to judge the relative size of two identical circles, 79 percent agreed with "the group" on an arbitrary and incorrect answer. Though Crutchfield found that his subjects resisted conformity pressure with respect to personal artistic preferences, later research has shown that even this type of response can be influenced by group pressure (Allen and Levine, 1971).

Factors Affecting Conformity

Once it had been convincingly demonstrated that a group can exert powerful pressure, many investigators began to examine the details of the conformity process. It was important to determine the conditions under which conformity is most likely and least likely to occur. For example, it is usually found that the larger the group, the greater the tendency of the individual to conform (Gerard, Wilhelmy, and Conolley, 1968). At the theoretical level, the question was, "Why do people conform at all?" We will examine some of the research that has dealt with such issues.

Reinforcement and Conformity. As with any other behavior, conformity varies as a function of rewards and punishments. For example, if other people like you better when you conform to their beliefs and judgments, such reinforcement makes you more likely to conform in future situations.

In one experiment (Endler, 1965), subjects were reinforced by the experimenter when they agreed with the incorrect group, and conformity was found to increase. On the other hand, when the reinforcement was given for resisting group pressure and disagreeing, conformity decreased. In addition, it has been found that conformity is greater when subjects are reinforced every time they agree with the group than when they are reinforced only half the time (Endler, 1966). Since conformity increases and decreases as a function of reinforcement and since there is generally a strong tendency for experimental subjects to conform, it follows that in real life people must usually be rewarded when they conform. Common observation suggests that people treat you nicely when you do so. As we saw in Chapter 5, studies of attraction consistently indicate that there is a positive response to others who are similar. From the viewpoint of the individuals exerting pressure, the person who conforms is simply agreeing—and most everyone likes those who agree.

Self-esteem, Competence, and Conformity. It must be kept in mind that some people do *not* conform. This suggests that some people have been rewarded for conforming while others have been rewarded for acting independently. One personality characteristic which is related to such differences is *self-esteem.* That is, the individual high in self-esteem is relatively sure of himself and independent; such a person is not as responsible to normative social influence. The low self-esteem individual, in contrast, seeks support from others and tries to please them. To test this idea, Stang (1972) measured the self-esteem of a group of subjects and predicted that those with the highest self-esteem would conform the least. The task was a series of visual judgments, presented on the Crutchfield apparatus. As expected, the higher the individual's self-esteem, the less the tendency to conform. In a similar way, those who feel very competent at a particular task are unlikely to conform to the group because, for them, informational social influence is relatively weak (Wiesenthal et al., 1976).

When an individual is made to believe that he or she is unusual or deviant, feelings of self-esteem or competence tend to decrease. Similarly, when someone is embarrassed or uncomfortable, there is less confidence in making decisions or judgments. An experiment by Duval (1976) could be interpreted as demonstrating the effect of such variables on conformity, even though the experimenter was working within a different conceptual framework (the theory of objective self-awareness which we discussed in Chapter 2). Subjects were told that their responses on ten attitudinal dimensions were like those of 95 percent, 50 percent, or 5 percent of a normative group of 10,000 individuals. Afterward, they took part in a conformity experiment during which half of the subjects were exposed to the live image of themselves on a television monitor. Both the possession of supposedly unusual attitudes and the presence of the TV monitor increased conformity. It seems possible that embarrassment and/or lowered self-esteem could account for their conforming behavior.

It is interesting to note that the experience of being deviant in a conformity experiment can lead an individual to be more conforming in a subsequent experiment. Darley et al. (1974) conducted such a two-part experiment and found that individuals who were given the experience of deviating from the majority on one task then tended to conform on a second task. Even if they did not conform the first time, they were more likely to conform afterward than were control subjects, which suggests that the nonconforming individual can be affected by the experience of being different from the group.

Ingratiation: Agreement with Others as a Social-influence Technique. One way to think about conformity is to consider it as a technique that can be used to try to induce others to like you. From this perspective, people who conform are simply trying to be **ingratiating** and hence popular (Jones, 1964). If someone wants to please a prospective employer, customer, date, or teacher, it is probably wise to agree with that person's opinions. If a boy wants a girl's parents to approve of him, he may try to dress in a way and behave in a way that conforms to their view of what is acceptable. Undoubtedly, many beards have been shaved, many haircuts endured, and many faded bluejeans set aside in the hope of getting a job, impressing a jury, or getting on the good side of a rich relative. Even elementary school children express the idea that tests and term papers will receive higher grades if the content expresses ideas with which the teacher agrees. A college student recently turned in all her assignments to one of the authors in brown folders because she had decided that was a color he liked. Thus, normative social influence operates in many situations.

Jones (1965) points out that such ingratiation also has a negative meaning to most of us. Negative terms such as "apple polishing" and "brown nosing" are applied to blatantly obvious efforts to be ingratiating. When agreement is perceived as insincere, the usual positive effect may be reversed. No one likes the idea of being told lies by someone trying to win him over. The character of Eddie Haskel on the old "Leave It to Beaver" television show was depicted as someone who behaved in a nauseatingly and falsely positive manner to adults only so long as they were in earshot. For conformity and ingratiation to be effective, the target person must be convinced that agreement is based on honesty. For this reason, conformity can be a tricky procedure for winning friends and influencing people. "In order to be successful, the ingratiator must complicate his tactics and inject some subtlety. One obvious way to increase subtlety is to convey the impression of agreeing in a discerning way" (Jones, 1965, p. 145). For example, agreement about something very important might be more believable if it occurred right after disagreement about something trivial. In other words, to be ingratiating, agree with the other person about God and communism after you firmly stand up for your true opinion about applesauce.

In one experiment dealing with these processes (Jones, Gergen, and Jones, 1963), the effect of status differences on ingratiation was investigated. The subjects were freshmen in a naval ROTC unit. Each subject exchanged written messages with an upperclassman in the same naval unit, expressing opinions on various issues, some relevant to the Navy, some of intermediate relevance, and some totally irrelevant. Actually, the experimenters collected the messages and substituted notes that had been prepared in advance. Among the fake notes were several very deviant opinions; conformity would be indicated if the subject's opinion shifted toward the deviant view the other person appeared to hold. Half the subjects were told that the experiment dealt with accuracy of judgment and half were told that it involved the ability to be compatible with others. As may be seen in Figure 6-3, the more relevant the topic to the relationship, the more the conformity of these low-status subjects to their high-status partners. Also, there was greater conformity when the subjects believed the experiment involved compatibility. It can be inferred that these individuals were trying to make themselves liked by conforming. Interestingly enough, when the responses of the high-status subjects were examined, there was much less conforming behavior—least of all on the topics most relevant to the Navy. We might safely

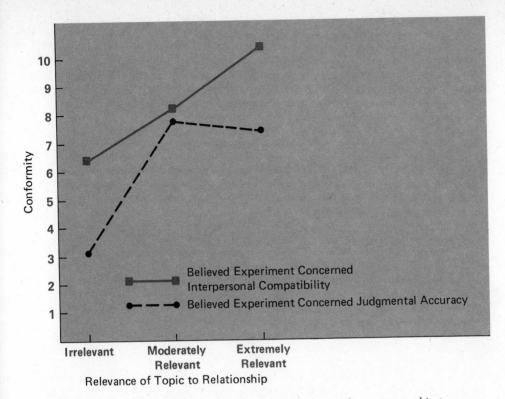

FIGURE 6-3. *Conformity can be an ingratiation tactic. Low-status subjects were more conforming to the opinions of high-status partners on issues relevant to their relationship than on irrelevant issues. In addition, conformity was greater when subjects believed the experiment dealt with interpersonal compatibility than when they believed it dealt with accuracy of judgment. (Source: Based on data from Jones, Gergen, and Jones, 1963.)*

guess that an employee would be more inclined to conform to his boss's opinions than vice versa, and that the boss would most strongly resist being influenced with respect to job-related topics.

Despite the fact that ingratiation is usually looked down upon, it is used sufficiently often that it must be effective. Why? For one thing, it is easiest to see ingratiation when it is directed at someone other than ourselves. If another person has the good sense to agree with me, he can't be all bad. In addition, flattery and positive statements are liked, even when the person receiving them knows that they are probably not true (Byrne, Rasche, and Kelley, 1974). It seems that ingratiation tactics are perceived negatively mainly by those observing them happening to someone else.

Attraction and Conformity. In conformity experiments the "group" is almost always composed of someone similar to the subject. That is, students are found to conform to other students, ROTC members to other ROTC members, and so forth. It is not reasonable, however, to expect individuals to conform to just any group of people. The minister quoted at the beginning of this chapter would most probably not find himself influenced by any group of bearded, long-haired young men wearing ragged jeans. A college student might not have much desire to conform if he found himself at a meeting of the Rotary Club. Conformity, then, tends to be toward our own *reference group*—those individuals we like and to whom we compare ourselves. Most often, an individual chooses a reference group because it is composed of people like himself or because it is composed of people he wishes to be like. Thus, each of us finds ourselves attracted to certain groups of individuals (an informal circle of friends, those in a particular fraternity or sorority, rock musicians, a street gang, professional colleagues, or whatever) and gradually become identified with that group. From then on, there is strong pressure to conform to the group's norms. All of this suggests that conformity occurs primarily when there is attraction (Sakurai, 1975).

In an early study of attraction and conformity in married-student housing units, Festinger, Schachter, and Back (1950) found that a couple's conformity to the norms of each living area was positively related to the number of friends they had within that area. Mere exposure to the group did not lead to conformity unless the students' social life was also centered there. Though we all conform to our reference groups to some degree, it is also true according to reactance theory (see Chapter 2) that we want to believe that we are free. For this reason, strong and obvious conformity pressures from those we like can have precisely the opposite effect, because individuals react against the perceived loss of freedom and assert their independence (Brehm and Mann, 1975). Have you ever had friends or relatives TELL YOU just how to dress or how to behave? If so, you may have experienced reactance and then asserted your independence. Less obvious pressure, however, leads to conformity. Kiesler (1963) has pointed out that conformity may occur if an individual is strongly attracted to a group even if the group is scarcely aware of his existence. For example, those who aspire to move upward in society often adhere to the moral values, customs, and lifestyles of those with higher socioeconomic status despite being unknown to those they try to resemble.

Several well-known early social psychological studies dealt with the power of reference groups to influence individuals. For example, Newcomb (1943) studied the way in which attitudes at Bennington College were altered by group influence. Students from relatively conservative families became increasingly liberal each year they were in school. It seems that the underclassmen tended to conform to the opinions of the most popular upperclassmen, and these in-group leaders were relatively liberal in their views. Some may think that college students *always* become more liberal over their four undergraduate years, but that is not the case. Students at Stanford University who moved into dormitories containing relatively conservative residents were found to become more conservative over time (Siegal and Siegal, 1957). Interestingly enough, these ideological changes that occur in college have been found to persist a quarter of a century later as indicated by follow-up studies (Newcomb et al., 1967).

If attraction toward a group affects conformity, it follows that attraction toward an individual would work the same way. It is found that a person is more likely to conform to the judgments of someone who has been agreeing with him or her than to someone who has been disagreeing (Savell, 1971). It is also found that after an individual has experienced agreement, conformity increases toward other people as well. It is possible that attraction generalizes to others and that those who experience positive feelings are more likely to conform than those whose feelings are negative (Macaranas and Savell, 1973).

Why Do We Conform?

Conformity tends to be perceived as an undesirable activity in which other people engage more than we ourselves. When students simply observe a conformity experiment, they predict that the subjects will be more conforming than they actually are, but predict that they themselves will be less conforming than is actually the case (Wolosin, Sherman, and Cann, 1975). Despite such misperceptions, we and they *do* conform. Why?

Social Comparison. In 1954, Leon Festinger proposed a **social comparison theory** that is helpful in explaining conformity as well as several other aspects of social behavior. He assumes that there is a basic drive within each of us to evaluate our own opinions and abilities. It is sometimes dangerous, and always embarrassing, to be incorrect and to misperceive what is going on around us. Have you ever thought you were good at some game or sport and then performed miserably? Have you ever confidently announced the answer to a question on a TV quiz show and been ridiculously wrong? Have you ever greeted a stranger warmly only to find out the person just looked like someone you know? It hurts to be caught in public mistakes. In an attempt to avoid such social disasters, we constantly seek relevant evidence. Thus, Festinger stresses informational social influence. For some things, the evidence is directly available in our contacts with the physical world. If you are not sure whether today is Thursday, you look at the morning newspaper for verification. If you are not sure whether you are able to do fifteen push-ups, you can get down on the floor all by yourself and find out. For most of our opinions, perceptions, and abilities, however, there is no objective, nonsocial way to evaluate oneself. All we can do is turn to other people. If you are not sure of whether Heaven and Hell exist, you find out what others say or what they have written. If you are not sure about how well you sing, you ask others to listen and give you feedback. Because we must depend a great deal on how others respond, this **social reality** becomes as important as, and sometimes more important than, **physical reality.** When people are confronted by ever-changing norms in a complex society, they turn to those around them to help determine how to respond.

We all want to do the "right" thing, and the group informs us as to what this means. Once a person is part of a group, any deviancy or discrepancy is threatening, in part because it raises doubts about how correct the group may be in making sense out of the world. For this reason, the group seeks to alter anyone who is deviant, and, if that fails, to reject him or her. In a classic study of the way in which groups respond to deviancy, Schachter (1951) created a series of small groups in which three confederates participated as if they were ordinary subjects. Each group was given a problem to discuss and to resolve. Group members each gave their opinions; then one of the confederates agreed with the majority while the other two deviated from the group. It was found that group members, especially when they were highly cohesive, first would exert pressure to try to get a deviant to change his mind. If such social pressure was not effective, the deviant was then rejected. Phrases such as "shape up or ship out" reflect just this process. Thus, the group tries to impose conformity in order to maintain a sense of reality. From the point of view of the deviant, he is motivated to conform both because the group may be correct and because he does not want to be rejected. When change is possible (as with opinions, judgments, or clothing styles), conformity is very likely to occur. When it is not possible to change (as with physical appearance, intelligence, or athletic ability), the person tends to seek a new reference group similar to himself.

Attribution and Conformity. Another approach to understanding the conformity situation has been offered by Ross, Bierbrauer, and Hoffman (1976). They point out that the subject in an Asch experiment is confronted by a very puzzling situation in which the correct answer is a matter of objective reality and yet a group of fellow subjects agrees in giving what seems to be an incorrect answer. This conflict between what the subject perceives and what a peer group apparently perceives creates uncertainty and very uncomfortable feelings. What does a subject think in that baffling situation and how does he explain it to himself? If he disagrees with them he runs the risk of appearing stupid, incompetent, or crazy *and* he is implicitly challenging the group's intelligence, competency, or sanity. The safe thing to do, therefore, is to conform.

In real-life situations, when we disagree with others we tend to make attributions about their motives. We see that different payoffs are involved, and this can explain what others do and what they believe. The man convicted of murder is against the death penalty because he fears losing his life. The general favors an increase in defense spending because such expenditures enhance his position and power. The cigarette smoker has doubts about the evidence linking cancer with smoking because she does not wish to consider her health as being in danger. Ross, Bierbrauer, and Hoffman (1976) reasoned that if such attributions could be made in an experimental situation, conformity would decrease. That is, the subject would be able to *explain away* the responses made by others.

In still other real-life situations of disagreement, the payoffs may be the same for ourselves and others, but disagreement occurs because different priorities are assigned. For example, few of us are in favor of organized crime, but some would be willing to tap the telephones of all suspected criminals and others would not. That is, some of us would give a high priority to stopping crime while others would place a higher priority on protecting individuals against the invasion of privacy.

To compare the way in which these different situations affect conformity, an experiment was designed in which some subjects were in a typical Asch experiment in which there was no reasonable explanation for the responses of the other individuals. Other subjects were in a condition in which the group members were told that extra points would be given to some subjects (the confederates) for particular responses—thus providing an explanation for why they might respond as they did. Still other subjects were given instructions that emphasized different priorities (taking a risk for extra points versus playing it safe). As expected, conformity was greater in the regular Asch situation than in the other two conditions. When it was possible to attribute the responses of others to differing payoffs or differing priorities, there was less tendency to be influenced by their behavior. In general, then, it was proposed that conformity pressures are greatest when the individual can find no rational explanation for why the judgments of others differ from his own.

The Value of Independence. It has been proposed that the more important the topic in question, the stronger is the tendency within the group to seek uniformity and to reject those who deviate. The cartoon in Figure 6-4 indicates

"And now apparently we have to listen to some sort of dissent."

FIGURE 6-4. *Within most groups, dissent is not really welcomed, and it is often very difficult to behave in an independent manner. (Source: Drawing by Handelsman; © 1975 The New Yorker Magazine, Inc.)*

TABLE 6-1. *Hollander (1975) has suggested six barriers to independent behavior. Conformity and lack of independence clearly represent safety and the avoidance of risks. Unless there is encouragement of independent behavior, however, a society loses its freedom and its ability to change, to be innovative, and to improve.*

Barriers to Independent Behavior	The Way the Barriers Work
Risk of Disapproval	People want to be liked and accepted, and, too often, deviation from the group leads to dislike and rejection.
Lack of Perceived Alternatives	Unless someone speaks out and offers alternatives, most individuals feel they have no choices—"What can I do?"
Fear of Disruption	In order to "get things done," it usually seems wise to stick to old, successful procedures from the past and not "rock the boat."
Absence of Communication	Without publicly expressed independence of ideas, each individual may privately dissent but nevertheless act like the citizens who did not risk embarrassment by saying anything about the naked Emperor's "new clothes."
No Feeling of Responsibility	With respect to much that goes on, many of us seem to agree with Chico—"That's not my job, man." If an individual does not feel responsible, why should he stick his neck out?
Sense of Powerlessness	If the prevailing feeling is that nothing can be done, that no one is listening, that no one cares, the resulting apathy leads to a self-fulfilling prophecy—and nothing *is* done.

the unpleasant response that dissent may evoke. As President Kennedy (1956) was told when he first was elected to Congress, "To get along, go along." At its worst extreme, this tendency is expressed in a totalitarian state which seeks to control the appearance, the behavior, and even the thoughts of its citizens. But, as Hollander (1975) points out, a free society with a free exchange of ideas is ideal for producing anything new and creative. Freedom and diversity may be upsetting at times, but that is the price we pay to avoid stagnation. Hollander notes that research on conformity has seldom stressed the value of independence and the difficulties involved in acting in an independent manner. Independence does not imply simply nonconformity or always opposing the group, but rather the freedom to be different.

As summarized in Table 6-1, there are six major hurdles to independent behavior: risk of disapproval, lack of perceived alternatives, fear of disruption, absence of communication, no feeling of responsibility, and the sense of powerlessness. Though it is difficult to create a general climate in which independence is encouraged, or even tolerated, Hollander proposes that we direct more research toward this goal and that those who act independently be rewarded for such behavior. It is important that they serve as models for others. It is interesting to note that from the viewpoint of outside observers, those who dissent are described in more positive terms (dynamic, confident, alert) than those who go along with the incorrect majority (Morris and Miller, 1975b). Perhaps there would be more support for independent behavior than most of us ordinarily expect.

EXPERIENCING CONFORMITY PRESSURES

In conformity research, one of the observations commonly made is that the subjects feel uncomfortable, puzzled, and anxious as they find themselves in disagreement with the majority position. Keep in mind that the "group" in such studies either consists of confederates who do nothing to challenge the subject's position or of blinking lights which record how others are supposedly responding. In real life, the pressures are much more severe because other people may ridicule the person who dissents, argue with him or her, and even become belligerent. It seems probable that the expression of independent judgments is more difficult outside the laboratory than within.

If you would like to examine such reactions at first hand, the following demonstration will provide you with a relatively mild sample of how conformity pressures operate. You can be the subject. Ask four of your friends if they would be willing to help you with a brief course assignment involving group decisions. When the group has gathered, explain that you have a series of factual questions that the five of you are supposed to answer. Say that the group is expected to reach some kind of consensus and that you are supposed to observe the process by which each person arrives at an answer. Prepare a series of questions which most people would be able to answer, but not something that is too obviously simple. For example, name the

two U. S. Senators from your state, the president of your university, the automobile manufacturer who produces the Cordoba, the names of two movies made by the Beatles, the name of Steve Canyon's wife, and so forth. After playing it straight for the first two questions, on the third one let your friends answer first and then you supply an incorrect, though plausible, answer. (If they don't agree on the correct answer, wait until the next question before you dissent.)

Your task is to determine how the other individuals react to your nonconforming answer. What do they say? Do they try to convince you to change your mind? Even though you set up the situation yourself and know that it is make believe, how do you feel about their comments toward you? What would your feelings be if this were a genuine situation, and they were responding to what you said about your political values or your religious beliefs? Can you appreciate how difficult it usually is to resist such pressures?

After you have made your observations, explain to your friends what you were doing and why. You might tell them something about the conformity studies described in this chapter. Finally, it is important for each of you to consider the difference between a factual disagreement in an experimental setting and an opinion disagreement in a genuine interaction. Do you think that independence is difficult to achieve or relatively easy?

Social Support as a Deterrent to Conformity: I Can Resist with a Little Help from My Friends. We have suggested that people conform when they are faced with a unanimous majority both because they doubt their own opinions and because they fear rejection by the group. The information provided by other people is uniform, and it may be accepted as social reality. What happens, though, when the majority is not uniform? What if at least one other person in the group differs from the majority and hence provides support for the subject's perception? It seems reasonable to expect that conformity would be reduced because of such social support, and research confirms that expectation (Allen and Levine, 1969).

An interesting question is whether the timing of the support makes a difference. When a majority is against an individual, would that person feel greater support if he learned of an ally right at the beginning or only later after the majority had spoken up? Morris and Miller (1975a) hypothesized that finding an ally at the end would provide the most support, because such a person would break up the consensus and demonstrate that other opinions were possible. By conducting an experiment to test this proposal, they discovered that the opposite is true. In groups of five in the Crutchfield apparatus, subjects made perceptual judgments about the number of dots presented briefly on photographic slides. On six critical trials on which the subject responded last, he was confronted by a majority who gave the incorrect answer. Three conditions were compared: all four of the others were incorrect, or the subject was given one dissenting group member who either responded before the incorrect three or after them. You can see in Figure 6-5 that conformity on the critical trials was greatest when there was total agreement among the other four group members, and that social support from one other person reduced conformity. Contrary to their original expectations, the least conformity occurred when the "deviant" partner responded first. It was suggested that initial support is effective because it provides immediate validation of the subject's first impression before there is time for any doubts to set in.

The quality of social support also seems to be a factor. If you were in a history class and found yourself all alone against everyone in the room in arguing about a given issue, it would strengthen your position if at least one of them agreed with you. But what if your lone support came from the dumbest person in class? It seems plausible that this individual's agreement would be less comforting than having a fairly intelligent person agree with you. Allen and Levine (1971) assumed that a supporter reduces the tendency to conform only to the extent that he provides an independent evaluation of reality. They hypothesized that a supporter who could not provide a valid evaluation would be less effective in reducing conformity than would an able supporter. To test this idea, they used a visual-perception task with an incorrect majority of three. A supporter responded in the fourth position, and the subject was fifth. Before the experiment began, the subject met the person who was to be his supporter. In the *nonvalid* support condition, the confederate wore glasses with extremely thick lenses, indicated that he could not see except at close range, and made it obvious that he could not read an easily legible sign on the wall any better than Mister Magoo. Nevertheless, he took part in the visual task. When the confederate was a *valid* supporter, he did not wear glasses nor indicate any visual problems. In the control condition, all four members of the group were unanimous in giving an incorrect response, and there was no support for the subject. The results are shown in Figure 6-6; conformity is greatest when the subject is faced with a unanimous majority, less when there is invalid social support, and least when there is valid social support. The most interesting aspect of these findings is that even invalid social support (from a stranger who presumably could not even see the stimulus clearly) was somewhat effective in reducing conformity. As it turns out, perhaps it would be better to have the dumbest person in your history class agree with you than to have no support at all.

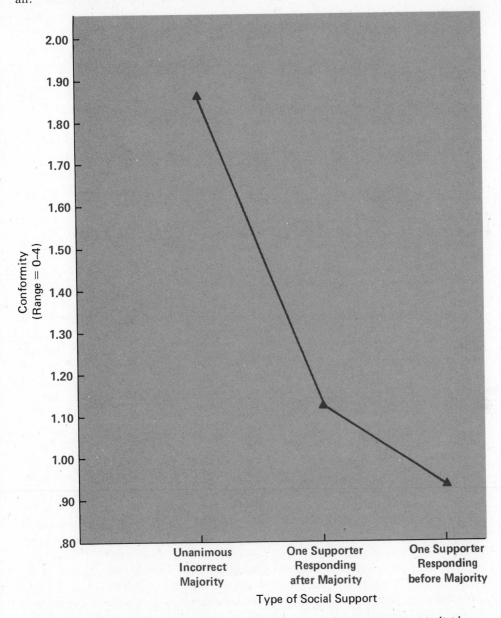

FIGURE 6-5. *When social support is provided in a conformity situation, individuals are less likely to conform to an incorrect majority. The effect of one additional dissenter is greatest, however, when that person responds before the majority rather than after. (Source: Based on data from Morris and Miller, 1975a.)*

Beginning with the very first experiments on conformity, individual differences in this behavior were observed. Attempts to relate personality variables to conforming tendencies have not been terribly successful, but the factors of

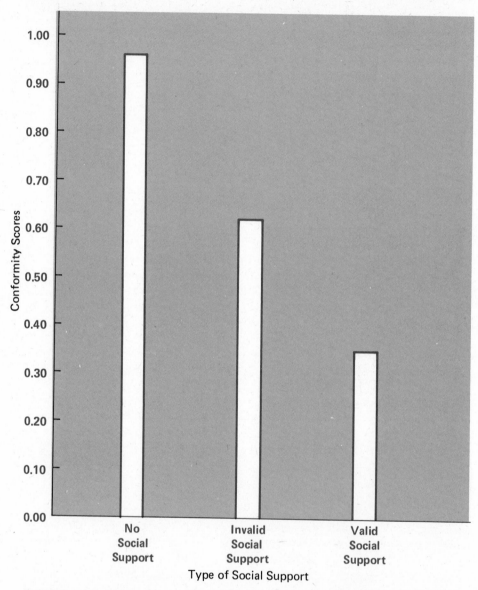

FIGURE 6-6. *Conformity is reduced by the presence of another individual who provides social support, but this reduction is less when the supporter cannot provide a valid assessment of reality than when the support is valid. (Source: Based on data from Allen and Levine, 1971.)*

chronological age and the subject's sex are frequently reported as correlates of conformity.

Age Differences. Though there have been a number of studies attempting to relate conformity and age (Hartup, 1970), the findings have not been entirely consistent. In fact, contrasting possibilities seem equally convincing. On the one hand, if conformity is learned, it should increase with age; there seems to be a progression from independent preschool children who are oblivious to what others do on up through high school students who feel that they must not deviate from their peers in dress, language, or values. On the other hand, the developmental process can be seen as one of growing independence—young children rely completely on the ideas and standards of their family, but there is a rebellion by adolescence in which each individual comes to have "a mind of his own." Probably both descriptions are correct. Whether conformity increases or decreases with age seems to depend on the specific behavior in question, the sex of the individual, and the identity of those exerting conformity pressure (Allen and Newtson, 1972).

Sex Differences and Sexism. In numerous studies with both children and adults, females have consistently been found to conform more than males. Interpretations of these results usually center on the idea that our culture traditionally has encouraged females to be docile, compliant, and submissive. When an occasional study reported no sex differences (for example, Costanzo and Shaw, 1966), the finding tended to be set aside as an unexplained exception to the general rule.

These conclusions and occasional exceptions were not accepted, however, by Sistrunk and McDavid (1971). They proposed that sex differences in conformity could be explained simply on the basis of the type of task used in the experiments. Most of the experimenters had been males, and it was possible that they had inadvertently selected tasks and opinion items which involve male-related activities rather than female-related activities. If so, what had seemed to be sex differences in "conformity" actually may have reflected only male-female differences in *familiarity* with the material to be judged and hence differences in how *confident* an individual would be of his or her correctness. To test this intriguing possibility, experiments were conducted using judgmental items more familiar to males, other items more familiar to females, or still other items equally familiar to each sex. Conformity pressure was applied by providing false information about the responses of "200 college students."

You can see in Figure 6-7 that conformity is not a matter of one's sex, but instead it depends on whether the material to be judged is sex-related. Females were more conforming on the masculine items, males were more conforming on the feminine items, and the two sexes were equally conforming on the neutral items. The authors concluded that previous generalizations about sex differences in conformity were incorrect and unfair to females. This work provides a very good example of the way in which a subtle bias such as sexism can accidentally influence research methodology and, as a result, the conclusions drawn from that research.

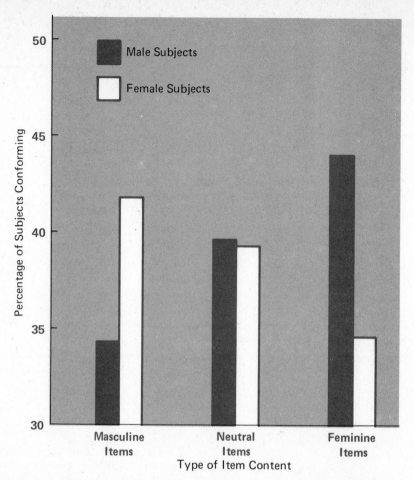

FIGURE 6-7. *Mean percentage of conformity by males and females as a function of the sex-related content of the items to be judged. Females conform more on masculine items, males conform more on feminine items, and the two sexes are equally conforming on neutral items. (Source: Based on data from Sistrunk and McDavid, 1971.)*

COMPLIANCE

As we have just seen, people tend to conform to the judgments of others even though there is no overt pressure to do so. If unspoken pressure is that effective in affecting behavior, what happens when the influence is made explicit? How do individuals respond when they are *asked* to do something?

One effect which at first seems a bit puzzling is that overt requests for compliance frequently arouse resistance. It is one thing to decide to go along with the group, seemingly of one's "own free will." It is something else to feel that another person is deliberately and obviously pressuring you to do something you may or may not wish to do. Interestingly enough, strong pressure in the form of threats is not usually as effective as promises in bringing about compliance (Heilman, 1974; Heilman and Garner, 1975). Each of us has had countless experiences in which someone tried to get us to comply. One familiar technique to obtain compliance is to suggest that a favorable response to a request is the norm—"everyone else is doing it." In one study dealing with this effect, female college students were asked to read and review some sex-education pamphlets. In the control condition, the mean number of pamphlets accepted for review was seven. When other subjects were told by the experimenter that "she was pleased that most women in the previous groups" had complied, the mean number accepted was seventeen (Schofield, 1975).

The variety of requests we receive each day is impressive. We are asked to sample a new kind of potato chip, to vote for a political candidate, to donate money to this and that charity, to fasten our seat belts, to recycle our newspapers, to rub our hands together briskly under the blower-dryer in the rest room, and to prevent forest fires. Even in one's home life, there are a multitude of requests to take out the garbage, mow the lawn, turn on the TV, pass the salt, and so on. Perhaps it is not surprising that we have learned various ways to resist at least some of these requests. From the other perspective, we also are busy asking that others comply with our requests, and we develop techniques to get others to give in to our wishes. If you want someone to do you a favor, what strategy do you use? Much of the research on compliance has dealt with the conditions under which compliance is obtained despite fairly strong tendencies to resist.

Reciprocation of Favors:
I'll Scratch Your Back—Then You Scratch Mine

Equity theory (Homans, 1961) proposes that interpersonal relationships tend to be structured in such a way that all of the participants feel that they are being treated fairly. We grow up being taught to take turns on the slide, to share the cookies equally, and to give someone a gift if they give one to us. This learned norm of behaving in an equitable fashion can sometimes be manipulated by those who want you to comply. Too often, when someone does you a favor, presumably out of the goodness of his heart, he afterwards expects you to want to reciprocate by doing *him* a favor. When a male in our society spends money entertaining a female on a date, the desire for an equitable response from her has been known to lurk in the back of his mind. At all levels of the business world, prospective clients are taken out to eat and drink in restaurants and (in some business circles) supplied with willing sexual partners (Jeffers and Levitan, 1972). There is some indication that members of the United States Congress have been involved in such activities. Even if you miss out on such fancy manipulations, you can hardly escape being the recipient of the economy version of the same technique when you get a toothpaste sample through the mail, a gift notebook from an insurance company, or a new brand of sausage on a toothpick as you walk through the supermarket. There is, of course, "no obligation" when you accept such favors. But of course, they'll get you to reciprocate if they can. After all, fair is fair.

Attraction theories can also be used to explain why it is that doing someone a favor might increase compliance. As was described in Chapter 5, a reward such as a free meal or a gift should increase attraction, and an individual should be inclined to comply with the request of a liked other. Salesmen sometimes make this connection explicit—"As a favor to you, just because I like you, tell you what I'm gonna do. . . . " Attraction does seem to increase compliance. In one experiment, attraction toward a confederate was manipulated, and then this person made a request of the subject. When the request involved a lot of time and effort (for example, return several books to the library), compliance was much greater when the confederate was liked than when she was disliked (Baron, 1971). In a related study, this time in a field setting, student experimenters approached other students and said, "Excuse me, could I borrow a dime for a long-distance phone call? It's kind of important." The person making the request was most likely to get the dime if he or she were dressed in the same style ("straight" versus "hippie") as the one being asked (Emswiller, Deaux, and Willits, 1971). Thus, compliance seems to be greatest in response to a similar, liked other.

Regan (1971) wanted to compare the equity versus attraction explanations of why favors lead to compliance, and he hypothesized that equity is more important than attraction. If another person does something nice for you, his "costs" in the relationship have increased while your "rewards" have increased. The relationship is no longer equitable, and you feel bad because the other person has been left holding the short end of the stick. You will feel much more comfortable and equity will be restored if you do him a favor to "pay him back." Undergraduates took part in an experiment that was described as one dealing with art appreciation. The subject found himself waiting with another student who was actually a confederate. In response to a telephone call, the confederate behaved either in a pleasant or an unpleasant manner to the caller in order to make himself liked or disliked by the subject. In the unpleasant condition he said, "Look, I don't work here, lady, for chrissake . . . Just call later . . . ," as he hung up in the middle of the conversation. In the pleasant condition he responded to the caller in a friendly, polite manner. The experimenter then appeared, and the subject and confederate rated several paintings. During a "pause in the experiment," the confederate either did a favor for the subject (brought him a soft drink) or did nothing. In still another condition, the experimenter performed the favor by bringing cokes. Later on, the confederate made a request. He asked the subject to buy raffle tickets to help his home town high school build a new gym (and to help him win a prize for selling the most tickets). The number of tickets bought was the measure of compliance.

The results are shown in Figure 6-8. Subjects were most likely to comply with the request to buy raffle tickets if the confederate had earlier performed a favor. There was also a tendency for the liked confederate to obtain more compliance than the unliked one. In this situation, then, both the attraction

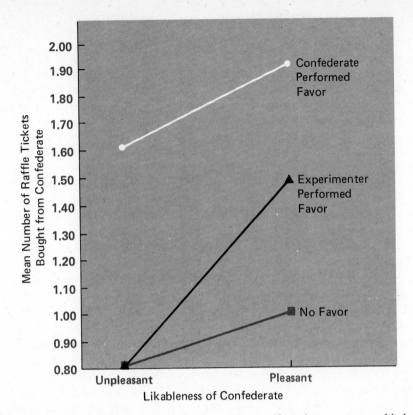

FIGURE 6-8. *Compliance with a request to buy raffle tickets was most likely to occur if the one making the request had performed a favor. Presumably, subjects felt that compliance to the request of such a person was equitable. Attraction and positive feelings also affected compliance in that more raffle tickets were bought from a pleasant confederate than from an unpleasant one. (Source: Based on data from Regan, 1971.)*

hypothesis and the equity hypothesis received support. When the experimenter performed the favor, compliance to a liked confederate also increased, presumably because of increased positive affect. Doing a favor clearly had the greatest effect, and it appears that compliance is strongly increased when an individual feels obligated to the one who makes a request. When you want someone to comply with your request, you might remember that a prior favor on your part will increase your chances of success. When you want to resist the requests of others, however, beware of a potential social influencer bearing gifts.

Making Multiple Requests: The Old One-Two Punch

A familiar and practical technique for getting a person to comply with a large request is to get him first to comply with a very small and simple request.

Salesmen have long utilized this technique. The trick is to "get your foot in the door" by persuading the potential customer to do something such as answer a simple question—"I am conducting a poll and would like you to name your three favorite magazines." In a recent newspaper interview, a very successful panhandler revealed that before asking a passerby for money, he first gets the person to give him directions or to respond to some other seemingly innocent request. A more ominous use of such techniques was reported by Schein, Schneier, and Barker (1961), who studied the way brainwashing was accomplished during the Korean War. The interrogator would first talk prisoners into signing noncontroversial documents or to agree about something that was obviously true; at that point, it proved easier to get compliance with a request to sign a damaging confession or an anti-American statement. Such accounts suggest, then, that compliance with a large request should be more likely following compliance with a small request.

Small Request First, Large Request Second: The Foot-in-the-door Technique. Freedman and Fraser (1966) designed a field study to determine the effectiveness of the **foot-in-the-door technique.** First, housewives were contacted by telephone and a small request was made—they were asked to answer a few questions about the soap they used. Three days later, a large request was made of these same individuals; each housewife was asked to permit a survey team to come into her home for two hours to classify the household products she used. Of those who were willing to answer the simple question about soap, over half (52.8 percent) later complied with the large request. Among other housewives who had not been the target of the foot-in-the-door (or mouth-in-the-telephone) technique, less than a fourth (22.2 percent) agreed to the large request.

In a follow-up study, the same experimenters wanted to determine whether a small initial request would increase compliance as a function of whether it was similar to the later large request or different. The large request this time was that homeowners install a gigantic sign on their front lawns which read "DRIVE CAREFULLY." Only 16.7 percent of a control group were willing to put such a sign in front of their houses. An experimental group received a preliminary small request before being asked about the sign. They were asked either to put a small sign (same type of request) or to place their signatures on a petition (different request). Similarity was also manipulated by having the issues involved in the two requests either the same (safe driving) or different (keeping California beautiful). When the issue and the type of task were the same for the two requests, 76 percent of the subjects were willing to place the large sign on their lawns. Even with a different issue and a different task, however, the foot-in-the-door technique led almost half the subjects to comply with the large request. Later research has replicated these findings (Pliner et al., 1974).

Foot-in-the-door and Self-perception: If He Complies Once, Will He Comply Again? Freedman and Fraser explained their findings on the basis of self-perception. That is, once an individual has agreed to a small request, he sees himself as someone who does that sort of thing (takes action on matters he

In order to obtain compliance with a request, it helps to make a small request first, thus getting your "foot in the door." Salesmen often use this technique by asking the prospective buyer a simple question or two before making their real sales pitch.

believes in, cooperates with good causes, etc.) and, to be consistent, must go along with the next request that is encountered. Snyder and Cunningham (1975) decided to test this explanation by inducing people to perceive themselves either as someone who does or who does not comply with requests.

In a field study, subjects were first approached with a small request that most people would not refuse (answer eight survey questions on the phone) or a large but not incredible request that most people would refuse (answer fifty survey questions on the phone). Two days later each person was called again by a different experimenter who made a moderate request that the person answer thirty survey questions. A control group was given only the thirty-question request.

The results are shown in Figure 6-9. Compliance with the moderate request was greatest when the subjects had previously complied with a small request and least when they previously refused to comply with a large request. These findings provide support for the idea that people like to be consistent in the way they perceive themselves. It seems that relatively simple procedures can determine one's self-perception as a complier or as a noncomplier.

In order for self-perception to be affected by prior compliance, the first request must be sufficiently large that the individual can clearly perceive himself or herself as having complied. Seligman, Bush, and Kirsch (1976) conducted a two-part telephone study to establish this relationship. In the first call, the person answering the phone was requested to respond to a survey consisting of 5, 20, 30, or 45 questions. Two days later, those who had complied were called again and asked to participate in a 55-question survey; the larger the size of the first request complied with, the greater the compliance with the second request. Thus, compliance to a very small request does not necessarily lead to subsequent compliance to other requests.

Compliance Following Transgression: The Guilty Should Pay for Their Sins

It is commonly observed that compliance increases when the individual has done something "bad." For example, when a mother finds that her children are being unusually helpful and doing exactly as she wishes, her suspicions are aroused. She reasons that if the children are being extra good, they must be trying to atone for having done something wrong. Adults, too, seem to feel that if they have, even inadvertently, caused someone harm or even hurt their feelings, it is only fair to make up for it by doing the injured party a favor.

Guilt: You Always Help the One You Hurt. One explanation for compliance following a transgression is based on the concept of guilt. That is, the individual feels uncomfortable (guilty) about having done something wrong and can relieve this unpleasant feeling by complying with a request. In an experimental test of the guilt hypothesis, Carlsmith and Gross (1969) gave subjects the role of teacher in a learning task. The one being taught (actually a confederate) went through several trials on the task, and the subject was supposed to pull a switch each time a mistake was made. For some subjects, the switch simply sounded a buzzer, but other subjects were made to believe that it

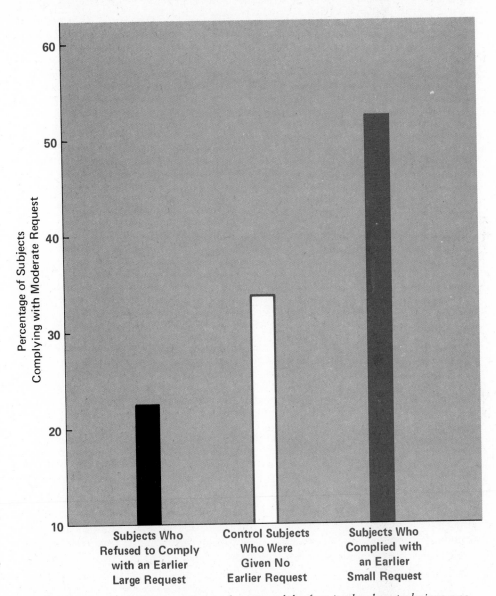

FIGURE 6-9. *A self-perception explanation of the foot-in-the-door technique was supported by an experiment in which subjects were first induced to comply or not to comply. Compared to a control group, those who first complied to a small request were more likely to comply later to a moderate request; those who failed to comply to a large request were less likely to comply later to a moderate request. (Source: Based on data from Snyder and Cunningham, 1975.)*

FOCUS ON RESEARCH

THE DOOR-IN-THE-FACE TECHNIQUE:
IF YOU WON'T MOVE MY MOUNTAIN,
WILL YOU GIVE ME A HAND WITH THIS MOLEHILL?

Though the foot-in-the-door technique is well documented as a social-influence device, is it possible that an opposite procedure might sometimes be effective? For example, if a stranger asks you to help him push his stalled car for a couple of miles to a gas station and you refuse, what would you say if he then asked you to let him have a dime so he could call the station? It seems possible that your refusal to go along with the large request might make your compliance to the smaller one more likely, as the young man in the cartoon in Figure 6-10 has learned.

This possible way of obtaining compli-

FIGURE 6-10. *When a large, unreasonable request is refused and then followed by a smaller one, compliance with the second request is likely. This door-in-the-face technique seems to be based on the fact that the requester has made a concession by scaling down his demands, so compliance seems like a fair way to reciprocate. (Source: © King Features Syndicate 1972.)*

delivered an electric shock to the learner. When the experiment seemed to be completed, the confederate casually mentioned that he was on a committee attempting to stop the construction of a freeway through a redwood grove in Northern California. He needed volunteers to man a telephone and request people to sign a petition. In the buzzer condition, only 25 percent agreed to help. In the shock condition, 75 percent complied with the request. Thus, guilt about shocking the person seemed to increase compliance with his requests.

Public Sin and Private Sin. Guilt alone may not be as powerful a variable as the embarrassment that is caused when the transgressor gets caught. Wallace and Sadalla (1966) proposed that efforts to atone for a transgression may be in large part a desire to look good to other people.

They put undergraduates in an experimental situation in which the subject

ance has been labeled the *door-in-the-face technique* by Robert Cialdini and his associates (Cialdini et al., 1975). The reasoning is somewhat like that of equity theory. If an extreme request is made and refused and the requester then backs down to a much more modest request, the one who refused might feel that he should make a concession, too, and meet the other person half way.

In a series of experiments, it was found that when subjects rejected an extremely large request, they were likely to comply with a modest second request. For example, when university students were stopped on the sidewalk and asked to chaperone a group of delinquents on a two-hour trip to the zoo, only 16.7 percent agreed to do so. When other students were first asked to act as non-paid counselors at the detention center for two hours a week for two years, no one agreed to do so; 50 percent of them were then willing, however, to comply with the zoo-trip request.

This general technique does not work, by the way, unless the two requests are made by the same person; it appears that the one making the large request must be perceived as backing down or conceding in settling for the small request. The authors point out that this technique is a powerful one in that the person who desires compliance with a particular request can greatly increase the odds of success by first asking the person to do something preposterous—when he really knows that it will be refused—and then hitting him with the genuine request.

In putting together the foot-in-the-door and the door-in-the-face studies, you may feel that there is some inconsistency, but apparently both procedures work, depending on the details of the situation. Cann, Sherman, and Elkes (283) point out that when a small request is made first, compliance with a second request seems to increase no matter what. Here, self-consistency explains the effect. If, however, a large, unlikely request is made first, a second, more moderate request is likely to be granted if it is made right away; when they tried the door-in-the-face technique with a week to ten days between the two requests, compliance did not increase. It seems that the need to be equitable and meet someone halfway fades over time. Thus, self-consistency operates against the door-in-the-face phenomenon *unless* a single individual makes both the original large request and the follow-up smaller request immediately afterward. Under those conditions, the requestor is perceived as having made a concession and the subject reciprocates by complying.

and a confederate were left in a room with pieces of complicated apparatus. The confederate fooled around with one piece of equipment and induced the subject to turn on one of the switches. What followed was a rigged "accident" in which there was a flash of light, white smoke, and the odor of burning wire. When the experimenter returned and viewed the make-believe disaster, the confederate either told him what had happened (the subject was thus "caught") or he lied and said the apparatus blew up all by itself (the subject got away with his sin). In a control condition, the apparatus was supposedly already broken before they got there. In all three conditions, the experimenter then requested the subject to take part in an unpleasant alternative study involving pain.

The effects of a transgression on compliance and the importance of getting caught are shown in Figure 6-11. In the control group, only 15 percent of the subjects agreed to take part in the unpleasant substitute study. Among the

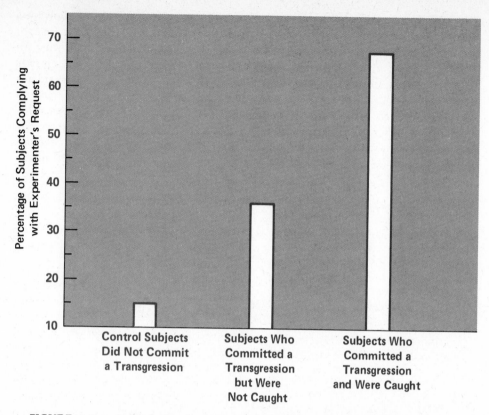

FIGURE 6-11. *Individuals who believed that they had broken a piece of experimental apparatus were more likely to comply with the experimenter's request to take part in a painful task than were control subjects. Among the transgressors, compliance was much greater for those who were caught than for those who were not. (Source: Based on data from Wallace and Sadalla, 1966.)*

subjects who committed a transgression but were not caught at it, 38 percent complied with the experimenter. The individuals who transgressed and were caught, however, were most likely to comply—69 percent of them did so. Guilt, then, seems to increase compliance, but public embarrassment does so even more.

Self-esteem and Compliance. McMillen (1971) proposed that compliance following transgression provides a way of raising one's self-esteem. Thus, the person is not necessarily feeling guilty about the victim as much as he is unhappy about his own self-image. This reasoning led to an experiment in which the transgressor was given a boost to his self-esteem by being told that he performed extremely well on some personality tests (McMillen and Austin, 1971). Under these conditions, the transgression-compliance effect was eliminated. Subjects did not have to comply to make themselves feel good; the positive test results did it for them.

If lowered self-esteem is the explanation for greater compliance following a transgression, it follows that any situation in which an individual feels foolish, awkward, or embarrassed would have the same effect. In other words, an individual need not transgress and feel guilty; compliance might increase just as much if he slipped on a banana peel. Apsler (1975) pointed out that most studies of embarrassment have found that embarrassed individuals tend to behave in various ways to try to create more favorable images of themselves. He hypothesized that compliance with a request might be one way to try to recover loss of face (see Chapter 11). Apsler created an unusual experimental situation in which a subject who was being observed was instructed to do each of the following:

1. Turn on the tape recorder and then dance to the music.
2. Laugh for thirty seconds as if you had just heard a funny joke.
3. Sing the *Star Spangled Banner.*
4. Imitate a five-year-old having a temper tantrum because he does not want to go to kindergarten.

Needless to say, the subjects felt quite embarrassed by the time their performance was over. At this point, the confederate who had been observing asked the subject to help in an assignment which required that a questionnaire be filled out each day for up to twenty days. Those who had just been embarrassed agreed to help for an average of fifteen days, while unembarrassed individuals volunteered only five days of help. A follow-up study showed that embarrassed individuals complied more than unembarrassed ones even if the request came from someone who had not observed their dancing, laughing, singing, and acting. It seems, then, that the primary reason for increased compliance in such situations is that the individual feels very uncomfortable and can make himself or herself feel better by doing a favor for another person.

Another example of the way in which lowered self-esteem affects compliance is provided by an experiment by Steele (1975). A real-life observation was the basis for the study. Steele told of a liberal who was called a racist and who felt very hurt by such a charge. Shortly afterward, this person received a request to donate time and money on a project for disadvantaged members of another race—he agreed readily, presumably because this action made him feel better about himself. The experimenter designed a two-part telephone study to determine whether that sort of name calling was generally effective in reducing self-esteem and hence increasing later compliance. A representative of what was supposed to be a polling institute called, and subjects were insulted with such statements as, "Isn't it accurate to describe you as predominantly self-oriented and apathetic about the welfare of others? Wouldn't you say that you tend to your own needs and ignore the needs of others even when helping them would entail little effort on your part?" Different subjects received a positive communication, saying that they were concerned, cooperative, and helpful; another group received no initial telephone call. Two days later a second person phoned to request help in getting information for a proposed neighborhood food cooperative. Of those who had heard negative things about themselves, 93 percent were willing to help the second caller, while only 46 percent of the control group complied. A positive message had some effect also, in that 65 percent of that group was willing to help. Once again, it seems clear that people will comply with requests if compliance provides a way to raise their self-esteem and make them feel better.

A final way in which self-esteem has been manipulated involved giving subjects fake feedback about their performance on a battery of personality tests. Filter and Gross (1975) administered a series of five tests and afterward provided fake information as to how the subject compared with a normative group of a thousand other college students—half of the subjects were told that their test responses were quite deviant. A fellow subject (actually a confederate) either knew or did not know about the subject's supposed deviancy. After all of this, the confederate made a request of the subject for assistance in writing letters for a committee to improve undergraduate education. The compliance measure consisted of how many letters the subject agreed to write. As expected, those who had just been told they were deviant agreed to write about twice as many letters as those who believed themselves to be normal. Interestingly enough, there was even greater compliance when the subject's deviancy was a secret from the confederate. Presumably, complying with the request made the subjects feel better and perhaps helped convince them that they were not behaving in a deviant manner. Rest assured, by the way, that the subjects were quickly informed that their test performance was not actually deviant and that the fake feedback was simply part of the experiment.

OBEDIENCE

One of the test items used to measure the personality trait of authoritarianism is worded, "Obedience and respect for authority are the most important virtues children should learn." A great many people agree with that statement. In fact, many aspects of our society are based on this most direct and explicit social influence process—obedience. Children are expected to obey their parents. Pupils are expected to obey their teachers. Enlisted men are expected to obey their officers. We are all expected to obey the law.

The way in which obedience is obtained seems straightforward enough. If one person has power over another, obedience can be demanded. If the one receiving the order fails to obey, power is exercised in the form of negative sanctions such as spankings, demerits, demotions, fines, imprisonment, and even death. Those who refuse to go along with the authority figures are labeled as bad, rebellious, uppity, or psychopathic. Troublemakers, anarchists, and criminals are dealt with severely by society.

These processes are such a common part of our lives that they usually are not questioned. It is increasingly obvious, however, that there are many possible negative consequences of blind obedience. Authority figures and the orders they give may be morally questionable. What then? If unthinking obedience to authority can lead to despicable behavior, this implies that individuals should

Obedience can be demanded by those with power, and disobedience leads to negative sanctions, including the use of force.

judge the goodness or badness of the orders they receive and then obey only the good ones. Such defiance of authority is difficult under the best of circumstances, and it can be very dangerous. Under what conditions do people obey and under what conditions are they willing to run the risks involved in not obeying?

These questions are not simply idle and irrelevant speculations—they are of vital importance to each of us. Perhaps the most chilling example of the evil results of blind obedience was provided by the Nazi experience in Germany. A great many otherwise decent individuals acquiesced to the demands of an authoritarian government in the 1930's and 1940's. As a result, they engaged in unthinkable crimes against fellow citizens who happened to belong to an "unacceptable" religious, ethnic, or political group. Beatings, confiscation of property, imprisonment, torture, and murder were carried out because someone issued orders to engage in such acts. In the United States, the war in Vietnam provided us with a more personal opportunity to question the wisdom of unthinking obedience. The best known single atrocity of the Vietnam War was the massacre of civilians in the village of My Lai. One of the participants was contacted by CBS reporter Mike Wallace, and a portion of that interview went as follows:

Q. How many people did you round up?
A. Well, there was about forty, fifty people that we gathered in the center of the

village. And we placed them in there, and it was like a little island, right there in the center of the village, I'd say . . . And . . .

Q. What kind of people—men, women, children?

A. Men, women, children.

Q. Babies?

A. Babies. And we huddled them up. We made them squat down and Lieutenant Calley came over and said, "You know what to do with them, don't you?" And I said yes. So I took it for granted that he just wanted us to watch them. And he left, and came back about ten or fifteen minutes later and said, "How come you ain't killed them yet?" And I told him that I didn't think you wanted us to kill them, that you just wanted us to guard them. He said, "No, I want them dead." So . . .

Q. And you killed how many? At that time?

A. Well, I fired them automatic, so you can't—You just spray the area on them and so you can't know how many you killed 'cause they were going fast. So I might have killed ten or fifteen of them.

Q. Men, women, and children?

A. Men, women, and children.

Q. And babies?

A. And babies . . .

Q. Why did you do it?

A. Why did I do it? Because I felt like I was ordered to do it, and it seemed like that, at the time I felt like I was doing the right thing, because, like I said, I lost buddies . . .

Q. What did these civilians—particularly the women and children, the old men—what did they do? What did they say to you?

A. They weren't much saying to them. They [were] just being pushed and they were doing what they was told to do.

Q. They weren't begging, or saying, "No . . . no," or . . .

A. Right. They were begging and saying, "No, no." And the mothers was hugging their children, and . . . but they kept right on firing. Well, we kept right on firing. They was waving their arms and begging . . .

—*New York Times*, Nov. 25, 1969

For psychologists to study such behavior and to see why immoral orders sometimes are followed and sometimes resisted, it was necessary to devise a laboratory situation that was to some extent analogous to the awesome events that have taken place in Nazi Germany, Vietnam, and in countless other places in every part of the world. Though even a mild simulation of such events raises ethical questions in the minds of many psychologists, the questions at issue are critical ones. Some commentators feel that it is wrong to create an experimental situation which places individuals in the uncomfortable position of having to choose between defying an authority figure or causing apparent harm to a stranger. Still others defend such research on the grounds that the problem is one of grave practical importance; they feel that it is vital for us to understand the causes of blind obedience and to devise ways to prevent its occurrence. Though this moral dilemma is still being debated, experiments *have* nevertheless been conducted. How can individuals be induced to obey an order to harm an innocent victim and what factors make it possible to resist such a command?

Consider the fact that " . . . Ordinary citizens are ordered to destroy other people, and they do so because they consider it their duty to obey orders. Thus, obedience to authority, long praised as a virtue, takes on a new aspect when it serves a malevolent cause" (Milgram, 1974, p. 2). To pursue this behavioral characteristic, Stanley Milgram (1963) developed a unique experimental procedure. As part of what was described as a learning experiment, a subject was ordered to administer electric shock to a victim. The research was supposedly testing the effect of punishment on memory, but the victim really was a confederate instructed as to how to respond. The shock generator, shown in Figure 6-12, is an impressive (though false) apparatus with thirty voltage levels ranging from "Slight Shock" to "Danger; Severe Shock" and on up to an ominous level marked "XXX." In each experimental session, the experimenter commands the subject to administer stronger and stronger shocks to the victim, up to and including the XXX level. At various points along the way, some subjects will refuse to go on, terminating the experiment. Obedience was measured by recording the shock level a subject reaches before he refuses to obey any further. Since the authority figure (the experimenter) had no real power over the subjects and no way to punish them for disobedience, you might wonder whether anyone would obey.

FIGURE 6-12. *The simulated shock generator used by Stanley Milgram to study obedience. (Source: Copyright 1965 by Stanley Milgram. From the film* Obedience, *distributed by the New York University Film Library. Reprinted by permission of the author.)*

The first subjects were males from the New Haven area who responded to newspaper advertisements for research subjects. They ranged in age from twenty to fifty, and they included postal clerks, high school teachers, salesmen, engineers, and laborers. The role of the experimenter was played by a stern thirty-one-year-old high school biology teacher dressed in a white technician's coat. The victim was played by a pleasant forty-seven-year-old accountant, shown in Figure 6-13. It appeared that the roles of teacher and learner in the task were decided on the basis of a random drawing, but it was actually rigged so that the subject would end up as the teacher and the accountant as the learner. In an adjoining room, as depicted in Figure 6-14, the learner was strapped into a chair "to prevent excessive movement when he was shocked." Electrodes were applied to his wrists with paste "to avoid blisters and burns." The experimenter announced that "although the shocks can be extremely painful, they cause no permanent tissue damage." The subject then received a mild sample shock to aid in convincing him that the apparatus was real. He was supposed to shock the learner each time an answer on the "learning task" was incorrect. Each participant was told to begin with fifteen volts and to increase the shock intensity by one level on each successive wrong answer. The number of wrong answers was, in fact, prearranged, and the learner did not actually receive any electrical shocks.

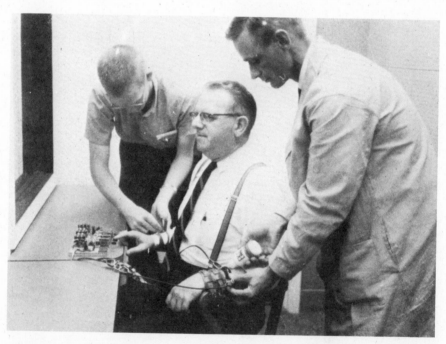

FIGURE 6-13. *Would you hurt this man? This individual played the part of the victim in Milgram's initial experiments. Subjects were ordered to administer electrical shocks of greater and greater intensity to him. (Source: Copyright 1965 by Stanley Milgram. From the film* Obedience, *distributed by the New York University Film Library. Reprinted by permission of the author.)*

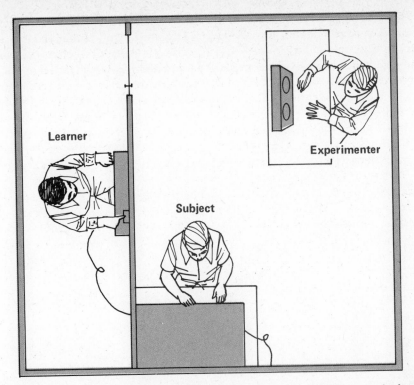

FIGURE 6-14. *The arrangement of the experimental room in Milgram's obedience studies. The subject believes he is delivering painful shocks to the learner (actually a confederate) in the adjoining room, while the experimenter is there to urge him to continue. (Source: From* Obedience to Authority *by Stanley Milgram. Copyright © 1974 by Stanley Milgram. Reprinted by permission of Harper & Row, Publishers, Inc.)*

When the shock level reached 300 volts, the learner pounded on the wall next to the chair to which he was confined. From then on, he stopped pushing the buttons and gave no more answers on the learning task. At this point, most subjects were puzzled as to what to do next. The experimenter said to treat the absence of a response as a wrong answer and to continue giving stronger and stronger shocks. The learner pounded on the wall once again at the 315-volt level, and then made no more sounds. Whenever the subjects were unwilling to continue, the experimenter had a set series of statements to prod him on:

1. Please go on.
2. The experiment requires that you continue.
3. It is absolutely essential that you continue.
4. You have no other choice, you *must* go on.

What do you think a subject would do in that situation? When a group of college students was asked to predict the outcome, the majority guessed that the subjects would refuse to administer the extremely strong shocks to an innocent victim. As may be seen in Figure 6-15, however, most participants *did* obey the command to continue shocking the victim all the way up to the maximum level. After the victim pounded on the wall and stopped responding, only 12.5 percent of the subjects defied the experimenter and stopped. Even when the shock level reached "danger" and beyond, well over half the subjects were still administering shock to the now silent victim. As might be expected, those who continued to obey the experimenter's orders tended to have higher scores on a measure of

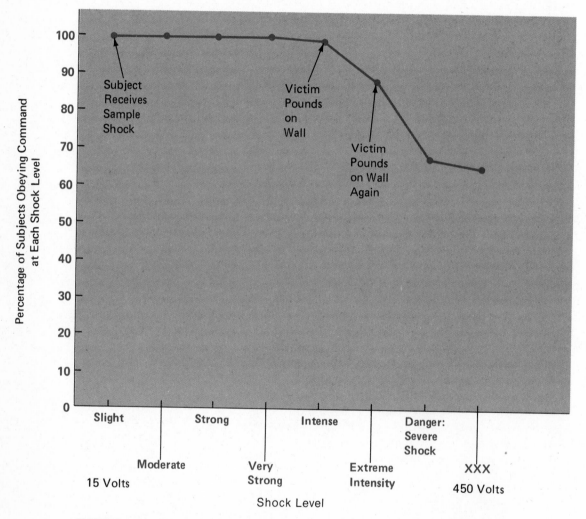

FIGURE 6-15. *Percentage of subjects who obeyed commands to continue shocking victim at various levels of shock intensity. Even when the victim reacted as if in pain and stopped responding to the memory task, almost two-thirds of the subjects obeyed the experimenter and administered shocks at the level of "danger" and beyond. (Source: Based on data from Milgram, 1963.)*

authoritarian personality characteristics than those who defied him (Elms and Milgram, 1966).

How did the subjects react as they were carrying out an order to hurt the man in the next room? They were not indifferent or cold-blooded torturers. Rather, they seemed to be very nervous and the tension appeared to be extreme These obedient individuals perspired, trembled, stuttered, bit their lips, groaned, and dug their fingernails into their palms. Over one-third of them laughed nervously and smiled. "The laughter seemed entirely out of place, even bizarre. Full-blown, uncontrollable seizures were observed for three subjects. On one occasion we observed a seizure so violently convulsive that it was necessary to call a halt to the experiment" (Milgram, 1963, p. 375). Subjects afterward were embarrassed about the laughter and explained that it was not under their control and certainly did not indicate enjoyment on their part. Those subjects who defied the experimenter and broke off the experiment often did so with an emotional and angry outburst such as:

I think he's trying to communicate, he's knocking. . . . Well it's not fair to shock the guy . . . these are terrific volts. I don't think this is very humane. . . . Oh, I can't go on with this; no, this isn't right. It's a hell of an experiment. The guy is suffering in there. No, I don't want to go on. This is crazy.

In effect, this experimental task places subjects in a conflict between their moral values about harming others and their tendency to obey an authority's command. The findings are especially frightening in their implications because this particular authority figure could obviously do nothing to make them obey and would not be in a position to punish them—in fact, they were unlikely even to see him again. Perhaps it is not surprising that obedience occurs in real-life situations in response to much more cruel orders than those given by Milgram's experimenter. Incidentally, most of these experiments used male subjects. When females *are* used, they tend to resist harming the victim more than do males (Kilham and Mann, 1974).

It was noticed, by the way, that subjects tended to avert their eyes so they could not see the victim through the window in the next room. This suggested that obedience to the experimenter might decrease if the victim's suffering was made more salient to the subject. Milgram (1974) created several different experimental conditions, varying the obviousness of the unhappy victim. Some subjects could hear the victim moan and complain, some were in the same room with him and so could hear and see him clearly, and others were not only with him but had to force his hand onto the metal shock plate. As expected, obedience decreased as proximity to the suffering increased. When they could hear the suffering, 37.5 percent of the subjects defied the experimenter, 60 percent were defiant when the victim was in the room with them, and 70 percent refused to obey when they had to hold the man's hand down on the electrified plate. In a way, such findings are encouraging in that these individuals found it much more difficult to be cruel when the results of the cruelty were made obvious. They can also be viewed in a negative light. Consider that when subjects were instructed to force the reluctant victim's hand onto a plate to receive painful high-voltage shocks, almost one-third continued to obey! It is also sobering to consider that much of the suffering in modern warfare is by victims who are unseen and unheard by those who launch the bombs and missiles. Another way to be personally removed from the harmful act is to be the one who simply transmits the orders rather than the one who actually carries them out. When subjects must pass on the experimenter's orders to harm the victim, they are more obedient than when they actually must pull the shock switch (Kilham and Mann, 1974).

Going Along with the Group

If an experimenter can induce subjects to cause pain to someone else, what happens when group pressure is involved, and peers urge an individual to administer shock? In order to determine whether subjects could be induced to administer more pain at the group's urging than they would do alone, Milgram (1964) used the same general procedure as in the previous experiments. As a control condition to determine what subjects would do in the absence of any social pressure to hurt the victim, other individuals were placed in the situation without any assistants and told to select any shock levels they wished. In the experimental condition, in addition to the subject and the confederate who played the learner, there were two additional confederates whose supposed job was to assist the subject, as shown in Figure 6-16. The level of shock to be administered after the learner made each mistake was to be suggested by the subject and his two helpers—the learner would receive the lowest of the three levels suggested. If the subject wished, therefore, he could give the mildest possible shock each time by sticking with the fifteen-volt level.

On every trial, the assistants proposed increasing the level of shock. The learner in the adjoining room indicated he was in pain as the shock increased. He groaned and shouted that the shocks were becoming painful. At 150 volts, he cried out that he wanted to be released from the experiment, complaining of a heart condition. At 180 volts, he cried, "I can't stand the pain." At 285 volts, there was an agonized scream. After 300 volts, he said that he would give no more answers in the learning task.

Figure 6-17 shows the shock levels administered by the subjects who were alone and by those who were urged on by the confederates. You can see that much more intense shocks were given by those receiving group pressure than by those who were alone. When subjects were by themselves, only 5 percent went past the 150-volt condition in which the learner asked to be released because of a heart condition; with group pressure, 67.5 percent went past this shock level. Looking at both this and the previous experiments, you might note that group pressure seems to be less effective in inducing the subject to shock the victim than were the commands of an authority figure. In both instances, nevertheless, it was shown that ordinary citizens can rather easily be influenced to inflict pain on another person.

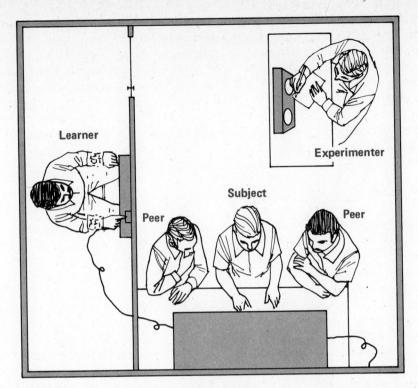

FIGURE 6-16. *The arrangement of the experimental room in the obedience studies when the subject has two "assistants" to help him by suggesting the level of shock to be administered to the learner. (Source: From* Obedience to Authority *by Stanley Milgram. Copyright 1974 by Stanley Milgram. Reprinted by permission of Harper & Row, Publishers, Inc.)*

Counteracting Obedience: What If They Gave a Command and No One Obeyed?

In this chapter on social influence, it may appear that conformity to the group is always bad and that it is always a mistake for an individual to be affected by what others say or do. Actually, what your peers do in real life may be good or bad, correct or incorrect, wise or foolish. If an authority figure gave you an immoral command and those around you urged you to defy him, group influences under those circumstances would be a force for good.

Commands are not necessarily irresistible (Michener and Burt, 1975), and obedience depends in part on the authority figure and in part on the responses of the group getting the orders. As mentioned earlier, people do tend to obey teachers, policemen, and military officers. At the same time, we all know that there can be student revolts, riots in the streets, and mutinies. A poster of the 1960's asked the question, "Suppose they gave a war, and nobody came?" It seems that the power of any authority to command others to obey can actually be

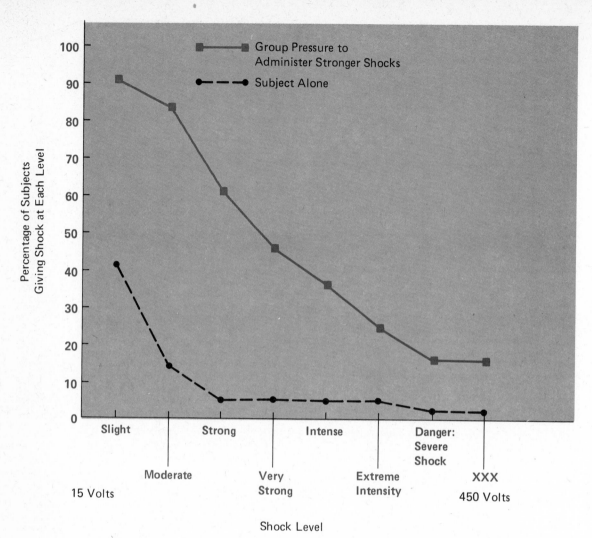

FIGURE 6-17. *Level of shocks given by subjects who were alone and by subjects who were urged by two confederates to give an increasingly higher voltage. More intense shock was administered when group pressure was exerted than when subjects were alone. (Source: Based on data from Milgram, 1964.)*

a fragile entity and that conformity pressures can sometimes come into conflict with obedience pressures.

Milgram (1965a) points out the large discrepancy between what subjects believe they would do in his experimental situation and what they actually do. When the experiment was described to potential subjects and they were asked to predict how they would respond, most saw themselves defying the experimenter—they estimated a maximum shock of 135 volts before stopping the experiment. When actual subjects were confronted by an experimenter who told them to continue, the average maximum shock level was 368 volts. The

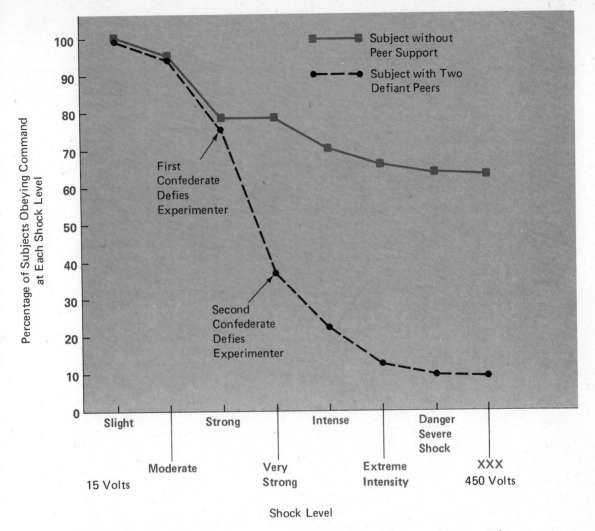

FIGURE 6-18. *Group pressure as an influence in defying authority. When subjects do not have peer support, 65 percent continue to obey the experimenter's commands to give stronger and stronger shocks throughout the experiment. When subjects are with peers who defy the experimenter, only 10 percent continue to obey the experimenter's commands. (Source: Based on data from Milgram, 1965a.)*

difference between what subjects say and what they do may be caused in part by judgments as to the immorality of hurting someone. One subject who had only heard a description of the experiment wrote, "I would say that one should not even start the shocks, but, rather, forcibly withdraw the moment that the outline of the experiment becomes evident. . . . I have internalized the view that hurting a man is wrong, and no amount of intellectual reasoning can shake this belief." So, subjects know the behavior is wrong and believe that they would behave in accordance with their moral values. In the actual situation, however, they tend to knuckle under to the authority unless the moral side of the conflict receives some additional support. What might tip the balance toward moral behavior?

In an experiment to test the usefulness of having peers present to help in defying authority, Milgram (1965a) again set up the situation with the subject and two "assistants." This time, however, the experimenter played his authoritarian role, and the two confederates went along with him only through the 150-volt level. At this point, one of them said he did not wish to participate any further because of the learner's complaints. Despite the experimenter's insistence, he got up and went to another part of the room. The experiment was then continued, but, after 210 volts, the second confederate also decided not to continue. He said, "I'm willing to answer any of your questions, but I'm not willing to shock that man against his will. I'll have no part of it."

The comparison of how subjects behave when alone with the experimenter and when they are accompanied by two defiant peers is shown in Figure 6-18. With the help of the two defiant ones, 90 percent of the subjects were able to disobey the experimenter at some point and stop shocking the victim. Without such support, only 35 percent did so. With two peers who refused to go along with the commands, the average maximum shock level was about 240 volts, compared with about 370 volts when the subject was alone with the experimenter.

Milgram suggests that in the alone condition, moral pressures probably lead many individuals to come close to defiance, but the final step is a very difficult one. Pressure from peers makes it possible to go over this threshold. As one subject said, "Well, I was already thinking about quitting when the guy broke off." For others, though, it was as if the defiant peers had suggested something new. "The thought of stopping didn't enter my mind until it was put there by the other two." Interestingly enough, most subjects denied that the confederates' behavior had anything to do with their own defiance. The data clearly indicate, of course, that they are incorrect. The confederates had a powerful influence. In real-life situations, if only a few individuals speak out and refuse to engage in behavior they know to be wrong, their influence may prove to be crucial. We all have greater freedom to defy immoral commands than we ordinarily realize, and the defiant behavior of others can make that fact obvious.

SUMMARY

Social influence occurs whenever our behavior, feelings, or attitudes are altered by what others say or do.

Conformity involves the way in which we are influenced by what others do, and by our implicit assumption that behaving like those around us will elicit approval while dissimilar behavior will bring disapproval. Sherif investigated the development of social norms by using the autokinetic phenomenon—the apparent movement of a stationary point of light in a dark room. The range of such perceived movement is strongly influenced by the responses of others, and subjects will conform to the norms set by other individuals. Asch devised a situation in which a subject must make a series of judgments in a group; the rest of the group consists of confederates who present a unanimous incorrect majority, and it is found that many subjects conform by going along with the incorrect responses. Crutchfield devised an improved methodology for studying conformity, in which the responses of other "group members" actually consist of material controlled by the experimenter. Conformity increases when group size increases, when conforming behavior is reinforced, when the subject is low in self-esteem, when subjects are attempting to be ingratiating, and, generally, when the subject is attracted to the group. Theoretical explanations of conformity have rested on Festinger's social-comparison theory and on the assumption that there are usually negative responses to independent behavior and dissent. When an individual receives social support from at least one other member of the group, conformity is reduced. Studies of individual differences in conformity indicate that age differences vary with the type of task and that the common finding of greater female than male conformity may be entirely attributable to the type of task used.

Compliance refers to behavior influenced by direct requests. Compliance is greater toward liked, similar others than toward disliked, dissimilar others. It increases after someone has received a favor, probably because favors create inequity. The foot-in-the-door technique refers to the procedure of getting people first to agree to a small request so they will then be more likely to comply with a large one. The door-in-the-face technique refers to the procedure of making a large request which will be refused and then backing down to a smaller one which is then more likely to be successful. Compliance also increases after an individual has committed a transgression, especially if he has been caught, if the person is embarrassed, and if self-esteem has been lowered.

Studies of obedience deal with effects of direct commands as a social-influence process. Much of the research on this behavior suggests that most of us have learned to obey authority figures even if they do not control powerful negative sanctions to punish us. Milgram devised an experimental procedure in which subjects are ordered to administer what they believe to be increasingly strong electric shocks to another individual. Most subjects will continue to obey such orders even though the victim is suffering and they personally are emotionally upset about continuing. They also respond to the urgings of peers to shock the victim. Obedience decreases if there is group support for disobedience.

GLOSSARY

Autokinetic phenomenon. The apparent movement of a single, stationary source of light in a dark room.

Compliance. Behavior which is in accord with direct requests made by others.

Conformity. Behavior which is like that of the individuals in one's group.

Crutchfield apparatus. A means for studying conformity in which five subjects believe they are receiving the responses of one another but are actually getting information programmed by the experimenter.

Door-in-the-face technique. The compliance strategy in which a large, unlikely request is made first, then is quickly followed by a more modest one.

— **Equity theory.** Homans's formulation that proposes that interpersonal relationships tend to be structured in such a way that the participants feel that each is being treated fairly.

Foot-in-the-door technique. The compliance strategy in which a small request is made first, followed by a larger one.

— **Informational social influence.** Pressures to go along with the group in order to be correct.

Ingratiation. The techniques individuals use in an attempt to make themselves liked by others.

Normative social influence. Pressures to go along with the group in order to conform to the positive expectations of others.

— **Obedience.** Behavior which corresponds to that ordered by an authority figure.

Physical reality. The actual world in which we live.

Reference group. The group used by an individual as the standard against which to evaluate himself or herself.

— **Social-comparison theory.** Festinger's formulation that posits a basic drive to evaluate one's own opinions and abilities which leads to comparisons between oneself and other people.

— **Social influence.** The alteration of one's behavior, feelings, or attitudes by what others say or do.

— **Social norms.** The various behaviors that define what is appropriate and acceptable within a given group.

— **Social reality.** The world as defined by human beings.

SUGGESTED READINGS FOR CHAPTER 6

Cialdini, R. B., Vincent, J. E., Lewis, S. K., Catalan, J., Wheeler, D., and Darby, B. L. Reciprocal concessions procedure for inducing compliance: The door-in-the-face technique. *Journal of Personality and Social Psychology*, 1975, *31*, 206–215. The basic description of the door-in-the-face technique along with experiments testing its operation.

Freedman, J. L., and Fraser, S. C. Compliance without pressure: The foot-in-the-door technique. *Journal of Personality and Social Psychology*, 1966, *4*, 195–202. The basic description of the foot-in-the-door technique along with experiments testing its operation.

Hollander, E. P. Independence, conformity, and civil liberties: Some implications from social psychological research. *Journal of Social Issues*, 1975, *31*, 55–67. An important discussion of the barriers to independent behavior and the reasons that society should actively encourage independence and dissent.

Kiesler, C. A., and Kiesler, S. B. *Conformity.* Reading, Mass.: Addison-Wesley, 1969. A very good coverage of the basic ideas and findings in the area of conformity.

Milgram, S. *Obedience to authority.* New York: Harper and Row, 1974. A very readable and nontechnical description of the obedience studies and their implications for society.

MODELING: UNINTENTIONAL SOCIAL INFLUENCE

7

It's late one blustery Tuesday afternoon when you arrive for an appointment with your academic advisor. You are about fifteen minutes early, and she is still talking to another student, so you take a seat outside in the hall and wait. Because it has been several hours since lunch, you begin to munch on a bag of heavily salted peanuts. After you finish, you discover that you are very thirsty. The only water fountain nearby, though, has a large sign over it reading DO NOT DRINK FROM THIS FOUNTAIN, with the first two words underlined in red for added emphasis. Since you usually make it a practice to obey signs, and because you're afraid that any attempt to drink from the fountain may produce unpleasant results (the water might be dirty or rusty, you might get squirted by a broken pipe), you sit and wait, growing thirstier and thirstier. After a few minutes, another person approaches and, without hesitation, stops at the fountain and takes a long drink. You watch with interest, half expecting that he will be drenched by a wild spray, or will find the water totally undrinkable. But nothing out of the ordinary happens, and he soon continues on his way, obviously refreshed by his cooling drink. After a moment of conflict, you decide that if this person could violate the prohibition with such ease and safety, you can too, and so you get up to quench your own thirst.

You are sitting in your car at a busy intersection waiting for the red light to turn green. As you wait, your mind wanders to the upcoming Christmas holidays and all the things you have planned for your two weeks in the sun. As you daydream about the fun you will have away from the daily grind of lectures, exams, and labs, you notice that the driver on your left has begun to move. Seeing him move off, you too step on the accelerator—and almost crash into the back of the car ahead of yours, which is still sitting perfectly still. Fortunately, you ram on your brakes and just manage to avoid a rear-end collision. You are about to honk angrily at the driver in front of you when you realize what has happened: the motorist on your left was waiting in a turn lane, and drove off when the green arrow came on. The traffic signal for your own lane, though, is still red. Embarrassed by having nearly caused a serious accident, you shrink down into your seat, trying to ignore the amused looks of the other drivers who witnessed your actions.

X-rated movies have never done much for you, so you are far from enthusiastic when your roommate suggests going to see one. Since she accompanied you to the last film you wanted to see, and since this particular movie has been discussed a great deal on campus, you finally *agree. As the movie proceeds, you find that, in general, it is quite boring. Watching other people make love is fun for a few minutes, but after that it tends to get very repetitious. Just when you have about given up and lost interest completely, the action on the screen takes a surprising new turn. You've never seen this particular form of love-making before, and it looks so appealing that you sit up in your seat and watch with growing interest. The techniques being shown seem a bit complicated, but after watching for a few minutes, you think you understand them quite well. Later, after the film is over, you think about what you have seen and decide that under the right conditions, and with the right partner, you might just be willing to try it out yourself.*

At first glance, these incidents may seem totally unrelated. In reality, though, they all point to an important fact: *in many cases, our feelings, behavior, and thoughts are strongly affected by exposure to the actions of the persons around us, and the outcomes they experience.* Having read Chapters 3 and 6, you will probably not find this too surprising. In these earlier discussions, we examined a large number of techniques through which individuals attempt to influence one another. Thus, adding still another to the list may not seem very important. Yet, there is a very important difference between the forms of social influence we have already considered and those we wish to examine here. In all of the others discussed earlier, the persons involved *intended* to affect other persons. In the examples described above, however, this was not the case. The person who drank at the fountain had no interest in getting you to drink also; the driver who turned left certainly had no desire to cause a serious accident; and the couple on the screen had no intention of causing you to adopt their style of loving. In fact, they could not even be aware of your existence. In short, in all these cases, one or more persons exerted strong effects on your behavior without intending to do so.

Instances of such **unintentional social influence** are very common. To mention just a few obvious examples, we often tend to laugh when we hear others laughing, to applaud when we hear others clapping, to look in the direction in which we see others gazing, and to sit or stand at social gatherings when we see those around us taking seats or rising to leave. Moreover there is growing evidence that exposure to the actions of others affects even such important forms of social behavior as aggression on the one hand, and altruism on the other.

Generally, instances in which the behavior, feelings, or thoughts of one person are strongly affected by exposure to the actions and outcomes of others are termed **modeling,** and it is with this important process that the present chapter is concerned. We should hasten to add that modeling is far from the only form of unintentional social influence. For example, we are often affected by the mere presence of others, rather than their actions or words—an important phenomenon we will consider in Chapter 12. But it is our impression that modeling is the most common and therefore perhaps the most important form of unintentional social influence. Thus, we believe that it merits careful attention here.

As we mentioned earlier, this particular type of unintentional social influence is very common and takes a number of different forms. To avoid getting mired in a wealth of details and many interesting, but secondary, issues, we will adopt the following general plan. First, we will examine the theoretical framework for understanding such effects that has been devised in recent years by Albert Bandura and his colleagues (Bandura, 1973, 1974). Next, we will turn to the role of modeling in several important forms of social behavior, including aggression, altruism, and the internal regulation of behavior. Third, we will consider the topic of **vicarious emotional arousal,** the process through which signs of emotional arousal in one person induce heightened arousal in others. And finally, we will focus upon the application of modeling principles to the treatment of several behavior problems. Here, we will see that in contrast to the techniques of intentional social influence we have already considered (e.g., compliance, obedience, persuasion, etc.), modeling has often been employed for the benefit of the persons toward whom it is directed rather than the individuals who use it.

UNINTENTIONAL SOCIAL INFLUENCE: A THEORETICAL FRAMEWORK

Early attempts to understand the manner in which exposure to the actions of others **(social models)** can influence the feelings, behavior, and thoughts of observers focused largely on *imitation*—instances in which observers directly matched the behavior of their models. Imitation, in turn, was generally explained within the context of learned, instrumental behavior. That is, it was usually assumed that individuals acquire a tendency to imitate the actions of others because, quite simply, they are rewarded for doing so (Gewirtz and Stingle, 1968; Miller and Dollard, 1941).

Evidence for this general view was obtained in a number of experiments in which subjects—both children and adults—were provided with various forms of reinforcement (candy, money, praise) for imitating the behavior of a model. Results generally indicated that under these conditions, subjects quickly acquired a strong tendency to match the actions of this person (Miller and Dollard, 1941; Rosenbaum and Tucker, 1962). As might be expected, though, they learned to imitate some models more readily than others. For example, most studies reported that subjects acquired a tendency to match the behavior of attractive, successful, and friendly individuals much more quickly than that of unattractive, unsuccessful, and unfriendly ones (Baron, 1970; Yarrow and Scott, 1972; see Figure 7-1).

Although research on imitation continued for many years, it generally left most social psychologists "cold." The main reason for the lack of widespread interest in this topic seems quite straightforward: although direct imitation may in fact be the sincerest form of flattery, it is relatively rare among adults. Indeed,

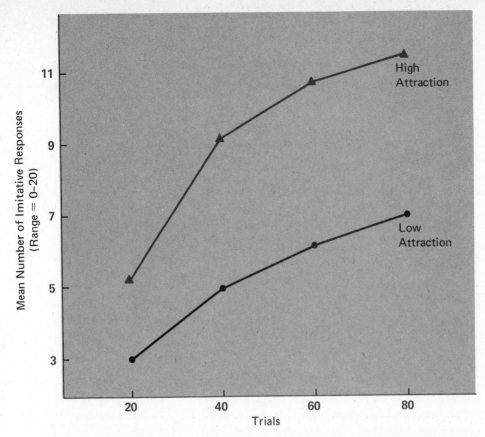

FIGURE 7-1. *As shown above, individuals generally learn to imitate the actions of persons they like more quickly than those of persons they dislike. In this study, subjects were made to like or dislike the model by receiving either favorable or highly unfavorable personal evaluations from him. (Source: Based on data from Baron, 1970.)*

as you probably know from your own experience, there are often strong norms—or even legal sanctions—against the performance of such behavior. For example, cheating on exams, literary plagiarism, or stealing the ideas of others are all strongly frowned-upon activities. As a result of such restrictions, direct imitation is not a very common form of behavior in our society. In view of this fact, many social psychologists dismissed imitation as being relatively unimportant, and turned their attention to other topics, including the many forms of intentional social influence described in Chapters 3 and 6.

In recent years, however, there has been a dramatic change in this state of affairs. It has become increasingly apparent that imitation is only the tip of the iceberg, so to speak—only one of many ways in which individuals can be affected by exposure to the actions and outcomes of others. Moreover, there has been a growing realization that the impact of various modeling processes on social behavior is far greater and more general than was previously assumed. The individual most directly responsible for calling these facts to the attention of social psychologists has been Albert Bandura—a former president of the American Psychological Association well known for his research on this important type of unintentional social influence. Because Bandura's views regarding the nature and impact of modeling have been extremely influential, we will begin with a summary of his proposals.

The Social-learning Theory of Modeling Processes

After years of careful study, Bandura (1973, 1974) has concluded that the influence of social models on observers may be categorized under three general headings: **inhibitory** or **disinhibitory effects, response-facilitating effects,** and **observational-learning effects.** Although these labels may be unfamiliar, we are quite sure that you will have no difficulty recognizing the processes to which they refer.

Response Inhibition or Disinhibition: Social Models as a Source of Encouragement or Restraint. Turning first to inhibitory and disinhibitory effects, it is apparent that exposure to the actions of others and the consequences they experience may often serve either to strengthen or weaken an observer's restraints against engaging in similar acts. Thus, witnessing another person receive a severe reprimand for violating some rule or prohibition may serve to strengthen our own inhibitions against breaking the same restriction. Similarly, observing another person "get away" with some prohibited act may serve to weaken our restraints against engaging in similar behaviors.

The occurrence of such inhibitory and disinhibitory effects have been demonstrated in a number of laboratory and field experiments. In one, which you will find quite similar to the water-fountain example presented earlier, Kimbrell and Blake (1958) first induced three levels of thirst among college students by feeding them salty crackers treated with Mexican hot sauce, plain crackers, or no crackers at all. Subjects were then asked to wait in the hall with another individual (a confederate of the experimenter) until summoned. Nearby was a water fountain over which was placed a sign reading "Do Not Use This Fountain." The confederate then either obeyed this prohibition, or violated it by taking the drink anyway. Results indicated that as expected, the thirstier the subjects were, the more frequently they disregarded the sign and took a drink. In addition, and more important in the context of our present discussion, subjects were much more likely to drink from the fountain when they had observed the confederate violate this prohibition than when they had not (see Figure 7-2). Thus, exposure to this individual's violation sharply weakened their own restraints against engaging in similar behavior.

A second interesting illustration of the strong inhibitory or disinhibitory effects which may result from exposure to the actions of a social model is provided by an experiment conducted by Walters, Leat, and Mezei (1963). These

THE EFFECTS OF BEING IMITATED: RECIPROCATION OR REJECTION?

As we have already noted, "common sense" suggests that being imitated by others is a flattering, and therefore pleasant, state of affairs. Presumably, this is the case because when others imitate our actions, they are expressing implicit approval of them, and we find such endorsement to be quite rewarding. But is this actually true; do we really enjoy being imitated by others? And if so, what effects do such reactions exert on our later behavior? Systematic information regarding these and related questions has recently been collected by Mark Thelen and his colleagues (Thelen, Dollinger, and Roberts, 1975; Thelen and Kirkland, 1976).

In the first of their studies on this topic, Thelen, Dollinger, and Roberts (1975) placed young children in a situation where their actions on simple tasks were imitated by one adult, but not imitated by another. For example, in one task, the children were shown four crayons, asked to choose one, and then to draw a circle with it. The imitating confederate always matched their choices in this respect, while the nonimitating person did not. Following such exposure to imitating and nonimitating adults, conditions were arranged so that the children could now choose to match the actions of either of these individuals (i.e., the confederates were selected to perform first on another simple task). It was expected that subjects would show greater imitation of the confederate who had previously imitated *them*, and this prediction was confirmed. Indeed, fully 72 percent of the children showed greater imitation of the confederate who had previously matched their behavior than of the confederate who had not. Further, when asked to express their preference for one or the other of these two persons, the children generally reported greater liking for the imitator than for the nonimitator (more than 82 percent chose the former). In short, being imitated by another individual led to reciprocal imitation of *his* actions, and to greater reported liking for him.

Additional studies (Bates, 1975) have extended these results to adults, who also seem to enjoy being imitated by others, and who also generally report greater liking for those who match their behavior than for those who do not. Not surprisingly, though, there appear to be certain limitations on the occurrence of such effects. In particular, it seems that being imitated by a person lower in status than ourselves is *not* rewarding. In fact, imitation from such persons may be unpleasant, and can lead to lessened liking for them (Thelen and Kirkland, 1976). Such effects are reminiscent of many real-life situations in which low-status persons attempt to improve their relative standing by imitating the actions and preferences of high-status ones—who then react negatively to such "social climbing" by persons they consider to be their subordinates. In sum, being imitated by others may well be a positive experience, but only, it seems, when such emulation stems from the "right" kind of persons.

investigators prohibited young boys in two groups from playing with a number of attractive toys, and then showed them films in which another child was either rewarded or punished by his mother for violating a similar prohibition. The experimenter then left the room, and the speed with which the children violated the restriction against playing with the toys was observed. Subjects in a third group were also left alone with these objects and prohibited from playing with

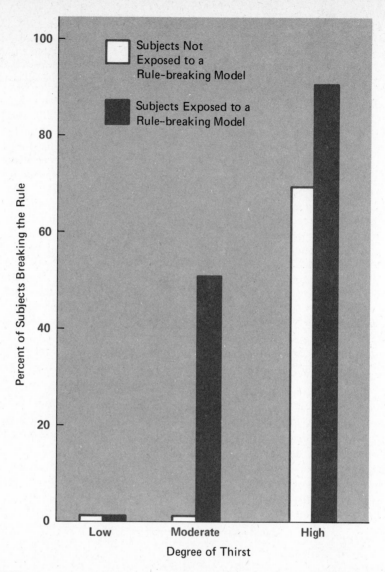

FIGURE 7-2. *When individuals are exposed to the actions of another person who breaks or violates a prohibition, the likelihood that they, too, will engage in such behavior is often increased. In the study represented above, subjects exposed to a model who violated a restriction against drinking at a water fountain were more likely to break this rule too than subjects not exposed to such a model. As might be expected, their tendency to violate the prohibition also increased with their degree of thirst. (Source: Based on data from Kimbrell and Blake, 1958.)*

them, but never witnessed any film in which a similar restriction was violated. The results of the experiment revealed both strong inhibitory and disinhibitory effects on subjects' behavior (see Table 7-1). Children who observed the film in which the model was rewarded for violating the prohibition disobeyed the

TABLE 7-1. *Inhibitory and disinhibitory effects induced by exposure to social models. Subjects who witnessed a peer model rewarded for breaking a prohibition against playing with attractive toys violated this rule more quickly than those not exposed to any model. Similarly, subjects who witnessed the model punished for such behavior violated this rule much more slowly than those not exposed to a model. (Source: Based on data from Walters, Leat, and Mezei, 1963.)*

	Experimental Condition		
	Model Rewarded for Breaking a Prohibition	No-Model Control Group	Model Punished for Breaking a Prohibition
Median Number of Seconds to First Violation	85	285	900

experimenter's command regarding the toys much more quickly than subjects in the control group who saw no film, while those who witnessed the movie in which the model was punished for his actions disobeyed much more slowly (if at all) than those in the no-film control group.

If inhibitory and disinhibitory effects were restricted to prohibitions against playing with certain toys or drinking at specific water fountains, they would be of little practical importance. Growing evidence suggests, however, that they may also play a role in the occurrence and spread of far more significant forms of behavior. In many situations, individuals are motivated to engage in some prohibited actions, but do not do so because of strong social norms, fear of punishment, or other internal restraints. In such cases, the individuals involved may be "pushed over the line," so to speak, by exposure to the actions of others who successfully violate the relevant prohibitions.

Wheeler (1966) has termed such effects **behavioral contagion**, and suggests that they play an important role in the spread of socially prohibited behaviors. While conclusive evidence regarding this suggestion is not yet available, it seems quite possible that this particular form of unintentional social influence may contribute to the occurrence of such disapproved behaviors as cheating on exams, drug abuse, speeding in traffic, marital infidelity, and even collective violence (Bandura, 1973). That is, in all these cases, individuals' restraints against engaging in such actions may be sharply reduced when they observe others performing—and getting away with—prohibited behaviors. Indeed, if the number of persons who violate a restriction is sufficiently large, the actions they perform may no longer even be viewed as wrong or inappropriate (see Figure 7-3).

Response Facilitation: Yawn and the World Yawns with You. A second type of modeling effect, response facilitation, occurs in situations where some action by another person cues or triggers similar behavior by observers in what often seems to be a totally automatic manner. In such cases, the behaviors involved are not prohibited or forbidden—they are simply not occurring prior to the model's action.

"If everybody's doing it, is it still a sin?"

FIGURE 7-3. *When a large number of persons engage in some form of prohibited behavior, the restrictions against its performance may be sharply weakened. In fact, the behavior itself may soon no longer be viewed as wrong or inappropriate. (Source: Copyright 1970 by permission of Saturday Review and Robert Censoni.)*

One good example of such response-facilitating effects is provided by the manner in which yawns spread from one person to another with remarkable ease. Here, a simple form of behavior which is not usually under the control of strong restrictions or controls, is greatly facilitated by mere exposure to others engaged in its performance.

A second illustration of response-facilitating effects has already been presented in the traffic-signal example on p. 304. There, we described a situation in which the actions of one driver (moving forward in response to a green signal) served as a cue for similar behavior by another motorist—with nearly disastrous results. Still another illustration of response facilitation is provided by our strong tendency to look in the direction in which we see others gazing. Again, a type of behavior (looking or orienting in a particular direction) which is not usually forbidden or prohibited is strongly facilitated by mere exposure to others who are exhibiting it. A simple experiment by Milgram, Bickman, and Berkowitz (1969), provides a clear illustration of this type of effect. These investigators arranged for varying numbers of individuals (1, 2, 5, 10, or 15) to stop on a busy Manhattan street and gaze intently at a window on the sixth floor of a nearby building. The incidence with which passersby also looked up, or both stopped and looked in this direction, was then recorded by filming the area during the sixty seconds immediately following the confederates' actions. As can be seen

When we see others gazing in some direction, we usually look there too. This is an example of response facilitation. (Photo: Talbot Lovering.)

in Figure 7-4, the percentage of passersby who demonstrated these behaviors tended to increase as the number of confederates who stopped and looked increased. Thus, the greater the number of models present on the scene, the stronger the response facilitating effects produced.

Although yawning, gazing in a specific direction, and responding to the actions of other drivers may not seem to be particularly significant forms of social behavior, you should not jump to the conclusion that response-facilitating effects are limited to simple actions of this type. In fact, a number of recent experiments suggest that such effects may also play a role in the occurrence of such important forms of behavior as donating to charity (Rushton, 1975), aiding others in distress (Bryan and Test, 1967), and even asking particular types of questions (Rosenthal, Zimmerman, and Durning, 1970). As a result, the importance of this particular form of unintentional social influence may be considerably greater than you might at first suspect.

Observational Learning: When Seeing Is Knowing. When observers are exposed to the behavior of a social model, a third and especially important type of effect may occur: they can acquire new forms of behavior merely by observing his or her actions. Such effects are usually described as *observational learning,* and can be readily noticed in a wide variety of contexts. For example, recall the movie-goer we described on p. 305, who acquired exotic new love-making techniques from the X-rated film she watched. Similarly, consider the case of a new employee who begins to learn the tools of his or her trade by observing the actions of more experienced workers. As a final illustration, imagine a situation in which a group of young men and women acquire the idea for a daring and

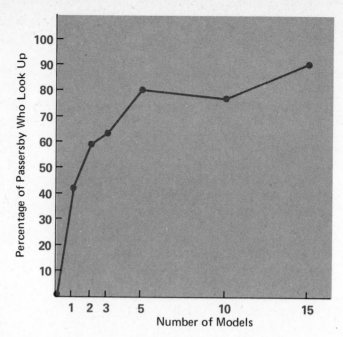

FIGURE 7-4. *The response-facilitating effects of social models. Passersby on a busy Manhattan street gazed upward when they saw others doing so. The greater the number of models present, the greater their tendency to glance in the same direction as these persons. (Source: Adapted from Milgram, Bickman, and Berkowitz, 1969.)*

unusual crime from a detailed report of similar events presented on the evening news. (Unfortunately, such effects appear to be more real than hypothetical: often, reports of unusual crimes on network television are followed by an outbreak of similar events in widely scattered geographic locations; see Bandura, 1973). In these and countless other instances, individuals acquire new responses not previously at their disposal simply by observing the actions of others.

Because of its important implications for many forms of social behavior, observational learning has been the focus of considerable research in recent years. The findings of such work suggest that this process is largely a function of four related factors. First, there is the problem of *attention*. Obviously, one person cannot hope to acquire new responses from another unless he or she observes it with some care. Thus, observational learning is often strongly determined by the degree to which observers have paid close attention to the actions of social models.

Second, there is the important process of *retention*—the extent to which observers can recall a model's behavior after watching his or her performance. Such retention appears to be largely determined by two major factors: the degree to which observers succeed in summarizing (coding) the model's actions in some convenient form, and the extent to which they immediately rehearse it. That is, to the extent that we are able to form some summary representation, either verbal or visual, of another's behavior, and rehearse it either overtly or implicitly, our memory of his or her actions will be enhanced (Bandura and Jeffery, 1973; Gerst, 1971).

A third important factor affecting observational learning is that of *motoric reproduction*. This refers to the fact that the rate at which observers can master complex behaviors demonstrated by a model depends, at least in part, on their prior knowledge of the necessary component responses. If these components are present, they may be readily combined into new and complex patterns as a result of exposure to the model, while if they are lacking, the development of such patterns will be slowed. For example, if you already know how to carry out each of the substeps involved in solving a complex mathematical problem, your ability to solve it may be improved by watching another person work it correctly. If you are unable even to add or subtract, however, seeing another complete it will probably be of little help.

Finally, *incentive* or *motivational* factors play an important role. Behaviors acquired through observational learning will generally be put into actual use only under conditions where individuals anticipate reward—or at least the absence of punishment—for their performance. For example, a bank teller who has acquired the combination to the vault by watching from a carefully concealed location as his employer opens it, may wait for weeks or even months until an especially large shipment of cash is on hand before putting this information to use. Similarly, a child who has acquired a new and potent way of aggressing from observing his favorite action-packed television show will probably not attempt to use it on his mother—an act which will almost certainly bring swift and severe punishment. But he may well use it to terrorize his younger brother or even some of his playmates. In view of the fact that behaviors learned through observation of others are usually only performed under conditions where observers expect them to work—that is, to be rewarded—it is important to draw a clear distinction between the *acquisition* of a model's actions and their actual *performance* (Bandura, 1965). In short, observational learning is no exception to the general rule that knowing is not necessarily doing.

Observational Learning and Socialization. Before concluding our discussion of observational learning, we should comment briefly on its crucial role in **socialization.** By this term we mean the process through which children acquire all of the attitudes, skills, values, and behaviors needed to function effectively as adults in their own society. For many years, it was widely assumed that socialization was based largely on instrumental learning, in which parents rewarded or punished their children for performing what they considered to be appropriate or inappropriate behaviors. Recently, though, there has been growing recognition of the importance of observational learning in this process. We have already examined the major influence of such learning on the formation of attitudes in Chapter 3. But this is only part of the picture. It now appears that children can acquire everything from language to moral values, and from sexual identity to a knowledge of the social norms of their society through observational learning (see Dorr and Fey, 1974; Sternglanz and Serbin, 1974). This is not to

IN SEARCH OF SOCIAL MODELS

If you are willing to expend just a small amount of effort, you can easily observe the three types of modeling effects we have been describing. A good spot at which to observe disinhibitory effects is any busy intersection where large numbers of pedestrians cross the street. If you watch closely, you may notice that if one person starts across while the light is red or the sign says "Don't Walk," many others will jaywalk, too. In fact, it often appears that the actions of a single individual are sufficient to induce an entire crowd of waiting pedestrians to step blindly into the path of oncoming traffic. In such cases, the first jaywalker may be viewed as a social model who, by violating a clear prohibition, reduces the restraints of other bystanders against engaging in similar behavior.

Instances of response facilitation are also quite common. One place where they are especially easy to observe, however, is the theater. Here, there is often a moment of silence at the end of scenes or acts during which no one applauds. Then, one or a few persons begin to clap, and, almost as if on cue, the rest of the audience joins in. It seems reasonable to view these events as a situation in which the first few persons clapping act as social models for the others, facilitating their performance of the appropriate and certainly nonprohibited action of applauding the actors.

Unfortunately, because of the gap between acquisition and performance we mentioned earlier, instances of observational learning are a bit more difficult to notice. However, you can readily observe this process in your own behavior by noting instances in which you acquire new acts, words, or even ideas simply by watching the behavior of others. In such cases, these persons serve as social models for you, and, depending on the behavior they demonstrate, you can acquire responses or information ranging in nature from trivial and useless to valuable and important.

say that instrumental learning or direct instruction are unimportant. They too, play a crucial role. An increasing number of developmental and social psychologists, however, have become convinced that observational learning probably lies very close to the heart of the socialization process.

At this point, we should hasten to add that the role of observational learning in socialization in no way contradicts our earlier suggestion that modeling be viewed as a form of unintentional social influence. It is true, of course, that parents often demonstrate particular forms of behavior in the hope of transmitting these actions to their offspring. And in such cases, the influence they exert, if successful, is anything but unintentional. Most of their actions, however, are *not* directed toward this goal. Yet, as you can probably guess, children are still strongly affected by their parents' behavior, even in such cases. Indeed, it is through such unintentional influence that mothers and fathers teach their children many patterns of behavior they would prefer them to avoid. Further, as you also probably realize, children are often strongly affected by exposure to the actions of many persons other than their parents. Teachers, friends, relatives, and even characters in stories, television shows, or movies can all exert a powerful effect on their behavior, feelings, or thoughts. And of course, in many cases, these persons are not at all concerned with wielding such influence. For example, do you remember any of your childhood heroes or heroines? The chances are good that they affected your behavior to an important degree, even if they were totally unaware of your existence. For these reasons, we feel it is often quite reasonable to view observational learning as a form of unintentional social influence, even with respect to its role in the important process of socialization.

THE PERVASIVE INFLUENCE OF SOCIAL MODELS: HURTING, HELPING, AND SELF-CONTROL

In our discussion of modeling processes up to this point, we have learned that exposure to the behavior and outcomes of others may (1) strengthen or weaken our inhibitions against engaging in similar actions, (2) facilitate our performance of a variety of responses not typically subject to strong restraints, and (3) allow us to acquire new and important forms of behavior not previously at our disposal. There can be little doubt, therefore, that others can exert extremely important effects on our behavior, even in cases where they have no intention of doing so. Obviously, we could not hope to mention all—or even a significant portion—of these effects in the present discussion. What we can do, though, is to provide you with some notion of the truly sweeping nature of such influence by examining the impact of social models on three diverse but significant forms of behavior: aggression, altruism, and self-regulation or control.

Social Models and Aggression: The Impact of Witnessed Violence

Can exposure to the behavior of others who act in a highly aggressive manner serve to elicit similar actions on the part of observers? Two distinct aspects of this important question have been the subject of extensive interest and attention. First, it has been suggested that the presence of live aggressive models may facilitate the initiation and spread of violent acts in many tense and threatening situations, thus playing a major role in the occurrence of tragic instances of collective violence. The findings of a considerable body of research suggest that this may well be the case (Baron, 1974; Baron and Bell, 1975). Since these investigations will be examined in some detail in a later chapter, however, we will not focus upon them here.

Second, it has frequently been suggested that exposure to a steady diet of violence in the mass media—particularly television—may significantly increase children's (and possibly adults') tendencies to behave in a similar manner. We have already encountered this issue in Chapter 1 where, as you may recall, we examined several studies concerned with the possible effects of televised violence as a means of illustrating the nature of social psychological research. We have decided to return to it here for two reasons. First, this issue provides an especially interesting illustration of the potential impact of models on social behavior. And second, the general question of whether televised violence adversely affects young viewers has been the center of one of the most heated and bitter controversies involving psychologists in recent years. As such, it seems well deserving of very careful attention.

Basically, research concerned with the effects of filmed or televised violence on observers may be viewed as having been conducted in three distinct waves or "generations." As you might guess, each successive generation grew out of criticisms of the research which preceded it, so that, in general, the investigations performed have become increasingly sophisticated and convincing with the passing years. Thus, in addition to providing you with information about the impact of televised or filmed violence on viewers, a summary of this research also offers one concrete example of the course of scientific progress within social psychology.

Phase One: The "Bobo Doll" Studies. The earliest research relating to this general issue was conducted by Albert Bandura and his co-workers (Bandura, 1965; Bandura, Ross, and Ross, 1963a, 1963b). In these studies, young children of nursery school age were exposed to short films (often projected onto the screen of a television set) in which adult models aggressed in very unusual ways against a large inflated toy clown (a "Bobo doll"). Thus, in one particular study (Bandura, Ross, and Ross, 1963a), the model performed such unusual acts as sitting on the doll and punching it repeatedly in the nose, pommeling it on the head with a toy mallet, kicking it about the room, and making such statements as "Sock him in the nose . . . ," "Hit him down . . . " and so on. Following exposure to these scenes, the children were placed in a room containing a variety of toys, several of which had been used by the model in his aggressive behavior, and allowed to play freely for a brief period of time (e.g., twenty minutes). During this interval, their behavior was carefully observed in order to determine whether and to what degree they would match the novel actions of the model. In general, the results of these studies revealed strong imitative effects (see Figure 7-5). Indeed, in some instances, the children actually appeared to become veritable "carbon copies" of the adult models they had observed.

Since the specific acts performed by the model were ones which were very rarely demonstrated by children not exposed to the films, these findings were usually interpreted as indicating that children may acquire new forms of physical and verbal aggression through the observation of such actions on the part of others. This is a reasonable conclusion, and one which was seldom called into question. However, some investigators, impressed by the fact that similar findings were obtained over and over again in a large number of studies (for example, Grusec, 1972; Hanratty, O'Neal, and Sulzer, 1972; Rice and Grusec, 1975) went one step further. Specifically, they employed such findings as grounds for concluding that televised violence not only teaches children new ways of aggressing, but also encourages them to participate in such behavior.

While this is certainly a very thought-provoking suggestion, and one which was soon to be supported by additional research, it rested, at that point in time, on shaky logical grounds. As we noted earlier, there is often a considerable gap

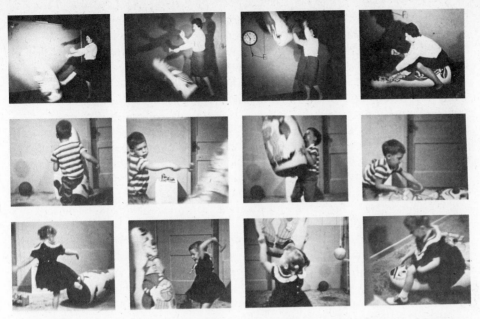

FIGURE 7-5. *Imitative aggression in young children. After witnessing an adult model (top row) engage in unusual aggressive acts directed toward a large inflated toy (a "Bobo doll"), children often performed such actions themselves. (From Bandura, Ross, and Ross, 1963a, p. 8. Copyright 1963 by the American Psychological Association. Reprinted by permission.)*

between knowing how to perform a particular action and actually performing it. Thus, the fact that children can acquire new ways of aggressing from popular television shows in no way guarantees that they will become more aggressive in their dealings with others as a result. The possibility for such effects exists, of course, but they are far from assured.

In addition to this logical problem, critics soon called attention to several aspects of the "Bobo doll" studies themselves which raised serious questions about the meaning of their results (Klapper, 1968). First, it was noted that the subjects in these experiments aggressed against inflated plastic toys specifically designed for such treatment rather than against another human being. As a result, it is not entirely clear that their behavior may reasonably be termed aggression—after all, no one was actually hurt in any manner. Second, the films viewed by subjects differed in several important ways from standard TV fare. For example, they failed to include a plot, provided no cause or justification for the model's behavior, and showed adults engaging in actions highly unlikely to appear on TV or anywhere else. Finally, the children in this research were provided with an opportunity to aggress in precisely the same manner as the models they observed, whereas viewers who witness violent acts by television characters rarely attain similar opportunities. For example, children are rarely able to take part in a military battle, or engage in a showdown with an outlaw after witnessing such incidents on TV.

For these reasons, it seemed unwise to interpret the findings of Bandura's early research as providing strong evidence for the suggestion that filmed or televised violence encourages interpersonal aggression. The fact that children can acquire new ways of aggressing from even brief exposure to televised models certainly pointed in this direction, but the evidence left too many gaps to be viewed as conclusive.

Phase Two: Laboratory Studies of Hurting. Confronted with the criticisms outlined above, many researchers quickly began to both plan and execute studies designed to eliminate these problems. Basically, these experiments sought to accomplish three major goals. First, they attempted to employ more realistic measures of aggression in which subjects' attacks would be directed against other human beings rather than mere plastic toys. Second, they exposed participants to more realistic violent materials—ones quite similar to or actually taken from TV shows or movies. Finally, they sought to eliminate the precise similarity present in earlier studies between the aggressive programs watched by subjects and the context within which they themselves could aggress.

We have already considered an example of such research in Chapter 1 where we discussed an investigation conducted by Liebert and Baron (1972). As you may recall, subjects in that experiment (young boys and girls) were first exposed either to a violent excerpt from an actual television show ("The Untouchables") or an equally exciting but nonviolent track race. Following this experience, they were provided with an opportunity to aggress against another child by means of a special red button which supposedly burned this individual each time it was pushed. (In reality, there was no victim, and no one was harmed in any manner during the study.) As we noted in Chapter 1, results indicated that subjects exposed to the violent program did in fact choose to deliver stronger attacks to the imaginary victim than those exposed to the nonaggressive race.

Similar findings have also been reported in a number of related studies conducted with both children and adults (see Tannenbaum and Zillmann, 1975). Basically, in all these studies, subjects were first exposed either to realistic scenes of aggression or other, nonviolent materials, and then permitted to aggress against another person by means of electric shock, heat, or intense noise (Berkowitz and Alioto, 1973; Geen and Stonner, 1972). In general, results have supported the view that exposure to filmed, televised, or even verbal descriptions of aggression may facilitate similar behavior by observers (Wilkins, Scharff, and Schlottmann, 1974). There do appear to be some limiting conditions on such effects, however.

First, it appears that exposure to filmed or televised violence may facilitate similar actions by observers only when the aggression they witness seems justified (Berkowitz and Alioto, 1973). If it appears unjustified, aggression may fail to be increased. Second, there is some indication that while actual aggressive behavior may be enhanced by exposure to scenes of violence, feelings of anger or hostility may sometimes be reduced (Manning and Taylor, 1975). In general, though, such "second generation" research on the effects of observed violence pointed to the conclusion that exposure to such materials may actually increase the level of overt aggression shown by observers.

While these experiments seemed to eliminate several of the problems raised about the early "Bobo doll" studies conducted by Bandura and others, they too were open to criticism on several grounds. First, it was noted that the measures of aggression employed in such investigations, although improved over hitting a plastic toy, were still far from perfect. Human beings rarely aggress against specific persons by pushing a button to burn or shock them (although they do often push buttons to aggress in more destructive ways, e.g., launching missiles or dropping bombs). As a result, there is some question as to whether participants in such experiments always believed that they were actually hurting another person through these actions. Second, although the programs shown to subjects were quite realistic in content, they were artificially brief—usually lasting only a few moments. Since most filmed or televised aggression is of a much longer duration, it is quite possible that such materials actually exert markedly different effects upon observers. And finally, only the immediate impact of observed violence on subjects' behavior was assessed. No information regarding possible long-term effects was obtained in these studies. In order to take account of such criticisms, a number of researchers have recently conducted what might be termed "third generation" experiments concerning the effects of witnessed aggression.

Phase Three: Long-term Field Studies. In these experiments, subjects have been exposed to full-length films, complete television shows, or even to controlled diets of violent or nonviolent materials for several days or weeks. And then their actual aggressive behavior in naturalistic settings has been observed over similarly extended periods of time. In this way, most criticisms of earlier research on this topic have been largely eliminated.

Despite all the differences between these sophisticated field studies and earlier laboratory experiments, their findings have usually pointed to the same general conclusions: exposure to filmed or televised violence increases the likelihood that viewers will themselves engage in such behavior (Leyens et al., 1975; Parke et al., 1975). We have already reviewed one of these studies in Chapter 1 (Leyens et al., 1975), and you may recall that in this investigation, boys exposed to several violent movies tended to become more aggressive in their interactions with others than boys exposed to nonviolent films (see pp. 25–26).

In general, such effects have been viewed as stemming from three major factors. First, individuals often learn new ways of aggressing from exposure to scenes of violence *(observational learning)*. Second, they undergo a sharp reduction in the strength of their restraints against such behavior *(disinhibition)*. And finally, they experience a gradual **desensitization** to aggression and signs of suffering on the part of others, so that after watching a great deal of violence, they no longer experience negative reactions to such behavior. This last process was demonstrated in an experiment by Cline, Croft, and Courrier (1973), in which children who watched a great deal of TV (25 hours a week or more) and children who watch very little TV (4 hours or less each week) were exposed to a violent boxing match. As expected, the heavy viewers demonstrated far less emotional reaction to the aggressive scenes than the light viewers (see Figure 7-6). Although far from conclusive (heavy and light TV viewers may have differed in a number of ways), such findings suggest that continual exposure to scenes of violence may lessen our negative reactions to such behavior, and so make it easier for us to engage in it ourselves.

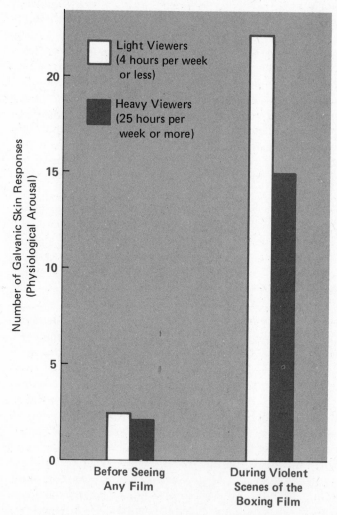

FIGURE 7-6. *When exposed to a brutal boxing match, children who usually watch a great deal of TV (25 hours a week or more) showed lower levels of physiological arousal than children who watch very little TV (4 hours a week or less). These findings suggest that constant exposure to televised violence may desensitize viewers to aggression, and so make it easier for them to engage in such actions themselves. (Source: Based on data from Cline, Croft, and Courrier, 1973.)*

At this point, we should hasten to add that not all results have pointed toward an aggression-facilitating effect of observed violence. In fact, there have been two notable exceptions to this otherwise consistent pattern of findings. First, Feshbach and Singer (1971) found that boys exposed to a steady diet of aggressive TV programs actually demonstrated *lower* levels of aggression in their interactions with others than boys exposed to nonaggressive shows. And Milgram and Shotland (1973) reported neither an increase nor a decrease in various antisocial behaviors (such as stealing or making abusive phone calls) as a result of viewing or not viewing such actions on an actual television program.

Because both these studies (and especially the Feshbach and Singer experiment) have been criticized on methodological grounds, it is our impression that the weight of existing evidence favors the view that exposure to scenes of violence does increase the tendency of observers to behave in a similar aggressive manner. But please take heed: this does *not* mean that after watching their favorite action-packed (and aggression-packed) program, adults or children are likely to rush out and launch blind attacks against anyone unfortunate enough to cross their path. What it does mean, we believe, is that this particular type of unintentional social influence may be contributing, along with many other factors (see Chapter 9), to the occurrence of overt aggression.

Social Models and Helping: Exposure to Hypocrites and Saints

In several respects, helping and other forms of prosocial behavior fall at the opposite end of the social continuum from aggression and violence. Yet evidence collected in recent years suggests that these behaviors, too, may be strongly influenced by exposure to the actions of social models.

In the case of adults, a number of interesting field experiments have demonstrated the impact of helping actions by others on observers' tendencies to engage in similar behavior (Piliavin, Rodin, and Piliavin, 1969). For example, in one early study, Bryan and Test (1967) arranged conditions so that motorists driving along a busy thoroughfare were exposed to one of two experimental conditions. In the first, they passed two "ladies in distress"—two young women whose cars were pulled over to the side of the road with flat tires. A male confederate was changing the tire on the first car, while no one was as yet assisting the second young woman. Thus, in this condition, subjects observed a helping model and were then provided with an opportunity to offer assistance themselves. In the second experimental group, only the second car was present. As a result, passing motorists were not exposed to the actions of a helping model before obtaining an opportunity to help another person (see Figure 7-7).

The main question under study was whether motorists exposed to the helping model would be more willing to aid the second lady in distress than drivers not exposed to such a model. As can be seen in Table 7-2, this was actually the case. In two additional studies, Bryan and Test moved their research to busy shopping centers in order to determine whether shoppers who witnessed a model drop coins into a Salvation Army kettle would make more donations

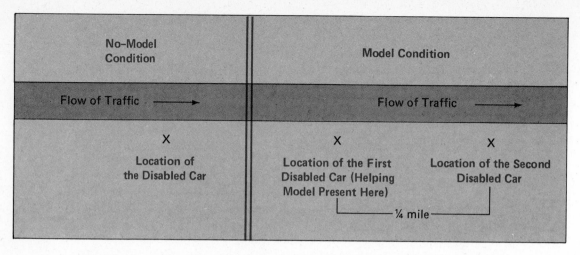

FIGURE 7-7. *The physical arrangement used by Bryan and Test (1967) to investigate the effects of exposure to a helping model on motorists' willingness to stop and assist a "lady in distress." In the no-model condition, drivers passed only one young woman in need of assistance, while in the model condition, they passed two, one of whom was already obtaining aid from a helping model.*

themselves than individuals not exposed to such actions by a model. Again, results supported these predictions (refer to Table 7-2). Similar findings regarding the influence of helping models on the behavior of observers have also been obtained in laboratory experiments (Krebs, 1970). That is, in these studies, too, exposure to others who act in a generous or helpful manner has been found to increase subjects' tendency to offer aid to persons in need of assistance. Further, exposure to selfish models has been shown to sharply *reduce* helping and generosity by observers (Wagner and Wheeler, 1969). Indeed, so powerful do the effects of such models appear to be, that subjects are strongly influenced by their actions even under conditions where they (subjects) express strong disapproval of the model's selfish actions, and deny any intention of imitating them (Masor, Hornstein, and Tobin, 1973).

If adults are strongly affected by exposure to generous or selfish models, it seems only reasonable to expect that children will be influenced to an even greater degree by such experience. That this is actually the case has been demonstrated in a number of recent studies. In most of these experiments, subjects have been asked to perform, along with another person, on a miniature bowling alley of the type shown in Figure 7-8. It is explained to them at the start of the session that each time either player attains a particular high score (for example, 20), he or she will receive several tokens which can later be exchanged for one of several attractive prizes. The experimenter further explains that each time one of the players wins some tokens, he or she has the option of keeping them all, or donating as many as he or she wishes to charity. (A special bowl or container for this purpose is placed nearby.)

TABLE 7-2. *The effects of a helping model on prosocial behavior. Subjects exposed to a model who helped a motorist with a flat tire or donated to charity were more likely to engage in such behaviors than those not exposed to helping models. (Source: Based on data from Bryan and Test, 1967.)*

	Experimental Condition	
	No Model	*Model*
Number Helping a "Lady in Distress" (out of 2,000 passing drivers)	35	58
Number Donating to Charity (out of several hundred passing shoppers)	43	69

During the game, conditions are arranged so that both the model and subject win on a number of trials. The actions shown by the model on such occasions are then systematically varied so that he either demonstrates generosity, donating to charity on each winning occasion, or demonstrates greed, making no contributions whatsoever. In general, the results of studies employing these procedures indicate that subjects' own behavior is strongly affected by the actions of the model. That is, those exposed to generosity donate more of their winnings than subjects in a control group not exposed to any actions by the model, while those exposed to selfish actions donate *less* than those in a no-model control group (Grusec, 1972; White, 1972).

Words versus Deeds: Practicing What You Preach. One interesting question which has often been raised with respect to the influence of models on children's behavior is the relative impact of the words and deeds of such persons: if children are exposed to models who verbally recommend one type of behavior, but then demonstrate another, which of these conflicting cues will they follow?

This question, of course, is by no means restricted to the impact of models upon helping. As you probably know from your own experience, hypocrisy is far from rare, and both children and adults are often exposed to others whose words and deeds are inconsistent (see Figure 7-9). Since most research on this topic has been conducted within the context of the effects of social models on children's prosocial behavior, however, we will also focus on this issue here.

A series of initial studies conducted by James Bryan and his colleagues (Bryan and Walbek, 1970; Bryan, Redfield, and Mader, 1971) seemed to suggest that, in general, a model's deeds are far more important than his or her words in

FIGURE 7-8. *A miniature bowling alley of the type often used in studies concerned with the effects of helping models upon children's prosocial behavior. Players receive tokens for "winning" scores which can later be redeemed for various prizes. Subjects exposed to helping models observe these individuals donate part of their winnings to charity. (Courtesy of Dr. Robert M. Liebert.)*

influencing children's behavior. In these experiments, youngsters were exposed either to models who failed to practice what they preached—urging generosity while practicing greed, or urging greed while practicing generosity—or to models whose verbal preachings and overt behavior were consistent. Results indicated that, in general, subjects were influenced to a far greater extent by the model's actions than by his or her words (see Table 7-3).

More recent studies indicate, though, that a model's verbal preachings *can* be effective in influencing observers' behavior under some conditions (see Rushton, 1977). For example, in one recent experiment, Rushton (1975) argued that perhaps verbal preaching proved ineffective in earlier studies because it was employed in a manner which tended to weaken its impact. Often, in these previous studies, the model's comments were not directed specifically to the subject, but were stated in a more general manner, almost as if she were talking to herself. Similarly, the model was usually a person subjects never expected to see again. In view of these facts, it is not at all surprising that her verbal recommendations had little effect on their behavior.

In order to determine whether verbal preaching might be more effective under other, more favorable conditions, Rushton (1975) conducted a study using the bowling alley procedures outlined above, in which the model was described to

FIGURE 7-9. *As shown above, there is often a considerable gap between parents' actual behavior and their verbal preachings to their children. (Source: "The Family Circus," by Bil Keane, reprinted courtesy of* The Register and Tribune Syndicate, *1975.)*

subjects as a future teacher in their school, and directed her preaching specifically to them. Surprisingly, even under these conditions, the model's verbal comments failed to exert an *immediate* effect upon subjects' behavior—only her actions (greed or generosity) influenced their behavior. However, when the children were retested in the same setting two months later, an effect of the model's preaching did emerge (see Figure 7-10). Subjects exposed to a model who preached generosity donated more of their winnings to charity than subjects exposed to a model who recommended selfishness.

In view of the fact that parents have considerable power over their children, and usually do direct their verbal suggestions to their youngsters in a highly specific manner, the findings of Rushton's study suggest that verbal preaching may sometimes prove effective. However, there is little doubt that the most powerful effects will be produced under conditions where a model's words and deeds are consistent and point in the same direction. Thus, our recommendation to parents wishing to direct their children's behavior into specific, desired patterns is as follows: always be careful to practice what you preach, and to preach what you practice.

Social Models and the Internal Regulation of Behavior

In many situations, we are prevented from behaving in the manner we would prefer or from obtaining various rewards we would like to possess by the

TABLE 7-3. *The impact of a model's words and deeds on children's willingness to donate to charity. In general, subjects are more strongly affected by the model's acts than by his or her words. Thus, they make larger donations when the model acts in a generous manner, and smaller donations when the model acts in a selfish manner, regardless of his or her verbal statements. Numbers shown represent the percentage of their winnings donated by subjects to charity. (Source: Based on data from Bryan and Walbek, 1970.)*

Model's Verbal Preachings	Model's Overt Behavior	
	Charity	Greed
Charity	33.1	14.7
Greed	37.4	18.7

presence of external forces and restraints. For example, we may be prevented from speeding on the highway by the presence of state troopers, from gaining entry to a football game by guards who will not let us pass without a ticket, and from purchasing some item we desire by a lack of money. In these and many other cases, it is safe to predict that if such barriers were removed, we would quickly shift to more preferred modes of responding.

In a number of other situations, however, such external obstacles or restraints are lacking, yet we still avoid acting in a totally self-indulgent manner. For example, suppose you visited the office of one of your professors and saw a copy of next week's final exam lying on her desk. Would you steal it? The temptation to do so might be strong, but quite probably you would resist, and quickly leave the room. Similarly, imagine that you could obtain a desirable job by circulating false but damaging rumors about the person who now holds it. Would you do so? Again, the temptation to follow such an approach might be strong, but your feeling that such tactics are morally wrong might well prevent you from actually adopting them. In such situations, our behavior is clearly under the control of certain internal standards—rules we impose on ourselves. In some cases, we adopt such standards willingly and with ease, while in others we can maintain them only by means of a difficult and continuous struggle. In both cases, however, the outcome is usually much the same: our behavior is markedly changed from what it might otherwise be—and often from patterns we would prefer.

Such internal regulators of behavior take many different forms, but among the most important are the capacity to resist temptation, and the ability to delay gratification—to put off small rewards today, in order to obtain larger ones at a later time. Both are important in situations where we are not subject to constant surveillance, and both have been shown to be strongly influenced by the actions of the persons around us, even when they are *not* specifically attempting to produce such effects.

Resistance to Temptation: Learning from the Mistakes (and Punishments) of Others. We have already considered some evidence relating to the influence of social models on resistance to temptation in our discussion of the experiment by Walters, Leat, and Mezei (1963). You may recall that in this study young children were left alone in a room with a display of attractive toys they were

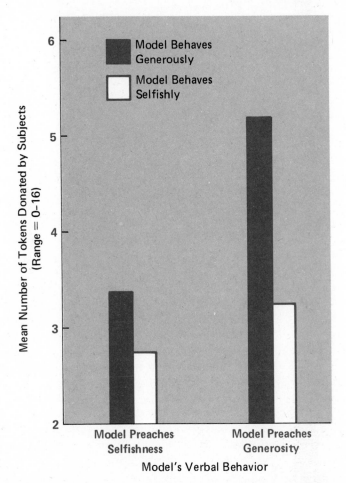

FIGURE 7-10. *The effects of a model's words and deeds on children's delayed willingness to donate to charity. Subjects contributed more of their winnings when the model preached generosity than when she preached selfishness, and also donated more when she acted generously than when she acted selfishly. Note that these effects of the model's verbal statements became visible only several weeks after subjects were exposed to her behavior; no immediate impact of the model's preachings was observed. (Source: Based on data from Rushton, 1975.)*

The Pervasive Influence of Social Models: Hurting, Helping, and Self-Control

forbidden to touch after witnessing films in which another child received either reward or punishment for violating a similar prohibition. Results indicated that, as expected, subjects exposed to the model-punished film were much more reluctant to violate the experimenter's prohibition against playing with the toys than subjects exposed to the model-rewarded film. In short, subjects' ability to resist even this powerful temptation was greatly increased by exposure to scenes in which another person suffered negative outcomes as a result of breaking the rule.

Similar findings in other studies (Bandura, 1974) point to the conclusion that whenever individuals are tempted to behave in some prohibited fashion but witness others being punished for such actions, their own inhibitions against breaking these rules may be greatly increased. Experiences of this type, of course, are far from rare, both for children and adults. For example, many popular TV shows and movies contain plots in which persons who yield to temptation are punished, sooner or later, for their transgressions (the familiar "crime-does-not-pay" message). And this theme is repeated in many fairy tales and stories parents present to their offspring. For example, do you remember Pinnochio's punishment for lying? Together, the findings of laboratory research and such informal evidence suggest that resistance to various types of temptation is based largely on inhibitions acquired through exposure to real or imaginary social models. Basically, we learn to resist because we fear the negative outcomes we have seen others experience after yielding.

Delay of Gratification: Waiting for Rewards. The ability to forego present rewards in order to obtain larger ones at some point in the future is both important and useful. Without it, individuals would be unable to complete the years of formal training required for entry into highly skilled professions, to put aside some money for a rainy day, or even to avoid snacks in order to save their appetite for a later delicious meal. Early attempts to account for such **delay of gratification** often suggested that it stemmed from the development of the *superego* (conscience), the resolution of personality conflicts, and other purely internal events (see Mischel, Ebbesen, and Zeiss, 1972). More recently, though, it has become apparent that modeling plays a crucial role in its development.

Specifically, it appears that exposure to the actions of others—parents, friends, relatives—who demonstrate a preference for either immediate or delayed gratification strongly affects our own orientation in this respect. Evidence for the occurrence of such effects has been gathered in several experiments (Bandura and Mischel, 1965; Stumphauzer, 1970), but among the most informative of these is a study conducted by Stumphauzer (1972).

In this investigation, male inmates at a state institution for youthful offenders were first tested in a special way to determine whether they held a preference for small but immediate, or larger but delayed, rewards. The test, which was based on procedures used in previous studies (Bandura and Mischel, 1965), required subjects to choose between fourteen pairs of rewards—one small but immediate and the other larger but delayed. For example, one of the fourteen pairs offered subjects a choice between $.35 now and $.50 in a week.

Only subjects who expressed a marked preference for immediate rewards were chosen for participation in the remainder of the study. In a second session, these individuals were either exposed or not exposed to the choices of a peer model (another prisoner who was working for the experimenter) before making their own selections on the delay-of-gratification test. As you might guess, the model chose the larger but delayed reward on all occasions.

Results indicated that when subjects then made their own choices on a new set of items, those exposed to the model showed a dramatic increase in their preference for delayed rewards (see Figure 7-11). Indeed, they moved from

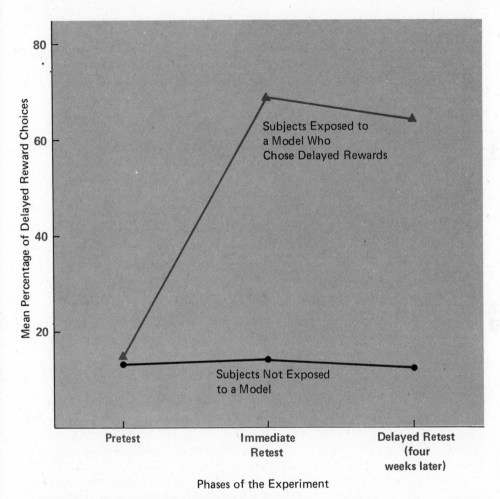

FIGURE 7-11. *The effects of social models on delay of gratification. Subjects who strongly preferred immediate, small rewards over delayed but larger ones reversed this preference following exposure to another person who consistently chose delayed rewards. Further, they did not revert to their initial preference for immediate gratification when retested four weeks later. (Source: Based on data from Stumphauzer, 1972.)*

selecting such alternatives only 15 percent of the time to choosing them on more than 70 percent of the trials. (Individuals in a control group not exposed to the model, of course, showed no similar alterations.) Further, when subjects were retested four weeks later, these changes still persisted: those exposed to the model's choices continued to show a marked preference for delayed but larger rewards. When it is recalled that the subjects in this study were in their early twenties and had had many years in which to practice a preference for immediate rewards, these findings seem doubly impressive. Apparently, even a few moments' exposure to an appropriate social model may be sufficient to reverse a long-standing, self-indulgent pattern of behavior.

As we have already noted, the ability to choose larger, but delayed rewards over smaller but immediate ones has many important implications. In fact, such delay of gratification seems to be essential for the attainment of many kinds of success in our complex, technological society. In this respect, it is interesting—but a bit unsettling—to note that while individuals from middle-class backgrounds, who are exposed to many high-delay models, are usually quite accomplished at deferring gratification in this manner, those from lower socio-economic levels, who are not exposed to such models with similar frequency, are not (Mischel, 1958, 1976). Such differences suggest that an orientation toward immediate or delayed gratification acquired through exposure to varying social models may ultimately be one of the major forces operating to "lock" individuals into various levels of the existing economic order. To the extent that this is true, such modeling represents an especially crucial form of unintentional social influence.

VICARIOUS EMOTIONAL AROUSAL: REACTING TO THE FEELINGS OF OTHERS

In Chapter 2, we discussed the manner in which we use the facial expressions, posture, and body movements of other persons as clues to their present emotional states. At that time, we noted that such nonverbal communication is very common, and that we are often quite adept in its use. However, we ignored an important and closely related question to which we now wish to turn: once we have succeeded in "reading" the emotions of others, does this knowledge have any impact on our own emotional states? As you probably know from your own experience, the answer is certainly "yes." In many cases, seeing other persons demonstrate signs of anger, sorrow, joy, or despair strongly affects our own feelings.

At first, you might assume that exposure to signs of emotional arousal in others always induces similar reactions in us—an occurrence usually known as **empathy.** However, while such effects *are* quite common, they do not occur in every case. Two other possibilities also exist. First, seeing signs of positive emotions on the part of others (for example, happiness) may sometimes serve to induce negative feelings in us (for example, anger). You are probably already quite familiar with such reactions under the heading of **envy.** Second, exposure to signs of negative emotional arousal on the part of others (for example, pain) sometimes induces positive responses in us (for example, joy). Such reactions are generally described as **sadism,** and, again, are far from rare in human interaction. (A summary of these three types of vicarious emotional arousal is provided in Table 7-4).

In the past few years, social psychologists have become increasingly aware of the important role of such reactions in many forms of social behavior. For example, it is now widely recognized that signs of pain on the part of a victim may often serve to inhibit further aggression against this person (Baron, 1974; Geen, 1970); that signs of pleasure on the part of other donors can strengthen altruistic tendencies (Midlarsky and Bryan, 1973); and that signs of fear on the part of several others can contribute to the development of dangerous panics (Gross et al., 1972). Since we will return to the influence of vicarious emotional arousal on such behaviors in later chapters, we will not focus on them here. Rather, we will first review some of the direct, physiological evidence for the occurrence of vicarious emotional arousal, and then examine the manner in which (combined with basic forms of learning) it contributes to the development of strong fears and intense racial or ethnic prejudice.

The Social Communication of Emotion: Evidence for the Occurrence of Vicarious Emotional Arousal

Informal evidence for the existence of vicarious emotional arousal is very easy to acquire—simply visit any nearby movie theater and discreetly observe members of the audience during the feature. In all probability, you will soon notice many persons reacting in a highly emotional manner to signs of grief, anger, fear, or other emotions on the part of actors on the screen. More formal evidence regarding the occurrence of such arousal is a bit more difficult to come by, for it involves the task of demonstrating heightened physiological arousal among subjects exposed to signs of emotion on the part of others. However, evidence of

TABLE 7-4. *Three forms of vicarious emotional arousal. In all three cases, exposure to signs of emotional arousal on the part of another person induces emotional reactions in us. As shown below, though, the relationship between his or her emotions and our own may vary greatly. (Based on proposals by Berger, 1962.)*

Type of Vicarious Arousal	Other Person's Emotional Reaction	Our Emotional Reaction
Empathy	Positive (joy) Negative (sorrow)	Positive (joy) Negative (sorrow)
Envy	Positive (joy)	Negative (anger)
Sadism	Negative (pain)	Positive (delight)

SOCIAL MODELS AND PAIN: EXTERNAL INFLUENCES ON INTERNAL REACTIONS

Pain is a very personal experience; in fact, it seems so much an internal, subjective event that it is hard for us to imagine it being influenced by the actions of other persons. Yet, evidence collected in recent years suggests that this is actually the case. In fact, several experiments by Kenneth Craig and his colleagues (Craig and Weiss, 1971, 1972; Craig and Neidermeyer, 1974) indicate that even our reactions to pain-producing stimuli may be strongly determined by the behavior of the persons around us.

For example, in one of these studies (Craig and Weiss, 1971), male college students were exposed to a series of increasingly painful electric shocks. Their task each time they were shocked was that of throwing one of five switches labeled "undetectable," "slightly detectable," "detectable," "questionably painful," and "painful" to indicate their subjective reactions. It was further explained that as soon as they reached the "painful" category, the session would be ended, and no further shocks administered. Before reacting to each shock, subjects saw another person (actually an accomplice of the experimenter) indicate *his* reactions to what they believed to be shocks identical to the ones they received. In one condition (the *pain-intolerant model* group), this person indicated high and increasing levels of pain; in fact, his reactions were always stronger than those of the subject on the preceding trial. In a second group (the *pain-tolerant model* group), his reactions were relatively low and although they increased, always remained below those of the subject. Finally, in a third, *control* group, the model's reactions were moderate and were based on the actual reactions of naive subjects to the same shocks.

The results of the experiment were quite straightforward: exposure to the pain-tolerant model sharply raised the level of shocks subjects would tolerate before throwing the "painful" switch, while exposure to the pain intolerant model sharply lowered this level, relative to the control condition (see Figure 7-12). In short, the amount of pain reported by subjects in response to identical shocks was either raised or lowered by exposure to the reactions of another person.

Although these results provide convincing evidence for the view that even such subjective, internal reactions as pain may be influenced by social models, they are open to question in one important respect: it is impossible to determine whether subjects actually *experienced* greater or lesser degrees of pain as a result of viewing the model's reactions, or merely *reported* such shifts. While it is impossible to get inside another person's head and measure the amount of pain he or she is experiencing, it *is* possible to get at this problem in a less direct manner. Specifically, it seems reasonable to argue that if subjects exposed to the pain-tolerant model were merely describing the strong shocks they received as nonpainful, but were actually experiencing high levels of discomfort, their degree of physiological arousal would be higher than that of subjects exposed to the pain-intolerant model, who accepted only much lower levels of shock.

In order to examine this suggestion, Craig and Neidermeyer (1974) conducted a study in which subjects' physiological reactions (as measured by heart rate and skin conductance) as well as their subjective reactions to shock were measured. As before, subjects received a series of shocks of increasing intensity after witnessing the reactions of pain-tolerant or pain-intolerant models. Results indicated that consistent with previous findings, subjects' *reported* reactions to the shocks were strongly influenced by the model's behavior: those exposed to the pain-tolerant model accepted higher levels of shock before throwing the "painful" switch

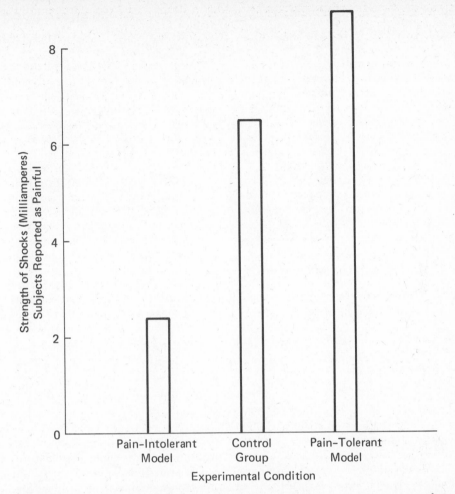

FIGURE 7-12. *The effects of social models on reported pain. Exposure to another person who demonstrated high tolerance for pain (a pain-tolerant model) increased the level of shock subjects were willing to tolerate themselves. Similarly, exposure to another person who showed little tolerance for pain (a pain-intolerant model) reduced the level of shocks subjects were willing to tolerate. (Source: Based on data from Craig and Weiss, 1971.)*

than those exposed to the pain-intolerant model. In addition, and of even greater interest, subjects exposed to the pain-tolerant model did *not* demonstrate higher levels of physiological arousal than those exposed to the pain-intolerant model, despite the fact that they accepted much stronger shocks than these latter individuals. In short, it appeared that the model's behavior affected not only subjects' reported reactions to the shocks, but their actual levels of physical discomfort as well. If unintentional social influence can alter even such internal, private reactions as these, it is hard to imagine any aspects of our behavior which will prove totally immune to its powerful impact.

When we are exposed to strong signs of emotion on the part of others, we often experience heightened emotional arousal ourselves.

precisely this type has actually been obtained in a series of experiments conducted by Richard Lazarus and his colleagues (Lazarus et al., 1962; Lazarus, Speisman, and Mordkoff, 1964).

In these studies, adult subjects were exposed to a film depicting a frightening religious ritual conducted by members of a primitive society. During the course of this ritual, a boy approximately thirteen or fourteen years of age was physically restrained by three or four older men, and the underside of his penis was cut open by means of a piece of sharpened stone. While subjects watched this stress-inducing scene, several measures of their level of emotional arousal (skin conductance, heart rate) were continuously recorded in order to determine whether the amount of arousal they experienced would be related to the events shown on the screen. In general, such a relationship was clearly indicated, with subjects' emotionality rising to extremely high levels at points in the film where the victim showed signs of pain and suffering, but dropping to much lower levels when the events depicted were of a less upsetting nature (see Figure 7-13).

Additional evidence for the existence of vicarious emotional arousal has been obtained in several experiments conducted by Robert Miller and his co-workers (Miller, Caul, and Mirsky, 1967; Miller, Levine, and Mirsky, 1973). In these investigations, monkeys exposed to a televised image of another monkey showing intense emotional upset tended to become emotionally aroused themselves. However, this was true only for animals raised in the wild or together with other monkeys in the laboratory: those raised in social isolation showed little reaction to the emotional expressions of a partner (Miller, Caul, and Mirsky, 1967). These latter findings suggest that responding emotionally to signs of emotional arousal on the part of others is *not* an innate ability. Rather, it seems to be acquired through social-learning experiences.

In all probability, you do not find the existence of vicarious emotional

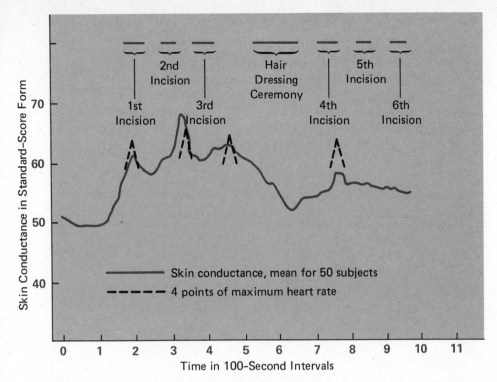

FIGURE 7-13. *Vicarious emotional arousal in response to the reactions of a filmed model. Subjects watching a movie in which a boy was cut with a stone knife showed maximum physiological arousal at times when the victim evidenced signs of intense pain and suffering. As might be expected, they showed lower levels of arousal at other times during the film. (Source: Adapted from Lazarus et al., 1962. Copyright 1962 by the American Psychological Association. Reprinted by permission.)*

arousal very surprising. Your own informal experience may well have convinced you, long before reading our comments, that emotions can be communicated in this manner. Even if this is the case, though, it is our view that scientific evidence regarding the occurrence of vicarious arousal is still important. Before it was available, we merely *suspected* that such social communication of emotion occurred. Now we know with some degree of certainty that it does.

While the simple existence of vicarious emotional arousal is not in itself unexpected, the role of this process in certain kinds of social learning—especially the development of strong fears and intense racial or ethnic prejudice—is not quite so obvious. Thus, it is to these topics that we turn next.

Vicarious Classical Conditioning: A Basis for Fear and Hate?

According to well-established psychological principles, if an initially neutral stimulus incapable of evoking a particular response is repeatedly paired with another stimulus which *is* capable of evoking this response, it too may soon acquire the ability to do so. This process of *classical conditioning* is usually illustrated in psychology texts by means of the familiar example involving a bell (the conditioned stimulus) which is at first incapable of inducing salivation from hungry dogs, but gradually acquires the ability to do so through repeated pairings with food (the unconditioned stimulus). But it also occurs in many other contexts as well. For example, you may recall that we commented in Chapter 3 on the role of classical conditioning in the formation of many attitudes. Similarly, evidence collected by clinical psychologists suggests that classical conditioning may play an important role in several forms of sexual disorder (Davison and Neale, 1974). To mention only one possibility, articles of clothing (high-heeled shoes, black lace negligees) which are repeatedly paired with stimuli capable of inducing strong sexual arousal (for example, the nude body of one's lover) may gradually come to elicit such feelings themselves. In this way, the seeds for a strong sexual fetish may be planted (see Figure 7-14).

Returning to vicarious emotional arousal, you may already be able to see how the principles of classical conditioning can be extended to this phenomenon. Basically, it seems possible that neutral stimuli initially incapable of eliciting strong emotional reactions from observers may gradually acquire the ability to do so when they are repeatedly paired with signs of strong emotional reactions on the part of social models. In short, we may come to react emotionally to stimuli which initially had little or no effect on our feelings simply because they are repeatedly paired with signs of emotional arousal in others. The occurrence of this process of **vicarious classical conditioning** has actually been demonstrated in a number of experiments.

In perhaps the most famous of these investigations, Berger (1962) placed subjects in a situation where they watched while another person (a confederate of the experimenter) appeared to receive a number of strong electric shocks. On each occasion when he was supposedly shocked, the model jerked his arm as if in pain, and provided a convincing demonstration of mild discomfort. In reality, however, he never received any jolts during the experiment. While subjects watched, the electrical conductivity of their skin was monitored, and as you might expect, this measure of physiological arousal showed large changes on many of the occasions when the model was supposedly shocked. That is, subjects demonstrated signs of vicarious emotional arousal in response to the model's apparent pain. In contrast, subjects in a control group who were informed that the model would receive no shocks, but would merely jerk his arm voluntarily on several occasions, showed fewer indications of emotional arousal (see Figure 7-15).

In order to determine whether vicarious emotional arousal could be conditioned to an initially neutral stimulus, a buzzer was sounded one second before each apparent shock to the model. According to the principles of classical conditioning, it was expected that this stimulus would gradually acquire the ability to elicit strong emotional reactions from observers as a result of its repeated pairings with the model's signs of emotional arousal. To see if this was actually the case, several *test trials* on which the buzzer was sounded but the

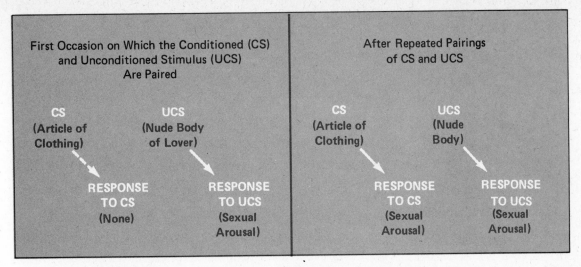

FIGURE 7-14. *The role of classical conditioning in the acquisition of one type of sexual "hang-up." At first, some article of clothing (the conditioned stimulus) is incapable of eliciting sexual arousal. Through repeated pairing with an unconditioned stimulus, however, it gradually acquires this ability.*

model showed no reaction were conducted. As shown in Figure 7-15, the buzzer did in fact come to evoke strong emotional reactions among subjects on these occasions. Thus, the arousal induced among observers as a result of witnessing the model's apparent pain could in fact be conditioned to an initially neutral stimulus.

More recent investigations have both confirmed and extended the findings of Berger's research. First, it has been found that vicarious classical conditioning may take place even under conditions where the signs of arousal on the part of the model are less obvious or pronounced than those shown in Berger's research. For example, in one study, Kravetz (1974) found that apparent changes in another person's heart rate in response to supposed electric shock were sufficient for the occurrence of vicarious conditioning.

Second, it has been found that such conditioning can be established on the basis of positive as well as negative emotional reactions on the part of a model (Venn and Short, 1973). And finally, it has been shown that vicarious classical conditioning—like many other forms of learning—may occur most efficiently at moderate rather than extremely high levels of arousal (Bandura and Rosenthal, 1966).

Together, these and other studies provide convincing evidence that vicarious classical conditioning does in fact occur. But what, precisely, is the significance of this process? Basically, we feel that its importance lies in its impact on two related forms of social learning: the acquisition of strong, irrational fears, and the development of intense racial or ethnic prejudices. Since the crucial events involved in both of these processes appear to be very much the same, we will

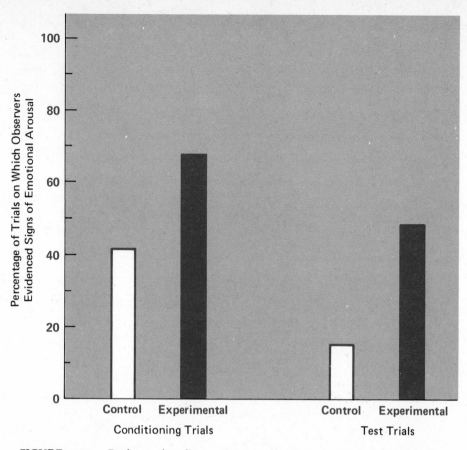

FIGURE 7-15. *Evidence for the occurrence of vicarious classical conditioning. Subjects showed heightened arousal on occasions when another person jerked his arm as if in pain when supposedly shocked (conditioning trials). In addition, they gradually came to react emotionally to a neutral stimulus (a buzzer) which was repeatedly paired with this person's signs of pain (test trials). Control subjects told that the model would move his arm voluntarily rather than in response to shock showed lower levels of arousal in both phases of the experiment. (Source: Based on data from Berger, 1962.)*

focus only on the development of racial prejudice. Briefly, such reactions may often be acquired by young children in the following manner.

In an initial step, children observe their mothers and fathers demonstrating signs of anger, hatred, or disgust when in the presence of members of certain groups they dislike. At first, the youngsters probably react strongly to their parents' signs of arousal, but demonstrate little or no reaction to members of the racial or ethnic groups in question: at this point, such persons are still relatively neutral stimuli for them. As such incidents are repeated, however, members of these groups—or at least certain of their characteristics such as skin color—are paired with their parents' signs of emotion over and over again. As a result of such association, conditioning occurs, and the children begin reacting negatively to such persons even when their parents are absent from the scene (see Figure 7-16).

A final step in the development of a full-blown prejudice may then involve the adoption of supporting beliefs which help the children "explain" the strong, negative emotions they feel when in the presence of such persons. For example, they might remark to themselves "I hate them because they are ugly, mean, and stupid." By means of this subtle process of vicarious classical conditioning, parents who do not specifically attempt to indoctrinate their children with hatred and prejudice may manage, nevertheless, to transmit such feelings to them in a highly effective manner.

We should hasten to add that the process just described is only a possibility, and has not been conclusively demonstrated. However, the facts that people *do* react emotionally to signs of emotion in others, and that such reactions can be readily conditioned to neutral stimuli suggest that it may actually occur in many situations.

MODELING AND BEHAVIOR DISORDERS: UNINTENTIONAL SOCIAL INFLUENCE AS A SOURCE OF POSITIVE CHANGE

Psychology, as you undoubtedly know, has something of a dual nature. First, it is a social science whose major goals are those we noted in Chapter 1: the prediction, understanding, and control of behavior. At the same time, it is also a member of what have often been termed the "helping professions." That is, many psychologists, like physicians, nurses, dentists, social workers, and many others, attempt to assist people in a number of ways.

Consistent with this dual nature, research on modeling has proceeded in two distinct directions. First, many studies have sought to investigate the nature of modeling and to establish its limits. At the same time, many attempts have been made to apply the knowledge acquired in these studies to the treatment of serious behavior disorders. The success attained in this respect has been so great, we believe, that it merits brief mention even in a text on social psychology. Thus, in this final section we will review recent applications of modeling principles to the treatment of two serious, personal problems: strong, irrational fears (phobias), and extreme social withdrawal.

Vicarious Extinction of Fear: Social Models and Courage

You may recall that in our earlier discussion of vicarious emotional arousal, we noted that intense fears are often acquired through a process of classical conditioning. That is, objects or persons which are initially neutral to observers gradually acquire the ability to elicit strong fear as a result of repeated association with signs of terror on the part of others. Regardless of the precise origin of such fears, however, their existence poses serious problems for the individuals they afflict. For example, a person who is terrified of snakes may avoid picnics in the woods, visits to scenic spots in the country, or even the purchase of a home in the

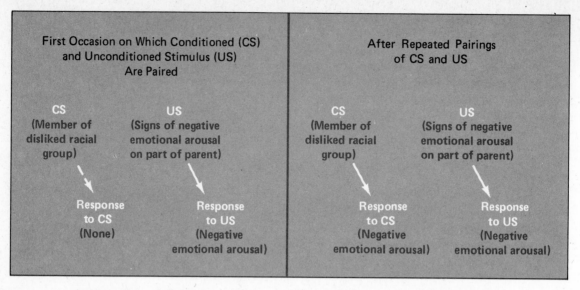

| First Occasion on Which Conditioned (CS) and Unconditioned Stimulus (US) Are Paired | After Repeated Pairings of CS and US |

FIGURE 7-16. *The role of vicarious classical conditioning in the development of a strong racial prejudice. At first, members of the disliked group are neutral stimuli to the child, and elicit little or no response. As a result of repeated pairing with signs of anger, hatred, or other negative emotions on the part of their parents, however, such persons come to elicit negative reactions themselves. A final step in the process may involve the adoption of supporting beliefs (e.g., "I hate them because they are ugly, mean, and stupid") which help the child "explain" his or her negative reactions to these persons.*

suburbs because of his or her intense anxiety over meeting such reptiles in chance encounters. Similarly, an individual who suffers from an extreme fear of heights may often be prevented from carrying out normal business or social acitivites because they require her to travel to meetings in high-rise buildings. Traditional methods of alleviating such fears have usually involved long and costly therapy, and have often proven to be quite ineffective. Fortunately, though, a number of recent studies indicate that simple procedures based on modeling may be readily adapted to the treatment of such problems (Bandura, Blanchard, and Ritter, 1969; Bandura, Jeffery, and Wright, 1974; Meichenbaum, 1971). A good illustration of the basic nature of this research is provided by a study conducted by Bandura and Menlove (1968).

In this investigation, the experimenters began by administering a behavioral test for fear of dogs to all the students in a particular nursery school. The reason for this test, of course, was that of identifying those children who were extremely frightened of such animals. The test consisted of a set of fourteen graded acts requiring increasingly intimate contact with a live dog, and all children were asked to perform them in the same predetermined order. The first behaviors in the set involved simple approach to the dog, looking at it from nearby, and petting it, while later acts involved walking the dog on a leash, scratching it on the stomach, and feeding it. The final act in the series required the child to enter a playpen with the dog and to remain in this enclosure while the experimenter left the room. Children were credited with two points for each of the fourteen acts they performed without hesitation, and one point for each act they performed only with some reluctance. As a result, scores on the test could range from 0 for children who were unable to perform even the simplest and least frightening acts, through 28 for those able to carry out all fourteen behaviors in a fearless manner.

On the basis of this test, the experimenters selected forty-eight children who demonstrated strong fear of dogs (they attained scores of 7 points or less) for participation in the experiment. These subjects were then divided into three groups, and exposed to different experimental treatments. Those individuals assigned to a *single-model* group observed eight brief three-minute films (two a day for four days) which depicted a five-year-old male model engaging in progressively bolder interactions with a live dog. Subjects assigned to a *multiple-model* group observed similar films, except that, in this case, the movies showed several different models of both sexes interacting with a number of different dogs ranging in size from quite small to relatively large. Finally, subjects in a third, *control,* group viewed an equal number of films of Disneyland and Marineland of the Pacific. As a result, they received no exposure to fearless models.

Following the completion of the last film, the behavioral test for fear of dogs was readministered to all subjects in order to determine whether exposure to the fearless models would result in any decrease in children's fear. As you can see in Figure 7-17, this was actually the case: subjects in both the single and multiple-model groups demonstrated a marked improvement in their ability to approach and interact with a live dog. In contrast, subjects in the control group showed no reduction in fear from the pretest to the posttest phases of the experiment.

In order to determine whether the reductions in fear induced among the children would remain stable over time, subjects were retested one month later. As indicated by Figure 7-17, there was no return to their former high levels of fear. Indeed, subjects in the multiple-model group even showed a slight, further increase in willingness to engage in contacts with live dogs at this time. (Once again, children in the control group showed no appreciable change in this respect.) When it is recalled that children in the two modeling groups observed a total of only 24 minutes of film, these results appear to be quite impressive. In fact, they suggest that even long-standing phobic reactions can be readily extinguished by a few moments' exposure to the behavior of fearless social models.

Equally dramatic reductions in fear resulting from brief exposure to nonfearful models have also been reported with adults (Bandura, Jeffery, and Wright, 1974; Meichenbaum, 1971). For example, in one of these investigations, Bandura, Blanchard, and Ritter (1969) found that fully 92 percent of a group of individuals who had initially demonstrated strong fear of snakes were later willing to allow one to crawl freely over their hands, neck, and arms after only two hours of exposure to fearless models (see Figure 7-18). Given the fact that many of these persons were at first so frightened of snakes that they could not

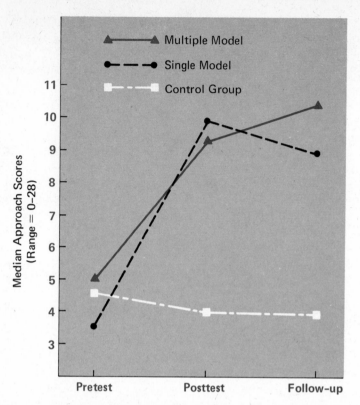

FIGURE 7-17. *The vicarious extinction of fear. Subjects exposed to fearless models (the multiple and single-model groups) showed a marked reduction in their fear of dogs. Moreover, these changes persisted, and were still present in a follow-up test conducted one month after their exposure to the models. Subjects in a control group not exposed to fearless models did not show any reduction in fear during the study. (From Bandura and Menlove, 1968, p. 102. Copyright 1968 by the American Psychological Association. Reprinted by permission.)*

even bear to look at them, it is hard to imagine a more impressive demonstration of the great success of modeling techniques in eliminating phobic reactions.

The Elimination of Severe Social Withdrawal:
When Isolation Hurts

In almost every neighborhood and classroom, there are one or more children who show little or no tendency to interact with their peers. Instead, these pathetic individuals play, work, and study in virtual isolation from others. Given the importance assigned by many psychologists to the role of social interaction in normal personality development (Mischel, 1976), such isolation appears to represent a potentially serious problem for the individuals involved. Thus, it would be very helpful, in many cases, if effective techniques for the elimination of such withdrawal could be devised. Fortunately, the results of several recent

FIGURE 7-18. *Exposure to fearless models who demonstrate increasingly intimate interactions with a live snake is highly effective in reducing even powerful snake phobias among observers. In fact, after only two hours of exposure to such models, persons formerly unable to even look at a snake without experiencing fear often become willing to both touch and handle them. (From Bandura, Blanchard, and Ritter, 1969, p. 179. Copyright 1969 by the American Psychological Association. Reprinted by permission.)*

investigations by Robert O'Connor (1969, 1972) suggest that modeling procedures may be highly successful in this regard.

In one of the more recent of these studies, O'Connor (1972) exposed nursery school children showing a very low level of social interaction with others to one of several conditions. One group was rewarded for interacting with their classmates by means of praise and attention from an adult experimenter. Such procedures were continued over a two-week period, until subjects had received a total of five hours of reward. A second group viewed a brief modeling film in which children of their own age interacted with others. In each scene shown, a child model first observed the interaction of others, then joined in, and finally received reinforcement for his or her social behavior. In contrast, subjects in a third, control condition benefited from neither of these procedures.

Following completion of the various experimental treatments, subjects' behavior in their nursery school classroom was observed on several occasions approximately one week apart. The results obtained in this manner were both straightforward and revealing (see Figure 7-19). First, exposure to adult praise

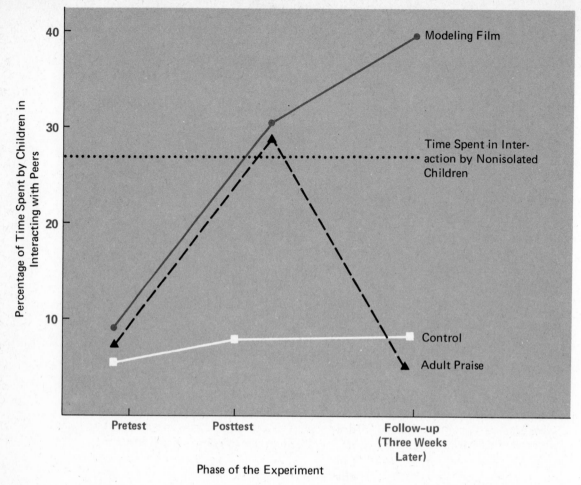

FIGURE 7-19. *Models and the elimination of severe social withdrawal. Socially withdrawn children who witnessed a modeling film in which other children demonstrated social interaction readily overcame their isolation. Moreover, they maintained these changes over a period of several weeks. Subjects praised by an adult for engaging in social interaction showed an immediate increase in such behavior, but soon reverted to their former isolation. Subjects in a control group demonstrated little change over the course of the study. (Source: Based on data from O'Connor, 1972.)*

and approval did increase subjects' level of social interaction up to that shown by normal, nonisolate children. However, once such procedures were ended, they returned to their former solitary state. In contrast, exposure to the brief modeling film served to produce more permanent shifts in subjects' behavior. In fact, individuals who witnessed this film were still demonstrating a level of interaction as great as that of nonisolate children three weeks after seeing it! Interestingly—and perhaps contrary to what common sense might suggest—the combination of modeling and reinforcement was *not* superior in changing children's behavior to modeling alone. Thus, the provision of adult praise and approval seemed to add little to the impact of the model. Finally, as would be expected, the behavior of subjects in the control group remained essentially constant during all phases of the study. Without the benefit of the experimental procedures, these children persisted in their unfortunate pattern of social isolation.

While many questions remain to be answered—for example, is modeling *always* superior to direct reinforcement in the manner observed here—the major implications of O'Connor's research seem clear: even strongly established tendencies to avoid contact with others can be readily countered by exposure to appropriate social models.

Other Applications . . . and a Concluding Comment on Social Influence

Our decision to focus on the application of modeling principles to the reduction of intense fears and the elimination of social withdrawal has made it impossible to consider other uses of such procedures—there is simply too much ground to cover. However, we can at least mention a few of these other applications in passing. A partial list includes the following: (1) teaching seriously retarded individuals to speak (Butz and Hasazi, 1973); (2) modifying the behavior of juvenile delinquents so that they are better able to stay out of trouble (Sarason and Ganzer, 1971); (3) training individuals who seem unable to stand up for their rights to be more assertive (McFall and Twentyman, 1973); (4) helping overweight individuals establish better self-control (Cautela, 1972); and (5) assisting individuals addicted to alcohol or drugs to resist these forms of temptation (Gotestam and Melin, 1974). In short, modeling procedures have been adapted to the alleviation of a wide range of problems. And in most cases, we should add, they have proven to be highly effective in helping to solve them.

By way of conclusion, we wish merely to call your attention to a fact which, though obvious, is frequently overlooked. Social influence, whether intentional or unintentional, is essentially neutral in nature. Like any other powerful force in the world around us, it can be used for beneficial or harmful purposes. On the one hand, it can be employed to induce slavish conformity, destructive obedience, or mass acceptance of false propaganda. On the other, it can be used to induce positive social change, teach individuals important new skills, and help them to overcome serious personal problems. The choice, in the final analysis, lies very much in the hands of those who wield it.

SUMMARY

It has long been observed that the behavior, feelings, or thoughts of one individual may be strongly affected by exposure to the actions and outcomes of others, even when these persons are *not* attempting to produce such effects.

Early attempts to examine such unintentional social influence focused on *imitation,* instances in which one individual matches the behavior of one or more others. In recent years, however, attention has shifted to a number of different modeling processes, including: the acquisition of new responses by observers *(observational learning),* the strengthening or weakening of restraints against various forms of prohibited behavior *(inhibitory* or *disinhibitory* effects), and the facilitation of various nonprohibited behaviors *(response-facilitating* effects). The influence of these processes is extremely pervasive, and has been found to play an important role in the occurrence of such diverse forms of behavior as aggression, altruism, and the internal regulation of behavior.

Exposure to signs of strong emotional arousal on the part of others may often serve to induce heightened emotional reactions in us. Such *vicarious emotional arousal* may then take one of three distinct forms: empathy—when the emotional reactions we experience closely resemble those of another person; envy—when we react negatively to signs of positive emotional arousal on the part of another; or sadism—when we react positively to signs of negative emotions in others. Recent findings suggest that vicarious emotional arousal may be classically conditioned to neutral stimuli present at the time it is induced. In this manner, it may play an important role in the transmission of strong fears or prejudices from parents to their children.

The principles uncovered in research on modeling have often been applied to the treatment of serious behavior problems. For example, social models have been successfully employed to eliminate strong, irrational fears, to alleviate extreme social withdrawal, and to modify the maladaptive behavior of juvenile delinquents. In these and many related instances, social influence is used to benefit the persons toward whom it is directed rather than benefit those who decide to employ it.

GLOSSARY

Behavioral contagion. Refers to situations in which the spread of socially prohibited behaviors is encouraged by the presence of individuals who perform such actions.

Delay of gratification. Refers to the ability to choose larger but delayed rewards over smaller but immediate ones.

Desensitization. A process whereby negative reactions to filmed or televised violence are reduced by continued exposure to such materials.

Disinhibitory effects. A weakening of observers' restraints against the performance of prohibited forms of behavior resulting from exposure to the actions of others who successfully violate such restrictions.

Empathy. A form of vicarious emotional arousal in which the emotional reactions of observers are similar to those shown by a social model.

Envy. A form of vicarious emotional arousal in which the emotional reactions shown by a model are positive (e.g., joy), and those by an observer negative (e.g., anger).

Inhibitory effects. A strengthening of observers' restraints against the performance of prohibited behavior resulting from exposure to the actions of other persons who refrain from such behavior, or are punished for performing it.

Modeling.   Any effects on the feelings, behavior, or thoughts of one individual resulting from mere exposure to the behavior and outcomes of others.

Observational learning.   A process whereby individuals acquire new responses not previously at their disposal simply by observing the actions of others.

Response-facilitating effects.   Refers to instances in which the actions of one person serve as a stimulus or cue for similar, nonprohibited actions by others.   One example of response facilitation is the spread of yawns from one person to another.

Sadism.   A type of vicarious emotional arousal in which the emotional reactions of the model are negative (e.g., pain), and those of the observer are positive (e.g., pleasure).

Socialization.   The process through which children acquire all of the attitudes, values, information, skills, and behaviors they require to function as adult members of their society.

Unintentional social influence.   Refers to instances in which one or more individuals alter the behavior, feelings, or thoughts of one or more others without intending to do so.

Vicarious emotional arousal.   The process through which signs of emotional arousal in one individual arouse heightened emotional arousal in another.

Vicarious classical conditioning.   The process through which neutral stimuli repeatedly paired with signs of strong emotional arousal on the part of others gradually acquire the ability to elicit emotional reactions from observers.   Such vicarious classical conditioning may play an important role in the development of racial prejudice and strong, irrational fears.

Vicarious extinction.   A process through which strong and often irrational fears on the part of an individual are reduced through exposure to fearless social models.

SUGGESTED READINGS FOR CHAPTER 7

Bandura, A.   *Social learning theory.*   Morristown, N.J.: General Learning Press, 1971.   A relatively brief, but thorough, discussion of Bandura's theory of modeling and related processes.

Bandura, A.   *Social learning theory.*   Englewood Cliffs, N.J.: Prentice-Hall, 1977.   A thorough discussion of recent developments in social learning theory.   Special attention is directed to the impact of social models, and the self-regulation of behavior.

Comstock, G.   *Television and human behavior: The key studies.*   Santa Monica, Calif.: Rand, 1975.   Presents brief descriptions of what the author considers to be the "key" studies regarding the impact of televised violence on viewers.   The experiments covered are organized into eleven separate sections, each dealing with a specific aspect of television's influence on viewers (e.g., the contents of TV shows, methods of studying their impact, etc.).

Liebert, R. M., Neale, J. M., and Davidson, E. S.   *The early window: Effects of television on children and youth.*   Elmsford, N.Y.: Pergamon Press, 1973.   A review of current evidence regarding the impact of television on children's behavior.   Recommendations concerning various ways of changing television programming in order to produce more positive effects are discussed.

PROSOCIAL BEHAVIOR: ALTRUISM AND HELPING

8

One evening after attending a movie, you walk toward the parking lot to get your car. It is rather cold and you walk fast to keep warm. Just before you reach your car, you hear what seems to be a sort of moaning sound. You look in the direction from which it came and see a man lying on his back beside the curb. Nearby, a torn paper sack has spilled its contents on the sidewalk, and you notice a broken bottle that is spreading a red circle of wine around the mess. The man's eyes are closed; he is breathing heavily and groaning from time to time. The dilemma faced by a bystander in such a situation was posed in the poem "The City Question" by R. Froman (1971):

<pre>
                        Wino?
             sidewalk.   Junkie?
                on   Hurt?
               face   Sick?
                on   Knife
               Man   in
                                  pocket?
                                     Danger?
                                 Medicine
                                    in
                                  pocket?
                            May
                        die
                     without
                       it?
                     Forget
                     Him?

                     Leave
                      him
                      to
                      the
                     cops?

            Or try to help?
</pre>

What would you do? Would you stop and try to find out what is wrong? Would you try to help him up? Would you call a doctor or a policeman, possibly try to get the man into a taxi? Would you drive away in your car and mind your own business? In recent years, a great many social psychologists have been studying situations such as this in an attempt to discover why a stranger in distress is sometimes helped and sometimes ignored. If you actually found yourself in the situation just described, what might be the reasons for your helping this man? We have all learned that it is good to help those who need help, that compassion for others is an admirable characteristic, and that we should try to treat others in the way that we hope they will treat us. There are some other considerations, though. When you notice the man by the curb, you are cold and in a hurry; stopping to help can only delay you and perhaps be very unpleasant as well. If the man is bleeding, you might mess up your clothes. Worse, maybe he is drunk and will throw up all over your shoes. Maybe he's a mugger who uses this trick to lure a victim close enough to bash him in the head. Maybe it's even a joke, and Allen Funt will jump out of the shadows telling you to "Smile, you're on Candid Camera!"

When you consider all the possible pitfalls, it seems as though you would never be inclined to help a stranger. An act of kindness might provide you with a clear conscience and a stranger's gratitude, but you also might lose something—anything from your wallet to your life. Despite this argument, we know that people often do help perfect strangers (and even imperfect ones). Individuals will sometimes risk great danger to guide someone they don't know out of a burning building, to save a child from drowning, or even to interfere with an armed robbery. Attempts to explain why these things sometimes occur and sometimes do not are part of a growing concern in psychology and in our society with questions of morality and social responsibility (Kelley, 1971; Staub, 1974).

In this chapter, we will examine the way in which social psychologists are attempting to identify the conditions under which altruistic behavior occurs and to explain this seemingly unlikely human tendency. First, we will consider *theories of* **prosocial behavior** and contrast two general approaches which stress either an internal mechanism such as conscience or the external stimulus conditions which influence the individual. Second, we will examine some of the *conditions under which people engage in prosocial behavior,* including the effects of multiple bystanders. Third, we will examine *internal factors influencing prosocial behavior* such as mood and the perceived costs of helping. Fourth, we will examine some *characteristics of the helper and the one who is helped,* including personality characteristics and sex. Finally, we will suggest some answers to the question, *how can the incidence of prosocial behavior be increased?*

THEORIES OF PROSOCIAL BEHAVIOR

In defining prosocial behavior (or altruism or moral behavior), we need to take into account both the individual's actions and why they are carried out. Consider a few contrasting examples.

A boy helps an elderly lady cross the street when she offers him $1.00 to do so.	A boy interrupts his game of ring toss to help an elderly lady cross the street when he sees that

she is having difficulty; she
thanks him.

A woman notices smoke coming
from the apartment directly
below her own and calls
the fire department.

A woman happens to be passing
an apartment house in a strange
neighborhood, notices smoke
coming from one of the windows,
and calls the fire department.

A man gives $1,000 to a local
charity and arranges for
a newspaper photographer to
be on hand when he presents
the check.

A man gives $1,000 to a local
charity with the stipulation that
he remain anonymous.

The right-hand example in each pair is likely to be labeled as an instance of prosocial behavior while the left-hand one is not. What is the difference? The outcome is the same in each instance: the lady gets across the street, the fire is reported, and the charity receives a helpful contribution. Skinner (1971, p. 45) points out that "the amount of credit a person receives is related in a curious way to the visibility of the causes of his behavior. We withhold credit when the causes are conspicuous." Thus, if you provide help to someone when you obviously benefit from the act, you are seen as behaving in your own self-interest; therefore you don't deserve any special credit. In contrast, if you provide help when you gain nothing from it, you are seen as altruistic and deserving of admiration. Even more, if the help you give involves a threat to your own self-interest, the resulting admiration and praise are increased. Children as young as first graders are found to make precisely these same distinctions in evaluating a person who helps another when expecting to be rewarded or expecting to be punished (Suls and Gutkin, 1976). Skinner would argue that behavior in each situation is determined by past and present reinforcements, but that some reinforcements are simply more obvious than others. It could be said that the study of prosocial behavior is the study of responses guided by nonobvious reinforcers. In a similar vein, our definition states that *prosocial behavior consists of those responses which have no obvious benefits for the responder but which are beneficial to the recipient.* We will now examine the major theoretical explanations of such behavior.

Guidance Systems
That Control Prosocial Behavior

Throughout most of human history, prosocial behavior has been considered to be something that varies among individuals, presumably as a function of differences among them in developing an internal guidance system. Those who engage in altruistic acts are said to do so because they are good, moral individuals who have

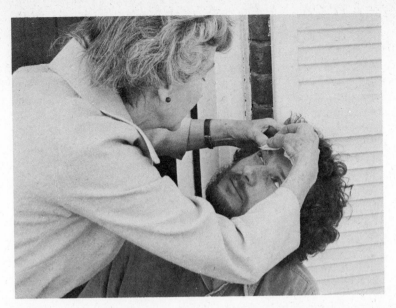

When an individual provides help to someone else and receives no obvious rewards for doing so, such behavior is labeled "prosocial." (Photo: Phil Carver & Friends.)

developed the right values and strength of character. At the opposite extreme from prosocial saintliness are the bad, immoral individuals with despicable values and weak characters. Many religions teach that each of us can choose to engage in either good or bad behaviors and that our eternal fate depends on which choice is made. Our laws follow the same general reasoning, except that the punishments for evil behavioral choices are applied during the individual's lifetime rather than in the hereafter.

When personality theorists first tried to explain prosocial and antisocial behavior, they tended to reject the notion of a simple choice of good versus bad; instead, they sought reasons for each type of behavior. The regulation of good or bad behavior was still conceptualized as the product of internal mechanisms, but it was thought that these processes could be identified along with the laws governing them. We will briefly describe two such theoretical explanations of how these internal mechanisms come to be: the superego and levels of cognitive development.

The Superego: Always Let Your Guilt Be Your Guide. In his pioneering efforts to make sense out of human behavior, Sigmund Freud (1933) tended to rely on a series of internal processes. His formulation of three personality structures (id, ego, and superego) has not only influenced the thinking of psychologists for many decades, and those concepts have also become a familiar part of our language and culture. Prosocial behavior was thought to be determined by one of these structures—the **superego.** In effect, Freud borrowed the commonly accepted idea of "conscience," and then tried to explain its origins and its functioning in psychological terms.

Of the other structures, *id* processes were described as involving the unrestrained desire to obtain pleasure and avoid pain, and *ego* processes were said to involve reality-oriented ways to obtain the same goals. The third structure, the *superego,* develops if the child learns a set of values from its parents. These values are internalized and incorporated as part of himself. They serve as an inner source of reward and punishment. Attempts to live up to an ideal standard of conduct and to avoid misconduct make the individual feel righteous. The demands of the superego can be stronger than the demands of id and ego—a person may flunk out of school rather than cheat, lose a job rather than lie, and even choose to die rather than violate a crucial moral standard.

The necessary conditions for such strong internalization of values include exposure to a set of standards in the context of a close, loving parent-child relationship (Staub, 1975a). If the parents' love is overwhelmingly important to the child, he or she will do anything and believe anything in order to maintain that love. Over time, the child develops a personal set of imaginary parents who administer internal punishment (in the form of guilt and anxiety) whenever behavior strays from the straight and narrow path. If you want a personal example of how such inner mechanisms operate, consider the following situation. The master of ceremonies on a kinky new TV game show offers you $1,000 to take off all of your clothes and dance an Irish jig. Even if your parents never got around to mentioning to you that "It's not nice to appear in the nude in public," the odds are that your values are such that you could not do it. It is just this sort of powerful internal restraint which characterizes the superego.

Cognitive Development: Growing toward Moral Maturity. An alternative way of conceptualizing the growth of a conscience and internal standards is through cognitive development. Both Piaget (1932) and Kohlberg (1969) have proposed that as a child grows and interacts with the environment, there is a natural progression from primitive notions of morality to highly sophisticated ones. Piaget observed, for example, that small children are confused about the difference between their own perspective and that of others. When a doll is placed on its back *looking up* and a child is asked to indicate what the doll sees, he responds with what he himself sees *looking down*. This egocentrism is not compatible with behavior involving altruism and empathy for others. As children grow older, they begin to grasp the fact that there are other perspectives besides their own. It has been suggested (Rushton, 1976) that this process can be speeded up if the child has the opportunity to engage in role-playing behavior and thus gain the ability to see the world from different perspectives. The rules defining morality also change as the child develops. Very young children perceive them as fixed, natural phenomena, while older children begin to realize that the rules are variable, man-made ideas about conduct. It should be noted that these stages of development are found to be influenced to some degree by the culture in which the child is raised (Salili, Maehr, and Gillmore, 1976).

Kohlberg identified a series of six **developmental stages** which include three different levels of morality. These stages and levels are shown in Table 8-1. As we mature, we understand more, grasp the consequences of our acts, and accept general principles of morality. Research supports the notion that as children grow older they progress to higher levels of cognitive development and different sorts of moral reasoning, but these cognitive differences do not seem to be particularly helpful in predicting actual altruistic behavior (Emler and Rushton, 1974; Rushton and Wiener, 1975).

Sex differences in prosocial tendencies have been considered by both Freud and Kohlberg. Though Freud (1925) postulated that the superego in females was never as well developed as with males, work within Kohlberg's framework suggests that just the opposite may be true, that females have stronger internal moral standards than males. For example, Hoffman (1975b) presented children and their parents with a series of items asking about such acts as stealing, cheating, and hit-and-run driving. He found that females more than males associated moral transgressions with feelings of guilt. The males, in contrast, were simply afraid of getting caught and being punished. Also, females showed more concern for the feelings of others.

A theory of moral conduct developed by Hogan (1973) combines the idea of cognitive development and the kind of internalization process emphasized by Freud. Hogan describes several dimensions of morality based on development and internalization; he points out the consequences of the various patterns that can emerge when some dimensions are stronger than others. For example, one individual may rigidly follow society's rules of conduct, but be unconcerned about the resulting harm to individual human beings—the bureaucrat who follows the

---

TABLE 8-1. *Kohlberg's stages of moral development. Lawrence Kohlberg has proposed that human beings progress through six stages of moral development that comprise three levels. The preconventional level is predominant in early childhood and only begins to be superseded by the conventional level of thought at about age 11. The postconventional level becomes fairly common in the late teenage years, but many individuals never reach that level.*

Preconventional Level

> A young child is primarily influenced by the consequences of what he or she does.

Stage One

> The child obeys because adults are powerful and can punish those who misbehave.

Stage Two

> The child attempts to obtain need satisfaction in a way that will lead to rewards.

Conventional Level

An older child becomes aware of and concerned about what others expect and tries to behave in a conventional way to meet these expectations.

Stage Three

There is a desire to be a good boy or girl so that others will offer approval.

Stage Four

There is a developing notion of doing one's duty, respecting authority, and preserving the social order because such things are accepted as right and proper.

Postconventional Level

As maturity approaches, an individual becomes oriented toward abstract moral values and toward what he or she personally believes to be right.

Stage Five

The person begins to think about the rights of others, the general welfare, and the laws adopted by the majority.

Stage Six

One's self-chosen standards of justice and one's own conscience have more effect on behavior than society's actual rules and laws.

letter of the law in planning a freeway that causes hundreds of families to lose their homes. Another individual with a different pattern of moral development may feel free to break society's rules but would never consider causing harm to another person—the high-living swinger who engages in socially unacceptable sexual practices but would never cause physical harm to anyone. Hogan thus describes prosocial behavior as a somewhat complex combination of independent characteristics.

Though it has been traditional to view morality and prosocial behavior as entirely dependent on internal mechanisms, there is another way to explain such characteristics. Our actions may be influenced to a large extent by the specific situation we are facing at the moment. If so, prosocial behavior would not depend on inner strength but on the variables operating in the immediate environment. From this perspective, it is not the individual who is prosocial; rather, the situation determines the likelihood of prosocial behavior occurring. The way an altered situation can change behavior without any change in internal mechanisms may be seen in the following example.

In describing Freud's concept of superego, we suggested that most individuals would refuse to dance in the nude before an audience for $1,000. A person who is presented with that choice and refuses to disrobe might well be characterized as being "good," as having well-developed moral values, and as having a strong conscience or superego. Let's change the situation and see what happens to morality. What if the $1,000 were given for killing a cow on stage? Though few individuals have ever personally killed a cow or perhaps even touched one, most of us during a lifetime are indirectly responsible for the slaughter of a good-sized herd (even if it's only one Big Mac at a time). It would not, therefore, seem to be a terrible sin to kill one such animal directly, especially with $1,000 as the reward. Would the killing of the cow be an immoral act? It depends on the culture in which you were raised. Thus, to the average American, cows are acceptable victims, and public nudity is taboo, but those moral distinctions are accidents of birth. To a Hindu in India, killing a cow is analogous to killing one's mother. To many Australian aborigines, nudity is the only reasonable response to hot weather. Your killing of the cow would be a moral disgrace to a Hindu observer, while your refusal to take off your clothes would be incomprehensible to those living in Arnhem Land. It seems that your moral behavior and how it is defined depend on the details of the situation and on the cultural beliefs you have learned.

Let's consider the power of the situation in a different way. What if you are offered not $1,000 to engage in a naked dance, but $1,000,000—tax free? If that money were carefully invested, you could have a substantial income for the rest of your life and do as you please without ever having any economic worries. Wouldn't a few minutes of embarrassed discomfort on the stage be worth it? After all, there's nothing really wrong with exposing your body: models, dancers, and actors do it all the time. Do you think you might accept the offer? Is the act of public nudity any different when the benefits involve a million dollars, a thousand dollars, or thirty-five cents? The act is not different and you are not different, but the likelihood of your doing it would most probably vary as the situation varies.

There are two major theoretical approaches to prosocial behavior that stress the power of the situation—a reinforcement explanation of why people sometimes help others and a cognitive analysis of the way perceptions and judgments influence behavior.

Reinforcement Theory: Rewards and Punishments for Prosocial Behavior. From the point of view of learning theory, prosocial responses occur because they have been rewarded in the past. If an individual goes to the aid of a stranger in distress, for example, he does so because such responses have been associated with positive reinforcement. Thus, altruistic behavior simply depends on the individual's reinforcement history. In addition to direct experience, people are also influenced by expectations about future rewards and punishments. Examples include concerns about being considered a hero or a coward and beliefs about spending eternity in heaven or hell. Such concerns and beliefs can be as powerful in determining behavior as the rewards and punishments in the immediate situation. Because altruistic intentions can arouse unpleasant expectations, one's perceptions of this unpleasantness may interfere with prosocial actions. For example, in a campus drive to obtain blood donors, those students most likely to refuse were those who most strongly believed that donating blood would be painful, anxiety evoking, fatiguing, time consuming, and that it would lead to feelings of faintness (Pomazal and Jaccard, 1976).

One prediction that stems from the reinforcement conceptualization is that prosocial behavior can be increased or decreased by associating rewards or punishments with it. In order to test this possibility, Moss and Page (1972) conducted a field experiment in which they manipulated the positive and negative consequences of a helping response in an effort to alter subsequent helping behavior. They arranged a situation in which unsuspecting subjects were asked to help a female confederate and then were rewarded or punished for their efforts. On the main street of Dayton, Ohio, the confederate would approach an individual who was walking alone and ask for directions to a local department store. After the subject explained the store's location, the confederate responded in one of three ways:

> Positive—She would smile and say, "Thank you very much, I really appreciate this."
> Negative—She would interrupt rudely and say, "I can't understand what you're saying. Never mind, I'll ask someone else."
> Neutral—She would simply say, "Okay."

About 75 feet farther down the street, a second female confederate stood looking in a store window, waiting. When the subject was six feet away, she began walking toward him, "accidentally" dropped a small bag, and then continued on as if she were unaware of what had happened. At this point, the subject could either offer to help her or he could just ignore the problem. The results, shown in Figure 8-1, indicate that positive reinforcement for one act of helping leads to a much greater tendency to help a second person than if the first helping behavior elicits a negative response. It seems clear, then, that helping can be made to vary as a function of reinforcement. Findings consistent with these were

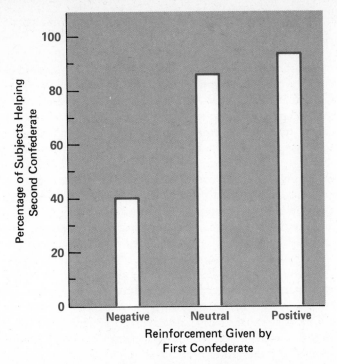

FIGURE 8-1. *Almost all subjects who helped one confederate and received a positive reinforcement were found to offer help to a second confederate. When subjects were treated negatively by the first confederate, less than half as many offered help to the second confederate. (Source: Based on data from Moss and Page, 1972.)*

reported in a laboratory investigation by McGovern, Ditzian, and Taylor (1975a). A single "thank-you" from a female victim significantly increased the helping behavior of male subjects during a series of subsequent interactions.

In the Moss and Page study, you may have noticed that the individuals receiving neutral feedback from the first confederate were almost as helpful to the second confederate as those who received positive feedback. That finding suggests that most people have been reinforced in the past for helping others. If so, through the process of conditioning, the act of helping should itself be positively reinforcing. When we see another human being in pain, most of us feel very uncomfortable. Subjects are found to respond more quickly to help someone apparently suffering great pain than someone experiencing mild discomfort (Baron, 1970). The act of helping should relieve the individual of the uncomfortable feelings and be a positive experience. Thus, any activity which relieved another person's suffering should be rewarding. Weiss et al. (1971) devised an experimental setting in which a subject interacted with a confederate who pretended to feel intense pain as he supposedly received an electric shock while performing a task. After each trial, the subject's job was to push a lever to "get the apparatus ready for the next trial." It was explained that the lever shut off the electric current between trials, thus giving the other person a brief respite from his suffering. If the sight of the stranger in pain was unpleasant, helping would act as a reward for the subject; if so, the speed with which the lever was pressed should increase over a series of trials (see Figure 8-2.) A control group went through a similar procedure but without any indication that the confederate was in pain or that the lever resulted in pain relief; therefore, for these subjects, speed of lever pressing should not have increased rapidly over trials because no reinforcement was involved. The hypothesis was confirmed. When lever pressing seemed to relieve someone's suffering, speed increased dramatically over the twenty-two trials. When button pressing had no relationship to helping another person, speed showed only a slight increase over trials (simply a little improvement due to practice). It seems that the act of helping another person can function just like other, more traditional rewards.

Though helping in general may be reinforcing, what about helping someone you dislike? If, for example, someone insulted you badly and then suddenly needed your help, you might be kind enough to provide the needed assistance but you probably wouldn't enjoy it. Kelley and Byrne (1976) used the Weiss et al. procedure to determine whether helping another person is always reinforcing or whether such behavior is reinforcing only when there are no negative feelings about the sufferer. Before the pain and lever-pressing portion of the experiment, the subject and confederate exchanged information, including an evaluation of the subject by the other person. Some subjects received positive evaluations and were informed that the confederate found them to be intelligent, well adjusted, and likable. Others received negative evaluations and were told that the other person saw them as stupid, maladjusted, and unlikable. A control group received no evaluations. As would be expected, a person who gave positive evaluations was liked much better than one who gave negative evaluations. Next, the experiment got underway with the confederate supposedly in pain and the subject supposedly bringing relief after each trial by pressing the lever. In Figure 8-3, you can examine the results. Over the twenty-eight trials, the control group's speed increased just as in the Weiss et al. experiment, indicating that helping behavior is generally reinforcing. When the victim is liked, however, the performance level is considerably higher, indicating that helping under these circumstances is even more reinforcing. When the suffering person is disliked, however, lever-pressing speed does not increase at all! It can be seen that coming to the aid of someone you dislike may not be in the least reinforcing.

Cognitive Analysis: What's Going On and What Should I Do? In a series of experiments to be described shortly, Latané and Darley (1970) have focused on the kind of situation in which there is some sort of emergency that presents the subject with the opportunity either to aid a stranger in distress or to ignore him. The theoretical question is, "What must go on in the individual's mind before a prosocial response can take place?" In these experiments, there is usually some emergency situation that has been staged by the experimenter. The unsuspecting subject is suddenly and unexpectedly confronted with a stranger who seems

A   B   C

FIGURE 8-2. *In the investigation of helping as a reinforcing activity, one experimental procedure involves a confederate who pretends to be receiving a painful electric shock. (A) The male subject and female confederate are given instructions about the experiment. (B) The confederate seems to be in pain as the subject evaluates her performance under stress. (C) The confederate slumps in apparent relief as the subject presses the lever that supposedly shuts off the electric shock.*

to have had an accident or with a thief who has taken someone else's property. The "right" thing to do in each instance seems clear. The person having the accident should be helped and the thief should be reported. In order for any of us to make such prosocial responses, however, a series of decisions must be made. These decisions are determined by many aspects of the situation and by one's past experiences.

We will take one example of this kind of situation and outline the sequence of perceptions and judgments that are necessary for prosocial behavior to occur. Let's say that you are spending the night alone in a hotel room. At ten in the evening while you are watching television, the occupant of one of the adjoining rooms returns from dinner and finds a burglar rummaging through his suitcase. Before he can call for help, he is struck down and knocked partially unconscious. The intruder quickly gathers up his loot and runs down the hallway. Your obvious prosocial responses would be to try to help the injured man, call a doctor, and summon the police. It takes several steps to reach that point, however.

Step I. Before you can respond, you first must notice that something is happening—you must perceive it and attend to it. You were concentrating on the TV program, and under those conditions many stray noises from outside the room are ignored. One of the authors sat typing in his office at the University of Texas one day as a sniper shot down dozens of people from the nearby library tower; the very loud gunshots made no impression at the moment. Only later were they vaguely remembered. In the example here, unless the sounds of scuffling or the later moans of the victim catch your attention, you will obviously take no action to help the other person.

Step II. You have to interpret what you hear. There are many logical explanations for the sound of a thump and moaning. Perhaps your neighbor is watching a mystery on television. Perhaps a man and his wife are having a fight. Perhaps someone dropped a Gideon Bible on his foot. Perhaps some children have made up a game. Perhaps your imagination is playing tricks on you. Perhaps someone has been hurt. Only the last possibility is an emergency requiring you to

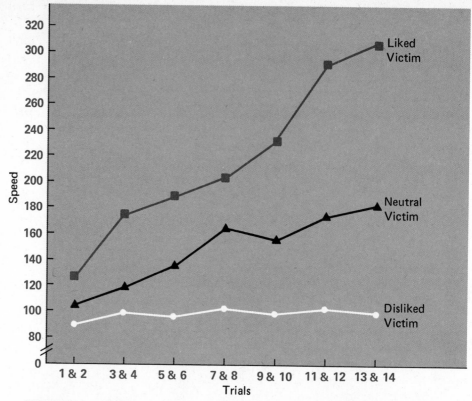

FIGURE 8-3. *When subjects press a button that supposedly relieves the suffering of a confederate over s series of trials, increasing speed is evidence that the helping response is reinforcing. It may be seen that such reinforcement is greatest when the victim is liked and absent when the victim is disliked. (The speed measure is calculated by dividing the number of seconds taken to push the button into 100.) (Source: Kelley and Byrne, 1976, by permission of Academic Press.)*

take action. If one of the other alternatives were correct, your intervention would be unwelcome and you would feel foolish.

Step III. If you perceive the noises and are correct in interpreting them as indicating an emergency, the next step is to assume personal responsibility for providing help. After all, you don't know the person, and there are other guests in other rooms who could help just as well as you could. Besides, it's the hotel's responsibility, so one of the employees really should be the one to do something. Thus, a key determinant in the situation is whether or not you decide that it's any of your business.

Step IV. You must decide what to do. Should you run next door and try to provide direct aid? Should you call the police? Notify the manager? Run down the hall after the assailant? Stand outside your door shouting for help? You must consider each alternative that occurs to you and decide which is the most reasonable.

Step V. You must actually engage in the behavior you decide on. This final step, then, depends on the preceding series of cognitive activities. This descriptive framework of Latané and Darley suggests the way in which research might be directed toward identifying the crucial variables at each step. For example, at the fourth step, it is found that the person needing help and the potential helper often have very different interpretations of the problem; if so, their different cognitions may result in "help" that is not really helpful (Batson, 1975).

CONDITIONS UNDER WHICH
PEOPLE ENGAGE IN PROSOCIAL BEHAVIOR

If the situation is a powerful determinant of how people treat one another, it is important to find out exactly what aspects of the situation serve to encourage or discourage prosocial acts. As is often the case in social psychology, one of the current lines of active research began with an actual incident that took place a few years ago—the murder of a young lady in New York:

> Kitty Genovese was set upon by a maniac as she returned home from work at 3 A.M. Thirty-eight of her neighbors in Queens came to their windows when she cried out in terror; none came to her assistance even though her stalker took over half an hour to kill her. No one even so much as called the police.

Unfortunately, that is not an isolated and unusual incident. You can find examples yourself almost every day such as these described by Huston and Korte (1976):

> Carmen Colon, a ten-year-old kidnapped while she was on an errand for her mother, temporarily escaped from her captor along a busy highway near Rochester, New York. Half-clad and obviously distraught, she cried out for help. More than a hundred motorists passed her by. Shortly thereafter, Carmen was murdered.
> Herman Glaser, a 56-year-old lawyer, was mugged and robbed on the streets of New York City before scores of onlookers, none of whom came to his aid. Glaser, recounting the experience at Lenox Hill Hospital said: "It was like a jungle. . . . I can't understand the apathy of all the people on that street."

The question in these and all such incidents is—why didn't the bystanders do something? What prevented Kitty Genovese's neighbors, the motorists passing Carmen Colon, and the pedestrians around Herman Glaser from providing some kind of help? It has been suggested that people have become apathetic and that most of us do not want to get involved in the problems of others. Cities often are blamed for the indifference, because people feel alienated and helpless among millions of strangers in New York, Chicago, Los Angeles, and all such metropolitan areas. Some see such behavior as the last gasp of a crumbling society which has lost its moral values (because of communist subversion, because of our imperialistic government, because of permissive parents, because of materialism, because of drugs, or whatever combination of causes you care to name). The nonresponsive bystanders in the situations just described must be apathetic, indifferent, or immoral—why else would they stand back and fail to act? We will now turn to a series of experiments that sought different answers to that question.

Darley and Latané (1968) proposed that individuals who are alone when an emergency situation occurs will behave differently from individuals in a group. If only one person witnessed a murderous attack, a child calling for help, or a man being mugged, that person would be likely to do something about it. At *Step II* of their cognitive analysis of such situations, an individual must interpret correctly what is going on; when several people are there, each one wonders how the others are reacting and whether his or her own interpretation is the correct one. At *Step III,* the individual must decide to assume responsibility to provide help; when other people are around, the possible responsibility is shared and does not clearly belong to anyone. This **diffusion of responsibility** is depicted by the cartoon in Figure 8-4; in real life, too, each person can ask, "Why doesn't somebody do something?" In general, when there are potentially negative consequences, an individual will readily deny his or her personal responsibility and instead share it with others (Mynatt and Sherman, 1975). This idea about the inhibiting effects of multiple bystanders suggests the possibility of a very simple relationship. It was hypothesized by Darley and Latané that as the number of bystanders increased, the likelihood of any one of them engaging in prosocial behavior would decrease.

Response to an Epileptic Seizure. In their initial investigation of the effect of bystanders on prosocial behavior, Darley and Latané (1968) created an interesting experimental situation. Students were told that they were to take part in a discussion of college problems. The experimenter left each subject alone after the instructions had been given, and the participants were in contact with one another only through an intercom. The subject believed that he was interacting with one other student, two other students, or five other students. In reality, no other students were present; there was only the subject and the appropriate number of tape recordings.

As the discussion began, the participants introduced themselves, and then, without warning, the person on one of the recordings began to gasp as he apparently underwent an epileptic-like seizure. In the two-person condition, the subject believed he was the only bystander who knew of this emergency. In the three-person condition, the subject assumed he was one of two bystanders; he was one of five apparent bystanders in the six-person condition. Would the subject's tendency to help be influenced by the number of bystanders?

The results are shown in Figure 8-5. The number of bystanders had a strong effect on the way the subjects responded to the emergency—the more bystanders, the less likely the subject was to do anything. Not only that, even when help was given, the more bystanders, the more time it took before anything was done. Subjects who were alone responded in less than a minute; those who thought they were one of five bystanders took almost three minutes to

DUNAGIN'S PEOPLE

by Dunagin

"LOOK, THERE'S ANOTHER MUGGING OUT THERE! WHY DOESN'T SOMEBODY DO SOMETHING?"

FIGURE 8-4. *When more than one bystander witnesses an emergency, responsibility is shared, and each individual is less likely to respond. (Source: DUNAGIN'S PEOPLE, by Ralph Dunagin, Courtesy of Field Newspaper Syndicate.)*

respond.* It seems to be true that prosocial behavior is inhibited by the presence of others. When these students were interviewed after the experiment, they did not believe that their failure to help was a function of the number of bystanders. Instead, they said they didn't know what was happening *(Step II)* or what exactly they should do *(Step IV)*. The failure to provide aid or lack of speed in doing so was not a matter of indifference or apathy. Actually, the subjects who did not respond seemed to be upset about their own behavior. They were caught in a conflict between a genuine desire to help and the fear that they would do the

---

*It should be noted that with multiple bystanders, even though each one is less likely to respond and each one takes longer to respond, the victim is more likely to receive help from *someone* in a large group of bystanders than in a small group.

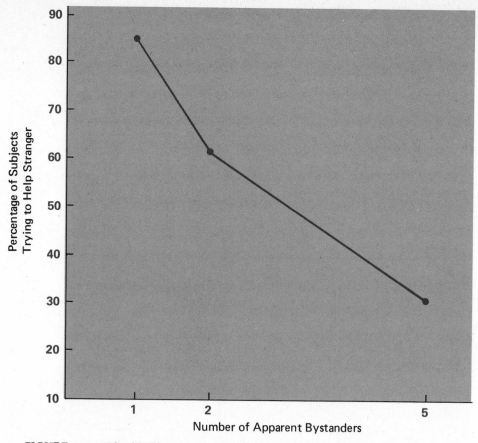

FIGURE 8-5. *The likelihood of a stranger receiving help when he seems to be having an epileptic seizure depends on the number of bystanders. As the number increases, fewer individuals respond to the emergency. (Source: Based on data from Latané and Darley, 1968. Copyright 1968 by the American Psychological Association. Reprinted by permission.)*

wrong thing and look foolish to the other bystanders. Most people do not want to be in the position of Charlie Brown when his classmates laugh uproariously at his blunders.

Fire! Reacting to the Reactions of Others. The "Charlie Brown hypothesis" is that our prosocial tendencies are inhibited by the presence of others because we are afraid of how they might evaluate what we do. As was discussed in Chapter 6, social influence can strongly affect one's behavior. Latané and Darley (1970) proposed that each individual in a group attempts to behave in whatever way will best protect him against embarrassment. In order to respond to an emergency, a person must stop whatever he or she is currently doing and then do something out of the ordinary. For example, in the study just described about reactions to a seizure, the subjects had to decide to abandon the experimental procedures they had been instructed to follow, get up and leave the experimental room, and then seek out either the student who had been heard gasping or the experimenter in charge. If an individual is alone, he tends to go ahead and engage in all of those unexpected, though necessary, activities. If others are there, he tends to hold back because of fears about having made the wrong interpretation of what was heard or of doing something inappropriate. When others are around, the safest thing to do to avoid making an ass of yourself is to "keep your cool" and not respond. It seems that most people in a group will give up the chance of being a hero rather than risk being ridiculed.

If this general idea is correct, it follows that individuals respond not only to the fact that others are present but also to what they do. If fellow bystanders can be seen to do nothing about an emergency, that should strongly inhibit anyone's tendency to take the initiative. Latané and Darley (1968) tested this hypothesis. Male students were recruited purportedly to be interviewed about college life. When each subject arrived, he was shown to a waiting room and left there to fill out a questionnaire. A few minutes later, smoke began to billow from a wall vent. Would the individuals keep on working despite the smoke or would they respond to the apparent emergency by reporting it? The subjects were either in the room alone, with two other genuine subjects, or with two confederates who had been instructed to continue working on the questionnaires, ignoring the smoke. After six minutes, the experiment was stopped even if the subject had not responded, because the smoke was so thick that it was difficult to see across the room.

As strange as it may seem, the presence of others had a dramatic effect on how an individual responded, as may be seen in Figure 8-6. When subjects were alone, 75 percent left the room and reported the smoke. When three naive subjects were there, there was a response by at least one of the three in only 38 percent of the groups. With seemingly unconcerned confederates, only 10 percent of the subjects responded. In that last condition, subjects found themselves with strangers who ignored the emergency, and 90 percent of them "coughed, rubbed their eyes, and opened the window—but they did not report the smoke" (Latané and Darley, 1968, p. 218). Presumably, these individuals felt that they could avoid possible embarrassment by following the actions of others. If strangers appear unconcerned about a room filling with smoke, most people seem willing to go along with the group, just as in the conformity studies described in Chapter 6.

There is another aspect of behavior influenced by the presence of strangers. The experimenters watched the subjects through a one-way mirror when the smoke was released. When others were in the room, subjects actually took longer to notice the smoke (Step I) than when alone. With strangers present, there was less of a tendency for the subject to look around the room than when alone. In our culture, it is not quite acceptable to be caught looking at strangers—it is better to keep your eyes to yourself. On a bus, in an elevator, in a doctor's waiting room, people do not generally stare at one another. This means, of course, that an individual in a group is less likely to perceive an emergency than an individual who is alone. It is interesting to note that when

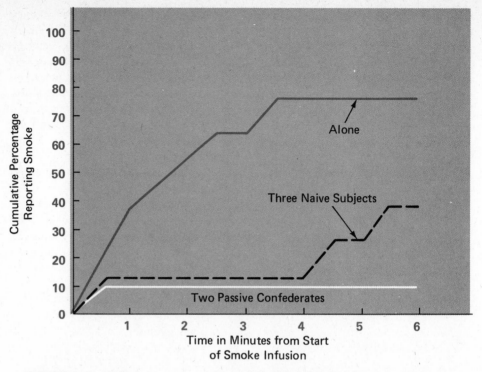

FIGURE 8-6. *Subjects in a room that rapidly filled with smoke were much more likely to leave and report the emergency when alone than when two others were present. When the strangers were two confederates who deliberately ignored the smoke, only 10 percent of the subjects responded to the emergency. (Source: From Latané and Darley, 1968, p. 218. Copyright 1968 by the American Psychological Association. Reprinted by permission.)*

the smoke experiment was repeated with a nonresponding *blind* confederate, subjects responded as frequently and as rapidly as when they were alone (Ross and Braband, 1973).

Friends as Fellow Bystanders: What Do You Think Is Happening? If prosocial behavior or any other active response to an emergency is inhibited by fear of how others might react, any communication among bystanders should be useful in reducing ambiguity. Strangers tend not to communicate about their perceptions, and there is no way to make accurate guesses about one another's perceptions or probable responses. Latané and Rodin (1969) reasoned that the presence of friends as fellow bystanders should serve to eliminate such difficulties. Friends would be expected to communicate with one another, compare their ideas, and decide what to do about any problem that arose.

In an experimental test of the effect of friends, male undergraduates were recruited for what was described as a market research study and were shown to a waiting room by a female experimenter. Each subject was either alone in the room, with a friend, with another subject who was a stranger, or with a confederate who had been instructed not to respond when the emergency occurred. When the experimenter left, she went behind a curtain which separated her office from the waiting room. For four minutes, she could be heard going about her routine work—opening desk drawers and moving papers about. Then an emergency was staged, presented by means of a stereo recording. The experimenter could be heard climbing up on a chair. Suddenly, there was a crash and the sound of a falling body. She exclaimed, "Oh, my God, my foot. . . . I . . . I can't move it. Oh . . . my ankle. I . . . can't get this . . . thing . . . off me." Next there were cries and moans, which eventually stopped.

Again, the question was whether each subject would respond. Do you think you would go behind the curtain and see if you could help? The effect of the various experimental conditions on helping behavior is shown in Figure 8-7. Most subjects who were in the room alone responded by going to the aid of the person who seemed to be hurt. Most subjects in the room with one other person did not. Nevertheless, the presence of a friend was less inhibiting than the presence of a stranger. A nonresponsive stranger was the most inhibiting of all;

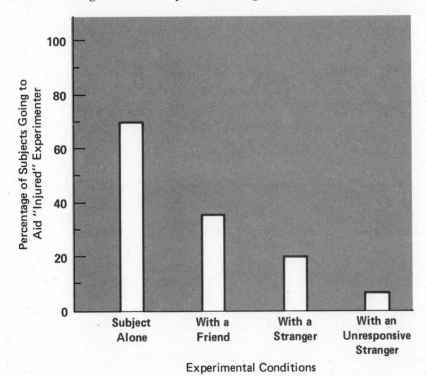

FIGURE 8-7. *Subjects who were alone when an experimenter seemed to have been injured in the next room were most likely to try to help her. The presence of one other bystander inhibited this helping response, but a friend was less inhibiting than a stranger. The least amount of help was given by subjects who were with a deliberately unresponsive confederate. (Source: Based on data from Latané and Rodin, 1969.)*

less than one person in ten made a move to help when a stranger sat there ignoring the problem. Though individuals with a friend were less responsive than individuals alone, there were clear differences between being with a friend and being with a stranger, as described by Latané and Rodin (1969, p. 200):

> When strangers overheard the emergency, they seemed noticeably confused and concerned, attempting to interpret what they heard and to decide on a course of action. They often glanced furtively at one another, apparently anxious to discover the other's reaction yet unwilling to meet eyes and betray their own concern. Friends, on the other hand, seemed better able to convey their concerns nonverbally, and often discussed the incident and arrived at a mutual plan of action.

When strangers *do* communicate, subjects are found to be strongly influenced by the way other people interpret the situation. Bickman (1972) staged an emergency in which a female was overheard to scream as something fell off a bookcase and crashed down on her. If a confederate suggested that the problem was not serious, half the subjects decided that the girl was not hurt. If the confederate said the person was hurt, almost all of the subjects decided the same thing. Interpretations of what is going on in an emergency seem to depend in large part on the reactions of others.

Children as Bystanders: Do They Inhibit Adults, Too? If you and several preschool children saw an elderly man lying on an icy sidewalk, would you be less likely to help him than if you were alone? The idea that inhibition is caused by the fear of appearing ridiculous leads to two opposite hypotheses concerning the effects of children. On the one hand, you could argue that children would not inhibit adult behavior because adults have more knowledge about what to do in an emergency. On the other hand, children might be even more inhibiting than adults—out of the mouths of babes might come the strongest ridicule of all.

Ross (1971) assumed that the first of these two possibilities was likely and hypothesized that children would not inhibit the responses of adults and might even make them act more responsibly in an emergency. In an experiment, college students were exposed to a simulated emergency either alone, with two other college students, or with two children (aged four and six). After about twenty minutes of working on a problem-solving task, the emergency was presented. Some subjects heard a nearby accident in which a workman seemed to have fallen and hurt his leg. Other subjects found that smoke was billowing into the experimental room.

When subjects were alone, almost all of them responded to either type of emergency. When two fellow college students were present, very few (16 percent) made any response. The effect of the children was, somewhat surprisingly, about halfway between being alone or being with fellow adults. That is, 50 percent of the subjects responded when they were in the room with two children. Ross proposed that both ideas about the effect of children had some validity. They inhibit an adult less than do other adults because the grown person feels some responsibility for taking charge, but they are more inhibiting than when one is alone because they are there to witness any potential blunders.

The net effect of children on the prosocial behavior of adults is, then, a combination of these two opposing trends.

In the research discussed so far, the experiments on prosocial behavior have involved situations in which an individual could help someone else (as when another person seems to be hurt) or himself (as when there seems to be a fire). If we shift our attention briefly to illegal acts, are there any differences in the general situation? One possible problem is that the individual who *helps* the victim of a crime at the same time *hurts* the criminal. Most of us have learned since childhood to place a negative connotation on being a tattletale or a snitcher, and as adults we hear equally negative characterizations of stool pigeons and police informers. There is, of course, another reason not to take action against someone who does something illegal; that person might retaliate against you. A 1976 newspaper story told of a middle-aged New York man, Fred Pirone, who was driving with his family when he saw a young black girl being beaten by twenty white female teenagers. He stopped the car, got out, and disbanded the white girls. While his family walked the victim to safety, Mr. Pirone returned to his car. His body was found an hour later. He had been slugged and stomped: his ribs were broken and his face was smashed in. Officially, he died of heart failure. It seems that the girls and their male companions had returned to the scene in order to "pay him back" for interfering with their earlier attack.

Despite such terrifying incidents, some individuals continue to take spontaneous action against those who commit crimes. An incident with a happier ending occurred on January 7, 1976 in Amboy, Indiana, when two housewives (Casey Bowland and Becky Griggs) broke up a bank robbery by taking the ignition keys and letting the air out of the tires of the robbers' car, chasing one of them on foot, and then tying his hands with a belt as they sat on him. Earlier, we described incidents in which bystanders were seemingly indifferent to a murder, a kidnapping, and a mugging. It seems possible that the same variables that determine whether an individual responds to an emergency such as an accident also determine responses when a person is a witness to a crime.

Witnessing a Theft: The Inhibiting Effect of Bystanders. The bystander effect was extended to the likelihood of reporting a crime by Latané and Darley (1970). Male undergraduates were supposedly waiting to be interviewed. A confederate, identified as another subject, went to the receptionist's desk when she left the room, removed about $40 from an envelope, and placed the money in his pocket. The subject was either the sole witness of the theft or one of two witnesses. The only two possible alternatives were to report the theft or to remain silent. Sadly enough, most individuals said absolutely nothing about the money being stolen after the thief left the room, even when they were the sole witness. Nevertheless, more subjects in the alone condition told the receptionist about what had happened than in the two-witness condition. Even though the theft was an obvious one and hidden observers felt confident that all subjects saw what had happened, the individuals who remained silent about the crime tended to deny having seen it or to deny knowing that the money was actually being stolen. One felt that the thief was only "making change," and another thought that the money had ended up in his pocket "by accident." It seems that this kind of illegal act is easily tolerated, especially when there is more than one witness.

The presence of fellow bystanders also inhibits the tendency of individuals to report stolen property. Latané and Darley (1970) arranged a series of apparent robberies at a discount store. When there was either a single customer in the store or two customers, a confederate would ask the clerk (who was, of course, participating in the experiment) to indicate the name of the most expensive beer they carried. The answer was Lowenbrau, and the clerk at this point had to go to the back of the store to determine how much he had in stock. When he left, the confederate picked up a case of beer on display, said, "They'll never miss this," and left, driving away with the loot. No customers tried to interfere with the robbery itself, but the majority of them did tell the clerk about the crime. Just as in the helping experiments, however, fewer people said anything about the theft when there were two witnesses than when there was just one. In this and subsequent studies of theft (Howard and Crana, 1974), the presence of multiple bystanders was found to inhibit prosocial behavior.

Shoplifting: Where Were the Witnesses Raised? Many of the newspaper accounts about bystander indifference reveal that the incident took place in a large city. As we indicated earlier, many of the explanations of such behavior place the blame on the city itself; those who live there are sometimes characterized as having become used to and unconcerned about an atmosphere of crime and brutality. Gelfand et al. (1973) propose that there *are* certain aspects of city life that might give rise to particular attitudes about individual responsibility in doing anything about those who commit illegal acts. People who live in rural areas and in very small towns are dependent on one another to provide help and to cope with emergencies. In a large city, the giving of help becomes specialized and professional; rather than having neighbors who pitch in and provide a helping hand, city dwellers depend on policemen, firemen, ambulance drivers, and so forth. Anyone raised in a community such as that depicted on the TV program, *The Waltons,* would be less likely to ignore a crime than someone raised in the big city environment depicted on the program, *Welcome Back, Kotter.*

The crime studied by this group of experimenters was shoplifting, a type of theft that retail merchants claim is responsible for the loss of nearly 50 percent of their potential profits. It is found that only two to eight percent of college students who observe such a theft will report it, even after a massive advertising campaign stressing what should be done (Bickman, 1975). In another study there was an attempt to make a female shoplifter unlikable—in the check-out line at a grocery store she bumped the shopping cart of a customer and snapped, "Keep your cart to yourself!" She then stole two items in full view of the customer, but this rude shoplifter was no more likely to be reported than either a nice or a neutral one (Bickman and Green, 1975).

In a field study in a drug-variety store (Gelfand et al., 1973), a female confederate played the role of a shoplifter who first caught the attention of a real shopper by dropping something, then stuffed several items of merchandise into her handbag. She then hurried out the front door without paying the cashier. The shopper was observed to determine whether the thief would be reported and then was interviewed before he or she left the store. Among the questions asked in the interview was the size of the community in which each person was raised. As may be seen in Figure 8-8, those who were raised in large cities (population 100,000 or more) were much less likely to report the shoplifter than those raised in small towns (population under 100,000) or in rural areas. Interestingly, in the Darley and Latané (1968) study of responses to an epileptic seizure, it was reported that the smaller the community in which a subject was raised, the faster the individual was in trying to help the victim. Similarly, a stranded female motorist was found to be more likely to receive help from rural residents than from urban dwellers (McKenna, 1976). Still other research supports the same general finding. A stranger was more likely to get help in making a phone call, in being told he had overpaid a store clerk, and in having someone mail an apparently lost postcard in a small-town setting than in a big city (Korte and Kerr, 1975). Gelfand and her colleagues suggested that we attempt to find out just what factors associated with country life lead to the development of helpful citizens. At that point, we could try to build these same factors into the social environment of cities.

Clarity of the Situation: Uncertainty, Not Indifference

Many of the experiments described so far suggest that people feel very uncertain in emergency situations—uncertain about what is going on, who should have the responsibility of helping, and what to do. Rather than having a weak superego or an undeveloped sense of morality, again and again the apathetic bystander turns out really to be the confused and uncertain bystander. Such findings suggest that the more ambiguous the emergency situation, the less likely prosocial behavior would be; thus, anything that clarified what was happening should increase the amount of prosocial behavior.

Ambiguity. It seems that any factor that creates ambiguity inhibits bystanders from engaging in effective action (Clark and Word, 1974). Earlier in this chapter, we mentioned an incident involving a sniper at the University of Texas. Some of the people who were shot had actually heard the shooting when it began and a few saw the bodies of the earliest victims as they lay dead or injured on the sidewalks and lawns surrounding the tower. Rather than take cover, however, a surprising number of people simply continued on their way to wherever they were going and thus became victims themselves. Some who were

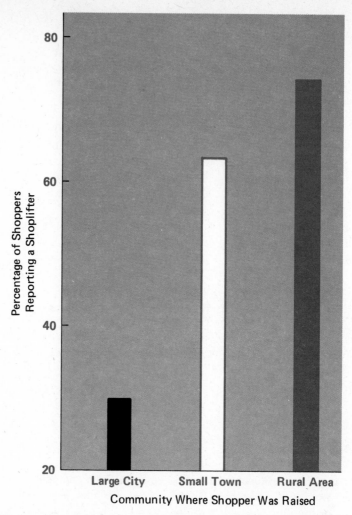

FIGURE 8-8. *In a field study of shoplifting, it was found that shoppers who were raised in rural areas were most likely to report the crime. Those raised in large cities were least likely to do so. (Source: Based on data from Gelfand, Hartmann, Walder, and Page, 1973.)*

only wounded described their reactions in terms of feeling confused about what was going on—some thought the rifle shots were sounds made by construction workers, the dead and wounded were perceived as actors in a fraternity stunt, and the puffs of gunpowder visible at the top of the tower were interpreted as evidence of a small fire. One wounded graduate student said afterward that he decided it would be silly to interrupt his lunch plans when he wasn't sure what was going on. If he postponed lunch and hid behind a wall just because of some noise from a construction site or because some undergraduates were putting on a skit, he would have felt totally ridiculous. Instead, he was shot and badly

Chapter 8   Prosocial Behavior: Altruism and Helping

wounded because the situation was too ambiguous for him to consider taking any action.

The effect of ambiguity on prosocial behavior has been demonstrated by Yakimovich and Saltz (1971). After an experimenter provided the instructions, each subject sat by himself in a deserted and isolated campus building. After a few minutes, a confederate posing as a window washer pretended to have an accident. The ladder and pail fell to the ground, the workman screamed, and he lay on the pavement clutching his ankle and moaning. All of the subjects went to the window to see what had happened, but only 29 percent did anything to help him. As in other situations of this type, the seeming cold-blooded indifference of the majority of the witnesses may only have reflected confusion in response to ambiguity. For other subjects, the situation was clarified by the addition of a single element—the fallen workman called out for assistance. Under those conditions, 81 percent provided help. This dramatic difference in altruism was apparently a function of a small difference in the ambiguity of the situation. It has also been found that helping increases if the victim stares at the bystander, but only if the situation is not ambiguous (Ellsworth and Langer, 1976).

Such findings suggest that the effect of bystanders on inhibiting prosocial behavior might disappear if there were no confusions about the nature of the problem. For example, Clark and Word (1972) created either a clear or an ambiguous situation in which a subject was alone, with one other subject, or with four others when an emergency occurred. A workman carrying a ladder and a venetian blind walked through to the next room; shortly afterward there was the sound of the ladder and venetian blind falling. The situation was made ambiguous by having the confederate say nothing or made clear by having him cry out that he was hurt. In the ambiguous condition, the usual bystander effect was obtained, and subjects were more likely to help when alone than with fellow bystanders. When ambiguity was low, however, subjects went to the aid of the victim *every time!*

Familiarity with the Situation. When you are in a new and unfamiliar setting, how do you feel? Think of your first day at a new school or the first time you took a trip by yourself. Most people seem to be somewhat anxious and confused when they first encounter unknown surroundings. Latané and Darley (1970) proposed that these feelings and the uncertainty about what to do should interfere with prosocial behavior. They chose two settings, a subway station and an airport, to provide different degrees of familiarity. Most individuals in a New York City subway station have been there countless times. Most individuals at LaGuardia Airport on any given day are likely to be relative strangers to that setting, and many of them are there for the very first time. At which place would a stranger in distress be more likely to receive help? An emergency was created by a male confederate who had a bandaged leg and walked with crutches. He moved slowly through the crowd until he spotted a male stranger sitting alone. As he drew near, the young man pretended to trip; he fell to the ground, holding his knee as if in pain. When this accident occurred in a subway station, 83

THE ROLE OF COMMITMENT:
CONVERTING APATHY TO INVOLVEMENT

In the Latané and Darley (1970) analysis of prosocial behavior, *Step III* requires that an individual assume personal responsibility for providing help. We have described how, with multiple bystanders, each person seems to feel less responsible. What might be done to increase the feeling of responsibility? One clue is provided in an experiment dealing with obedience, such as those of Milgram described in Chapter 6. In one such study, Tilker (1970) found a way to eliminate the blind obedience of subjects. When an individual was told that he was *totally responsible* for the well-being of the person receiving the painful shocks, he was not only likely to disobey the experimenter but to disrupt the experiment entirely. Some subjects who were given such responsibility threatened violence if the experiment was not halted, and one went so far as to wreck the shock apparatus. If the same idea could be applied to the witnessing of crimes, would responsibility work in a similar way?

Moriarty (1975) proposed that any conflicts about taking responsibility and intervening in an emergency would be resolved if an individual were committed ahead of time to assume responsibility. He also suggested

that such commitment is relatively easy to obtain. The site of his field study was Jones Beach in New York during several summer days. The confederate selected an individual who was settled on a blanket to be a subject; he would place his own blanket nearby and turn on his portable radio to a local rock station. Shortly afterward, he spoke to the subject and either asked for a match or said, "Excuse me, I'm going to the boardwalk for a few minutes . . . would you watch my things?" All subjects agreed to do so, thus committing themselves as responsible bystanders. In both conditions, the confederate then walked away, and a second confederate entered the scene, picked up the radio that was still playing, and hurried away with it in the opposite direction.

Of those subjects who had been simply asked for a match and had made no commitment, only 20 percent did anything about the theft. Most watched the thief disappear with the radio and then went back to whatever they were doing. Once again, it might appear that people are indifferent and apathetic about helping. When subjects made a commitment to watch the stranger's belongings, however, 95 percent intervened. These individuals

A   B

C

D

E

FIGURE 8-9. *When a radio was "stolen" on a beach in a field experiment (A), few bystanders did anything about it—they just passively watched the thief (B). When the victim had previously asked the bystander to watch his things, this simple commitment led almost all bystanders to chase the thief (C and D) and even to restrain him physically (E), as shown in these movie stills taken at the scene. (Source: Dr. Thomas Moriarty.)*

stood up, ran up to the thief, and demanded an explanation. As may be seen in Figure 8-9, some did something physical to the thief such as grabbing him, holding him, and taking the radio back. When the same basic study was repeated in a New York automat with a suitcase being stolen while the "victim" ate, very similar results emerged. All the committed subjects responded to the theft, while only about 10 percent of the uncommited ones did anything.

Moriarty points out that what appears to be an apathetic public can rather quickly be changed into very responsible individuals. All that is needed is a simple commitment to be helpful. Such behavior can nevertheless be inhibited when other witnesses are in close proximity. Thus, even with commitment, the presence of an apathetic bystander decreases the likelihood of interventions to stop a thief (Shaffer, Rogel, and Hendrick, 1975).

percent of the strangers came over to help him up; in the airport, only 41 percent helped. Familiarity with the setting seemed to be the primary reason for the difference—in the subway station, help was found to be given more by regular users than by those for whom a subway was an unusual experience.

One reason that unfamiliar situations may have a negative effect on prosocial behavior is that you must pay a great deal of attention in order to figure out what to do, where to go, and how to behave. You have to read signs, listen for announcements, ask directions, and pay attention to what others are doing—in other words, there is *stimulus overload.* Sherrod and Downs (1974) created an analogous situation in a laboratory by having subjects perform complex tasks while listening to confusing auditory messages. The basic task was to proofread a passage underlining each error while listening to a taped voice read random numbers and noting each time a "2" was said. A stimulus-overload condition was created by having some subjects carry out these tasks while also listening to a loud Dixieland jazz recording *and* a voice rapidly reading a passage from Aristotle. Surprisingly, both groups did about equally well with the proofreading. Just afterward, when they left the laboratory and the experiment was seemingly over, a confederate asked a favor of each subject. Those in the overload condition were much less helpful than those in the regular condition. The experimenters suggested that the overloaded subjects were much like urban dwellers who adapt to fairly unpleasant conditions and get their work done, but they are then less apt to behave in a prosocial manner.

Implicit Rules: What Can I Do? Among the things that must be learned in any culture are the implicit rules that define what we can and can't do in each situation. A few of the rules have been suggested in the research on prosocial behavior. Don't stare at strangers. Be cool and do nothing rather than risk making a fool of yourself. Don't interfere unless it's your responsibility. Help a stranger in distress if you're *sure* he's in distress. Some of these rules have been found to interfere with our ability to deal with emergencies and to be helpful. Bryan and London (1970) indicate that children tend to follow such cultural norms more and more closely as they grow older.

In a study of helpfulness among children, Staub (1970) found that very young children were actually more likely to help another child in distress than were older ones; helping behavior declined from third grade on through the sixth grade. Children who failed to help were interviewed, and they indicated that they were afraid of doing something they were not supposed to do, afraid that the experimenter would not approve. For them, learning society's norms meant primarily learning taboos, inhibitions, and what not to do. Once children are old enough to learn to mind their own business, to respect the privacy of others, and so forth, they are less inclined to offer help when an emergency arises.

To determine whether such factors can be altered, Staub (1971) placed seventh graders alone in a room with instructions to draw a picture. In the next room another student was also working alone. Soon after the experimenter departed, there was the sound of a crash and a girl crying. Only 15 percent of the subjects made any move to help—the rest kept on working. Other subjects were placed in an identical situation except that the experimenter said, "If you need more drawing pencils, you may go into the other room and get some. There are some in there on the windowsill." With this brief indication that it was OK to enter the other room, 50 percent of the subjects went next door in response to the crash and the crying. One student provided a very good demonstration of the importance of rule-oriented behavior. She listened to the sounds coming from the other room, quickly broke the points of her two pencils, and then went to the aid of the victim. She seemed to be covering all bases to make sure that she had a justifiable reason to enter the room where the accident had taken place.

INTERNAL FACTORS INFLUENCING PROSOCIAL BEHAVIOR

Most of the research on prosocial behavior has concentrated on those aspects of the situation which increase or decrease the likelihood of individuals engaging in an act of helping. Even though there has not been much research dealing with concepts such as conscience or superego, there are other internal processes that influence altruistic behavior. We will now examine a few of these.

Mood and Prosocial Behavior

Our feelings influence many of the things we do, and prosocial responses seem to vary in part as a function of whether we are "up" or "down." Imagine that you see a stranger having difficulty opening her car door. Do you think your tendency to lend a helping hand would be the same if you had just received an "A" on a final as it would if you had just received an "F"? In Chapter 5, it was shown that we like other people better when our mood is positive than when it is negative. For that reason, it seems probable that one's affective state would be a determinant of prosocial responses. In that earlier chapter, one experiment was described in which attraction was increased after subjects listened to good news and decreased after they heard bad news. In a similar way, a positive news broadcast has been found to increase prosocial behavior (Hornstein et al., 1975).

The Warm Glow of Success. Evidence to support the general idea that feelings determine helpfulness was first provided by Isen (1970). She proposed that an individual's feeling state at any given moment would affect prosocial responses toward a stranger. In an experimental test of this idea, school teachers were given either a success or a failure experience in order to manipulate their feelings. It was hypothesized that subjects who did well on the experimental task would feel a "warm glow of success" and hence be friendly and generous to others. Presumably the cool gloom of failure would lead to unfriendliness and stinginess. Just after the success or failure experience, a confederate came into the room with a can labeled "Junior High Air-Conditioning Fund," supposedly a money-raising scheme for making the school's library more comfortable in the summertime. The can was left in the room with the subject, and the confederate went out again. Individuals who had just had the success experience placed an average of 46 cents in the can; those who had failed donated an average of 7 cents each.

In a subsequent experiment with children, Isen, Horn, and Rosenhan (1973) found that success led to increased generosity while failure led to decreased generosity among children as well as adults. Because such behavioral effects are theoretically attributed to positive and negative feelings, it was important to demonstrate that success and failure are not required for such findings, but that other ways of manipulating feelings lead to similar results. Rosenhan, Underwood, and Moore (1974) were able to show this by asking second and third graders to sit and think about past experiences that made them feel happy or sad. The children were "paid" 25 cents for taking part in the experiment, and it was mentioned to each subject that it might be nice to share some of the money with those children who did not take part. Subjects who thought of sad experiences donated 3.2 pennies to the other children; those who thought of happy experiences gave 7.4 pennies. Thus, there seems to be a definite relationship between an individual's feeling state and the tendency to be generous in helping others.

Lucky Me! The mood studies discussed so far have involved generosity as a function of feelings. What about other types of prosocial behavior, such as offering help to an individual who needs assistance? Isen and Levin (1972) devised a very clever and surprisingly simple way to manipulate mood in a field experiment. The setting was a series of telephone booths in shopping malls in San Francisco and Philadelphia. To create positive feelings, the experimenters simply placed a dime in the coin-return slot for the next telephone user to find. They compared the prosocial responses of these subjects with the responses of other telephone users who were not lucky enough to find a dime. Lurking near the phone booth was a female confederate. Just after the subject finished the telephone call, the confederate happened to drop a folder full of papers directly in the subject's path. Do you think that the positive feelings associated with finding an unexpected dime would be strong enough to cause him or her to stop and help pick up the scattered papers? As you can see in Figure 8-10, less than 5 percent of the shoppers helped with the papers if they were in the no-dime condition; among those who found a dime, almost 90 percent stopped and helped.

In subsequent research, Levin and Isen (1975) pointed out two possible problems with the dime study. First, perhaps those who found a dime were not being more helpful, but were just paying more attention which could explain how they spotted the accident. After all, they had just been rewarded for paying close attention in the phone booth, so perhaps they were looking around for more good fortune when they saw the dropped folder. Second, the relationship between affect and attraction suggests that their good feelings may have led them to seek a positive interpersonal interaction. In other words, maybe they were

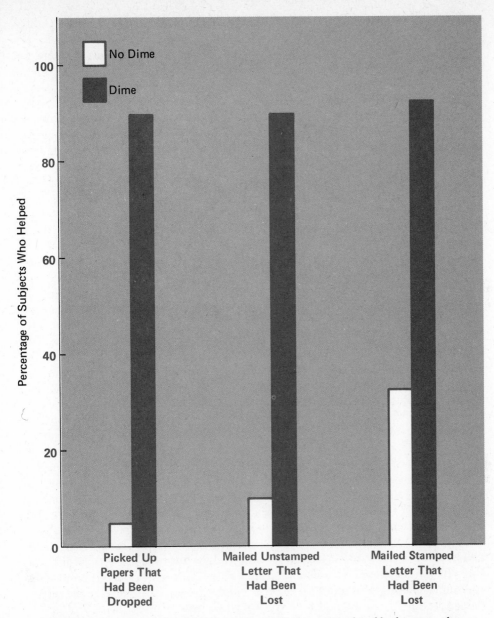

FIGURE 8-10. *In a series of field studies, mood was manipulated by leaving a dime in the coin-return slot, in a public telephone booth. Compared to phone users who found only an empty slot, those who had just found a dime were more likely to help a stranger who had dropped her folder of papers and more likely to mail either a stamped or an unstamped letter "accidentally" left in the booth. (Source: Based on data from Isen and Levin, 1972, and Levin and Isen, 1975.)*

looking for a friendship rather than just being altruistic. To rule out such possibilities, the dime–no dime manipulation was repeated in a railroad station in Philadelphia. This time, the helping involved a letter which the experimenter "accidentally" left in the telephone booth just before the subject entered. All letters were addressed, and half of them were stamped and half unstamped. Observers watched to be sure that each subject saw the letter (most picked it up and read the address), so the possibility of differences in attention could be ruled out. Second, helping involved simply taking the letter to a mailbox or not, so the possibility of differences in desire for interpersonal interactions could be ruled out. Nevertheless, as shown in Figure 8-10, those who found a dime were much more likely to mail the letter (with or without a stamp) than those who had not made such a find. It seems safe to conclude, then, that positive feelings increase the probability that a person will engage in prosocial behavior.

The Perceived Cost of Helping

In discussing a reinforcement theory of prosocial behavior earlier in the chapter, we indicated that such behavior will increase if it results in rewards and decrease if it results in punishment. In examining complex human behavior outside the laboratory, it is always difficult to determine just what the rewards and punishments for each person might be. One approach is to attempt to analyze each situation from the viewpoint of the individual whose behavior is of interest. We will now describe such an analysis of prosocial behavior.

Why Does Anyone Help? Piliavin and Piliavin (1976) have proposed a model of bystander behavior that attempts to integrate a number of the findings we have described in the present chapter. They believe that the observation of an emergency is physiologically arousing in an unpleasant way, and that the individual will seek some means to reduce this aroused state. Consistent with this idea, individuals are found to respond physiologically when someone like themselves is being shocked and the greater the physiological response, the greater their altruism toward the victim (Krebs, 1975). In a similar way, an individual who is under experimentally created stress (expecting electric shock) is more likely to help someone in the same situation than when stress is absent (Dovidio and Morris, 1975). The specific response that is chosen is whatever behavior will most rapidly and most completely reduce the arousal but in a way that will maximize the rewards and minimize the "costs" (or punishments). As was indicated at the beginning of this chapter, there are many costs when a person decides to be helpful and these include loss of time, the risk of getting hurt, the expenditure of effort, and possible exposure to disgusting experiences. There are also some rewards for helping—increased self-esteem, being thanked by the victim, and sometimes receiving praise, honor, and glory. In addition, there are some costs for failing to help, such as self-blame, guilt, and criticism from those who are aware of your behavior. Each individual must weigh these potential costs and rewards for himself or herself.

What happens in a emergency situation is described as a kind of **bystander calculus** which is illustrated in Table 8-2 in a form suggested by Walster and

TABLE 8-2. *Using bystander calculus to predict an observer's response to an emergency. When arousal increases, there is increased probability that an observer will make some response to an emergency. With the level of arousal held constant, the probability that an observer will provide direct help to a victim depends on bystander calculus, which refers to the relative strength of the costs for providing direct help and the rewards for providing such help.*

		Costs for Providing Direct Help	
		Low	High
Rewards for Providing Direct Help	High	Direct help will be given.	Indirect help will be given along with excuses for not helping directly.
	Low	Response will be determined by personality factors rather than by the situation.	Escape behavior will take the observer away from the situation.

Piliavin (1972). Assuming that the arousal level is held constant, if the cost of helping is low and the rewards high, most people will respond readily and provide help. If the cost of helping is high and the rewards low, help is less likely, in that the bystander may decide that someone else should take responsibility and then he is free to run away from the emergency. For example, Darley and Batson (1973) increased the cost of helping a victim slumped over in an alleyway by telling subjects they had to hurry to make an appointment or that there was plenty of time; the less time the subjects believed they had, the less likely they were to stop and help. It follows, then, that whenever the costs are increased, prosocial responses are not as likely to occur. We will now describe two experiments that have been conducted in which the costs associated with helping were manipulated.

The Limits of Benevolence: When Helping Costs Too Much. Piliavin and Piliavin (1972) varied the unpleasantness, or cost, of helping in an emergency situation on a Philadelphia subway car. The victim, walking with a cane, entered the car, began moving toward the other end, and suddenly collapsed on the floor. Half the time this scene was enacted, in addition to falling, the victim also released a flow of red-colored diet liquid that had been concealed in his mouth. It appeared that a trickle of thick blood was running down his chin. Presumably, it would be perceived as more costly to help a bleeding victim than a nonbleeding one. It was found, as predicted, that fewer people helped and that those who did help responded more slowly when blood was present than when it was absent. It seemed that, even though a bleeding victim might be in the greatest need of help, the bystanders were repulsed by the sight of blood and afraid of getting involved in such a messy problem. In that situation, it might seem justifiable to let a trained professional assume responsibility for a high-cost victim.

One aspect of the Piliavins' formulation is that only in a high-cost situation will some of the other bystander-inhibition effects be observed. For example, it

When helping is too "costly" (for example, when the victim is bleeding), bystanders are more reluctant to provide aid than when the problem is less serious. They are also more inclined to feel that another, more able bystander (such as someone with medical training) should have the responsibility to help. (Photo by Bill Saidel; Stock, Boston.)

has been found that the presence of a bystander does not inhibit helping behavior in a low-cost situation—that is, when the subject is actually better able to provide help than the other person (Bickman, 1971). When the cost is high, however, it is easy to hold back and assume that someone else is better able to help and should have the responsibility. Piliavin, Piliavin, and Rodin (1976) predicted that this diffusion of responsibility would occur *only* when costs were extremely high; otherwise, the subject would not need to dodge the responsibility. This time using a New York subway, the experimenters manipulated both the cost of helping the victim and the presence of a more able fellow bystander.

The confederates who played the role of victim were white male undergraduates. The high-cost condition consisted of a victim with a physical stigma that would cause feelings of distaste and revulsion; theatrical makeup was used to create a large and unattractive "port wine stain" birthmark on the victim's left cheek. Another male confederate sat in one of the four seats nearest the victim; this bystander either wore a sport coat and tie or (in the "more able bystander" condition) he wore a white medical jacket and looked like an intern. The emergency occurred between two subway stops. The victim staggered several feet, fell with a moan, and remained on the floor, curled up on his side, eyes closed. As is shown in Figure 8-11, the predictions were confirmed. In the low-cost (no birthmark) condition, a high percentage of bystanders tried to help the victim, and the presence of the able intern had little effect on this prosocial response. When, however, the cost was high (birthmark condition), fewer

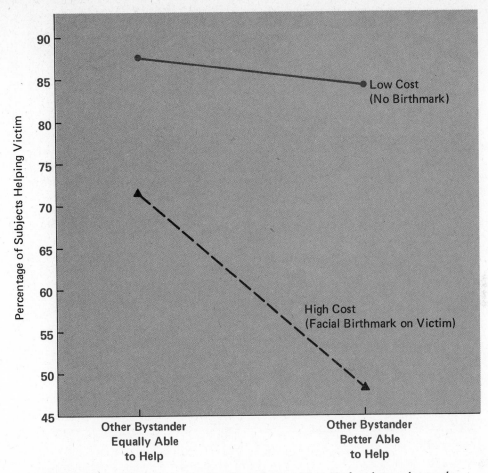

FIGURE 8-11. *When a "victim" collapsed on a New York subway, bystanders were less likely to help when the "cost" increased (the victim had a large, red facial birthmark). In the high-cost situation, bystanders were also more likely to stand back and let a more able bystander (a medical intern) take responsibility. (Source: Based on data from Piliavin, Piliavin, and Rodin, 1976.)*

people helped, and the presence of the intern clearly made a great difference. Under these circumstances, the majority of the bystanders were presumably willing to let the intern do something about the problem. Altogether, it seems reasonable to assume that a number of variables that have been found to inhibit bystander responsiveness are more likely to function in a high cost than in a low cost emergency situation.

CHARACTERISTICS OF THE HELPER
AND THE ONE WHO IS HELPED

Are some individuals more likely to help than others? Are some individuals more likely to receive help than others? How do the helper and the victim

THE ETHICS OF RESEARCH ON PROSOCIAL BEHAVIOR

Increasingly, those conducting psychological research have become sensitive to the ethical issues involved in conducting experiments with human subjects. Most psychology departments have committees that review all proposed projects and eliminate or modify those that might possibly cause any harm to the individuals taking part. Most often, potential subjects are informed of the general nature of the experiment and of what they will be doing; in this way, they can decide freely to participate or to refuse. Subjects have the right to change their minds and withdraw from an experiment if they find it objectionable in any way.

By its very nature, research on prosocial behavior has not tended to follow these guidelines. In order to create an emergency situation, it is necessary to deceive subjects and make them believe that they are taking part in a particular type of experiment—then, suddenly something unexpected occurs, and they are confronted by an accidental fall, a room filling with smoke, or whatever. Only afterward do they learn the true nature of the experiment. In field

studies, the "subjects" are not even research volunteers who are deceived—they are ordinary citizens who are going about their business riding a subway, walking down a sidewalk, buying beer, and so forth. They, too, are unexpectedly confronted by what seems to be an emergency. Is it reasonable to intrude on these individuals with a false accident or the enactment of a fake robbery?

Some critics of this research would definitely say that all such experiments are unethical and should be stopped. Unsuspecting and possibly unwilling subjects are being upset, having their privacy invaded, and being embarrassed by such experiments. Those who help and respond in a prosocial manner must feel at least a little foolish when they discover that there really was no emergency at all. Those who fail to help and afterward are asked why not may feel guilty and ashamed of their unresponsiveness. There is also the very real possibility that those who participate in these studies and maybe even those of us who read about them will be less likely to respond to real

perceive one another and how do they perceive themselves? In this section we will examine some recent research that attempts to deal with such questions.

The Helper's Needs and Beliefs

Most of the initial attempts to relate personality differences to helping behavior were unsuccessful (for example, Schwartz and Clausen, 1970), but more recent studies have revealed that it is possible to identify a few such variables that are associated with the tendency to help or not to help. For example, McGovern (1976) has found that those who receive high scores on a "fear of embarrassment" test are less likely to help than those with low scores. As we indicated earlier in this chapter, helping seems to be inhibited by the fear of making a fool of oneself in public. What other personality characteristics are related to prosocial behavior?

Need for Approval. We have suggested earlier that one of the rewards for emergencies in the future. If next week you saw someone collapse on a subway, or witnessed a fall in an airport, or heard the crash of a workman's ladder, might you think back to this chapter and wonder whether a social psychologist could be watching you from some hiding place?

The opposing argument is that these studies deal with a vitally important aspect of human behavior. For one thing, they seem to dispel the pessimistic view that people have become indifferent to the suffering of others and are deliberately unwilling to help. People are very willing to help if the conditions are right. Further, knowledge growing out of this research may make each of us realize that we should assume responsibility and make a decision to come to the aid of those in need. Greenwald (1975) points out that when seminary students in an earlier experiment were asked to read the parable of the Good Samaritan just before encountering a shabbily dressed stranger "by the side of the road," it increased the odds in favor of their helping him by more than 50 percent. Perhaps reading altruism research has a similar effect. After going through this chapter, do you think you would stand idly by while Kitty

Genovese was being murdered and decide to do nothing, not even make a phone call? We do not know as yet whether behavior becomes more prosocial among those aware of this body of research, but an anecdote provides a homely hint. During the period when one of the authors was in the middle of writing the present chapter, he was in a grocery store one afternoon when a female shopper across the aisle pulled out a roll of paper towels and caused an avalanche of other towels and paper products to cascade to the floor. Though the author was in a hurry and not terribly eager to help a stranger restack the merchandise, he thought, "How could I go back to write about and think about prosocial behavior if I walked away from this poor lady? Besides, how could I look Bibb Latané and the others in the eye?" His prosocial impulses easily won out.

What do you think? Is the knowledge gained by this research useful? Is it worth the momentary embarrassment experienced by a few subjects? Do you think your behavior will be more prosocial as a function of what you now know? We hope so, and those conducting this research hope so, too.

engaging in prosocial behavior is the social approval that an altruistic person receives. Individuals are found to differ, however, in the extent to which they are motivated to seek such approval. For example, Satow (1975) hypothesized that those individuals with high approval needs would be more likely to help others than individuals whose need for approval was low and that such differences would be greatest when others witnessed the act of helping.

Female subjects were given a test measuring need for approval (Crowne and Marlowe, 1960) and divided into high- and low-need groups. They were paid $1.50 for taking part in the experiment. Subjects were told that the money came from a university research fund, and, if they wished to make a donation to that fund, they could place their money in a jar containing other contributions that was conveniently available on the table. Some subjects were left alone to work in private and contribute anonymously, and some were told that the experimenter would be observing them through a one-way mirror.

As can be seen in Figure 8-12, much more money was contributed in the public condition when subjects were being observed than in the anonymous condition. **Need for approval** exerted a strong effect on the tendency to be

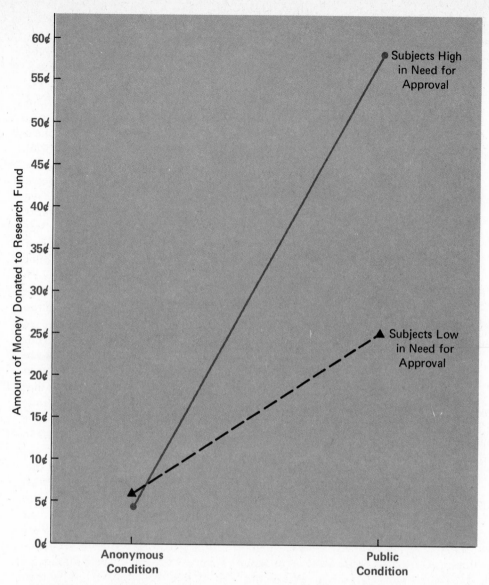

FIGURE 8-12. *Subjects who were high or low in the need for approval were given the opportunity to donate money to a research fund anonymously or publicly (being observed by the experimenter). Both groups donated more money in the public condition, but this difference was greatest for individuals with a high need for approval. (Source: Based on data from Satow, 1975.)*

charitable, but only in the public condition. In other words, those subjects who strongly needed social approval behaved in a prosocial manner to the greatest extent when such behavior could be seen and applauded by another person. Whether this need influences other types of prosocial acts remains to be discovered in future research.

Belief in a Just World. Lerner, Miller, and Holmes (1976) point out that the idea of justice and of getting what one deserves pervades our entire society. Both our ancient myths and our current ones tend to stress that justice will always triumph—the good guys will be rewarded while the bad guys will get their comeuppance. Despite these beliefs, we all are aware that each day people are victimized by wars, crimes, and natural disasters, humiliated by loss of jobs, and killed by disease, accidents, and starvation. From time to time, we get glimpses of such events on our television sets in living color. In order to reconcile one's belief in a just world and one's observation of widespread suffering, Lerner (1970) suggests that an individual may either work to restore justice by helping the victims or rationalize things as they are by deciding that the victim must deserve his fate. Blaming a victim may seem odd, but, after all, those terrible things have not happened to me, and I am a good person. I am safe because such events only happen to bad people, undeserving people, inferior people—those who "got what was coming to 'em." It has been found that individuals who attribute their own successes and failures to their ability and hard work are less likely to offer help, money, understanding, and sympathy to victims than are individuals who feel their own successes and failures are due to external factors such as luck (Phares and Lamiell, 1975). In Chapter 11, we will return to this topic and the tendency people have to place the blame for misfortune on the victim. Here, we will describe how the **just-world hypothesis** can bring about increased altruism.

Though the desire to believe in a just world is a very common one, there are still individual differences in its strength, and a Just-World Scale has been constructed to measure this characteristic (Rubin and Peplau, 1973). Using that scale, Zuckerman (1975) has conducted a series of experiments showing how, under certain conditions, altruism increases among individuals who strongly believe in justice. He hypothesized that at a time when they themselves are in need, those who most strongly believe in a just-world behave in a more prosocial manner than people whose belief is weak. The idea is that believers feel that when they behave in a good way to help others, they will be rewarded—that is, your good deeds will be "paid back" by subsequent success. The subjects were college students, and they were approached either five months or two days before an exam—those with an upcoming midterm only two days away were presumably in greater personal need than the group studied five months before their exam. All subjects were phoned and asked to volunteer to help a graduate student with his research. The high and low just-world subjects differed in their willingness to help only when they were called two days before their test—at that time, those high in the belief volunteered to assist with more experiments than those low in the belief. In a similar follow-up study, it was also found that when their own needs were high, individuals who strongly believed in a just world were more willing to serve as readers for blind students. Zuckerman interprets the behavior of the high just-world individuals not as altruism but as trading one favor (altruistic behavior) for something expected in return (success on the exam).

With respect to both need for approval and belief in a just world, it may be seen that these characteristics lead to an increase in prosocial behavior under specific circumstances. As was suggested at the beginning of the chapter, however, once the benefits of altruism are identified, that behavior is likely to be interpreted as self-serving. It is possible, of course, that all prosocial behavior may contain just such elements. For example, a charitable appeal that provides the donor with something in return for a contribution (e.g., a broom, light bulbs, cookies, a candle) is more successful than an equally deserving appeal for a straight contribution, so long as the exchange appears to be fair (Holmes, Miller, and Lerner, 1974).

The Victim's Sex

As we have noted in Chapter 4, we have traditionally been taught that males and females are different, that they act differently, and that they should be treated in different ways. In our culture, for example, females have been assumed to be the weaker sex, and males have been expected to help them whenever possible, whether in carrying their books to school, lighting their cigarettes, or changing their flat tires. If these values and customs still have any influence, it would be expected that female victims would receive help from males to a greater extent than males would receive help from females.

On the Road: Helping a Gentleman or a Lady in Distress. Most of us at one time or another find ourselves on the side of a highway, stuck with a car that won't function. At such times, we are the victims and badly in need of help. In this situation, does the sex of the victim affect the likelihood of being helped, and are men or women more likely to provide the help? Pomazal and Clore (1973) parked a car near the road at two locations near Champaign-Urbana, Illinois, raised the trunk, and propped a spare tire against the car. Either a male or a female confederate pretended to be jacking up the car, but the victim did not look in the direction of the passing cars or make any gestures for them to stop. When the victim was a female, approximately one car out of every four that passed stopped to offer assistance. When the victim was a male, only one car out of fifty stopped. Also, those who helped were almost all males. The typical male who stopped was over thirty-five years old, alone, and driving either a camper or a pick-up truck. A later study conducted in Tallahassee, Florida, used a stalled car by the side of the road with the hood raised; females were helped much faster than males and again almost all of those who stopped to assist were males (West, Whitney, and Schnedler, 1975).

Another type of person needing help on the highway is a hitchhiker. Does sex determine who gets or who offers a ride? Again, Pomazal and Clore (1973) placed confederates on Illinois highways, but this time without a car. Once more, females in need had better luck than males. Out of each 100 passing cars, 19 stopped for a female hitchhiker and only 6 for a male. Also, those offering the rides were almost all males; only one female stopped. The person who offered the ride tended to be alone, as in the flat-tire study, but the drivers were younger (between 20 and 25) and riding in cars rather than campers or trucks. Another investigation of hitchhiking was conducted in and around Palo Alto, California, and compared the help offered to a female, a male, and a couple; the lone female had by far the greatest success in getting picked up and once again most of the rides were offered by males (Snyder, Grether, and Keller, 1974). These investigators also found that when a hitchhiker was able to catch the driver's eye and stare at him, more rides were offered than when no eye contact was made. They raised the possibility of sexual overtones when a lone male stops to pick up a lone female who has looked him directly in the eye. This interpretation is strengthened by the fact that, in an emergency, males offer more help to a physically attractive victim than to an unattractive one (West and Brown, 1975). Thus, the possibility is raised of a selfish motive for altruism among the roadside Samaritans.

In the Elevator: Chivalry Above and Below the Mason-Dixon Line. Though the familiar male-female roles are changing in the United States, not all parts of the country are changing at the same rate (Latané and Dabbs, 1975). These experimenters hypothesized that the traditional sex roles would influence behavior more in the South than elsewhere in the country. The stereotypes of the Southern Gentleman and the Southern Lady would still seem to be powerful enough to affect behavior. Southern men are supposed to be gallant and chivalrous; Southern women are supposed to accept male courtesies with charm and grace.

To test this general idea, male and female experimenters entered a variety of public buildings and took about 1500 elevator rides, staging a small accident in the presence of a total of almost 5,000 bystanders in Atlanta, Seattle, and Columbus. The accident consisted of dropping a handful of pencils or coins, and the investigators were interested in the relationship between the sex of the victim and of those who helped pick up what had been dropped.

As in the highway studies, females were more likely to receive help than males, and males were more likely to give help than females. Of greatest interest, as shown in Figure 8-13, is the extent to which help was received from a member of the opposite sex in relation to the section of the country where the incident took place. In general, males were more likely to help females than the reverse, and this sex difference was much greater in Atlanta than in the two northern cities. It appears that chivalry (or benevolent sexism) is alive and well in the South, has waned in the Northwest, and seems to be nearly nonexistent in the Midwest. It was also found once again that group size influenced helping behavior—as the number of bystanders on the elevator increased, the willingness of each individual to help decreased.

Some aspects of sex-role behavior apparently maintain themselves without respect to geographic location. If a male were placed in a situation in which he had the choice of watching another person receive an electric shock *or* directing that shock to himself, do you think the sex of the other person would influence his decision? In Ohio (at Kent State University) McGovern, Ditzian, and Taylor (1975b) confronted undergraduate males with that choice situation. It was found that when the potential victim was a fellow male, subjects chose to be shocked

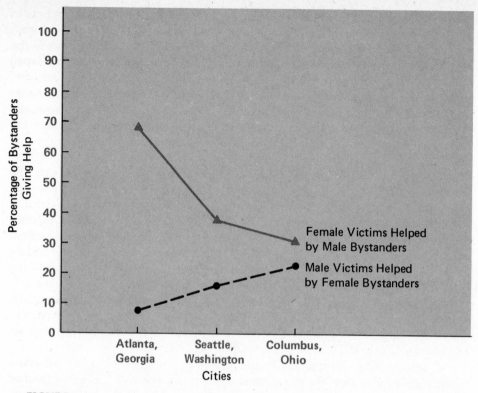

FIGURE 8-13. *A female who drops a handful of pencils or coins on an elevator receives help from a male bystander to a greater extent than a male victim receives help from a female bystander. The effect of sex on helping behavior is strongest in the South and weakest in the Midwest. (Source: Based on data from Latané and Dabbs, 1975.)*

themselves only about 18 percent of the time. With a female victim, however, males sacrificed their own comfort and received the shock almost 60 percent of the time. Why this difference? When subjects were asked to rate the confederate who had posed as the victim, it became clear that a male and a female are seen as different on several dimensions. In a very traditional way, a female victim compared to a male was perceived as weaker, more cowardly, more of a follower than a leader, more submissive, and more dependent. In this type of interaction, at least, such sexual stereotypes seem to be powerful enough to influence helping behavior.

It Sometimes Hurts to Be Helped

Most of the research on prosocial behavior has been directed at the helper or potential helper. It is generally taken for granted that the person in need of help wants assistance, is pleased to receive it, and feels undying gratitude to the person who offered it. It was pointed out earlier that it is rewarding to engage in altruistic behavior. Those who help feel good about their prosocial activities, whether as individuals assisting a stranger, professionals offering help to the needy, or, at another level, wealthy nations providing aid to underdeveloped countries. Individuals, professionals, and governments are usually surprised to find that those who receive aid are sometimes ungrateful and often resentful (Gergen et al., 1975; Gergen, Morse, and Bode, 1974). Americans especially seem to have assumed that aid will elicit love and respect; to our amazement, the reaction is frequently resentment and contempt.

Resources, Threat, and Self-esteem. Research has shown that those who receive aid may respond either positively or negatively, depending on several specific aspects of the situation (e.g., Morse and Gergen, 1971). In general, if the one who provides aid is seen as liking the victim and as being truly interested in his welfare, then the person who is helped feels good about the interaction. One variable determining such reactions is the degree to which the one providing aid can afford to do so (Gergen, Morse, and Kristeller, 1973). For example, if a wealthy nation provides foreign aid, the recipients might feel that it was the only fair thing for the donor to do, that people in such a country are more successful and hence must feel superior, and that help from such a source is not deserving of gratitude. On the other hand, if a poor nation acts as a donor, they should get much more credit for straining their budget in order to be generous.

A similar process should operate at the individual level, and Fisher and Nadler (1976) designed an experiment to test this possibility. They reasoned that a person who receives help that represents a high cost to the donor should respond positively and should feel good about himself because such aid indicates that the donor likes him and is concerned. In contrast, help that represents a low cost to the donor should be threatening and make the recipient feel that he failed and must be dependent on someone who is succeeding. The experimental task was a game-like situation in which each subject was supposedly interacting with a partner. After the first two sessions of the game, it was arranged that each subject was doing very badly, whereas the partner was either doing slightly better or extremely well in terms of the number of playing chips (representing money). Then, the partner either donated some of his chips to the subject (so he wouldn't be eliminated during the subsequent sessions) or he donated no chips. At this point, a measure of self-esteem was administered to determine how the subject felt about himself with respect to his intelligence and self-confidence. As can be seen in Figure 8-14, aid which represented a high cost to the donor resulted in positive self-feelings in the recipient, but low-cost aid led to a relatively negative self-image in the recipient. Thus, it appears that the total resources of the donor are important in determining whether help from that person provides a boost to the ego or whether it represents a threat.

Attraction toward the One Who Helps. Much of the research on reactions to being helped deals with how well the helper is liked. For example, it seems that the person who is helped feels at a disadvantage (in terms of equity), and he

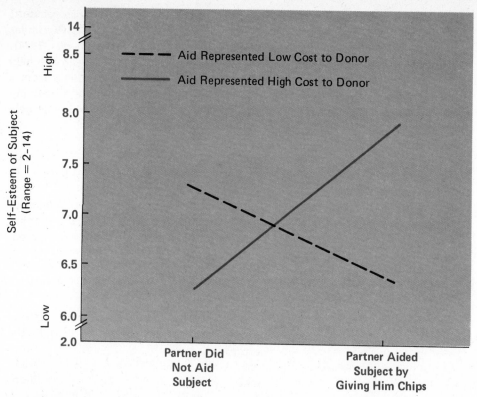

FIGURE 8-14. *When aid represents a high cost to the donor, the recipient's self-esteem is enhanced. In contrast, when aid represents a low cost to the donor, the recipient's self-esteem is relatively low. (Data from Fisher and Nadler, Effect of Donor Resources on Recipient Self-esteem and Self-help.* Journal of Experimental Social Psychology, *1976, 12, p. 145.)*

or she is uncomfortable unless there is an opportunity to reciprocate. Thus, the recipient likes the donor better if there is a chance to return the favor at a later time or even to do someone else a favor (Castro, 1974; Gross and Latané, 1974). It is also found that people respond more positively to help that is offered spontaneously than to help that is given only after it is requested. In one such experiment (Broll, Gross, and Piliavin, 1974), subjects were given an almost impossible problem in logic, but they could enlist the aid of a female helper. For half the subjects, the helper offered her assistance frequently during the session. For the other half, help was given only when the subjects asked for it. Attraction toward the voluntary helper was greater than toward the one who simply responded to requests.

If the person in need of help has an existing relationship with the helper, what is the response to receiving aid? How would you feel about being helped by a good friend versus an enemy? Offhand, it appears likely that help from a friend might be positive while an enemy's help might raise suspicions about his

Chapter 8   Prosocial Behavior: Altruism and Helping

motives, and some research supports this idea (Nadler, Fisher, and Streufert, 1974). Also, people are more willing to accept help from someone who is similar and liked than from someone who is dissimilar (Clark, Gotay, and Mills, 1974). There are, however, some negative aspects to such situations. For example, help from a similar other lowers self-esteem and self-confidence while help from a dissimilar other has a positive effect—presumably because it is more threatening for someone like yourself to be in a superior position and able to provide help (Fisher and Nadler, 1974).

HOW CAN THE INCIDENCE OF PROSOCIAL BEHAVIOR BE INCREASED?

Most of us would agree that in the best of all possible worlds, prosocial behavior should occur whenever a fellow human being is in need. The research that has been conducted so far suggests a few ways to increase its occurrence in our society.

Raising Children with Prosocial Values

One of the important outcomes of theorizing about internal determinants of prosocial behavior has been an interest in child-rearing behavior. Despite the power of situational variables, some people *do* help more than others. Aronfreed (1968) stresses the importance of determining how internal controls might be built into our children so they would be less dependent on external conditions and more dependent on their own internal standards.

Many investigators have found that there are crucial elements in the interaction between parents and children that influence conscience development. For example, altruistic children are found to have at least one parent who is also altruistic (Hoffman, 1975a). Many studies indicate that children are most likely to develop internal controls if they are raised in an atmosphere of emotional warmth and love, and if they are not disciplined by physical punishment. Children who are taught only to respond to rules and regulations, and who receive punishments for violating the rules, seem to learn to respond primarily to external cues. If the rules change, the behavior changes, too. In Chapter 6, we discussed the way in which a great many people were able to carry out antisocial orders in German extermination camps, in the village of My Lai, and in Milgram's laboratory. An individual can be a law-abiding bank clerk one day and a torturer the next, so long as the external rules are clear. Without strong internal constraints, one can go through life dependent on others to indicate what is right and wrong.

What about those who refuse to act against their fellow human beings? What might their early experiences be? Withdrawal of love seems to be an effective disciplinary device when used in an atmosphere of genuine emotional closeness. Essentially, the child becomes dependent on the parents' love, and the possibility of losing that love is traumatic. The child learns to behave and even to think in such a way as to maintain this loving relationship. The parents' values are accepted and believed. It is just such solidly ingrained values which can cause an individual to become a religious martyr, to risk life itself to support a cause such as civil rights, or to stand up against the powerful forces of an unjust or immoral government.

Possessing internal standards of morality has some drawbacks, by the way. Among the consequences of strong conscience development are anxiety and feelings of guilt. Some people experience agonies of self-torture as they attempt to act and to think in acceptable ways. For some, the moral standards are unrealistically high, and psychotherapy may be needed to help relax some of the inappropriate internal standards. We need to develop child-rearing techniques that produce strong but nevertheless realistic prosocial values.

Reducing Environmental Ambiguity and Teaching Responsible Behavior

Research on prosocial behavior repeatedly indicates that the "indifferent" bystander actually is one of several very concerned bystanders trying to figure out what is happening. Among the variables identified as having a positive effect on prosocial behavior, the most pervasive seems to be the ambiguity of the situation. Individuals hesitate to take action when the situation is ambiguous; they are afraid of making a mistake and becoming objects of ridicule. This suggests that society could benefit from educational efforts that expose each of us to varied settings and to the types of emergencies likely to arise there. Another important variable is the perceived responsibility of the bystander—which may simply mean that there is sometimes ambiguity about what to do. That, too, can be taught.

Only one educational effort to deal with emergencies seems to be a firmly established part of our culture and that is the fire drill practiced in schools. Besides the joy of having your classes interrupted, the fire drill taught you over and over again what it meant when the alarm sounded and what to do in such a situation—how quickly and in what order to leave your classroom, where to exit the building, and where to stand when you got outside. This training served to make an unusual, and unlikely, emergency situation into a familiar possibility that we knew just how to handle.

We need to identify a wide variety of such emergencies in diverse settings and to prescribe the most appropriate responses to each. What *should* you do if you see someone bleeding on a subway, drop a handful of pencils on an elevator, or stop beside the highway with a flat tire? Some of these events probably occur only rarely in our lives, and some may never occur. It is not surprising that we tend to hold back and to try to decide what is happening and what should be done.

It may sound farfetched, but why couldn't we develop simulation devices of the kind that are used to train pilots? In a realistic version of a cockpit, the trainee is exposed to the sights and sounds and movements he would experience

SUGGESTED READINGS FOR CHAPTER 8

Latané, B., and Darley, J. M. *The unresponsive bystander: Why doesn't he help?* New York: Appleton-Century-Crofts, 1970. A very readable description of the original experiments on unresponsive bystanders and an explanation of their behavior.

Lerner, M. J., Miller, D. T., and Holmes, J. G. Deserving versus justice: A contemporary dilemma. In L. Berkowitz (Ed.), *Advances in experimental social psychology.* New York: Academic Press, 1976. An interesting view of the just world phenomenon and how it relates to the perception of a victim and the way the victim is treated.

Lickona, T. (Ed.). *Moral development and behavior: Theory, research, and social issues.* New York: Holt, Rinehart, and Winston, 1976. A collection of original chapters describing several aspects of moral behavior and its antecedents.

Staub, E. *The development of prosocial behavior in children.* Morristown, N.J.: General Learning Press, 1975. An excellent brief summary of the research dealing with the way in which children learn or fail to learn to behave in a prosocial manner.

Wispé, L. (Ed.). *Positive forms of social behavior.* Cambridge, Mass.: Harvard University Press, 1976. An up-to-date collection of original chapters covering both research and theory relevant to prosocial behavior.

AGGRESSION: ITS NATURE, CAUSES, AND CONTROL

9

My Lai; Bangladesh; Angola; the Symbionese Liberation Army; terrorism in the Mideast; senseless violence on the streets of our major cities; murder; rape; child abuse—the list of human cruelty goes on and on. Indeed, so common do instances of violence appear to be at the present time that it is virtually impossible to pick up a daily newspaper, leaf through a popular magazine, or tune in the evening news without learning of the occurrence of some shocking new atrocity. Given this unsettling state of affairs, it often seems that we must live during a period when the "evil side" of human nature is stronger and less well controlled than at any time in the past. Yet, history reveals a long and uninterrupted record of war, invasion, torture, and destruction stretching back to the shadowy beginnings of organized society. In the face of such evidence, we can only conclude that the twentieth century holds no monopoly on widespread violence.

When human beings aggressed against others by means of spears, bows and arrows, or other primitive weapons, their assaults were quite destructive and led to much needless suffering. Yet, these attacks were generally restricted to one locale, and never threatened the existence of the entire species. The power of modern weaponry, however, has radically changed all this. Today, at least two nations—and probably soon others as well—possess the capacity to decimate all life on earth. Moreover, we are now moving into a period when nuclear weapons can be produced at what amount to "bargain basement" prices, a development which threatens to hasten their spread among even the less advantaged countries of the earth. In view of these unsettling trends, there can be little doubt that the unchecked spread of violence and conflict must be numbered among the most serious problems facing humanity today.

But why do people aggress? What causes human beings to turn on their fellow men and women with a savageness unmatched by even the fiercest predators ever to stalk the earth? And what steps can be taken to prevent or control such behavior? For many years, attempts to answer these questions focused on the needs, motives, and conflicts of individual aggressors. It was widely held that human beings engaged in such behavior because they were somehow driven or impelled in this direction by dark forces within their own nature. More recently, however, it has become increasingly apparent that violence, like many less dramatic forms of behavior, is strongly influenced by social factors and conditions. In fact, it now appears that the occurrence, direction, and specific form of aggressive acts are as much a function of the social context in which they occur as of the motives, needs, and urges of individual aggressors. In short, growing evidence suggests that we must search for the roots of violence in prevailing—and often complex—social conditions, as well as within the "psyches" of violent men and women.

As the social nature of aggression has become increasingly apparent, psychologists have devoted growing attention to this timely topic. As a result, we now possess a far more thorough and accurate understanding of this dangerous form of behavior than was true even a decade in the past. Because the volume of recent research concerned with aggression has been very great, it would be impossible for us to present anything approaching a complete summary of it within the confines of the present chapter. Largely out of necessity, therefore, we have chosen to limit the scope of our discussion in two distinct ways. First, because it is human rather than animal aggression which threatens humanity's continued survival, attention will be focused primarily on this topic. Second, rather than attempting to examine all lines of current investigation concerning aggression, a smaller number of central issues have been chosen for consideration. Briefly, our discussion will proceed as follows.

First, we will examine several contrasting *theoretical perspectives* regarding the origins and nature of aggression. Among the views considered here will be those suggesting that such behavior results from (1) inborn urges or instincts, (2) externally stimulated drives, or (3) social-learning experiences. Next, we will shift our attention to several *situational antecedents* of aggressive acts, including such factors as frustration, attack, and general arousal. Third, we will consider various *individual determinants* of aggression, including personality characteristics which predispose particular persons toward such actions, and one genetic pattern—the XYY syndrome—which has been linked to similar effects. Finally, we will focus on various means for *preventing or controlling* aggression, such as punishment, catharsis, and the induction of responses incompatible with anger or overt violence among aggressors.

As you probably know from your own experience, such terms as "aggression" and "aggressive" have several different meanings in everyday speech. For example, the actions of a brutal murderer and those of a highly successful salesman may both be described as "aggressive," but for very different reasons. A similar situation exists within psychology, where the term aggression has also acquired several different meanings. As a result, we would quickly become mired in confusion if we did not begin by carefully specifying the meaning we will attach to this term in the pages which follow. Before turning to any of the interesting topics mentioned above, therefore, we must first complete one important preliminary task—the formulation of a clear, working definition of aggression.

AGGRESSION: A WORKING DEFINITION

Although many different definitions of aggression have been offered, none has as yet been universally adopted. One which would probably be acceptable to many social psychologists, however, is as follows: **aggression** *is any form of behavior directed toward the goal of harming or injuring another living being who is motivated to avoid such treatment.* At first glance, this definition seems both simple and straightforward. Closer examination reveals, however, that it actually contains several features demanding careful attention.

Aggression as behavior. First, it suggests that aggression is a form of behavior rather than emotion, need, or motive. As such, it must be distinguished from emotions which may or may not accompany it (for example, anger), motives which may or may not underlie it (for example, the desire to inflict pain or suffering on others), or negative attitudes which sometimes facilitate its occurrence (for example, racial or ethnic prejudice). Further, as a specific type of overt behavior, aggression can take many different forms. It can be *physical,* consisting of attacks against others by means of fists, teeth, or weapons, or *verbal,* consisting instead of insults, taunts, or threats. Similarly, it can be *direct,* involving assaults against the target person himself, or *indirect,* involving actions against this person's property, possessions, or even loved ones. Finally, it can be *active,* consisting of overt harm-doing behaviors by the aggressor, or *passive,* involving instances in which harm is produced in the absence of overt attacks (e.g., through the withholding of some reward or refusal to perform some essential action). Regardless of the precise form taken, aggression may always be viewed as involving forms of behavior in which one person attempts to harm or injure one or more others.

Aggression and intention. Second, our working definition limits application of the term aggression to acts in which the aggressor *intends* to harm the victim. Unfortunately, the inclusion of such a criterion of intent to harm raises a number of serious difficulties. As pointed out by several experts in this field (Bandura, 1973; Buss, 1971), intentions are private, hidden events not open to direct observation. As a result, they must be inferred from events which both precede and follow alleged acts of aggression. In some cases, establishing the presence of an intention to harm is relatively simple. Aggressors often admit their desire to injure their victims, and even express regret if their attacks have failed to produce the intended effects. Similarly, the social context within which harm-producing behavior takes place often provides strong evidence for the existence of such intentions on the part of aggressors. For example, imagine a scene in which one individual in a bar is taunted verbally by another until, unable to stand further verbal abuse, he picks up an empty beer bottle and beats his tormentor senseless. Here, there would be little reason to doubt that the person administering such attacks fully intended to harm or injure the recipient, or that his actions should be labeled as aggression. In other situations, however, it is much more difficult to establish the presence or absence of aggressive intent. For example, consider a situation in which, while cleaning a gun, one individual shoots and kills another. If the person involved expressed deep remorse and proclaimed over and over again that his friend's death was purely accidental, it might at first appear that intention to harm was lacking, and that his behavior—while extremely careless—did not represent an instance of interpersonal aggression. If further evidence then revealed that he owed the victim a great deal of money and that the so-called accident occurred immediately after a heated argument over its repayment, we might begin to suspect that perhaps a strong motive for aggression existed.

Despite the difficulties involved in determining the presence or absence of aggressive intent, however, there are several compelling reasons for retaining such a criterion in our definition of aggression. First, if all reference to such intent were eliminated, it would be necessary to classify *accidental harm* or *injury* to others as aggression. In view of the fact that people do sometimes hurt each others' feelings, close doors on each others' fingers, and even strike each other with their automobiles quite by accident, it seems important to distinguish such actions from aggression—and this can only be accomplished through reference to the intentions behind such behaviors.

Second, if the notion of intention to harm were excluded from our definition of aggression, it would be necessary to describe the actions of surgeons, dentists, and even parents when disciplining their children as aggressive in nature. In view of the fact that the acts performed by these individuals are carried out with at least the apparent purpose of helping rather than harming the persons involved, it seems unreasonable to term them aggression (see Rule and Nesdale, 1976c).

Finally, if the notion of intent were excluded from our definition, instances in which attempts to harm or injure others are made, but fail, would not be labeled as aggression, even though the availability of better weapons, more accurate aim, or greater skill on the part of the aggressor would have resulted in serious injury to the victim. For example, imagine a situation in which a hired assassin fires a rifle at a political leader, but misses her target. It seems necessary to view such instances of *accidental noninjury* as aggression, even though they fail in their intended purpose. For all these reasons, it is essential to define aggression not simply as behavior which inflicts harm or injury on others, but rather as any actions *directed toward the goal* of inflicting such negative, aversive consequences.

Aggression is directed toward living beings. A third major aspect of our definition which requires some comment involves the contention that only actions that harm or injure living beings may be viewed as aggressive in nature. While it is obvious that individuals often strike, kick, or hit various kinds of inanimate objects (e.g., furniture, dishes, walls), such behavior will not be considered to be aggression *unless* it causes some form of harm or injury to another living organism. In many instances, of course, this is actually the case. For example, the proud owner of a priceless antique or beautiful new automobile is certainly harmed when an aggressor destroys this loved possession. In many other cases, however, attacks against inanimate objects cause no harm or injury to other persons (e.g., kicking a tin can down an empty street, hurling rocks against a brick wall, or repeatedly punching one's pillow). Although such actions may often closely resemble aggressive behaviors in physical form, they are best viewed as primarily emotional or expressive in nature, and will not be considered to represent instances of overt aggression throughout the present chapter.

Aggression involves an avoidance-motivated victim. Finally, our definition notes that aggression may be said to have occurred only when the recipient or victim is motivated to avoid such treatment at the hands of the aggressor. This is often true, for the victims of harmful physical or verbal assaults usually wish to steer clear of such unpleasant or injurious experiences. In other instances, however, the recipients of harm-inducing actions are *not* motivated to avoid such consequences. For example, some individuals seem to enjoy being hurt in various ways by their lovers and make no efforts to shun such treatment. Similarly, but in a more dramatic manner, persons who commit suicide actively *seek* the fatal injuries they suffer. According to our working definition, such events should not be viewed as instances of aggression, because there is no apparent motivation on the part of the victim to avoid the harm inflicted.

Aggression defined: A recapitulation. In sum, throughout the remainder of this discussion we will define aggression as any form of behavior directed toward the goal of harming or injuring another living being who is motivated to avoid such treatment. While such actions may take many different forms and can be directed against a wide variety of targets, all are similar in the crucial sense of representing intentional efforts to inflict unpleasant, harmful consequences upon unwilling victims.

THEORETICAL PERSPECTIVES: SEARCHING FOR THE ROOTS OF AGGRESSION

That human beings frequently engage in dangerous acts of aggression is hardly open to question—the tragic events of recent history as well as the alarming crime statistics issuing from our major cities leave little room for doubt on this particular score. The question of *why* they engage in such activities, however, has long been open to serious dispute. Although many explanations for the widespread occurrence of human violence have been proposed over the years, most seem to fall into one of three distinct categories which attribute such behavior primarily to (1) innate urges or dispositions, (2) externally elicited drives, or (3) present social conditions coupled with previous social learning. Each of these contrasting perspectives will now be examined.

Aggression as Human Destiny: Inborn Urges toward Death and Destruction

The oldest and probably best known view concerning the nature of aggressive behavior is one suggesting that violence occurs because human beings are somehow "programmed" for such actions. As you may already know, the most famous early proponent of this position was Sigmund Freud, who held that aggression stems mainly from the operation of a powerful *death instinct* possessed by all human beings. According to Freud's theory, hostile impulses generated by this instinct build up gradually over time, and unless released periodically in relatively safe, noninjurious ways, soon reach dangerous levels capable of inducing harmful violence (see Figure 9-1). Thus, within the framework proposed by Freud, human beings are constantly being driven or pushed in the direction of aggressive actions, and can only be prevented from engaging in such behavior with the utmost difficulty.

A surprisingly similar view regarding the nature of human aggression has been proposed in more recent years by the Nobel prize winning ethologist Konrad Lorenz (1966, 1974). According to Lorenz, aggression springs primarily from an innate *fighting instinct* which man shares with many other animal species. Presumably, such an instinct developed during the long course of evolution because it yielded many benefits. For example, fighting often serves to disperse animal populations over a wide geographic area, thus ensuring maximal utilization of available food resources. Similarly, since it is often closely related to mating, such behavior frequently helps to improve the genetic makeup of various species by guaranteeing that only the strongest and most vigorous individuals manage to reproduce.

Although the theories of Freud and Lorenz differ in many important details, both have similar pessimistic implications with respect to the prevention or control of human aggression. That is, the suggestion—so central to both—that aggression arises largely from instinctive drives or urges, leads logically to the conclusion that it is probably impossible to entirely eliminate such reactions. Neither the satisfaction of all material needs, the elimination of all social injustice, nor any other positive changes in the structure of society will succeed in preventing the generation—and ultimate expression—of aggressive impulses. Rather, these and other attempts to control such behavior can only serve to lower the intensity of aggression when it occurs, or to channel it into forms less dangerous to life and limb. Freud did, in the end, hold out some slight hope that, with the production of stronger and stronger internal controls over aggression, human beings might eventually become incapable of acts of violence. Similarly, Lorenz (1974), like other ethologists, has recently shown greater

FIGURE 9-1. *The view that aggressive impulses increase over time and must be periodically released if dangerous acts of violence are to be avoided remains quite popular. As we shall soon see, however, recent evidence casts serious doubt on its validity. (Source: Copyright King Features Syndicate, 1971.)*

recognition of the important role of learning and environmental factors in the occurrence of aggression and many other forms of so-called instinctive behavior (Mason and Lott, 1976). However, both theorists retained their basic assumption that human beings are genetically programmed for violence, and so offered little hope for its total elimination.

Aggression as an Elicited Drive: Motivation to Harm or Injure

Given the pessimistic implications of the instinct views proposed by Freud, Lorenz, and others, you should not be surprised to learn that this perspective was never widely adopted by social psychologists. An alternative approach which gained much greater support centered around several related proposals often known as **drive theories of aggression.** Basically, such theories held that human aggression stems mainly from the arousal of a drive to harm or injure others, which is itself elicited by various environmental conditions. The most famous statement of this general perspective is found in the famous **frustration-aggression hypothesis** proposed several decades ago by Dollard et al. (1939). Because we will return to this proposal in some detail in a later section, it will be mentioned only briefly at this point, primarily as a means of illustrating the general nature of drive theories of aggression.

Basically, this hypothesis suggests that **frustration**—the blocking of ongoing, goal-directed behavior—leads to the arousal of a drive whose primary goal is that of harm to some person or object. Such **aggressive drive,** as it is often termed (Berkowitz, 1970, 1974), then leads to the performance of overt aggressive acts. In short, aggression is assumed to stem from exposure to particular environmental conditions which elicit strong motivation to engage in such behavior.

Because drive theories of aggression attribute such behavior to the presence of specific environmental conditions (i.e., frustrating events) rather than to innate tendencies toward violence, they are somewhat more optimistic with respect to the prevention or control of such behavior than instinct theories. That is, they seem to suggest that the removal of all sources of frustration from the environment would go a long way toward eliminating dangerous forms of interpersonal aggression. Unfortunately, though, frustration in one form or another is probably such a frequent occurrence for most individuals that its total elimination is quite impossible. For this reason, drive theories, too, seem to leave human beings burdened with a continuous and largely unavoidable source of aggressive impulses, despite the fact that in this case these urges stem mainly from external rather than internal sources.

Aggression as Learned Social Behavior: Training for Violence

In recent years, a third distinctive theoretical perspective regarding the nature of aggression has received increasing support. Basically, this point of view regards aggression primarily as a specific form of social behavior, which is both acquired and maintained in much the same manner as many other forms of activity. Although this general position has been supported by several noted authorities on aggression (Berkowitz, 1974; Buss, 1971), perhaps its most outspoken proponent has been Albert Bandura (1973).

According to Bandura, a comprehensive analysis of aggressive behavior requires careful attention to (1) the manner in which it is acquired, (2) the factors which instigate its occurrence, and (3) the conditions which maintain its performance. Since we will turn to a detailed examination of the situational and individual antecedents of aggression in later sections, we will focus here on the acquisition and maintenance of such actions.

We have already considered one important manner in which individuals acquire various aggressive responses in our discussion of modeling processes (see Chapter 7). At that time, we noted that both children and adults often learn new forms of behavior—including aggression—by observing the actions of others. Since we examined considerable evidence pointing to such conclusions in Chapter 7, we will not review it here. You may recall, however, that the results of many different experiments indicate that both adults and children can learn new and often deadly forms of violence simply by observing the actions of friends, relatives, schoolmates, or even characters in TV shows or Hollywood epics.

A second manner in which individuals may acquire aggressive responses is through experiences in which they are directly rewarded for such behavior. Evidence for the occurrence of such effects has been obtained in a number of experiments conducted with animals. For example, Ulrich et al. (1963) found that initially docile rats quickly learned to attack their cagemates when they were deprived of water and could obtain a drink only through such behavior. Similarly, several studies performed with human subjects have reported that aggression is facilitated when participants are rewarded for such behavior (usually through verbal praise from the experimenter) (Geen and Pigg, 1970, Geen and Stonner, 1971). In sum, existing evidence suggests that individuals can readily learn to behave in an aggressive manner when such actions yield desired outcomes.

Turning to conditions which serve to maintain patterns of overt aggression once they are acquired, Bandura has called attention to a number of different factors. First, it is often the case that successful aggression against others results in the attainment of various tangible (i.e., material) rewards. For example, a child who aggresses successfully against his or her playmates may soon claim the most desirable toys available. Similarly, as noted by Buss (1971), aggression may also "pay" handsomely for adults. Thus, the rulers of organized crime continue to reap huge fortunes from the expert use of violence, while nations which employ their military might to exploit their weaker neighbors often gain valuable trade or territorial concessions.

Aggression may also be maintained by various forms of social reward and approval. For example, during time of war, soldiers often receive medals and gain special privileges for killing a large number of enemy troops. Similarly, the

MEASURING PHYSICAL AGGRESSION: HURT WITHOUT HARM

Before considering various antecedents of aggression, we should address a question you may have already begun to consider: how can aggression—and especially physical aggression—be studied under safe, laboratory conditions? Obviously, psychologists wishing to accomplish this task face a puzzling dilemma. On the one hand, they wish to study individuals' tendencies to attack and harm others, while on the other, they cannot possibly permit the participants in their research to suffer any actual harm. For many years, this dilemma seemed insoluble, and research on aggression was restricted to studies of verbal rather than physical assaults. In the early 1960's, however, a simple but effective solution emerged. Essentially, this solution centered around the strategy of somehow convincing subjects that they could physically harm another person when, in fact, they could not. Under such conditions, it was reasoned, their intentions to inflict pain and suffering on others could be studied without the risk of any actual injury to participants. The first psychologist to hit upon this approach was Arnold Buss (1961), and the procedures he devised have been widely adopted by other researchers concerned with the nature of aggressive behavior. Briefly, Buss's method is as follows.

When subjects arrive for their appointment, they are informed that they will be participating, along with another individual (actually a confederate) in a study concerned with the effects of punishment on learning. It is further explained that in order to investigate this topic, one of the two persons present will serve as a *teacher* and the other as a *learner*. The teacher will have the task of presenting various materials to the learner, who will then attempt to master them. On each occasion when the learner makes a correct response, the teacher will reward him by indicating that he has responded appropriately, while whenever he makes an error, the teacher will punish him by means of electric shock. Both rewards and punishments are to be administered by means of a device such as the one shown in Figure 9-2, an apparatus which has generally come to be known in psychology as the *aggression machine*. As you can see, this equipment contains ten buttons, and it is explained that on each occasion when the learner makes an error, the teacher will choose one of these switches, and deliver an electric shock to the learner by depressing it. The first button is described as delivering very mild shock, the second as delivering somewhat stronger punishment, and so on, up to the tenth, which presumably delivers extremely powerful jolts. In order to convince the subject that the apparatus actually works in this manner, sample shocks are then delivered from several of the buttons.

As you can probably guess, the actual subject is always chosen to serve as the teacher, and the confederate to serve as the learner. The confederate then makes a prearranged series of errors, thus providing the subject with several opportunities on which to shock him. The strength of the subject's tendencies to aggress against the confederate are then measured by recording both the intensity and duration of the shocks he chooses to deliver. Needless to say, the learner never receives any of these painful jolts; subjects are merely led to believe that this is the case.

By this point, you may have noticed that the procedures devised by Buss are quite similar in general nature to those used by Milgram to study destructive obedience (see Chapter 6, pp. 289–294). There is one crucial difference between them, though, which should not be overlooked: in Milgram's procedures, subjects are *ordered* by the experimenter to deliver increasingly severe shocks to the victim, while in Buss's procedures, they are provided with complete freedom concerning the strength of the shocks to be employed.

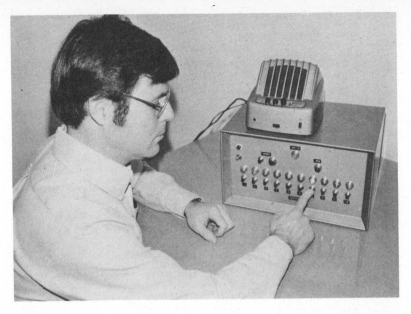

FIGURE 9-2. *An "aggression machine" similar to the one devised by Buss (1961). Note that the individual shown is pushing button 7 and is, therefore, behaving in a highly aggressive manner.*

As a result, studies using the methods outlined by Milgram provide evidence regarding obedience to the commands of an authority, while those employing the procedures developed by Buss yield information on what is usually interpreted as voluntary aggression.

Before concluding our discussion of Buss's procedures, one final—and crucial—issue must be considered: does this method actually provide a valid means for studying aggressive behavior? More specifically, does subjects' behavior on the "aggression machine" really reflect the strength of their desires to harm the victim? Or does it merely indicate their response to implicit pressure from the experimenter to use high-numbered buttons (i.e., demand characteristics)? Although this issue has not as yet been totally resolved, existing evidence seems to support the first of these two possibilities. For example, in one study concerned with this topic, Wolfe and Baron (1971) reasoned that if the aggression machine actually measures sub-

jects' willingness to harm another person, individuals with a previous history of violent acts will tend to push higher numbered buttons than persons without such experience. In order to test this prediction, they compared the behavior (on this apparatus) of college students and a group of prison inmates of the same age who had been convicted of such violent crimes as murder, manslaughter, or assault with a deadly weapon. As predicted, the prisoners did in fact select and use significantly higher buttons. Together with the findings of several related studies (e.g., Shemberg, Leventhal, and Allman, 1968), these results lend support to the view that the procedures devised by Buss provide a reasonably valid means for studying physical aggression under safe, laboratory conditions. In short, it seems possible to examine individuals' intentions to harm or injure others, and the factors which affect them, without permitting the possibility of any actual harm to research participants.

toughest teenager in the neighborhood may receive a considerable amount of status and prestige, in addition to various tangible rewards, as a result of successful attacks against others. A particularly grizzly illustration of the use of social reinforcers to maintain and encourage a high level of aggression is provided by the records of Nazi concentration camps during World War II. Here, medals, promotions, and many other benefits were distributed to those most successful in the mass murder of inmates, and camp commanders and their staffs often competed vigorously for such rewards (Bandura, 1973).

Before concluding our discussion of the **social-learning theory of aggression,** we should note that it is much more optimistic with respect to the possibility of preventing or controlling human aggression than either the drive or instinct views considered previously. This is the case for two basic reasons. First, according to this perspective, aggression is a learned form of social behavior. As such, it is open to direct modification, and can be readily reduced through such procedures as the removal of those conditions tending to maintain its occurrence. Second, in contrast to the drive and instinct theories, the social-learning approach does not view human beings as constantly driven or impelled toward violence by built-in internal forces or ever-present external stimuli (i.e., frustrating events). Rather, it suggests that individuals aggress only under appropriate social conditions which facilitate such behavior. Alter these conditions, it is argued, and aggression may be readily prevented or reduced. Given the basic optimism of this general perspective, and the growing body of empirical evidence for its basic accuracy, it is not surprising that the social-learning view outlined by Bandura (1973) and others has gained rapid acceptance among social psychologists in recent years.

SITUATIONAL DETERMINANTS OF AGGRESSION: VIOLENCE IS WHERE YOU FIND IT

Aggression rarely occurs in a "social vacuum." Rather, it usually seems to stem from particular conditions and events which pave the way for its occurrence. In many instances, the aggression-eliciting nature of such conditions is readily apparent. For example, one person may attack another because he has previously been provoked by the victim, or because he is urged to do so by others who are also present on the scene (Borden and Taylor, 1973; Gaebelein, 1973). In other cases, however, the factors leading to violence are more complex and harder to recognize. As an illustration of this fact, consider the following incident:

YOUNGSTERS BEAT TOT TO DEATH

HOUSTON (AP)—Police quoted the three children, aged 9, 11, and 12, as saying "Punkin" was bad, so they pounded him with their fists and feet and whipped him with belts until he died.

"Punkin" was Robert Hillard Battles, 4. He was found dead Sunday from blows to the head, chest, and abdomen, an autopsy showed.

The victim's brother, Daven, 5, also was beaten, investigators said. He was listed in fair condition in a hospital Monday night. . . .

Police officer G. C. Montgomery said the beatings occurred over a two-week period with the last one late Saturday night. . . .

Police quoted the three children as saying they beat Robert "for being bad," and that the Saturday night assault followed the breaking of a model car. . . .

Why did the children in this situation behave in the way they did? Clearly, there are no simple or obvious answers. Yet, even casual inspection of this tragic incident suggests a number of reasonable possibilities. To mention just a few, they may have aggressed in this deadly manner because of provocation from the victim (perhaps he was a nasty, quarrelsome little boy), because they had repeatedly witnessed similar events on TV, because it was uncomfortably hot (as it often is in Houston) and they were quite irritable, or because they knew they could "get away" with such actions as a result of the absence of adult supervision and the victim's small size. Of course, in the absence of further information, it is impossible to determine whether these or other factors actually led to the attacks which occurred. What does seem clear, though, is that even in such bizarre and unsettling instances as this one, the occurrence, strength, direction, and form of aggression is often strongly determined by various situational factors. In the discussion which follows, we will examine several of these conditions.

Frustration: Preventing Others from Getting What They Want

For many years, it has been widely assumed that the most important single antecedent of aggression is *frustration*—the blocking of ongoing, goal-directed behavior. That is, it has been suggested that the most potent means of inducing human beings to aggress is that of preventing them from obtaining various goals which they seek. Acceptance of this suggestion seems to stem primarily from the famous *frustration-aggression hypothesis* already mentioned earlier. Basically, this hypothesis suggests that:

1. Frustration always leads to some form of aggression.
2. Aggression is always the result of frustration.

Thus, according to the initial supporters of this view (Dollard et al., 1939), frustrated persons always engage in some form of aggression, and every act of aggression is the result of some type of frustration (see Figure 9-3).

As noted recently by Bandura (1973), these assertions are highly appealing, partly because of their boldness, and partly because of their simplicity: if they are accepted, a highly complex form of social behavior is explained in one daring stroke. In view of this fact, it is not at all surprising that they soon attained widespread acceptance among laymen and scholars alike. Unfortunately, though, careful analysis of both proposals indicates that they are probably far too sweeping in scope.

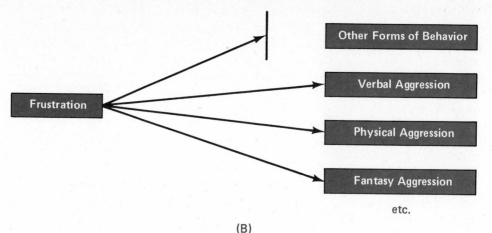

(A)
Frustration always leads to some form of aggression.

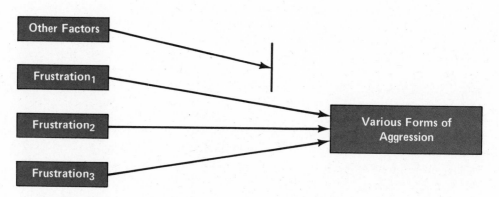

(B)
Aggression is always the result of frustration.

FIGURE 9-3. *As shown above, the famous frustration-aggression hypothesis (at least in its original form) proposed that (A) aggression always leads to some form of aggression (not to other forms of behavior), and (B) aggression is always the result of frustration (no other factors play a role in its occurrence). Unfortunately, recent findings suggest that both proposals are far too sweeping in scope.*

First, it is quite apparent that frustrated individuals do not *always* turn to aggression either in their thoughts, words, or overt deeds. Rather, they may demonstrate a wide variety of reactions, ranging from resignation and despair on the one hand, to active attempts to overcome the obstacles in their paths on the other. For example, an individual whose amorous advances toward a member of the opposite sex are rejected and who, as a result, experiences strong and bitter frustration, is probably more likely to weep, feel depressed, or crawl into bed and sleep than to aggress against his or her would-be lover or other persons. Similarly, a student whose applications to medical or law school are all rejected is more likely to experience discouragement and dejection than anger or rage. In

view of such considerations, Neal Miller (1941), one of the original formulaters of the frustration-aggression hypothesis, quickly amended it so as to
suggest that frustration leads to many different forms of behavior, only one of
which is aggression. In short, the strong and sweeping suggestion that
frustration *always* leads to some form of aggression was quickly abandoned even
by one of its originators. Despite this fact, however, this assumption continues
to enjoy a surprising degree of acceptance even to the present day. Indeed, you
may often encounter it during casual conversations with your friends at parties,
or even in other college courses. Hopefully, our comments up to this point will
lead you to at least question its accuracy whenever you hear it voiced.

Turning to the second proposal, that aggression always results from
frustration, it is clear once again that the formulaters of this view went too far.
There can be little doubt that aggression often stems from factors other than
frustration and can, in fact, occur even in the total absence of such conditions.
For example, consider the actions of a prize-fighter who enters the ring and
immediately begins raining blows on the head and body of his opponent, even
though he has never laid eyes on this individual before. In this case it makes
more sense to attribute his aggressive behavior to such factors as a desire to win,
and so claim the available rewards, than to frustration. Similarly, consider the
actions of a pilot who, although in the best of spirits and not feeling frustrated in
the least, bombs and strafes an enemy position, killing a number of innocent
civilians as well as soldiers. Here, such factors as direct orders from his
superiors, the promise of various rewards for successfully completing his
mission, and perhaps a sense of duty or patriotism probably play a greater role in
influencing his aggressive actions than frustration. In sum, the suggestion that
all acts of violence result from the blocking or thwarting of goal-directed behavior
does not bear up well under close examination.

In the face of such considerations, few social psychologists presently believe
that frustration always leads to aggression, or that all aggressive behavior stems
from frustrating events. Instead, many have adopted a more moderate view
which proposes that frustration is simply one of many different determinants of
aggression, and sometimes—but by no means always—leads to such behavior
(Berkowitz, 1969). Although this general position appears much easier to defend
on logical grounds than the sweeping generalizations of the original frustration-
aggression hypothesis, evidence regarding even *its* validity has been quite mixed
in nature. On the one hand, several experiments have reported that frustration
often fails to enhance aggression (Buss, 1963, 1966; Taylor and Pisano, 1971).
Indeed, a few studies have even found that under some conditions, at least,
frustration may actually tend to *reduce* the level of aggression shown by subjects
(Gentry, 1970). In sharp contrast to these negative findings, other investigations have reported that frustration may indeed facilitate aggression against
others (Geen, 1968; Geen and Berkowitz, 1967; Pastore, 1952; Zillmann and
Cantor, 1976). While the issue is far from resolved, careful comparison of these
two sets of experiments suggests that whether frustration increases or fails to
increase subsequent aggression may depend largely on two important factors.

First, it appears that frustration will lead to heightened aggression only

Situational Determinants of Aggression: Violence Is Where You Find It   417

Aggression can result from many factors other than frustration. For example, the individuals shown above are probably aggressing, not because they have been exposed to severe frustration, but because—quite simply—it is their job to do so. (UPI photo by Nguyen Thanh Tai.)

when it is quite intense. When it is of low or even moderate strength, in contrast, little or no effect upon aggression will be observed (Harris, 1974). Second, the results of several different studies suggest that frustration will lead to increased aggression only when it is perceived as *arbitrary* or unreasonable; when it is viewed as justified or reasonable, however, little or no aggression may be induced (Rule, Dyck, and Nesdale, 1976; Worchel, 1974; Zillmann and Cantor, 1976). For example, returning to an illustration we examined previously, consider the case of an individual who applies to twenty-five different medical schools, only to be rejected by all. If she perceives that this severe frustration is due to the fact that other, more qualified candidates have applied, it is unlikely that she will react with anger or overt aggression. However, if she concludes that she has been rejected on the basis of such unreasonable or arbitrary grounds as her sex, race, or religion, considerable hostility may well be aroused.

In sum, recent research concerning the influence of frustration on aggression seems to point to the following general conclusions. Frustration is only one of many different determinants of such behavior, and is probably neither the most important nor the most powerful of these factors. However, it can indeed facilitate subsequent aggression under conditions where it is quite severe, and is perceived as arbitrary or unjustified by the persons experiencing it. While Dollard et al. (1939) greatly overstated the case, preventing individuals from getting what they want (i.e., interfering with their goal-directed behavior) does seem to be one way of inducing them to aggress.

Verbal and Physical Attack:
Aggression Breeds Aggression

A second situational factor which seems to exert a strong effect on aggression— and as we shall see, perhaps a much stronger impact than frustration—is physical or verbal **attack.** Informal observation suggests that aggression often occurs in situations where one individual directly provokes another through either words or deeds. And, unfortunately, once such an aggressive interchange is begun, it frequently escalates, with each side delivering stronger and stronger attacks against the other. The following description of "playing the dozens," a ritualized trading of provocations common among ghetto teenagers, illustrates this dangerous process quite clearly (Berdie, 1947, p. 120):

> One of the tormenters will make a mildly insulting statement, perhaps about the mother of the subject, "I saw your mother out with a man last night." Then he may follow this up with "She was drunk as a bat." The subject, in turn, will make an insulting statement about the tormenter or some member of the tormenter's family. This exchange of insults continues . . . until they eventually include every member of the participants' families and every act of animal and man. . . . Finally, one of the participants, usually the subject, who has actually been combating the group pressure of the observers, reaches his threshold and takes a swing at the tormenter, pulls out a knife, or picks up an object to use as a club. That is the sign for the tormenter and sometimes some of the observers, to go into action, and usually the subject ends up with the most physical injuries.

Evidence for the powerful influence of verbal or physical attack on the occurrence of aggression has also been obtained in a number of laboratory experiments. For example, a series of investigations by Stuart Taylor and his colleagues (Borden, Bowen, and Taylor, 1971; O'Leary and Dengerink, 1973) indicates that most individuals will usually respond to physical provocation from another with strong counterattacks. In these studies, subjects compete with an opponent on a reaction time task under conditions where the slower player on each occasion receives an electric shock. The magnitude of these shocks is set in advance by both players, so that each supposedly controls the strength of the jolts received by the other. Generally, though, the opponent is fictitious, and subjects are made to lose on a set proportion of the trials. The strength of the shocks they receive on these occasions is then made to rise steadily, thus indicating that their partner is behaving in an increasingly aggressive manner. In general, subjects respond to such provocation by raising the strength of their own shock settings (see Figure 9-4), retaliating in kind rather than "turning the other cheek."

That human beings often respond aggressively to indications of an *intention*

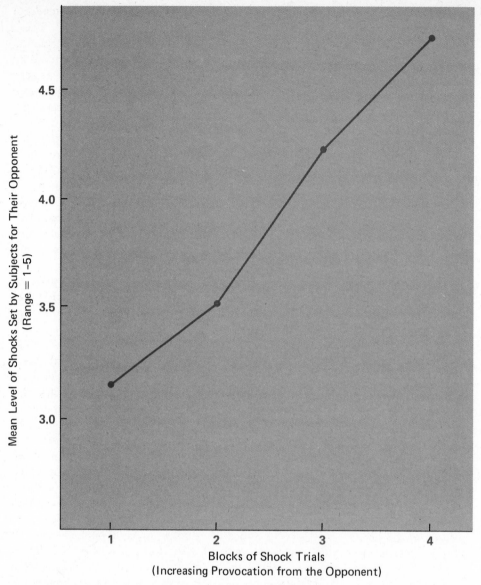

FIGURE 9-4. *Physical attack as an elicitor of aggression. Subjects respond to increasing provocation from others with stronger and stronger counterattacks of their own. (Source: Based on data from Taylor and Pisano, 1971).*

on the part of others to harm them, as well as to actual physical attacks, is suggested by the findings of an additional investigation by Greenwell and Dengerink (1973). In this study, subjects received information suggesting that their opponent was increasing the strength of the shocks he was directing against them. In reality, however, the intensity of these assaults remained constant over time. Despite this fact, subjects reacted to their partner's apparent intentions, sharply raising the strength of their own counterattacks. These findings lend support to our earlier suggestion that instances of "accidental noninjury," in which one person attempts to harm another but fails, should be viewed as aggressive in nature. Apparently, most individuals view attacks launched against them, but which somehow miss their mark, as sufficient grounds for retaliation, despite the fact that they have managed to escape any actual injury.

Informal observation suggests that verbal as well as physical attacks may have strong, aggression-eliciting properties. As you probably know from your own experience, "cutting" or sarcastic remarks from others may often hurt as much—and perhaps sometimes more—than actual physical assaults. Further, it is clear that they represent a much more common form of aggression, at least among middle-class individuals, than assaults involving fists or weapons. Not surprisingly, laboratory studies have readily demonstrated the ability of verbal insults or taunts to elicit strong counterattacks (e.g., Wilson and Rogers, 1975). In addition, the findings of such investigations have also yielded two less obvious results. First, they suggest that verbal attacks may often lead to physical retaliation. Thus, as noted above, incidents which begin with verbal taunts may quickly escalate into violent brawls. Second, it appears that verbal assaults may actually be more effective in eliciting overt aggression than several types of frustration. For example, in perhaps the best-known study on this issue, Geen (1968) exposed subjects in three different groups to *insult* (totally unprovoked, nasty comments from a confederate), *personal frustration* (a confederate prevented them from completing an assigned task), or *task frustration* (subjects were unable to complete the task because it was, quite simply, impossible to do so). Subjects in a fourth, *control* group, were exposed neither to insult nor frustration. Following these procedures, participants in all four conditions were provided with an opportunity to aggress against the confederate by means of electric shock within the teacher-learner paradigm described previously. Results indicated that verbal attack produced the highest level of aggression against the victim, followed by personal and then task frustration (see Figure 9-5). As expected, subjects in the nonprovoked control group delivered the weakest attacks of all. In sum, it appeared that verbal provocation was a more powerful elicitor of subsequent aggression than either of the two forms of frustration. The fact that similar findings have been reported in other studies (e.g., Rule and Hewitt, 1971) lends support to this general suggestion. However, it is important to note that in these studies, no attempt was made to equate the *magnitude* of the frustrations and verbal attacks employed. As a result, it is by no means certain that the same pattern of results would be obtained at all values of these two factors. (For example, would mild insult always be more effective in eliciting subsequent aggression than extremely strong frustration?) All that can be safely concluded, therefore, is that within the relatively restricted range of attack and frustration which can ethically be employed in the laboratory experiments, direct physical or verbal provocation may well be a stronger elicitor of overt aggression than several types of frustration.

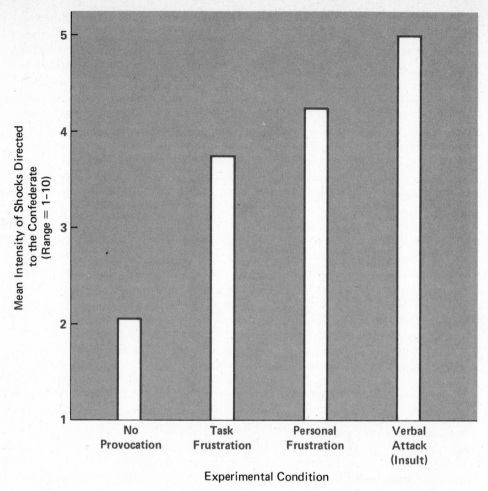

FIGURE 9-5. *The effects of verbal attack (insult) and two types of frustration on aggression. While both types of frustration increased subjects' tendencies to aggress, insult seemed to be even more effective in producing such effects. (Source: Based on data from Geen, 1968.)*

Exposure to Aggressive Models: The "Contagion" of Violence

You may recall that in our previous discussion of modeling processes, we summarized a large body of evidence suggesting that exposure to filmed or televised aggressive models often exerts strong effects on the behavior of viewers (see Chapter 7, pp. 317–323). In particular, we noted that exposure to highly aggressive actions by characters in the mass media may lead both children and adults to (1) acquire many new ways of aggressing, (2) experience a sharp reduction in the strength of their own restraints against engaging in such behavior, and (3) undergo a "desensitization" to signs of pain and discomfort on the part of others. Since we have already examined such effects in some detail, we will not return to them here. Instead, we wish to call your attention to the fact that exposure to live as well as filmed or televised **aggressive models** can exert a similar impact upon observers. Indeed, growing evidence now suggests that live aggressive models may play an important role in the occurrence and spread of collective violence. Eye-witness accounts of such incidents often report that large-scale aggression fails to develop even in extremely tense situations until one or more "hot-headed" individuals commits an initial act of violence (Lieberson and Silverman, 1965; Momboisse, 1967). Prior to such events, angry muttering and a general "milling about" may predominate. Once the first blow is struck, the first rock hurled, or the first weapon fired, however, a destructive riot may quickly follow. It seems reasonable to view the individuals who initiate violence in such situations as aggressive models who, by their overt acts of violence, sharply reduce the restraints of other bystanders against engaging in similar behavior. The following description of the events immediately preceding the initiation of one of the tragic riots of the late 1960's provides a clear illustration of such effects (Conot, 1967, p. 29):

> Without conscious thought of his action he darted into the street and hurled the empty pop bottle in his hand toward the last of the departing black-and-white cars. Striking the rear fender of Sgt. Rankin's car, it shattered, and it was as if in that shattering the thousand people lining the street found their own release. It was as if in one violent contortion of the bonds of restraint were snapped. Rocks, bottles, pieces of wood and iron—whatever missiles came to hand—were projected against the sides and windows of the bus and automobiles that, halted for the past 20 minutes by the jammed street, unwittingly started through the gauntlet. . . . It was 7:45 P.M. Amidst the rending sounds of tearing metal, splintering glass, cries of bewilderment and shouts of triumph, the Los Angeles uprising had begun.

Of course in this and related cases, the individuals present on the scene had been made "ready" to aggress by strong prior provocation, or powerful frustrations stemming from continued social injustice. Yet, despite these strong instigations toward aggression, an initial act of aggression often seems to be required before large-scale violence will erupt.

Further evidence for the ability of live aggressive models to elicit similar actions from observers has been provided by a number of laboratory studies (Baron, 1972; Baron and Kepner, 1970; Wheeler and Caggiula, 1966). In these studies, subjects exposed to the actions of a confederate preprogrammed to behave in a highly aggressive manner have been found to direct stronger levels of aggression against others than subjects not exposed to such conditions. Considered together with evidence concerning the impact of filmed or televised violence on viewers, such findings suggest that the actions of aggressive models may often play an important role in eliciting overt aggression. In short, witnessing aggression on the part of others—whether these persons are present in the flesh or merely shown on a screen—may represent still another important way in which aggression tends to breed further aggression. (For further information on this general topic, please see our earlier discussion of the effects of televised violence, pp. 317–323).

Heightened Arousal and Aggression: "Energizing" Violence

Suppose that a few minutes after taking a hard, uphill bicycle ride, another person insulted you in a highly obnoxious manner. Do you think you would be more likely to aggress against this individual under these conditions than you would be if he insulted you at some other time? The results of a number of experiments suggest that this might well be the case. In particular, it appears that heightened physiological arousal—whatever the source—may sometimes serve to facilitate overt aggression. Indeed, heightened arousal stemming from such sources as loud and unpleasant noise (Geen and O'Neal, 1969), competitive activities (Christy, Gelfand, and Hartmann, 1971), and even vigorous exercise (Zillmann, Katcher, and Milavsky, 1972) has been found to facilitate aggression under some conditions. The words "some" should be emphasized, however, because it is now clear that increased arousal will exert such effects only under relatively specific circumstances.

First, in order for heightened arousal to facilitate overt aggression, such behavior must represent a strong or dominant tendency on the part of the persons involved. If aggression is not strong or dominant, increased arousal may well facilitate the performance of other reactions, and so even reduce the frequency or intensity of aggressive behavior (Bandura, 1973). This fact has been demonstrated in a number of different studies (Geen and O'Neal, 1969; Tannenbaum and Zillmann, 1975; Zillmann, Katcher and Milavsky, 1972), but as an example of such research, let us consider an experiment conducted by Konecni (1975b).

In this study, male and female college students were first either insulted or treated in a less provocative manner by a confederate of the experimenter. Following these procedures, they were provided with a number of opportunities to deliver electric shocks to this person, under the guise of evaluating the creativity of his responses on a word-association task. On each of these occasions, some subjects were exposed to loud, arousing sounds, others were exposed to soft, nonarousing sounds, while still others heard no sounds at all. On the basis of the suggestion that increased arousal facilitates aggression only under conditions where such behavior is a strong or dominant response tendency among subjects, we would expect the loud, arousing sounds to facilitate subjects' tendencies to shock the confederate only when they had previously been insulted by this person; if, instead, he had treated them in a friendlier manner, aggression would represent only a weak response tendency, and might fail to be enhanced by increased arousal. As you can see in Figure 9-6, results supported these predictions. That is, subjects exposed to the loud, arousing sounds delivered more shocks to the victim than those exposed to the soft, nonarousing sounds, or

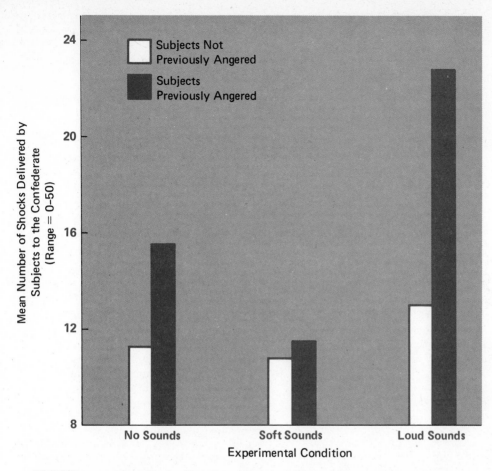

FIGURE 9-6. *The effects of heightened arousal on aggression. As shown above, increased arousal stemming from exposure to loud sounds facilitated later aggression only when such behavior represented a strong or dominant response (i.e., only when subjects had previously been provoked). See text for further explanation. (Source: Based on data from Konečni, 1975b.)*

to no sounds at all only when they had previously suffered strong insult at his hands. When he had previously behaved in a civil manner, heightened arousal failed to enhance their aggression.

A second factor which seems to exert a strong effect on whether heightened physiological arousal will lead to increased aggression is the manner in which individuals label or interpret such feelings. A series of ingenious studies conducted by Zillmann and his associates (Zillmann and Bryant, 1974; Zillmann, Johnson, and Day, 1974) suggests that heightened arousal will facilitate later aggression when subjects misinterpret this arousal as feelings of anger, but will fail to exert such effects when they correctly attribute it to its original source. Apparently, the crucial factor in such cases is the ease with which individuals can

FOCUS ON RESEARCH

SEXUAL AROUSAL AND PHYSICAL AGGRESSION:
FACILITATION OR INHIBITION?

While many forms of arousal might be expected to influence the occurrence of aggressive behavior, none has been the focus of as much recent attention as the sexual excitement stemming from exposure to erotic stimuli. Within the past few years, many investigations have been conducted to determine whether individuals exposed to such stimuli will later demonstrate higher or lower levels of aggression than subjects not presented with sexually arousing materials. Surprisingly, the results of these studies have been quite inconsistent. On the one hand, several investigations have reported that heightened sexual arousal may indeed facilitate overt attacks against others (Jaffe et al., 1974; Meyer, 1972; Zillmann, 1971) while on the other, several experiments have reported that heightened sexual arousal may actually reduce later aggression (Baron, 1974a; Baron and Bell, 1973; Frodi, 1977). At first, the contradictory nature of these findings seemed quite puzzling. How could sexual arousal both enhance and inhibit physical aggression? Fortunately, one initial hint concerning this mystery was provided by a careful comparison of these two sets of studies. Briefly, it appeared that those reporting an increase in aggression following exposure to erotic stimuli employed relatively explicit materials of a highly arousing nature (e.g., films of young couples engaged in actual love-making; highly explicit and arousing erotic passages). In contrast, studies reporting a reduction in later aggression generally employed much milder stimuli (e.g., *Playboy* nudes; pictures of attractive young women in bathing suits or revealing negligées). In short, there was some indication that mild erotic stimuli might inhibit aggression, while more arousing materials of this type might increase such behavior. But why, in turn, should this be the case? One explanation has been provided by Donnerstein, Donnerstein, and Evans (1975).

Basically, these investigators propose that erotic stimuli actually produce two distinct effects upon the individuals who view them. First, they increase the level of arousal experienced by these persons, and, second, they distract their attention away from any provocations they have previously experienced. Whether such stimuli will enhance or inhibit later aggression, then, may depend primarily on which of these two effects predominates. Since mild stimuli would be expected to have only minimal effects upon arousal, their major impact might be that of distraction. Thus, they would be expected to reduce later aggression. In contrast, more explicit stimuli would be quite arousing, and as a result, might well increase later aggression under conditions where such behavior is a strong or dominant response among subjects (e.g., following severe provocation).

In order to examine the accuracy of these suggestions, Donnerstein and his colleagues conducted an experiment in which male subjects were first insulted or not insulted by a confederate of the researchers, and then exposed to either mild erotic stimuli (*Playboy* nudes), stronger erotic stimuli (explicit pictures of sexual activities taken from X-rated magazines), or neutral, nonerotic stimuli (ads for book clubs, soft drinks, etc.) Following these procedures, they were provided with an opportunity to aggress against the confederate within the teacher-learner paradigm devised by Buss. On the basis of the reasoning outlined above, it was predicted that among insulted subjects, mild erotic stimuli would inhibit later aggression, while highly erotic stimuli would fail to inhibit aggression, and might even enhance it. (No similar effects were predicted for noninsulted individuals, who were expected to show a uniformly low level of aggression.)

As you can see in Figure 9-7, results provided support for these predictions. Mild erotic stimuli did indeed inhibit aggression

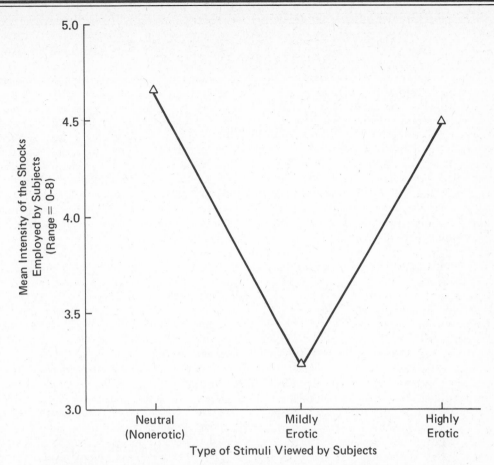

FIGURE 9-7. *The effects of sexual arousal on aggression. While exposure to mild erotic stimuli seems to inhibit later aggression, exposure to more explicit (and arousing) materials seems to enhance such behavior. (Source: Based on data from Donnerstein, Donnerstein, and Evans, 1975.)*

by previously angered subjects, while more arousing stimuli returned such behavior to the levels shown by subjects exposed to neutral materials. Similar results have also been obtained in a more recent study (Baron, 1976a), in which male subjects were exposed to five different types of stimuli: neutral pictures of scenery and furniture, "cheesecake" pictures of young women in bathing suits and negligées, *Playboy* nudes, explicit pictures of sexual activities, and highly arousing erotic passages. As in the research by Donnerstein, Donnerstein, and Evans (1975), mild erotic stimuli inhibited later aggression. In this case, however, the most arousing stimuli (i.e., the erotic passages), slightly facilitated such behavior. On the basis of such evidence, it seems reasonable to conclude that there is indeed a link between sexual arousal and aggression. The nature of this bond, however, is somewhat more complex than was at first assumed.

become confused about the source of the arousal they are experiencing. If it is clear that such feelings stem from exercise, competitive activities, unpleasant noise, or similar sources, increased arousal will fail to increase aggression. However, if the source of such feelings is no longer easily identified, for example, because some time has elapsed since the arousing event, they may become "confused," and attribute it to feelings of anger. In such cases, heightened aggression may result.

In sum, it appears that increased arousal stemming from such diverse sources as exercise, loud noises, and competition with others can indeed facilitate subsequent aggression under certain circumstances. In order for such effects to occur, however, two conditions must usually be met: (1) aggression must be a relatively strong or dominant response among the individuals in question, and (2) they must interpret their feelings of arousal as anger or annoyance.

The Role of Aggressive Cues:
Does the Trigger Pull the Finger?

Suppose that you were intensely angered by an acquaintance while sitting in a room containing his large and varied gun collection. Do you think that you might be more likely to aggress against him in these surroundings than you would be if he angered you to a similar degree somewhere else? (Assume that all the guns are unloaded!) According to Leonard Berkowitz (1969, 1974), a noted authority on aggression, this might well be the case. Specifically, Berkowitz has proposed that one important determinant of aggression is the presence of what he terms **aggressive cues** in the immediate environment. Such cues, he reasons, "pull" or elicit aggressive responses from persons who have been angered or otherwise made ready to aggress, so that the greater their presence on the scene, the higher the level of aggression shown. Going further still, Berkowitz has also proposed that both people and objects can acquire such aggressive cue value through repeated association with anger arousal, witnessed violence, or aggression generally. In short, he has suggested that any stimuli which are repeatedly associated with aggressive activities—whether people or objects—may gradually acquire the ability to elicit such behavior themselves.

Support for Berkowitz's views concerning the acquisition of aggressive cue value by specific persons has been obtained in a number of related studies (see Berkowitz, 1974; Berkowitz and Turner, 1974). For example, it has been found in these experiments that individuals whose first names associate them with the characters shown in a brutal boxing film later elicit stronger attacks from subjects they have angered than persons whose first names do not associate them with witnessed violence in this manner. These findings suggest that particular individuals are often chosen as the targets of aggression because they possess a high degree of aggressive cue value.

Perhaps even more intriguing than such results is evidence concerning the possible aggression-eliciting influence of weapons. According to Berkowitz's theory, such objects should acquire strong aggressive cue value because of their regular and repeated association with aggression. As a result, their mere physical presence on the scene should often facilitate the occurrence of overt aggression, even when they themselves are not used in this regard.

Support for these suggestions has actually been obtained in a well-known study conducted by Berkowitz and LePage (1967). In this experiment, subjects were either angered or not angered by a confederate and then provided with an opportunity to retaliate against this person by means of electric shock either in the presence or absence of weapons (a 12-gauge shotgun and a .38-caliber revolver). Consistent with Berkowitz's proposals, results indicated that angry subjects did in fact deliver more shocks to the victim in the presence of the weapons than in their absence. In short, it appeared that the mere physical presence of weapons facilitated the occurrence of overt aggressive acts.

While similar results have been obtained in other investigations (e.g., Frodi, 1975), they have failed to emerge in several additional studies (Buss, Booker, and Buss, 1972; Page and Scheidt, 1971). Indeed, more recent evidence suggests that the effects uncovered by Berkowitz and LePage may only be observed under conditions where subjects are totally naive with respect to the hypothesis under investigation, and have little or no concern about the experimenter's evaluation of their behavior (Turner and Simons, 1974). These findings suggest that while weapons may indeed sometimes tend to facilitate the occurrence of aggression, such effects may be quite difficult to demonstrate under controlled laboratory conditions because of problems of growing subject sophistication. Regardless of the validity of the controversial "weapons effect," however, there can be little doubt that Berkowitz's more general proposal that aggression is "pulled" from without rather than merely "pushed" from within has attained widespread

 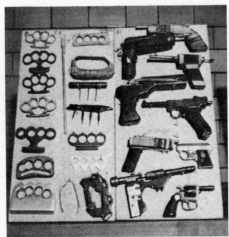

Can the mere physical presence of weapons facilitate aggression even when they are not used in its performance? Some experimental findings suggest that this may be the case.

acceptance. In fact, it seems safe to say that his views in this respect have been extremely influential in causing social psychologists to shift their search for the determinants of aggression largely from internal conflicts and motives to external, environmental factors.

The Impact of Drugs: Alcohol, Marihuana, and Aggression

As you probably already know, various drugs exert important effects on human behavior. For example, tranquilizers tend to produce a calming effect, reducing emotionality and slowing reactions, while stimulants exert the opposite effect, increasing activity, energy, and emotional responsiveness. Given their often wide-ranging impact upon behavior, it seems only reasonable to expect that drugs will also play a role in the occurrence of overt aggression. While many substances might exert such effects, two—alcohol and marihuana—have been the subject of most attention in this respect.

The first (alcohol) has long been viewed as a releaser or stimulator of aggressive actions. Drink too much, common knowledge holds, and the chances of your becoming involved in hostile interactions with others are increased. In contrast, marihuana has often been held to be an inhibitor of overt aggression, presumably because it places its users in such a relaxed or pleasant state that aggression is the farthest thing from their minds.

Interestingly, support for both of these suggestions has recently been obtained by Stuart Taylor and his associates in a series of ingenious laboratory studies (Taylor and Gammon, 1975; Taylor et al., 1976). In these experiments, male subjects have been provided with special "cocktails" consisting of ginger ale, peppermint oil, and either small or large doses of alcohol or THC—the active substance of marihuana. (Subjects in control groups receive only the ginger ale and peppermint oil mixture.) After receiving their special drinks, subjects participate in the type of competitive reaction time task described earlier, in which the loser on each trial receives a shock from the winner. Since the level of these shocks is set in advance by each player, aggression can be measured in terms of the strength of the shocks set by each participant for his opponent. The results of these investigations have been both clear and informative.

First, with respect to alcohol, findings indicate that small doses tend to inhibit aggression, while larger doses tend to facilitate such behavior, relative to a no-drug control condition. Thus, experimental evidence lends support to the informal observation that one cocktail or a couple of beers may put people in a happy frame of mind and so reduce the likelihood of aggression, while a larger number of drinks serves to weaken their inhibitions and so increases the probability of dangerous attacks on others. Further evidence suggests, however, that even individuals who have consumed a large amount of alcohol do not necessarily respond with heightened aggression. Rather, they seem to demonstrate such behavior only when provoked or threatened in some manner by others (Taylor, Gammon, and Capasso, 1976).

Second, with respect to marihuana, results suggest that small doses have little impact upon aggression, while larger ones tend to produce an inhibiting effect (see Table 9-1). Further, there is some indication that even larger doses of this drug would be more effective in producing reductions in overt violence.

Considered together, the findings of Taylor's research suggest that both alcohol and marihuana are capable of exerting important effects upon the tendency of human beings to inflict harm or injury upon others. However, the direction and magnitude of these effects seems to differ greatly between the two drugs.

Additional Antecedents of Aggression:
Orders, Heat, and Crowding

Although frustration, attack, and the other factors we have considered so far have probably received most attention as determinants of aggression, several additional factors also seem to play an important role in eliciting such behavior. We have already considered one such condition in our earlier discussion of *destructive obedience* (see Chapter 6, pp. 289–294). At that time, we noted that many individuals can readily be induced to inflict pain and suffering on others by the commands of an authority figure. Indeed, such blind, unthinking submission seems to play a crucial role in tragic instances where soldiers or police machine gun unarmed civilians, massacre helpless captives, or murder thousands in gas chambers and concentration camps. In these and many other cases, aggression stems more from a sense of duty or obedience than from hatred or anger toward the target persons. In short, the phrase "orders are orders" may go a long way toward explaining the occurrence of a great deal of organized, collective violence.

Two additional factors which seem to play an important role in the occurrence of aggressive actions are the environmental factors of *heat* and *crowding*. Since we will return to the influence of these conditions in some detail

TABLE 9-1. *The effects of alcohol and marihuana upon physical aggression. As shown below, small doses of alcohol seem to inhibit aggression, while larger doses facilitate such behavior. In contrast, small doses of marihuana have little effect upon aggression, while larger doses reduce it. Numbers shown represent the average strength of the shocks set by subjects for their opponent. (Based on data from Taylor et al., 1976.)*

	Dose		
	Small	*Large*	
Drug			
Alcohol	2.1	5.4	(No Drug = 3.9)
Marihuana	3.1	1.0	

in Chapter 13, we will merely mention here that while both seem to influence the frequency and intensity of overt aggression, their impact in this respect is much more complex than common sense suggests (Geen and O'Neal, 1976; Rule and Nesdale, 1976b). The "long hot summer" may indeed be hot, and the crowd may well be "maddening," but only under certain and quite specific circumstances.

INDIVIDUAL DETERMINANTS OF AGGRESSION: VIOLENCE, PERSONALITY, AND GENES

Are there specific characteristics that predispose individuals toward or away from acts of violence? Informal observation suggests that this is certainly the case. With a little effort, you can probably bring to mind persons you have known who, because of unusually high or low "boiling points" tended to become involved either in far more or far less than their fair share of aggressive interactions. More formal evidence for the existence of important individual differences in the tendency to aggress have been obtained in a number of laboratory experiments (Dengerink, 1971; Wilkins, Scharff, and Schlottmann, 1974). For example, in one recent study, Carver and Glass (1977) found that individuals scoring high on a psychological test related, in part, to aggression and hostility, directed stronger shocks to a confederate who had provoked them than subjects scoring low on the same inventory. Findings such as these suggest that individuals do differ greatly in their tendencies to aggress, and, further, that such differences can be readily measured by appropriate personality scales or inventories.

Going further, other researchers have attempted to determine what factors underlie such differences in aggressiveness. That is, they have sought to determine *why* some individuals fly off the handle at every little annoyance, while others show great restraint even in the face of very strong provocation. Because such investigations have yielded a great deal of new—and often surprising—information concerning the personal dynamics of aggression, they seem well deserving of our careful attention.

Inhibitions and Violence: Undercontrolled and Overcontrolled Aggressors

MAN HURLS CHILDREN FROM 14th FLOOR
MOTHER CHARGED IN BRUTAL CHAIN-SAW MURDERS
SNIPER SHOOTS MOTORISTS FROM BRIDGE
VICTIM TURNED INTO HUMAN TORCH

Headlines such as these have appeared with increasing frequency in recent years on the front pages of our morning or evening newspapers. In general, our reaction to these tragic events is one of profound bewilderment. How, we ask, could anyone commit such brutal crimes? What type of crazed or deranged monsters are responsible for these violent and often senseless acts? Until quite recently, the answer to these questions provided by most psychologists, psychiatrists, and other professionals emphasized a breakdown in the normal, internal restraints against aggression. It was suggested that the perpetrators of such acts are dangerously lacking in internal inhibitions, and that it was this basic disturbance which accounted for their frighteningly violent behavior.

Within the past decade, however, it has become increasingly apparent that often the individuals responsible for such crimes are not the type of violent, assertive person we might expect; rather, they turn out instead to be passive, retiring, mild-mannered men and women, totally lacking in a past history of overt aggressive acts. Indeed, far from being impulsive or easily provoked, they appear to exhibit extraordinary levels of restraint and control. The following example clearly illustrates this important point (Schultz, 1960, p. 106):

> Then Jim came home by surprise one day and discovered his wife in bed with a neighboring farmer. He said he did not know what to do and merely closed the door and returned to the fields and cried. He added that he could have done "something" as there was a loaded rifle in the room adjoining the bedroom. Jim never brought up his wife's infidelity, and she, seeing so little objection, became more bold in her affair. The paramour began staying for meals, and on several occasions stayed overnight. Jim voiced no objections and even lent the paramour money, seed, and farm equipment, as well as labor. Finally, after this arrangement had gone on for three years, the paramour took a truck to Jim's farm while the latter was away, loaded up his household goods and livestock, as well as Jim's wife and four children, and took them away. Jim, though surprised at his wife's and children's absence, did nothing to find out where she was or to attempt to bring her back, nor did he ever approach his wife's lover.

Certainly, it is hard to imagine a more amazing example of restraint in the face of repeated provocation. Despite the actions of his wife and her lover, Jim did nothing, failing to offer any type of protest during several long years. Only later, when he remarried and discovered that his second wife, too, was unfaithful, did he finally explode into violence, murdering her and her lover in a particularly brutal fashion.

After carefully analyzing a number of such cases, Edwin Megargee (1966, 1971), has reached the conclusion that many of the perpetrators of extreme acts of violence are individuals of this type (**overcontrolled aggressors**)—that is, persons possessing powerful inhibitions against the performance of aggressive acts. Going even further, he has proposed that because of their rigid internal controls, such men and women usually show little reaction to provocation, choosing instead to hide their anger or resentment behind a cloak of extreme passivity. Over the course of time, however, provocations mount until even *their* excessive inhibitions are overcome. And then, these seemingly docile individuals erupt into sudden violence which often catches their victims totally by surprise. Following the completion of their aggressive outburst, they quickly revert to their former, passive state, appearing once again to be persons without a temper, totally incapable of mild, let alone extreme, acts of violence.

Evidence for these suggestions has been obtained in several investigations conducted by Megargee and his colleagues (Megargee, 1971). For example, it has been found that after their arrest, many of the individuals responsible for brutal acts of violence settle down, and become cooperative, model prisoners. Such behavior, of course, is consistent with the view that they possess unusually strong inhibitions against aggression, and demonstrate such behavior only on relatively rare occasions. Similarly, it has been found that such individuals score higher than other prisoners and several groups of nonprisoners on a psychological test designed to measure the presence of unusual restraints against aggression. Together, these findings and additional evidence suggest that in many cases, the most likely candidates for the performance of extreme acts of violence may not be the "hot-headed" individuals who go about looking for trouble with the proverbial chip on their shoulder, but rather quiet, docile, retiring men and women who at first glance seem totally incapable of such acts. Apparently, such persons are, in a sense, walking "time bombs" with a fuse of indeterminate length; and woe to the friends or acquaintances who happen to be on the scene when the fuse finally runs out!

Violent Men and Women: Some Identifying Characteristics

In sharp contrast to the overly restrained type of individuals just considered, are many other persons who seem to go—quite literally—from one hostile interchange to another. Because such men and women account for a much larger proportion of the violence in their societies than their actual numbers would suggest, they have long been the center of much interest and concern. Perhaps the most revealing information regarding the personality characteristics related to their high level of aggression, however, has been gathered by Hans Toch (1969).

In order to study the personality structure of violent individuals, Toch arranged for the conduction of extensive interviews with a large number of prisoners and recent parolees. On the basis of this data he concluded that violence-prone persons generally fall into a number of fairly distinct types, who turn to aggression for markedly different reasons. Among the major categories Toch uncovered are the following.

Self-image Compensators: Violence and Self-esteem. Perhaps the largest single group of violent individuals are those whose aggression stems from pronounced feelings of insecurity and lack of self-worth. Basically, these persons hold a very low opinion of themselves, and are extremely worried that others will share such a view. As a result, they turn to aggression as a means of both defending and promoting their self-image (i.e., as a means of demonstrating their power and worth to themselves and others). In short, they seek to hide their feelings of insecurity behind a mask of bravado and daring.

Bullies or Sadists: Hurting Others for Pleasure. Some individuals appear to take great pleasure in inflicting pain and suffering on others, and persons of this

Some individuals seek to conceal basic feelings of insecurity and low self-esteem beneath a mask of bravado and toughness. (Photo by Donald Deitz; Stock, Boston.)

type represent a second distinct group of "violent men." In general, they choose for their targets others who are uniquely susceptible to their attacks. However, if such a victim cannot be located, they will seek to arrange conditions so that they have an unfair advantage and are sure to win. Thus, there appears to be no "honor" among bullies. But merely getting the upper hand is not enough for these persons, for they actually seem to *enjoy* the suffering of their victim. Indeed, once this person is down, they often redouble their efforts to harm or injure him, relishing his cries of pain and pleas for mercy. Clearly, individuals of this type represent a particularly dangerous kind of aggressor—one to be avoided at all costs.

Self-defenders: Mistrusting the World. A third group of aggressive individuals seem to turn to violence largely out of intense fear of others. Basically, these people are afraid that if they do not strike first, they will soon be victimized themselves. Feeling this way, they seek to eliminate danger by destroying its source—other people! Consider the following illustration (Toch, 1969, p. 164):

This man shows a pattern which is dominated by . . . the conviction that others are trying to kill him. He sees in many of the personal exchanges that he has become involved in as threats upon his life. . . . He seems to resort to violence as a way of being assured that the other party is not going to kill him—at least, that is the way he feels.

In short, Toch's research suggests that predispositions toward repeated aggression seem to stem from many different sources. There is not simply one type of personality which makes men or women aggressive, but several, each with its own distinctive characteristics. As a result, it will probably not prove possible to develop a single set of procedures for modifying the behavior of all—or even most—violent men and women. Rather, different techniques will be required for dealing with each type described above, and probably several others as well. It would appear, therefore, that psychologists hoping to develop methods for altering the behavior or perennial "trouble makers" face a long and difficult task.

AGGRESSION: ITS PREVENTION AND CONTROL

If, perhaps while preparing a term paper for this course, you were to conduct a survey of all the articles published by psychologists about aggression during the past ten years, you would probably discover a surprising fact: while many reports have been concerned with factors tending to *elicit* overt aggression (frustration, attack, aggressive models, etc.), a much smaller number have dealt with means for controlling such behavior. Although many reasons have probably contributed to this unsettling state of affairs, one of the most important has been a persistent belief among psychologists that they already knew the best means for preventing aggressive outbursts. In particular, it was widely believed that two techniques, actual or threatened **punishment** and **catharsis,** were the best means for controlling overt aggression. Unfortunately, evidence collected within the past few years suggests that neither of these procedures is quite as effective in accomplishing this goal as was once believed. After examining the effects of punishment and catharsis on aggression, therefore, we will turn to one additional approach which appears to be quite promising as a means of controlling such behavior—the induction among aggressors of responses incompatible with anger or overt attacks against others.

Punishment: An Effective Deterrent to Human Aggression?

Common sense suggests that either punishing aggressors for their violent behavior or merely threatening to do so may be a highly effective means of preventing these persons from engaging in such activities. On the basis of this general belief, most societies have established—and exacted—severe punishments for murder, rape, assault, and similar aggressive crimes. That psychologists too, have generally accepted the suggestion that actual or threatened punishment is an effective deterrent to human violence is readily apparent. For

Down through the ages, most societies have sought to deter aggressive actions by their members through the threat of severe penalties for such behavior. (Photo by Cary S. Wolinsky; Stock, Boston.)

example, Dollard et al. (1939, p. 33), the formulators of the famous frustration-aggression hypothesis, held that:

> The strength of inhibition of any act of aggression varies positively with the amount of punishment anticipated to be a consequence of that act.

And more recently, but in a similar vein, Richard Walters—a noted developmental psychologist—has stated (1966, p. 69):

> It is only the continual expectation of retaliation by the recipient or other members of society that prevents many individuals from more freely expressing aggression.

That punishment is sometimes quite effective in deterring overt aggression is obvious. Indeed, the results of several studies conducted with children suggest that the frequency or intensity of such behavior can often be sharply reduced by even such mild forms of punishment as social disapproval (e.g., Deur and Parke, 1970; Brown and Elliott, 1965). Despite such findings, though, there are several grounds for doubting that punishment will *always* or even usually serve as an effective deterrent to human aggression.

Turning first to actual punishment, it is clear that the recipients of such disciplinary action may often interpret it as an *attack* against them, and so respond with heightened rather than lessened aggression. In fact, severe punishment may often be more likely to instill a desire for revenge than

CAPSULE CONTROVERSY

HEREDITY AND VIOLENCE: THE XYY SYNDROME

Normally, the cells of the human body possess 46 chromosomes, two of which—"X" and "Y"—play a crucial role in the determination of sex. More specifically, men possess one "X" and one "Y" (XY), while women possess two "X's" (XX). On relatively rare occasions, however, men possessing an extra "Y" chromosome (XYY) are encountered. Although the existence of this unusual pattern was recognized for many years, it was viewed as merely an interesting but relatively unimportant departure from normality until the mid-1960's. At that time, a team of researchers (Jacobs, Brunton, and Melville, 1965) reported that this unusual chromosomal pattern was much more common among individuals imprisoned for various crimes than among the general population. Further, they described an XYY "syndrome" presumably shown by such persons, consisting of (1) excessive height, (2) mental retardation, and (3) occasional outbursts of extreme violence.

These early findings received a great deal of attention, and were soon followed by a number of additional studies conducted in several countries around the world. Although the results of individual experiments were not always totally consistent, most tended to confirm the original findings reported by Jacobs, Brunton, and Melville (1965), indicating that the XYY chromosomal type does indeed occur more frequently among prisoners than among other groups of individuals. That is, while the rate of occurrence of this abnormality is approximately one in a thousand for newborn baby boys or normal adult males, it is more than fifteen times higher in the case of prison inmates (Jarvik, Klodin, and Matsuyama, 1973; see Table 9-2).

On the basis of such evidence, many researchers concluded that possession of an extra "Y" chromosome predisposes individuals toward aggression. Indeed, some went even further, suggesting that the high level of violence often demonstrated by such individuals impli-

cates the single "Y" chromosome possessed by normal males in the occurrence of such behavior. As stated by one group of researchers (Jarvik, Klodin, and Matsuyama, 1973, p. 80):

. . . The increased frequency of XYY individuals among perpetrators of such crimes suggests that an extra Y chromosome predisposes [individuals] to aggressive behavior. If an extra Y chromosome can lead to excessive aggression or hostility, it is possible that the single Y chromosome with which each normal man is endowed may itself be the genetic root of "normal" aggressiveness. . . .

While such conclusions are quite intriguing, they were greeted with skepticism by other scientists, who pointed to several important grounds for exercising caution in their acceptance. First, as you might already have guessed, it was noted that most crimes of violence are committed by individuals possessing the normal XY chromosome combination. Thus, possession of an extra "Y" does not in itself seem to be a necessary condition for the performance of violent acts. Second, closer study of the XYY individuals found in prisons revealed that most were arrested not for attacks upon others, but for far less dramatic offenses, such as theft or robbery (Price and Whatmore, 1967). Similarly, there is some indication that, as is the case with normal XY individuals, only a small percentage of XYY's ever commit or are convicted of criminal activities. Findings such as these suggest that the possession of an extra "Y" chromosome is not, in itself, sufficient to produce heightened levels of aggression.

Finally, it was suggested that any tendency on the part of XYY individuals to become involved in violence more frequently than normal XY persons may stem primarily from social rather than genetic factors (Bandura, 1973). For example, being quite large for their age, such individuals may often associate with older children or teenagers, and so be exposed to violent, delinquent models at an earlier stage of development. Similarly, being both tall and

TABLE 9-2. *The incidence of XYY individuals in prison and nonprison populations. Persons showing the XYY chromosomal pattern are more than fifteen times as common among prisoners as among newborn babies or normal (nonprison) adult males. (Source: Based on data from Jarvik, Klodin, and Matsuyama, 1973.)*

Population	Number in Sample	Number of XYY's in Sample	Percent XYY's in Sample
Prisoners	5,066	98	1.93
Newborn male babies	9,904	13	.13
Normal adult males	6,148	8	.13

well-developed for their age, they may be rewarded for aggressing more frequently than comparable XY individuals, and so quickly acquire such patterns of behavior. In sum, it seems possible that any strong or unusual tendencies toward violence on the part of XYY individuals may stem from experiences during socialization rather than from genetically encoded dispositions toward such activities.

While controversy concerning the possible role of the XYY syndrome in violent behavior has continued to the present time, the arguments just considered have led most psychologists to reject the view that possession of an extra "Y" chromosome automatically disposes individuals toward aggression. Instead, a majority believe that human aggression—like other forms of social behavior—stems more from situational factors which elicit its occurrence, and social learning experiences which shape its forms of expression, than from direct genetic causes.

permanent restraints against violence among its recipients. Second, the persons who administer punishment may often serve as *aggressive models* for those on the receiving end of such discipline. For example, consider the case of a parent preparing to spank his or her child as punishment for previous aggressive acts, who shouts "I'll teach you to hit other children!" What the child may learn in such cases is that it is indeed appropriate to aggress against others, but that one should always select a victim smaller than oneself! Finally, there is some indication that under most conditions, punishment induces only temporary reductions in the incidence or strength of aggressive behavior; once it is discontinued, such acts will quickly reappear with all their previous force and vigor. For all these reasons, it seems likely that direct punishment often backfires and actually tends to enhance the aggressive acts it is designed to prevent.

Shifting to threatened punishment, a number of recent studies (Baron, 1973; Donnerstein et al., 1972; Knott and Drost, 1972) suggest that this procedure, too, may often be of only limited effectiveness. Indeed, in one recent experiment, the threat of imminent punishment for aggressive acts has been found to *increase* rather than reduce subjects' tendencies to attack at least some victims (Wilson and Rogers, 1975). Taken together, the findings of this and other research on the effects of threatened punishment suggest that such treatment will only be effective in deterring later aggression when (1) the persons preparing to aggress are not very angry; (2) these individuals have relatively little to gain by aggressing; (3) the magnitude of punishment they anticipate is great; and (4) the probability that punishment will actually be delivered is high. Since violence often occurs under conditions where the individuals involved have a great deal to gain from their attacks on others, anger runs high, and the likelihood of being caught and brought to justice is minimal, it is not at all surprising that threats of punishment often prove ineffective in preventing such behavior. Unfortunately, crimes of violence often "pay" if one can avoid the punishments set up to deter their performance.

Catharsis: Does Getting It Out of Your System Help?

Suppose that one of your friends or acquaintances did something that made you very angry. If you then threw your pillow about the room, kicked a tin can down the street, or hit a punching bag over and over again, would you be less likely to aggress against this person than would otherwise be the case? Until quite recently, most psychologists believed that this would indeed be so. In fact, it was widely assumed that providing angry individuals with an opportunity to "blow off steam" through participation in such activities would (1) cause them to "feel better" (i.e., lower their level of arousal), and (2) weaken their tendency to engage in dangerous acts of interpersonal aggression (see Figure 9-8). Although both suggestions have attained widespread, general acceptance, the findings of a number of recent experiments suggest that only the first may be true.

Evidence for the tension-reducing properties of various types of aggressive acts has been obtained in a series of investigations conducted by Jack Hokanson and his colleagues (Hokanson and Burgess, 1962; Hokanson, Burgess, and Cohen, 1963). In these studies, subjects were first angered by the experimenter, and then provided with an opportunity to aggress against this person or another individual either physically (by means of electric shock), verbally (on a questionnaire), or in their imaginations (on a projective psychological test). Measures of physiological arousal (heart rate, blood pressure, etc.) were taken throughout the study in order to determine whether and to what extent various forms of aggression would be successful in reducing the heightened tension induced by anger arousal. In general, results indicated that relatively direct attacks (physical or verbal) against the anger instigator or persons closely related to this individual were effective in reducing such arousal. However, more indirect forms of aggression (assaults only in one's own imagination) or attacks against innocent victims unrelated to the source of anger failed to produce similar reductions in overall tension.

As noted by Hokanson (1970, p. 85), these findings agree with our strong subjective impression that we often "feel better" after aggressing against someone who has provoked us. But please take note: since the reductions in

"Feel better, dear?"

FIGURE 9-8. *The suggestion that permitting angry individuals to "blow off steam" in some safe manner will reduce their tendency to aggress against others has long enjoyed widespread, popular support. Unfortunately, recent evidence suggests that it may be far less effective in this respect than has previously been believed. (Source: Drawing by Barsotti; © 1974 The New Yorker Magazine, Inc.)*

tension produced in this manner are often quite pleasant, they may serve as a form of reward, and so actually *strengthen* our tendencies to engage in similar behavior on later occasions. Given such possibilities, it seems unwise to assume that reductions in arousal resulting from successful attacks against others will automatically lessen the probability of subsequent aggression.

Turning to the suggestion that the performance of relatively "safe" aggressive acts reduces the likelihood of more dangerous forms of such behavior, existing evidence is quite discouraging. In particular, it appears that such cathartic effects may be observed only under highly specific circumstances—if at all—and do not occur in many situations where they were previously assumed to take place.

First, a growing body of research suggests that angry individuals cannot be restrained from aggressing through exposure to scenes of violence involving persons other than the ones who have annoyed or provoked them (Berkowitz and Alioto, 1973; Goranson, 1970). Indeed, as we have already noted above, and in Chapter 7, aggression is often strongly enhanced by such procedures.

Second, allowing angry individuals to aggress against inanimate objects does not seem to be effective in reducing the strength of their tendencies to direct such behavior toward persons who have provoked them. In fact, there is some indication that subsequent aggression is actually *facilitated* by such activities (Mallick and McCandless, 1966). Although kicking furniture, punching a pillow, or throwing objects against a wall may cause many persons to "feel better," it is doubtful that such activities are effective in preventing them from aggressing against others.

Third, it appears that verbal aggression against others will often fail to reduce the tendency to assault them on later occasions. In fact, the results of several studies suggest that quite the opposite may be true (Ebbesen, Duncan, and Konecni, 1975; Mallick and McCandless, 1966). That is, the opportunity to "sound off" against others may actually enhance rather than reduce our tendencies to aggress against them on subsequent occasions.

Together, the findings that later aggression is not reduced by exposure to scenes of violence, the chance to attack inanimate objects, or an initial opportunity to engage in verbal aggression all argue against the widespread occurrence of catharsis. However, it might still be suggested that such effects will occur under conditions where we can either inflict or witness direct physical harm to the persons who have annoyed us. That is, having "evened the score," we may be less likely to attack them on later occasions. Unfortunately, even the evidence regarding this more limited occurrence of catharsis is quite mixed in nature. On the one hand, several experiments have reported that opportunities to harm the objects of our anger do indeed reduce the tendency to attack them on later occasions (Doob and Wood, 1972; Konečni, 1975a). In sharp contrast, though, the findings of several other studies suggest that such actions either fail to reduce later aggression, or even tend to facilitate its occurrence. For example, in one experiment conducted by Geen, Stonner, and Shope (1975), male college students were first provoked or not provoked by a confederate. Next, one-third were given an opportunity to deliver electric shocks to this person, a second-third witnessed the experimenter shock him, while the final-third merely waited for an equivalent period of time. Finally, subjects in all three conditions were provided with an opportunity to shock the confederate within the teacher-learner paradigm. If catharsis occurs under such conditions, it would be expected that individuals given a chance to shock the victim themselves during the second phase of the study would show the lowest level of aggression in the final phase. Yet, as you can see in Figure 9-9, this was definitely not the case. In fact, subjects in this group delivered stronger shocks to the confederate than those in any of the others. (We should hasten to add that these findings—which seem to argue strongly against the occurrence of catharsis—have recently been called into question by the results of an additional study which *did* obtain evidence for catharsis under similar conditions [Konečni and Ebbesen, 1976]. Thus, the results reported by Geen and his colleagues must be viewed as somewhat controversial in nature.)

At the present time, there is, unfortunately, no simple or straightforward explanation for the seemingly contradictory results obtained by Doob, Konečni, Geen, and others. Taken together, though, existing evidence concerning the

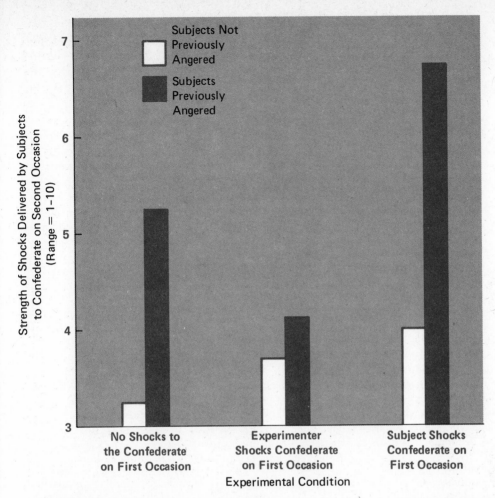

FIGURE 9-9. *Evidence inconsistent with the notion of catharsis. Angry individuals permitted to aggress against the person who had provoked them on one occasion actually directed stronger—not weaker—attacks against him on a second occasion than individuals not provided with an initial opportunity to aggress. (Source: Based on data from Geen, Stonner, and Shope, 1975.)*

occurrence of catharsis seems to point to three conclusions upon which most, if not all, researchers would agree. First, if catharsis occurs, it does so only under highly specific conditions, and is not the widespread or general phenomenon previously believed. Second, under some circumstances, at least, the opportunity to harm individuals who have angered or provoked us may lead to heightened—not lessened—aggression against them on other occasions. And finally, while participation in cathartic activities may sometimes succeed in reducing overt aggression, the potential benefits of such procedures have probably been somewhat overstated in the past.

INCOMPATIBLE RESPONSES AND AGGRESSION: A FIELD STUDY

While most studies bearing on the impact of incompatible responses in reducing overt aggression have been performed within the laboratory, one recent—and somewhat controversial—experiment has been conducted in a more naturalistic setting (Baron, 1976b). The location chosen for this study was a moderately busy intersection near a major university. Conditions were arranged so that male drivers who happened to approach this intersection would encounter a mildly frustrating or annoying situation. Specifically, they were delayed by a male confederate who failed to move his car for 15 seconds after the light turned green. Subjects' reactions to this delay—and their tendency to aggress against the confederate—were then noted by two hidden assistants who observed participants' behavior and tape-recorded the speed and frequency with which they honked at the delaying driver (Turner, Layton, and Simons, 1975).

In order to determine whether incompatible responses would reduce subjects' tendencies to agress in this situation, three experimental procedures were instituted during the period while the light was still red (i.e., prior to the irritating delay). In one of these conditions (the *empathy* group), a female confederate wearing a bandage on her leg hobbled across the street on crutches. In a second condition (the *humor* group), she crossed the street wearing an outlandish clown mask. Finally, in a third (the *mild sexual arousal* condition), she crossed wearing a very brief and revealing outfit. In addition to these experimental groups, two control conditions were also included. In one (the *distraction* group) the confederate crossed the street while dressed in normal, conservative attire. In the second, she was entirely absent from the scene. (Please note that in all conditions, the confederate's walk was carefully timed so that she was completely out of sight by the time the traffic light turned green.) Conditions existing in the empathy, humor, sexual arousal, and distraction groups are illustrated in Figure 9-10.

It was predicted that exposure to the three experimental treatments would induce responses incompatible with anger or irritation among subjects, and so reduce their tendencies to honk at the confederate. Consistent with these predictions, results indicated that subjects in the empathy, humor, and mild sexual arousal groups honked significantly less frequently, as well as more slowly, and evidenced significantly fewer overt signs of

A

B

C   D

FIGURE 9-10. *Conditions existing in the distraction (A), empathy (B), humor (C), and mild sexual arousal (D) groups of the Baron (1976b) study. Exposure to the treatments shown in Photos B, C, and D significantly reduced the tendency of passing motorists to honk at another driver who delayed them in traffic.*

irritation than those in the distraction and control groups. That these effects were actually produced by the influence of incompatible responses was suggested by further, careful observation of subjects' behavior during the period when the confederate was present. At this time, those in the humor group frequently laughed out loud as she passed, those in the sexual arousal condition frequently made sexually oriented comments, and those in the empathy group often looked closely at the confederate and then quickly away, as if to avoid further exposure to the sight of another person experiencing discomfort. Thus, there was suggestive evidence that participants were, in fact, experiencing the anticipated reactions.

In sum, the findings of this study tended to confirm the results of previous laboratory experiments in suggesting that overt acts of aggression may often be inhibited through the induction of incompatible responses among potential aggressors.

Incompatible Responses: Empathy, Laughter, and Lust

The evidence we have considered so far suggests quite strongly that the most widely accepted deterrents to human aggression—punishment and catharsis—may actually be less effective in controlling such behavior than has previously been assumed. In view of these findings, it seems necessary that other means for preventing such behavior be determined. Although a number of different techniques have been suggested for this purpose (Singer, 1971), among the most promising is one based on the simple fact that all organisms, including human beings, are incapable of engaging in two **incompatible responses** at once. For example, it is impossible to both daydream and read, to study for an exam and watch television, or to drive a car and make passionate love (although some people often attempt to combine these last two activities). Extending this basic principle to the control of aggressive behavior, it seems possible that any conditions serving to induce responses or emotional states among aggressors which are incompatible with anger or the performance of violent acts will be highly effective in preventing such behavior. Although many responses might prove to be inconsistent with aggression, two which have been the subject of growing attention in this regard are *empathy* and *feelings of amusement* or overt laughter.

Empathy: Reactions to the Suffering of Others. Turning to **empathy** first, a number of experiments point to the conclusion that when aggressors are exposed to signs of pain or suffering on the part of their victims, they often sharply reduce the strength of their attacks against these unfortunate persons (Geen, 1970; Rule and Leger, 1976; Savitsky et al., 1974). That is, in these studies, individuals exposed to indications of pain or discomfort on the part of the persons they attack have been found to demonstrate a lower level of aggression than subjects not exposed to such feedback. One interpretation of such results is that they stem from the fact that groans, shouts, or pleas for mercy from their victims cause aggressors to experience strong feelings of empathy which make it more difficult for them to continue their assaults (Berger, 1962). That is, hearing the cries of these persons and seeing the injuries they have inflicted, aggressors experience negative emotional reactions which they may label as guilt, sorrow, or remorse. In order to reduce or eliminate such unpleasant feelings, they may then cease their attacks or even decide to leave the scene.

Unfortunately, as you might well guess, aggressors do not always react in this manner to signs of pain on the part of their victims. Sometimes they are relatively unaffected by such feedback, and on other occasions, may actually respond by raising the frequency or strength of their attacks (Baron, 1974b; Feshbach, Stiles and Bitter, 1967; Swart and Berkowitz, 1976). This latter type of reaction seems to occur only under conditions where they have been subjected to extreme provocation, and so enjoy the suffering of what they consider to be their deserving victims. Under conditions where anger is only mild or even moderate, empathy may occur, and act to inhibit further aggression.

Humor and Laughter. A second form of activity which appears to be quite incompatible with aggression is that of laughter or feelings of amusement. Informal observation suggests that once angry individuals have been induced to smile, the probability that they will engage in overt acts of violence may be sharply reduced. More formal evidence that this is indeed the case is provided by the findings of several experiments (Donnerstein and Mueller, 1976; Landy and Mettee, 1969; Leak, 1974). For example, in one of these studies (Baron and Ball, 1974), male college students were first either angered or not angered by a confederate, and then provided with an opportunity to aggress against this individual by means of electric shock within the familiar teacher-learner paradigm. Before attacking the confederate, half the subjects in each of these groups were exposed to a series of amusing cartoons (e.g., The Lone Ranger, shown wearing a ridiculous Groucho Marx mask, turns to Tonto and says "Next time, I'll get the mask myself.") In contrast, the remaining half examined neutral pictures of scenery, furniture, or abstract art. In accordance with the view that feelings of amusement would be incompatible with overt aggression, it was predicted that angry subjects exposed to the cartoons would direct weaker attacks against the confederate than those exposed to the neutral pictures, and as you can see in Figure 9-11, this was actually the case. These and similar findings in other studies (Landy and Mettee, 1969) suggest that with respect to the prevention of human aggression, at least, laughter may indeed be one of the best medicines.

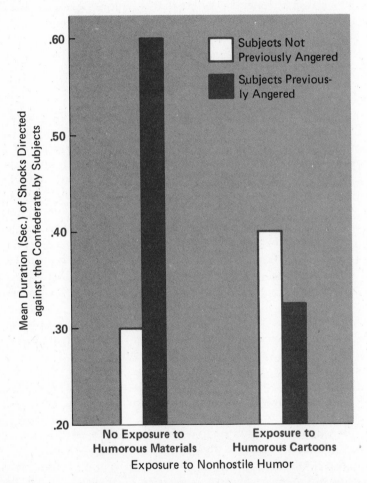

FIGURE 9-11. *Humor as a technique for reducing overt aggression. Angry individuals exposed to humorous cartoons directed weaker attacks against the person who had previously provoked them than angry individuals not exposed to such materials. In fact, their level of aggression dropped below that of persons who had never been angered. (Source: Based on data from Baron and Ball, 1974.)*

Of course, many other reactions besides empathy and feelings of amusement may also prove to be incompatible with anger or overt aggression. For example, as we noted above, the mild sexual arousal or "titillation" stemming from exposure to certain types of erotic stimuli may often exert such effects. Similarly, the fact that both human beings and many animals often become "frozen with fear" when facing extreme danger suggests that feelings of anxiety may also play such a role. Third, strong feelings of guilt concerning the performance of aggressive actions may serve to prevent or reduce such behavior. Finally, even participation in absorbing cognitive tasks (e.g., attempts to solve mathematical problems) may induce reactions incompatible with feelings of anger or overt aggression (Konecni, 1975a). Although many practical problems remain to be overcome, it seems possible that techniques based on the induction of incompatible reactions among aggressors may one day prove to be of major use in attempts to prevent or control the occurrence of human violence.

SUMMARY

Aggression has often been defined as any form of behavior directed toward the goal of harming or injuring another living being. Although many theoretical explanations for the occurrence of such actions have been offered, most fall into one of three distinct categories. According to the first, or *instinct* view, aggression stems from innate tendencies toward such activities—that is, human beings aggress because it is their "nature" to do so. According to the second, or *drive* view, aggression is the result of an externally elicited motive to harm or injure others. Finally, the *social learning* perspective suggests that aggression is simply a learned form of behavior, acquired in much the same manner, and maintained by many of the same types of reinforcers as other forms of activity. This final point of view is much more optimistic than either the instinct or drive positions with respect to the possibility of preventing or controlling such behavior.

Aggression does not occur in a "social vacuum." Rather, it is often elicited by specific situational factors. For many years, it was held that frustration—the blocking of ongoing goal-directed behavior—was the most powerful antecedent of aggression. Recent evidence suggests, however, that it may actually be a relatively weak determinant of such behavior. Among the factors which seem to exert a somewhat stronger impact on aggression are verbal or physical attack from others, exposure to aggressive models, and heightened physiological arousal. Environmental factors such as crowding and heat also seem to play a role in the initiation of such behavior.

The occurrence of aggression is also influenced by characteristics of the specific individuals involved in its performance. For example, it now appears that many of the persons who perform extreme acts of violence possess unusually strong inhibitions against aggressing. As a result, they refrain from such behavior until repeated provocations overcome even *their* powerful restraints and they literally explode into violence. Many other individuals possess only weak inhibitions against aggression, and so frequently adopt such behavior as a basic strategy for interacting with others. The fact that individuals possessing an extra "Y" chromosome (XYY's, as they are often termed) are found with a higher-than-expected frequency among prison populations has led some researchers to suggest that this genetic abnormality predisposes such persons toward violence. However, additional findings suggesting that possession of an extra "Y" chromosome is neither a necessary nor a sufficient condition for the performance of violent acts tend to weaken the strength of this argument.

It has generally been assumed that *punishment* (either actual or only threatened) and *catharsis* provide the most effective means for preventing or controlling human aggression. However, recent evidence suggests that neither technique is as effective in this regard as was previously believed. An additional procedure based upon the induction among aggressors of responses incompatible with anger or overt aggression seems to offer an alternative means for controlling such behavior. Among the responses which have been found to reduce aggression in this manner are *empathy* (induced through exposure to the suffering of aggressors' victims), and *feelings of amusement* (induced through exposure to humorous cartoons or similar materials).

GLOSSARY

Aggression. Any form of behavior directed toward the goal of harming or injuring another living being who is motivated to avoid such treatment.

Aggression machine. A device employed in laboratory studies of physical aggression. By pushing any one of several buttons on this apparatus, subjects can presumably deliver electric shocks of various intensity to another person. In reality, however, this individual is a confederate of the experimenter and never receives any shocks.

Aggressive cues. Stimuli having the capacity to elicit aggressive behavior from angry individuals. Both persons and objects can acquire aggressive cue value through repeated association with anger, witnessed violence, or aggression generally.

Aggressive drive. The motive to harm or injure others.

Aggressive models. Individuals who behave in a highly aggressive manner and so induce others to act in a similar fashion.

Attack. A physical or verbal assault by one person against another. Existing evidence suggests that attack is a powerful elicitor of counteraggression.

Catharsis. Reductions in emotional upset and/or the tendency to aggress presumed to result from participation in relatively "safe" aggressive actions. Recent evidence suggests that the occurrence of such effects is much less widespread or general than had previously been believed.

Drive theories of aggression. Theories which attribute the occurrence of aggression to the arousal of drives or motives to harm or injure others.

Empathy. Emotional reactions induced by exposure to signs of emotion on the part of others. Feelings of empathy toward the victim often serve to inhibit futher attacks against this person by aggressors.

Frustration. The blocking of ongoing, goal-directed behavior. Frustration has long been held to be one of the major elicitors of aggression, but recent findings suggest that it may play a smaller role in this respect than was previously suspected.

Incompatible-response theory.   Refers to the proposal that aggression may be inhibited through the induction among aggressors of responses incompatible with anger or overt violence.   Among the reactions found to be effective in this regard are empathy toward the victim, feelings of amusement, and mild sexual arousal.

Instinct theory of aggression.   The view that aggression stems from innate tendencies toward such behavior.   Among the most noted supporters of this perspective have been Sigmund Freud and Konrad Lorenz.

Overcontrolled aggressors.   Individuals possessing unusually strong restraints against aggression.   As a result of their powerful inhibitions, such persons usually turn to aggression only after enduring a long series of provocations.   When they finally do aggress, however, their attacks against others may be quite severe.

Social-learning theory of aggression.   The view that aggression is simply a specific form of social behavior which is both acquired and maintained in much the same manner as other forms of human activity.

"Weapons" effect.   Refers to the possibility that the physical presence of weapons tends to facilitate aggressve behavior, even when they are not used in its performance. Evidence regarding the existence of such effects has been inconclusive.

XYY syndrome.   Refers to the suggestion that individuals possessing an extra "Y" chromosome are particularly prone to outbursts of violence.   Although initial findings seemed to support this proposal, more recent evidence casts doubt on its accuracy.

SUGGESTED READINGS FOR CHAPTER 9

Bandura, A.   *Aggression: A social learning analysis.*   Englewood Cliffs, N. J.: Prentice-Hall, 1973.   An in-depth treatment of the nature and causes of aggressive behavior. The chapters on theoretical perspectives and techniques for preventing or controlling aggression are especially interesting.

Berkowitz, L.   The control of aggression.   In B. Caldwell and H. Ricciuti, eds.   *Review of child development research.*   Chicago: University of Chicago Press, 1973, pp. 95–140. In this article, a noted researcher discusses various techniques which might be used to prevent or control human aggression.

Geen, R. G., and O'Neal, E. C., eds.   *Perspectives on aggression.*   New York: Academic Press, 1976.   A collection of specially prepared articles dealing with several different aspects of aggression.   Among the topics included are the influence of environmental factors (heat, crowding, noise, etc.) on aggression, moral judgments of aggressive behavior, and the nature of interracial aggression.

Lunde, D. T.   Our murder boom.   *Psychology Today*, 1975, *9*, 35–42.   An interesting discussion of some of the factors leading up to murder and related acts of violence. For a more detailed discussion of this topic, you may wish to see Lunde's full-length book, *Murder and madness.*   San Francisco: W. H. Freeman, 1975.

SEXUAL BEHAVIOR

A THEORETICAL FRAMEWORK
Reproduction: Maintaining the Species
Learning: Variety and Imagination
Emotions: Good Sex and Bad Sex

EXTERNAL INFLUENCES ON SEXUAL BEHAVIOR
Erotic Stimuli: Look at What That Couple's Doing Now!
Variety Is the Spice of Life (at Least for Males)

INDIVIDUAL DIFFERENCES IN SEXUAL BEHAVIOR
Personality Variables: Different Strokes for Different Folks
Sex Differences: Are Females Less Sexual than Males?

THE EFFECTS OF EROTIC STIMULATION
Sexual Arousal
Overt Behavior Following Exposure to Erotica

10

It was late in the twenty-second century when the Starship Enterprising *first visited the galaxy containing the planet Eros. Reports of that space contact were of immediate interest to we people of Earth for two reasons. First, Eros was found to be inhabited by a species almost identical to ourselves in appearance and in many aspects of their civilization. Second, the most notable difference between our people and theirs was one which greatly surprised our explorers: the attitudes of the citizens of Eros about sex and about food were found to be more or less the reverse of our own.*

In their culture, sexual activity is totally accepted both as a natural bodily function and as a source of pleasure to be cultivated by those with imagination and good taste. Children are taught about sex from their earliest years and encouraged to enjoy their bodies by masturbating. Young people engage in sexual games with their playmates and are regularly exposed to the sexual activities of the adults around them.

Almost all of the movies, plays, and TV shows contain explicit sexual scenes. On educational TV a middle-aged lady has a popular show that teaches advanced sexual techniques and variations. So much is known about sex in that society that schools devote very little class time to it, although there is an elective sex course, complete with laboratory, beginning at the junior high level. In a somewhat chauvinistic fashion, housewives are encouraged to buy sex magazines and fancy sex books with lavishly illustrated "recipes" for special treats with which to please their mates when they return home from work. Sexual supermarkets are conveniently located in each city and stocked with a wide variety of sexual paraphernalia, including vibrators, dildoes, special lotions and creams, and some devices that the visiting astronauts were never able to figure out. Because of the central role that sexuality plays in the lives of the people, they frequently seek entertainment or celebrate special occasions by going to public establishments, called sexaurants, where both males and females are sexually served by courteous employees who work primarily for tips. Many of these establishments are decorated in such a way as to provide a foreign atmosphere; some charge outrageously high prices; a few are made to revolve slowly on the top floor of tall buildings, thus providing a spectacular view of the city below while the patrons are engaged in sexual pleasures. More economical establishments also are commonly seen in each town—fast sex franchises which provide the basic sexual gratifications but dispense with all the frills of the fancier places.

The Earthmen were, of course, startled by the sexual atmosphere of Eros, but there was an even bigger surprise. When inquiries were made about the eating habits of these people, most of those interviewed refused even to talk about the subject, a few blushed when the word "food" was mentioned, and some of the more conservative members of the community wanted to have the visitors prosecuted for violating the obscenity laws and creating a public nuisance. One Earthman was unexpectedly arrested while eating a Milky Way candy bar in public and charged with committing an abominable crime against nature. The captain of the starship was able to secure his release by promising that the man would never again set foot on Eros. Near the end of the visit, it became possible to obtain information about eating from a few individuals who had become friendly enough to talk about intimate matters. These informants indicated that while everyone acknowledged that eating is a physical necessity, most people would be embarrassed to discuss openly the fact that they do it, or even worse, enjoy it. There seemed to be a difference between the sexes in that men are more likely than women to joke about the subject; they sometimes even try to persuade women to share a meal with them. Many females, on the other hand, reported that they had never enjoyed a meal in their lives. The tradition is to eat alone or in pairs in darkened rooms, and there is a strong taboo against being seen eating or seeing anyone else eat. Occasionally, a deviant is arrested for peeping in a dining room window. Children are taught very little about the whole process; if a child is caught putting food in his mouth publicly, he is told that such practices will rot his brain and cause blindness. Words for items such as "knife" and "fork" or functions such as "chewing" and "swallowing" occur only in obscene jokes or among the individuals at the fringes of society. No one is permitted to write about eating unless it can be shown that the total work has some socially redeeming value and is not designed simply to make people hungry. Public displays of anything dealing with food in the theater or on television are illegal. It is widely agreed that those who read or view hard-core nutrition material will be incited to run wild in the streets, committing unspeakable food crimes.

In adulthood, it is expected that each person will take meals only with a spouse, though it is known that some people fool around and share a snack or two with someone else's mate. In the more progressive communities, there are food-education courses in the schools; these are taught to sexually segregated classes and deal primarily with the technical details of digestion plus sections on the dangers of obesity and food poisoning. There is no indication in such courses that eating can be fun. The visitors from Earth found a number of crude pictures drawn on the walls of some of the eating cubicles which depicted people consuming ice cream sundaes; also, there frequently are scrawled messages such as "Mary likes succotash," followed by a telephone number. Despite the taboos, there is a flourishing underground business in selling pictures and stories about food, rundown movie theaters in the larger cities show 16-mm films of people consuming an eight-course meal, and the *audiences are mainly males who sit quietly watching and chewing gum. There are a few shady establishments (called dental parlors) where men may go and order a gourmet meal prepared by a sordid young lady; during election campaigns, there is usually a police crackdown on such activities. There are persistent rumors of analogous outlets for women, where males do the cooking, but this may only represent a masculine fantasy.*

This science fiction version of a culture different from our own may seem impossible or improbable, but perhaps it is only a historical accident that our society treats the need for food and the need for sex in such different ways. Because of the negative view of sex throughout much of our history, scientific knowledge about sexual behavior has not been as advanced as our knowledge in other areas. Though attitudes are changing rapidly, there is still a great deal of resistance to conducting this type of research, and any applications of the research findings are almost certain to arouse controversy. Nevertheless, much progress is currently being made. Perhaps on the planet Eros, a social psychology text would include a chapter on eating behavior, while there would be no reason to include a special section on sex.

In the present chapter, we will first present *a theoretical framework,* suggesting some of the variables that seem to be important in studying sexual behavior. Then we will examine what is known about *external influences on sexual behavior* with respect to the stimulus conditions that affect sexual arousal. *Individual differences in sexual behavior* will then be considered with respect to personality variables and male-female differences. Finally, the *effects of erotic stimulation* will be described with studies of physiological responses and the influence of pornography on sexual behavior.

A THEORETICAL FRAMEWORK

Most theoretical approaches to sexuality have dealt with very specific and limited concerns such as how guilt develops or with the role of sexual conflicts in some types of abnormal behavior. Most of the research on sexual behavior actually has not been based on theory; rather, there are descriptive surveys asking people what they do and think, and there are empirical experiments that examine particular problems.

A framework within which to describe this research has been suggested elsewhere (Byrne, 1974) and will be presented briefly here. The basic idea is to describe sexual behavior in terms of three phases of the sexual act in a way analogous to Masters and Johnson's (1966) outline of physiological responses. In the present context, we will deal with (1) the *stimulation* of sexual desire by external and internal cues, (2) the *behavior* motivated by this sexual arousal, and (3) the culmination of sexual activity in *orgasm*. Each of these three phases is described at three levels of human development. The simplest level, *reproduction,* is characteristic of most animal behavior and probably of the earliest human beings as well. With our high degree of cognitive ability, however, sexual behavior gradually became quite complicated and varied, as will be seen in a description of the *learning* level. Finally, as human culture evolved, sexuality took on still more complex meaning with taboos, customs, laws, and religious injunctions which are reflected in the third level, that dealing with *emotions.* These three levels and their effects on the three phases of sexuality will now be described.

Reproduction: Maintaining the Species

In prehistoric times, at least, human sexual behavior was probably as uncomplicated as was eating behavior. A physiological need became aroused, and an act took place which satisfied that need. Such a pattern evolved because it served to maintain the species. We will examine some of the aspects of this basic level of sexuality.

Stimulation Phase. For mammals, including ourselves, sex arousal is a joint function of internal cues regulated by hormones and external cues associated with a potential sexual partner. For most animals, if the necessary hormonal state is present, the organism is likely to be receptive to the external cues when they appear. In many species, hormonal readiness occurs only at particular seasons of the year or only at specific time intervals; other species such as human beings are in a continual state of sexual readiness from adolescence through adulthood. The sexual behavior of human males seems to be relatively unrelated to normal variations in hormone level (Raboch and Starka, 1972). In fact, there is some evidence that the amount of male hormone in the blood is *negatively* related to orgasm frequency—the more sexually active the man, the lower his average testosterone level tends to be (Kraemer et al., 1976). Though a number of self-report studies suggests that the sexual desires of human females, at least, are controlled by hormonal factors (Udry and Morris, 1968), experimental studies find no relationship between phases of the menstrual cycle and how aroused an individual becomes in response to erotica (Griffith and Walker, 1975).

The external cues to arousal can be visual (a female primate bends over and exposes her genitals to the male), olfactory (the odor of a female dog in heat attracts males from all over the surrounding area), auditory (animals such as the moose respond to mating calls), tactual (the "fighting" of cats ends when the male grips the skin on the back of the female's neck between his teeth to begin the sexual act), and kinesthetic (rhinoceroses must run at one another over a space of several acres in order to prepare for intercourse).

The **stimulation phase** can be a prolonged affair, as when squirrels engage in an elaborate, teasing chase, or a brief interlude, as when a bull approaches a cow. Sometimes, a combination of cues is required for sexual arousal, but smell seems

TESTING YOUR KNOWLEDGE ABOUT SEX

Given our history of taboos about anything having to do with sex, it is not surprising that there is a great deal of variability with respect to what each of us knows about the topic. Until recent years, even physicians were relatively lacking in knowledge about sexual matters. Despite the availability of courses on sex education and a flood of books on every aspect of sexuality, most people still acquire the basic facts about sex from friends and acquaintances.

In order to get a sample of some of the things you and your classmates know about various aspects of sexuality, the following test can be used. Right now, why don't you take it yourself? Mark each answer True or False by circling the appropriate response.

Sex Knowledge Test

1. *Nocturnal emissions ("wet dreams") are a normal phenomenon.*   T   F

2. *Women do not ejaculate, as men do, when they have an orgasm.*   T   F

3. *Simultaneous orgasms are necessary for a sexually happy marriage.*   T   F

4. *As women mature, they tend to have vaginal rather than clitoral orgasms.*   T   F

5. *Athletic performance is not impaired by sexual intercourse or masturbation a few hours before the event.*   T   F

6. *The larger a male's penis, the more sexually potent he is.*   T   F

7. *Sterilization does not reduce the sex drive of either males or females.*   T   F

8. *Sexual desire and ability to perform decrease markedly after an individual reaches age 40 or 50.*   T   F

9. *If a female urinates following intercourse, pregnancy is usually prevented.*   T   F

10. *Women who are frigid are as likely to become pregnant as women who climax easily.*   T   F

11. *A woman who is raped really wants it to happen or else a man could not force himself on her.*   T   F

12. *People are born with a tendency to be totally homosexual or totally heterosexual.*   T   F

to be the most usual sense mode for stimulation. Females of many species have been found to produce a sex attractant (called **pheromones**) in the vagina which serves to stimulate the male of her species. The power of these substances has been shown experimentally; when vaginal secretions from a female rat are placed on a male rat, other males will attempt to mount him sexually (Connor, 1972). Such cues are very important in species below the human level; when experimenters interfere with the sense of smell of male rhesus monkeys, these males no longer respond sexually to females (Michael, Keverne, and Bonsall, 1971). It seems reasonable to suppose that human beings should respond sexually to similar cues, but research suggests that we do not (Doty et al., 1975). There are, however, numerous commercials for aftershave lotions, perfumes, and deodorants that try to convince us that the natural smells are offensive, while certain artificial smells will drive the opposite sex wild.

13. Both males and females masturbate, and this practice has never been found to cause insanity, warts, acne, or hairy palms. T F
14. Women who have strong sex drives, climax easily, and sometimes have multiple orgasms are classified as nymphomaniacs. T F
15. Transvestites (those who dress in the clothes of the opposite sex) are not usually homosexuals. T F
16. Sex offenders typically are atheists. T F
17. Research has not found that pornography stimulates people to engage in sex crimes. T F
18. When a white female receives a blood transfusion from a black male, any child she later conceives may be partially black. T F
19. Enjoyment of oral sex does not indicate suppressed homosexual tendencies. T F
20. Conception is not prevented by intercourse in a standing position. T F

When you have finished the test, turn to the answer key below and mark each question that you missed. If your instructor would like to do so, it might be interesting to look at how your class as a whole responded to this test. Names should not be used—simply indicate on a sheet of paper whether you are a male or a female, record your total score, and list the items that you marked incorrectly. When the entire class has done this, separately for males and females, determine the average score, the range of scores (lowest to highest), and the number of people who missed each item. Do males and females differ in their total scores or in the specific items they marked incorrectly? Do you think that your class is more or less informed about sex than most college students or than people in general?

Though some of these points are covered in the present chapter, the test questions were adapted from material presented in McCary (1973). You might want to read that book or Sexual Myths and Fallacies (McCary, 1971) to find out more about these topics.

Answer Key

1-T, 2-T, 3-F, 4-F, 5-T, 6-F, 7-T, 8-F, 9-F, 10-T, 11-F, 12-F, 13-T, 14-F, 15-T, 16-F, 17-T, 18-F, 19-T, 20-T.

Whatever the sense mode, all of the sexual cues serve (1) to create sexual excitement as evidenced by an increased flow of blood in the genitals and the secretion of lubricating fluids and (2) to motivate the male and female to move into close physical proximity.

Behavioral Phase. Once the pair is sufficiently close, excitement is maintained and enhanced by behavior such as biting, licking, and touching. As this interaction continues, the penis is inserted into the vagina. Depending on the species, intercourse may consist of one violent thrust (cattle), several periods of rapid thrusting interrupted by dismounting (rats), or a series of thrusts of quickening intensity (chimpanzees)—whatever the pattern for a given species, the movements ensure genital friction. We can only guess about the **behavioral phase** of prehistoric man, but studies of relatively primitive groups suggest that their sexual practices were probably as limited and as unchangeable as those of our primate cousins.

Orgasm Phase. There are two aspects of the **orgasm phase.** One is based on evolutionary necessity: the survival of the species requires that the male sperm and female ovum come in contact within the female's body so that conception can occur. In addition, it appears that orgasm is a pleasurable experience in each mammalian species, at least among males. Though female orgasm is rare or nonexistent in other animals, human females have been found to surpass males in this respect. The external behavior of the animal at the point of orgasm tends to be relatively uniform for each species. For example, when they ejaculate, stumptail monkeys have a series of muscular spasms, display a frowning round-mouthed look, vocalize with a high-pitched breathy sound, and often gently bite their partner's neck (Chevalier-Skolnikoff, 1975).

Learning: Variety and Imagination

It seems a safe guess that primitive human beings approached both food and sex in the simplest fashion possible. Hunger led to eating, and sexual desire led to intercourse, and there was probably little refinement or variety in either activity. The human species is comparatively bright, however, so our ancestors eventually learned to prepare a wide variety of foods, to cook some of them, to combine ingredients, to add spices, and so forth. What effects did human intelligence have on sexual behavior?

Stimulation Phase. The sexual behavior of human beings has been greatly affected by out intellectual ability. Because of our learning skills, any stimulus can theoretically be associated with arousal and, through simple conditioning, become sexually exciting. The way in which we can learn to associate new cues with arousal has been shown in numerous experiments. For example, Rachman (1966) has demonstrated that subjects can learn to become sexually excited by footwear. Male subjects were shown a photographic slide of a pair of women's black boots, and then slides of attractive, naked girls. After several such trials, the subjects became sexually aroused, as indicated by erections, in response to the picture of the boots. In addition, there was generalization in that they also were aroused by pictures of other boots and of shoes. Thus, individuals who initially had no sexual response to such stimuli easily learned to become aroused by them.

Beyond such laboratory studies, common observation and case-history material clearly indicate that human beings have learned to respond sexually to many kinds of stimuli in addition to members of the opposite sex. Possibly through accidental conditioning experiences, individuals learn to become excited in response to articles of clothing, parts of the body that have nothing to do with sex, members of their own sex, being humiliated, drive-in movies, a particular song, the smell of grass, being whipped, taking an enema, dogs, the taste of champaign, and Holiday Inn signs. Despite the evidence for a simple conditioning process, there is also reason to believe that some stimuli are more easily associated with sexual arousal than others. For example, Gebhard (1969) has reported that the most common **fetish** objects (those which have special sexual meaning for an individual and which elicit excitement) include spiked high heel shoes, leatherware, and underclothing. If nothing more than conditioning were involved, you might expect to find that ceilings, pillows, ears, and hands would be high on the list of fetishes. Since they are not, it is possible that human beings are somehow programmed to associate a given emotional state with certain types of stimuli rather than others (Seligman, 1971).

Human intellectual development provides us with another source of stimulation as well—the imagination. Beach (1969) has pointed out that hormones have less and less effect on sexual behavior as animals progress up the evolutionary scale; in the primates, such as monkeys and people, it is the brain rather than the glands that has the greatest influence. The effects of castration illustrate the difference. The sexual behavior of lower mammals such as rats quickly ceases if the male's testes are removed, whereas apes, monkeys, and especially human males can remain sexually active for many years after being castrated (Luttage, 1971).

The difference between a castrated rat and a castrated primate is, in popular terminology, what goes on in their heads. We know that people do not have to wait for a given level of hormone concentration and an appropriate external stimulus to create sexual excitement; the stimulus can be one's own thoughts. In one experiment, married couples were asked to look at erotic photographs, read erotic passages, or just to think about such scenes (Byrne and Lamberth, 1971). As may be seen in Figure 10-1, those who used their own imaginations reported being much more sexually aroused than those who actually were given erotic material. The power of the imagination as a sexual stimulus is such as to suggest that many of the differences among people in "sex drive" may actually be a function of whether the individuals have learned to create sexual fantasies for themselves. In a similar way, sexual activity in old age need not cease if individuals utilize their imaginations. In addition, the existence of erotica from the earliest cave drawings to the most recent hard-core pornographic movie suggests that pornography has long been a way to express sexual fantasies, to communicate them to one another, and to utilize them to create excitement (Byrne, 1976).

Behavioral Phase. Our intellectual ability not only permits us to be stimulated by a wide variety of internal and external images, it also permits human beings to engage in a wide variety of sexual activities. The behavior that maintains and increases sexual excitement need not be limited to simple responses featuring the contact of male and female genital organs. Over the centuries, by trial and error, by observation, by instruction, and sometimes by sheer inventive creativity, human beings have learned that the same kind of genital friction that characterizes sexual intercourse can be obtained in an almost limitless number of ways. Though other species can and do learn sexual variations, they ordinarily do not. At the simplest level, we became the only mammals who frequently have intercourse in other positions beyond that of the male entering the female from the rear. In addition, human beings masturbate,

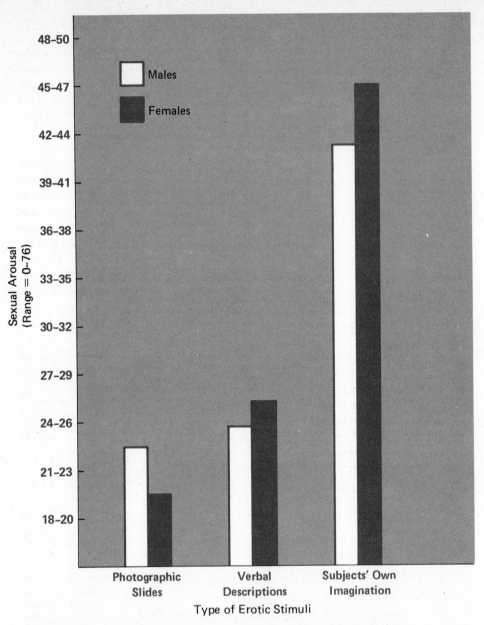

FIGURE 10-1. *The effects of different types of erotic stimuli on sexual arousal. Subjects who were asked to imagine various sexual acts were much more aroused than subjects who saw photographs or read descriptions of such acts. (Source: Based on data from Byrne and Lamberth, 1971.)*

engage in oral sex, anal sex, and, in fact, receive sexual gratification from contacting any part of the partner's body. The sexual object can be oneself, a member of the opposite or same sex, multiple partners, members of other species, or an inanimate object such as a battery-powered vibrator.

Thus, human imagination and learning have enormously increased the range of stimuli which elicit sexual excitement and the range of the sexual behaviors which then occur. An example of the varied stimuli and varied behavior which are common in some sections of our society can be found in the advertisements of any sexual publication, such as the ones selected from a New York newspaper and reproduced in Figure 10-2.

Orgasm Phase. Intellectual ability can also have a few effects on orgasm. Individuals can learn to delay orgasms, to enhance them by means of accompanying fantasies, and to intensify them with drugs. Those who have difficulty in having orgasms can learn to do so by means of sexual therapy (Hartman and Fithian, 1974). The most important implication of this level for the orgasm phase is the fact that the variations in sexual activity are such that the final step in the sexual sequence is not necessarily the depositing of sperm in the vagina. The fact that sexual acts need not involve reproduction has had a profound effect on the meaning of sex to different individuals, as we shall see in the following section.

ATTENTION!!!
GENTLEMEN IN NEED OF DISCIPLINE
are invited to our house of
expertly trained mistresses,
some of whom will accept novices;
but we demand full respect and
ONLY OBEDIENT MEN!
If you're a serious submissive
Call Mistress Manson

TWO GUYS YOU'VE
NEVER SEEN BEFORE!
Jan, 18 Dave, 20
together or
separately
for sincere,
enjoyable pleasure!

ATTENTION FIREMEN! Male, 35, with great film collection would like to meet firemen with rubber coat & boots. I am generous & privacy is guaranteed.

PANTIES: THEY'RE SOILED AGAIN. $5.00 each. With pic $7. Personal note included. Janis

CALIFORNIA STUD
Young, blonde, blue-eyed athlete new in town. Muscular, well-endowed. Any scene, any time.
MIKE

DOMINANT
FEMALES
LIVE OUT YOUR FANTASY
ENEMA, TV, and BONDAGE
MY PLACE OR YOURS
Call PEARL

FOR A SPANKING
GOOD TIME
a
BAG full of fun. Come to the therapy studio of Belle de Jour. Where all your DRESS UP fantasies get BOUND UP into realities.

MOTHER
&
19-YEAR-OLD
DAUGHTER
WILL PERFORM

THREE IS NOT A CROWD!
We're two young, beautiful girls who love each other and are eager to share our love. Are you the liberated, virile male we're looking for? Are you willing to let us pamper you while you enjoy and satisfy the passion we arouse in one another? We'll take you beyond your wildest dreams as we caress and kiss each other (and you, too!) into a frenzy of desire; then, as we devote all our attention to you, we'll give you pleasure you never thought possible. Are you man enough to handle it? Of course, you can always try one of us and then come back to see what two can do. Call us at our private apartment:

A GENUINE SUBMISSIVE GIRL
TINA
I have been a very bad girl and I need a strong man to discipline me. So: tie me, gag me, chain me, chase me, whip me, beat me, rape me

JANE
Wild jungle beauty. I will do anything you want. Fully equipped.

FIGURE 10-2. *An an example of the variety of sexual stimuli to which individuals respond and of the variety of interpersonal acts in which individuals engage, a sample of some of the milder advertisements from one issue of a sexual publication is presented here. Note the way in which some of the ads utilize specific types of fantasies to appeal to different customers. (Telephone numbers and addresses have been removed.) (Source:* Screw, *January 19, 1976.)*

Though the biological function of sexual intercourse is the creation of offspring, that is not usually the reason that individuals engage in such behavior. Instead, there is simply a strong motive to stimulate the genitals, and the activity happens to be extremely pleasurable. The strength of this biological drive can be demonstrated in animal research; when male rats are deprived of food for up to six days and then given a choice between food and a receptive female, they choose the female (Sachs and Marsan, 1972). Sex, then, in nature should represent a strong need which is pleasurable to satisfy.

As knowledge grew, people gradually learned of the relationship between sexual intercourse and the birth of offspring. That may not seem to be a complex problem to solve, but anthropologists have described a number of primitive groups who were unaware of a connection between intercourse and birth even in the twentieth century. Whenever that fact has been learned, however, sex becomes complicated. The sexual act no longer is just a strongly desired behavior that feels good; it takes on added meanings. As societies evolved, all of the rules and regulations involving the good of the group, ideas of morality, conceptions of the meaning of duty and pleasure, and notions of property rights and of individual rights were inevitably applied to the realm of sexual behavior.

The Regulation of Sexual Behavior. We can only guess at the way in which some of the ideas about sexual morality originated, but the eventual outcome was the attempt to regulate sexual behavior by means of customs, religious taboos, and laws. For example, if it were to the tribe's advantage to increase in size, any sexual behavior that did not result in conception would constitute a threat to the group; thus, there would be rules against masturbation, contraception, oral sex, homosexuality, anal sex, and bestiality. Many of these efforts at regulating sex continue to exist in the form of laws. For example, oral sex is still illegal in several states and is defined as "the abominable and detestable crime against nature." That law is still enforced at times—a physician in Indianapolis was recently convicted as a "criminal sexual psychopath" for engaging in such acts. And, in January of 1976, the Vatican issued a declaration which described masturbation as a "seriously disordered act." Besides encouraging reproduction, there are other reasons for regulating sex. If a society developed in which women and children were assumed to need male protection, some generally accepted bond such as matrimony could evolve as a requisite for intercourse; thus, there would be rules against premarital sex. When the idea of property rights and inheritance of property arose, any confusion over parentage would be undesirable, so there would be rules against adultery. In the last century in England, a law was introduced to make adultery punishable by death (Taylor, 1954). When the idea of individual rights arose, any attempt to take advantage of weakness or ignorance would be seen as wrong; as a result, there would be rules against rape and against intercourse with anyone too young or otherwise incompetent to give their informed consent to engage in sexual acts. Whatever the reasons and whatever their validity, there came to be a complex set of rules governing sex in every society.

Such rules have given rise to two problems, which influence each phase of sexual behavior emotionally. First, even though the situation may change and make a given rule obsolete, the rule is nevertheless often retained. For example, with overpopulation as one of mankind's great disasters, laws and moral codes condemning contraceptive techniques are not only unnecessary to society—they actually become a threat to its well being. Technological advances such as the contraceptive pill and simple sterilization procedures for each sex make it possible to separate the pleasure of sex from the goal of parenthood, but many of our existing attitudes, laws, and moral precepts are not based on such present realities. Second, throughout history, each generation has had the task of teaching the next generation that some sex is bad while other sex is good. Frequently it has been taught that sexual desire and sexual pleasure in intercourse with a spouse are good while any other type of sexual desire or sexual pleasure is bad. Very often there are efforts to prevent "bad" sexual desires and activities among children and adolescents by communicating the idea that all aspects of sex are somehow wrong, as in the myths about masturbation illustrated in Figure 10-3. Such myths are learned very effectively; a surprisingly large portion of college students still believe that masturbation is shameful, disgusting, and potentially harmful (Abramson and Mosher, 1975.) Children and teenagers learn that certain words are not to be said and certain parts of the body are not to be seen—even on dolls. Young people are often left in ignorance about the details of intercourse and conception as long as possible by means of a curtain of silence, embarrassment, and censorship. As one parent expressed it:

> I try to keep them from knowing too much; I approach it the same as my parents did. My parents did not tell me about it. I don't discuss it either. I think sex education corrupts the minds of 15–16 year olds! There is absolutely *no* communication between parents and kids about sex. Kids know too much already. I just tell them to behave and keep their eyes open. (Libby and Nass, 1971, p. 233).

What happens, then, when these negative emotional responses become attached to all aspects of sexual behavior?

Stimulation Phase. Emotional reactions influence the way we evaluate the experience of sexual arousal—whether such arousal is something positive to be sought or something negative to be avoided. It is obvious that individuals can acquire very different attitudes about sexuality when we note that some spend time and money to attend erotic movies in order to become aroused while others advocate cold showers and vigorous exercise to take one's mind off sex. It seems that each of us, through a lifetime series of emotional experiences, has come to associate sex with varying degrees of positive and negative feelings.

Wallace and Wehmer (1972) measured these different attitudes toward sex

2 MASTURBATION

Masturbation is a form of sexual release for most males and females. You won't injure your body by masturbating -- no matter how often.

If masturbation has become a habit that makes you feel guilty, it is more like self-punishment than self-enjoyment. Just about the only way to break a strong habit is to somehow manage to put up with the tension that

results when you don't do it (masturbate, smoke, overeat, or whatever). The tension will decrease as you get used to the change.

Many people of all ages get pleasure from masturbating. Still, if you have religious or moral objections, then don't do it. A person doesn't have to masturbate in order to be sexually healthy.

FIGURE 10-3. *Negative information about sex is communicated to both children and adolescents. Masturbation has traditionally been described as something harmful, evil, shameful, and to be avoided at all costs. The material here is part of a sixteen page comic book for young people which is designed to counteract many of these unpleasant and inaccurate teachings. (Source: Ten Heavy Facts about Sex, Institute for Family Research and Education, Syracuse, New York.)*

among Detroit residents and classified them as sexual liberals or sexual conservatives. When these individuals were shown a series of photographic slides depicting several sexual themes, the two groups responded in quite different ways. For the sexual liberals, the most arousing pictures were judged to be the most entertaining. For the sexual conservatives, the most arousing pictures were seen as the most offensive and least entertaining. Both groups were sexually aroused, but they differed greatly in whether that arousal was labeled and experienced as something pleasurable or as something disgusting.

In an attempt to identify these emotions, married couples were exposed to a series of explicit erotic themes and asked to indicate their feelings immediately afterward (Byrne et al., 1974). There were two distinct types of emotional responses to these arousing stimuli—positive feelings such as entertainment and curiosity, and negative feelings such as disgust and nausea. The somewhat surprising finding was that there were not just the two opposite emotional reactions (positive versus negative) but all possible combinations of the two. That is, some people found sexual arousal to be very positive and not at all negative, some found it to be both positive and negative; and so forth. The four extreme patterns of emotional reactions are shown in Table 10-1, and the four corresponding types of individuals have been labeled as sexually liberal, conservative, ambivalent, and indifferent. Such varied emotional reactions lead to very different attitudes about sex. For example, erotic stories and pictures are most likely to be classified as "pornographic" by those whose emotional responses place them in the sexually conservative category. Those same individuals tend to favor government censorship of the sexual content of books, magazines, and movies. The sexual liberals, in contrast, feel that very few erotic themes are pornographic, and they are against censorship for adults. It seems likely that many arguments about censorship, sex education, and morality are based on these very different emotions rather than on logic or factual information.

Behavioral Phase. Do such emotional responses have an effect on actual sexual behavior? It appears that the more negative the emotional response, the more narrow the range of "acceptable" sexual acts. Among married couples, sexual conservatives are much more likely to judge acts such as masturbation, oral sex, and intercourse in unusual positions as obscene and offensive (Byrne et al., 1974). Though these self-reports are not necessarily accurate reflections of actual behavior, it seems probable that the liberals engage in more varied sexual activities than the conservatives. Another study with married females found that negative emotional responses (such as those expressed by conservatives) were associated with less sexual desire, less enjoyment of intercourse, and lower frequency of intercourse (Kutner, 1971).

Among unmarried college students, emotional responses also influence sexual behavior. Mosher (1968) has developed a measure of sex guilt which asks

TABLE 10-1. *When subjects indicated their feelings on several positive and negative scales after being exposed to erotic stimuli, four patterns of emotional responses were found. Some individuals expressed primarily positive feelings (Liberal), some expressed primarily negative feelings (Conservative), some felt both emotions (Ambivalent), and some felt neither (Indifferent). (Source: Based on data from Byrne et al., 1974.)*

Positive Emotional Responses to Erotica	Negative Emotional Responses to Erotica	
	Low	*High*
High	LIBERAL—those who enjoy being sexually aroused	AMBIVALENT—those who are in emotional conflict about sexual arousal
Low	INDIFFERENT—those who are not emotionally responsive to sexual arousal	CONSERVATIVE—those who dislike being sexually aroused

subjects to indicate their positive and negative reactions to their own sexual desires and experiences. Among both male and female undergraduates, the greater their guilt the less sexual experiences they have had. Low-guilt individuals were much more likely than those high in guilt to have petted to orgasm, experienced **cunnilingus,** or had intercourse (Mosher and Cross, 1971).

In the behavioral phase, it seems clear that emotions influence what people do sexually, how often they do it, and how much they enjoy it.

Orgasm Phase. There are two ways in which emotional responses influence orgasm. First, because of differences in the desire for sex and enjoyment of it, it is not surprising that those who react negatively, at least among females, are likely not to have orgasms at all—to be **frigid** (Kutner, 1971). Second, even when orgasm occurs, it can be experienced either as an intense pleasure or as a source of anxiety, depending on one's general emotional response to sex. Fisher (1972) has reported that women with orgasmic difficulties indicate that they are afraid of letting go and abandoning themselves to a sexual climax; this holding back seems to be based on feelings of anxiety. Males who have problems with impotence or with ejaculation may also experience some of these same negative feelings about orgasm as something frightening, involving a loss of control and a "weakening" of the body.

This general description of sexual behavior in terms of three phases as they operate at three levels is summarized in Table 10-2. We will now examine a variety of factors that influence human sexuality.

EXTERNAL INFLUENCES ON SEXUAL BEHAVIOR

Because there are ethical and legal restrictions attached to every aspect of sexual expression, the investigation of human sexual behavior has frequently been limited to verbal reports about past and present behavior. Except for the highly specialized and sometimes controversial work of Masters and Johnson (1966), there has been very little *direct* study of this very important aspect of human behavior. Most of the research represents a compromise between what investigators are actually interested in learning and what it is feasible to do in our culture at this time. In experiments, for example, sexual arousal is not obtained by having subjects kiss and caress and engage in foreplay—instead, erotic stories and pictures are used as sources of stimulation. It is assumed that arousal to such material is the same as arousal in a real sexual interaction and that the laboratory findings can be generalized to what happens sexually outside of the laboratory.

Erotic Stimuli: Look at What That Couple's Doing Now!

We know that human beings can become sexually stimulated when they read about or see the sexual activities of others. In the same way, hunger can be

TABLE 10-2. *A framework for conceptualizing human sexual behavior in terms of stimulation, behavior, and orgasm at three levels of development: reproduction, learning, and emotions. (Source: Based on Byrne, 1974.)*

	Phases of Human Sexual Behavior		
Levels of Development	Stimulation Phase	Behavioral Phase	Orgasm Phase
Reproduction	Sexual excitement is elicited by a sexual partner.	The sexual act involves contact with the partner which leads to intercourse.	Semen is ejaculated into vagina.
Learning	Through conditioning, other stimuli acquire the power to arouse the individual; imagination and fantasy become powerful cues that elicit arousal.	Individuals learn a wide variety of possible sexual behaviors.	Orgasm for either sex can be brought about in many different ways.
Emotions	Internal and external sexual cues can evoke positive and/or negative feelings.	Any sexual act can evoke positive and/or negative feelings.	Orgasm can evoke positive and/or negative feelings.

aroused by seeing others eat or by looking at a magazine's color photograph of a slice of apple pie. Except for sex, however, viewing or reading about our bodily functions does not seem to be in great demand—do you know of any books or movies that people seek out primarily to make themselves hungry or sleepy or thirsty? There is a great demand for erotica, however, and the production and sale of sexually stimulating material has become a major business in the United States and in several other nations around the world. The Commission on Obscenity and Pornography (1970) estimated that Americans alone spend about $600,000,000 each year on books, magazines, and movies depicting explicit sexual acts. We will examine three questions about this flood of erotica. What sort of material do people find arousing? Why is it arousing? Why do people want to be exposed to erotica?

What Stimuli Are Sexually Arousing? In many of the first sex experiments, it was simply assumed that any photographs or stories with sexual content would be sexually arousing. In more recent research, many investigators have become interested in determining specifically what kinds of erotic material are most and least arousing.

MY PARENTS WOULDN'T DO THAT!

It seems to be generally agreed that the emotions associated with sexuality are sufficiently strong that parents and their offspring find it very difficult to communicate about sexual matters. Though parents often express the idea that they, rather than the schools, should teach their children about sex, few actually do so. Among others, Spanier (1975) has found that parents typically teach little beyond warning their kids about dangerous consequences; most people learn what they know from friends. Why do parents fail to carry out this seemingly important function? Most people would suggest that the problem lies in their being more uptight about sex than their offspring, more conservative about sex, and more emotionally negative toward the topic.

An alternative possibility is proposed by Pocs and Godow (1977) who suggest that the younger generation is just as uptight in communicating to parents about sex as their par-

FIGURE 10-4. *It is difficult for parents and children to communicate about sex. Although the "blame" has frequently been placed on parents because they are seen as uptight, recent research indicates that their offspring are also very uncomfortable in this situation. They do not want even to think of their parents as sexual beings. (Source: Copyright, 1976, G. B. Trudeau / Distributed by Universal Press Syndicate.)*

ents are in communicating to them. In fact, most people don't like to think of their parents as having any interest in sex. The investigators decided to get at this issue by asking a large group of college students to make estimates about several aspects of their parents' sexual activity. How do you think you would respond to such questions?

Their first finding was that students were very negative to the idea of even considering their parents' sexuality. Many refused to answer. Others wrote comments indicating that "this questionnaire stinks" or asked if the experimenters were "perverts." A great many did answer, however, and their estimates of their parents' behavior were compared with the data from survey studies of people the same age as their parents. In every instance, students tended to underestimate the sexuality of their parents. For example, only 33 percent of the females thought

their fathers had engaged in premarital intercourse, whereas about 90 percent of the males of their fathers' generation actually had done so. Only 2 percent of the males thought their mothers had ever engaged in extramarital sex, whereas the survey studies suggest the figure should be about 26 percent.

With respect to their parents' current sex life, the estimates were even more discrepant with reality. About one-fourth of the students felt that their parents never had intercourse or did so less than once a year. In Figure 10-5 are their average estimates of the frequency of intercourse per month along with the comparable survey data of Kinsey and his associates (Kinsey et al., 1948, 1953). (Note, also, that because married couples are actually having intercourse more frequently today than when Kinsey's data were gathered (Hunt, 1974), the students really are underestimating their parents' sex life more than

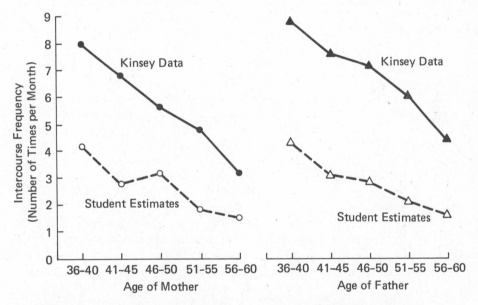

FIGURE 10-5. *When college students were asked to estimate the frequency with which their parents engaged in intercourse, they greatly underestimated. Most individuals seem to think of their parents as relatively uninterested in sex. (Source: Based on data from Pocs and Godow, 1977.)*

these figures suggest.) Another finding with respect to the students' perceptions of their parents was that close to 90 percent thought that their mother and father were in love and happily married. Nevertheless, their love and happiness were seen as having very little to do with sex.

Why should most of us like to think of our parents as relatively nonsexual beings? One possible reason lies in the parent-child relationship. Parents primarily teach negative things about sex (don't masturbate, don't engage in intercourse, don't get pregnant, don't get VD, etc.), so it is not unreasonable for their children to assume that sex must be distasteful and unpleasant to their parents.

The fact that most parents effectively hide their own sexual activities and desires from their offspring is consistent with the idea that they don't like it and don't do it. Beyond that, however, there is probably a more general prejudice against thinking about older people having anything to do with sex. When college students were asked to make a recording in which they read an explicit sexual passage, they felt the most uncomfortable when the prospective audience was a middle-aged person (Miller, Byrne, Fisher, and White, 1976). It is apparently much easier to deal with sexual matters with someone of one's own age group.

One reasonable guess would be that the more explicit and the more varied the depicted behavior, the more arousing it would be to the viewer. Schmidt and Sigusch (1970) have created a series of color movies in which the same two individuals are shown entering a bedroom and then engaging in various sexual acts. What the couple does is different in each movie, so it is possible to determine whether arousal is affected by the specific activity being shown on the screen. When different groups of male subjects viewed each movie, it was found that some themes were more arousing than others. For example, subjects were least aroused by a movie in which the male and female partially undress, caress one another, and pet without reaching orgasm. Most arousing was a movie in which they completely undress, caress, engage in cunnilingus and **fellatio,** have intercourse in various positions, and reach orgasm. Such findings confirm the suggestion that the more explicit and varied the depicted behavior, the more aroused is the viewer.

Because movies are relatively complex and contain many scenes, it is not really possible to specify exactly which elements are arousing and which are not. In order to make that kind of analysis, Miller, Byrne, and Fisher (1976) prepared a set of forty slides made from the Schmidt and Sigusch movies and presented them in various sequences to groups of male and female undergraduates. Because the two sexes responded in much the same way, their arousal ratings were combined, and their responses to eleven of the slides are shown in Figure 10-6. Though it is clear that the greater the degree of nudity the more arousing the slide, the relative eroticism of the various scenes do not seem to fall along any immediately obvious dimension. It is interesting to note, however, that some of the scenes that were rated only moderately arousing (ejaculation on breasts and cunnilingus) were also rated as the most disgusting.

The similar responses of these male and female students may seem surprising. Actually, when the results of different investigations in different

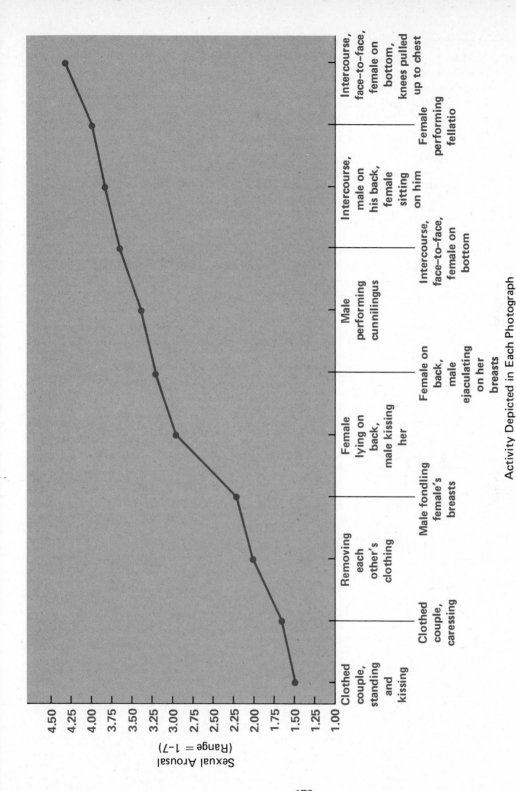

FIGURE 10-6. *When male and female undergraduates were asked to indicate how sexually aroused they felt in response to a series of explicit photographs, the various scenes were rated as shown here. (Source: Based on data from Miller, Byrne, and Fisher, 1976.)*

parts of the world are combined, as shown in Table 10-3, there is considerable agreement about erotica. Both males and females, married and unmarried, Americans and West Germans, are found to be most aroused by pictures of intercourse, petting, and oral sex. The least arousing themes include sadism, individuals of one's own sex, and males engaged in homosexual acts. Though heterosexual subjects are most aroused by seeing males and females interacting sexually, it is found that homosexual males are most aroused by pictures of two males engaged in fellatio and anal intercourse (Abel et al., 1975). It appears, then, that people are most aroused by seeing others engage in sexual acts that they, themselves, would normally experience.

Why Are Erotic Stimuli Sexually Arousing? This may seem to be an obvious and unnecessary question until you try to answer it. It seems that erotic material induces the individual to think about the scene in question. In fantasy, the viewer becomes an imaginary participant in the activity. The feelings of

TABLE 10-3. *In studies conducted with both married and unmarried males and females in the United States and West Germany, there is a surprising amount of agreement about how arousing particular types of erotic photographs are. (Based on data reported by Byrne and Lamberth, 1971; Griffitt, 1973; Levitt and Brady, 1965; Sigusch et al., 1970.)*

MALE SUBJECTS

Most Arousing Themes	Least Arousing Themes
Sexual intercourse in various positions	Female physically hurting male
Genital petting	Male masturbating
Female engaging in oral sex with male: fellatio	Two males engaged in anal intercourse
	Nude male
Male engaging in oral sex with female: cunnilingus	Male in undershorts
Female masturbating	Male engaging in oral sex with male: homosexual fellatio
Group oral sex	
Male caressing female's breast	

FEMALE SUBJECTS

Most Arousing Themes	Least Arousing Themes
Male engaging in oral sex with female: cunnilingus	Male physically hurting female
	Male in undershorts
Sexual intercourse in various positions	Female physically hurting male
Genital petting	Two males engaged in anal intercourse
Male caressing female's breast	Clothed female
	Male engaging in oral sex with male: homosexual fellatio
	Nude female
	Nude male

arousal and the accompanying physiological responses are like those that would occur if the viewer were actually taking part in the scene.

There is some evidence that indicates that individuals are most aroused by seeing activities that they have actually experienced personally. At times, then, an erotic stimulus may elicit memories that add to the effects of imagination. Griffitt (1975) obtained information about the sexual experiences of a group of undergraduates. Based on the data in Figure 10-7, these college students seem relatively representative with respect to the kinds of sexual behavior they have experienced. These same subjects were also shown photographic slides of individuals engaging in each of these activities (the masturbation slide was of someone of their own sex), and they were asked to indicate how arousing each picture was. It was found that the more sexual experience an individual had had, the more arousing the scenes were. For females, there was a striking relationship between experience and arousal. Those who had had intercourse with the male above the female (the traditional "missionary" position) were more aroused by a photograph of such intercourse than those who had not, those who had performed fellatio were more aroused by a fellatio photograph than those who had not, and so forth. Such findings cannot be conclusive evidence that experience causes the reaction to the erotica—perhaps those who find a particular act exciting are the ones who have been motivated to go out and do it. Nevertheless, it seems to be a plausible explanation of why particular themes are arousing to particular people.

Why Do People Expose Themselves to Erotic Stimuli? We know that **pornography** is widely distributed and that such material has been produced throughout recorded history and before. As soon as our ancestors learned to draw, some of the drawings were of sexual acts. In fact, the development of each type of communication from writing to photography to movies to videotape has been quickly followed by the use of each medium to communicate erotica. Why do people in all parts of the world create this material and why do people want to expose themselves to the erotic creations of others? Those who condemn this sort of sexual expression tend to see it as a conspiracy by some outside force. For example, in the Middle Ages erotic images, fantasies, and even dreams were damned as the work of the devil. Currently in the United States, pornography has been condemned as a communist plot to undermine our nation and/or as a Mafia plot to destroy our morals. In the USSR, it has been condemned as a capitalist plot to destroy the morale of the socialist working class. Though it has been disclosed that the CIA made a movie supposedly depicting the president of Indonesia in sexual acts, in an effort to discredit him with his followers, we suspect that most erotica exists not because of plots but because it serves at least two important functions (Byrne, 1977).

One function, strangely enough, is sex education. A great many people report that they first learned the anatomical details of the opposite sex and the intracacies of various sexual acts from reading or viewing erotica. Thus, young people often seek out sexual material because they are curious and are seeking otherwise unavailable information. Beyond the simple facts of sexuality, how-

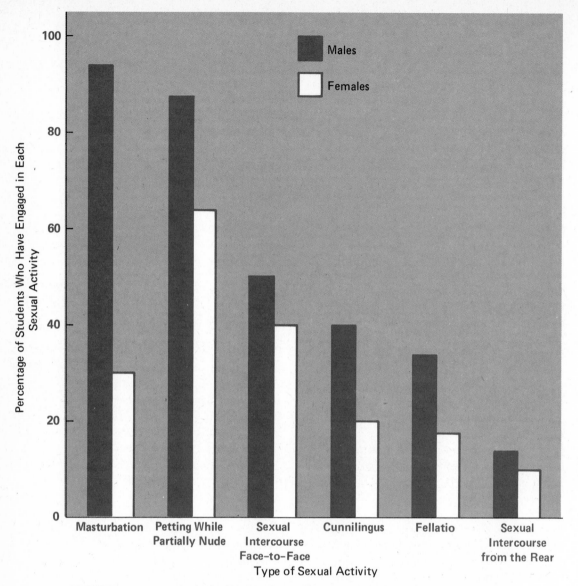

FIGURE 10-7. *A group of college undergraduates was asked to indicate whether or not they had ever engaged in each of six types of sexual activity. When they were shown photographic slides depicting each activity, those who were more experienced were more strongly aroused by the erotic pictures. (Source: Based on data from Griffitt, 1975.)*

ever, this material also provides us with a way to compare ourselves with others. Festinger's (1954) social-comparison theory (see Chapter 6) proposes that we have a need to evaluate our abilities and our opinions in comparison with those of other people. Since sex organs and overt sexual activities do not tend to be displayed in public, it is primarily by means of scientific research and hard-core pornography that anyone is able to make such sexual comparisons. In part, then, people read the Kinsey reports and attend a Linda Lovelace movie for the same reason.

A second function of erotica is to serve as an **aphrodisiac** and to enhance pleasure. Despite the centuries-old legends of various foods and spices and drugs that will cause instant excitement, there is none. The only true aphrodisiac is in the power of human beings to create internal fantasies, and these can be helped along by external fantasies created by others. The power of erotica to induce excitement is used not only by those who want to stir themselves up, but it has also been employed for hundreds of years in attempts to excite others— usually by males attempting to seduce females. For example, Mosher (1971) reports that, in a sample of college males, 16.1 percent said that they had shown pornographic material to females as a seduction technique; 41.5 percent further indicated that it had the desired effect. Besides just the power to arouse, erotic materials provide a way to enhance pleasure during the behavioral and orgasm phases. Research indicates that most people have fantasies while they masturbate (Hunt, 1974) or have intercourse (Hariton and Singer, 1974), and it seems that many of these fantasies are based on erotic scenes and images that are unrelated to their actual life experiences.

Variety Is the Spice of Life (at Least for Males)

Experiments with Animals. In studies of animal behavior, it has long been known that males respond very positively to unfamiliar sexual partners. After males have ejaculated, they tend to be uninterested in further sexual activity. This unresponsiveness, called the *refractory period,* increases in length if there has been more than one **ejaculation** during a sexual encounter (Beach, Westbrook, and Clemens, 1966). In a similar way, after the need for food or for liquid has been satisfied, a satiated animal is temporarily uninterested in eating or drinking.

With sex, however, male behavior can be altered dramatically by the introduction of a new and unfamiliar female partner. The seemingly depleted and satiated male is suddenly and surprisingly eager to engage in renewed sexual activity (Clemens, 1967). Thus, the male is too pooped to be interested in his familiar mate but is hot to trot with someone new. With rats, the mechanism seems to be controlled by the sense of smell. A male rat spends much more time investigating a container that has the odor of a novel female than one which smells of his regular sex partner (Krames, Costanzo, and Carr, 1967).

Female animals show a somewhat different pattern. They, too, tend to lose interest in sex immediately after intercourse, though not as completely as males (Pierce and Nuttall, 1961), and there is little evidence that a novel male has any special appeal. Also, the odor of novel males holds no strong allure for females (Krames, Costanzo, and Carr, 1967). In fact, female rats, if anything, prefer a familiar partner (Law and Gerbrandt, 1967). Not only are females disinterested in novelty, it is found that female dogs will actually refuse to mate with certain males (Beach and LeBouef, 1967). Thus, male animals are found to respond positively to any receptive female, but especially to a new girl in town, while female animals are much more discriminating and show some tendency to prefer a tried and true partner.

Parallels to Human Behavior. How relevant to human sexuality are these findings about sexual novelty among such animals as rats and dogs? The notion of sex differences fits in well with anecdotes and common observations about promiscuous males as opposed to females who wish to form a permanent relationship. Despite changes in sexual attitudes and customs, it is still true that husbands are more likely to engage in extramarital intercourse than are their wives (Hunt, 1974). It is impossible to determine, of course, whether such differences represent basic biological differences in sexual preferences or simply the current realities of a male-dominated culture.

Experimental research on actual sexual behavior is not feasible in seeking the answer, because of the obvious ethical problems in conducting research in which satiated human males are perked up by the presence of a female stranger. There is some indirect evidence provided, however, by studies of mate swapping. A great many couples have indicated that the problem of sexual boredom in the traditional marriage relationship was solved for them by engaging in relatively well-organized **swinging** groups (Denfeld and Gordon, 1970). The number of people who have participated in such activity is unknown. For example, Breedlove and Breedlove (1964) estimate that 8,000,000 couples in the United States have tried mate swapping while Bartell (1971) places the estimate at no more than 1,000,000; a survey of the readers of *Forum* magazine (December, 1975) revealed that one couple out of five had swapped, while Hunt (1974) found that only one couple out of fifty had done so. Whatever the actual numbers, most studies agree on several aspects of mate-swapping behavior. It is almost always the sexually bored husband who initiates the idea and persuades his wife to participate. Observers at such get-togethers report that some aspects of the interactions are consistent with the animal experiments—while spouses at home most often engage in one sexual act and stop, the majority of individuals at a mate-swapping party usually engage in multiple acts to the point of orgasm with more than one partner (O'Neill and O'Neill, 1970). Incidentally, it is also frequently reported that males eventually feel threatened by this activity and talk their wives into giving it up. The threat seems to be based on the fact that many females are able to continue engaging in sexual acts and experiencing repeated orgasms long after their mates are satiated and unable to continue.

There is one type of human experimentation that may provide more direct answers to the question of whether human beings respond as animals do to novel sexual cues, and that is the study of response to erotica. Though only male subjects have been used so far, results suggest that familiar erotic stimuli become progressively less arousing and that the introduction of a novel stimulus leads to renewed excitement (Howard, Reifler, and Liptzin, 1971). Male volunteers were exposed to ninety minutes of pornographic movies, pictures, magazines, and novels each day for ten days. Arousal was measured physiologically by means of urine analysis—it has been found that urinary **acid phosphatase** increases following sexual excitement (Barclay, 1970). As shown in Figure 10-8, the acid-phosphatase level rose sharply on the first day of exposure to the pornography and then gradually dropped during the following days as the same material was seen over and over. Then, on the eleventh day, new erotic stimuli were provided, and the arousal level once again rose. It appears that human males, at least, become sexually bored with familiar erotica but then show renewed arousal in response to novelty. It remains to be seen if responses to actual sexual partners is at all analogous to this and whether or not female subjects respond in a similar fashion.

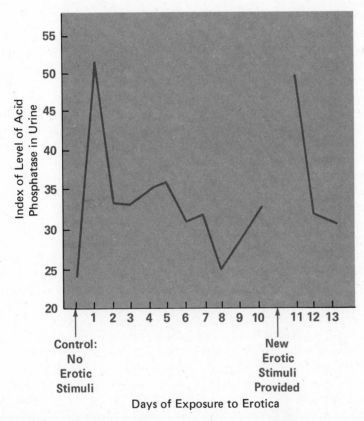

FIGURE 10-8. *When male subjects were exposed to pornography each day for ten days, they showed a large initial increase in the level of acid phosphatase in the urine and then a decline in this index of arousal with repeated exposure to the same stimuli. When novel erotic material was introduced on the eleventh day, acid phosphatase levels again showed a large increase and again declined with repeated exposure. (Source: Adapted from Howard, Reifler, and Liptzin, 1971, p. 117.)*

In discussing the three aspects of sexuality, it was pointed out that the learning ability of human beings results in vast differences among individuals in what is sexually stimulating, in the kind of sexual behavior that occurs, and in the emotional responses attached to various aspects of sex. We will now describe how such differences are associated with identifiable personality variables and with differences between males and females.

Personality Variables: Different Strokes for Different Folks

Sex Guilt. In discussing emotional effects earlier, it was noted that **sex guilt** is associated with less sexual desire, lower frequency of orgasms, and relatively unenjoyable sex. Mosher (1968) defines sex guilt as a general tendency to punish oneself by means of anxiety whenever sexual standards are violated in thought or deed. For example, if a male had been taught that it is unwholesome to become excited while kissing a female, he would feel guilty if he experienced an erection in such a situation or even just thought about the possibility. Thus, sex guilt operates as an internal control device or conscience, as was described in Chapter 8. The only reason that guilt about sexual acts is of special interest is that there are such dramatic variations in what people have learned is right or wrong about sex. Most of us would agree that if a woman feels guilty about her murderous feelings toward her husband, it is fortunate that she has enough guilt to inhibit any overtly aggressive behavior. On the other hand, if she feels guilty about wanting to engage in cunnilingus with her husband, many would conclude that it is unfortunate that she is too anxious to be able to do as she wishes.

Since guilt involves self-punishment, anyone high in guilt might be expected to avoid any thoughts or situations that could possibly lead to guilt arousal. For example, those high in sex guilt were found to have greater difficulty in remembering the details of a lecture on birth control than were low-guilt individuals (Schwartz, 1973). In other research to be described next, the results are also consistent with these expectations.

Guilt and the Perception of Sexual Meanings. One way of getting at thought processes is through the word-association test. For example, if you hear the word "screw," your first thought may be of a small metal device used to fasten things together, or it may be of a common slang word for sexual intercourse. Galbraith and Mosher (1968) proposed that such associations are determined both by the extent to which an individual is sexually aroused and by the extent to which he feels guilty about sex in general.

Male undergraduates were given a sex-guilt test and were then divided into those with high and low scores. Some of each group were then placed in a sexually arousing situation in which they sorted through a series of nude female photographs to select the one who was most sexually appealing, the one most likely to be a **nymphomaniac,** the one most likely to be a prostitute, and so forth.

The remaining subjects were placed in a nonarousing situation. Afterward, all subjects were given a word-association test containing neutral words such as "chair," "tobacco," and "table" mixed in with words having a double meaning such as "nuts," "piece," and "cherry." Whenever a subject's association to one of the latter words indicated that he was responding to the sexual rather than the nonsexual meaning, one point was scored.

As may be seen in Figure 10-9, sexual responses to the word-association test were given more often by sexually aroused than by nonaroused subjects and much more often by low-guilt than by high-guilt individuals in both conditions. Not only were the high-guilt subjects less likely to respond to the sexual meanings of the words, they were even found to be less aware of those meanings

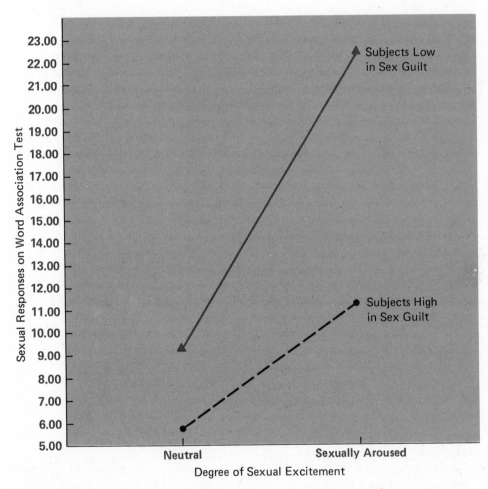

FIGURE 10-9. *The effects of sex guilt and sexual arousal on word-association test responses. Subjects high in sex guilt gave fewer sexual responses to words with double meanings under both neutral and arousing conditions than did low-guilt subjects. (Source: Based on data from Galbraith and Mosher, 1968.)*

than were subjects low in sex guilt. It appears that as sex guilt increases, thoughts of sexual matters decrease.

Sex Guilt and Interest in Sexy Magazines. Since high guilt seems to lead individuals to avoid sexual thoughts, it should also lead them to avoid situations that might arouse sexual thoughts. Schill and Chapin (1972) compared the casual reading habits of high- and low-guilt male college students. When a subject reported for the experiment, he was told that the experimenter was still working with a previous subject. The individual was asked to wait for five minutes in an assistant's office in which there were four magazines piled loosely on the desk; two were sexual in content and two were not. Most subjects picked up a magazine to look at while they waited, and their choices were observed through a one-way mirror. Those low in sex guilt were most likely to choose *Playboy* or *Penthouse* while the high-guilt subjects selected *Outdoor Life* or *Newsweek*. There seems to be a very general tendency to avoid sexual stimuli when sex guilt is high.

Repression and Sexual Avoidance. A measure of individual differences in defense mechanisms yields results very much like those of sex guilt. The **Repression-Sensitization** Scale (Bell and Byrne, 1976) measures an individual's general tendency to avoid and repress anything that evokes anxiety versus the tendency to approach and be overconcerned about the source of anxiety. Subjects with different defenses respond to the sexual meanings on a word-association test in the same way as those who differ in sex guilt. Under both neutral and aroused conditions, the sensitizers who tend to approach threat gave more sexual responses than the repressers who generally avoid anything involving anxiety (Galbraith and Lieberman, 1972).

Sex Differences: Are Females Less Sexual than Males?

Two basic questions have been asked by those investigating sex differences in sexuality. First, do men and women differ in their desire for sex, in how much they are aroused by erotic stimuli, and in their enjoyment of sex? Second, when male-female differences *do* occur, is the explanation to be found in underlying biological differences or in what the two sexes have been taught within a particular culture?

Do the Sexes Differ in Sexual Behavior? To most people, the difference between males and females in sexuality is obvious, and it would seem ridiculous to have to ask such a question. Gordon and Shankweiler (1971) examined the best-selling marriage manuals of the past twenty years and found that the writers of such books uniformly assumed that women are less interested in sex than men; in fact, a major task of a husband is to arouse the wife so that she can at least participate in the sexual act. In a similar vein, but with a different solution, in his syndicated newspaper column physician-psychologist George

Crane frequently states that males need more "sexual calories" than females and that a smart wife will pretend to be an ardent lover—a good actress who serves "boudoir cheesecake" on a regular basis can hold onto her mate. Much of our culture's sexual lore seems to agree that only males are sexually aggressive, easily aroused, and almost insatiably driven by desire. "Male sex response is triggered easily . . . like putting a quarter in a vending machine" (Comfort, 1972, p. 73). In contrast, females are stereotyped as being passive, hard to arouse, and interested in meeting the sexual demands of males only as a way to obtain children or find security. After the male is lured into marriage, of course, sex is supposedly avoided by the female whenever possible by resorting to such excuses as the proverbial headache. There have always been a few females who actually like sex, and we have a great many terms that describe such undesirable individuals—nymphomaniacs, whores, cheap bitches, tramps, round-heels, easy makes, and so forth. Decent women are obviously not like that, thank goodness.

There are several kinds of data consistent with this general picture of sexually disinterested females. We mentioned earlier that females are less likely than males to engage in extramarital sex; the same is true of premarital sex (Hunt, 1974). Males and females are also different in their tendency to seek sexual stimulation in pornography and erotica. For example, the customers of adult book stores and pornographic movie houses are predominantly male (Nawy, 1971). Survey studies have consistently reported male-female differences in how much erotica they have seen and in whether they are aroused by it. Kinsey and his coworkers (1953, p. 662) suggested that it is " . . . likely that most females are indifferent to the existence of such material because it means nothing to them emotionally." Though there have been many changes in society's attitudes about sex since Kinsey's time, males still report more interest in and exposure to erotic pictures, movies, and books than is true for females (Abelson et al., 1971).

Until fairly recently, there was no reason to question this general picture, and then suddenly new information of several types became available. First, the long-accepted psychoanalytic myth of the mature vaginal orgasm versus the immature clitoral orgasm was laid to rest by the work of Masters and Johnson (1966). The only physiological differences between an orgasm brought about by manipulating the clitoris (as in masturbation) and one brought about by penetration of the vagina (as in intercourse) is that most women have a more intense experience by way of clitoral friction. Anatomically, the clitoris is analogous to the head of the penis, with the same type of nerve endings and the same potential for pleasurable sensations. A major implication of such findings is that females can no longer be characterized as helplessly dependent on males for bringing them the gift of an orgasmic experience; rather, the two sexes seem to be very much alike in their ability to enjoy themselves sexually. Even the subjective experience of orgasm seems to be similar in the two sexes. Vance and Wagner (1976) asked college students to describe what an orgasm felt like. These descriptions were then given to medical students, gynecologists, and clinical psychologists who were asked to guess the sex of the person who wrote

Males are the primary customers of adult book stores and pornographic movies, but experimental research suggests that females are equally responsive to erotica. (Photo: Phil Carver & Friends.)

each one—their guesses were at the chance level; males and females describe the experience in the same way!

Second, as the women's liberation movement in its various forms began to raise the consciousness of many females, attitudes about the role of women in our society began to change. Except in *The Stepford Wives* (Levin, 1972), in which mindless female robots catered to their husbands' wishes, few women today can still accept the notion that they should passively serve men rather than express desires of their own (Masters and Johnson, 1974). In addition, the finding that women are capable of engaging in sustained sexual activity and of having multiple orgasms added new elements to the image of female sexuality. The tables were now turned—for the first time, men were described as frail sexual performers who could ordinarily achieve only one or sometimes two orgasms per session, while females were described as sexual superwomen with an almost unlimited ability to engage in repeated sexual acts and, furthermore, to enjoy them with gusto.

The third type of information was that new patterns of behavior are emerging in which males and females are becoming less and less different sexually. While males are becoming even more permissive and more sexually active than previously (Finger, 1975), similar changes among females are occurring at a much more rapid rate (Curran, 1976). For example, sex differences have been noted in that females historically were less likely than males to engage in premarital intercourse. That pattern is changing, however, for younger females in our society. As you can see in Figure 10-10, the gap between male and female premarital sexual activity has been steadily growing smaller (Hunt, 1974). In a much less dramatic way, a similar trend is occurring for extramarital sex. Such changes across generations sometimes make it difficult for parents to communicate with their offspring (as in Figure 10-11). One possible reason for the change, of course, is that the availability of effective contraceptives makes it feasible for females to satisfy their sexual needs without the fear of pregnancy. It seems quite possible that male-female differences in sexual behavior will disappear entirely, at least in the highly developed industrialized nations.

The fourth source of new information came when experimenters began for the first time in the early 1970's to use female subjects in studies of response to erotica. Several such experiments have been noted in this chapter, and it has repeatedly been found that males and females are remarkably similar in responding with sexual excitement to erotic stimuli. In one of these experiments (Schmidt and Sigusch, 1970), male and female students looked at erotic movies and photographic slides and then answered questions about their physiological responses to this material. Figure 10-12 indicates that most individuals, regardless of their sex, reported some physiological reaction. Most males said that they had an erection, while most females reported some genital sensations such as a feeling of warmth. Over a fourth of each sex also reported the emission of genital lubricating fluids. This and other research suggests that there are striking similarities between males and females in responding to sexual cues.

How can we resolve the contradictions between what has been "known" for centuries about female sexuality and the most recent data which stress a very different picture? We will briefly look at some possible explanations.

Why Should There Be Any Sex Differences? Studies of animals indicate that there is a biological basis for minor differences between the sexes but not for extreme differences. For example, there are data indicating that female animals have strong sex drives; they will learn a response that is reinforced by sexual intercourse, and they will risk leaving a safe place when mating is offered as a reward (Bermant, 1961; Pierce and Nuttall, 1961). There are two primary differences between male and female animals in sexuality and these have been mentioned previously. Female sexual needs tend to vary periodically as regulated by their hormonal state while most male mammals tend to remain more or less constantly ready; the other difference is that females are more discriminating than males and do not show a preference for novel mates.

If human females have a strong sex drive, can have multiple orgasms, and are as aroused by sexual cues as males, how is it that females have been less sexually motivated than males? The obvious answer is that the differences have been learned. For example, girls are much more likely than boys to be taught

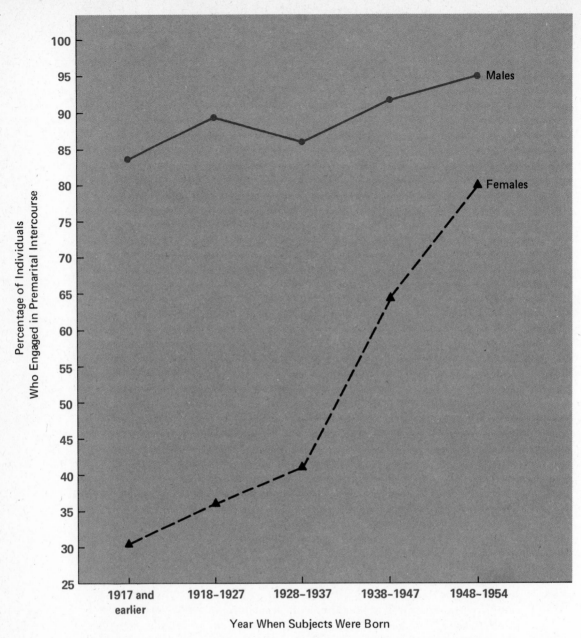

FIGURE 10-10. *The sexual behavior of males and females in the United States is becoming increasingly similar. Each decade there has been an increase in premarital sex among females, so that now they are almost as likely as males to engage in intercourse prior to marriage. (Source: Based on data from Hunt, 1974.)*

that sex is a source of danger, that they should avoid sexual excitement in a dating situation so they won't get carried away by lust, and that nice girls aren't interested in dirty books and dirty pictures. Our society does not have "dirty old women" visiting the adult bookstores and theaters because most women have been taught that it is not acceptable to do such things. The next question is *why* has female sexuality been suppressed? No one can answer that question with certainty, but one possibility is that males have utilized sex as a way of dominating females. If women actually enjoy sex, they may not keep themselves in an "undamaged" condition prior to marriage, they may not be faithful to their husbands, and they may even become pregnant by other men, which, among other things, would add confusion about inheritances. There is some evidence that men sometimes fear female sexuality, and there are a number of African and Middle Eastern cultures in which the clitoris of all females was traditionally removed at puberty in order to prevent them from having sexual pleasure. Among the Somali, an even more selfish masculine motive was involved in the clitoral operation; it was felt that a female who had no interest in sex would be better able to concentrate on pleasing the male. Whatever the explanation for such practices, there is obviously no justifiable reason for suppressing female sexual expression.

For anyone who believes that males and females have inborn differences in

"Of course we're delighted to have you bring home a
college friend for the holidays, dear—we just feel
Mr. Brenner would be more comfortable in a room of his own."

FIGURE 10-11. *Sexual attitudes and sexual behavior have been rapidly changing for the past several decades, especially for females. These changes sometimes make it difficult to communicate across the "generation gap." (Source: Reproduced by special permission of PLAYBOY Magazine; copyright © 1968 by Playboy.)*

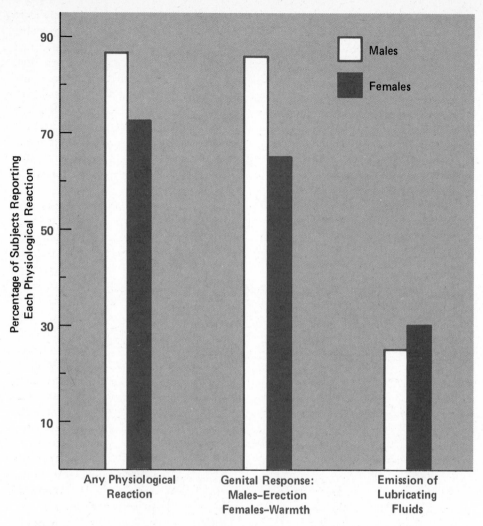

FIGURE 10-12. *When male and female students were shown erotic movies and slides, most individuals of each sex reported having physiological reactions. Such experiments suggest that the sexes are quite similar in responding to erotica. (Source: Based on data from Schmidt and Sigusch, 1970.)*

sexual needs, anthropologists have had contrary evidence for some decades now. In 1935, Margaret Mead described marked differences among various primitive groups in their sexual behavior. In some tribes, neither males nor females seemed to be terribly interested in sex while in others both men and women pursued such goals aggressively. In some tribes the male and female roles were very much like our own, while in the Tchambuli tribe the roles were reversed; the woman was the dominant sexual partner, and the man was passive and emotionally dependent. Over the past several decades, anthropological studies continue to reveal that male and female behavior can vary tremendously from culture to culture (Marshall and Suggs, 1971). Other evidence is provided by the work of those who have done extensive research with the relatively rare individuals who have been raised as members of one sex even though their genetic characteristics and sexual glands were of the opposite sex (Money and Ehrhardt, 1972). For example, a male infant's penis was accidentally destroyed during a minor operation, and it was decided to raise him as a girl. Individuals like this who are raised as females adopt a typically female orientation, appearance, and behavior while females raised as males are clearly masculine in their characteristics. Thus, cultural influences seem to be powerful determinants of what we often have assumed to be "basic differences between the sexes."

Sex Differences? Love, Exploitation, Female Dominance, Rape, and Masturbation. The fact that males and females are much more alike sexually than most people have believed does *not* mean that they are *identical*. For example, even when there is the same degree of arousal in response to erotic stimuli, females often express more negative feelings than males, perhaps because females tend to receive more negative warnings than males do about the dangers of sex and sexual excitement. How else might the sexes differ?

In legal battles, there is usually an attempt to distinguish hard-core pornography from erotic literature. It is said that there is no real character development in pornography, only ever-ready bodies panting from one orgasm to the next. It also used to be assumed that pornography was exciting only to males and that females could be aroused, if at all, only by stories containing affection and a loving relationship (Kinsey et al., 1953). The first real test of this long-accepted assumption was in an experiment by Schmidt, Sigusch, and Schäfer (1973). Two parallel stories were created. In each, the sexual activities of a young couple were described—petting, foreplay, oral sex, and intercourse in a variety of positions. One story blatantly described what they did in the style and language of hard-core pornography. In the other story, affection was expressed, and it was made clear that the two individuals were real people who had a tender, loving relationship. College students read one or the other story and then indicated their degree of sexual arousal. It was found that both stories were equally arousing and that males and females did not differ in their reactions. It appears that the distinction between the two types of erotic writing is not a particularly meaningful one and that the idea of sex differences in response to love versus lust is not an accurate one.

Occasionally, sex differences are reported, as when Izard and Caplan (1974) asked undergraduates to read one chapter out of *Eternal Fire* by Calder Willingham and found that males were more sexually aroused than females and had more positive emotional reactions as well. One problem with such findings was pointed out by Herrell (1975) who suggested that the content of the chapter might be responsible for the sex differences. In fact, the episode dealt with the seduction of a virgin girl by a sexually experienced young man, and it seemed possible that females were being turned off by the theme of sexual exploitation rather than by the erotic content. So, Herrell repeated the study and added a condition in which other subjects read a positive sexual scene from *Lady Chatterly's Lover* in which the two participants enjoyed the experience to an equal degree. Males were again found to be more aroused by the selection from *Eternal Fire* than were females, but with *Lady Chatterly* the sex differences disappeared. Such findings suggest that while males and females respond to erotica in a generally similar way, the specific theme of the sexual material might be crucial in determining whether sex differences occur.

A topic about which there has been much discussion and little research is the meaning to each sex of the position assumed in intercourse. Traditionally in our culture, the male plays a dominant and active role in intercourse while the female plays a submissive and relatively passive role. Among the various possible intercourse positions, nevertheless, are some in which the male lies passively on his back while the female places herself above him and assumes the active and thus dominant role. It has been asserted from time to time that males tend to feel threatened by this reversal of positions. To examine possible male-female differences in such reactions, Allgeier (1976) exposed undergraduates to sexually explicit photographic slides and asked them to evaluate the man and woman in the photographs. Half of the subjects saw a couple engaging in intercourse with the man in the dominant role either above the woman or entering her from the rear. The other half saw the same couple but with the woman in the dominant role, sitting and lying on her reclining partner. Surprisingly, the male subjects rated the couple in a similar way regardless of position, though they were somewhat more positive if the woman was dominant. Female subjects, however, responded *negatively* when the woman was above the man. They evaluated such a sexually dominant female as less clean, respectable, moral, good, and as less desirable as a wife and mother; also, they rated the submissive man as less clean, respectable, moral, and masculine. These negative reactions by females were equally true for traditional and nontraditional individuals in terms of their own sex role identification. Whether these striking sex differences in responding to photographic depictions of intercourse are related to evaluations of personal sexual experience in real life remains to be determined.

One topic that might be expected to have different effects on the two sexes is rape. Schmidt (1975) presented subjects with a movie depicting a girl being raped by a group of men. Such a movie might be especially negative to women because rape is the ultimate sexual exploitation and degradation. On the other hand, rape fantasies are commonly utilized by both sexes as a means of becoming excited; also, some studies have found that aggression can be a stimulus to sexual feelings (Barclay, 1971). As it turns out, males and females were both quite aroused by the rape movie; in addition, there were some accompanying negative feelings—helplessness in females and guilt in males (Schmidt, 1975). Both sexes expressed anxiety and anger after viewing the depicted rape.

Response to masturbation was also studied by Schmidt (1975), and males and females saw a film and slides that either depicted a male or a female masturbating to orgasm. This is an interesting stimulus because masturbation is an especially taboo topic for most people and because the sight of another person engaged in this behavior is not a common experience. How do you think the two sexes would respond? As shown in Figure 10-13, both males and females were aroused by seeing a person of the opposite sex masturbate. It was less arousing to see someone of their own sex, but this was more so for males than females. Not only were males not aroused by seeing a male masturbate, they also expressed very negative feelings about the experience. The sex difference in response to same-sex masturbation was attributed to the arousal of homosexual anxieties among males and/or to the greater freedom females have in expressing bisexual tendencies. Females, for example, find it more socially acceptable to hold hands, embrace, or kiss one another in our culture than is true for males. Mosher and Abramson (1977) reported very similar findings with respect to male-female differences. They also administered a test that measures attitudes toward masturbation; both males and females who feel most negatively about

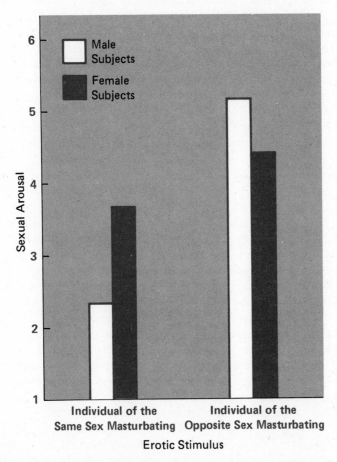

FIGURE 10-13. *When males and females viewed films and slides of an individual masturbating, both sexes were most aroused when viewing an opposite-sex individual. When the masturbator was of the same sex, males were much less aroused than females. (Source: Based on data from Schmidt, 1975.)*

this practice report the most disgust, guilt, shame, and anger after viewing someone of their own sex masturbating in a movie.

In general, then, there are a few sex differences in responding to erotica with respect to specific sexual themes. While love and affection are irrelevant factors to both sexes, females are less aroused by a theme of sexual exploitation, females respond more negatively to a sexually dominant female, males are less aroused by seeing someone of their own sex masturbate, and both sexes are aroused by rape but with somewhat different negative emotions accompanying the arousal.

THE EFFECTS OF EROTIC STIMULATION

One of the greatest sources of concern about erotica has to do with the effect of such material on what people do. The censorship laws are usually based on the idea that erotica has harmful effects—especially on young people—and that society should protect itself against these effects. The underlying assumption seems to be that exposure to any kind of erotic stimulus leads to a change in behavior. Interestingly, though most of the subjects in a large nationwide sample expressed the opinion that explicit sexual movies should not be made available to anyone, regardless of age, most of these same individuals had themselves been exposed to such explicit erotica—presumably with no ill effects (Wilson and Abelson, 1973). The most lurid fear is that sexual stimulation excites the imagination, arouses uncontrollable sexual urges, and precipitates violent sexual crimes such as rape. If this were found to be true, even the most enthusiastic champions of free speech would be likely to agree that censorship of pornography was a necessity. A less dramatic possibility is that erotic presentations increase the general level of sexual excitement and hence induce viewers to engage more frequently in ordinary sexual activity. If this were found to be true, reactions to such an effect would depend on questions of moral values and one's evaluation of the possible consequences such as increased masturbation as well as a greater incidence of premarital, marital, and extramarital sex.

It should be noted that arguments about pornography or sex education are not likely to be resolved by research. Attitudes about erotica are firmly entrenched and seem to be based on the kind of learned emotional responses that are associated with sex. For some, erotica would be a source of personal pleasure even if it were shown to have negative consequences for other individuals. Others would favor legal restrictions even if erotica were shown to have no harmful effects (Wallace, 1973). Knowledge about the nature of such effects would seem to be necessary, however, if decisions about pornography are ever to be based on intellectual rather than emotional grounds.

Sexual Arousal

We have already indicated that when subjects read or view erotic material, they describe themselves as being sexually aroused. It was noted that this effect is

Public concern about pornography is based on fears about the effects of such material on behavior, especially for young people. Only by means of research can we determine whether sexual stimulation brings about "uncontrollable" sexual desires. (Photo by Daniel S. Brody; Stock, Boston.)

revealed by self-ratings, by descriptions of a person's own physiological responses, and by physiological measures such as changes in urinary acid phosphatase and changes in penis size. We will now examine the direct physiological measures more closely.

The Physiological Response of Males. The most direct approach to measuring the response of males to erotic stimuli involves a device that is attached to the penis to detect changes in volume or in circumference. Freund, Sedlacek, and Knob (1965) first reported the use of this **penile plethysmograph** which provides a sensitive measure of the male's response to sexual stimulation. Several versions of such instruments have been used in research.

In one experiment, this device was used to compare the effects of a pornographic movie on males who had and had not been exposed to a great deal of pornography prior to seeing this particular erotic film (Howard, Reifler, and Liptzin, 1971). Some of the subjects had been exposed to pornography for an hour and a half each day for fifteen days while a control group had not had this experience. Each individual was then shown an erotic movie while a penile plethysmograph recorded any changes in his penis size. As shown in Figure 10-14, both groups had a rapid erection response when the movie began, there

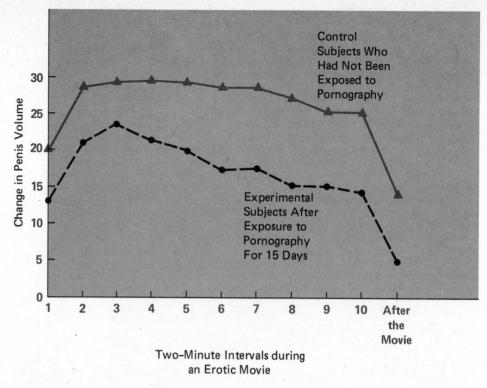

FIGURE 10-14. *Male subjects responded to an erotic movie with an increase in penis volume, and their erections decreased when the movie was over. Subjects who had been exposed to pornography each day for fifteen days showed less of a sexual response to the movie than subjects who had not had this experience. (Source: Adapted from Howard, Reifler, and Liptzin, 1971.)*

was a gradual decline in excitement as the movie progressed, and both groups returned toward a normal state after the movie ended. You might also note that those who had been exposed to several days of pornography were less aroused throughout the film than were the control subjects. The difference between the two groups suggests that a sexual response to erotic stimuli is dampened by repeated exposure to such material.

Another experiment which used the penile plethysmograph provides interesting data as to the role of imagination in responding to an erotic stimulus (Geer and Fuhr, 1976). It was suggested earlier that erotica is presumably arousing because it stimulates fantasies and that individuals probably imagine themselves as participants in the activity. These experimenters decided to test this general proposition by means of a procedure that makes it difficult to pay attention and think about a stimulus. It was hypothesized that as such interference increased, the sexual response to an erotic stimulus should decrease. The instrument to measure arousal was attached to each subject's penis, and (through a headset attached to one ear) they listened to an erotic tape with a woman's voice describing a sexual experience with explicit descriptions of sex play, oral-genital sex, and intercourse. Four different conditions were created to produce increasing degrees of interference with attention and fantasy. In the other ear, all subjects heard a random number spoken every three seconds. One group just listened to the erotic tape and were free to ignore the numbers. A second group had to write the numbers down as they were spoken. The third group had to add each successive pair of numbers. The fourth group with the most complex task had to consider each pair and classify it as above or below fifty, odd or even. The results are shown in Figure 10-15, and they are an impressive indication of the way in which alternate thought processes can interfere with the effect of erotica

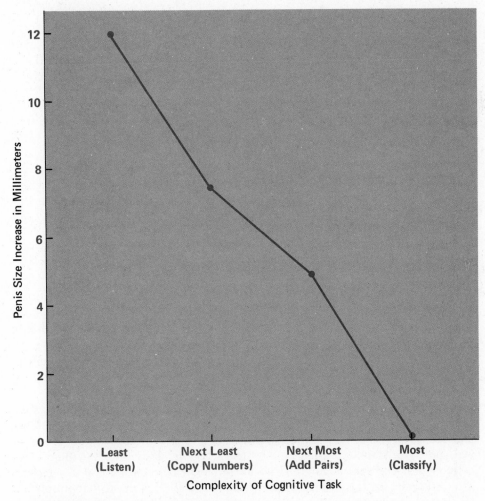

FIGURE 10-15. *Male subjects listened to an erotic story while carrying out one of four types of increasingly complex cognitive tasks. The more complex the task, the less aroused they were (as measured by a penile plethysmograph). (Source: Adapted from Geer and Fuhr, 1976.)*

on arousal. It can be seen that the group with the most difficult cognitive task was not aroused at all by the story. This is the clearest demonstration yet of the role played by thought processes when individuals are exposed to an erotic stimulus. It also suggests the way that an individual's thoughts and worries might interfere with a sexual response in intercourse.

The Physiological Response of Females. The female's sexual response is not as overtly obvious and easy to measure as that of the male, but several means have been developed to solve the problem. For example, Jovanovic (1971) devised a balloon-like instrument which detects vaginal contractions; he also has recorded changes in the temperature of the clitoris during sexual excitement.

Geer (1975) noted that the work of Masters and Johnson indicates that there is a markedly increased flow of blood in the genitals of both sexes when they are aroused. It makes sense, then, to utilize this fact in attempting to measure sexual excitement in females. An instrument, the **vaginal plethysmograph**, has been developed that uses reflected and diffused light as a way to detect vaginal blood volume (Sintchak and Geer, 1976). This is a vaginal probe made of clear acrylic, and it is the shape and size of a menstrual tampon. Imbedded in the acrylic is a light source and light sensing device. The amount of blood in the walls of the vagina affects the amount of light that is reflected and hence provides an indication of sexual excitement.

Research with this device has shown that it is a very sensitive measure of arousal in females. For example, undergraduates were shown a nonsexual film about the crusades and an explicit erotic movie; the vaginal plethysmograph clearly revealed vaginal responses during the erotic movie (Geer, Morokoff, and Greenwood, 1974). In another study, female students volunteered to masturbate while their responses were monitored by this instrument (Geer and Quartararo, 1976). The plethysmograph detected the excitement associated with masturbation and also revealed a dramatic decrease in blood volume when orgasm occurred. It should be noted, by the way, that this type of research is conducted in such a way as to minimize any embarrassment to the participants. All subjects are fully informed volunteers. They insert the measuring device themselves and are in a room alone during the experiment and in contact with the experimenter only through earphones.

These studies of female physiological responses are consistent with previous findings which suggest the similarity of males and females in their sexual responses. Experiments with both sexes indicate that the physiological responses to erotic stimuli are the same as the physiological responses to a sexual partner. Our bodies respond to depictions of erotic sexual activities in the same way as in the stimulation phase of a sexual interaction. The next question is whether this excitement induces individuals to engage in overt sexual acts.

Overt Behavior Following Exposure to Erotica

As we have seen, erotic stimulation initiates a series of bodily responses that would ordinarily lead the individual to engage in a sexual act and to have an orgasm. Except in those private instances where such stimuli are used to enhance the pleasures of masturbation or intercourse, the arousal caused by erotica cannot ordinarily be satisfied. That is, if you read an erotic magazine in a barber shop or a beauty parlor and become aroused, you must necessarily inhibit or postpone any tendency to engage in the physically appropriate behavior. What are the consequences of such exposure and such increases in arousal level? Opinions from politicians, ministers, columnists, and citizens' groups about possible consequences are extremely negative and stress the multiple dangers that might be caused by unrestrained erotica. Even among college students, a 1972 *Playboy* poll indicated that over half the respondents felt that pornography was harmful to society. At this point, facts would seem to be needed more than opinions.

Sex Crimes. Is it possible that some individuals are impelled by exposure to pornography to engage in sexual crimes? You will remember our discussion in Chapter 9 of the link between sexual arousal and aggression. Can the level of unsatisfied sexual arousal reach a point at which the individual is compelled to commit rape, peep into windows, expose himself in the park, or whatever? These are difficult questions to answer conclusively, but there are two types of data that are relevant.

Studies of convicted sex criminals have been conducted in an effort to find out whether they, in fact, have had an unusual amount of contact with pornography. Occasionally, a newspaper headline announces that an arrested rapist was found to have a collection of erotic magazines in his room, and it is implied or even stated that the magazines are responsible for the sexual activities. Since some policemen, newspaper reporters, and bank clerks also read erotic magazines, it is important to determine whether rapists differ from nonrapists in the extent of their contact with erotica. It has been found, strangely enough, that sex offenders have *less* contact with erotica during adolescence than do nonoffenders (Goldstein, Kant, and Hartman, 1974). Moreover, there is evidence that the early family experiences of offenders include restrictiveness and repression with respect to sexual matters. Those who commit sexual crimes have heard less, seen less, read less, and talked less about sex than comparable individuals who do not commit such crimes. For example, one study found that by the time the average male is fourteen years old, he has seen a picture of a couple engaged in intercourse; for the future sex offender, the average age for first seeing this kind of picture is eighteen (Eysenck, 1972).

The fact that sex criminals do not appear to have excessive experience with erotica does not necessarily prove that there is no connection. It is conceivable that some individuals are so weak that even a small amount of stimulation provokes them to engage in offensive acts. If this were true, it might be argued that without the protection provided by antipornography laws and censorship, a few people in every community might be overwhelmed by sexual urges as a result of such exposure. An interesting kind of "experiment" dealing with the effects of unrestrained pornography has been provided by the decision in Denmark in the 1960s to allow all forms of explicit sexual material to be sold. If erotic stimulation leads to sex crime in even a small percentage of the population, we could expect a dramatic increase in Danish sex offenses once the citizens were freely exposed to hard-core pornography in magazines, books, movies, and live sex shows on stage. Instead, sex crimes decreased dramatically, and this decline has continued in the succeeding years. All classes of sex crimes occurred less frequently, including rape, Peeping Tom activity, and homosexual offenses (Commission on Obscenity and Pornography, 1970). Various types of data analyses led a Danish investigator, Berl Kutchinsky (1973), to conclude that for one type of offense—child molestation—a marked decrease was directly attributable to the availability of hard-core pornography; the number of crimes dropped from 220 cases annually to 87. While no one can legitimately argue that all the facts are known, the available evidence leads to the conclusion that erotic stimulation does not cause sex crimes and, in fact, an increase in the availability of erotica might have precisely the opposite effect.

Increased Sexual Activity. The other major concern with behavioral effects involves the possibility of a general increase in the frequency of sexual acts, including behavior that many in the community would consider immoral. Two considerations make it seem logical to expect that exposure to erotica would increase both the amount and the range of sexual behavior. First, it has been shown that such material is sexually arousing. With a higher level of sexual motivation, we might expect a greater amount of sexual activity. Second, as we have discussed in Chapter 7, individuals often tend to imitate or model the behavior of others. If, for example, movies freely depict themes of premarital intercourse, group sex, and oral sex, movie patrons might be inclined to adopt these patterns of behavior whenever the opportunity arises. The possibility that the incidence of such sexual acts would be increased by the presence of public erotica can be seen as a welcome move toward a freer society or as the final decadent stage of our nation's moral collapse, depending on one's point of view. To some degree such changes *are* occurring, though of course, we do not know the reason for sure; young people especially are expressing a more permissive sexual ideology in the United States (Hunt, 1974), in Canada (Hobart, 1972), and in Europe (Schmidt and Sigusch, 1972).

While research cannot answer moral questions as to the goodness or badness of more permissive sexual standards, it can determine whether erotic stimuli actually do have any effect on such behavior. In correlational research, it has been found that males who report having been exposed to a considerable amount of pornography before age 14 also report such adult sexual experiences as group sex, sex without love, homosexuality, and a high frequency of heterosexual intercourse (Davis and Braucht, 1973). The existence of such relationships cannot, of course, establish cause and effect in that pornography may have been responsible for such later sexual patterns, or highly sexed individuals may simply be strongly motivated to seek out pornography in their youth. Thus, experimentation is needed in order to determine whether behavior actually changes as a function of exposure to erotic stimulation.

The typical experimental approach has been to determine specific details about the sexual behavior of subjects (sometimes married, sometimes single), present them with erotic material, and then at a later time (twenty-four hours, two days, a week) ask them again about their sexual behavior. Comparisons are then made between the preexperimental and postexperimental behavior. Any changes are attributed to the effects of the erotic presentations. Sometimes a comparison is made with a control group that was given nonerotic material. There have been at least a dozen such experiments, and the results are somewhat surprising. In general, exposure to erotica is found to have very little effect on overt behavior, and any increases in sexual activity seem to involve only behavior that was already part of the individual's sexual pattern.

In one experiment, when married males were shown erotic slides, 56 percent reported having sexual relations with their wives that evening; in a control group that had seen slides of geometric forms, only 24 percent reported having intercourse that night. In addition, the more arousal reported by an individual in the experimental group, the more likely he was to have coitus (Cattell, Kawash, and De Young, 1972). With a group of Canadian undergraduate males, the only significant behavioral change after seeing erotic slides was an increase in the frequency of masturbation (Amoroso et al., 1971). Married students in Denmark reported more intercourse after exposure to pornographic films, magazines, and an audio presentation of an erotic story (Kutschinsky, 1971). When such behavior is studied over a period of time, it seems that the effects of erotic stimulation are specific and limited. For example, Mann et al. (1974) showed either erotic or nonerotic films to married couples for four weeks and obtained daily reports of their sexual behavior during this time and also for the following four weeks; those who saw the erotic films reported greater sexual activity on the night they saw the film, but there was no general increase in sexual behavior on the other nights. Also, in successive weeks there was a decline in the effect of the erotic movies. It appears that any fears (or hopes) that concentrated presentations of pornography are likely to instigate unrestrained sexual expression seem to be unfounded.

Interpersonal Behavior. You might expect individuals in a social setting to react differently to members of the opposite sex partly as a function of their level of sexual arousal. In a study supposedly dealing with blind dates, sexually aroused males tended to rate females as more physically attractive and as more sexually receptive than did nonaroused males (Stephan, Berscheid, and Walster, 1971). The aroused males felt that the prospective date was amorous, immoral, willing, promiscuous, and uninhibited—it seems possible that a male with those perceptions of a female would behave differently on a date than one who was not sexually aroused.

Sometimes arousal leads to an avoidance of relevant interpersonal situations. For example, Brehm and Behar (1966) found that aroused students were inclined to avoid members of the opposite sex and approach someone of their own sex. Moreover, there are individual differences in such social effects. Subjects who were shown erotic slides and then reacted with positive emotions afterward were found to spend more time looking at a member of the opposite sex and to sit closer to such an individual; aroused subjects who had a negative emotional reaction to the slides tended not to approach the opposite sex by gazing or sitting close (Griffitt, May, and Veitch, 1974).

Individual Differences: Eroticaphobes and Eroticaphiles. The effects of erotic stimuli on sexual behavior might be quite different for different individuals. In one experiment, it was decided to examine those who differ in their emotional responses to sex and to determine whether the generally prosex and the generally antisex individuals differ in how they are influenced by erotic stimuli. Undergraduate males and females were given a series of questionnaires dealing with their sexual attitudes, family background, and sexual behavior (Fisher and Byrne, 1976). They were then shown an erotic movie in which a male and female undress, play with one another's genitals, and then engage in cunnilingus and fellatio until each has an orgasm. The subjects were divided into those who responded to the movie with negative feelings **(eroticaphobes)** and those who responded positively **(eroticaphiles).** Both groups were equally aroused by the film, but they differed in how it affected their subsequent behavior. Unexpectedly, a comparison of their sexual behavior just before the experiment and during the two days afterward revealed that only the eroticaphobes showed an increase in sexual behavior! Though the eroticaphiles behaved in the same way before and after the movie experience, male and female subjects who were most negative about sex reported an increase in heterosexual activity—including petting, oral sex, and intercourse. After seeing the movie, the eroticaphobes became as sexually active as the eroticaphiles had been *before* they saw the movie. Interestingly enough, there were no effects on masturbation or on such fantasy activities as thinking or dreaming about sex.

In an attempt to learn more about these prosex individuals who are not affected by pornography and the antisex ones who are, the questionnaire responses of these two groups were compared. As you might guess, eroticaphobes are higher in sex guilt than eroticaphiles. You can see in Table 10-4 that they are also quite different in their background experiences, in their feelings about the film they had seen, and in their general attitudes about sex. Such differences suggest that the eroticaphobes increased their sexual activity following the movie because they were not experienced with respect to dealing with sexually explicit material and their own resulting excitement. Subsequent research has replicated these general findings and provided a possible explanation for such differences among individuals (Fisher, 1976). Though both types of viewers were equally aroused by an erotic movie, eroticaphobes denied that the film would affect their sexual desires or sexual behavior while eroticaphiles did not; it is conceivable that an inability to recognize one's own needs results in less control over their expression in subsequent interactions.

One of the ironic aspects of such findings is that those individuals who are most negative to sexuality and most alarmed about the effects of pornography are the ones who are most likely to be influenced by it.

TABLE 10-4. *Individuals who were most negative to an erotic movie (eroticaphobes) were found to increase their sexual activity following the movie while those who were most positive (eroticaphiles) showed no behavioral effects. Analysis of questionnaire responses revealed many differences between these two types of people in their background experiences, their reactions to the film, and in their general attitudes toward sex. (Source: Adapted from Fisher and Byrne, 1976.)*

	Eroticaphobes	Eroticaphiles
Differences in Background Factors	Rarely heard sex discussed at home	Heard sex discussed at home
	Rate sex knowledge as inadequate	Rate sex knowledge as adequate
	Rate selves as sexually and politically conservative	Rate selves as sexually and politically liberal
	Attend church frequently	Attend church infrequently
	Have had fewer premarital sex partners	Have had more premarital sex partners
	Intercourse occurs infrequently	Intercourse occurs frequently

	Eroticaphobes	Eroticaphiles
Differences in Response To Film	Negative feelings aroused	Negative feelings not aroused
	Actors rated as abnormal and immoral	Actors rated as normal and moral
	Believe such films should be banned	Believe such films should not be banned
	Unwilling to volunteer for another experiment of this type	Willing to volunteer for another experiment of this type

	Eroticaphobes	Eroticaphiles
Differences in General Attitudes about Sex	Premarital sex is bad	Premarital sex is good
	Sex must be linked with love	Sex not necessarily linked with love
	Sex rated as unimportant aspect of their lives	Sex rated as important aspect of their lives
	Dislike oral sex	Like oral sex
	Believe the law should regulate sexual behavior	Believe the law should not regulate sexual behavior
	Disapprove of erotica and believe it is harmful	Approve of erotica and believe it is not harmful
	Disapprove of college health clinics dispensing contraceptive devices	Approve of college health clinics dispensing contraceptive devices
	Disapprove of abortion	Approve of abortion

SUMMARY

Research on human sexual behavior deals with the special problems involved in expressing this biological need as compared with the expression of other needs such as hunger.

A theoretical framework was suggested as a way to conceptualize the research on sexuality. Three phases of sexual expression (stimulation, behavior, and orgasm) were considered with respect to reproduction, learning, and emotions. In the simple reproductive process, stimulation is a joint function of internal cues regulated by hormones and external cues associated with a member of the opposite sex. The male and female engage in a few preliminary interactions and then intercourse begins, culminating in orgasm as the male ejaculates in the female's vagina. With our intellectual ability, human beings can learn to be stimulated by many different stimuli: including imaginative fantasies, to engage in many kinds of sexual behavior besides simple intercourse, and to have orgasms that need not involve depositing semen in a vagina. As our ancestors discovered the relationship between intercourse and reproduction and as complex societies developed, many rules, taboos, laws, moral restrictions, and customs developed as ways to regulate sexual acts. One result is that negative emotions often become attached to each phase of sexuality. Partly as a function of these strong feelings, parents and their offspring often find it difficult or impossible to communicate with one another about sex.

Much of the research on human sexuality has utilized erotic stimuli to create arousal. Heterosexual individuals are most aroused by themes of intercourse, petting, and oral sex; in general, people are most aroused by seeing others engage in sexual acts that they themselves normally experience. Erotic materials stimulate fantasies, and they have been produced throughout mankind's history. People utilize them to learn about sex, to satisfy the need for social comparison, and as an aphrodisiac to enhance pleasure. With other mammals, males are especially stimulated by a novel mate while females prefer a familiar partner. Among human males, familiar erotic stimuli become progressively less arousing, while novel erotica are much more exciting.

People differ greatly in their feelings about sex. For example, compared to those low in sex guilt, high-guilt individuals desire sex less, find it less enjoyable, engage in it less frequently, and tend to avoid coming in contact with stimulating cues or stimulating thoughts. Though it has long been assumed that females were considerably lower in sexual motivation than males, recent research suggests that females respond to clitoral stimulation with intense, and sometimes multiple, orgasms and that they can be more sexually robust than males. Survey studies show that sex differences in behavior are rapidly disappearing, and experimental studies show that males and females respond in a surprisingly similar way to erotic stories and pictures. Apparently, differences in learning experiences account for what was long believed to be biological differences between the sexes. Some specific erotic themes *do* elicit sex differences: females are less aroused by a story of sexual exploitation, males are less aroused by a same-sex individual masturbating, females are more negative toward a sexually dominant woman, and both sexes are aroused by rape but with different accompanying negative emotions.

The most immediate effects of erotica involve physiological changes in both males and females as measured by the penile plethysmograph and the vaginal plethysmograph. Despite fears to the contrary, there is no evidence that pornography leads to sex crimes. In fact, studies of sex criminals and of the effects of removing censorship in Denmark suggest that the opposite may be true. Laboratory research indicates only limited effects of exposure to erotica; there tends to be a small increase in the frequency of one's usual sexual behavior immediately following exposure, but no long-range effects. Interestingly, those who are most negative toward pornography and sex in general are found to be behaviorally affected by pornography more than those who feel positively.

GLOSSARY

Acid phosphatase. A substance in the urine that increases following sexual excitement.

Aphrodisiac. Any substance which brings about sexual excitement.

Behavioral phase. In the Masters and Johnson schema, the sexual activity that follows stimulation and leads to orgasm.

Cunnilingus. Oral stimulation of the female genitals.

Ejaculation. The expulsion of semen from the penis.

Eroticaphile. Those who like pornography and explicit erotica.

Eroticaphobe. Those who dislike pornography and explicit erotica.

Fellatio. Oral stimulation of the male genitals.

Fetish. A stimulus which has special sexual meaning for an individual and which elicits excitement.

Frigidity. The inability of a female to have orgasms.

Nocturnal emission. A spontaneous emission that can occur while a male is asleep.

Nymphomaniac. A female who engages in intercourse with abnormal frequency but without being able to reach orgasm.

Orgasm phase. In the Masters and Johnson schema, the apex of sexual activity.

Penile plethysmograph. A device that measures sexual excitement in males by recording increases in the volume or circumference of the penis.

Pheromones. Vaginal secretions that are sexually arousing to male animals who smell them. The existence of pheromones in human beings has not been established.

Pornography. Pictures or stories whose primary purpose is to cause sexual arousal.

Repression-sensitization. The dimension of defense mechanisms ranging from avoidance of anxiety-evoking stimuli to approaching such stimuli.

Sex guilt. The general tendency to punish oneself whenever sexual standards are violated in thought or deed.

Stimulation phase. In the Masters and Johnson schema, the initial phase in which various cues lead to sexual excitement.

Swinging.   The practice of "swapping" partners for sexual purposes.

Vaginal plethysmograph.   A device that measures sexual excitement in females by recording increases in the volume of blood in the vaginal walls by means of a light source and a light sensing device.

SUGGESTED READINGS FOR CHAPTER 10

Byrne, D., and Byrne, L. A., eds.   *Exploring human sexuality.*   New York: Harper & Row, 1977.   A collection of new and reprinted articles covering current research and theory dealing with human sexuality.   Each selection is especially edited to make it comprehensible to the nonprofessional reader.

Commission on Obscenity and Pornography.   *The report of the Commission on Obscenity and Pornography.*   Washington, D.C.: U.S. Government Printing Office, 1970. The nontechnical summary of the findings, conclusions, and recommendations of the President's Commission which conducted the first large-scale research on pornography and its effects.

McCary, J. L.   *Human sexuality.*   New York: D. Van Nostrand, 1973.   An excellent undergraduate text which covers the major aspects of sexual anatomy and sexual behavior.

Money, J., and Musaph, H., eds.   *Handbook of sexology.*   Amsterdam: Excerpta Medica, 1977.   The most complete and up-to-date coverage of all aspects of sexuality with chapters by a collection of scientists and practitioners from many nations.

Wilson, S. T., Roe, R. L., and Autrey, L. E., eds.   *Readings in human sexuality.*   St. Paul: West, 1975.   A wide-ranging and easy to read collection of material on sexual behavior, including such diverse topics as contraception, vasectomy, venereal disease, sodomy, love, and sex differences.

SOCIAL EXCHANGE: COMING TO "TERMS" WITH OTHERS

11

It's one of those days on which you and your boyfriend can't seem to agree about anything. All afternoon, you've had your mouth set for a delicious Chinese meal, but now you discover that he wants to eat at an Italian restaurant instead. And for more than a week you've been looking forward to visiting a local nightspot where one of your favorite groups is performing—only to discover that he wants to see a movie instead. As you discuss your conflicting plans, tempers grow short, and it begins to seem as if you will have to go your separate ways. After some embarrassing and tense moments, though, he suggests a compromise: he'll agree to visiting the nightclub, if you'll agree to an Italian-style dinner. Although you're reluctant to miss out on an oriental banquet, you realize that this is the only way to salvage any of your plans, so you agree, and with a great deal of relief, the two of you set off on what you hope will turn out to be a pleasant evening after all.

Graduation day is drawing near, and it's time to part with your old and faithful car. There's nothing seriously wrong with it; it's just that you've accepted a job in a city more than a thousand miles away, and have decided that you need a newer and larger car to make this trip and move all of your belongings. You've placed an ad in the paper, and the first person to answer it seems quite interested in buying your old vehicle. After kicking the tires, listening to the motor, and test driving the car, he offers you a figure somewhat lower than the one you had in mind. Actually, it's not that far off, but you pretend shock at his low bid in hopes of getting him to raise it substantially. After hesitating for a few minutes, you come back with a counter offer. He chuckles at your suggestion, and points out the numerous dents and scratches you car has suffered over the years of hard use. You respond by calling his attention to the new set of tires you installed only a few months earlier. At this point, he stops laughing and makes another offer, closer to your original goal. You counter with one of your own, and when he suggests splitting the difference, you agree and the deal is closed.

You approach the list of grades posted outside one of your classes with a great deal of anxiety. You've worked very hard in the course, and were on the borderline between an A and a B before the final. A wave of disappointment sweeps over you as you find your score, and discover that you received a B. You're still standing in front of the list when a friend approaches and begins to search for her own grade. You know that she did very little work for the course, and did not score as high as you did on the exams. But she volunteered a lot in class, and always stayed for a few minutes after the bell to talk to the instructor. After a quick search, she finds her grade on the list and breaks into a broad smile—it's an A. Upon hearing this outcome, your blood begins to boil. It doesn't seem at all fair that she should get a higher grade than you for much less effort, just because she managed to get into the instructor's good graces. As you turn and walk away, you feel yourself growing angrier and angrier. In fact, you become so upset that you half decide to confront your professor in an attempt to gain the simple justice you feel you so strongly deserve.

It's a dismal winter day, and as you return to your car from the store where you've been shopping, you notice that the ground—which was only wet when you entered—has now turned into a solid sheet of ice. This causes you some concern, because you remember that you parked in a spot which sloped downward, and you're afraid that you won't be able to pull out. As it turns out, your worst fears are confirmed, and try as you may, you can't get enough traction to back out of the parking spot. After a few frustrating moments, you notice another driver parked a few spots away who is having the same problem. Almost at the same moment, he notices you, and quickly you both hit upon a solution to your mutual dilemma: he will push as you attempt to back out, and then you will do the same for him. Your plan works, and in a few minutes, you are both back on level pavement, ready to go your separate ways. As you drive off, you wave to each other in a friendly manner. You've never met before, and probably won't again, but by working together you've managed to help each other out of a very annoying and unpleasant situation.

Have you ever been involved in situations such as these? In all probability, you have. That is, you have probably often found it necessary to compromise with others, to bargain with them over items you wished to buy or sell, or to cooperate with them in order to obtain some mutually desired goal. And unless you've been extremely fortunate, you have almost certainly found yourself in situations where you felt that you received the "short end of the stick"—lower payoffs for more effort than someone else. In all these cases, you have gained first-hand experience with the important process of **social exchange**— interactions in which we agree to trade something we possess or can provide, for something another person possesses or can offer. Because many of the exchanges into which we enter are largely economic in nature—for example, buying or selling various items, working for wages or other forms of compensation—we often think of social exchange largely in these terms. But in reality, individuals often exchange many commodities on which it is impossible to place a monetary or economic value. For example, lovers provide each other with a wide range of physical and emotional rewards, friends exchange many types of assistance and support, and even casual acquaintances may supply each other with information, an opportunity to voice their opinions, and other desirable social outcomes. Moreover, many exchange relationships are implicit rather than explicit in nature. To mention one example, a dominant and a submissive individual may become fast friends and provide each other with important psychological benefits without ever reaching formal agreement about who will do most of the talking, make most of the decisions, and so on. In short, individuals exchange a much wider range of benefits, and do so in a much more subtle and complex manner than you might at first imagine.

That social exchange is quite common and plays an important role in our relations with others is obvious. The reasons why individuals so often enter into this process, however, may be less apparent. Basically, such relationships seem to stem from two important facts. First, as you probably know from your own experience, we are generally unable to satisfy all of our physical and emotional needs by ourselves. Rather, we are usually dependent upon others in this respect to at least some degree. Second, as you also probably realize, other persons are generally quite unwilling to provide us with the resources, products, or services we desire totally "free of charge." Instead, we must usually offer them something in return for such benefits.

Together, these two facts virtually guarantee that social exchange, in one form or another, will be an everyday occurrence for most individuals; indeed, it is the only way in which most of us can hope to satisfy all of our basic needs and desires (Simpson, 1972; Thibaut and Kelley, 1959).

While an element of exchange or trading enters into many forms of social interaction (do you recall our comments in Chapter 8 and 9 about the importance of reciprocity in both helping and aggression?), perhaps it is most clearly represented in two important types of activity—**cooperation** and **bargaining.** Thus, it is on these forms of behavior that our present discussion will focus. In addition, because feelings on the part of one or more parties to a social exchange that they have somehow been shortchanged or cheated can strongly affect the nature of their later behavior, we will also direct considerable attention to the important role of **perceived fairness** in such relationships, as well as social interaction generally.

COOPERATION AND COMPETITION: WORKING WITH—AND AGAINST—OTHERS

In our earlier discussion of helping (refer to Chapter 8), we noted that under some conditions, individuals will offer aid or assistance to others, even in the absence of any immediate or direct reward for such actions. Although such one-way assistance occurs in a wide range of settings, it is probably less common than another type of behavior in which two or more individuals work together or coordinate their actions in such a manner that the outcomes received by each are enhanced. Such mutual, two-way assistance is generally known as *cooperation,* and represents a basic and important form of social exchange.

We have already described one instance of cooperative behavior in the parking-lot example mentioned above, and you can readily observe many others in everyday life. To mention just a few examples, two or more persons can work together to wash a huge stack of dishes, paint a house, score points against opponents in an athletic contest, write a report, or win an election. In short, cooperation appears to be a very common form of social behavior, and occurs in a wide range of situations. Indeed, it often develops in settings where its occurrence is considered to be undesirable or inappropriate—as during classroom exams!

Given the obvious benefits that may often result from cooperative behavior, it might be expected that such actions would quickly develop in any situation where two or more individuals seek the same goal. After all, two heads *are* often better than one, and many people working together can often accomplish what one or a few cannot (see Figure 11-1). And, in fact, in cases where the goals

"Many hands make light the work."

FIGURE 11-1. *When individuals work together or coordinate their efforts, they can often accomplish tasks beyond the reach of any one person. In the example shown above, of course, cooperation is forced rather than voluntary. (Source: Drawing by O'Brian; © 1971 The New Yorker Magazine, Inc.)*

sought by several persons can be shared among them once obtained, cooperation does often seem to be the rule. Unfortunately, though, there is one important reason why it cannot occur in every situation where individuals seek the same rewards: in many cases, such goals cannot be shared among the persons who pursue them. For example, it is impossible for athletes participating in various events at the Olympics to share the gold medal—only one can carry off this valuable prize. Similarly, it is impossible for two young women seeking an attractive job to both obtain it—only one position is available, and it cannot be shared. In such cases, cooperation between the participants is impossible, and an alternative form of behavior known as **competition** often develops. Here, each individual strives to maximize his or her own outcomes, often at the expense of others. Indeed, in some cases they actually attempt to block or sabotage the efforts of their opponents to reach the desired goal, and so increase their own chances of success. Because it is usually the case that attractive goals are sought by a larger number of persons than can actually hope to attain them, competition is also a common pattern in social interaction, and as you well know, can often reach very fierce levels.

Although there are some situations in which the individuals involved have little choice but to cooperate or compete with each other, many others exist in which either of these two forms of behavior can develop—where the participants have the option of working with or against each other. In such cases, a large

Because many attractive goals cannot be shared, and are sought by a much larger number of persons than can actually hope to attain them, competition is a very common form of social behavior. (Photo, right: Phil Carver & Friends.)

number of factors seem to determine whether cooperation or competition will ultimately occur, and it is with such factors that social psychologists have been primarily concerned. The remainder of our discussion, then, will focus upon the conditions which tend to tip the balance toward one or the other of these contrasting patterns of behavior. Before turning to such factors, however, we should say a few words about the technique developed by social psychologists to investigate cooperation and competition under controlled laboratory conditions. Thus, we urge you to examine the insert on pages 514–517 very carefully before proceeding.

Situational Determinants of Cooperation: Tipping the Balance

Is cooperation more likely to develop under some conditions than others? Common sense suggests that this will certainly be the case. For example, it seems likely that such behavior will occur more often when the persons involved both know and like each other than when they are total strangers. Similarly, it appears reasonable to expect that cooperation will develop more quickly when the rewards to be gained through such actions are large than when they are small. Fortunately, we do not have to rely solely upon informal evidence in evaluating these and similar suggestions (Kahn, Hottes, and Davis, 1971; Gallo and Sheposh, 1971). A large and growing number of experiments have been conducted to examine the influence of situational factors upon the development of cooperative behavior. Although the findings of such investigations point to the impact of many different conditions (e.g., Brauer and Barnett, 1976), among the most important seem to be (1) the behavior of other persons—do *they* act in a cooperative or competitive manner? (2) the apparent power of such persons—to what extent do they control important resources? and (3) the availability and use of various forms of communication, including threats.

Reactions to Cooperation from Others: Reciprocity or Exploitation? Moral teachings urge us to follow the golden rule and "do unto others as we would have others do unto us." Despite such suggestions, though, most of our interactions seem to be governed by a strong adherence to the principle of *reciprocity.* That is, in many situations, we behave toward others in a manner that is highly similar to their past treatment of us. For example, when another individual helps or assists us in some manner on one occasion, we generally reciprocate his or her help at a later time. Similarly, if an acquaintance treats us in a hostile manner, we rarely "turn the other cheek." Instead, we generally respond with counterattacks of our own (see pp. 419–421). In short, our relations with others often seem to be strongly affected by a search for reciprocity.

Given the apparently general nature of our commitment to this principle, there are no obvious grounds for doubting its importance in the process of social exchange. We might expect, then, that the level of cooperation demonstrated by a given individual will often be strongly determined by the extent to which others have cooperated with *her.* Unfortunately, though, informal observation sug-

FOCUS ON RESEARCH

COOPERATION AND COMPETITION IN THE LABORATORY: THE GAMES SUBJECTS PLAY

Imagine the following hypothetical, but potentially real situation: two individuals have been arrested by the police on suspicion of a serious crime (for example, armed robbery). Although it appears that they are the guilty parties, the district attorney does not have enough evidence against them to be certain of a conviction. As a result, he is faced with the task of getting one, or preferably both, to confess. In order to attain this goal, he orders them placed in separate rooms, and interviews each in isolation from the other. While questioning each suspect, he carefully explains that each man has only two choices: he (the suspect) can confess, or stick to his alibi. The district attorney further explains that if both men refuse to confess, he will book them on a relatively minor charge, and both will receive a sentence of one year. On the other hand, if they both confess, he will charge them each with the more serious crime, and each will receive a much stiffer sentence. Since they have ad-

mitted their guilt, however, he will recommend leniency, and they will receive less than the maximum sentence (eight years instead of ten). Finally, he indicates that if one confesses while the other does not, the confessor will receive a very mild sentence of three months as a reward for turning "state's evidence," while the other will suffer the full weight of the law, and receive ten long years in jail. All these possible outcomes are represented in Figure 11-2. In this diagram, the behavior of each suspect is shown along the edges of the matrix, while within each of the four boxes, the outcomes for Prisoner 1 are indicated below the diagonal line, and those for Prisoner 2 above it. For example, if Prisoner 1 confesses but Prisoner 2 sticks to his alibi, the first man will receive a three-month sentence, while the second will be sent "up the river" for a ten-year stretch.

After explaining all the possibilities to each of the two men, the district attorney withdraws so that they can think things over

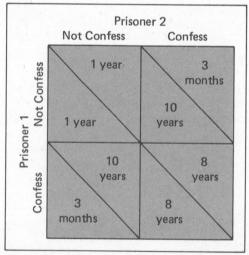

FIGURE 11-2. *The Prisoner's Dilemma. Within each box, outcomes for Prisoner 1 are indicated below the diagonal and those for Prisoner 2 above it.*

and decide whether to confess or continue to insist on their innocence. During this time, they are still kept apart so that they cannot communicate before reaching a decision. What, then, should the suspects do? As you can probably see, this is far from an easy decision. On the one hand, it is to their mutual benefit to refrain from confessing—in that way, each will receive only a one-year sentence. Thus, pressures in the direction of mutual trust and cooperation are strong. On the other hand, however, each man is also tempted to betray his partner by turning state's evidence, and so gain the minimum three-month sentence. In short, pressures in the direction of mutual betrayal and suspicion are also quite powerful.

Because it involves the arousal of conflicting tendencies toward cooperation and competition, this situation—generally known as the "Prisoner's Dilemma"—seems to provide an interesting context within which to examine factors serving to tip the balance in favor of one or the other of these contrasting patterns of behavior. As you can probably see, however, there appears to be one major problem standing in the way of its use: how, you might ask, can the outcomes shown in Figure 11-2 be translated into laboratory studies of cooperation and competition? Social psychologists, after all, do not have the power to sentence individuals to jail, and subjects, of course, are far from suspected criminals. The answer to this puzzle lies in a simple but important fact. In reality, the outcomes in the matrix shown above bear a specific mathematical relationship to each other. As a result, it is possible to replace the numbers representing months and years in jail with numbers representing almost anything else, provided the mathematical relationships between them remain the same. Given this fact, it is actually quite simple to adapt the Prisoner's Dilemma to laboratory studies of cooperation and competition.

Basically, such experiments begin with the construction of a matrix such as the one shown in Figure 11-3. Then, during the

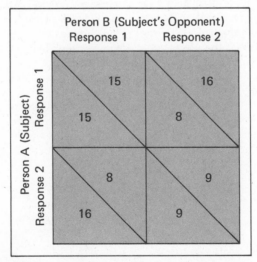

FIGURE 11-3. *An outcome matrix of the type often employed in laboratory studies of cooperation and competition. The numbers in the matrix represent the outcomes which will be obtained by subjects and their opponents each time they both choose one of the two responses. In each box, outcomes for the subject are shown below the diagonal line, and those for his or her opponent above it.*

actual experiment, subjects are presented with these values, and informed that the numbers shown in each quadrant represent the outcomes that can be obtained by their partner and themselves each time they both choose one of the two available responses. For example, in the matrix shown, if they both choose Response 1, each will receive an outcome of 15. In most cases, the numbers in the matrix are described as referring only to arbitrary points, but in some studies, they are described as corresponding to varying amounts of money (for example, each point = 1¢). In either case, subjects' task is precisely the same: choose one of the two available responses each time they are signalled to do so by the experimenter. As you can see, Response 1 is the cooperative choice in this situation, for if both individuals select it, they each receive relatively favorable outcomes. In contrast, Response 2 represents the competitive alternative, since by choosing this behavior, each person attempts to maximize his or her own gains at the expense of the partner. As you might guess, individuals usually play not against another subject, but against a confederate, or even a nonexistent person whose responses are supplied by the experimenter. Regardless of the precise details followed, subjects' tendencies to cooperate or compete are measured in terms of the pattern of responses they select: the greater their choice of alternative 1, the more cooperative their actions are interpreted as being.

Before concluding our description of the Prisoner's Dilemma and its use in the systematic study of cooperation and competition, we should address one additional question: do procedures based on this situation actually yield valid measures of cooperative and competitive behavior? Although there is relatively little in the way of direct information concerning this issue, three lines of evidence suggest that they do. First, subjects participating in such research often become highly involved in their task, growing angry when their partner fails to cooperate, showing signs of relief when he does, and so on. Such informal observation suggests that participants become so absorbed in the game that they often behave as they would in other, less artificial settings. Second, large individual differences between participants are often observed. Some compete, others choose to cooperate, and still others waver back and forth between these approaches (Kuhlman and Marshello, 1975; NcNeel, 1973). Further, there is some indication that such strategies reflect subjects' general orientations toward social exchange, and that they behave in corresponding ways outside the laboratory as well (Kelley and Stahelski, 1970). And finally, experiments employing such procedures have often yielded expected differences between various cultural groups. That is, individuals from highly competitive cultural backgrounds do in fact show higher levels of competition than those from more cooperative groups (McClintock, 1974). Together, these separate lines of evidence suggest that situations based on the Prisoner's Dilemma do indeed provide a useful means for studying cooperation and competition under controlled laboratory conditions. In short, subjects' behavior in the games they are asked to play may actually reveal much about the nature of social exchange in other, more realistic settings.

gests that this may not always be the case. While cooperative gestures to others are sometimes returned, they are also often ignored. Indeed, there appears to be a fairly widespread belief that acting in a totally cooperative manner toward others may yield exploitation and mistreatment at their hands far more often than a return of trust and assistance. "Stick your neck out for others," the saying goes, "and you will be sure to get it chopped off." Regrettably, these pessimistic sentiments have been at least partially confirmed by the findings of several laboratory experiments (Bixenstine, Potash, and Wilson, 1963; Black and Higbee, 1973). Perhaps the most unsettling demonstration of such effects is provided by a study conducted by Shure, Meeker, and Hansford (1965).

In this investigation, subjects participated along with another person in a game where only one player at a time could perform an assigned task (moving "messages" through a simulated communication system). Thus, the best strategy was for the two individuals involved to alternate turns. One interesting and important feature of the game involved the fact that the first player to complete the task successfully (i.e., the first to transmit a "message") would gain the use of a "Jolt Back" option through which he could, at will, both interrupt his opponent's performance, and deliver a painful electric shock to this person. As a result, it was clear that the player possessing this option would actually gain complete domination of the game.

On the first and crucial trial, subjects' opponent (whose responses were actually simulated by the experimenter), acted in a completely trusting manner, standing idly by while the subject successfully completed the task and seized control of the "Jolt Back" maneuver. In this manner, he (the opponent) seemed to demonstrate complete faith that the subject would treat him in a fair manner during the remainder of the session. Unfortunately, such trust was far from justified: fully 129 out of the 143 subjects participating responded to this cooperative and trusting gesture with exploitation, using the "Jolt Back" option to completely dominate their helpless and presumably suffering opponent. Moreover, this was the case even when the fictitious opponent was described as a Quaker who was morally committed to principles of nonviolence and fair play, when he refused to take advantage of an opportunity to acquire the shock option for himself, and even when he sent written messages to subjects pleading for fair treatment. In short, when faced with an opponent who adopted a pacifistic and totally cooperative strategy, most individuals chose to exploit rather than cooperate with this person.

The fact that several additional studies have yielded findings similar to those obtained by Shure, Meeker, and Hansford leaves little doubt that many individuals will often choose to take advantage of an opponent who behaves toward them in a totally cooperative manner (Black and Higbee, 1973; Solomon, 1960). But why is this the case? What accounts for the apparent willingness of so many persons to exploit others who offer them nothing but trust and confidence? Many possibilities exist, but we will consider only two.

First, it may well be the case that individuals exposed to total cooperation on the part of another become suspicious about the motives behind his or her behavior. Is this individual genuinely cooperative, or is she merely "setting them up for the kill?" Unfortunately, most of us have experienced situations in which we were induced to trust another person, only to find our confidence later betrayed. And we are quite familiar with reports concerning the activities of professional confidence artists, who often begin by establishing a high level of trust among their victims, only to fleece them thoroughly once it has been established. With such information and memories before them, it is not at all surprising that most persons adopt a cautious and wary approach to others who seem to offer unlimited cooperation. Second, total cooperation on the part of another person may be interpreted as a sign of weakness, or even stupidity. After all, anyone who continues to behave cooperatively regardless of our own actions must not care very much about his or her own outcomes. And if he or she doesn't care, why should we? Together with other factors, these processes may account for the strong tendency of many persons to exploit totally trusting others.

If we were to end our discussion of reciprocation in social exchange at this point, it would be on a very pessimistic note. Fortunately, though, other findings serve to considerably brighten this dismal picture. First, a recent investigation by Enzle, Hansen, and Lowe (1975a) suggests that under conditions where subjects believe that their partner fully intended to cooperate with them, and did not simply blunder into this strategy by accident, reciprocity is sharply enhanced. Specifically, these researchers found that subjects were more likely to cooperate with their partners when they received hand-written notes from this person indicating that she had fully intended to cooperate with *them,* than when they received only automated feedback to this effect from the experimental apparatus. In short, reciprocity was facilitated when subjects believed that their partner's cooperation had been deliberate and planned.

Second, you may have noticed that up to this point, we have been discussing only the reciprocation of *total* cooperation. That is, subjects' opponent in the Shure et al. study and similar investigations continued to cooperate with them no matter how they behaved. What might happen, you may ask, if subjects were presented with an opponent who offered them a high level of cooperation, but only in a *contingent* manner—continuing to cooperate only so long as *they* cooperated with him? Such conditions are much closer to most real-life situations, for we rarely meet individuals who continue to offer us unlimited trust in response to repeated betrayal. The effects of such a strategy of conditional cooperation have been examined in a number of different experiments, and in general, results have been quite reassuring (Kuhlman and Marshello, 1975). In particular, it appears that when confronted with an opponent who offers cooperation on a contingent basis, most individuals do in fact reciprocate his trust, and adopt a cooperative strategy themselves. Indeed, there is some indication that cooperation may be higher and more consistent under these conditions than under any others (Rapaport, 1973). In view of such results, we can end our discussion on a much more positive note than might otherwise be the case. It appears that while total and seemingly unintentional cooperation toward others may invite exploitation in return, conditional and fully intentional cooperation may well foster a repayment of such behavior. In short, cooperation may indeed be reciprocated, but only under certain limited conditions.

Cooperation and Social Power: When Weakness Is Strength. Suppose that in a situation involving social exchange, you found yourself facing a vastly more powerful opponent—someone who could exert much greater effects upon your outcomes than you could exert on his. How would you expect this person with **social power** to behave, and how might you yourself choose to act? In all probability, you might expect this individual to behave in a somewhat demanding manner, requiring more from you than he or she returned in any social exchange. And you yourself would probably act in a highly cooperative manner, for only in this way could you expect to salvage any rewards at all. In short, common sense suggests that in an exchange relationship where the opponents differ considerably in available power, the stronger person will usually be able to behave in a more exploitative and demanding manner than the weaker, who has little choice but to cooperate (see Swingle, 1970a).

But now consider what might happen in such a situation if the powerful party failed to use his or her influence, always behaving in a cooperative manner; how would the weaker individual react? At first, he or she might continue to offer cooperation, fearful that any other form of behavior might anger the dominant person, and cause him to retaliate strongly. Over time, however, the weaker party might begin to form the impression that his or her powerful adversary was not making use of his available power because of an inability to do so. And then, emboldened by this thought, the weaker person might actually begin exploiting the more powerful one!

Situations such as this have actually developed in the sphere of international relations in recent years, where both the United States and the Soviet Union have frequently found themselves the victims of continual "nose-tweaking" by smaller and much weaker nations. Apparently, these relatively powerless countries realize that the two superpowers are greatly reluctant to bring their superior forces into play, and take full advantage of this fact. Indeed, as a result of their obvious unwillingness to resort to direct military force, both powers have had to suffer quite humiliating treatment at the hands of countries they could easily crush in a few hours—provided they were willing to bring their full military might into play. Such events suggest that the failure to make use of available power may often serve as a signal to weaker opponents that they can "get away" with exploitation, and so encourage them to engage in such actions. The occurrence of such effects has actually been demonstrated in several laboratory experiments.

For example, in one study conducted by Black and Higbee (1973), subjects played a Prisoner's Dilemma game with an opponent under conditions where (1) they held more power than this person, (2) they and their opponent held equal power, or (3) the opponent held more power than they. (Power was defined in terms of the ability of each person to control the other's payoffs; thus, the opponent was said to be in power when he could strongly determine subjects' outcomes, while they could not affect his, and so on.) In all three conditions, the opponent—whose responses were actually simulated by the experimenter—acted in a highly cooperative manner, choosing to cooperate 95 percent of the time. On the basis of the reasoning outlined above, it was predicted that subjects would be more likely to exploit the opponent when he held a power advantage but failed to use it than when they themselves held the "edge." As you can see in Figure 11-4, these predictions were strongly confirmed. Together with the

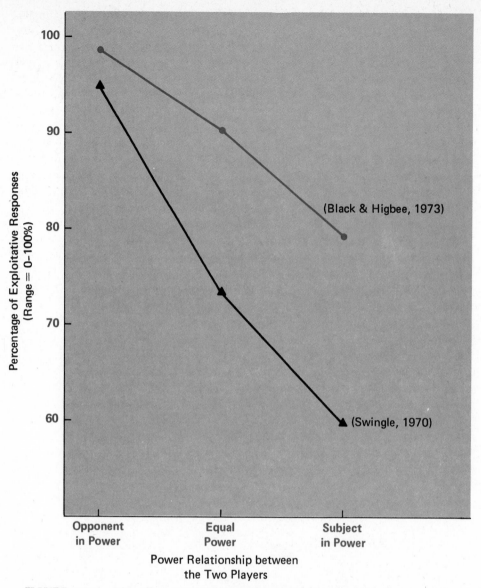

FIGURE 11-4. *The effects of failure to use available power in an exchange relationship. As shown above, the results of several studies indicate that subjects attempt to exploit their opponent more frequently when he holds a power advantage, but fails to use it, than when they themselves hold such an advantage. (Source: Based on data from Black and Higbee, 1973, and Swingle, 1970a.)*

results of other studies (Swingle, 1970a), such findings suggest that individuals—and possibly nations—who are treated in a cooperative, friendly manner by a powerful adversary will often fail to respond to such treatment with gratitude or trust. Rather, they may react with scorn for their opponent's apparent "weakness," and attempt to exploit this person.

Communication and Cooperative Behavior: Coordination through Threats?
Common sense suggests that providing potential opponents with an opportunity to communicate with one another may facilitate the occurrence of cooperative behavior. That is, discussion of the relevant issues and contingencies may lead them to conclude that cooperation is, after all, the best strategy for both sides, and so lead to the development of such behavior. By the same token, it may actually be impossible for individuals to coordinate their actions in a mutually rewarding manner unless they can communicate with, or at least signal, each other in some fashion. On the basis of such considerations, powerful nations have established "hot lines" between their capitals, over which heads of state can communicate in times of emergency. And large organizations such as government agencies and giant corporations often schedule endless rounds of meetings and issue huge piles of memoranda in an attempt to facilitate communication—and so, presumably, cooperation—between their various departments.

That some forms of communication do indeed facilitate cooperation has been amply demonstrated in laboratory studies. For example, in one study (Wichman, 1970) female subjects played a Prisoner's Dilemma type game under conditions where they could (1) both see and hear their opponent, (2) hear but not see her, (3) see but not hear her, and (4) neither see nor hear her. Not surprisingly, cooperation tended to increase as the level of contact between these individuals increased. Unfortunately, however, not all types of communication between the parties to a social exchange seem to produce such effects (Swingle and Santi, 1972). In fact, one type of contact between potential opponents—**threats** directed by one against the other—actually seem to backfire, and *reduce*

Because of the widespread belief that communication facilitates cooperation—and can often head off conflict—the Soviet Union and the United States have established special "hot lines" which can be used by their respective heads of state during times of emergency. (Photo: United Press International.)

rather than enhance cooperative actions. The impact of this factor upon the development of cooperation was first studied in a systematic manner by Deutsch and Krauss (1960).

In order to examine the effects of implicit threat on cooperation, these researchers devised an ingenious task which has since been employed in many other studies. In this situation—often known among social psychologists as the *trucking game*—subjects were asked to imagine that they were in charge of two different companies whose task it was to move some merchandise from one point to another. Their profits in the game (which were described to them as being only imaginary) would then be determined by the speed with which they managed to accomplish this task. Thus, on each trial, both players started with sixty cents, and "operating expenses" were subtracted from this amount at the rate of one cent per second until they managed to reach their destinations. As shown in Figure 11-5, each of the two players (known, respectively, as Acme and Bolt) could follow either a short, direct route to the goal, or a longer, alternate route. Since winnings in the game would be determined by the amount of time needed to arrive at these points, the direct route was clearly the preferred one for

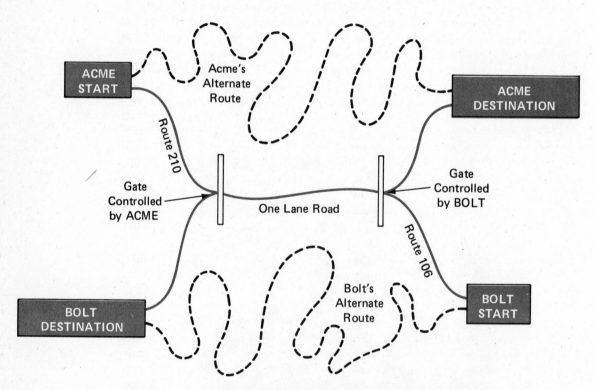

FIGURE 11-5. *The "trucking game" used by Deutsch and Krauss to study the effects of threat on cooperative behavior. Note the presence of gates which could be used by one or both players to threaten their opponent and block his or her progress toward the appropriate destination. (Source: Adapted from Deutsch and Krauss, 1960, p. 183.)*

both players. Unfortunately, though, as you can see from Figure 11-5, it involved a stretch of one-lane road through which only one truck at a time could pass. It was obvious, then, that the best strategy for the two players was a cooperative one in which they alternated turns in using the short, preferred route. And in fact, this was the pattern of behavior which actually developed in most instances when the game was played as we have just described—that is, in the absence of threats from either opponent.

To determine whether providing one or both players with an opportunity to implicitly threaten their opponent would facilitate or interfere with the development of cooperative behavior, Deutsch and Krauss then added another feature to the game. Specifically, they provided subjects in two experimental groups with *gates* (refer to Figure 11-5) which they could close at will, in order to prevent their partner from moving her truck through the one-lane road. In a *unilateral-threat* condition, only one of the players (Acme) possessed a gate, while in a *bilateral-threat* condition, both players were provided with gates. (In a no-threat control group, neither player possessed a gate.) The possession of a gate, of course, posed an implicit threat to that player's opponent: after all, their progress toward the goal could now be blocked at any time if this person decided to use it.

Before describing the results of the study, we should emphasize again that the threats posed by the gates were only *implicit* ones—it was not required that persons possessing them actually put them into use. Thus, if subjects were willing to trust their partners, cooperative behavior could still develop. However, if each player assumed that individuals possessing gates would tend to use them, cooperation would be prevented as each attempted to "strike" first, and reach his destination. In reality, this is precisely what seemed to occur: possession of a gate by either player led to considerable conflict, and substantial losses for both participants. Moreover, losses were even greater under conditions where *both* players had gates at their disposal (see Table 11-1). In this case, both individuals would typically slam their respective gates shut at the start of each trial, and then sit idly by as their potential profits evaporated with each tick of the clock. In sum, providing subjects with an implicit means of threatening their opponent sharply reduced the occurrence of cooperative patterns of behavior.

You have probably noticed that in the experiment conducted by Deutsch and Krauss, the closing of a gate by one player automatically prevented the other from moving toward the goal in the most direct manner. Thus, in addition to serving as a *threat*—a signal by one player that she intended to reduce the other's winnings—this action also necessarily *produced* these negative outcomes. In many life situations, in contrast, threats are separated from actual harmful consequences. For example, one person may warn another that he will cease cooperating unless certain actions are taken. In view of this fact, it seems possible that when threats are separated from actual negative effects, they may sometimes serve to enhance cooperative behavior.

This possibility has actually been examined in several experiments (Shomer, Davis and Kelley, 1966; Smith and Anderson, 1975) and indeed, it does appear that when threats are separated from actual negative outcomes, they may

TABLE 11-1. *Joint outcomes earned by subjects in the no-threat, unilateral-threat, and bilateral-threat conditions of the Deutsch and Krauss (1960) experiment. Positive numbers indicate winnings, while negative numbers reflect losses. (Source: Based on data from Deutsch and Krauss, 1960.)*

Condition	Joint Outcomes
No threat	+203.31
Unilateral threat	−405.88
Bilateral threat	−875.12

sometimes facilitate cooperation. However, such effects seem to occur only when no other form of communication between opponents is permitted. Under such conditions, threats may serve as a primitive type of communication, and so aid subjects in coordinating their behavior. When other forms of communication are permitted, however, threats seem to sharply reduce cooperation, perhaps because individuals resent being threatened when less provocative means for obtaining coordination are available. Evidence pointing to this conclusion has been obtained in a recent study conducted by Smith and Anderson (1975).

In this investigation, subjects played the trucking game under conditions where some could first threaten their opponent (by lighting a "threat" light on a panel in front of him) and then "fine" him (by deducting forty cents from his winnings) if he failed to heed this warning. (Other subjects did not have these responses at their disposal.) In one experimental condition, players could communicate freely with each other in any way they wished, while in a second they were forbidden to communicate in any manner. As expected, results indicated that the presence of the threat and fine options facilitated cooperation when no other means of communication was available, but actually inhibited such behavior when opponents could converse freely (see Figure 11-6). While these findings suggest that threats may occasionally foster the development of cooperation, it should be recalled that in most instances of social exchange, participants can communicate freely with each other in several different ways. Thus, it seems probable that under normal conditions, threats are more likely to produce resistance and conflict than cooperation and mutual trust.

Individual Determinants of Cooperation: Cooperators, Competitors, and Individualists

Are there individual (personality) characteristics that predispose specific persons toward cooperation or competition? Informal observation suggests that there certainly are. Often, we characterize our friends and acquaintances as cooperative and reasonable, or as hard-driving and competitive. Further, there is a

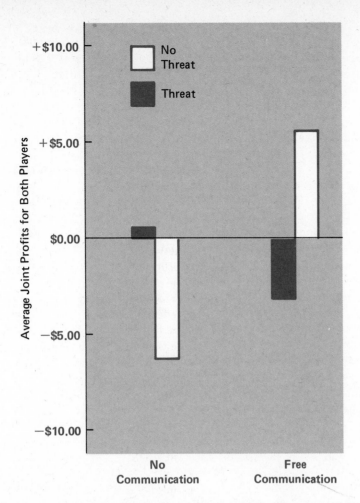

FIGURE 11-6. *The effects of threat on cooperation. When no other form of communication was available, the presence of responses through which subjects could both threaten and then fine their opponent increased cooperation, and led to higher payoffs for both players. When subjects could communicate freely in other ways, however, the presence of threat sharply reduced joint winnings. (Source: Based on data from Smith and Anderson, 1975.)*

persistent, widespread belief that competitive, "aggressive" persons will usually come out on top in any social exchange.

These suggestions concerning large individual differences in cooperative or competitive orientations are supported by the findings of many experiments. Generally, such studies suggest that individuals *do* differ greatly in their tendencies toward cooperation or competition, and that in many instances, these differences will strongly affect their behavior toward others (Kelley and Stahelski, 1970; Kuhlman and Marshello, 1975; NcNeel, 1973). Basically, it appears that most individuals can be categorized as falling into one of three major "types."

First, there are **competitors,** persons who seek to maximize their own gains relative to others. These individuals are primarily concerned with doing better than the others around them, regardless of the payoffs at stake. Indeed, they are often far more interested in this goal than in that of obtaining positive outcomes, and will sometimes settle for negative results, as long as their outcomes are better than those of others. Existing evidence suggests that often, we may recognize such persons by virtue of the fact that they choose to behave competitively even in situations where it would be to their advantage to adopt a cooperative strategy (Enzle, Hansen, and Lowe, 1975b). Second, there are **cooperators,** individuals concerned with maximizing both their own gains and those of others as well. Such persons are interested in assuring that both they and their partners in a social exchange obtain positive results, and are usually quite satisfied when all participants obtain equal payoffs. Third, there are **individualists.** These persons are primarily concerned with maximizing their own gains, and have little concern for the outcomes of others one way or the other. Whether they do better or worse than their opponents, and whether these persons obtain positive or negative results is of little interest to them; only their own rewards seem to matter.

As you might expect, individuals showing these different orientations often behave in contrasting ways during social exchange. For example, in situations such as the Prisoner's Dilemma, competitors usually attempt to exploit their opponent, cooperators usually seek to cooperate with him, and individualists adopt whichever strategy will maximize their own outcomes. Perhaps the largest and most interesting differences in the behavior of these three "types" of persons are seen in their reactions to various patterns of behavior on the part of their opponent. Thus, cooperators often attempt to cooperate with this person, regardless of his behavior, unless it is obvious that such a strategy is impossible. Competitors usually respond competitively regardless of their partner's behavior, and individualists will either cooperate or compete, depending on which of these approaches will yield the largest outcomes. Such differences in the behavior of cooperators, competitors, and individualists have been observed in several recent experiments (McClintock et al., 1973; McNeel, 1973). For example, in one study by Kuhlman and Marshello (1975), subjects first completed a task which allowed the experimenters to classify them as largely competitive, cooperative, or individualistic in orientation. (You might be interested in learning that among a fairly large group of undergraduates, 26 percent turned out to be individualists, 28 percent cooperators, and 21 percent competitors; the remainder could not be readily classified as one type or another.)

Following these procedures, all subjects played a Prisoner's Dilemma game against a partner who adopted one of three basic strategies: 100 percent cooperation, 100 percent competition, or conditional cooperation, in which he always matched subjects' own choices. It was expected that under these conditions, cooperators, competitors, and individualists would show sharply different reactions to their partner's behavior, and as you can see in Figure 11-7,

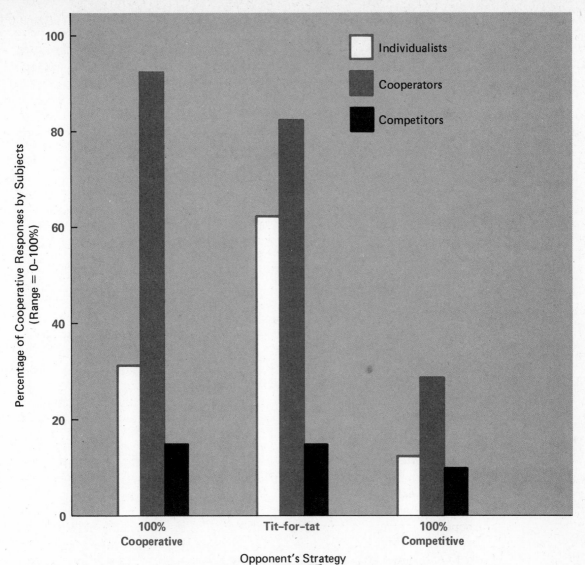

FIGURE 11-7. *Individual differences in cooperative behavior. As shown above, individuals previously classified as "cooperators," "competitors," and "individualists" reacted differently to several patterns of behavior by their opponents. Cooperators behaved cooperatively except when their partner attempted to always exploit them, competitors behaved exploitatively in all cases, and individualists cooperated only when their partner adopted a tit-for-tat strategy. (Source: Based on data from Kuhlman and Marshello, 1975.)*

this was clearly the case. That is, competitors attempted to exploit their partner regardless of his behavior, cooperators cooperated with him except when it was clear that such behavior was impossible (i.e., when the partner was competitive 100 percent of the time), and individualists cooperated only with the conditionally cooperative opponent. In short, subjects' different motivational orientations strongly affected their reactions to their partner's three strategies.

Perhaps the most surprising finding in this and related research has been the strong tendency by competitors to attempt to exploit their opponent, regardless of his or her reactions. Such behavior is quite puzzling in at least one respect: why, after all, should they continue to behave in a competitive manner even when this strategy proves largely ineffective? The answer appears to lie primarily in their perceptions of other persons (Kelley and Stahelski, 1970). Basically, competitors seem to assume that everyone they meet shares their orientation, and will, therefore, behave competitively. Given this belief, it is not at all surprising that they often attempt to strike first, and show little if any trust in others. This is in sharp contrast to cooperators, who appear to realize that other persons differ markedly in their orientation toward social exchange, with some being cooperative, others competitive, and still others somewhat in between (see Table 11-2).

Unfortunately, the firm belief by competitors that they are surrounded by other, equally competitive persons, tends to operate in a self-fulfilling manner. Since they refuse to cooperate with others, they more or less force competition upon them, thus confirming their perception that the world is a "dog-eat-dog" kind of place. In a sense, they more or less assure through their own actions that the bulk of their social interactions will be highly competitive in nature.

BARGAINING AND NEGOTIATION: RESOLVING INTERPERSONAL CONFLICT

Unfortunately, conflict seems to be an all-too-common part of life. Individuals, groups, organizations, and even nations often find themselves at odds over opposing interests and goals. The issues at stake can very from relatively trivial (e.g., who will take out the garbage each evening?) to quite momentous (e.g.,

TABLE 11-2. *Expectations of individuals possessing a cooperative, neutral, or competitive orientation concerning the orientation of others. Subjects with a cooperative orientation expect other individuals to show a considerable amount of variability in terms of their orientations, while subjects with a competitive orientation expect most persons to share their own preference for competition. (Source: Adapted from Kelley and Stahelski, 1970.)*

Subject's Orientation	Expected Orientation of Others		
	Cooperative	Neutral	Competitive
Cooperative	40%	14%	46%
Neutral	16%	31%	53%
Competitive	7%	9%	84%

the shape of national borders), but the strong negative feelings generated tend to be surprisingly similar in all cases. One possible solution to conflict, of course, lies in the use of force; and as we are constantly reminded by newspapers and telecasts, such actions are far from rare. As we noted in Chapter 9, however, the use of force often tends to breed counterforce, with the result that in many cases, such an approach may turn out to be largely self-defeating.

Perhaps a much better solution to interpersonal conflict is provided by the process of *bargaining* or *negotiation*. In this important form of social exchange, individuals or their representatives meet to engage in a mutual trading of offers and, hopefully, concessions. If this process is successful, an agreement acceptable to both sides may be obtained, and further conflict avoided. If it fails, however, discussion may be abandoned, and other, less desirable approaches adopted. The fact that negotiations have begun, then, in no way guarantees that an agreement will actually be reached.

As you can probably guess, bargaining is a very complicated process. Indeed, it is probably safe to suggest that it involves many of the forms of social behavior we have already considered. For example, persuasion and other forms of social influence almost certainly play a role, as each side attempts to sway and wring concessions from the other. Given such complexity, it is not at all surprising that at present we are far from a total or complete understanding of this process. Yet considerable progress toward this goal *has* been made. Several of the factors which exert a major impact upon the course and final outcomes of bargaining have been uncovered, and a number of techniques for increasing its effectiveness in resolving interpersonal conflict have been developed. It is on these factors and procedures that we will focus in the present discussion.

Extremity of Initial Offer: When It Pays to Be Unreasonable

All negotiations must begin with an initial offer by each side; after all, until such opening bids have been made, there is nothing to discuss. But what type of opening offer is best from the point of view of maximizing one's own outcomes? Should an individual seeking to obtain a favorable agreement begin with an extreme offer that is almost certain to be rejected by his or her opponent, or with a more moderate bid that demonstrates "good faith" and a strong desire to attain agreement? Informal observation suggests that in most cases, bargainers seem to follow the former strategy. For example, automobile dealers generally advertise the vehicles on their lots at prices several hundred dollars above their actual market value, and real-estate brokers generally begin by offering houses at prices much higher than the one they hope to obtain (see Figure 11-8). That the strategy of beginning with a relatively extreme initial offer may often be an effective one is suggested by the findings of several studies (Benton, 1971; Yukl, 1974a).

For example, in one interesting experiment, Chertkoff and Conley (1967) asked undergraduate women to play the role of either a buyer or a seller in a

PERSONAL EFFECTIVENESS IN SOCIAL EXCHANGE:
HIGH MACHS AND LOW MACHS

Before proceeding any further, please enter your reactions to each of the statements listed in Table 11-3. That is, indicate the extent to which you agree or disagree with each by circling one number.

You have just completed a short form of a psychological inventory designed to measure

the belief that other persons can be readily manipulated—swayed or influenced for our own purposes. Because this belief lies at the heart of suggestions for obtaining and holding power offered several centuries ago by the Italian philosopher Niccolo Machiavelli, the psychologists who devised these items

TABLE 11-3. *Please indicate your reactions to the statements shown above by circling one number for each. If you agree strongly with a particular statement circle 5, if you agree, but to a lesser extent, circle 4, and so on. Then, when you are finished, read further to find out about the relationship of these statements to social exchange. (Courtesy Dr. R. Christie.)*

	Disagree		Neutral	Agree	
	A Lot	A Little	Neutral	A Little	A Lot
1. The best way to handle people is to tell them what they want to hear.	1	2	3	4	5
2. When you ask someone to do something for you, it is best to give the real reasons for wanting it rather than giving reasons which might carry more weight.	1	2	3	4	5
3. Anyone who completely trusts anyone else is asking for trouble.	1	2	3	4	5
4. It is hard to get ahead without cutting corners here and there.	1	2	3	4	5
5. It is safest to assume that all people have a vicious streak and it will come out when they are given a chance.	1	2	3	4	5
6. One should take action only when sure it is morally right.	1	2	3	4	5
7. Most people are basically good and kind.	1	2	3	4	5
8. There is no excuse for lying to someone else.	1	2	3	4	5
9. Most men forget more easily the death of their father than the loss of their property.	1	2	3	4	5
10. Generally speaking, men won't work hard unless they're forced to do so.	1	2	3	4	5

(Christie and Geis, 1970a) chose to name their inventory the Mach scale. But what, you may be wondering, can the possession or lack of such a Machiavellian orientation have to do with the process of social exchange? Potentially, a great deal.

In particular, it seems reasonable to assume that in many cases, individuals who believe that others can be readily manipulated will seek to put this belief to actual use. And given that practice does indeed often make perfect, it might be expected that they will soon come to master this subtle art. As a result, they will often tend to be more successful in situations involving social exchange than persons not holding such views. That high scorers on the Mach scale do indeed often do better in social exchange than those scoring low has been demonstrated in several interesting experiments. For example, in one study (Christie and Geis, 1970b), ten one-dollar bills were placed on a table in front of groups of three subjects, who were then informed that this money would belong to any two of them who could agree on how to divide it. One of the three persons present during each session was a high scorer on the Mach scale, one a medium scorer, and one a low scorer. It was predicted that in general, high-Mach individuals would tend to do best in this type of exchange, and in fact, results supported this expectation. In every single case, the high-Mach person was a member of the winning coalition. Further, these individuals succeeded in talking their partners out of more money than medium or low Machs: average winnings for the high, medium, and low-Mach players were $5.57, $3.14, and $1.28, respectively. Similar results have been obtained in many other situations, including ones based on the Prisoner's Dilemma (Christie, Gergen, and Marlowe, 1970). Thus, it does appear that in many cases, high-Mach individuals are more successful in instances of social exchange than others. Further findings suggest that their success is primarily due to two factors.

First, high Machs tend to show a pattern of cool detachment in exchange situations. They do not become emotionally involved with their opponents, or even with their own beliefs and actions. Rather, they operate in a largely pragmatic fashion directed consistently toward the goal of positive outcomes. Thus, while others are becoming excited or upset, they retain their "cool," and continue to behave in a manner calculated to yield the best possible results. Second, high Machs appear to be both highly resistant to social influence from others and also quite skilled at using such techniques themselves. Thus, they are not easily swayed by arguments from their opponents and instead, often manage to influence them. Together, these patterns of behavior generally ensure that high Machs both dominate and control many social interactions, often at the expense of their opponents.

Now that we have considered the meaning of Machiavellianism and its relationship to social exchange, please go back and compute your own score on the Mach scale. For questions 1, 3, 4, 5, 9, and 10, simply add the numbers you have circled. For questions 2, 6, 7, and 8 reverse the scoring so that 5 becomes 1, 4 becomes 2, and so on. Then add the values for these two sets of questions. An average score on this short form of the Mach scale is 25, so if you scored substantially above this value, you are a high Mach, while if you scored substantially below it, you are a low Mach. Given the evidence we have already reviewed, it seems possible that if you qualify as a high Mach, you may be quite adept at manipulating others, and so tend to succeed in instances of social exchange. If you are a low Mach, however, you may be somewhat less successful in such situations. Please note, though, that many other factors influence our outcomes in social exchange, so scoring high or low on the Mach scale does not in any sense guarantee—or rule out—success in such interactions. Moreover, even if you believe that other people can be readily hypothetical situation involving the sale of a used car. If they played the role of buyer, they were informed that the particular type of auto in question usually sold for $1,500, so under no circumstances should they agree to pay more than this amount. If they played the role of seller, they were told that they could be certain of obtaining at least $1,000 for the vehicle from almost any used-car dealer, so they should never agree to sell it for less than this amount.

After receiving these instructions, subjects exchanged written bids and counterbids with another individual whom they believed to be a subject like themselves. In reality, though, they actually exchanged bids with the experimenter, who played the appropriate role. Because the experimenter served as the opponent for each subject, it was possible to systematically vary the initial offers they received. In one group (the *moderate initial-offer* condition), the experimenter's opening bid was quite moderate in nature, while in a second group (the *extreme initial-offer* condition), it was much more extreme. For example, when playing the role of seller, the experimenter opened with an initial asking price of $1,500 in the moderate-offer condition, but with a far less reasonable demand of $2,000 in the extreme-offer group.

Bargaining then continued by means of the exchange of written offers between the experimenter and subjects until agreement was reached. Chertkoff and Conley reasoned that subjects would fare more poorly in the exchange when facing an opponent who began with an extreme offer than when facing one who started with a moderate position, and as you can see in Figure 11-9, this was actually the case. Participants did offer more for the car when playing the role of buyer, and received less for it when playing the role of seller under conditions

FIGURE 11-8. *Opening with a relatively extreme initial offer may often prove to be an effective strategy in interpersonal bargaining. (Source: THE WIZARD OF ID by permission of Johnny Hart and Field Enterprises, Inc.)*

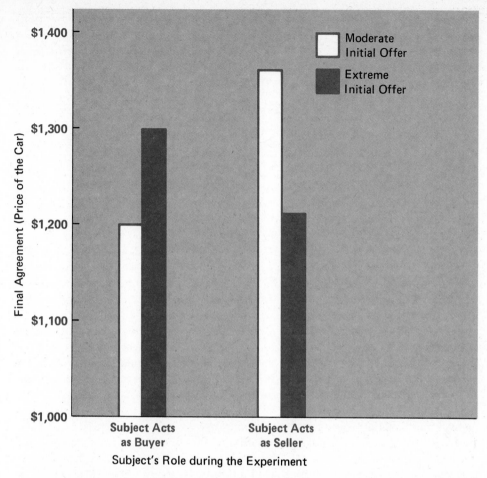

Final Agreement (Price of the Car)

$1,400

$1,300

$1,200

$1,100

$1,000

☐ Moderate
Initial Offer

■ Extreme
Initial Offer

**Subject Acts
as Buyer**

**Subject Acts
as Seller**

Subject's Role during the Experiment

FIGURE 11-9.   *The effects of initial (opening) offers on bargaining.   Subjects fared more poorly against an opponent who started with an extreme initial offer than against one who opened with a moderate initial offer.   That is, they paid more for the car when playing the role of buyer, and received less when playing the role of seller.   (Source: Based on data from Chertkoff and Conley, 1967.)*

where the experimenter began with an extreme initial offer.   In short, they fared more poorly against an opponent who adopted a "tough" initial stance than against one who assumed a more reasonable opening position.

Before proceeding further, we should note that the strategy of beginning with an extreme initial offer can easily be overdone, and so backfire on its users. That is, starting with a totally outlandish bid may sometimes serve only to anger or irritate one's opponents, so that they break off the negotiations before they actually get started.   Short of this point, though, the findings of the Chertkoff and Conley study, as well as those of several others, suggest that assuming a relatively extreme initial stance can often be an effective strategy in interpersonal bargaining.

While several mechanisms probably contribute to such effects, additional research suggests that the most important involves changes in the aspirations held by one's opponents (Yukl, 1974a, 1974b). After receiving an extreme initial bid, many individuals seem to lower their expectations, and no longer hope to do as well in the exchange as they had originally planned. This reduction in ambitions, in turn, leads them to make larger concessions than might otherwise have been the case, with the end result that the "tough" bargainer emerges with a highly favorable settlement. In short, the impact of taking an extreme initial position seems to stem primarily from the fact that it serves to discourage or demoralize one's opponents.

Making a Profit While Breaking Even: The "Big-lie" Technique in Social Exchange. Closely related to the tactic of taking an extreme initial position in negotiations is the procedure of announcing a highly favorable break-even point. Bargainers using this technique inform their opponents that their outcomes will be negative below a particular point—when in fact they will actually be positive. For example, a saleswoman may seek to convince a potential customer that if she agrees to sell an automobile, appliance, or house for the price suggested, she will actually lose money on the deal. Similarly, a prospective employee may attempt to persuade his new employer that it would not be worth his while to shift jobs unless certain benefits are provided when in fact this is not the case. If used effectively, this **big-lie technique** can be quite successful. Convinced that they must at least equal their opponent's break-even point, bargainers may raise their offers to levels where this person is actually obtaining very favorable outcomes (Chertkoff and Baird, 1971). From the point of view of maximizing one's outcomes in a social exchange, then, it is often beneficial to announce a break-even point far higher than reality dictates.

The Role of Concessions in Bargaining: When It Pays to Be Reasonable

As our discussion up to this point suggests, many bargaining sessions seem to begin with the adoption of relatively extreme initial positions by both sides. That is, each party quickly assumes a position he or she knows full well is unacceptable to the other, and negotiations proceed from this point. If agreement is ever to be reached in such cases, of course, it is necessary for at least one side, and perhaps both, to make some concessions to their opponent. In the absence of such movement, discussions will probably grind to a halt, and may even collapse altogether. Given the fact that negotiators are often faced with strong and mounting pressures to reach agreement (e.g., the costs rise rapidly for both sides in prolonged labor disputes or armed military conflict), it might be expected that the individuals involved would turn quickly to a pattern of mutual concessions in order to resolve their differences in a rapid and efficient manner. Unfortunately, as you probably know, history reveals that this is frequently not the case, and that important negotiations do often become deadlocked. Further, your own experience probably suggests that a similar pattern of stubborn inflexibility often develops in personal disputes between friends, relatives, and even lovers. Several reasons seem to account for such unwillingness to compromise.

First, individuals involved in a social exchange are often reluctant to grant concessions to their opponents because they realize that once these are offered, they cannot be readily withdrawn. In short, bargainers are afraid that by behaving in a conciliatory manner, they may actually weaken their own position. Second, and perhaps even more important, they are concerned that any concessions on their part will lead to unfavorable changes in the image they convey to their opponent. For example, they fear they will lose the appearance of inflexibility that may cause their opponent, instead, to give ground. Or similarly, they worry that by granting concessions they will be made to seem "weak," with the undesirable result that their opponent will actually increase his or her demands in the present or future situations (Pruitt, 1971a). To put it simply, if you give in to another person's demands today, it may be very difficult to refuse them on other occasions.

To some degree, such concerns seem justified. Research findings suggest that in many cases, individuals who make few concessions, or concessions of small magnitude often obtain better outcomes in social exchange than individuals who grant many concessions or ones of large magnitude (Chertkoff and Conley, 1967; Komorita and Brenner, 1968). Once again, however, such tactics can readily be overdone to the point where they anger one's opponents and cause them to become equally unyielding themselves. Thus, other findings suggest that perhaps the best bargaining strategy is one of offering one's opponents a relatively large number of concessions, but keeping the magnitude of these concessions quite small (Yukl, 1974a, 1974b). In this manner, little will actually be conceded, but at least the appearance of being reasonable and willing to compromise can be maintained.

Resolving Interpersonal Conflict: Strategies for Compromise

The evidence we have considered so far seems to suggest that from the point of view of maximizing our own outcomes in social exchange, a "tough" bargaining strategy is often best. In general, we can obtain more favorable settlements or terms by adopting a relatively extreme initial position, announcing an artificially high break-even point, and making only small concessions than by following an opposite, conciliatory strategy. Unfortunately, though, as noted above, such procedures often tend to backfire. As long as our opponents can be persuaded to give ground, a "tough" approach may be successful. Once these persons have decided to stiffen their own resolve and stand firm, however, continued use of this strategy may yield only deadlock, and turn out to be largely self-defeating. In such cases, both sides refuse to budge, and further progress toward a settlement is impossible. Indeed, each side may loudly condemn the other for its unreasonableness and inflexibility, with the result that feelings run high, and the chances of an agreement are further reduced.

Regrettably, instances of this type are far from rare. For example, they can be seen in peace talks which drag on for years while mutual blood letting continues, and in bitter labor disputes which persist for months while both sides suffer painful economic losses. Given the seriousness of such situations, it would be very beneficial if techniques for reducing conflict and encouraging trust and compromise could be developed. Fortunately, several such procedures have been proposed, and we will consider two of the more promising.

The first, usually known as the **graduated reciprocation in tension reduction** approach, was proposed some years in the past by Charles Osgood (1962). This strategy for inducing mutual trust and reducing persistent conflict is based largely on the performance by one side to a dispute of an initial small, and unilateral conciliatory action. That is, one side first announces and then carries out a small concession, without requiring any guarantee of reciprocal action by the other. Presumably, such a move puts pressure upon the second party to grant a similar concession. This can then be reciprocated by the first, and gradually, through a series of small, conciliatory gestures, trust is restored and tension reduced.

Informal evidence for the effectiveness of such a strategy is provided by actual events in the field of international relations between the Soviet Union and the United States which took place during the months following the Cuban missile crisis. Some of the steps in this graduated reciprocation in tension reduction were as follows. First, President Kennedy announced on June 10, 1963, that the U.S. was unilaterally ceasing to test nuclear weapons in the atmosphere. Thus, he took the first step toward conciliation between the two nations. Premier Khrushchev responded to Kennedy's initiative by praising his decision, and announcing that he had ordered a halt to the production of strategic bombers. Additional small steps followed, leading finally to the signing of a formal test ban treaty on August 5, 1963. Through a series of unilateral conciliatory gestures, then, tensions between the two superpowers were reduced, and some degree of trust restored.

More formal evidence for the effectiveness of Osgood's strategy has been obtained in several experiments (Komorita, Sheposh, and Braver, 1968; Pilisuk and Skolnick, 1968). For example, in a study conducted by Hamner (1974), subjects bargained against an opponent (whose responses were simulated by the experimenter) over the price of an imaginary product. The session began with a stalemate, in which the subjects' opponent refused to make any concessions. Then, in a second phase, he made a number of unilateral concessions. Finally, following this, he adopted one of three distinct strategies: he either matched the magnitude of any concessions made by subjects (a "soft" approach), made slightly smaller concessions than subjects (an intermediate approach), or made concessions only half as large as those made by subjects (a "tough" approach). As expected, results indicated that the "soft" strategy was most effective in ending the stalemate, and restoring movement toward agreement. In fact, when the opponent adopted this strategy, agreement was ultimately reached 100 percent of the time (see Figure 11-10). The results of this study, and those of other experiments, seem to suggest that, following a stalemate, procedures based on Osgood's proposals may indeed be highly effective.

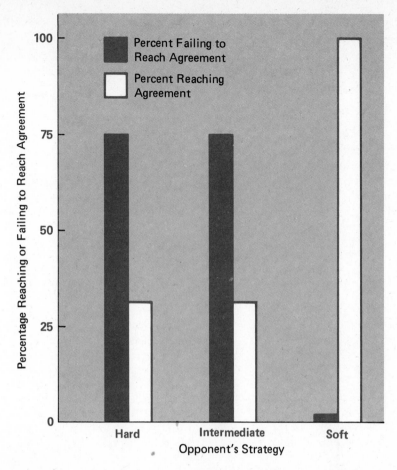

FIGURE 11-10. *The effects of concessions on bargaining. Following a stalemate, the adoption of a "soft" strategy, in which each side matches the other's concessions, may be much more effective in producing an agreement than a "hard" strategy in which each attempts to make smaller concessions than the other. (Source: Based on data from Hamner, 1974.)*

A second major strategy which may prove effective in helping to resolve interpersonal conflicts has been suggested recently by Pruitt and Lewis (1975). Basically, these researchers argue that *integrative solutions*—ones in which both sides achieve highly favorable outcomes—can be strongly enhanced by a **problem-solving orientation** to social exchange. In such an orientation, both opponents view the exchange situation as one representing a solvable problem in which, if appropriate steps are taken, both sides—not simply one—can obtain highly positive results. This is in sharp contrast to the more common orientation of bargainers that their major task is simply that of doing as well as they can, regardless of the outcomes of the other side. The problem with such an individualistic approach, Pruitt and Lewis argue, is that it often results in

SAVING "FACE": PROTECTING ONE'S IMAGE IN SOCIAL EXCHANGE

No one wants to look weak or foolish in the eyes of others. As you undoubtedly know from painful, personal experience, public embarrassment is a very negative occurrence—something to be avoided at all costs. Given this fact, it seems quite reasonable to suggest that most individuals possess a strong motive to avoid losing *face* in front of other persons. And indeed, the existence of such a motive has been confirmed in several different experiments (Brown, 1970; Garland and Brown, 1972). Not surprisingly, this desire to protect one's image appears to exert several important effects on the process of social exchange.

First, the motive to avoid losing "face" leads many persons to adopt a relatively firm stance in their dealings with others. That is, afraid that any concessions on their part will be interpreted as signs of weakness, bargainers often follow a "tough" strategy in which they refuse to make any conciliatory gestures. Unfortunately, as we have already noted, such tactics often result in stalemate, and negative outcomes for both sides. In many such cases, only the efforts of *mediators*—whose recommendations permit those involved to grant mutual concessions without losing face—are successful in breaking the deadlocks which develop.

Second, the motive to avoid losing "face" often leads individuals to sacrifice valuable gains in order to avoid public embarrassment. This conclusion is supported by the findings of several experiments conducted by Bert Brown and his colleagues (Brown, 1970; Brown and Garland, 1971). In these studies, subjects were offered considerable monetary payoffs for engaging in various embarrassing tasks. For example, in two studies conducted by Brown and Garland, they were offered pay at the rate of $7.20 per hour for singing the ballad "Love is a Many Splendored Thing" in front of an audience. As you might expect, subjects often chose to forego such rewards in order to avoid the public embarrassment and

possible loss of "face" they might experience as a result of performing such activities.

Finally, the motive to avoid losing "face" may often serve as the basis for vengeful behavior in social exchange. Persons who have been forced to lose "face" by an opponent often seem willing to sacrifice valuable gains—and even to accept negative outcomes—in order to get back at the person responsible for their embarrassment. Evidence for such effects has also been obtained in actual research. For example, in one study (Brown, 1968), subjects were first exploited by their opponent in a bargaining situation, and then received feedback from an audience who had watched these events informing them either that they had been made to look weak and foolish, or that they had done the best they could under the circumstances and had not lost "face." (Individuals in a third, control group received no feedback.) Conditions were then arranged so that participants could retaliate against their opponent and make *him* lose "face," but only at considerable monetary expense to themselves. As you can see in Figure 11-11, subjects were much more likely to engage in such behavior when they had previously suffered a severe loss of "face" than when they had not. In fact, it appeared that they were far more concerned with restoring their lost image than in obtaining the economic rewards available.

Together, such findings suggest that the motive to protect one's image—or restore it when damaged—may often play a powerful role in social exchange. Human beings are not simply concerned with economic considerations; social needs and motives are often of equal—if not greater—importance. The implications of these facts for effective dealings with others should be obvious: tactics which cause one's opponent to lose "face" should usually be avoided. For example, it may be very poor strategy to present final ultimatums to others; such actions place them

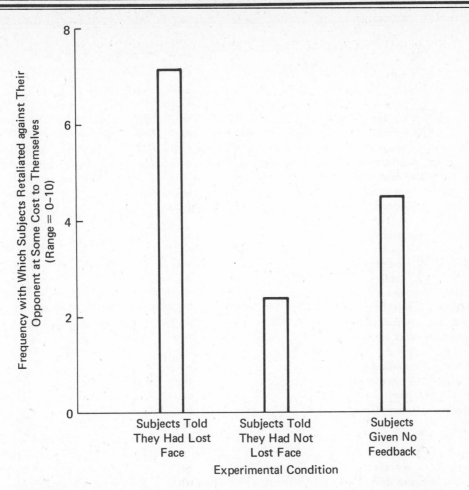

FIGURE 11-11. *"Revenge" following a severe loss of face. Subjects who had been exploited by an opponent and informed that he had caused them to look weak and foolish later attempted to retaliate against him (at considerable cost to themselves) much more frequently than subjects informed that they had not lost face in this respect, or those not provided with any feedback on this issue. (Source: Based on data from Brown, 1968.)*

in a position where to accept, guarantees a severe loss of face. Similarly, it is a mistake to goad one's opponents into statements to the effect that their position is firm or "nonnegotiable." Once such declarations have been issued, they may lock individuals into positions from which they can later escape or retreat only at the expense of a severe loss of "face." And finally, it is probably a serious error to gloat publicly over the retreat or surrender of one's adversaries—such actions may cause them to regret their concessions, and may even lead them to withdraw such offers. In sum, there appear to be very strong grounds for seeking to protect our opponents in any social exchange—as well as ourselves—from a public loss of "face."

settlements which are only barely acceptable to one side or the other. And, of course, such agreements hardly represent a firm or solid basis for lasting trust and cooperation.

In order to test the validity of these suggestions, Pruitt and Lewis (1975) conducted an experiment in which male undergraduates, playing the role of a buyer and seller, respectively, bargained over the price of various commodities (iron, sulfur, coal). In one condition, they were told to approach their negotiations as a solvable problem in which conflict should be avoided, and both sides obtain positive outcomes, while in a second, they were instructed simply to make as much profit for themselves as possible. In accordance with the suggestions outlined above, it was found that subjects did indeed make a larger joint profit under the problem-solving than individualistic instructions. Moreover, under a problem-solving orientation, subjects tended to show more concern for their opponent's welfare, transmitted more accurate and less false information, used fewer pressure tactics against their opponents, and made fewer outright demands for concessions on his part. In short, the bargaining sessions took on a distinctly cooperative flavor, in which both sides worked together to obtain a mutually beneficial agreement. Given such findings, it seems reasonable to suggest that to the extent individuals participating in social exchange can be induced to adopt such a cooperative, problem-solving orientation, conflict may not only be resolved and eliminated, but perhaps actually avoided.

PERCEIVED FAIRNESS IN SOCIAL EXCHANGE: GETTING WHAT WE DESERVE FROM OTHERS

Have you ever taken part in a social exchange which you felt was somehow unfair? In all probability, your answer is "yes," for such experiences seem to be a very common feature of our social relations with others. In most cases, feelings of unfairness center around the belief that we have somehow been cheated or shortchanged in the relationship—that we have received less than we deserve. For example, we may feel that we have done more for another person than they have done for us, or that we have worked harder on some project than others, only to receive the same or even smaller rewards than they. In other situations, though, such feelings stem primarily from the belief that we have received *more* than we deserve. For example, we may conclude that we have not earned the praise or prestige we receive from other persons, or that we have been too demanding in our relations with a friend or acquaintance. Regardless of whether such reactions arise out of having exploited others or having been exploited by them, it is the perception on our part of *unfairness* that is of primary importance.

At first glance, it might seem that the task of determining whether a given social exchange has been basically fair or unfair would be a simple one: presumably, we merely examine our outcomes and those of others, and determine whether all parties have received what they deserve. In reality, though, making such judgments turns out to be far more complex in nature.

Fairness can be defined in several different ways, and this definition itself can vary from situation to situation, and relationship to relationship. According to Gerald Leventhal (1976a, 1976b), a researcher who has spent almost ten years investigating the nature of fairness in social relations, our judgments in this respect appear to be strongly determined by three distinct rules, according to which we determine whether participants are getting what they deserve in such relationships or not. One of these rules is based on the contributions of each party to the exchange, another upon their respective needs, and the third upon equality of outcomes.

Judgments of Fairness in Social Exchange: The Role of Contributions, Needs, and Equality

The first rule we seem to follow in judging the fairness of any social exchange, and the one which has received by far the greatest attention, is based upon both the contributions and outcomes of all participants. According to this rule—which has often been termed *distributive justice* or **equity**—fairness exists when the outcomes of each participant match his or her contributions in a special manner. Specifically, fairness exists when individuals who have made large contributions receive relatively large rewards, those who have made small contributions receive small rewards, and so on. This type of special "justice" has often been represented by the following simple equation:

$$\frac{\text{Outcomes of Person A} - \text{Contributions of Person A}}{\text{Contributions of Person A}} =$$

$$\frac{\text{Outcomes of Person B} - \text{Contributions of Person B}}{\text{Contributions of Person B}}$$

Basically, what this equation implies is that fairness or equity will be seen to exist when the ratio of Person A's outcomes or benefits to his overall contributions approximate those of Person B (i.e., the ratio of this person's outcomes to *his* contributions). Equity, in short, is largely a relative judgment. What is important is not that the actual outcomes or contributions (inputs) of the individuals involved be equal, but that the *ratio* of these two factors match. Perhaps the nature of both equitable and inequitable social relations can best be illustrated by means of a specific example.

Imagine the case of two individuals, both of whom work for the same company. One is paid $10,000, shares an office and phone with several other persons, does not have the key to the executive washroom, and has no parking space in the company garage. The other, in contrast, receives a salary of $35,000, has a large private office, two private phones, enjoys all executive privileges, and possesses a reserved parking space with her name printed above it in large gold letters. Would these two individuals perceive that equity or **inequity** exists between them? So far, it is impossible to tell. Remember that judgments of this type are *relative* in nature; before we can determine whether the relationship between these persons will be perceived as fair or unfair, we must know what their contributions, as well as their outcomes, are.

Let us suppose, then, that the first individual above has a very easy job requiring only thirty-five hours of nondemanding work per week, had no prior experience before joining the company, and holds only a B.A. degree. In contrast, imagine that the second performs a much more difficult and technical job, involving over fifty hours of work per week, had fully twenty years of prior experience before gaining her present position, and holds the Ph.D. degree. Given this additional information, would you say that equity or inequity prevails? In all probability, the relationship between the two persons would probably be viewed both by outside observers and the individuals themselves as basically equitable or fair: the person providing large contributions to the company (long hours of work, a great deal of experience, advanced training) receives larger outcomes than the one providing smaller contributions (less work, little experience, no advanced training). This, of course, is as it "should be," and since the ratio of their positive outcomes to their contributions appears to be roughly in balance, fairness prevails (see Table 11-4 for a summary of these conditions).

But now consider the following situation. Imagine that the outcomes of the two persons remain as already described, and that the contributions of the first are also unchanged. However, the contributions of the second are much lower, so that they now involve performance of an extremely easy job requiring only twenty hours of relaxed work per week, one year of prior experience, and possession of only a B.A. degree. Would the two persons involved now perceive the relationship between them in a different light? Almost certainly they would. Both individuals—but especially the first—might now perceive that a high degree of inequity exists. This is the case because one provides relatively small contributions and receives relatively small rewards, while the other provides even *smaller* contributions (she works only twenty hours per week), yet receives fairly large payoffs. The equation representing their contributions and outcomes is badly out of balance, and feelings of unfairness would probably be aroused (refer to Table 11-4). Indeed, the first individual might speculate that the second has "something" on the boss, or is related to this person in some manner. In sum, one rule we follow in making judgments of fairness or unfairness—and perhaps the most important—is based upon the belief that the contributions and outcomes of all participants to an exchange should be in approximate balance. When this rule is violated, as is often the case, strong feelings of inequity or unfairness may be produced.

A second rule we seem to employ in making judgments about fairness in social exchange involves the relative *needs* of the persons involved. Often, we define fairness in terms of the extent to which each participant has his or her legitimate needs fulfilled. According to this rule, those with strong needs should receive more than those with weaker ones. Informal evidence for the operation of this principle can be observed in many situations. For example, it seems to

TABLE 11-4. *Conditions which would be expected to produce feelings of equity (fairness) or inequity (unfairness) on the part of a particular individual (Person A). In the first case (equity), Person B receives greater outcomes than Person A, but deserves these rewards because of his or her greater training, experience, and effort. In the second case (inequity), however, Person B receives greater benefits, but does not appear to be entitled to them.*

		Equity or Fairness	
	Person A		*Person B*
Outcomes	$10,000 salary Small, shared office Party-line phone No key to washroom No parking	Outcomes	$35,000 salary Large, private office Private phone Key to washroom Reserved parking
Contributions	Easy work No prior experience B.A. degree 35-hour work week	Contributions	Difficult work 20 years prior experience Ph.D. degree 50-hour work week

		Inequity or Unfairness	
	Person A		*Person B*
Outcomes	Same as Above	Outcomes	Same as Above
Contributions	Same as Above	Contributions	Easy work 1 year prior experience B.A. degree 20-hour work week

account for the fact that in times of accident or disaster, help is usually provided first to those who are most in need of assistance (the "women and children first" syndrome). It can also be seen in the actions of teachers, who often spend more of their time attempting to aid the slowest students in the class (those most in need of such help) than helping the faster pupils. The operation of this rule has also been demonstrated in several laboratory studies (Berkowitz, 1972; Leventhal, Weiss, and Buttrick, 1973). For example, in one recent experiment (Leventhal and Weiss, 1977), subjects were asked to divide monetary rewards between themselves and a partner whose need for money seemed to be either high or low. In accordance with the needs rule, subjects generally gave more to the former than to the latter individual.

A final justice rule according to which we make judgments of fairness in social exchange involves *equality* of outcomes for all participants. Basically, this rule suggests that all participants should obtain similar, if not identical payoffs, regardless of their contributions. As you might guess from your own experience, this principle often seems to play an important role in social exchange

Perceived Fairness in Social Exchange: Getting What We Deserve from Others

among adults. In addition, because of its relative simplicity, it is relied upon quite heavily by young children, who lack the sophistication needed to follow the contributions or needs rules with a high degree of consistency (Peterson, Peterson, and McDonald, 1974).

Not surprisingly, the relative weight or importance of each of these rules varies from situation to situation, and from one type of interpersonal relationship to another. For example, the contributions (equity) rule seems to be of great importance in cases where individuals are strongly concerned about getting their "fair share," such as in the type of employment setting described previously. Similarly, the equality rule is often followed in situations where the persons involved wish to maintain harmony and avoid conflict. That is, it is often believed that an equal distribution of outcomes will help accomplish such goals (Leventhal, Michaels, and Sanford, 1972). Finally, the needs principle seems quite important in various types of intimate relationships, such as those between lovers or close friends, in which the parties involved are strongly concerned that each other's needs be fulfilled. Regardless of which of these three principles is assigned the greatest weight, however, considerable evidence suggests that when one or more have been violated, and the parties to a social exchange conclude that it has somehow been unfair, two major effects generally follow. First, they experience negative emotional reactions, and second, they seek to reduce or eliminate such feelings (Adams, 1965; Walster, Berscheid, and Walster, 1973). Because the attempts by such persons to counteract feelings of unfairness often exert a strong effect upon the nature of their relationships with others, we will now examine several different strategies for accomplishing this goal.

Tactics for Restoring Fairness: Overcoming Injustice in Social Exchange

The first general strategy which can be employed by individuals to eliminate feelings of unfairness is that of altering their contributions to a social exchange. If they feel that they have received *less* than they deserve, they may reduce their contributions, while if they feel that they have received *more* than was fair, they may actually increase such inputs. An example of the first reaction is provided by the actions of a worker who, concluding that her wages are too low (given the demands of the job) reduces her productivity. An instance of the second type of reaction—increasing one's contributions to justify the receipt of large rewards— might be seen in the behavior of a pampered husband who, after having his "consciousness raised," realizes that his wife has been handling an unfairly large share of the household drudgery, and decides to take over several of these tedious chores. Evidence that individuals do often attempt to eliminate feelings of unfairness through adjustments in their contributions has been obtained in a number of different studies (Kessler and Wiener, 1972; Pritchard, Dunette, and Jorgenson, 1972). In such experiments, subjects led to believe that they were being underpaid often reduced their productivity in performing various tasks, while those led to believe that they were being overpaid often raised their work performance. Such findings suggest that under some conditions, at least, individuals often do attempt to eliminate feelings of unfairness by changing the nature of their contributions to a social exchange.

Closely related to this first strategy is a second, in which individuals seek to eliminate feelings of unfairness by altering their *outcomes* in an exchange relationship. That is, a person who feels *underrewarded* may attempt to gain a larger share of available rewards, while one who feels *overrewarded* may actually seek to lower his or her share of the benefits. Instances of the first type, of course, are extremely common. For example, workers who feel underpaid will often seek to increase their wages through strikes or other collective action, while friends, relatives, and even lovers who feel that they are not receiving their just rewards in a relationship may complain loudly and long about their mistreatment. As you can probably guess, instances in which individuals attempt to eliminate feelings of unfairness by *reducing* the size of their outcomes are far less common. Apparently, most persons are somewhat less sensitive to unfairness when it operates in their favor than then it operates to their disadvantage. However, the occurrence of this type of reaction has also been observed in several laboratory studies.

For example, in one investigation (Leventhal, Weiss, and Long, 1969), subjects were confronted with a situation in which a $2.00 reward earned by themselves and a partner could be divided by the two parties in any way they wished. Half then learned that their partner had decided to give them $1.40 while keeping only $0.60 for himself, while the remainder learned that he had

One strategy often adopted by individuals experiencing feelings of unfairness concerning a social exchange is that of attempting to change their outcomes in it. For example, workers who feel that their wages are too low may strike for higher pay. (Photo by Owen Franken; Stock, Boston.)

Perceived Fairness in Social Exchange: Getting What We Deserve from Others

decided to divide the rewards in precisely the opposite manner, taking the lion's share for himself. Subjects in both conditions were then told that they could alter this division by shifting any amount they wished up to a limit of $0.70, between their partners and themselves. In general, subjects took advantage of this opportunity, and altered the division imposed by their partner in the direction of equality. Those who had been offered only $0.60 added about $0.40 to their share, while those who had received $1.40 subtracted about $0.30 from their earnings. (Notice that persons in the latter group did not quite return all their excess winnings to their partner; apparently, a slight differential in their favor was quite acceptable!)

Interestingly, the tactic of restoring feelings of fairness through adjustments in the magnitude of one's outcomes may involve several exchange relationships rather than simply one. That is, an individual who feels cheated or exploited on one social exchange may attempt to make up for such treatment by taking more than he deserves in another. Similarly, a person who feels that he has received more than he deserves in one relationship may actually take less than his fair share in another (Austin and Walster, 1974, 1975). In short, feelings of equity or fairness can be restored by adjusting one's outcomes across several different relationships, as well as by changes within one.

A third strategy which can be adopted by individuals who perceive that they have been treated unfairly in social exchange is that of withdrawing from the relationship altogether. For example, a young man who feels that his college roommate has failed to pay for his fair share of the expenses may decide to move and seek other company. Similarly, a woman who feels that she has been exploited by her marriage partner may finally seek divorce as an effective—if drastic—means of eliminating such unfair treatment. Once again, laboratory evidence confirms the use of such a strategy. Indeed, experimental findings suggest that many individuals prefer smaller rewards in fair relationships to larger ones in unfair exchanges where they are exploited (Schmitt and Marwell, 1972).

A final technique for reducing feelings of unfairness—and perhaps the one which has received the greatest amount of attention from social psychologists— involves changes in one's perceptions of an exchange relationship. That is, individuals experiencing feelings of unfairness may simply alter their perceptions of the relationship in question, so that at least the illusion of justice, if not justice itself, is restored. Such distortions in perceptions or cognitions can take many different forms. For example, individuals who find themselves receiving the "short end of the stick" may rationalize this unpleasant state of affairs by concluding that the person who is exploiting them actually *deserves* his or her excessive share of the rewards by virtue of some special talent, ability, or other characteristic (Walster, Berscheid, and Walster, 1973). Or, in an even more bizarre manner, they may conclude that they are actually benefiting from the unfair treatment they receive—after all, a little suffering is "good for the soul," and may make them a better person! Perhaps the most unsettling type of perceptual distortion occurring in such situations, however, involves the tendency of persons receiving more than they deserve to derogate and devalue the persons they exploit. In fact, as we shall soon see, observers often seem to derogate such victims even in cases where they themselves are not responsible for their exploitation or suffering.

Derogating Innocent Victims: Justifying Injustice. Suppose that in order to fulfill a course requirement, you participated along with several other persons in a psychological experiment. By what appeared to be random choice, one of the participants was selected to perform a memory task, receiving painful electric shocks for her errors, while the others, including yourself, were simply asked to observe her reactions and emotional states. After watching this person receive a number of shocks, and react with what seemed to be strong pain, you were asked to evaluate her along several different dimensions (e.g., intelligence, likableness, cooperativeness, etc.). How do you think you would respond? Common sense suggests that you might experience sympathy for the innocent victim, and so perhaps evaluate her quite favorably. In reality, however, the results of a large number of experiments suggest that just the opposite would be true: you and the other persons present would actually tend to derogate her quite strongly, giving her low ratings on many of the dimensions (Lerner, 1970, 1974; Lerner and Simmons, 1966). Although several interpretations have been offered for the occurrence of such **victim derogation,** one centers around the feelings of unfairness you might experience in this setting, and the ways in which you might reduce them. Basically, the argument goes something like this. Because the victim has suffered quite a bit while you and the other participants have escaped totally unscathed, you might well view the situation as an unfair one—after all, why should one person receive all the shocks while the others merely watch? Since you can't offer the victim any help, it is impossible to eliminate these feelings by taking your fair share of the punishments. One way in which you *can* eliminate such feelings, though, is by perceiving her in a very negative light. That is, if she is not a very nice person, then perhaps she really *deserved* the suffering she experienced. Since it is relatively easy to lower your opinion of a stranger, you can readily eliminate your feelings of unfairness in this manner, and may well choose to do so. The result, of course, is that the innocent victim is derogated and devalued merely because she has suffered! (Needless to say, victims never receive any shocks in such studies; in fact, what subjects usually observe is merely a specially prepared videotape in which the supposed victim pretends to experience discomfort.)

While the reactions we have just described may strike you as quite surprising, they have been observed in so many studies, and under so many different conditions (Stokols and Schopler, 1973; Stein, 1973), that there is currently little doubt about their occurrence. Further, it has been found that this tendency to derogate and devalue persons who have somehow gotten the "short end of the stick" may be even greater in situations where we ourselves are directly responsible for their exploitation, rather than merely witnessing it (Leventhal, 1976a). This tendency to devalue such persons has many important implications. Perhaps most important is its potential role in the tolerance of social injustice. Specifically, many basically decent individuals may be willing to accept or overlook conditions in which one group is exploited and mistreated by another because, observing the victims suffer, they conclude that they must somehow *deserve* such abuse. If this is indeed the case, injustice may often carry with it the foundation for its own justification.

Fortunately, additional evidence suggests that the strong tendency to derogate the victims of exploitation can be counteracted by several different

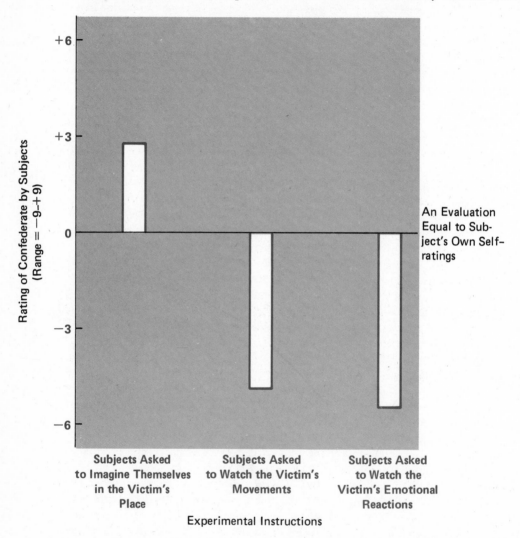

FIGURE 11-12. *Empathy and the derogation of "innocent victims." When subjects were asked to imagine themselves in the role of a person who received what seemed to be a series of painful electric shocks, they showed little tendency to derogate or devalue her. In fact, they tended to evaluate her more favorably than themselves. In contrast, when subjects were asked merely to observe this person's emotional reactions or movements, they derogated her strongly. (Source: Based on data from Aderman, Brehm, and Katz, 1974.)*

factors. First, it appears that such effects may be avoided when these persons have the capacity to retaliate for their mistreatment (Berscheid, Boye, and Walster, 1968). Second, derogation may fail to occur when the victims *choose* to be exploited in order to spare others from such treatment (Legant and Mettee, 1973). Here, feelings of gratitude may block devaluation of such persons. Finally, derogation may be prevented by feelings of sympathy or empathy for innocent victims. Evidence pointing to this conclusion has been obtained in a recent study by Aderman, Brehm, and Katz (1974). In this experiment, subjects watched an innocent person receive a series of seemingly painful electric shocks under conditions similar to those described above. In one condition, they were asked to observe her emotional reactions, as in the research conducted by Lerner and his colleagues (Lerner and Simmons, 1966). In a second group, they were asked to observe all her body, head, and arm movements as closely and carefully as possible. Finally, in a third condition, they were told to try to imagine themselves in the same situation—how they would react if *they* were the victim. It was predicted that these latter instructions would cause subjects to experience empathy toward the victim, and so prevent them from derogating her at a later time. As you can see in Figure 11-12, results confirmed these predictions. While subjects in the first two groups derogated the victim strongly, those in the final, empathy-enhancing condition actually evaluated her in a more favorable manner than themselves. Such findings suggest that derogation of innocent victims may occur only under conditions where empathy is absent, and may be readily prevented by the presence of such responses. Unfortunately, the development of empathic reactions can be blocked by a number of different conditions, including anger toward the victim, dislike for this person, or even simple distraction (Bandura and Rosenthal, 1966). Thus, it appears that in many cases, derogation may be a relatively simple and convenient means through which exploiting persons can lessen feelings of unfairness with respect to their victims.

SUMMARY

Because we cannot satisfy many of our most important needs by ourselves, we must often enter into a process of *social exchange* with others, offering them benefits in return for those we wish to obtain. This process is seen very clearly in *cooperation*—behavior in which two or more individuals work together or coordinate their actions in such a manner that the outcomes attained by each are increased. Cooperative behavior usually develops in situations where the goals sought by several individuals can be shared or divided once they are obtained. In many cases such divisions are impossible, and an alternative form of behavior known as *competition* develops. Here, each individual strives to maximize his or her own outcomes, often at the expense of others.

Research concerned with the occurrence of cooperation has indicated that it is strongly influenced by a number of situational factors including (1) the behavior of other persons (whether they behave cooperatively or not), (2) their apparent power to influence our outcomes, and (3) various forms of communication, including threats. In addition, large individual differences in the tendency to cooperate also exist. Most persons seem to fall into one of three distinct "types" in this respect: cooperators—who are concerned with the welfare of others as well as themselves; competitors—who are concerned primarily with doing better than others, and individualists—who are concerned only about their own outcomes. *Machiavellianism,* a tendency to view others as easily or readily manipulable, also seems to play an important role in several aspects of the exchange process.

Bargaining represents a somewhat more complex form of social exchange in which participants engage in a mutual trading of offers in an attempt to reach an agreement about issues of common concern. Many forms of behavior, including various techniques of social influence and persuasion seem to play a role in this process. Research findings indicate that taking an extreme initial position and making relatively small concessions to one's opponents may often be an effective bargaining strategy. However, such tactics can sometimes backfire and result in a deadlock. Once stalemate has occurred, other procedures involving willingness to make unilateral concessions, and adopt a problem-solving orientation toward negotiations, may be more useful. Most individuals are greatly concerned that they do not lose "face" in social exchange—be made to look weak or foolish by their opponents. Indeed, so strong is this motivation that many persons will give up large rewards in order to avoid public embarrassment.

In many cases, one or more of the participants to a social exchange may conclude that it was somehow *unfair.* Usually, such feelings stem from the belief that one has been cheated or shortchanged by others, but they can also arise when individuals perceive that they have received more than they deserve. Such feelings of unfairness are quite unpleasant, and individuals often actively attempt to reduce them by (1) altering the magnitude of their contributions to the exchange, (2) altering the magnitude of their outcomes from it, or (3) withdrawing from the relationship altogether. An additional strategy for reducing feelings of unfairness involves distortions of one's perceptions regarding the exchange, and can take many different forms. One particularly unsettling reaction of this type is the tendency to derogate or devalue persons who have been exploited. Through such reactions, individuals who have exploited or harmed others may convince themselves that these persons were actually deserving of such treatment, and so eliminate any feelings of unfairness.

GLOSSARY

Bargaining. A form of social exchange in which individuals trade offers and concessions in an attempt to reach agreement concerning some issue of mutual interest.

Big-lie technique. A bargaining tactic in which negotiators announce artificially high break-even points. (That is, they claim that they need better outcomes in the exchange to break even than they really do.)

Cooperation. A form of social exchange in which two or more individuals work together or coordinate their behavior in order to attain a shared goal.

Cooperators. Individuals who have a cooperative orientation toward social exchange. That is, they wish to maximize others' outcomes as well as their own.

Competition. A form of social exchange in which individuals attempt to maximize their own gains, often at the expense of others.

Competitors. Individuals who have a highly competitive orientation toward social exchange. That is, their main goal is that of doing better than their opponents.

Equity. Refers to perceived fairness in social exchange. Equity or fairness is seen to exist when the outcomes received by each participant and the contributions they supply are in approximate balance.

Face. Refers to the strong motive possessed by most persons to avoid appearing weak or foolish in front of others. When, despite their best efforts, individuals do suffer public embarrassment, a loss of face is said to have occurred.

Graduated reciprocation in tension reduction. A strategy for resolving conflict in which each side engages in a series of small, unilateral concessions. As a result, tension is reduced and progress toward agreement may be facilitated.

Individualists. Persons who have an individualistic orientation toward social exchange. That is, they are concerned only with maximizing their own outcomes; the results obtained by others are of little or no interest to them.

Inequity. Refers to the absence of perceived fairness in social exchange. Inequity or unfairness is seen to exist when the outcomes received by each participant and the contributions they supply are not in balance.

Reciprocity. An important principle of social interaction (often viewed as a social norm) suggesting that we should behave toward others in a manner similar to their past treatment of us.

Social exchange. A basic process of social interaction in which individuals provide each other with a wide range of benefits.

Social power. Refers to the ability of one individual to influence the outcomes obtained by another. Thus, in any social exchange, if one individual can affect the outcomes of the other to a greater extent than this person can influence *his* outcomes, the first person is said to have a power advantage.

Threats. A form of communication in which one individual warns another of negative actions he or she will take if the threatened person does not behave in some specified manner.

Victim derogation. Refers to the fact that often the innocent victims of exploitation or harm are derogated by persons who either witness or actually cause such negative outcomes.

SUGGESTED READINGS FOR CHAPTER 11

Brown, B. R. Saving face. *Psychology Today,* 1974, *4,* 55–59. An interesting discussion of the motive to save "face"—avoid appearing weak or foolish in the eyes of others—and the effects which may occur when, despite their best efforts, individuals experience a loss of "face."

Christie, R., and Geis, F. L., eds. *Studies in Machiavellianism.* New York: Academic Press, 1970. This book describes the role of Machiavellianism—a personal orientation based on the belief that others are easily manipulated—on various forms of social exchange. Chapter 1, which describes the nature of Machiavellianism, and Chapter 15, which provides an overview of the research conducted to study it, may be of special interest.

Leventhal, G. S. Fairness in social relationships. In J. Thibaut, J. T. Spence, and R. Carson, eds. *Contemporary topics in social psychology.* Morristown, N. J.: General Learning Press, 1976. A very readable discussion of the nature of perceived fairness in social interaction. Among the topics covered are the bases upon which individuals make judgments concerning the fairness of any exchange relationship, and various strategies they adopt to eliminate unfairness.

Simpson, R. L. *Theories of social exchange.* Morristown, N. J.: General Learning Press, 1972. A summary of several major theories of social exchange. The discussion of the framework proposed by Thibaut and Kelley is especially interesting.

Walster, E., Berscheid, E., and Walster, G. W. New directions in equity research. *Journal of Personality and Social Psychology,* 1973, *25,* 151–176. This article presents a very carefully organized and reasoned discussion of equity theory. In addition, applications of this theory to such topics as derogation of innocent victims and intimate (romantic) relations are included. (Since this paper is a bit more technical than several of the others listed here, you may wish to read it after completing the article by Leventhal.)

GROUPS AND INDIVIDUAL BEHAVIOR: THE CONSEQUENCES OF BELONGING

12

Your throat is dry, your stomach seems to be tied in knots, and icy chills run up and down your spine. It's your day to give an oral presentation in one of your courses and although you've prepared for many hours, you can't help feeling extremely nervous about the whole situation. Suddenly, the fateful moment is upon you, and you hear your instructor call your name. With shaking knees, you make your way slowly to the front of the room. Turning to face your audience, you spread your carefully prepared notes before you, and crossing your fingers for luck, plunge right in. At first, your voice quavers, and you feel as though you are about to pass out. As you continue, though, a remarkable transformation seems to occur. Your confidence grows with each passing minute, and soon you find yourself holding forth with considerable vigor and eloquence. So smoothly do things go that before you know it your time is up, and you are returning to your seat. Now that your ordeal is over, you feel downright elated, and can't imagine why you were so worried before. After a few minutes, the class is over, and as you pick up your books and leave, you find yourself wondering about the small miracle that has just taken place. How was it possible, you wonder, that you actually performed better *in front of a large and critical audience than you did the night before alone in the privacy of your own room? Why did the presence of many other persons actually seem to improve rather than impair the quality of your presentation?*

For the fifth night in a row, you sit down with your three roommates to a dinner consisting largely of beans. As you attempt to choke down one mouthful after another of this unpleasant meal, you find yourself pondering the circumstances that led you to this unfortunate state of affairs. Back at the beginning of the semester, you and your three friends were faced with a tough decision: you could rent either a small and rather plain apartment which you could easily afford, or a large and fairly luxurious one which would be certain to put a serious strain on your limited resources. One afternoon, you met to discuss these two possibilities. At the beginning of your conversation, it was obvious that all of you were mildly in favor of renting the luxurious suite of rooms, but that you also shared serious misgivings about being able to afford it. As your talks continued, though, a strange shift seemed to take place. Gradually, you all became increasingly enthusiastic about the extravagant choice, until finally, you unanimously agreed to adopt it. Now, several lean and hungry months later, you find this decision puzzling. How, you wonder, could you have made such a poor choice? What mysterious process caused the four of you to convince one another that you could afford an apartment which was actually far beyond your means?

Your school's football team has just won a dramatic victory. The score was tied until the last few seconds, when a long forward pass by the star quarterback saved the day. As soon as the whistle blows, happy fans stream down onto the playing field, elated at the victory. At first, the crowd simply mills about, but soon some daring fellows pull down the goalposts and break them up into small pieces. Within a few minutes, a roaring fire is going, and happy students, parents, and faculty are moving excitedly about, illuminated by the red glow. Gradually, emotions rise to a higher and higher pitch and soon other objects are being tossed into the flames. Paper plates, newspapers, and other forms of litter are the first to go. But as the minutes pass, larger and more valuable objects begin to make their appearance, and you notice books, programs, pennants, and even articles of clothing being thrown into the fire. By this time, many people are shouting in a hysterical manner, and still larger objects are being hurled into the flames. Stadium seats, the carts of hot dog and ice cream vendors, and even benches from the sidelines are all smashed and tossed into the huge bonfire. Things are really beginning to get out of hand when the sound of police sirens suddenly fills the air. With surprising speed, the crowd begins to scatter, leaving behind a scene of utter chaos and destruction. The next morning you read in the paper that over $100,000 worth of damages were inflicted on the stadium, and that it will have to be closed for several weeks for major repairs. Moreover, you are shocked to discover that more than a dozen persons were injured in the night's activities. As you fold the paper, you marvel over the frenzied events you observed. What process, you wonder, managed to convert a happy crowd of sports fans into a raging mob of vandals? How did this happy, if boisterous occasion turn into such a destructive and dangerous one?

It's Saturday morning, and you are enjoying the luxury of resting in bed. As you lie there, warm and snug under the covers, your thoughts return to the happy days of your childhood. You remember your old friends, and the many games you played. One person in particular stands out in your mind—Dave—the acknowledged leader of your neighborhood group. His opinions were always the most influential ones, and it was to him that the other members turned for advice and decisions. The group usually played whatever game he desired, and it was his style of dress, mannerisms, and expressions that everyone attempted to copy. As you remember his central role in your childhood group, you find yourself wondering how he attained this influential position. Dave was not the tallest or strongest member of the gang.

Nor was he the handsomest or brightest. Yet somehow he always seemed to be the one to whom everyone turned for direction and leadership. Why, you wonder, was this the case? Are some people born to lead and others only to follow? Or was Dave simply thrust into this position by virtue of the fact that he was the most effective at getting certain things done—the best person for the job, so to speak?

Although these incidents are quite varied in nature, they actually share two characteristics. First, in each one, you were part of a group, and second, your membership in that group—no matter how shortlived or fleeting—exerted strong effects upon your behavior. In the first of our examples, knowledge that the instructor and other members of the class were watching and evaluating your performance exerted a strong impact upon it. In the second, a discussion with your friends led to a bad decision for which you all paid dearly. In the third, being part of a large crowd seemed to influence the actions of many persons, somehow inducing them to behave in ways they would never show while alone. And in the fourth, the important impact of leaders on the behavior of other group members—including your own—was brought into focus. In all of these incidents, then, the feelings, behavior, and thoughts of the persons involved (you and others) were strongly affected by membership in various social groups.

Before proceeding further, we should pause to specify precisely what we mean by the term **group**. In social psychology, groups are usually viewed as possessing two major characteristics. First, their members generally recognize some degree of affiliation or connection with one another. That is, they experience a sense of *belonging* which, however fleeting, is not shared by nonmembers. Second, the fates of group members are somehow interdependent, so that the outcomes of each person are linked in some manner to those of others. Together, these two criteria allow us to distinguish between social groups on the one hand, and mere collections of individuals who happen to be present at some location on the other.

As we have already noted, membership in various groups can often exert important effects upon the individuals involved, shaping their behavior, attitudes, beliefs, and interests to a surprising degree. Because the effects of groups on their members are so far-ranging and profound, we could not hope to examine all of them here. What we can do, though, is focus our attention on several of the more interesting and important ones. Basically, then, our discussion will proceed as follows.

First, we will examine what is in some ways, at least, the simplest kind of group influence: effects stemming from the mere physical presence of others. While the presence of other persons has many effects upon our behavior (see Chapter 7, pp. 308–315), one of the most important seems to involve their impact on our performance of various tasks—a phenomenon often known as **social facilitation**. Thus, our main concern here will be with the question of whether performance is improved or impaired by the presence of others who can observe

A

B

True social groups (Photo A) are distinguished from mere collections of individuals (Photo B) by two facts: their members experience a feeling of belonging, and are somehow interdependent.

and possibly evaluate our behavior. Second, we will consider the impact of group membership on *complex decisions*. Are groups or individuals more likely to "go off the deep end" and adopt extreme positions? Recent experiments provide some intriguing answers to this age-old question. Third, we will examine the ability of groups to weaken the restraints of their members against engaging in various forms of dangerous antisocial behavior—a process usually termed *deindividuation*. And finally, because groups often seem to exert their most important effects on individual members through the actions or directives of *leaders,* we will also turn our attention to this topic. Here, two basic questions will be of primary interest: How do individuals rise to positions of leadership, and what factors then determine their effectiveness in such roles?

SOCIAL FACILITATION: BEHAVIOR IN THE PRESENCE OF OTHERS

It's a bright, sunny day in spring, and since the flowers are blooming, and the trees are cloaked in a new coat of brilliant green, you decide to take advantage of the beautiful weather and get some practice in your new hobby, painting. You have just set up your easel in an attractive spot and begun to paint, when another person walks by. Obviously interested in your work, he pauses, and after a moment asks whether you mind if he watches. Wishing to be polite, you indicate that you have no objections, and he takes a seat on the grass, watching over your shoulder as you work. A few minutes later, a young couple strolls by. They too stop and ask your permission to sit nearby. Again you agree, and now all three individuals watch as you paint. Similar incidents continue to occur at irregular intervals, and within half an hour, you find yourself surrounded by a circle of spectators, all intent upon observing your canvas take shape. Do you think that the presence of these persons will have any effect upon the quality of your work? That is, do you think that your picture will turn out to be better, worse, or very much the same as it would have been if no one else were present on the scene?

Interest in such questions has had a long history within social psychology. Indeed, many of the earliest experiments in the field were conducted to examine the influence of an audience upon performance (Triplett, 1897). Unfortunately, the results of these studies were quite confusing. On the one hand, a number of experiments conducted with human beings, animals, and even such unlikely

As common sense suggests, our performance of various tasks is often strongly affected by the presence of an audience. (Photo: Talbot Lovering; Stock, Boston.)

subjects as ants suggested that performance could be improved by the presence of others, either as passive spectators or as co-actors performing the same task (Chen, 1937; Dashiell, 1930; Travis, 1925). Such results were often labeled **social facilitation**—the enhancement of performance produced by the presence of others. On the other hand, however, an equally large number of investigations suggested that performance could actually be *impaired* by such conditions (Gates and Allee, 1933; Husband, 1940; Pessin, 1933). In fact, so inconsistent and contradictory were the results of these studies that early researchers literally threw up their hands in despair and turned their attention to other topics.

Somewhat surprisingly, this state of affairs continued essentially unchanged until quite recent times. In fact, it was not until the mid-1960's that an apparent solution to this old but persistent puzzle began to emerge. At that time, Robert Zajonc (1965), a well-known social psychologist, conducted a thorough review of all existing evidence relating to this issue. On the basis of this intensive analysis, Zajonc concluded that the conflicting experimental findings reported over the years could readily be resolved if it were assumed that the presence of others tends to produce an increase in individuals' level of motivation or general arousal. This suggestion agrees, of course, with the informal observation that the presence of other persons—especially in the form of an audience watching our behavior—often makes us feel tense, nervous, and excited. But how, you may ask, can it help us account for the fact that their presence sometimes serves to facilitate and sometimes to impair our performance on various tasks? The answer lies in two basic facts.

First, it is a well-established principle in psychology that increments in an organism's level of motivation or arousal often lead to an enhancement of its tendency to perform the strongest or most dominant responses in its behavior repertoire. Second, these dominant responses can either be correct or incorrect in any particular situation under study. Combining these two simple facts in a straightforward manner, it can readily be predicted that any increments in motivation induced through the presence of an audience or co-actors will facilitate subsequent performance when dominant responses are *correct* in a given situation, but will actually impair performance when such responses are *incorrect* or inaccurate. (The manner in which both of these predictions can be derived from Zajonc's proposals is illustrated in Figure 12-1, and we suggest that you examine it carefully before proceeding further.)

As you might suspect, Zajonc's theoretical suggestions were greeted with considerable enthusiasm by social psychologists: in one clean stroke, his proposals seemed to resolve more than sixty years of confusing and inconsistent results. Put very simply, his theory suggested that whether the presence of an audience will improve or interfere with performance depends primarily on which responses are dominant among the individuals involved. Applying this proposal to previous research, it seemed reasonable to suggest that studies which had demonstrated improved performance in the presence of an audience involved situations in which subjects' dominant responses were correct ones, while investigations which had yielded opposite findings probably involved situations in which participants' dominant responses had been incorrect.

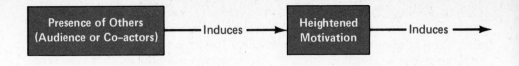

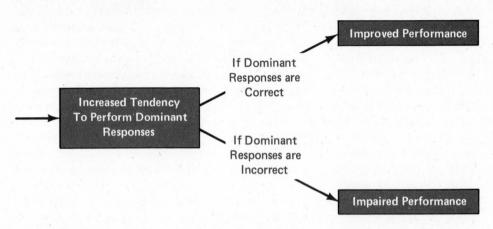

FIGURE 12-1. *Zajonc's theory of social facilitation. The presence of other persons induces increased motivation which, in turn, enhances the tendency to perform dominant responses. If these are correct, performance is improved, while if they are incorrect, it is actually impaired.*

While Zajonc's theory seemed to account both simply and elegantly for the findings of many previous studies, it could not be accepted with any great degree of confidence until it was itself subjected to careful experimental test. Fortunately, such tests were not long in coming, and as we shall soon see, quickly provided convincing support for the drive or motivational interpretation of social facilitation.

The Drive Theory of Social Facilitation: Some Initial Findings

Not too surprisingly, the first investigation designed to examine the suggestion that the mere presence of others increases motivation, and so enhances the emission of strong or dominant responses, was conducted by Zajonc himself (Zajonc and Sales, 1966). Basically, this study consisted of two distinct parts. In the first, subjects were asked to examine photographs of ten different words supposedly taken from the Turkish language, but actually constructed for experimental purposes (e.g., civadra, zabulon, lokanta). Each time a word was presented, it was pronounced by the experimenter and then by the subject. The frequency with which each word was exposed was varied systematically, so that some were shown only once, others twice, and still others four, eight, or sixteen times. In this manner, Zajonc and Sales hoped to control the extent to which subjects became familiar with or learned each of these strange, new terms, so that it would be possible to know which were relatively dominant and which relatively subordinate within their individual response hierarchies.

During the second part of the study, subjects were informed that the same Turkish words would be flashed on a screen for very brief periods of time, and that their task was that of attempting to recognize them. In reality though, the slides shown contained only wavy black lines. Zajonc and Sales reasoned that under these conditions, subjects' guesses concerning the words being presented would reflect the degree to which they had become familiar with them during the first part of the study. In short, subjects should now show a marked tendency to report "seeing" words they had previously examined eight or sixteen times more often than words they had seen only once or twice; indeed, they might not even remember the latter words well enough to say them. Zajonc and Sales further reasoned that if the presence of other persons actually enhanced our tendencies to emit dominant responses, the frequency with which subjects would report perceiving high-frequency words should be increased by the presence of others on the scene. In order to investigate this crucial suggestion, half of the subjects attempted to recognize the Turkish words supposedly being shown while alone in the experimental room, while the remainder performed the same task in the presence of two confederates who had supposedly requested permission to watch the experiment. It was predicted that subjects in the audience condition would emit more dominant, high-frequency words and fewer subordinate, low-frequency words than those in the alone condition, and as you can see in Figure 12-2, this was actually the case. Similar findings were soon reported in other investigations, some employing procedures similar to those we have described here, and some using quite different methods (Cottrell, Rittle, and Wack, 1967; Matlin and Zajonc, 1968). Together, the results of such studies provided convincing support for Zajonc's proposal that the presence of other persons enhanced the performance of dominant responses.

Zajonc's second major suggestion—that the presence of other persons produces an increase in motivation or arousal—was also soon confirmed. For example, in one study conducted by Martens (1969), subjects performed a complex motor task either while alone in the experimental room or while being observed by an audience of ten other persons. At various points during the study, a measure of their level of physiological arousal (based on the amount of perspiration present on the palms of their hands) was obtained. As expected, subjects who performed in front of an audience demonstrated a higher level of arousal than those who performed the same task while alone in the room. Thus, consistent with our informal observation that the presence of other persons often causes us to feel nervous or tense, research findings revealed that we do sometimes experience increased physiological arousal under such conditions.

Within a few short years, then, considerable support was obtained for both assumptions of Zajonc's theory (see Laughlin and Jaccard, 1975). The presence of other persons did seem to increase the tendency of individuals to perform their strongest or most dominant responses, and such effects did seem to stem from

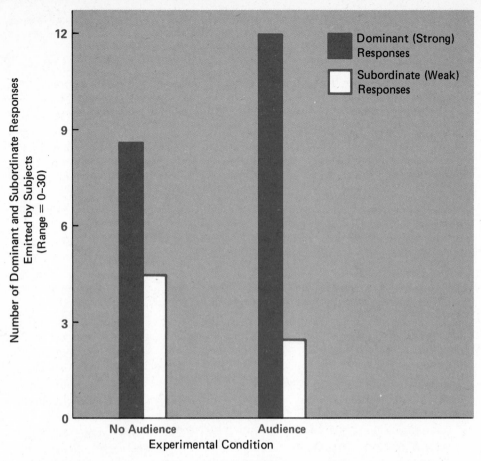

FIGURE 12-2. *The effects of an audience on the performance of dominant and subordinate responses. As shown above, subjects emitted more dominant responses and fewer subordinate responses in the presence of an audience than when alone in the experimental room. (Source: Based on data from Zajonc and Sales, 1966.)*

increased arousal or motivation. Unfortunately, though, these initial studies failed to address one important issue which may already have crossed your mind: do such effects stem from the mere physical presence of other persons, or from different and somewhat more complex factors? In all of the investigations we have described so far, the other persons present while subjects performed various tasks expressed interest in observing their actions, and actually watched while they behaved. As a result, it is impossible to determine whether the effects they exerted stemmed from their physical presence on the scene, or other factors such as subjects' concern about the impressions they were making on these individuals. It is precisely with this important issue that many subsequent studies of social facilitation have been concerned.

Suppose that you were performing some difficult and intricate task. Do you think that your execution of it would be more strongly affected by the presence of several soundly sleeping persons, or by an equal number of individuals who observed your actions very carefully, making detailed notes about them as you worked? Common sense suggests quite strongly that your performance might well be affected to a much greater degree by the latter conditions than by the former, despite the fact that Zajonc's original proposals make no mention of such factors. That is, it appears that social facilitation may occur only when others can observe our behavior, and perhaps evaluate it as well. That this is indeed the case has been demonstrated by several different experiments (Henchy and Glass, 1968; Martens and Landers, 1972).

First, it has been shown that the presence of others influences our behavior only when they are capable of observing our actions. Thus, in one well-known study (Cottrell et al., 1968), subjects performed a task similar to the one employed by Zajonc and Sales while either (1) alone in the experimental room, (2) in the presence of two other persons who wore blindfolds and could not see their performance, or (3) in the presence of two other persons who expressed interest in watching their behavior and wore no blindfolds. As expected, results indicated that social facilitation occurred only in the last of these conditions. Thus, contrary to Zajonc's original proposals, the mere physical presence of other persons—their warm bodies in the room—was not in itself sufficient to produce social facilitation. Such effects emerged only when they could observe subjects' behavior.

Second, it has also been demonstrated that social facilitation occurs only when subjects believe that the other persons present are judging or evaluating their behavior in some manner (Innes and Young, 1975; Martens and Landers, 1972). For example, in an experiment conducted by Paulus and Murdoch (1971), subjects performed the recognition task described previously either while in the presence of two other persons, or while alone in the experimental room. Half of the subjects who performed alone were informed that their actions would later be evaluated by two other individuals, while the remainder were not informed about any future evaluation. Similarly, half of those who performed before an audience were told that the persons watching would evaluate their performance, while the remainder were led to believe that no evaluation would occur. It was predicted that social-facilitation effects—the enhancement of subjects' tendencies to emit dominant responses—would occur only when evaluation was expected, and as you can see in Figure 12-3, this was actually the case. In short, it appeared that **evaluation apprehension** (concern over being evaluated or judged by others) and not their mere physical presence was crucial for the occurrence of social facilitation.

Together, the results of the studies conducted by Cottrell, Murdoch, and Paulus, and many other investigators seem to provide convincing evidence for

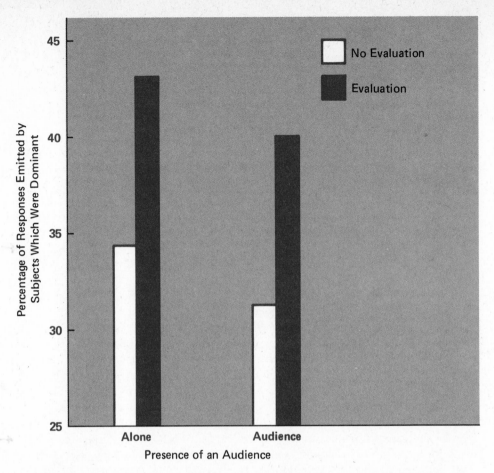

FIGURE 12-3. *The effects of anticipated evaluation on social facilitation. As shown above, subjects' tendencies to perform dominant responses were increased when they expected their perfomance to be evaluated by others. Moreover, this was the case whether these persons were physically present or not. (Source: Based on data from Paulus and Murdoch, 1971.)*

the view that social facilitation stems mainly from our concern over evaluations from others. Unfortunately, though, this relatively neat and orderly picture concerning the basis of such effects is somewhat clouded by one final set of findings: animals are affected in very much the same manner as ourselves by the presence of co-actors or an audience. Perhaps this surprising fact is most vividly illustrated by an intriguing study conducted by Zajonc, Heingartner, and Herman (1969).

In this unusual experiment, a very unlikely group of subjects—common household cockroaches—were placed in the two mazes shown in Figure 12-4. As you can see, the task represented at the top is quite simple, and subjects' dominant response—running straight ahead—is the correct one (it leads to

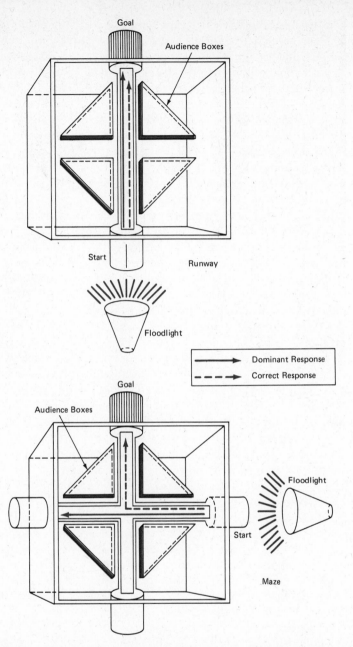

FIGURE 12.4. *The apparatus employed by Zajonc, Heingartner, and Herman (1969) in their investigation of social facilitation among cockroaches. Subjects' dominant responses (running straight ahead) were correct in the simple runway at the top, but were incorrect in the more complex maze, bottom. Note the boxes in which an audience of four other roaches could be placed in appropriate experimental conditions. (Source: Zajonc, Heingartner, and Herman, 1969. Copyright 1969 by the American Psychological Association. Reprinted by permission.)*

escape from the bright light). The task represented at the bottom, however, is somewhat more complex, requiring a turn to the right. Thus, subjects' dominant response is incorrect in this situation, and does not lead to escape from the light. Zajonc's theory leads to straightforward predictions in both situations. Basically, it predicts that the presence of an audience will facilitate performance in the case of the first maze, where subjects' dominant responses are correct, but will impair performance in the second, where their dominant responses represent errors. In order to test these predictions, subjects performed both tasks while alone in the apparatus, or while in the presence of four other roaches who were placed in the boxes shown in Figure 12-4. Results offered strong support for both expectations: the presence of an audience facilitated performance of the simple task, but interfered with performance of the more complex one. Thus, it appeared that roaches, like human beings, could be strongly influenced by the presence of an audience who could easily observe their performance.

These findings, and the results of other studies conducted with a wide variety of animal species (e.g., Rajecki et al., 1975, Rajecki, Kidd, and Iuins, 1976) raise serious questions for an interpretation of social facilitation in terms of evaluation apprehension. It seems quite awkward, after all, to attribute such concerns to chickens, roaches, or ants. (For example, do roaches as well as men and women worry about "looking good" in front of others?) In view of this fact, it appears that a truly satisfactory explanation for the occurrence of social facilitation must be based upon some simpler psychological mechanism common to human beings and many other species. Fortunately, one such mechanism has recently been proposed by Nicholas Cottrell (1972).

Social Facilitation: A Possible Resolution. Basically, Cottrell has suggested that social facilitation stems from the anticipation of positive or negative outcomes in the presence of others. More specifically, he suggests that both human beings and animals learn to anticipate various rewards and punishments while in the presence of other members of their own species, and that it is such anticipations which underlie the increased motivation and enhanced tendencies to perform dominant responses often observed under such conditions.

In the case of animals, such anticipatory reactions may be acquired through experiences in which the presence of others is linked with competition for food and mates, or with a battle for territory and other rewards. Among human beings, the presence of others is also frequently associated with positive or negative consequences, although in this case such outcomes may take a much wider range of forms, including praise, criticism, loss of "face," and so on. Whatever the particular consequences expected, however, Cottrell believes that it is the anticipation of their occurrence which underlies social facilitation.

As you can probably already see, these suggestions help explain why we are usually unaffected by the presence of other persons who cannot observe us or our performance: in such cases, we have little reason to anticipate positive or negative outcomes. Similarly, they shed some light on the question of why social facilitation is such a remarkably general phenomenon, occurring among roaches and birds as well as human beings. Briefly, it is based upon simple mechanisms of learning common to many different species. While there has not as yet been time for the full investigation of Cottrell's suggestions, initial findings do seem to support their accuracy (Good, 1973). Thus, when all the evidence is finally in, it may well turn out to be the case that this simplest type of group effect rests very much on processes and mechanisms we share with many other forms of life.

DECISIONS IN GROUPS: MODERATION OR POLARIZATION?

More than fifteen years in the past, at a time when John Kennedy had just become President and Vietnam was still an unfamiliar name to most Americans, James Stoner, a graduate student at M.I.T., planned an ambitious project for his master's thesis. Basically, he wanted to examine the popular belief that groups are more conservative in their decisions than individuals. In order to accomplish this task, he asked groups of college students to act as advisers to fictitious individuals supposedly facing choices between relatively risky but attractive courses of action, and relatively conservative but less attractive ones. For example, in one of these hypothetical situations, an individual faced the task of choosing between a secure but low-paying job, and a less certain, but higher-paying position with a new and untried company. In an initial phase of the experiment, subjects made their recommendations regarding these decisions alone. Then, in the main part of the study, they met in small groups where they discussed them until agreement was reached. In accordance with common-sense beliefs, Stoner expected that his results would show the group decisions to be more conservative than those reached by individuals. Yet, surprisingly, just the opposite was true: time and time again, groups made more risky or daring recommendations than their individual members had while alone.

Although the size of this difference was small, it quickly seized the attention of many social psychologists. This was the case for two major reasons. First, this apparent shift toward increased risk following group discussion ran directly counter to common sense and intuition. Decisions by groups, after all, must usually represent a compromise between the views of many different persons. Thus, it seems only reasonable to expect them to show a drab, middle-of-the-road quality (see Figure 12-5). Second, it was quickly realized that if groups were indeed more likely to "go off the deep end" than individuals, important implications for the decision-making activities of juries, military councils, government committees, and many other groups would be suggested.

In the face of these possibilities, many investigators turned their attention to this issue, and research on this phenomenon—which quickly came to be termed the **risky shift**—proceeded at full throttle for almost ten years. At first, researchers concentrated on demonstrating the reliability of such effects—showing that the risky shift actually occurred. Soon, however, they turned to the task of determining the reasons behind its existence (Dion, R. S. Baron, and Miller, 1970; Myers and Lamm, 1975, 1976). Several competing interpreta-

"Gentlemen, let us pool our expertise."

FIGURE 12-5. *Because decisions reached by groups must usually represent a compromise between the views of several persons, it has often been assumed that they will show a conservative, middle-of-the-road quality. (Source: Drawing by Stan Hunt; © 1975 The New Yorker Magazine, Inc.)*

tions were offered, and considerable heat was generated in arguments concerning the relative accuracy of each. Gradually, though, as such work continued, an important fact began to emerge: group decisions were not *always* riskier than individual choices. In fact, in some cases, they were actually more conservative (McCauley et al., 1973; Knox and Safford, 1976).

Thus, what had at first appeared to be a shift toward risk was soon revealed as a more general phenomenon: a *shift toward polarization*. In short, what seemed to take place during group discussion and decision making was this: group members became even more extreme in the same direction as their initial pregroup responses. That is, they came to hold their initial views or recommendations even more strongly than was at first the case. For example, if they were mildly in favor of a particular view or course of action prior to the group discussion, they came to favor it even more strongly after these procedures. Similarly, if they were mildly opposed to a particular view or course of action prior to group discussion, they came to be even more strongly opposed to it after the discussion was completed. (Both of these effects are illustrated in Figure 12-6).

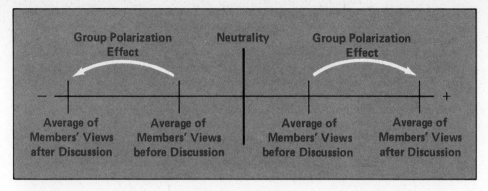

FIGURE 12-6. *Group-polarization effects. Following group discussion, members often shift toward positions more extreme than the ones they held initially, but in the same general direction (i.e., on the same side of the neutral point).*

As you can probably see, the existence of such shifts toward polarization has even broader and more important implications than the existence of a shift toward risk. Thus, not very surprisingly, they have recently become the focus of a great deal of interest and attention within social psychology. In the discussion which follows, therefore, we will touch on three major topics. First, we will examine some of the evidence relating to the occurrence of such effects—where and when they occur. Second, we will consider possible explanations for their occurrence—why group discussions often lead to polarization. And third, we will examine some of the implications of such shifts for group interaction, attitude change, and the quality of group decisions.

Polarization Is Where You Find It: The Generality of Group-induced Shifts

If group polarization effects occurred only with respect to a limited range of issues or views, they would be of little practical importance. In reality, however, they seem to take place in an extremely wide range of settings. Although we could not possibly hope to consider all of these here, we can at least focus upon two of the more important: the impact of group-induced shifts on attitudes, and jury or other court decisions.

Group Polarization and Attitudes: Enhancing Extremism. Perhaps one of the most important contexts within which group-induced shifts seem to occur is that of the discussion of attitudes. Several different experiments suggest that group members tend to become more extreme in their views following group discussion (Doise, 1969; Moscovici and Zavalloni, 1969). For example, in one study (Myers and Bishop, 1971), subjects first expressed their individual attitudes toward various courses of action which could be taken by another person (e.g., she could return home on vacation or go on a biology field trip). After expressing their favorability toward each action, subjects in one condition (the *discussion* group) met and discussed each item for three minutes. Those in a second condition (the *information-exchange* group) merely exchanged information regarding their initial positions without any discussion. Finally, those in a *control* group completed a brief anagram-solving task during this period of time. Following the completion of the appropriate activities, subjects in all three conditions expressed their own attitudes once again. It was predicted that only individuals who had met and discussed their attitudes with others would show a shift toward more extreme views, and as you can see in Figure 12-7, this was

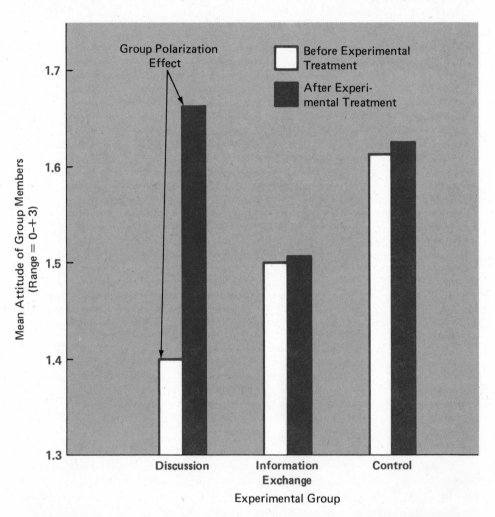

FIGURE 12-7. *Group polarization and attitudes. Individuals who discussed their views with others (the discussion group) shifted toward more extreme views. Those who merely exchanged information regarding their initial positions (the information-exchange group) or who performed unrelated tasks (the control group) failed to show similar shifts. (Source: Based on data from Myers and Bishop, 1971.)*

actually the case. Together with the findings of many other studies (Cvetkovich and Baumgardner, 1973; Myers and Bishop, 1970), these results indicate that group discussion does indeed frequently lead to shifts in the direction of polarization. In short, after discussing their views with others, individuals often seem to move toward and adopt more extreme views than they held initially.

Group Polarization and Court Decisions: Shifts toward Guilt or Innocence. One setting in which group-polarization effects would appear to be quite out of place is in the deliberations of juries or judges. Ideally, such discussions should center around the evidence presented by the defense and prosecution, with the final decision reflecting this information in as fair and impartial a manner as possible. Yet, somewhat unsettlingly, there is growing evidence that group-polarization effects occur in this context too.

First, several laboratory studies involving simulated juries (usually consisting of college students) indicate that subjects do indeed become more extreme in their views following a period of group discussion (Myers and Kaplan, 1976; Vidmar, 1972). Second, and even more disturbing, there is some indication that actual court decisions often develop in much the same manner. For example, in one interesting study, Walker and Main (1973) compared the decisions made by individual federal judges with those made by panels of three judges, in civil-liberties cases. Since the judges' initial views tended to be mildly pro-civil liberties, it was expected that group discussion might enhance or strengthen such views, and this was actually the case. While 30 percent of the decisions reached by individual judges were pro-civil liberties, fully 65 percent of those reached by the three-judge panels were in this direction.

In a related investigation, Kalven and Zeisel (1966) examined the court records for fully 225 trials. Not surprisingly, in the light of the evidence we have presented so far, they found that the initial majority position predicted the final outcome fully 90 percent of the time. Indeed, so strong was the evidence that jury deliberations served to strengthen initial judgments, that Kalvan and Zeisel (1966, p. 489) were led to make the following remark: "The deliberation process might well be likened to what the developer does for an exposed film: it brings out the picture, but the outcome is predetermined. . . . " In short, juries often seem to start with an initial, and relatively mild, tendency to hold the defendant guilty or innocent, and then, as a result of their discussion, become increasingly convinced of these views.

Other Instances of Group Polarization. Additional studies have demonstrated the occurrence of group polarization effects with respect to *risk taking* (Davis et al., 1974), *bargaining and negotiation* (Lamm and Sauer, 1974) *perceptions of other persons* (Myers, 1975), and even *judgments of physical dimensions* (Vidmar, 1974). In all these cases, individuals have been found to adopt more extreme positions or views following group discussion. Taken together, then, existing evidence seems to suggest that group-induced shifts toward polarization are a widespread and general phenomenon.

Group Polarization: Why Does It Occur?

As we noted earlier, when group-induced shifts were viewed primarily as involving movement toward increased risk, a number of competing explanations for their occurrence were suggested (see Dion, R. S. Baron, and Miller, 1970). As it became increasingly apparent that group-induced shifts were actually more general in nature, however, these interpretations were largely replaced by two somewhat broader views based, respectively, on **social comparison** and the **exchange of information** or **persuasive arguments.** Since these two approaches are now the most widely accepted, we will consider them in some detail.

Social Comparison and Group Polarization: The Desire to Be More Than Average. As you probably know from your own experience, we are constantly comparing ourselves with others. One reason why we engage in such activities so frequently is that often, it is difficult to evaluate many of our characteristics or accomplishments without reference to the people around us. Are we handsome or plain? Bright or average? Did we do well on an exam or poorly? Frequently, answers to such questions can only be obtained through a process of *social comparison* in which we relate our own traits, actions, and outcomes of those of others.

Although the relationship between this process and group polarization may not at first be obvious, social comparison has often been suggested as one potential explanation for such effects. Basically, the argument proceeds as follows. Most persons wish to maintain a positive self-image. As a result, they generally perceive their own views or inclinations to be more extreme—in the appropriate, valued directions—than those of others. For example, they perceive themselves as being more fair, open-minded, and unprejudiced than other persons. Yet, when they enter into discussions with such individuals, they often discover that, in reality, their own beliefs and preferences are relatively moderate—far more moderate than they initially believed. As a result, they then frequently shift in the direction of greater extremity in order to demonstrate strong adherence to the "right" values or views, and so reestablish a favorable position relative to others on these dimensions (Pruitt, 1971b, 1971c). As noted by Roger Brown (1974), the originator of this general approach: "To be virtuous in any of an indefinite number of situations is to be different from the mean—in the right direction and to the right degree." Evidence lending support to the social-comparison view stems from several different sources. First, as suggested by this interpretation, individuals do often tend to perceive themselves as being more extreme—in the "right" directions—than others. For example, in one study (Wallach and Wing, 1968), subjects were asked to fill out items similar to those contained in Table 12-1 two times, once as they would themselves, and again as they thought the majority of other students at their university would. As predicted by social-comparison theory, they tended to believe that these other individuals would be more conservative than themselves. (At this point, you may be able to demonstrate this fact for yourself. Simply compare your average scores for the Self and Others categories in the *Social Psychology in Action* insert above. Because larger scores indicate greater conservatism, social-comparison theory suggests that the score for the second category should be larger than that for the first.)

Second, individuals do often report admiring positions or views which are more extreme than their own—provided, once more, that they are extreme in the "right" or valued directions (Levinger and Schneider, 1969). (Once again, you may be able to demonstrate this for yourself by comparing your scores for the Self and Most Admired categories in the insert. In this case, the score for the first category should exceed that for the second.) Related to these findings is the fact that individuals do often perceive others who have responded more extremely than themselves more favorably than those who have not (R. S. Baron, Monson, and P. Baron, 1973; Jellison and Davis, 1973).

Together with other findings, such evidence seems to provide fairly strong support for an explanation of group polarization in terms of social comparison. However, we should hasten to add that not all experimental findings have been consistent with this general approach. For example, it has been found that subjects' tendencies to perceive others as less extreme than themselves seems to disappear when they estimate these persons' views *before* reporting their own (McCauley, Kogan, and Teger, 1971). According to social-comparison theory, the order in which such judgments are made should produce little or no difference. Second, an explanation of group polarization in terms of social comparison suggests that the larger the difference between their own views and those of others perceived by subjects, the greater should be their tendency to shift to extreme positions after group discussion. Yet this does not appear to be the case (Myers, Wong, and Murdoch, 1971). In the face of such negative findings many researchers have turned to a second explanation for group-polarization effects which we shall now consider—one based on an exchange of information or persuasive arguments.

Persuasive Arguments and Group Polarization: Loading the Dice in Favor of Group-induced Shifts. Basically, this second approach suggests that during group discussion, most of the arguments generated tend to favor the initially preferred view or alternative. That is, as might be expected, most of the arguments presented by participants offer support for their own initial beliefs. Since some of these arguments are almost certain to be ones which some members, at least, have not previously considered, the individuals taking part in the discussion literally convince one another that their initial views are indeed the best or most correct ones. As a result, there is a general shift toward more extreme positions. Several forms of evidence tend to confirm these seemingly reasonable suggestions.

First, it has been found that the greater the proportion of arguments favoring a particular point of view during a group discussion, the greater the shift in its direction (Morgan and Aram, 1975). For example, in one interesting study (Ebbesen and Bowers, 1974), subjects listened to specially prepared tape recordings of group discussions in which the proportion of arguments favoring risky and conservative courses of action varied from 90/10 percent (90 percent

SOCIAL PSYCHOLOGY IN ACTION

COMPARING YOURSELF WITH OTHERS:
GROUP POLARIZATION AND SOCIAL COMPARISON

Before proceeding any further, please stop for a few moments and complete each of the items shown in Table 12-1. First, complete them as you would yourself, by placing a check mark in front of the appropriate answer for each. Next, complete them as you
think most other readers of this book would by placing an X in front of one answer for each. Finally, indicate the answer you would most admire for each item by placing a + in the appropriate spot.

Table 12-1. *Complete these items in each of the ways described above. We will return to the relationship between your answers and group-polarization effects later. (Source: Adapted from Kogan and Wallach, 1964.)*

1. Ms. F is currently a college senior who is very eager to pursue graduate study in chemistry leading to the Doctor of Philosophy degree. She has been accepted by both University X and University Y. University X has a world-wide reputation for excellence in chemistry. While a degree from University X would signify outstanding training in this field, the standards are so very rigorous that only a fraction of the degree candidates actually receive the degree. University Y, on the other hand, has much less of a reputation in chemistry, but almost everyone admitted is awarded the Doctor of Philosophy degree, though the degree has much less prestige than the degree from University X.

Imagine that you are advising Ms. F. Listed below are several probabilities or odds that Ms. F would be awarded a degree at University X, with the greater prestige.
Please check the lowest *probability that you would consider acceptable to make it worthwhile for Ms. F to enroll in University X rather than University Y.*

____ Place a check here if you think Ms. F should not enroll in University X, no matter what the probabilities.
____ The chances are 9 in 10 that Ms. F would receive a degree from University X.
____ The chances are 7 in 10 that Ms. F would receive a degree from University X.
____ The chances are 5 in 10 that Ms. F would receive a degree from University X.
____ The chances are 3 in 10 that Ms. F would receive a degree from University X.
____ The chances are 1 in 10 that Ms. F would receive a degree from University X.

2. Mr. A, an electrical engineer, who is married and has one child, has been working for a large electronics corporation since graduating from college five years ago. He is assured of a lifetime job with a modest, though adequate, salary, and liberal pension benefits upon retirement. On the other hand, it is very unlikely that his salary will increase much before he retires. While attending a convention, Mr. A is offered a job with a small, newly founded company which has a highly uncertain future. The new job would pay more to start and would offer the possibility of a share in the ownership if the company survived the competition of the larger firms.

Imagine that you are advising Mr. A. Listed below are several probabilities or odds of the new company's proving financially sound.
Please check the lowest *probability that you would consider acceptable to make it worthwhile for Mr. A to take the new job.*

_____ The chances are 1 in 10 that the company will prove financially sound.
_____ The chances are 3 in 10 that the company will prove financially sound.
_____ The chances are 5 in 10 that the company will prove financially sound.
_____ The chances are 7 in 10 that the company will prove financially sound.
_____ The chances are 9 in 10 that the company will prove financially sound.
_____ Place a check here if you think Mr. A should not take the new job no matter what the probabilities.

3. Ms. G, a competent chess player, is participating in a national chess tournament. In an early match she draws the top-favored player in the tournament as her opponent. Ms. G has been given a relatively low ranking in view of her performance in previous tournaments. During the course of her play with the top-favored man, Ms. G notes the possibility of a deceptive though risky maneuver which might bring her a quick victory. At the same time, if the attempted maneuver should fail, Ms. G would be left in an exposed position and defeat would almost certainly follow.

Imagine that you are adivsing Ms. G. Listed below are several probabilities or odds that Ms. G's deceptive play would succeed.

Please check the lowest probability that you would consider acceptable for the risky play in question to be attempted.

_____ The chances are 1 in 10 that the play would succeed.
_____ The chances are 3 in 10 that the play would succeed.
_____ The chances are 5 in 10 that the play would succeed.
_____ The chances are 7 in 10 that the play would succeed.
_____ The chances are 9 in 10 that the play would succeed.
_____ Place a check here if you think Ms. G should not attempt the risky play, no matter what the probabilities.

4. Mr. B is a writer who is said to have considerable creative talent but who so far has been earning a comfortable living by writing cheap westerns. Recently he has come up with an idea for a potentially significant novel. If it could be written and accepted it might have considerable literary impact and be a big boost to his career. On the other hand, if he is not able to work out his idea or if the novel proves to be a flop, he would have expended considerable time and energy without remuneration.

Imagine that you are advising Mr. B. Listed below are several probabilities or odds that the novel will be a success.

Please check the lowest probability that you would consider acceptable for Mr. B to attempt to write the novel.

_____ Place a check here if you think Mr. B should not write the novel no matter what the probabilities.
_____ The chances are 9 in 10 that the novel will be a success.
_____ The chances are 7 in 10 that the novel will be a success.
_____ The chances are 5 in 10 that the novel will be a success.
_____ The chances are 3 in 10 that the novel will be a success.
_____ The chances are 1 in 10 that the novel will be a success.

5. Mr. D is the captain of College X's football team. College X is playing its traditional rival, College Y, in the final game of the season. The game is in its final seconds, and Mr. D's team, College X, is behind in the score. College X has time to run one more play. Mr. D, the captain, must decide whether it would be best to settle for a tie

score with a play which would be almost certain to work or, on the other hand, should he try a more complicated and risky play which could bring victory if it succeeded, but defeat if not.

Imagine that you are advising Mr. D. Listed below are several probabilities or odds that the risky play will work.

Please check the lowest probability that you would consider acceptable for the risky play to be attempted.

____ *Place a check here if you think Mr. D should not attempt the risky play no matter what the probabilities.*
____ *The chances are 9 in 10 that the risky play will work.*
____ *The chances are 7 in 10 that the risky play will work.*
____ *The chances are 5 in 10 that the risky play will work.*
____ *The chances are 3 in 10 that the risky play will work.*
____ *The chances are 1 in 10 that the risky play will work.*

When you have finished, add your answers for each of these three categories. That is, first add the numbers corresponding to each of your checks, then add the numbers for each of your X's, and finally add the numbers for each of your +'s. Next, take the average for each of these three totals by dividing by 5, *and enter these numbers in the spaces below.*

Self____   Others____

Most Admired____

Now continue with the text. We will return to the meaning of these numbers, and the significance of any differences between them, shortly.

favoring risk and 10 percent favoring caution), to 10/90 percent (10 percent favoring risk and 90 percent favoring caution). It was predicted that depending on the proportion of arguments they heard, subjects would demonstrate shifts toward either risk or caution, and that the magnitude of these shifts would vary with the proportion of the arguments they heard. As you can see in Figure 12-8, results offered strong support for these suggestions. Subjects who heard mostly risky arguments shifted in this direction, those who heard mostly conservative arguments shifted toward greater caution, and those who heard an equal number of both showed virtually no shift at all. These findings lend support to the view that group polarization is strongly influenced by the type of arguments presented during group discussion.

Additional support for the persuasive-arguments view is provided by the findings that (1) group-induced shifts occur even in the absence of actual discussion, provided subjects are exposed to arguments favoring one point of view over others, and (2) outside observers generally rate the arguments presented during actual group discussions which support participants' initial views as more persuasive than those supporting other positions (Vinokur and Burnstein, 1974).

Together, such evidence has led some investigators to conclude that it is the

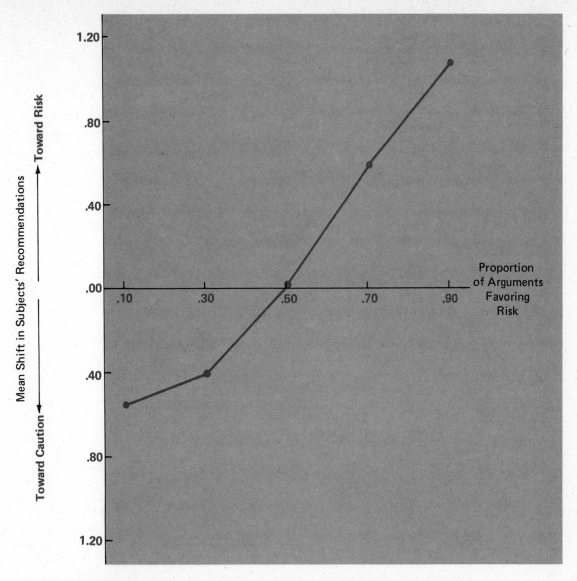

FIGURE 12-8. *Persuasive arguments and group polarization. Subjects' tendencies to alter their own views after overhearing a group discussion depended very strongly on the kind of arguments it contained. When most of the arguments favored risk, subjects shifted in this direction, while when most favored caution, they moved toward this strategy. (Source: Based on data from Ebbesen and Bowers, 1974.)*

exchange of persuasive arguments, and not social comparison, which accounts for the occurrence of group-polarization effects (Burnstein, Vinokur, and Pichevin, 1974). However, the fact that shifts of this type seem to occur even in situations involving simple perceptual judgments, where arguments and persuasion probably play little if any role, suggests that social comparison is also of some importance (R. S. Baron and Roper, 1976). At the present time then, it is probably most reasonable to assume that both social comparison and information exchange contribute to the occurrence of group polarization (Myers and Lamm, 1975, 1976). In short, individuals participating in group discussions probably shift toward more extreme positions both because they wish to demonstrate stronger adherence to the "right" views than other group members, and because they become increasingly convinced by the arguments they hear that the beliefs with which they started are indeed the best or most correct ones.

Group Polarization: Some Unsettling Implications

Regardless of the mechanisms involved in their occurrence, group-polarization effects appear to have many important implications. First, as you may have already guessed, they can contribute to the unsettling tendency of many decision-making groups to get further and further out of touch with reality, and so reach poor or erroneous conclusions. Such groups often meet repeatedly before making final decisions, and these meetings generally involve prolonged periods of group discussion. Thus, there is ample opportunity for the views held by members to become increasingly extreme and isolated from external circumstances. The result, of course, may well be inappropriate decisions with disastrous consequences. Did such effects contribute to the United States government's decision to escalate the Vietnam war, to the Japanese decision to ignore the threat of atomic weapons until they were actually used on Hiroshima and Nagasaki, and to other, similar tragic blunders throughout history? No direct evidence on such questions exists, but the possibility seems far from remote.

Second, the occurrence of group polarization may often contribute to the drift toward extremism which frequently seems to develop in political or social-action groups. Such organizations usually attract individuals who share basically similar views. Thus, when they meet to discuss these beliefs, members may soon become more and more convinced that *their* views are the only correct ones, and that all others are wrong or even evil. Since the same process may well be taking place simultaneously in groups holding sharply opposing views, the end result can often be a frightening degree of political polarization between as well as within groups (Myers and Bishop, 1970).

We should hasten to add, of course, that group discussion and resulting group-induced shifts in attitudes or beliefs can often have positive as well as negative consequences. Open discussion does provide individual members with a chance to have their "say," and bring potentially important facts or arguments to the attention of others. Further, a free exchange of views is essential for any democratic action. Finally, polarization effects may well produce beneficial results when the initial views held by members are indeed the best or most correct ones (assuming an objective means of assessing "correctness" exists). However, five years of intensive research on group polarization points to the conclusion that, contrary to popular belief, group discussion may not be the unmixed blessing it was once assumed to be. Indeed, under some circumstances, it seems capable of producing negative, harmful outcomes. As a result, we must always be on guard to protect against the development of dangerous forms of "groupthink" whenever individuals meet to discuss any one of a wide range of important decisions (Janis, 1972).

DEINDIVIDUATION: GROUPS AS RELEASERS OF ANTISOCIAL ACTIONS

Have you ever attended a crowded party where, after things "warmed up" sufficiently, many of the persons present began acting in ways they would normally never demonstrate (e.g., making passionate love in public, cracking one ridiculous joke after another, throwing food or other objects about the room)? Similarly, have you ever attended an exciting sports event at which you heard other fans shouting colorful phrases at the top of their lungs which they would probably never utter in the absence of a large crowd? If so, you have already observed first-hand evidence for the fact that the presence of many other people often seems to weaken our restraints against engaging in mild forms of socially prohibited behavior.

If the restraint-reducing influence of groups were limited to such relatively trivial instances, they would be of little interest or importance. Unfortunately, though, this is far from the case. Indeed, it appears that under certain conditions, groups may serve to weaken the restraints of their members against engaging in even such tragic and objectionable forms of behavior as destructive vandalism, mob violence, and gang rape. That such actions are indeed attributable (at least in part) to the restraint-reducing impact of large groups is suggested quite strongly by the fact that most of the persons taking part in such behaviors would never dream of acting in such a manner while alone, and are genuinely shocked and horrified by their actions when they later consider them in isolation during calmer periods. Thus, there seem to be strong grounds for suspecting that groups may sometimes induce their members to participate in activities they would never choose to perform as individuals. But why, you are probably wondering, do such effects take place? How can the presence of many other persons transform essentially peaceful, law-abiding individuals into wild-eyed killers capable of shocking and senseless acts of violence? According to Philip Zimbardo (1970), a social psychologist who has long been concerned with such questions, the answer lies in the important psychological process of **deindividuation.**

As outlined by Zimbardo (1970), the development of deindividuation seems to involve a complex chain of events. First, various social conditions, such as the presence of many other persons and the anonymity this affords, lead the persons involved to believe that they will no longer be observed or evaluated as individuals; instead, they will be "submerged" unrecognizably in the larger group. Such perceptions then lead to important internal changes, including a loss of self-awareness, reduced concern over evaluations from others, and a narrowed focus of attention. Together, these changes produce a sharp reduction in the strength of individuals' restraints against engaging in various forms of socially prohibited but potentially rewarding forms of behavior. Such actions are then initiated, usually in a cautious and tentative manner. Once they are begun, however, they are generally found to be so rewarding and pleasurable that any remaining vestiges of conscience or anxiety over disapproval from others are quickly eliminated. The end result is that truly wild, impulsive behavior is released, and tends to occur with increasing vigor and mounting emotional excitement. The words of an American soldier whose job in Vietnam involved the interrogation (and occasional torture) of Vietcong prisoners provide a vivid illustration of the progressive development of such behavior:

> First you strike to get mad, then you strike because you are mad, and in the end you strike because of the sheer pleasure of it. This is the gruesome aspect of it which has haunted me ever since I came back from Vietnam. (*Toronto Star,* November 24, 1967.)

A summary of some of the external conditioning leading to deindividuation, and the internal alterations which characterize this psychological state is presented in Figure 12-9; please refer to this figure before proceeding further.

In addition to being wild and impulsive in nature, behavior stemming from deindividuation is also characterized by one additional property: generally, it is unaffected by the kind of external stimuli which normally regulate other forms of social behavior. Thus, once it is initiated, it can usually be brought to a halt only by a marked change in existing conditions. Typically, then, deindividuated behavior is terminated only when there is a major alteration in (1) the state of the person enacting it (e.g., he or she becomes completely fatigued or passes out), (2) the state of the victim (e.g., he or she loses consciousness or actually expires), or (3) the state of some instrument being employed (e.g., a gun is emptied, a knife blade breaks off inside the victim). It is only in the face of such drastic

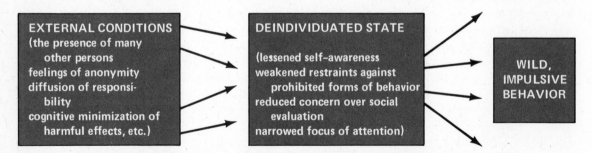

FIGURE 12-9. *According to Zimbardo's theory of deindividuation, various external conditions (e.g., the presence of many other persons and resulting feelings of anonymity) encourage development of a deindividuated state. This state (which is characterized by such internal changes as a lessening of concern over social evaluation) may then often facilitate the performance of wild, impulsive behavior.*

changes in the situation that the frenzied activities released by deindividuation come to a halt, and the persons performing them return to a more normal psychological state.

Since we have chosen to view deindividuation as one of the many effects stemming from group membership (it could, instead, have been quite reasonably considered in our discussion of aggression), we should take special care to describe the manner in which being part of a group can facilitate the occurrence of this state. First, the presence of many other persons may cause each member to perceive that he or she will be *anonymous*, and thus relatively immune to punishment for any antisocial actions. Very few members of rampaging mobs, after all, are ever captured and brought to trial, and most of the participants in such activities are well aware of this fact. Second, the presence of many other members may cause each individual to feel that the responsibility for any antisocial actions performed will be divided among a large number of persons, and will not rest solely with him. We have already met such *diffusion of responsibility* in Chapter 8 (see pp. 366–367), where we noted its role in the failure of many individuals to offer help in times of emergency. Here, we wish to note that the same factor may also contribute to the performance of many dangerous types of antisocial behavior. Third, the presence of other persons who act in a violent, destructive, or unrestrained manner may provide individuals with several *social models* for such behavior. As we saw in Chapter 7, exposure to such models often exerts very powerful effects upon observers, and a sharp reduction in the strength of their restraints against prohibited forms of behavior is one of the most common of these influences.

In these and possibly other ways as well, the presence of a large number of persons may often tend to facilitate the occurrence of a deindividuated state, and so increase the likelihood of wild, impulsive behavior. Given the potentially important and dangerous consequences of such actions, it is not surprising that deindividuation has been the subject of an increasing amount of research (Diener et al., 1973; Diener et al., 1976; Watson, 1973). Together, the findings of these studies point to the role of several additional factors in encouraging the development of this state.

First, it appears that such reactions are often strongly enhanced by feelings of anonymity (Diener et al., 1973). Perhaps the most dramatic illustration of this fact is provided by an experiment conducted by Zimbardo (1970). In this study, groups of four college women were asked, under the guise of an experiment concerning empathy, to deliver apparently painful electric shocks to another woman. (In reality, of course, she was an accomplice who never received any shocks during the study.) In one experimental group, conditions were arranged so as to maximize subjects' anonymity while participating in the study. Thus, each person dressed in an oversized lab coat and face hood immediately upon entering the laboratory (see Figure 12-10). Further, the room was dimly lit, and no names were ever used. In a second experimental group, in contrast, conditions were arranged so as to ensure that subjects would be anything *but* anonymous. No coats or hoods were used, the laboratory was brightly lit, and all participants wore large name tags which clearly identified each to the others.

FIGURE 12-10. *Subjects in the deindividuation group of Zimbardo's experiment. As you can see, when dressed in this manner, participants were totally anonymous. (From Zimbardo, 1970, p. 267.)*

In accordance with his theoretical assumptions, Zimbardo reasoned that deindividuation would be much more likely to develop under conditions of anonymity than under conditions favoring ready recognition. As a result, subjects would be expected to feel much less restrained against shocking the innocent victim in the first than in the second of these two conditions. As you can see in Figure 12-11, results provided strong support for these suggestions: subjects who felt completely anonymous during the study did in fact direct shocks of much longer duration against the helpless victim than those who felt that they were easily identifiable. In short, feelings of anonymity seemed to encourage at least one form of impulsive, dangerous behavior—attacks against another human being.

Additional factors which seem to facilitate the occurrence of impulsive, frenzied behavior (presumably by encouraging the development of deindividuation) have been uncovered by Ed Diener and his colleagues (Diener, 1976; Diener et al., 1973; Diener et al., 1975). For example, in one of these experiments (Diener et al., 1975), subjects were simply instructed to behave in any manner they wished toward another person they found sitting on the floor of a dimly lit room. (In reality, he was a confederate, specifically trained to remain passive throughout the session.) Various objects—including toy guns, sponge rubber bricks, plastic swords, and rubber bands—were also present in the room, and subjects' behavior while in this setting was observed very carefully. Before entering the room and interacting with the confederate, participants were exposed to three different factors expected to influence the occurrence of

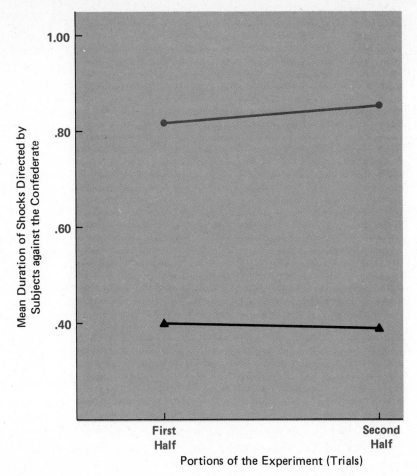

1.00

.80

.60

.40

Mean Duration of Shocks Directed by
Subjects against the Confederate

First
Half

Second
Half

Portions of the Experiment (Trials)

FIGURE 12-11.   *Deindividuation and aggression.   As shown above, subjects who
were made to feel anonymous—and so presumably experienced deindividuation—
directed longer shocks against an innocent victim than subjects not made to feel
anonymous.   (Source: Based on data from Zimbardo, 1970.)*

deindividuation, and thus the frequency of wild, impulsive behavior.   The first
involved *responsibility* for their actions.   In one condition, subjects were
informed that they would be responsible for their own behavior, while in a
second, they were told that the experimenter would take full responsibility for
their actions.   It was expected that deindividuation would be encouraged under
the latter conditions, with the result that subjects would behave in a more hostile
and impulsive manner toward the confederate.   Second, participants were asked
to think of the situation either as a game or as a test of aggression.   Diener and
his colleagues predicted that the first of these two sets of instructions would
provide subjects with a means for perceiving hostile behavior against the
confederate as moral or justified, and so tend to reduce their restraints against

such actions relative to the second set. Finally, subjects saw one of two brief films before interacting with the confederate. In one, another person behaved in a highly aggressive manner, while in the other he behaved in a nonaggressive fashion. As you can probably guess, it was expected that subjects who witnessed the first of these films would tend to behave more aggressively themselves than those who watched the second.

Observations of participants' behavior while in the room with the confederate offered support for all of these predictions. That is, as expected, they were much more likely to kick this person, drag him around the room, throw rubber sponges at him, or swing at him with the plastic swords when they felt little responsibility for their actions, thought of the situation as a game, and had seen the aggressive model, than when the opposite of each of these conditions prevailed. Zimbardo's (1970) theory, of course, would explain such differences through reference to the development of a deindividuated state. That is, it would suggest that feelings of deindividuation were encouraged under conditions where subjects felt little responsibility for their actions, viewed the situation as a game, and were previously exposed to an aggressive model. Further, it would propose that such reactions led to heightened attacks against the confederate. Somewhat surprisingly, however, questionnaires completed by participants at the end of the study failed to provide support for this view. That is, individuals in the various experimental groups did not report experiencing deindividuation to different degrees, despite the fact that they showed sharply contrasting levels of aggression. The absence of a strong link between the occurrence of deindividuation and wild, impulsive behavior in this and subsequent studies (Diener, 1976) raises questions concerning this portion of Zimbardo's theory. Specifically, the second link shown in Figure 12-9—the one between deindividuation and wild, impulsive actions—may not be as strong or straightforward as Zimbardo seems to suggest. Given the inconclusive nature of existing evidence, however, it is clear that further studies are needed before any definite conclusions regarding this point may be reached.

Regardless of the outcomes of such research, the findings of the studies already conducted by Diener and his colleagues, as well as those completed by other investigators (Cannavale, Scarr, and Pepitone, 1970; Watson, 1973) do seem to confirm the existence of a relationship between several external factors and the occurrence of wild, impulsive behavior. Under conditions where individuals are part of a large group, believe that they can "get away" with antisocial actions, and can somehow cognitively minimize the potential harm of such behavior, their restraints against dangerous and prohibited acts may be sharply reduced. And it is precisely in such settings that human beings may turn upon their fellow men and women with a savagery and brutality unmatched by any other living creature on earth.

LEADERS AND FOLLOWERS: PATTERNS OF INFLUENCE WITHIN GROUPS

In almost every group, there is one individual (or sometimes several) who seems to exert a considerable degree of influence over the others. Sometimes such persons are appointed from the outside by "the powers that be," as when a new officer is chosen to lead an army unit or command a ship, while in others, they are selected by the members themselves in a more democratic fashion. In many cases, the privileges and responsibilities of such persons are clearly stated—often in written documents—and they are given special titles such as President, Prime Minister, Director, or Chair. In others, however, the situation is far less formal, and their role and duties in the group, as well as the limits of their authority, are not clearly noted.

Regardless of the source of their power or the extent to which it is openly specified, such **leaders** often exert tremendous influence over other group members. Indeed, they are often so essential that the very existence of the groups they head may be threatened by their absence or removal. For example, whole nations are often thrown into turmoil when a powerful political leader dies or is assassinated, especially if no formal procedures for selecting a replacement exist. And informal groups often disband if a leader resigns, moves away, or joins another organization.

Given the powerful impact of leaders upon other members, no discussion of group influence on individual behavior would be complete without some attention to this important topic. Thus, we will conclude with a brief examination of the nature and scope of leadership. Over the years, social psychologists have sought to investigate many different aspects of this complex process. Two basic questions, however, have often dominated and guided their research. First, they have sought to determine why particular individuals rise to positions of power and authority. What, in short, makes some persons leaders and others only followers? And second, they have attempted to determine what factors influence leaders' degree of success once they have assumed such roles. Both of these questions will now be considered.

"Great Men and Women" or Technocrats: Who Becomes a Leader?

Why do some individuals rise to positions of leadership and power while others remain only noninfluential followers? Early attempts to answer this intriguing question focused primarily upon the personality characteristics that seem to distinguish leaders from nonleaders. Basically, it was suggested that certain persons tend to rise to positions of authority because they possess special charismatic traits not shared by others, which make them unusually well suited for such a role. In short, it was proposed that leaders owe their favored positions to the possession of rare, exceptional qualities, and are essentially born rather than made.

At first glance, this is a highly plausible suggestion. After all, common sense suggests quite strongly that persons who rise to positions of power and fame do indeed differ sharply in several respects from more average or typical individuals. World leaders such as Indira Gandhi, Mao Tse Tung, and Jomo Kenyatta, to mention only a few, all seem to share an unswerving will, boundless

A SIMULATED PRISON: GROUP INFLUENCE OR DEMAND CHARACTERISTICS?

Imagine that you are unlucky enough to experience the following chain of events. One peaceful Sunday afternoon, you hear a loud knock on your door. When you go to answer, you find yourself confronting several policemen. Without a word of explanation, they place you under arrest, and take you downtown where you are photographed, fingerprinted, and "booked." Next, you are blindfolded and driven to a prison whose whereabouts you can only guess. Once there, you are stripped of all your clothes and forced to dress in an uncomfortable, loose-fitting smock and a tight nylon cap. All of your personal possessions are removed, and you are given an I.D. number to use in place of your name. Then you are locked in an empty cell containing only the bare necessities of life. Your guards in the prison wear identical khaki-colored uniforms, and silver reflector sunglasses which make eye contact with them impossible. Moreover, they carry badges of authority appropriate to their role—billyclubs, whistles, and handcuffs (see Figure 12-12). As a prisoner, you are expected to obey a long set of rules, under the threat of severe punishment for failure to comply. For example, you must

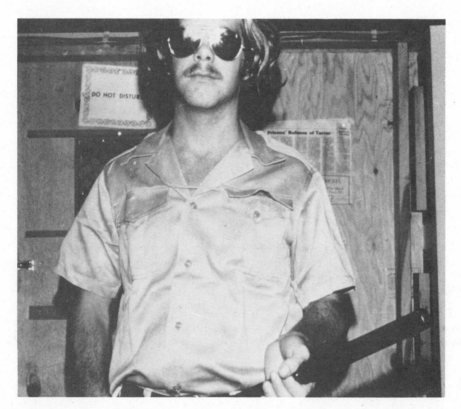

FIGURE 12-12. *A guard in the controversial Stanford Prison experiment. (Photo courtesy of Dr. Philip Zimbardo.)*

remain silent during rest periods and after the lights are turned out each night. You must eat only at mealtime, and must refrain from tampering with or defacing prison property. You must address other prisoners only by their I.D. numbers, and your guards as "Mr. Correctional Officer." And you must ask their permission to perform even the simplest acts such as writing letters, smoking, and going to the bathroom.

How do you think you might react to such circumstances? Would you obey the rules or rebel? Would you become angry and resentful, or depressed and resigned? And what if you were made into a guard instead? Would you treat your charges in a fair and kindly manner, or would you harrass and humiliate them? These intriguing questions were actually examined by Philip Zimbardo and his colleagues in a famous—and somewhat controversial—study widely known as the Stanford Prison experiment (Haney, Banks, and Zimbardo, 1973; Zimbardo et al., 1973). In this investigation, male college students who had previously volunteered to take part in a psychological study of prison life were arrested, confined to a mock prison located in the basement of the Stanford University Psychology building, and treated in the manner described above. Their guards, too, were paid volunteers who had also agreed to take part in the study. In fact, the assignment of individuals to these two roles—prisoner or guard—was entirely random. The major purpose of the study was that of determining whether, as Zimbardo and his colleagues suspected, the behavior shown by prisoners and guards in real prisons stems, to a large degree, from the situation in which they find themselves, rather than from special characteristics they bring with them to this setting. In short, the major goal was that of determining the extent to which these largely middle-class, highly educated subjects would come to act very much like real guards and prisoners when placed in an environment simulating actual prison conditions as closely as possible.

The results of the experiment were both dramatic and unnerving. Although the investi-

gation was originally planned to continue for two weeks, it was necessary to terminate after only six days. The reason for this change of plans was that even during this relatively brief interval, major—and quite alarming—changes developed in the behavior of both the prisoners and guards. At first, the prisoners were rebellious, and even attempted to take over the prison. Once their uprising was crushed (and quite ruthlessly!) by the guards, however, they became increasingly passive and depressed. Indeed, several began to show signs of serious psychological disturbance. One had to be released after only thirty-six hours in the prison when he began to demonstrate uncontrollable fits of crying and screaming, and two others were released shortly thereafter when they also showed symptoms of severe emotional disorder. The remaining individuals became increasingly passive, and soon reached the point where they responded only when forced to do so by the guards.

At the same time that prisoners were becoming increasingly disorganized and depressed, the guards were becoming increasingly brutal and sadistic. They harrassed the prisoners constantly, forced them to curse and derogate each other, and asisgned them tedious, senseless tasks such as moving cartons back and forth between closets in an endless manner. Moreover, they tended to dehumanize the prisoners, often coming to perceive them as somehow less than human. In the words of one participant:

I was surprised at myself. . . . I made them (the prisoners) call each other names and clean the toilets out with their bare hands. I practically considered the prisoners cattle, and I kept thinking: I have to watch out for them in case they try something.

On the basis of these dramatic results, Zimbardo and his colleagues concluded that to a surprising extent, prisons may actually create the brutal behavior of guards and the passive, despondent behavior of prisoners. Contrary to popular belief, these persons do not act in such a manner because it is their "nature" to do so;

rather, they adopt such patterns of behavior because of the social conditions around them.

Such conclusions are certainly quite provocative. Moreover, they have important implications for prison reform and related issues. But are they actually valid? Can we accept the findings of the Stanford experiment as an accurate reflection of the processes at work in actual prisons? As you might suspect, these questions have been the center of a lively and heated controversy. On the one hand, several critics have called the validity of Zimbardo's research into serious question (Banuazizi and Movahedi, 1975). First, it has been argued that the participants in this study knew full well that they were simply volunteers taking part in a psychological experiment. Thus, their behavior may merely have reflected their beliefs concerning the manner in which real prisoners and guards behave. In short, they may have simply played the roles they thought they should play under the circumstances. Second, it has been suggested that the procedures employed provided subjects with a great many cues concerning the experimenters' hypotheses and expectations. Thus, their behavior during the study may have been more reflective of demand characteristics than actual psychological processes.

In reply to such criticism, other investigators have noted that Zimbardo and his colleagues actually had no clearly defined hypotheses at the start of their study. They expected the prison experience to influence the behavior of their subjects, but were not sure precisely how (DeJong, 1975). Given this fact, it is hard to see how they could have caused participants to behave in the manner in which they did. Similarly, it has been noted that even if subjects were indeed attempting to play the roles of prisoner or guard, they were no different, in this respect, from individuals who actually enter these roles for the first time in real prisons. Such persons, too, bring expectations concerning "appropriate" behavior with them, and attempt to live up to these beliefs as best they can (Thayer and Saarni, 1975). Thus, even if role playing contributed to the results obtained, they may still provide us with important information about the processes at work in actual prisons.

As you can probably guess, the controversy concerning the validity of the Stanford Prison experiment will not be easily or readily resolved. Regardless of whether we choose to place confidence in its specific findings, however, the investigation itself serves to underscore a basic principle we have sought to emphasize throughout the present chapter: being part of a group (or larger social system) often exerts powerful effects upon the behavior of individual members. Indeed, in many cases, the impact of such factors may prove to be far greater than the unique dispositions or characteristics they carry with them into the group setting.

energy, and a certain degree of flamboyance not observed in most human beings. Thus, while they and other leaders have adopted radically different goals and political ideologies, they do seem to be quite similar in at least certain respects.

In the face of such informal observations, most of us have the strong subjective impression that given a few moments, we could easily generate an accurate list of the traits required for effective leadership. Carried to its logical extreme, this general belief leads to a view often known as the **great man–woman theory of leadership**—an approach which suggests that (1) leaders are distinguished from nonleaders by a relatively small number of crucial characteristics, and (2) these traits remain essentially unchanged at all times and in all situations. Thus, according to this view, the great leaders of history—Genghis Khan, Joan of

Arc, Alexander the Great, Julius Caesar, Queen Victoria and many others—all shared a number of central traits. Moreover, it was these traits which facilitated their rise to positions of power and world domination. Clearly, these are intriguing proposals, and it is easy to see why they stimulated many early researchers to launch a spirited search for the traits or dispositions serving to distinguish great leaders from the remainder of humanity.

Unfortunately, though, despite the best efforts of a number of skillful and ingenious investigators, early attempts to uncover these crucial characteristics met with repeated failure (see Bass, 1960; Mann, 1959). That is, try as they might, researchers could not construct a list of traits which served to distinguish leaders from followers in a clear and consistent manner. Indeed, in the end, there appeared to be almost as many different lists of such traits as there were investigators working in the area! In the face of this muddled state of affairs, social psychologists reluctantly surrendered their search for the crucial characteristics of leaders, and turned instead to a markedly different approach.

Are leaders born or made? The "great man–great woman" theory suggests that they are born to this role, and that all the famous leaders of history shared special, charismatic qualities. However, systematic research has failed to confirm this belief. (Phil Carver & Friends.)

Basically, this newer approach emphasized **situational** rather than personality determinants of leadership. That is, it was assumed that the individual most likely to become a leader in any given situation was not the awe-inspiring great man or woman whose charismatic qualities somehow hypnotized others into blind submission, but rather the grey *technocrat* whose special competence and skills assisted the group in attaining its goals. Who became a leader, then, depended more on such factors as the type of task faced by the group and the general situation within which it operated than on a few crucial qualities of its individual members (Hollander and Julian, 1970). According to this general approach, therefore, an individual who served effectively as a leader in one group or context might well be pushed into the background in some other situation or group. For example, an expert bowler might well lead her company's team in competition against other squads, but hold a low-status position on the job. Similarly, a mathematical wizard might well serve as the undisputed leader of a group of scientists or engineers, but take a distant backseat to others in planning or participating in various social functions. Certainly, this is a far cry from the view that leaders are more or less born to their positions of authority, and will quickly assume them in almost any situation (see Figure 12-13).

Carried to its logical extreme, the situational view of leadership suggests that virtually any individual can become a leader under conditions which favor his or her emergence in this role. The possession of various personality characteristics is of relatively little importance, provided the situation is appropriate. That this is actually the case is suggested by the results of several different experiments (Hastorf, 1965; Zdep and Oakes, 1967) in which even shy and retiring individuals have been induced to behave in a leader-like manner through social reinforcement for such behavior. (They received feedback indicating that they were acting in a beneficial manner whenever they took an active or directive role in the group's activities.) Such findings suggest that situational factors may often outweigh personal characteristics in determining who becomes a leader. However, as you can probably guess, personal dispositions *do* play a role, and cannot be entirely ignored. In fact, additional studies have reported that while virtually all individuals can be nudged in the direction of increased leadership behavior, some seem to adopt such a role much more readily than others (Nydegger, 1975). And consistent with what common sense suggests, there is growing evidence that individuals are quite aware of differences in their ability or willingness to assume the privileges and responsibilities of leadership (Beckhouse et al., 1975). In short, while different situations may call for different types of leaders, and special skills or knowledge are often more important than personal charisma in propelling specific persons to the "top," not all individuals seem capable of rising to the occasion with equal ease.

Who Becomes a Leader?
A Modern Perspective

Although the situational view of leadership was extremely valuable in pointing to the importance of several factors overlooked by the personality or trait approach,

"There are no great men, my boy—only great committees."

FIGURE 12-13. *In contrast to the "great man–great woman" theory of leadership, the situational view holds that it is those persons most capable of helping the group attain its goals—those with the appropriate technical skills—who generally rise to positions of power or authority. (Source: Drawing by Chas. Addams; © 1975 The New Yorker Magazine, Inc.)*

it too was open to several criticisms. For example, as noted by Hollander and Julian (1969), it tended to view leadership as a "one-way" street in which leaders influenced and directed their groups, but were not affected, in turn, by followers. Many investigations indicate that this is actually far from the case, and that leaders' behavior is often strongly affected by the demands and actions of other group members (Beckhouse et al., 1975). Similarly, the situational view often seemed to suggest that the leader is an extremely important element in the situation, and may readily change or alter it in many ways. Finally, it became

Leaders and Followers: Patterns of Influence Within Groups

FOCUS ON RESEARCH

HOW DO WE RECOGNIZE A LEADER WHEN WE SEE ONE?
RATE OF PARTICIPATION AND LEADER CHOICE

As we have already noted, there is frequently a fairly precise matching of group needs and member abilities, so that the person best suited to helping the group reach its goals often emerges in this role. But how, precisely, does such emergence take place? What actions does a potential or would-be leader take which cause the other members to recognize him or her as holding a position of authority? Obviously, this is a complex process involving many different factors (Stein, 1975). However, one relatively simple aspect of group members' behavior seems to exert a very powerful effect upon their emergence as a leader: the sheer volume of their participation in the group's activities. In short, the more one talks, the more one tends to be perceived as a leader by other group members (Borgatta and Bales, 1956; Regula and Julian, 1973).

In one sense, at least, this is not very surprising. By speaking a great deal, individuals may create the impression that they are experts at the task at hand, and so quickly gain acceptance as a leader (Gintner and Lindskold, 1975; Sorrentino and Boutillier, 1975). Much more surprising, however, is the fact that the sheer volume of their contributions often seems to be far more important in this respect than what they actually have to say. Individuals who hold the floor much of the time and make many comments quickly emerge as leaders and are recognized as such by the other group members, regardless of the overall quality of their statements. This fact is illustrated quite clearly in a recent experiment by Sorrentino and Boutillier (1975).

In this study, groups of four male undergraduates made a series of decisions regarding a matrix of payoffs according to which the group could win or lose imaginary points. One of the individuals present was actually a confederate who had been specially trained to

vary two aspects of his contributions in a systematic manner: the *quantity* of his verbal statements (high or low), and the *quality* of these comments (mostly correct choices or mostly incorrect ones). Following the decision-making phase of the study, all participants rated both themselves and the other members on leadership ability and several other dimensions, including perceived competence, confidence, influence over the group, and contributions to the group's goals. On the basis of previous research, it was predicted that the ratings of leadership ability received by the confederate from other members would be affected by the quantity, but not the quality, of his contributions. As you can see in Figure 12-14, these expectations were confirmed. While quality (correctness) of the confederate's choices did affect his ratings of competence and contribution to the group, it exerted virtually no impact on his perceived leadership ability.

At first glance, such findings seem quite puzzling. Why, you may ask, should we assign so much weight to the sheer volume of others' verbal statements and so little to the quality of these contributions in rating their leadership ability? One possible answer, suggested by Sorrentino and Boutillier (1975), involves the fact that these two aspects of another person's behavior seem to tell us somewhat different things about them. The sheer volume of another's participation in group activities may be indicative of his or her level of motivation. That is, high participation suggests strong motivation to help the group reach its goals, while low participation indicates low motivation in this respect. Since we tend to assign a great deal of importance to others' motives or intentions in attempting to predict their future behavior, it is not surprising that the volume of their contributions during group discussion turns out to

594   *Chapter 12   Groups and Individual Behavior: The Consequences of Belonging*

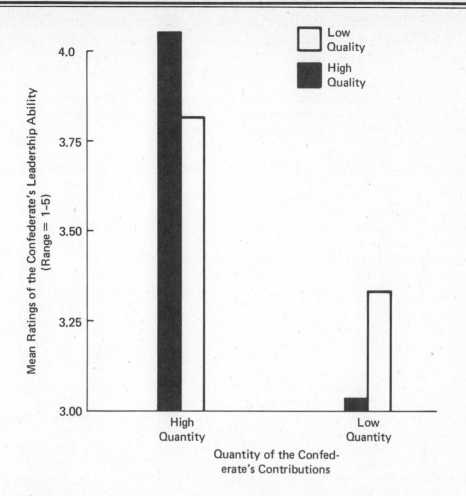

FIGURE 12-14. *Quantity and quality of contributions as determinants of leadership choice. As shown above, the sheer volume (quantity) of a confederate's verbal statements exerted a much greater impact on the ratings of leadership ability he received from other group members than the correctness (quality) of these statements. (Source: Based on data from Sorrentino and Boutillier, 1975.)*

be an important determinant of our willingness to recognize them as a leader. In contrast, the quality of others' contributions seems to be more indicative of their level of ability: high-quality statements suggest a high level of ability, while low-quality statements suggest lower levels of ability. In general, we assign less importance to such factors in attempting to predict others' behavior than to their level of motivation; after all, high-ability persons may or may not use their skills for beneficial purposes, while highly motivated ones can generally be counted upon at least to try to do their best. According to Sorrentino and Boutillier, then, it is for these reasons that we seem to pay more attention to the sheer volume of others' contributions than to the quality of their statements in recognizing them as leaders.

We should hasten to add that while this interpretation is consistent with existing findings (Gintner and Lindskold, 1975), it has not been subjected to independent study. Thus, it must be viewed as only tentative in nature. What *does* seem to have been clearly established, though, is the following generalization: If you wish to attain a position of influence and authority in a small, informal group, it is probably better strategy to concentrate upon speaking very frequently than upon making only eloquent, high-quality contributions. In short, being a "fast talker" may actually serve as one effective means for seizing and holding leadership in groups.

increasingly clear that the trait and situational approaches merely emphasize different parts of a single unitary process, and that any comprehensive theory of leadership must devote full attention to both of these components.

In the face of these arguments, the situational approach has given way, in recent years, to a newer and more sophisticated orientation to the study of leadership sometimes known as the **transactional view.** Within the context of this modern perspective, leadership is viewed as a reciprocal process of social influence in which leaders both influence followers, and are influenced, in turn, by them. Moreover, this new approach suggests that a thorough understanding of leadership must involve careful attention to the perceptions of both the leader and followers regarding the relationship between them (for example, do followers perceive the leader's position as legitimate?), as well as to various characteristics of the leader and the nature and requirements of the group task. In short, it argues for a far more sophisticated view of leadership than has prevailed in the past.

Although this view is a relatively new one, and has emerged only within the past decade, it has already stimulated a considerable amount of research (Hollander and Julian, 1970; Michener and Tausig, 1971). Perhaps it is most clearly represented, however, in a theory of leader effectiveness developed in recent years by Fred Fiedler and his colleagues (Fiedler, 1967, 1972; Fiedler and Chemers, 1974).

The Contingency Model of Leader Effectiveness: Matching Leaders with Demands

What are the determinants of a leader's effectiveness? That is, what factors influence the degree to which he or she will contribute to the productive functioning of the group? It is with questions such as these that Fiedler's theory is concerned. Basically, the theory may be described as a **contingency model of leader effectiveness,** because it assumes that the contribution of the leader to successful group performance is determined both by certain of his or her personality characteristics, and by various features of the situation. In one important sense, therefore, it represents an attempt to combine the trait and situational approaches we have already described.

Turning first to characteristics of leaders, Fiedler has focused primarily upon a disposition he terms *esteem for least preferred co-worker*—leaders' tendencies to evaluate the group members whom they like least in a positive or negative manner. Leaders who perceive this person in uniformly negative terms (low-LPC leaders in Fiedler's terminology), seem to be primarily motivated toward successful task performance. Thus, they usually adopt a directive, authoritarian approach. In contrast, leaders who perceive this person in a more favorable light (high-LPC leaders) seem to be mainly concerned with establishing warm, friendly interpersonal relations. As a result, they generally adopt a more relaxed, nondirective leadership style.

But which of these two approaches, you may be wondering, will be most effective? Since it is a *contingency* model, Fiedler's theory suggests that neither will be superior in every case. Instead, the success of both depends upon various situational factors. In particular, Fiedler contends that whether low-LPC or high-LPC leaders will prove more effective is strongly determined by the favorability of existing conditions to the leader—the extent to which present circumstances provide this person with influence and control over the group. Under conditions which are very favorable to the leader, a directive, task-oriented approach such as the one shown by low-LPC individuals should be best, for in such situations, group members anticipate ready attainment of their goals, and are probably ready to accept the leader's directives. Similarly, such a style of leadership should also be highly effective when conditions are highly unfavorable to the leader, for under these circumstances, the group will literally fall apart unless the leader exerts active control.

In contrast, a nondirective, relaxed approach such as the one provided by high-LPC individuals will probably be best under conditions that are moderately favorable to the leader, for in such cases conditions are quite mixed, and this type of orientation will help to smooth over differences and improve cooperation and morale. In sum, Fiedler suggests that low-LPC leaders will be more effective in facilitating group performance than high-LPC leaders under both extremely favorable and extremely unfavorable conditions, while high-LPC leaders will be more effective under conditions which are only moderately favorable to the leader. (These predictions are summarized in Figure 12-15.)

Going one step further, Fiedler has attempted to specify the situational factors which determine the degree of favorability to the leader. Basically, he believes that three factors are of greatest importance: (1) the leader's personal relations with other group members (ranging from good to bad), (2) the structure of the task faced by the group (ranging from structured to unstructured), and (3) the leader's power over the other group members (ranging from high to low). Presumably, the most favorable situation possible is one in which the leader enjoys extremely good relations with the other members, the task on which the group works is highly structured, and his power is relatively high. In contrast, the most unfavorable situation is one in which the leader's relations with other members are poor, the task is unstructured, and the leader's power is limited.

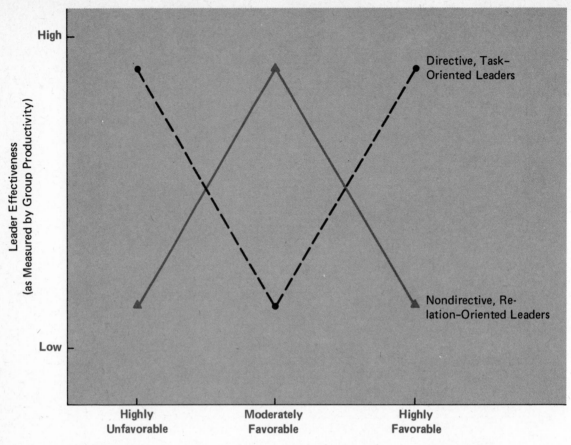

High ―

Leader Effectiveness
(as Measured by Group Productivity)

Directive, Task–
Oriented Leaders

Nondirective, Re-
lation-Oriented Leaders

Low ―

Highly
Unfavorable

Moderately
Favorable

Highly
Favorable

FIGURE 12-15. *The contingency theory of leader effectiveness. As shown above, the theory predicts that directive, task-oriented leaders will be more effective than nondirective, relation-oriented leaders under highly favorable or highly unfavorable conditions. Just the opposite will be true, however, under moderately favorable conditions.*

To repeat our previous comments, Fiedler predicts that low-LPC leaders will be more effective in both extremes than high-LPC leaders, while these latter individuals will be more effective when conditions are somewhere in between.

Attempts to test predictions derived from Fiedler's theory have generally yielded positive results (Hardy, 1971). Consistent with the theory, low-LPC leaders have been found to be more effective in facilitating group productivity than high-LPC leaders under extremely favorable or unfavorable conditions, while high-LPC leaders have been found to be more effective under mixed, moderately favorable conditions. For example, in one interesting study (Chemers et al., 1975), male students worked together in small groups on the task of deciphering coded messages. The appointed leaders of these groups were either high-LPC or low-LPC individuals. Moreover, before meeting with

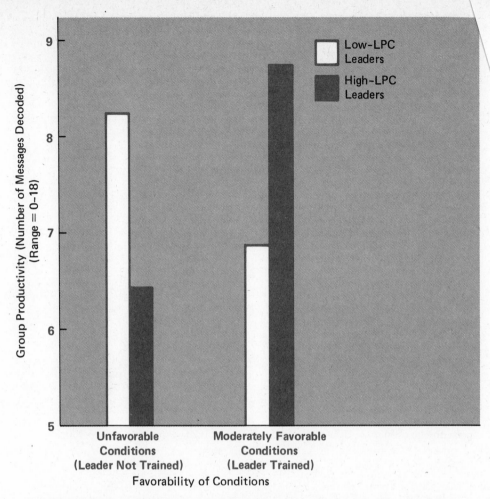

FIGURE 12-16. *A test of the contingency theory. It was predicted—and found—that low-LPC leaders would be more effective than high-LPC leaders under highly unfavorable conditions (in the absence of training), while the opposite would be true under moderately favorable conditions (when the leader had received special training). (Source: Based on data from Chemers et al., 1975.)*

their groups, leaders either received or failed to receive special training on the task the group would perform. Since leader-member relations were found to be fairly negative, it was assumed that when the leaders had not been trained, conditions would be quite unfavorable, and low-LPC individuals would prove more effective in enhancing productivity than high-LPC individuals. However, when leaders had received special training, conditions would be moderately favorable, and high-LPC leaders would prove to be more effective. As you can see in Figure 12-16, this was actually the case.

Together with the results of other studies, these findings provide support for

Leaders and Followers: Patterns of Influence Within Groups

the basic accuracy of Fiedler's model. However, we should note that not all evidence collected to date has been consistent with the theory (Graen, Orris, and Alvares, 1971). Moreover, there is still a considerable degree of ambiguity with respect to the classification of situations as relatively favorable or unfavorable to the leader. Although Fiedler has specified three factors which seem to play a role in this regard, many others not included in his model are probably also quite important (e.g., the extent to which group members feel that the leader is competent in his role). Until such factors are included in the theory, the placement of various situations along a continuum of favorability to the leader will remain somewhat ambiguous. And since predictions regarding the type of leader who will be most effective in a given situation depend very heavily upon such placement, this uncertainty represents a serious problem for the theory.

Despite these problems, it is obvious that the contingency model—and the general transactional approach it represents—have conbributed much to our understanding of leadership processes. The view that leader behavior and effectiveness stem from a complex interplay between personal characteristics and situational factors is more complex, and in some ways less dramatic, than the older "great man or woman" approach. However, there is currently little doubt among social psychologists that it is also much closer to the truth.

SUMMARY

Groups often exert a powerful influence upon the beliefs, values, motives, and behavior of their individual members. The simplest effect of this type has often been termed *social facilitation,* and refers to effects on performance stemming from the presence of other persons. Recent findings suggest that the presence of others is motivating or arousing, and enhances our tendency to perform dominant responses. If such responses are correct, performance may be improved, while if they are incorrect, performance may be impaired. Additional evidence indicates, however, that such effects seem to occur only when the other persons present can both observe and evaluate our behavior.

Common sense suggests that the decisions reached by groups are generally more conservative than those recommended by individuals. However, initial experimental findings seemed to suggest that group discussion may often lead to a *risky shift*—movement by the group toward more daring or risky decisions. Further research has now revealed, though, that the effects of group discussion are actually somewhat more general in nature, involving a movement toward *polarization.* That is, group discussion seems to cause individual members to shift toward views which are more extreme than their initial beliefs, but in the same general direction. Such effects are quite common, and seem to occur with respect to attitudes, bargaining, judgments of physical dimensions, and even court decisions. Two major explanations for their existence have been advanced, one based upon the desire of group members to outdo one another in the acceptance of the "right" views or values, and the other based on an exchange of persuasive arguments favoring their initial views. Evidence for both has been obtained, and each probably plays a role in group polarization.

In many cases, individuals who find that they are part of a large group seem willing to perform acts they would never dream of performing while alone (e.g., vandalism, gang rape, etc.). This seems to be due to the occurrence of *deindividuation*—a psychological state in which individuals' restraints against antisocial actions are sharply reduced. A number of factors, including the presence of many other persons, anonymity, lessened responsibility for one's acts, and the belief that one can "get away" with antisocial behaviors, all seem to encourage the development of deindividuation. And once it has been induced, wild, impulsive behavior may often follow.

In almost any group, there are certain individuals whose ability to exert influence and control over other members sets them apart as *leaders*. Early attempts to account for the rise of such persons to positions of power and authority focused upon their possession of special, charismatic traits which rendered them particularly well suited for such a role. A second, and sharply contrasting view, stressed the importance of *situational factors* which more or less thrust particular persons—those most suited to helping the group reach its goals—into positions of leadership. In the past decade, these two approaches have been combined in a more sophisticated framework which views leadership as a joint function of characteristics of the leader and the situation faced by the group. An example of this newer perspective is provided by recent research concerning the determinants of leader effectiveness.

GLOSSARY

Contingency model of leader effectiveness. A theory proposed by Fiedler which holds that leader effectiveness is determined both by characteristics of the leader and the favorability of the situation he or she confronts.

Deindividuation. A psychological state characterized by lessened concern over social evaluation, a narrowed focus of attention, and a reduction in restraints against prohibited forms of behavior. Deindividuation often leads to the occurrence of wild, impulsive actions.

Evaluation apprehension. Concern over evaluations from others. Evaluation apprehension seems to play an important role in the effects of audiences on performance.

Great man–great woman theory. A theory of leadership which holds that all great leaders share certain charismatic traits which distinguish them from nonleaders and which are largely responsible for their rise to positions of power and authority.

Group. In social psychology, this term refers to two or more persons who perceive that they are affiliated in some manner, and whose fates are interdependent in one or more respects.

Group-polarization effect. Refers to the fact that following group discussion, individuals often shift toward views which are more extreme—but on the same side of the neutral point—than the ones they initially supported.

Information-exchange theory. The view that group-polarization effects stem from the fact that during group discussion, most of the arguments presented favor or support the positions initially held by group members.

Leader. That member of a group who exercises the greatest amount of influence and authority over others. Leaders can be appointed from outside the group or chosen by its own members.

Persuasive-arguments theory. (See information-exchange theory.)

Risky shift. Refers to the fact that following group discussion, individuals often recommend riskier or more daring courses of action than they did prior to such discussion. Recent findings suggest that the risky shift is by no means a universal occurrence; shifts toward caution may often occur instead.

Situational view. With respect to leadership, refers to the suggestion that the persons who rise to positions of authority are those who can best help the group attain its goals.

Social-comparison theory. Refers to the fact that we often seek to evaluate our opinions, characteristics, and accomplishments by comparing ourselves to others.

Social facilitation. Refers to effects upon performance stemming from the presence of others. Since such conditions can both facilitate and interfere with performance, describing these effects as social *facilitation* is somewhat misleading.

Transactional view of leadership. A modern approach in which leadership is viewed as a reciprocal process of social influence where leaders both influence followers and are influenced, in turn, by these persons.

SUGGESTED READINGS FOR CHAPTER 12

Fiedler, F. E., and Chemers, M. M. *Leadership and effective management.* Glenview, Ill.: Scott, Foresman, 1974. A full-length discussion of the factors affecting leader effectiveness in many real-life settings. Evidence relating to the contingency model is reviewed in detail.

Myers, D. G., and Lamm, H. The polarizing effect of group discussion. *American Scientist,* 1975. A very clear discussion of the nature of group polarization, theoretical interpretations for its occurrence, and some of its important implications.

Zajonc, R. B. Social facilitation. *Science,* 1965, *194,* 269–274. Zajonc's initial statement of his theory of social facilitation. This paper provides an outstanding example of the manner in which conflicting experimental findings can be integrated and resolved by means of an effective theoretical framework.

Zimbardo, P. G. The human choice: Individuation, reason, and order versus deindividuation, impulse, and chaos. In W. J. Arnold and D. Levine, eds., *Nebraska symposium on motivation,* 1969. Lincoln: University of Nebraska Press, 1970. An intriguing discussion of the causes, nature, and effects of deindividuation. Some of the research reviewed is among the most fascinating ever conducted in social psychology.

Zimbardo, P. G., Haney, C., Banks, W. C., and Jaffe, D. A Pirandellian prison: The mind is a formidable jailer. *New York Times Magazine,* April 8, 1973, pp. 38–60. A very readable account of the controversial Stanford Prison experiment. Both the rationale behind the study and the investigators' interpretation of its results are discussed.

ENVIRONMENT AND SOCIAL BEHAVIOR

13

Imagine that you suddenly find yourself enclosed in a noisy moving cylinder, surrounded by hoards of people and hot, stuffy air. The array of smells (some pleasant, some awful) which are generated by the crowd billows over you in waves. You feel hot and crowded, since the personal space you ordinarily maintain between yourself and others is violated. Some of the people surrounding you are sitting and some are standing (apparently suspended from the ceiling by straps), but as the cylinder sways unpredictably during its movement, they brush against your body. When your container suddenly stops, as it does from time to time, you lurch forward trying to maintain your balance as your neighbors are thrown against you. Then the screeching noise suddenly subsides, leaving a shocking calm. The ordeal is not over, however, because a door swings open and more people enter, crowding you worse than before. Overall, you feel as if the unbearable conditions you are experiencing must be a new form of physical and psychological torture

One of the consequences of technological progress and urban living has been a steadily accumulating array of stressors which affect human behavior, including overcrowding, noise, and polluted air. (Photo: Phil Carver & Friends.)

designed to destroy your resistance and make you confess some un-
speakable crime. You have fantasies of escape to some quiet, calm,
uncrowded sanctuary. As a matter of fact, you hope you'll never have
to ride the New York subway during the rush hour again!

While the example above may seem a bit exaggerated, thinking about such discomfort should make you aware of the desire of each of us to maintain more or less optimal environmental conditions. Part of the problem is in our attributions. The same objectively uncomfortable subway conditions just described would be perceived quite differently and reacted to quite differently if they really constituted a deliberate effort by someone to cause us pain versus a necessary discomfort that enabled us to reach our work or a place of entertainment economically. Nevertheless, there *are* some aspects of the environment that represent relatively pleasant and relatively unpleasant realities. We want to have a sufficient amount of space between ourselves and others and a sense of control over the territory around us. Further, we value air conditioning when we're hot, and we like to be shielded from excessive noise. To the extent that these conditions are not present, we become upset, our performance may be impaired, and we are motivated to take steps to restore a comfortable equilibrium.

This chapter is devoted to **environmental psychology,** a newly emerging area of research which concentrates on the reciprocal relationship between the physical environment and human behavior (Altman, 1976). One important part of this relationship is the effect of the physical environment on behavior. For example, the behavioral consequences of crowded conditions (like those in the "cylinder" we described) are explored by environmental psychologists. But people are not merely passive respondents to environmental stimuli; many of our behaviors are directed toward the environment and significantly influence the physical conditions around us. Attempts to control the immediate environment (spatial and territorial behavior) as well as environmentally destructive behaviors such as littering are also studied by environmental psychologists. Since it deals with some of the most pressing problems society will face in the foreseeable future (crowding, pollution, the attractiveness of our surroundings), environmental psychology may play an increasingly important part in our lives. Its promise is especially great, because it cuts across many of the traditional divisions between the various areas of psychology, and between psychology and other sciences. To date, social psychologists, architects, ecologists, and others have made significant contributions to the development of environmental psychology.

In the first section of this chapter, we will consider *spatial behavior.* **Personal space** is the **bubble** or invisible boundary we maintain between ourselves and others. It moves with us wherever we go. Psychologists have been concerned with such issues as identifying factors which determine how much personal space we require between ourselves and others and studying how we respond when our personal space is "invaded." Next, we will discuss

territorial behavior, which involves the staking out and defending of a specific area against members of one's own species. Research in this area has surveyed territorial behavior of both humans and animals, and has considered such questions as "What are the functions of territory?" and "How is territory defended?" Next, we will look at *environmental effects on behavior.* Initially, we will consider the way in which we perceive the world around us. While it might seem surprising, our perception of the environment is determined by factors in addition to the physical characteristics of an environmental setting. We will also consider research on the behavioral effects of particular environmental stimuli (for example, population density, heat, and noise). In an already overcrowded world in which many people complain of excessive noise and pollution, studying the consequences of these environmental stressors is crucial. Since the "man-made" aspects of the environment such as interior decorating and architectural planning of buildings also affect our behavior, we will consider the consequences of man-made environmental settings on our responses. In the final section, we will discuss the possibilities for *environmental change* and the efforts being made by individuals, government agencies, and industrial concerns to restore and maintain a livable world.

SPATIAL BEHAVIOR

People engage in two forms of spatial behavior: personal space and territoriality. While both have evoked a great deal of interest, research on personal space has been especially active (Linder, 1974). In fact, over two hundred experiments have investigated personal space since 1959 (Altman, 1975).

Personal Space: Private, Keep Out

None of us likes to feel that others are "breathing down our necks." Thus, we all maintain an area around our bodies which has been characterized as *personal space.* Personal space is defined as an invisible boundary surrounding each individual, through which most other people should not pass. It moves about with us and has been found to expand and contract, depending on the situation in which we find ourselves (Sommer, 1966).

Why do we maintain such a portable bubble around ourselves, and how does it serve us? Our bubble has two primary purposes. First, it functions as a buffer against a series of real or perceived threats. For example, it keeps us a comfortable distance from potential emotional threats (e.g., too much intimacy, not enough privacy, general overstimulation) by enabling us to control the intensity of our relationships with the outside world and to protect ourselves. If space protects us from emotional stimulation, it follows that we should place the greatest distance between ourselves and those individuals who exhibit the greatest stimulus intensity. This idea was tested at an amusement park by Nesbitt and Steven (1974), who observed how far people waiting in line stood from the person directly in front of them. Any intense stimulus, such as brightly colored clothing, perfume, or after-shave lotion, led to increased interpersonal distance from that individual.

The second function of our personal space bubble is to facilitate communication (Pedersen and Shears, 1973). In one sense, a minimal personal space must be maintained or effective interpersonal communication will be hampered, since vision becomes blurred and our other channels of communication distorted when we are too close. In another sense, we communicate considerable information to others about the quality of our relationship with them by the size of the personal space we maintain.

Determinants of the Size of One's Personal Space. It is clear that people sometimes insist on a rather large zone between themselves and others, while at other times they are content to let their barriers down and interact with certain individuals at much closer distances. In addition, you have probably noticed that some individuals typically get very close to others in their everyday interactions, while some people habitually preserve very large interpersonal distances. Individual preferences for interpersonal distances seem to develop early in life and to be relatively stable over time (Eberts and Lepper, 1975). Thus, both *situational* and *individual difference* variables affect the size of personal space. While you may be aware of these factors through observation and everyday experience with others, you may be wondering how social psychologists formally explore the effects of these variables on personal space.

In past research on determinants of personal space, three different experimental methodologies have been employed, and they represent some of the fundamental methods of exploration in social psychology (see Chapter 1). Many of the studies have used *simulation methods* in which subjects manipulate the personal space between dolls or symbolic figures under various experimental conditions. *Laboratory methods* have also been used: in this approach the distance between subjects (who generally know they are being observed) is measured as a function of experimental conditions. Finally, a third series of studies has employed *field methods,* which involve observing interpersonal positioning in naturally occurring situations. Fortunately, most of the major relationships between situational and personality variables and the size of personal space have been consistent across different research approaches. We will now examine some of them.

In Chapter 5 it was shown that attraction affects the size of personal space. The greater the attraction between two people, the more physically close they desire to be, especially when they are of the opposite sex. You may also recall that when the interacting individuals are both of the same sex, the relationship between attraction and personal space becomes a bit more tricky. In one experiment (Heshka and Nelson, 1972), the investigators photographed pairs of adults as they walked down the street in London. After taking the photograph, the experimenter approached the unknowing subjects and asked them to describe the type of relationship they had. It was found that female-female pairs interacted at closer distances as the intimacy of their relationship increased, whereas male-male pairs did not interact at closer distances under conditions of greater friendship. In fact, females in general maintain closer distances than do males in situations ranging from playground interactions among children (Aiello and Jones, 1971) to structured interviews (Pellegrini and Empey, 1970). It is possible that such differences reflect the fear of the possible homosexual implications of a close interaction with someone of the same sex which tends to be more threatening to males than to females.

The research demonstrating that opposite-sex pairs generally interact at closer distances with increasing friendship suggests that closer personal space is a consequence of increased attraction. Are observers aware of the relationship between interpersonal attraction and physical closeness? Anyone who has ever seen an embracing couple walking down the street and thought "they must be in love," knows the answer: close distances are interpreted as indicators of attraction. This has been verified experimentally in several studies which have shown that observers infer greater attraction and generally more favorable interactions between individuals who interact at a closer distance than between people interacting at greater distances (Goldring, 1967; Haase and Pepper, 1972; Mehrabian, 1968).

Under some conditions, the relationship between attraction and physical closeness can be reversed; that is, if people can be induced to break through personal space barriers and touch, this can—under the right circumstances—lead to positive interpersonal feelings. In an encounter group situation, for example, structured exercises in which participants are instructed to touch one another (e.g., to administer a back rub) lead to an increase in positive feelings and friendly interactions (Dies and Greenberg, 1976). There are sometimes sex differences in response to being touched, however. Females can interpret (often correctly) a male's touch on some parts of her body as an unwelcome sexual advance (Nguyen, Heslin, and Nguyen, 1975, 1976). In a nonsexual interaction, in contrast, females are much more positive than males in response to being touched by a stranger. Fisher, Rytting, and Heslin (1976) instructed library clerks either to touch each subject on the hand or not to touch as books were being checked out. Under these conditions, males had mixed feelings about being touched, but females responded with positive affect to touches from a clerk of either sex.

Effect of Similarity on Interpersonal Distance. We know that attitude similarity leads to attraction, and that this results in closer interpersonal distances. How general is the similarity-closeness relationship? How do other types of similarity affect the size of spatial zones? You might guess that similarity along many dimensions would lead to closer interpersonal positioning. This proposition has been supported in a number of studies. It has been found that closer distances are maintained between individuals of similar rather than dissimilar age (Willis, 1966), race (Campbell, Kruskal, and Wallace, 1966), and status (Lott and Sommer, 1967). Finally, it is unfortunate to note that the nonhandicapped tend to interact at a greater than normal distance with individuals who have a physical handicap (Kleck et al., 1968).

Why should similarity lead to closer interpersonal positioning than dissimilarity? It has been found that people generally anticipate more favorable interactions with liked than with disliked others. If one of the functions of personal space is protection against perceived threats, then we should be willing to interact at closer distances with those who offer the least possible threat.

Type of Interaction and Interpersonal Distance. If situations can be placed on a pleasant-unpleasant dimension, such qualities should also affect the size of our personal space. This general line of reasoning is supported by studies which have varied the affective quality of the interaction situation and measured the effects on spatial positioning. In one experiment, Rosenfeld (1965) asked subjects either to appear friendly and to seek approval or to avoid being friendly when interacting with a confederate. He found that friendly subjects placed their chairs closer to the confederate than subjects instructed to avoid being friendly. Another bit of evidence further supports the proposition that the quality of the anticipated interaction affects spatial behavior. Sommer (1969) reported anecdotal evidence that twice as many people mysteriously fit into theater lobbies when erotic films are showing than when family movies are playing.

Some studies have shown that in addition to determining interpersonal distance, situational variables affect the body orientation which we maintain between ourselves and others. One such variable is the cooperativeness or competitiveness of the interaction. Sommer and his colleagues (Sommer, 1965; Norum, Russo, and Sommer, 1967) allowed cooperating or competing pairs to position themselves at a rectangular table. Cooperating pairs tended to sit side-by-side while competing pairs sat across from each other.

Racial and Cultural Determinants of Personal Space. It might be reasonable to expect that spatial behavior should vary for groups who, for various reasons, are subjected to dissimilar learning experiences early in life. For example, it would not be surprising to find cross-cultural differences in interpersonal distancing and dissimilarities between subgroups within a given culture.

The evidence relating to cross-cultural variation in spatial behavior is quite clear: cultural groups show consistent differences in the size of personal-space zones (Sommer, 1968). For example, Hall (1966), Watson and Graves (1966), and Little (1968) found that Latin Americans, French, Greeks, and Arabs use smaller interaction distances and are less rigid in their use of space than is true for citizens of the United States. Further, Sommer (1969) and Little (1968) found that English, Swedish, and Swiss people are similar to Americans in the size of their spatial zones.

When people differ in their preferred interpersonal distances, difficulties can arise when they attempt to communicate. Imagine, for example, an interaction at the United Nations between an Arab and an Englishman. The Arab stands close in what he judges to be a normal, friendly distance for a conversation. The Englishman is suddenly uncomfortable because of what seems to be an inappropriate degree of intimacy, and he therefore moves back a step. At this point, the

Arab misinterprets what has happened and assumes that he has been rebuffed. You can see that unless individuals are aware of such differences, serious misunderstandings can easily arise. Have you ever interacted with someone who preferred an interpersonal distance that was different from your own usual style?

The research on subcultural differences in personal space within our society is more confusing. There is evidence that individuals tend to interact at closer distances with members of their own group than with nonmembers (Willis, 1966). Findings of differences between groups regarding the typical distance range at which members interact with one another have been somewhat inconsistent. It has been suggested (Patterson, 1974) that socioeconomic status may be the best predictor of spatial behavior. While members of a subculture may vary greatly in their living conditions, members of a particular socioeconomic group tend to experience relatively similar conditions. Consistent with such expectations, Scherer (1974) found that both lower class blacks and whites interact at a relatively close distance while black and white middle-class children both interact at a greater distance.

Personality Determinants of Spatial Behavior. Since within any sex, race, or other category some people typically interact at closer distances than others, an attempt has been made to identify personality traits associated with differential concern about maintaining personal space. Surprisingly, this line of research has resulted in many contradictory findings, though individuals with a positive self-concept approach others more closely than do those with a negative self-concept (Stratton, Tekippl, and Flick, 1973).

One of the reliable relationships comes from a comparison of spatial behavior between nonviolent and violent prisoners (Kinzel, 1970). In one study, it was found that violent prisoners required nearly three times as much area around themselves to feel comfortable as did nonviolent prisoners. A second series of studies (Horowitz, Duff, and Stratton, 1964; Sommer, 1959) compared the spatial needs of schizophrenic patients and normals. It was found that schizophrenics required greater space.

A procedure recently adopted by Patterson (1974) may provide a way to show the effects of other personality characteristics. Instead of looking at single personality traits as predictors of spatial behavior, Patterson has conceptualized personality dimensions in more general terms. That is, he has looked at personality variables which suggest a general tendency to approach or avoid social situations rather than considering only single traits. This research has demonstrated that clusters of related personality variables which tap a central dimension are better predictors of interpersonal distancing than are any individual traits.

Consequences of Too Much or Too Little Personal Space

What happens when we interact with another person under conditions of "inappropriate" personal space? For example, what would be the effect on our relationship with a stranger if we spoke to him about the weather at a distance of three inches? Since we noted earlier that personal space serves some important functions, we can assume that inappropriate distancing may have negative effects.

Inappropriate Distance: Getting Our Signals Crossed. One formulation which specifies the consequences of inappropriate spatial positioning is Hall's (1963; 1966) work on **proxemics,** his term for the study of interpersonal distance. He observed that Americans use four ranges of personal space in their interactions with others. He labeled these **intimate, personal, social,** and **public** distance. According to Hall, the four zones vary in terms of the quality and quantity of stimulation which is exchanged. The particular spatial zone which is appropriate for an interaction between two individuals depends on the situation. Table 13-1 depicts the interpersonal relationships and activities characteristic of each spatial zone, as well as the associated sensory qualities of each.

Hall predicts that when two interacting individuals occupy an inappropriate spatial zone (that is, a zone which is too intimate or too remote for their relationship and the type of interaction they are having), negative effects occur. Deviation in either direction (too close or too far) elicits negative feelings, as well as negative inferences about the other. Hall's predictions concerning such reactions to inappropriate positioning are shown graphically in Figure 13-1.

TABLE 13-1. *Types of interpersonal relationships and activities, as well as sensory qualities characteristic of Hall's spatial zones.*

	Appropriate Relationships and Activities	Sensory Qualities
Intimate Distance ($0-1^{1}/_{2}$ feet)	Intimate contacts (e.g., making love, comforting), physical sports (e.g., wrestling), and aggression (e.g., slapping)	Intense awareness of sensory inputs (e.g., smell) from other person; touch overtakes vocalization as primary mode of communication
Personal Distance ($1^{1}/_{2}$–4 feet)	Contacts between close friends, as well as everyday interactions with acquaintances	Less awareness of sensory inputs than intimate distance; vision is normal and provides detailed feedback; verbal channels account for more communication than touch
Social Distance (4–12 feet)	Impersonal and business-like contacts	Sensory inputs minimal; information provided by visual channels less detailed than in personal distance; normal voice level (audible at 20 ft.) maintained; touch not possible
Public Distance (more than 12 feet)	Formal contacts between an individual (e.g., actor, politician) and the public	No sensory inputs; no detailed visual input; exaggerated nonverbal behaviors employed to supplement verbal communication, since subtle shades of meaning are lost at this distance

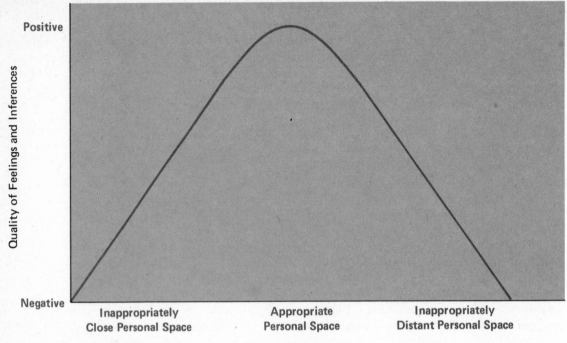

FIGURE 13-1. *Deviation from the "appropriate" interpersonal distance zone in either direction elicits negative feelings and inferences.*

Several studies have tested Hall's predictions about interactions in an inappropriate spatial zone. In an experiment on the effects of distance between a subject and a communicator, Albert and Dabbs (1970) hypothesized that negative feelings and attributions would occur if a communicator and a subject were not positioned at *social distance,* which is appropriate for such interpersonal contacts. Accordingly, the communicator (actually an experimenter) and the subject were constrained to interact at the appropriate distance (five feet) or at one of two inappropriate distances (either two or fifteen feet). Several effects were measured, and the findings basically support Hall's prediction. Selective attention was greater at the five-foot distance than at either of the other spatial zones. Further, inferred expertise of the communicator was judged greatest at five feet, and information recall tended to be greatest at this distance as well.

Boucher (1972) found similar results with schizophrenics as subjects, in a study which demonstrates that interpersonal positioning can have therapeutic implications. In this experiment, therapists sat down with patients for an interview at a distance which was inappropriately close, appropriate, or inappropriately distant. This distance manipulation was accomplished by bolting both chairs to the floor at one of three distances so that people in inappropriate positions could not adjust their proximity to a more comfortable zone. Following a ten-minute interview under these circumstances, several measures were employed to assess the subject's attraction to the interviewer. It was found that more attraction was expressed for the interviewer at the appropriate distance than at the distances which were too close or too far away.

In addition to negative evaluations, what other effects can inappropriate spatial positioning have? According to Argyle and Dean (1965), a series of nonverbal reactions should occur which act to restore a comfortable equilibrium. Specifically, Argyle and Dean argue that equilibrium will be achieved by adjustments in such nonverbal behaviors as the rate of eye contact and the directness of body orientation. While all of the implications of this proposition have not been tested, studies have provided support for Argyle and Dean's formulation. In one such experiment (Patterson, 1974), subjects interacted with an interviewer at both appropriate and inappropriate distance zones, and changes in both eye contact and body orientation were recorded. In support of the equilibrium hypothesis, it was found that body orientation became less direct and that percentage of eye contact decreased with inappropriate proximity.

Invasions of Personal Space: I Don't Like It When You Crowd Me. Hall's formulation and supporting research suggest that when ongoing interactions take place at inappropriate distances, they lead to lower attraction, negative inferences, and compensatory behaviors. What happens, however, when an individual is sitting alone, minding his own business, has no intention of interacting with anyone, and a total stranger sits down in inappropriately close proximity? You have probably been the target of such "invasions" and can formulate several hypotheses from your own experience. How did you feel and what did you do?

The first systematic study on the effects of personal space invasions was conducted by Felipe and Sommer (1966). At a mental institution where patients spent much time outdoors, a stranger (actually a confederate) approached lone patients at a distance of six inches. If the subject attempted to compensate by moving away, the confederate moved so as to maintain close positioning. The flight behaviors of the invaded individuals were compared with those of control individuals who were not invaded. As can be seen in Figure 13-2, after two minutes one-third of the invaded subjects and none of the control subjects had fled; after twenty minutes 65 percent of those who had been invaded had left their places; only 35 percent of the control subjects had moved away during the same time period. Is it possible that this retreat from an invading stranger was simply a function of the emotional state of the patients who were invaded? It has been found in other research that those who are the most disturbed prefer to place the greatest distance between themselves and others (Duke and Mullens, 1973). Would normally functioning individuals also retreat from an invading stranger?

Similar flight behavior in a non-hospital setting following an **invasion of personal space** was reported by Konecni et al. (1975). In this study (see Figure 13-3), it was found that both male and female pedestrians crossed the street faster if their personal space had been violated by a same-sex confederate than in a control condition. In addition to flight, Patterson, Mullens, and Romano (1971) reported that invaded subjects turn away, avoid eye contact, try to put some

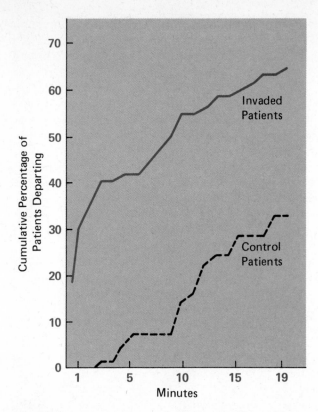

FIGURE 13-2. *What happens when a stranger invades one's personal space? When a confederate came within six inches of solitary hospital patients, these "invaded" individuals were much more likely to leave the area than comparable patients who were not invaded. (Source: Based on data from Sommer, 1969.)*

object between themselves and the invader, fidget, mumble, and display other coping reactions more than noninvaded control subjects.

Sex Differences in Responding to Invasions. As you may recall from some of the attraction studies described in Chapter 5, males tend to place themselves *across from* someone they like, while females prefer to sit *beside* a liked other. Going beyond such findings, Fisher and Byrne (1975) hypothesized that the *preferred* position for a friend would constitute the most *threatening* position for an invading stranger. In other words, females should respond more negatively than males to a side-by-side invasion of personal space by a stranger, but males should respond more negatively than females to a face-to-face invasion.

The scene for testing these ideas was a college library. You may have noticed that people in such a setting tend to get as far away from one another as space permits. The subjects were students who were each sitting alone at a table. As the individual sat working, a confederate took a seat at the same table, either in a chair beside the subject or in one directly across the table. This

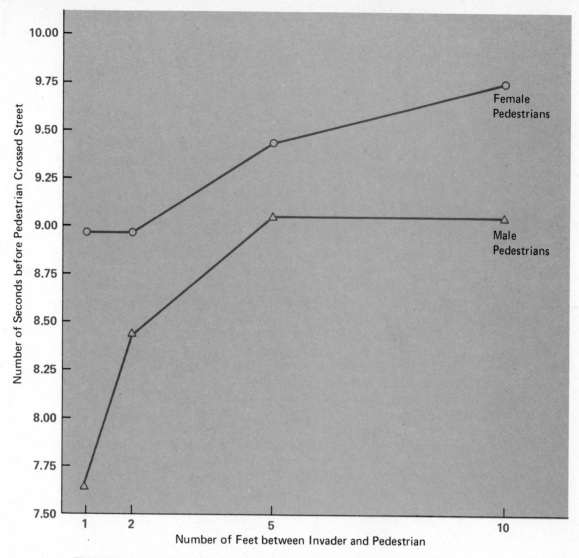

FIGURE 13-3. *When a same-sex individual approached a pedestrian on a sidewalk, the closer the approach the fewer number of seconds before the pedestrian crossed the street to escape. Also, males tend to escape more quickly from such invasions than females. (Source: Based on data from Konecni et al., 1975.)*

"invader" simply took notes from a book for five minutes and then, apparently finished, left the subject's table. At that point, an experimenter arrived and introduced himself as a student who was conducting a study for an introductory psychology class. He said that he noticed that another person had been working nearby, and he asked the subject to give his or her impressions of that person as well as some impressions of the library.

It was found that, regardless of the invader's sex, males responded negatively after a face-to-face invasion while females responded negatively after a side-by-side invasion—these effects included the subjects' present emotional state, their attraction toward the invader, their guesses as to that person's motives, and their perceptions of the beauty and crowdedness of the library.

These strong sex differences in responding to the specific seating location of an invader were further investigated in a follow-up library study. It was assumed that if males dislike being invaded by someone sitting across the table from them, they should try to protect themselves by erecting barriers when they first sit down. That is, they should place their books and personal effects between themselves and the empty seat facing them. Females, on the other hand, should erect barriers between themselves and an empty adjacent seat. Systematic observations of students working alone in a college library confirmed these expectations: males placed their belongings in front of them, while females placed theirs to the side.

Such male-female differences could possibly lead to misunderstandings between the sexes. A female who wants to make friends with an unknown male may be surprised to find that a nonthreatening (to her) eyeball-to-eyeball approach causes consternation and alarm. In an analogous way, a male who attempts to ingratiate himself with an unknown female by sitting down beside her in a nonthreatening (to him) position may not understand why he elicits a Miss Muffet reaction and unintentionally "frightens her away."

Though the sex of the invader made no difference in the context of a university library, male invaders have been found to cause victims to flee more rapidly in public settings such as a large suburban shopping mall (Bleda and Bleda, 1976).

Effects of Invading on the Invader: Pardon Me, but I Have to Intrude. We've described how it feels to be the victim of a personal space invasion but have not yet mentioned how it feels to be the invader. That can be unpleasant too. Picture yourself entering a crowded bus at the beginning of what is to be a long trip. All the seats are filled except for one, which is occupied by an elderly woman who has spread out over both sides of the seat. What do you do? Whether you barge your way into her personal space, stand the entire way, or take another bus, you realize how difficult it is to be cast in the invader role.

Recently, several investigators have been looking at just what does happen when people are placed in such dilemmas. In one study (Barefoot, Hoople, and McClay, 1972) a confederate was stationed one, five, or ten feet from a public water fountain. It was found that fewer passersby attempted to use the fountain when doing so would violate the confederate's personal space (at the one-foot distance) than when it wouldn't constitute such a violation (at the five or ten-foot distances). Thus, it appears that invading a lone individual's personal space is an aversive experience, to be avoided if at all possible. Several additional studies (Cheyne and Efran, 1972; Efran and Cheyne, 1973) have looked at the invader's reactions to violating the personal space of two interactants who are facing each other. If you are walking down a hallway and find part of your path blocked by two individuals, do you go around them, between them, go another route entirely, or what? In field studies, it has been found that people are less likely to invade if the individuals are conversing rather than not conversing, if the individuals are occupying Hall's personal distance zone rather than social distance, and if the two individuals are of the opposite rather than the same sex. Further, Efran and Cheyne (1974) found that the act of invading has affective consequences: subjects in invasion conditions indicated more negative feelings and displayed more unpleasant facial expressions than noninvading control subjects.

Several characteristics of the person being invaded seem to determine how likely others are to intrude on their personal space. In an interesting field study, Dabbs and Stokes (1975) filmed several hundred pedestrians as they walked past a confederate who stood on the edge of a sidewalk. The experimenters were able to measure how far each individual walked out of his or her way to avoid invading the confederate. Two general findings stood out—people went farther to avoid a male than a female, and they went farther to avoid a beautiful woman than an unattractive one. It was proposed that both masculinity and female beauty are equated with power in our society and that those passing by felt threatened by the possibility of walking too close to powerful others.

Territorial Behavior: This Land Is My Land

Anyone who has ever unknowingly passed a "no trespassing" sign on a country road and then come into contact with a rural dweller brandishing a rifle has first-hand experience with the concept of territoriality. Territorial behavior is engaged in by human beings and also by other animals. In general terms, territoriality involves the staking out and defending of space against members of one's own species. Unlike personal space which regulates *distance* between people (and moves about with the individual) territories regulate *who* will interact, and are often characterized by specified boundaries. Among animals, territory is important for such essential functions as mating, food gathering, rearing the young, and maintaining a proper level of population density. While territoriality doesn't serve such survival-related functions in man, it affords us control of inputs from the outside world (for example, a "Do not disturb" sign on the door of a motel room may keep unwanted visitors away), and it provides us with a sense of identity by helping us differentiate what is "ours" and "theirs."

Some individuals are more likely to display territorial behavior than others. For example, those who own their homes tend to erect signs that warn against entering the property and to have physical barriers such as a fence or hedge more than is true for renters; those with such territorial defenses also answer the doorbell more quickly than those without defenses (Edney, 1972). Presumably, the territorial individuals are more vigilant about possible trespassers and hence are alert to get to the door quickly.

FOCUS ON RESEARCH

PHYSIOLOGICAL EFFECTS OF SPATIAL INVASIONS: TOGETHERNESS AT THE URINAL

If a stranger's intrusion on one's personal space is an uncomfortable emotional experience, physiological indicators of arousal should be sensitive to such interactions. Several theorists (e.g., Evans and Howard, 1973; Sommer, 1969) have suggested that a victim engages in avoidance behavior precisely *because* invasions elicit high levels of arousal. Presumably, avoidance behavior or escape represents attempts to reduce such arousal.

How would one go about measuring physiological arousal in a real-life setting in which individuals were invaded by strangers? Offhand, this does not seem possible, but an ingenious field experiment by Middlemist, Knowles, and Matter (1976) provides some unusual data which support the arousal concept, using urination responses as the index of stress. Research indicates that any stress tends to delay the onset of urination and to shorten its duration. Therefore, if invasions are stressful, urinating time should be affected.

The unique research locale was a three-urinal men's lavatory. The authors point out that the use of a public restroom evokes concern for privacy among members of the middle class. For example, urinals are placed next to one another in a row, and males must stand shoulder to shoulder, so to speak, engaging in an ordinarily private act. This situation is unlike others in which invasions have been studied because an individual cannot comfortably defend himself by turning away or walking out. In the experiment, the unknowing subjects were restroom users who were forced to occupy the left-most urinal in one of three experimental conditions. In the close-invasion condition, a male confederate pretended to urinate at the middle urinal, and the right-most one was blocked by a sign reading, "Don't use, washing urinal," plus a

bucket of water and a sponge. In the moderate-invasion condition, the confederate stood at the right-most urinal, and the middle one was blocked off. There was also a no-invasion control condition in which there was no confederate; only the left-most urinal was free, because the other two were blocked off.

In order to determine how long it took each subject to begin urinating and then to complete the task, an experimenter sat in an adjacent toilet stall equipped with a periscope and two stopwatches to record the urination times. As can be seen in Figure 13-4, the hypothesized relationships were confirmed. The closer the interpersonal distance between confederate and subject, the greater the time required to begin urinating and the less the time required to complete the act. It might be noted that even though no one was physically harmed by serving as a subject in this experiment, critics of such research point out that personal privacy was being invaded even more than personal space. What is your opinion about the ethics of observing restroom responses?

Beyond the general stress of a spatial invasion and any special embarrassment associated with urination, is there any additional reason why males might react to this situation as being stressful? One possibility is a not quite conscious fear of the homosexual implications of someone getting too close in a lavatory. Morin (1975) reported that when he publicly announced that he was a homosexual, male colleagues tended to move away from him in the restroom—as if he might pounce on them at any moment. To explore this idea further, he had a male and a female confederate interview college students, half of the time wearing a button inscribed "Gay and Proud." Both male and

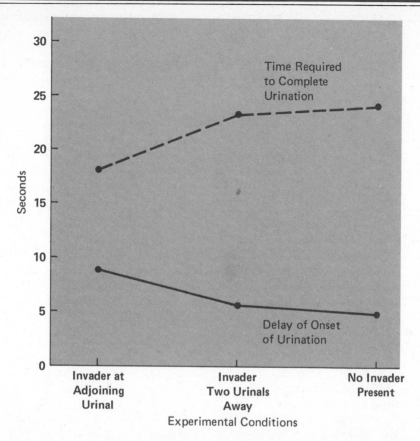

FIGURE 13-4. *Spatial invasions result in the physiological arousal of the invaded victim. One index of such arousal is the time required to begin urinating and the length of time required to complete the act. As the personal space of males in a public restroom was invaded by an experimental confederate at a nearby urinal, physiological arousal was indicated in that the onset of urination was delayed and the time required to complete urination was shortened. (Source: Middlemist, Knowles, and Matter, 1976. Copyright 1976 by the American Psychological Association. Reprinted by permission.)*

female subjects tended to sit farthest away from a same-sex confederate who was identified as gay, and this was especially true of males.

Whether or not homosexual fears are involved in the response to urinal invasions, it *is* clear that spatial intrusions can cause measurable physiological stress reactions.

Types of Territories. Altman (1975) describes three types of human territories which vary in terms of how central they are to everyday life, how long they are occupied, and the degree of control they afford. A **primary territory** is an area which is "owned" and personalized by an individual or group, who use it regularly and on a long term basis as an essential part of their everyday activities. Owners completely control access to these areas, and intrusion by unwelcome outsiders is a serious matter. An example of a primary territory is your home or apartment. The idea of criminals, government agents, or anyone else bursting into one's dwelling is extremely upsetting and is something we take steps to prevent.

A **secondary territory** is an area which is used regularly by a specific group of people who have less complete control, ownership, and power to regulate who comes and goes than in the case of primary territories. In general, a number of people have access to a secondary territory, it isn't identified as belonging to a specific individual, and the main users may vary over time. Examples of secondary territories include classrooms and seats in a theater which are understood to be reserved for particular groups at specific times. Also, (like Archie Bunker) your father probably has an armchair that is "his" in the evening but available to other family members when he is absent.

Finally, **public territories** are areas which are occupied only temporarily and which are available to almost anyone. Legitimate control over such space is especially difficult. An example of a public territory is your spot on the beach which can easily be lost if you walk away to buy an ice cream cone. Even in that setting, however, people attempt to mark off "their" area with personal belongings (Edney and Jordan-Edney, 1974).

Human Territoriality: Identifying Your Own Turf. Most of the research on territorial behavior has focused on animal populations, but several studies have

People, like other animals, tend to stake out territories as their own and to defend this area against intrusion by others. (Photo: Phil Carver & Friends.)

demonstrated that human beings frequently display territorial behavior. In one of these, Suttles (1968) observed the territoriality among various ethnic groups on Chicago's South Side. Each ethnic group claimed and defended a separate territory. In addition, there were shared territories in which certain community resources were used jointly in prescribed fashion. Have you ever observed high school or college eating facilities which were unofficially but regularly segregated as to where members of certain clubs sit, where the athletes sit, etc.?

Individuals also display **territorial behavior** in everyday social situations. We often adopt certain areas as our own and attempt to keep others out. For example, when you enter a cafeteria, you may place your jacket on the back of a chair so that you'll have a place to sit when you return with the food. How effective is this strategy? Do others interpret our possessions as a "private property—keep out" sign? Several studies have pursued this question.

In two such investigations, Sommer and Becker (1969) and Becker (1973) looked at the relative effectiveness of various territorial defense strategies in warding off territorial invasions. First, they found that people were less likely to sit down at tables with any kind of marker (a sandwich, a sweater, books) than at tables without such belongings. The greater the number of markers and the more personal they are, the more effective the barrier. Of course, the presence of an individual sitting at a table was the best signal of territory. Of interest as well was the finding that bystanders sitting near markers sometimes explained their meaning to potential intruders. This was most likely when the intruder directly questioned the bystander about the space in question ("Is someone sitting there?") and when the owner of the territory hadn't been away too long.

There's No Place Like Home. Is it true that people feel better when they're in their own territory than when they are visiting in someone else's territorial domain? Was Dorothy more comfortable in Kansas than in Oz? Being at home has been shown to have a number of advantages. In one study, Edney (1975) had Yale undergraduates participate in an experiment in pairs. The study was arranged so that it took place in the dorm room of one member of the pair, while the other member was a visitor. It was found that subjects who were in their own territory responded differently than visitors on a number of measures. Residents expressed greater feelings of passive control than visitors. In addition, visitors rated residents as being more relaxed than residents rated visitors, and residents rated the rooms as more pleasant and private than visitors.

The advantages of being "at home" have been shown in two other studies. Esser (1970) showed that psychotic patients were more successful at influencing others in their home territory than in other areas, and Martindale (1971) reported that dormitory residents were more successful at a negotiation task on their own turf than visitors. Thus, the speculation that a "home-court advantage" is a valuable asset appears to be true. It is interesting to note that research indicates that, for animals, winning or losing a fight is often better predicted by which animal is on home territory than by which is bigger and stronger (Leary and Moroney, 1962).

Areas which appear to be someone's territory have another positive feature.

CREATING INVISIBLE BOUNDARIES

It is possible to observe the effects of personal space on potential invaders at first hand. To do so, you might try a simple field experiment that is based on the research of Knowles, Kreuser, Haas, Hyde, and Schuchart (1976).

When you pass by a stranger in a public setting, there is a strong tendency to leave sufficient space between you so that your passage will not constitute an invasion of that person's space. What if more strangers are present? Would two strangers be avoided by a passerby at an even greater distance than a single person? Would four people have a larger boundary still?

To test the effect of varying numbers of people on the behavior of those who are passing near them, select a public hallway and place a bench against one wall, as shown in Figure 13-5. Directly in front of the bench place small strips of black tape, marking six-inch intervals from the front of the

bench to the opposite wall. You will need one person to serve as an observer, preferably in a location out of each subject's line of vision. Subjects should be strangers who are walking alone in a left to right direction. As they pass the markings, the observer should record the number of inches between bench and subject.

Three experimental conditions can be created. First, leave the bench empty and record the passing distances of a reasonably large number of individuals walking by (say fifty). Then, in the one-person condition, have a confederate sit quietly on the bench reading a book; this person should avoid making eye contact with the subjects. Again, record the passing distances of fifty subjects. Finally, create a four-person condition in which a group of confederates sit on the bench quietly talking and looking at one another; record the behavior of another fifty subjects who walk past this group.

When spaces have clear boundaries that signal they belong to somebody, less crime and vandalism occur. In a study of low-cost urban housing developments, Newman (1972) found that when areas had no clear symbols of ownership, they were more likely to be vandalized than when they had well-marked boundaries. Supportive evidence is also provided in a study which observed where cars were vandalized and stripped of parts in inner-city Philadelphia (Ley and Cybriwsky, 1974). It was found that more vandalism took place near abandoned houses, vacant lots, or public places such as factories and schools than in areas which signaled territorial ownership. In your own experience, are you more careless in the way you treat property in a public place than in a friend's home? In effect, people tend to respect properties which can be identified as territory more than properties that can't be easily identified.

ENVIRONMENTAL EFFECTS ON BEHAVIOR

Both personal space and territoriality may be viewed as attempts by individuals to control the level of stimulation they receive, and now we'll turn our focus to the behavioral effects of a number of environmental stimuli that confront us every

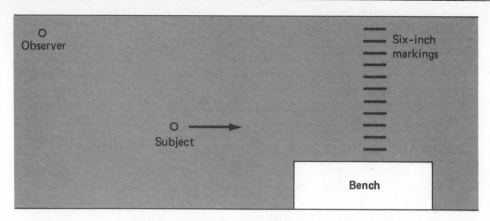

FIGURE 13-5. *Physical arrangement for field experiment to test the effect of social boundaries on the behavior of potential invaders.*

When the experiment is completed, obtain the average distance recorded in each of your three conditions. Your instructor may want you to test the group differences statistically or have you create a graph showing these effects. Why do you think people respond to such interpersonal boundaries? Do you think that the tendency to avoid intruding on others may serve some useful functions in society?

day. For example, we'll look at how such potential stressors as population density, heat, noise, and air pollution, as well as man-made aspects of the environment—such as high-rise buildings—affect our behavior. Before beginning our discussion of the behavioral effects of environmental stimuli, we'll first consider the way in which the environment is perceived.

Environmental Perception

How do we perceive the environment? We might be tempted to answer, "We see what's there," but this isn't actually the case. Over the years, psychologists have derived a variety of theoretical approaches to explain the processes involved in perception (Brunswik, 1956; Gibson, 1966). While the dynamics of such models are beyond the scope of this chapter, what is of interest is that the various approaches agree that what we see in the environment isn't merely a reflection of objective physical reality. The distinction between objective and perceived reality has been shown for many environmental stimuli. For example, it has been found that the objective state of high **density** differs from the experience of **crowding** (Stokols, 1972). The same number of people per square feet (density) may be experienced as crowded under some circumstances (a hallway between classes) and uncrowded under different circumstances (a rock concert). In a similar way, stimuli are classified as noise on the basis of more than just the objective qualities of the sound (Kryter, 1970). You and your mother, for example, may differ as to whether your phonograph or her dishwasher represents an obnoxious noise. In effect, environmental perception is a combination of objective physical stimuli, our personal characteristics (for example, background, values, needs), and situational conditions such as the context in which the stimulus occurs. Clearly, the environment as we see it is a better predictor of our behavioral reactions than is any straightforward measure of objective physical conditions.

Mapping Environmental Perceptions. One way of illustrating environmental perception is by considering studies which have been done on **cognitive mapping.** A cognitive map of an environment is one's mental image of that environment. Research on cognitive mapping shows that different people can perceive the same objective environment quite differently.

Lynch (1960) performed one of the first cognitive-mapping investigations. In one study, residents of Jersey City, New Jersey, were asked to sketch a map of

FIGURE 13-6. *Research indicates that our cognitive maps of the environment are not always precisely accurate and that different individuals may have very different maps of the physical world. Because of such differences, two people may have difficulty in communicating about locations or in giving directions—as the policeman and citizen in this cartoon demonstrate. (Source: Drawing by Stevenson; © 1976 The New Yorker Magazine, Inc.)*

their city, to provide detailed descriptions of a number of trips through the city, and to list and describe the parts which were most distinctive. Using these data, Lynch was able to construct a cognitive map of the area. By examining Figure 13-7, you will find that perceptions of the physical environment differ markedly from objective physical conditions. Many aspects of the objective environment are not represented, and some are distorted. In effect, it appears that some dimensions of the objective environment are more salient to city dwellers than others, and these are reflected in individuals' mental images of the city.

Other cognitive mapping studies by Saarinen (1969) showed that perceptions of the Chicago Loop were affected by an individual's familiarity with the area. The subjects were people who worked in the Loop plus students who did not work in the Loop but who lived nearby. The cognitive maps drawn by the two groups may be seen in Figure 13-8. Clearly, individuals displayed different cognitive images as a function of their degree of familiarity with the Loop. Workers within the Loop tended to map a more tightly defined area with more internal detail; those from outside tended to include a broader area with more emphasis on external landmarks (for example, Lake Michigan, Lake Shore Drive, and Soldiers Field).

Feelings and Perception. Situational variables have also been shown to affect environmental perception. In a laboratory study by Fisher (1974), individuals interacted with either an attitudinally similar or dissimilar confederate in an objective environment which was held constant. After their interaction, subjects were asked to make judgments of the overall environmental quality of the experimental room, as well as a rating of how crowded they felt while interacting with the similar or dissimilar confederate. Although the physical environment was the same under each condition, subjects perceived environmental quality to be lower and viewed themselves as more crowded when interacting with the dissimilar than with the similar other. These findings suggest that when situational qualities vary, perceptions and evaluations of the environment can be markedly affected.

Sonnenfeld (1964) demonstrated that favorability of environmental perception is in part a function of familiarity. In this experiment, subjects from Alaska and Delaware rated slides showing vegetation, landscapes, and bodies of water. Each group rated most positively the kind of environmental features with which they were familiar. "There's no place like home" is more than just a cliché .

We will now turn our attention to the behavioral effects of some important environmental stimuli—population density, noise, heat, pollution, and our man-made surroundings. When there is an imbalance between the demands imposed by the environment and the individual's ability to cope with them, the individual experiences stress and behaves accordingly (Lazarus, 1966). How do such stressful conditions affect behavior? Presumably, stress activates coping processes, whose aim it is to reduce or eliminate the negative effects of the stressor. If successful, coping processes result in adaptation. Adaptation to environmental stressors often requires changes in the organism, and such changes can sometimes have unpleasant consequences.

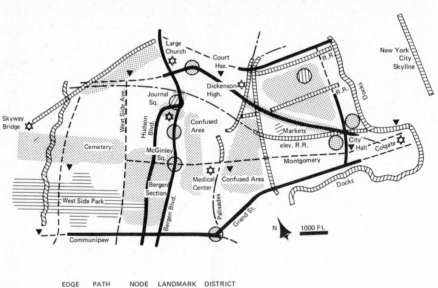

EDGE	PATH	NODE	LANDMARK	DISTRICT
major element 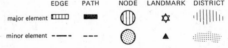			✡	
minor element			▲	

FIGURE 13-7. *A comparison of an aerial map of Jersey City, New Jersey, and a cognitive map of the same city indicates that those who live there have an inner picture of their environment that differs somewhat from objective reality. (Source: Lynch, K., The image of the city. Cambridge, MA.: M.I.T. Press, 1960.)*

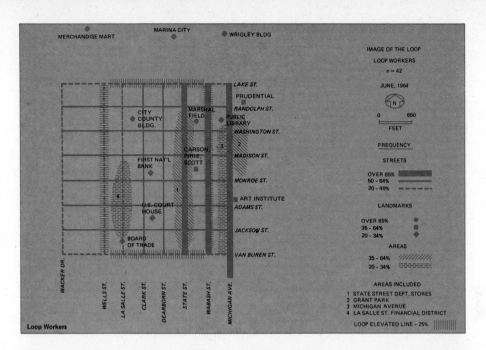

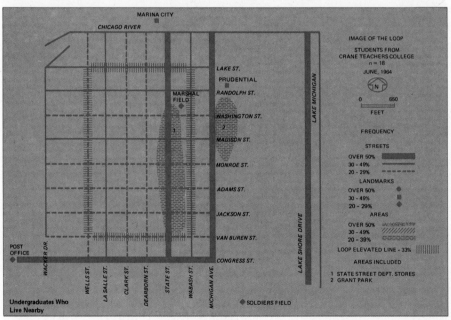

FIGURE 13-8. *Cognitive maps of the Chicago Loop as produced by individuals who worked there and by students who did not work in the Loop but who lived nearby. The student "outsiders" had less internal detail and more external landmarks. The percentages refer to how many subjects in each group included a particular street or location in drawing their cognitive maps. (Source: Saarinen, Perception of the environment. Resource paper 5. Assn. American Geographers, 1969.)*

Density among Animals: Packed Rats.   Regrettably, most of us have observed animals that were confined in tiny cages in zoos. Research suggests that high density is often sufficient to cause social disorganization and physiological ill effects among several species.

A number of studies illustrate that animal populations are unable to adapt to high density without destructive effects.   The classic experimental research in this area was done by Calhoun (1962; 1966; 1971).   In one of his studies, Calhoun built an apparatus which could comfortably contain forty-eight rats, and allowed the population to increase unchecked, providing the animals with adequate food and water.   When the population reached about eighty, a series of abnormal reactions were observed among the crowded occupants.   Specifically, the mortality rate of young rats became extremely high, and nest-building and maternal behaviors were disturbed, as were sexual and territorial behavior.   Some rats became hyperactive, hypersexual, homosexual, and cannabalistic.   In addition, several physiological disorders such as tumors and abnormalities of the kidneys, liver, and adrenal glands became common.

Calhoun's research with animals has been corroborated by a number of observational studies.   One interesting descriptive account is provided by Dubos (1965), who found that when the population of Norwegian lemmings becomes too high, they tend to migrate to the sea where many drown.   Dubos attributed this abnormal behavior to metabolic malfunctions involving the adrenal glands and the brain.   Do human beings respond to high density conditions as badly as rats and lemmings?

Crowded People: We Cope.   At first, there were a number of speculations generalizing from animal research to human behavior.   Thus, densely packed individuals in large urban centers might be expected to behave in disruptive and maladaptive ways.   Fortunately, our reactions to high density are not as uniformly negative as those of other animals.   In fact, when we're at the premiere of a new movie or at a football game, conditions of high density are experienced as favorable and even add to the fun.   In an attempt to specify the conditions under which density *is* experienced by man as stressful, psychologists have differentiated *density*—an objective physical state—from *crowding*—a psychological state of stress (Stokols, 1972).   Specifically, density is conceptualized as a physical state involving potential inconveniences such as restricted movement or lack of privacy which may or may not be important to individuals in the situation.   In contrast, crowding is conceptualized as a subjective experience characterized by feelings of stress.   Crowding occurs when situational conditions make the individual sensitive to the restrictive aspects of high density.

When does high density become crowding and thus result in negative behavioral effects?   Various theoretical perspectives propose somewhat different conditions as critical.   In a review of the literature Stokols (1975) identified three theoretical perspectives.   These are (1) **stimulus-overload models,** (2) **behavioral-constraint models,** and (3) **ecological models** as outlined in Table

13-2. Together, these models may be viewed as suggesting a number of conditions in which high density results in crowding which then motivates adaptive behavior.

Density and Interpersonal Behavior. Some of the studies of the effects of population density on human behavior are necessarily correlational. Usually, such investigations are designed to determine the association between population density and indicators of social and individual breakdown. Pressman and Carol (1969) have found that number of people per acre (outside density) is unrelated to crime and disease after the effects of other variables (such as socioeconomic status) were statistically controlled. However, even when such confounding factors are removed, there sometimes appears to be a persisting relationship between number of people per residence (inside density) and physical illness, emotional problems, and crime (Booth and Welch, 1973; Galle, Grove, and McPherson, 1972; Marsella, Escudero, and Gordon, 1970). Nevertheless, Freedman, Heshka, and Levy (1975) have been able to demonstrate that the crucial factors really are income level and ethnic group membership rather than density.

Experimental research on the effect of high density is relatively recent, but numerous studies have been conducted in the past few years. It is important to note that two types of density manipulations have been used in experimental research. Studies which have varied **social density** involve comparisons of groups of different sizes in a space of a single size. Research manipulating **spatial density** involves comparisons of a group of a single size in spaces of different sizes. To date, experiments have explored the effect of density on such variables as affective state, interpersonal attraction, altruism, task performance, and aggression. As with the correlational studies, experimental investigations also suggest that density does not invariably have negative effects on behavior.

TABLE 13-2 *Three explanations of crowding and the hypothesized feelings and behaviors that accompany this state. (Source: This table from "The Experience of Crowding in Primary and Secondary Environments," by Daniel Stokols is reprinted from* Environment and Behavior *Vol. 8, No. 1 (March 1976) p. 61 by permission of the Publisher, Sage Publications, Inc.)*

Model	Critical Determinant	Emotional Responses	Primary Adaptive Processes
Stimulus Overload	Excessive arousal	Confusion, fatigue	Escape from the stimulation, behavioral or psychological withdrawal, changing some aspect of the environment
Behavioral Constraint	Reduced behavioral freedom	Feelings of infringement	Leave situation, improve coordination and relations with others
Ecological	Scarcity of resources	Competition	Collective defense of group boundaries and resources, increased territoriality, exclusion of outsiders

For one thing, it matters whether an individual is interacting with friends or with strangers (McClelland, 1976).

In a similar way, a close positive interaction is more pleasant than a distant positive interaction while a close negative interaction is more unpleasant than the same interaction with the participants farther apart (Schiffenbauer and Schiavo, 1976). Thus, crowded conditions can *intensify* feelings that are already present. In addition, the type of activity is a factor: high density is perceived as positive at a party and as negative while studying (Cozby, 1973).

Several experiments indicate that high density elicits negative feelings. In one of these, Griffitt and Veitch (1971) varied social density and reported that subjects in high-density conditions experienced more negative affect than subjects in low-density conditions. This conclusion is also supported in a field study by Paulus et al. (1975), who had inmates at a federal correctional institution fill out a scale which tapped affective responses to their physical surroundings. Inmates resided either in single-occupancy cells (low density) or dormitories accommodating twenty-six to forty-four (high density). It was found that high-density subjects were more negative toward their immediate environment than low-density subjects. It is possible, however, that negative affective responses to high density are limited primarily to males. Ross et al. (1973) and Freedman et al. (1972) found that while males report more negative affect in high than in low-density conditions, the reverse is true for females.

Such sex differences have also been found in a classroom setting (Schettino and Borden, 1976). In classes ranging in size from 13 to 279 students, the experimenters determined density by dividing the number of individuals in each room by the total number of available seats. For males, the greater the classroom density, the more aggressive they felt; for females, high density was associated with feelings of nervousness and crowdedness. It was suggested that while females tend to internalize their discomfort in an overcrowded situation, males tend to externalize their negative feelings by expressing aggression. Such findings may reflect the fact that male socialization is relatively competitive, and they therefore see crowds as a source of threat.

Will we like a stranger more if we meet him while we're cramped in an elevator or when we're in a more spacious setting? The pattern of effects for density on attraction is similar to those of density on affect. Several experiments suggest that high density leads to a decrease in interpersonal attraction. In a study by Baron et al. (1975), dormitory residents living in "triples" (three students in a room designed for two) were compared on a variety of measures with residents living with one roommate in a room of similar size. Students living in triples were less satisfied with their roommates and perceived them to be less cooperative than students in doubles. Experiments by Valins and Baum (1973) and Baum and Valins (1973) provide corroborative evidence. Residents of high-density dorms avoided others on their floors, sat farther away from strangers in a laboratory setting, and experienced greater discomfort in the presence of strangers. It is as if high-density situations evoke defensive strategies in individuals that cause them to write off other people as undesirable.

Again, however, there is evidence that there may be sex differences in the effects of density (Freedman et al., 1972; Ross et al., 1973; Stokols et al., 1973). In one experiment, Freedman et al. had groups of males and females participate in a mock jury situation in either a small or large room. Subjects listened to a series of five courtroom trials and gave their verdict in each case. As shown in Figure 13-9, it was found that females were much more lenient in the high than in the low-density room, while males tended to be slightly more negative in the crowded than in the uncrowded room.

Is an old woman who needs directions to get to her daughter's house more likely to get help (a) in a high-rise building, (b) a low-rise building, (c) in a small town, or (d) in a large city? Recent studies have looked at the effect of population density on helping, and the findings are quite provocative. In

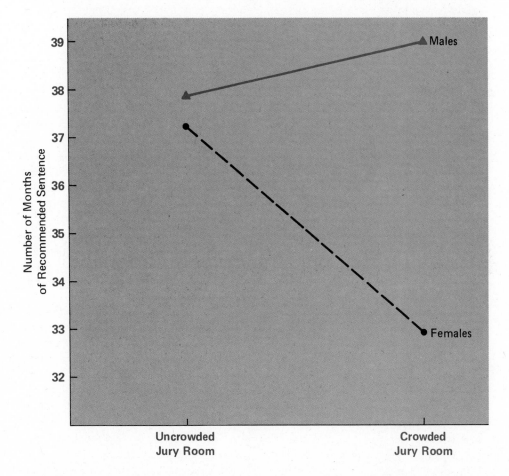

FIGURE 13-9. *Density has been found to have different effects on males and females. In a mock jury situation under either crowded or uncrowded conditions, males were slightly less lenient toward the defendant when crowded while females were much more lenient when they were crowded. (Source: Based on data from Freedman et al., 1972.)*

Chapter 8, it was reported that city residents are less helpful and less informative to strangers than rural dwellers in a number of different ways. Specifically, urban dwellers were less likely to admit a stranger into their dwelling to use a telephone, less likely to assist callers who had mistakenly called a wrong number, less likely to correct overpayments made in purchasing items, less likely to mail a lost postcard, and less likely to report a shoplifter. What about the incidence of helping in high rise as opposed to low-rise buildings? The overstimulation hypothesis would predict that low-density residents would be more helpful than high-density occupants. In a study by Bickman et al. (1973), the **lost-letter technique** was used to compare helping of residents in high, medium, and low-density living situations. In this technique, addressed, stamped envelopes were dropped in public areas of dorms. Helpfulness was measured in terms of how many letters were picked up and mailed by dormitory residents. The results suggested that high density conditions (58 percent returned) lead to less helping than medium density (79 percent returned), which leads to less helping than low density (88 percent returned).

The question as to whether population density affects performance is an especially crucial one. Early studies (e.g., Freedman, Klevansky, and Ehrlich, 1971; Rawls et al., 1972) rather consistently failed to show negative effects on performance under conditions of high density. Since many of us are forced to work daily under crowded conditions, the conclusion that we adapt to high density without cost to performance might have been a happy one to draw. Recent research, using more sensitive tasks, supports a somewhat different conclusion. For example, Paulus et al. (1975) performed three experiments in which they showed that high social and spatial density, and close interpersonal positioning all lead to poorer task performance on a maze task.

Do people become aggessive when they are forced to interact under conditions of high density? Under some conditions, density appears to lead to aggressive behaviors; under other conditions, it leads to withdrawal as a coping strategy. Recently, Baum and Koman (1975) have argued that aggression tends to occur under conditions of high *spatial density,* while withdrawal is chosen under conditions of high *social density.* For example, Rohe and Patterson (1974) varied spatial density in a day-care center. In this study, a group of constant size was subjected to conditions of both high and low spatial density. There were significant increases in destructive and aggressive behaviors as a result of increased density. Not surprisingly, the negative effects of high density were heightened if decreased room size was accompanied by a decrease in resources such as having fewer toys available.

Noise and Behavior

What is noise? Some of us who sing beautifully in the shower have actually been accused by others of making noise. Clearly, noise is different things to different people. In fact, one definition states that noise is simply "unwanted sound"

(Kryter, 1970). Technically, however, noise refers to a sound that is composed of many frequencies not in harmonious relation to one another. In terms of federal regulations, noise pollution is ordinarily defined with respect to how loud sound is at peak intervals plus the average loudness level over a period of time. To date, environmental psychologists have studied the effects of noise on performance, altruism, and aggression. In this research, it has been found that it is valuable to consider steady noise and unpredictable noise as being quite different environmental events.

Steady Noise versus Unpredictable Noise. How does steady noise affect performance? Experiments have found that individuals can adapt to steady noise fairly well except when they are performing complex tasks and when the noise level is particularly high (over 90 db) (Kryter, 1970). Steady noise does, however, often decrease responsiveness to incidental stimulation (Hamilton and Copeman, 1970; Hockey, 1970). For example, workers may learn to go about their jobs quite normally in a very noisy factory, but they may at the same time fail to perceive events in their surroundings that are unrelated to the work at hand.

The effects of unpredictable noise have been explored in an interesting series of studies by Glass and his associates. Glass, Singer, and Friedman (1969) reasoned that adaptation to unpredictable noise should require greater effort than adaptation to predictable noise. Further, it was assumed that the greater effort required to adapt to unpredictable noise might produce negative aftereffects. The hypotheses were supported. While adaptation occurred for both types of noise, subjects exposed to unpredictable noise showed less tolerance for frustration and made more errors on a proofreading test than subjects exposed to predictable noise.

An interesting field study by Cohen, Glass, and Singer (1973) generalized these findings beyond the lab and demonstrated that exposure to unpredictable noise can have particularly damaging aftereffects. The subjects were children who lived in a high-rise housing development in New York City. Their apartment development was built over a noisy expressway, and the lower floors were noisier than the upper floors. While children at both levels were able to adapt to the noise, adaptation was more costly for residents of lower floors. When they were tested for auditory discrimination and reading ability, it was found that residents of top floors did better than residents of bottom floors. Since the investigators ruled out the possibility that these results were due to other factors which could vary with height of a building such as social class or air pollution, it appears that the impairment in children at lower levels was due to greater unpredictable noise.

Why should exposure to unpredictable noise be worse than exposure to predictable noise? Glass, Singer, and Friedman (1969) suggested that unpredictable stressors make the individual feel that he cannot control his environment. They hypothesized that if this were true, the negative effects of unpredictable noise might be less severe if individuals were led to believe that they had control

FOCUS ON RESEARCH

LEARNED HELPLESSNESS:
THE EFFECTS OF EXPOSURE TO UNCONTROLLABLE EVENTS

As we have indicated, certain findings in Glass's research suggest that individuals find the inability to control their immediate environment quite disturbing. And, much that occurs around us in the environment *is* beyond our immediate control. That is, any of us can wake up any morning and be confronted with smog, the noise of a construction project, funny tasting tap water, a traffic jam, or whatever. Sometimes these unexpected occurrences can be very annoying and upsetting. The negative response seems to be most severe when individuals conclude that control is absent—that there is no contingency between the way they behave and the rewards or punishments they experience. We all wish to be the "masters of our fate," and to direct or influence events that befall us.

Attention was first drawn to such effects by research conducted with animal subjects. In several initial studies, Martin Seligman and his colleagues (e.g., Seligman and Maier, 1967) found that subjects exposed to a series of inescapable shocks, who then were given a chance to escape further punishment by the simple response of jumping from one compartment of an experimental apparatus to another, failed to learn this simple response. Instead, they often remained in the first compartment and "took their punishment." In sharp contrast, subjects who had not previously been exposed to inescapable shocks readily learned to escape by jumping from one compartment to another. Seligman (1975) termed such effects *learned helplessness,* and attributed them to the fact that the animals learned that their responses were independent of reinforcement—that nothing they did would be effective in terminating the shocks. As a result, he reasoned, they demonstrated lowered motivation, which caused them to make few responses in the new situation, and

experienced reduced cognitive functioning, which lowered their ability to learn an effective escape response.

That such effects also occur among human beings was soon established in further research. For example, in one well-known study (Hiroto and Seligman, 1975), subjects were first exposed either to a series of soluble or insoluble problems. Following this experience, both groups attempted to solve a series of anagrams. Consistent with Seligman's theory of learned helplessness, those who had been exposed to the insoluble problems in the first part of the study did much more poorly on the anagrams. Indeed, it was as if, having learned that nothing they did "worked," they largely gave up and made little further attempt to succeed. Further studies replicated these findings and also demonstrated that, as expected, the greater subjects' experience with insoluble problems or other uncontrollable events, the greater their feelings of helplessness, and the lower their performance on later tasks (Roth and Kubal, 1975). Thus, learned helplessness could be readily induced among human beings as well as the members of various animal species. It is as if we can easily learn to "give up."

Although initial investigations seemed to suggest that exposure to any uncontrollable events—either positive or aversive in nature—would lead to feelings of learned helplessness, recent investigations point to the conclusion that only unpleasant ones produce such effects (Benson and Kennelly, 1976). That is, individuals exposed to uncontrollable positive outcomes (e.g., being told that they are correct on a task regardless of their actual performance) do not show learned helplessness in other situations. Thus, only exposure to uncontrollable aversive events seems to produce such reactions. The opposite reaction can also be learned; exposure to controllable ones may lead to corresponding increments in performance—an effect sometimes termed *learned industriousness* (Eisenberger, Park, and Frank, 1976). Apparently, learning that one can control one's outcome in a given situation can lead to greater effort and better performance in other contexts.

If the effects of learned helplessness were restricted to decrements in performance on various learning tasks, they would certainly be quite serious. Learning, after all, is a central process in human behavior. Unfortunately, however, they appear to be far more general in nature. In particular, it appears that feelings of helplessness may be closely related to psychological depression and may, in fact, often underlie such reactions (Klein, Fencil-Morse, and Seligman, 1976). As noted by Seligman (1975), when individuals learn that they cannot control their environment or their own outcomes, it is not unreasonable to develop a sense of sadness and hopelessness. In short, there is some reason to believe that when individuals find themselves in situations where they experience intense feelings of helplessness and lack of control, profoundly detrimental effects may follow.

over this aversive stimulus. The results supported their contention; subjects who were told they could turn off unpredictable noise showed fewer aftereffects than subjects who did not think they had control of the stimulus.

Noise and Interpersonal Behavior. Two recent studies have examined the effect of environmental noise on helping behavior (Mathews and Canon, 1975). It was hypothesized that excessive noise would constitute overstimulation, which would lead to less attentiveness to environmental cues. A consequence of inattentiveness to environmental cues would be less inclination to help others. The first study was performed in a laboratory waiting room under normal, moderate, or high noise levels. When the subject and a confederate were called by the experimenter to begin the study, the confederate dropped a stack of books and magazines on the floor. As can be seen in Figure 13-10, fewer subjects volunteered to help the confederate pick up the books as the level of noise increased. These findings were replicated in a field experiment in which subjects observed a confederate drop his books on the sidewalk. In this study, a lawn mower either was operating nearby or was not operating. Again, less help was offered under conditions of high than low noise.

It is also not surprising to find that exposure to noise affects other interpersonal processes such as aggression. Geen and O'Neal (1969) exposed subjects to an aggressive boxing film or to a film depicting a nonaggressive sport. Each subject was then given an opportunity to aggress against a confederate. At the time the subject was delivering electric shocks to the confederate, he was either exposed to continuous noise or no noise. Both the film content and the presence of noise influenced aggression. It was found (see Table 13-3) that the greatest amount of aggression occurred for subjects who were exposed to noise after viewing the films which contained aggressive cues.

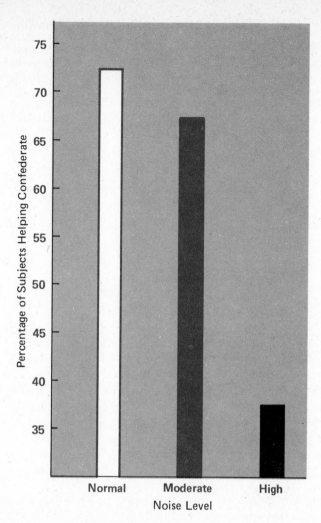

FIGURE 13-10. *At each of three levels of background noise, a confederate dropped a stack of books, seemingly by accident. The louder the background noise in the room, the less likely subjects were to help pick up the books. (Source: Based on data from Mathews and Canon, 1975.)*

Temperature and Behavior

In a general sense, people tend to express decided preferences with respect to the climate in which they wish to live. As Bass and Bass (1976, p. 158) note, "It is easier to attract professionals to work in Monterey, California, than in Pierre, South Dakota." There is even a "computer date" type of service that assesses your needs and preferences and then gives you the names of twenty cities that match you best (*Money*, July, 1976). Though there is much folklore dealing with positive reactions to the seashore and mountains and negative reactions to

TABLE 13-3. *Number of shocks given by subjects to confederate. In an experiment on noise and aggression, subjects first watched either an aggressive or a nonaggressive film. Afterward, each subject had the opportunity to aggress against a confederate by administering electric shock; during this interaction, there was either a continuous noise or no noise in the room. Aggression was increased by exposure to an aggressive movie and by exposure to environmental noise. (Source: Based on data from Geen and O'Neal, 1969.)*

Environmental Stimulation	Content of Movie	
	Aggressive Boxing Film	Nonaggressive Sport Film
Noise	4.58	3.50
No Noise	3.16	2.91

intense cold, most of the psychological research on the effects of climatic factors has focused on responses to uncomfortably high temperatures.

Anyone who has ever spent a hot summer night lying on a sweat-soaked sheet or driven across country on a July day with his or her back stuck to a vinyl car seat doesn't have to be convinced that extreme heat can have an aversive effect on one's disposition. In fact, our culture has come to accept a number of common-sense beliefs about the effects of heat on behavior. For example, it seems reasonable to believe that heat makes people aggressive. In the research to be reviewed in this section, we'll see that these popular assumptions are sometimes, but not always, true.

The Long Hot Summer Effect? Would you like other people better on a comfortably cool day or on an uncomfortably hot day? Griffitt (1970) hypothesized that high levels of heat would cause individuals to experience negative affect. As was explained in Chapter 5, if negative affect is elicited by heat, attraction toward others should be lower under hot conditions than when temperature is in the normal range. As can be seen in Figure 13-11, subjects in hot conditions responded more negatively to both similar and dissimilar strangers than subjects in "normal" temperature conditions. Among the implications of these findings is that a hot day would not be the ideal time to meet a blind date.

Beyond the dampening of interpersonal attraction, is it possible that high temperature elicits aggressive behavior? Actually, excessive heat has been suggested by the mass media as one of the causes of the violent urban disorders during the 1960's. This explanation is supported by an analysis by Goranson and King (1970) which suggests that much of the collective violence in American cities occurred during heat wave conditions, as shown in Figure 13-12.

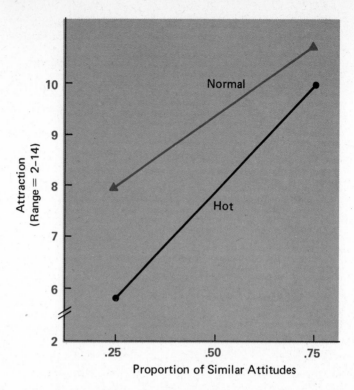

FIGURE 13-11. *Uncomfortably high temperatures lead to less positive interpersonal responses. At three levels of attitude similarity, subjects were more attracted to a stranger when the temperature was normal than when it was hot. (Source: Griffitt, 1970. Copyright 1970 by the American Psychological Association. Reprinted by permission.)*

Such evidence seems convincing with respect to the influence of heat on aggression, but subsequent research indicates that the long hot summer effect is not quite that simple. ˙

Cooling It with Excessive Heat. In a recent study, Baron and Bell (1975) placed half of their subjects in a comfortably cool experimental room while the remaining subjects were in an uncomfortably hot room. In addition, half of the subjects received negative evaluations from a confederate while the remaining subjects were evaluated favorably. It was initially expected that with oppressive heat and unfavorable evaluations (that is, with strong negative affect), more intense aggression would occur. However, this was not the case. Surprisingly, oppressive heat led to greater aggression by subjects who had received favorable evaluations, and to decreased aggression by subjects who had been evaluated unfavorably. This relationship was later replicated, so it would seem to be a consistent, though at first puzzling, phenomenon.

In attempting to explain these unexpected results, Baron and Bell proposed the existence of a curvilinear relationship between negative affect and aggres-

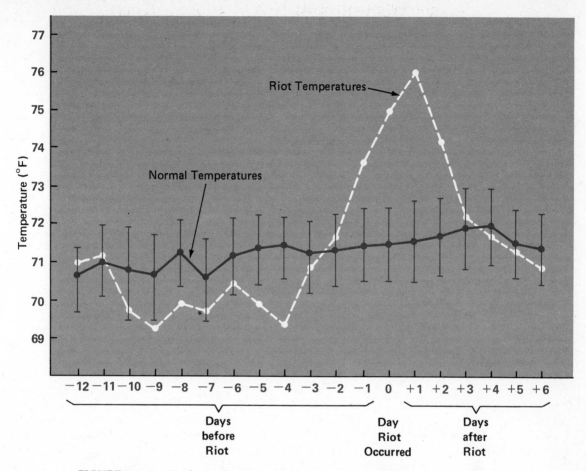

FIGURE 13-12. *Evidence that a rise in temperature precedes the outbreak of a riot was found in an investigation of the 1967 riots in the United States. Riots tended to break out following several days of above-average temperatures. (Source: Goranson and King, 1970. Reprinted with permission of the authors.)*

sion. According to this hypothesis, moderate levels of negative affect, such as those which would be produced either by negative evaluations from another person or by high temperature alone, cause individuals to feel irritated or annoyed, and so increase their willingness to aggress against others. In contrast, however, very high levels of negative affect, such as those which would be produced by the combination of high temperatures *and* negative evaluations from others, cause individuals to feel so miserable, that other responses—especially ones incompatible with aggression—become dominant instead. For example, the extremely uncomfortable individual might be more interested in escaping from the situation than in aggressing. The result, of course, is that overt aggression against others should actually be reduced under the most negative conditions.

In order to determine whether the influence of ambient temperature upon aggression could be understood within such a framework, Bell and Baron (1976) conducted an additional study. In this investigation, subjects in eight different groups were exposed to varying combinations of ambient temperature, positive and negative evaluations from another person, and attitudinal agreement or disagreement from this same individual. The most positive condition, then, was one in which subjects participated in the study under comfortably cool temperatures and received both a positive evaluation and agreement from the confederate. In contrast, the most negative condition was one in which they took part in the study under stiflingly hot conditions and received both a negative evaluation and disagreement from the confederate. On the basis of the curvilinear relationship that had been proposed, it was predicted that aggression would first increase as experimental conditions became more and more unpleasant, but that beyond some point, aggression would actually decrease as subjects came to concentrate on escape or on minimizing their discomfort in other ways. As can be seen in Figure 13-13, these predictions were strongly confirmed; when subjects were provided with an opportunity to aggress against the confederate by means of electric shock, the expected curvilinear relationship emerged.

The existence of such a relationship between negative affect and aggression leads to some interesting and surprising predictions concerning the impact of ambient temperature upon such behavior. For example, consider the case of an individual who finds himself in a very hot room, and who has been evaluated quite negatively by another person. As we have seen, he may feel so miserable that escape from the unpleasant surroundings becomes his strongest response tendency, so aggression is quite unlikely. But now imagine that we give such a person a cooling drink, and thus make him feel more comfortable; what might result? Strangely enough, the curvilinear relationship leads us to predict that the drink will reduce his negative feelings to more moderate levels and that, as a result, aggression may actually be increased! That is, he may stop concentrating upon escape and turn instead to attacks against others. Despite its unusual nature, this prediction has been confirmed in a recent study (Baron and Bell, 1976). Thus, contrary to common belief, the "pause that refreshes" may not always produce positive results; in fact, it may sometimes provide individuals with just enough relief to permit them to become aggressive in their dealing with others.

In conclusion, we can note that existing evidence regarding the effects of ambient temperature upon aggression suggests that there is indeed a link between these two factors. However, contrary to both common sense and informal observation, the nature of this relationship is far more complex and involved than is suggested by such phrases as "the long hot summer."

Pollution and Behavior

Without doubt, air pollution is a major concern in the 1970's. You may be surprised to learn, however, that the problem is not an entirely new one. In

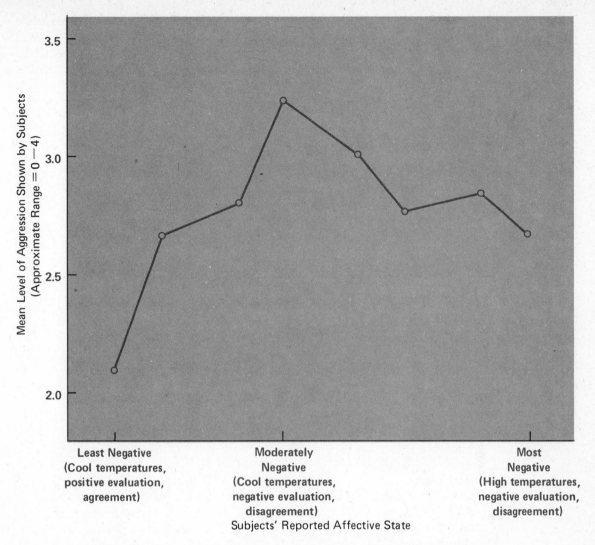

FIGURE 13-13. *An experimental demonstration of the curvilinear relationship between negative affect and aggression. Aggression first rose as negative affect increased from low to moderate levels, but then actually dropped as such feelings continued to increase to very high levels. (Source: Adapted from Bell and Baron, 1976.)*

1841, in *The Old Curiosity Shop,* Charles Dickens described the following scene that Little Nell and her grandfather encountered in their travels:

A long suburb of red brick houses, . . . some with patches of garden-ground, where coal dust and factory smoke darkened the shrinking leaves, and coarse rank flowers, and where the struggling vegetation sickened and sank under the hot breath of kiln and furnace. . . .

On every side, and far as the eye could see into the heavy distance, tall chimneys, crowding on each other, and presenting that endless repetition of the same dull, ugly form, which is the horror of oppressive dreams, poured out their plague of smoke, obscured the light, and made foul the melancholy air (p. 338).

In recent years government regulations have been invoked which have forced industries to control the smoke that they produce, automobile manufacturers to make substantial reductions in dangerous emissions from cars, and individuals to protect nonsmokers from the indoor pollution of tobacco smoke. While it is obvious that physiological damage occurs from long-term breathing of polluted air, we might expect there also to be some more immediate effects. Relatively little research has been done in this area, but a study done in England by Lewis et al. (1970) is illustrative of the potential effects of pollution on performance. These investigators had subjects carry out information-processing tasks while breathing air which was either pure and clean, or air obtained fifteen inches from the ground on a road which handled 830 vehicles per hour. It was found that subjects breathing polluted air performed relatively poorly on most of the tasks. Thus, in addition to damaging our bodies in a physiological sense, pollution may also be interfering with our ability to work effectively.

In one recent study of the psychological effects of air pollution, subjects were placed in an experimental room that had a normal atmosphere or in one that had an offensive odor caused either by butyric acid or by ammonium sulfide (Rotton et al., 1976). Compared to those in the ordinary room, college students in the foul-smelling rooms expressed negative feelings about themselves, their surroundings, and about other students. These unpleasant emotional responses also affected behavior—those in the polluted rooms actually finished the experiment faster, presumably so they could escape the negative environment.

Though the effects of water pollution on behavior have not yet been the subject of psychological research, one cannot but wonder about how most people might react to a presumably reassuring announcement on this topic such as the following newspaper story. It appeared in a small Massachusetts journal, the *Northampton Hampshire Gazette*:

> Residents of the North Amherst–Cushman area have been told the green slime in their water supply is nothing to worry about. According to Public Health Director Charles Drake the affected water has been traced to the Atkins Reservoir in Shutesbury but has so far defied bacterial and chemical analysis.

Man-made Environments

The way that one's house or apartment is designed can also affect behavior. Simply stated, some environments are much more livable than others. We will now consider the behavioral effects of a variety of design-related factors.

The View from the Top. One environmental setting that has been subject to intensive research is the high-rise building. A good deal of controversy has centered on whether skyscrapers are efficient means of housing large numbers of people when available land is scarce, or whether the social costs of this type of housing outweigh its benefits. A questionnaire survey done at the University of Maryland (Haber, 1975) illustrates some of the salient issues. It was found that people saw the spatial economy of tall buildings as a plus and enjoyed looking out at the scenery from the upper stories. However, concern was expressed about feeling insignificant as individuals in a vast setting, about safety and escape in case of fire (especially among students who had seen the film "The Towering Inferno"), and about the sameness among such buildings in their outside appearance.

Does high-rise living affect the actual behavior of residents? Although several studies have attempted to answer this question, results are not entirely consistent. While several investigations have found no harmful effects caused by high-rise living (e.g., Crantz and Schumacher, 1975; Newman, 1975), a recent study by Gelb (1975) suggests that high-rise buildings and the traffic they generate have a negative impact on neighborhood livability. In other words, tall buildings are an efficient way to house people but you wouldn't want to live there.

Pretty Rooms and Ugly Rooms. Manufacturers of home furnishings would like us to believe that we will feel better and perform better in aesthetically pleasant surroundings than in unattractive ones, and there is some support for their claims. In an early study, Maslow and Mintz (1956) created a pretty room, an ugly room, and an average room. The pretty room was painted beige, had indirect lighting, a mahogany desk, curtains, a large Navajo rug, and art objects. The ugly room was battleship grey, had an overhead light with a dirty and torn lampshade, and furnishings suitable for a janitor's storeroom. A professor's office was used for the average room. After placing subjects in one of the rooms, the experimenter asked them to rate a series of facial photographs. The aesthetic quality of the room clearly affected the ratings. Subjects in the beautiful room attributed the most energy and well being to the photographs, subjects in the average room made intermediate ratings, and subjects in the ugly rooms made the lowest ratings. Mintz (1956) also observed the assistants who conducted the experiment. He found that they actually took less time to run the experiment in the ugly room. The setting was so unpleasant that they wanted to leave as quickly as possible. Such findings might suggest that people always prefer the most beautiful of all possible environments, but more recent research indicates that that is not so.

An experiment by Krieger (1972) suggests that what is beautiful is not necessarily good. In this study, it was found that introductory psychology students participating in an experiment were somewhat less anxious when they were in an ugly room (which resembled a relatively low-status graduate student's office) than when they were in a pretty room (which resembled a high-status professor's office). Thus, it may be that relatively humble surroundings (just like home) are somewhat more comfortable for some individuals.

Back to the Soil. An environmental decoration which has recently become the subject of popular interest is that provided by house plants. Until a few years ago, most people were content to have one or at most a couple of plants in their homes. In the past few years, however, Americans have seemingly become plant crazy; many of us fill our homes and offices with a wide array of plants. In response to this mania, several studies have explored the behavioral effects of plants. Much of this research has been done by horticulturists and is relatively descriptive in nature.

It appears that plants have a number of positive effects. Lewis (1974) suggests that house plants satisfy a basic need to communicate with nature, and Kaplan (1973) has found that the recreation afforded by maintaining plants helps to relieve everyday stress. Several applied efforts have made use of the positive effects of plants on people. One very interesting application is in rehabilitative therapy. At present, over two-hundred institutions (including mental hospitals, prisons, and homes for the elderly) use horticulture as an added element in treatment. This type of therapy has been found to help patients assume responsibility, express emotions, and gain confidence (Lewis, 1974).

A second situation in which the introduction of plants has had positive effects has been in urban housing projects. In the past several years, programs have been introduced to encourage city residents to plant gardens and window boxes in New York, Philadelphia, and Chicago. It has been found that residents readily become involved in these programs and that such projects lead to a sense of community pride, cohesion among neighborhood residents, lower vandalism, and increased efforts by neighborhood residents to improve other aesthetic aspects of the environment (Lewis, 1974).

Behavioral Effects of Interior Design. In addition to studying skyscrapers, ugly rooms, and house plants, investigators have explored the effects of furniture design and arrangement on human interaction. Osmond (1957) has conceptualized space as **sociopetal** (encouraging social interaction) or **sociofugal** (discouraging social interaction). For example, a seminar room with seats around an oval table is sociopetal while a traditional classroom with seats facing forward is sociofugal. In a study which suggests the effects of sociofugal space, Sommer and Gilliland (1961) found that mental patients assigned to sociofugal space tend to be lonely and friendless while patients located in sociopetal space interact and make friends. Interestingly, a study by Sommer and Ross (1958) indicates that an effort to turn sociofugal space into sociopetal space can have important behavioral consequences. Initially, the investigators observed very low rates of social interaction among patients in a dayroom which was arranged in a sociofugal side-by-side position. To attempt to stimulate interaction in such an environment, they changed the arrangement of chairs to a more sociopetal one by placing the chairs around tables. After a few weeks, social interaction among patients had doubled, and patient morale increased dramatically.

Aside from affecting intensity of interaction among patients, qualities of the environment can affect patients' behavior in other ways. Sommer (1974) and Stainbrook (1966) have suggested that the cues provided by the environment to residents and practitioners in institutions convey information to them about the type of behavior that is expected. For example, it may be that seatless toilets, crude and rugged furniture, and bare walls communicate to both the patient and the staff that the resident is out of control and not to be trusted. Studies by Lee

(1965) and Greco (1965) have found that when supportive changes are instituted in the environment (for example, when breakable materials are introduced), the behavior of both patients and staff noticeably changes. The patients act more responsible, and the staff becomes more accommodating.

The observation that design-related features affect behavior suggests that when architects and designers fail to consider the behavioral effects of design, there can be disastrous consequences. One tragic example of such a failure is the Pruitt-Igoe public housing project in St. Louis, which was built in 1955 (Newman, 1972). This development contained thirty-three eleven-story buildings and almost 3,000 apartments. Although it was relatively expensive to construct and won design awards, it nevertheless was just that design that doomed it to failure. The buildings provided few places for residents to socialize, preventing the development of a social order. There were many stairwells, making it difficult to supervise children. In addition, the buildings were sterile, containing institutional wall tile, narrow hallways, indestructible but unattractive light fixtures, and vandal-resistant radiators. Rainwater (1966) has suggested that such features are psychologically damaging to residents because they convey a self-threatening message of inferiority and a lack of trust; they also challenge residents to destroy them. Within three years, the buildings had been defaced by their occupants, were physically deteriorated, and had become a hotbed of criminal activity. In 1972, the city of St. Louis had to destroy them. With further advances in environmental psychology, perhaps such expensive and self-defeating mistakes can be avoided in the future.

ENVIRONMENTAL CHANGE

In the preceding pages, you have seen a great deal of evidence which suggests that environmental stressors can have negative effects on human behavior. Why do we find ourselves in a world where pollution, noise, and crowding are causing us slowly to self-destruct?

While the answer is undoubtedly complex, the desire for progress has had many side effects which gradually have become obvious to everyone. Adherents of very different political philosophies have for some time agreed that a primary concern should be economic growth and material success. Now that there is an increased realization of the potential negative consequences of an unqualified acceptance of those criteria of the "good life," many people are striving to seek at least a compromise between economic goals and psychological ones in order to maximize feelings of well-being (Campbell, 1976). Alleviating environmental problems requires a willingness by many individuals to make sacrifices, a desire by government to legislate strict standards, and an agreement by the industrial sector to comply (as in the cartoon in Figure 13-14). Unfortunately, it has been shown that in many cases even though the public wants to improve environmental conditions, government and industry fail to respond. A study by Wall (1973) found that citizen attitudes were decidedly in favor of pure air in British towns which complied with a clean-air law and equally so in towns that failed to

DUNAGIN'S PEOPLE

"And this product offers the maximum protection
against wetness with minimum damage to the atmosphere."

FIGURE 13-14. *When individuals become sufficiently concerned about the environmental effects of specific products and technologies, industry can sometimes become responsive and develop appropriate new products and technologies. (Source: Dunagin's People by Ralph Dunagin, Courtesy of Field Newspaper Syndicate.)*

comply. Noncompliance was attributed to the negative attitudes and actions of a few individuals with decision-making power and to powerful special-interest groups.

It would seem that only organized and determined action on the part of citizens can hope to influence government and industry. Avoiding environmental disasters such as overpopulation and pollution also requires changes in behavior on an individual level. In order to have an optimum environment, critical decisions about change should be in the hands of those who are most directly affected (Insel and Moos, 1974). Because it illustrates the application of a number of psychological principles to an applied problem and demonstrates how social psychology may be utilized to help us solve our environmental problems, we will describe some recent research on litter control.

Reinforcing Responsible Environmental Behavior

Clearly, traditional methods, such as signs proclaiming "Do Not Litter" and the threat of heavy fines, have not led to a significant decrease in littering. In addition to the ugliness of bottles, cans, paper, and pop-tops wherever people gather, littering costs American taxpayers $500 million annually to clean it up. In an attempt to assess the effectiveness of a variety of antilittering strategies, Clark, Hendee, and Burgess (1972) conducted a field study using a movie theater. Various litter-control approaches were used, such as doubling the number of trash cans in the theater, showing a Walt Disney antilittering cartoon, distributing litterbags for use while in the theater, combining litterbags with instructions to use them, and providing money and movie tickets as rewards for filling such bags. To assess the effectiveness of each strategy, the proportion of the total litter which was deposited in trash cans was measured. As can be seen in Figure 13-15, doubling the number of trash cans or showing the antilitter film had no effect. The first noticeable behavior change appeared in the litterbag condition. Still more change is brought about by explicit instructions to use the bag, and the greatest change occurred when rewards were provided. Thus it appears that many traditional methods are relatively useless in eliciting compliance and that the use of reinforcements is very effective.

While the extremely potent effects of providing reinforcements for litter control have been shown in a forest campground as well as in a movie theater (Clark, Burgess, and Hendee, 1972), supplying rewards for each bit of litter collected could become an expensive enterprise. One solution is a procedure, called the "marked-item technique," that has been introduced by Hayes, Johnson, and Cone (1974). These investigators suggested that people would exhibit a high degree of litter control even when rewarded only occasionally if the potential rewards were sufficiently attractive. Specifically, marked items were scattered on the grounds of a correctional institution, amidst the litter which was habitually present. Residents were informed that some of the litter was marked in an indetectable fashion and that, if a marked item were among the litter they collected, they would win a prize. Thus, picking up litter is something like an Easter Egg hunt or a search for hidden treasure. Under these conditions, litter collection increased dramatically. The authors have suggested an unusual system for improving litter control throughout America. Litter marked with radioactive isotopes would be distributed all over the country along with automated trash bins which would deliver valuable rewards automatically whenever marked trash was deposited. This garbage lottery would induce people to pick up all the trash in sight in hopes of finding a valuable piece of litter and winning a prize! As odd as that may sound, perhaps behavioral science can use some version of that technique to improve the environment and make life a little more fun at the same time.

As with any attempt to alter human behavior, the most effective long-range approach is to teach children to respond in the desired way and then wait for a

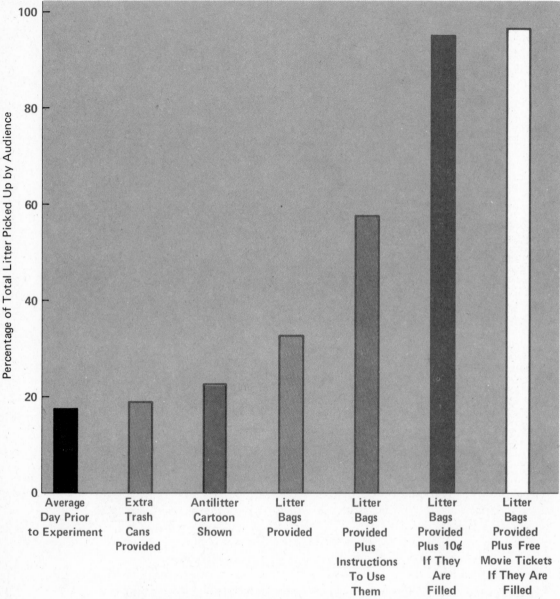

FIGURE 13-15. *In a movie-theater experiment, various techniques were used in an attempt to get patrons to pick up their litter rather than throw it on the floor. The use of litterbags, especially when combined with reinforcement to encourage their use, clearly had a positive effect on behavior. (Source: Based on data from Clark, Hendee, and Burgess, 1972.)*

new generation of responsible adults. How might one go about altering littering behavior among elementary school children? Miller, Brickman, and Bolen (1975) decided to compare two very different procedures in an effort to teach fifth-graders not to litter and to clean up after others who do.

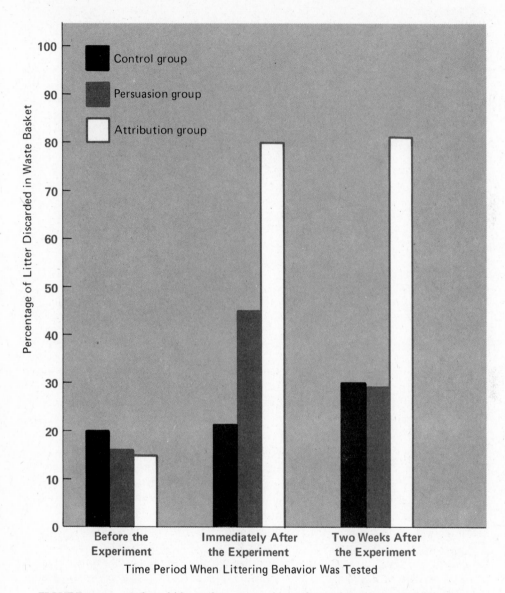

FIGURE 13-16. *When fifth-graders were subjected to techniques to persuade them not to litter, they temporarily became somewhat neater and then fell back a couple of weeks later to the level of the control group. Other children—to whom the attribution of neatness was made—improved greatly, and their class persisted in this new behavior even after the experimental period had ended. (Source: Data based on Miller, Brickman, and Bolen, 1975.)*

CAPSULE CONTROVERSY

IS OVERPOPULATION THE ULTIMATE ENVIRONMENTAL PROBLEM?

Whenever we consider such environmental problems as pollution, noise, overcrowding, or whatever, the crucial factor is that of people. Is it possible that there are too many people on our planet? Would the environment and would humanity be better off if there were a smaller number of human beings competing for dwindling resources, creating demands for technological growth, and pressing ever more tightly together in depressing high-density living areas?

Many individuals disagree with the idea that there is a population problem. There are numerous ideological barriers to the concept of family planning or the setting of limitations on how many children anyone can have. Various national, political, religious, and ethnic groups argue vehemently against population control— at least for themselves. Rosenman (1973) finds that blacks in the United States resist family planning for the black community because they mistrust the motives of the white-dominated

government. China's Ministry of Health denounced birth control as an imperialist plot against the underdeveloped nations (Forum, January, 1975). A conservative rabbi in New York City has organized the Jewish Population Regeneration Unit which rejects the idea of zero population growth for Jews and recommends that each Jewish couple produce four or five children (Time, July 14, 1975). The World Moslem League announced that "birth control was invented by the enemies of Islam" and succeeded in banning contraceptives in Saudi Arabia (Forum, October 1975). Few African nations perceive birth control as desirable, and they joined the Communists and the Catholics at the 1974 World Population Conference at Bucharest in resisting all proposals to limit population growth (Astrachan, 1974).

Is there a population problem? It is estimated that the total number of human beings on our planet 10,000 years ago was about five million—less than are now residing in the Met-

In one class, *persuasion* was used. The children were told about ecology, the dangers of pollution, and how litter contributes to the problem. On other days they were told about garbage and flies, appeals were made on behalf of the janitor, both the teacher and the principal lectured on the importance of clean, tidy classrooms, and a large Peanuts poster ("Don't be a litterbug") was placed on the bulletin board. This campaign went on for eight school days.

In another class, an *attribution* approach was tried for eight days. Instead of being told to be neat and tidy, these youngsters were in effect told that they *already were* that way. The teacher passed on the janitor's alleged comment that their class was one of the cleanest in the building. Individuals were praised as being ecology-conscious. A row was commended for being exceptionally neat. The principal visited and commented on how orderly the room appeared— afterward the children spontaneously criticized the teacher for having the only messy desk in the room. *Their* Peanuts poster read, "We are Andersen's Litter-Conscious Class."

In a third class, as a control, nothing was done to encourage non-littering.

Littering behavior was measured before the experiment began, just after the persuasion and attribution treatments were completed, and then again two weeks ropolitan Chicago area (Ehrlich and Ehrlich, 1971). It took from that ancient time until the year 1800 to reach the one billion mark (Demeny, 1974). On a Sunday late in March of 1976, the world population reached four billion. Right now, this figure increases by 80 million human beings each year, and the situation is getting rapidly worse. The worldwide growth rate is slightly over two percent per year. That may sound very small, but it means that the population will double in less than thirty-five years, and then again in another thirty-five years. And again, and again, and again. Another 350 years at the present growth rate will produce a world population of more than four trillion individuals (Coale, 1974). It is not only unwise and irresponsible for people to continue this present pattern of behavior, it is impossible. If current trends continue for the next 6,700 years, the entire mass of the known universe will consist of human bodies (Asimov, 1975). Since that obviously cannot happen, what are the alternatives open to us?

There seem to be four obvious ways in which population growth can be halted. One possibility is an educational attempt to increase awareness of the problem in the hope that knowledge will lead to voluntary behavioral changes (Buckhout, 1972; Fischer, 1972). A second approach is that of a benevolent central government which could manipulate positive incentives to influence the desired behavior; for example, monetary bonuses or free vacations could be given to couples who restrict the number of children they conceive (Kangas, 1970). Third, an authoritarian central government could make contraception, sterilization, and/or abortion mandatory with severe penalties invoked against those who disobey (Callahan, 1972). Finally, if nothing is done, existing populations will be reduced in the way predicted by Malthus through starvation, disease, and war (Heilbroner, 1974).

Do you believe that overpopulation is the ultimate environmental problem? If so, what approach do you favor in seeking a solution? What do you think is actually going to occur in the coming decades?

later. At each testing, the students were given something that was to be discarded, and the question was whether the children would use wastebaskets or simply discard their litter elsewhere. For example, in one test all three classes were given free candy and each piece was wrapped in one of three different colors of cellophane (one color for each class). Thus, the experimenters could later search the wastebaskets and the schoolyard to find out what each class had done to dispose of its candy wrappers.

The results are shown in Figure 13-16. First, you will note that before the experiment the majority of the children in all three classes were clearly litterbugs. After the experimental manipulations were completed, both the attribution and persuasion groups showed an improvement, though the attribution group was obviously superior. Even more impressive was the post-experimental test two weeks later in which the persuasion group had reverted to the littering level of the control group while the majority of the children in the attribution condition were now behaving in an environmentally responsible fashion.

It seems that, in many respects, we are what we believe we are. With environmental behavior, perhaps it would be of great value if we all began to attribute responsibility to ourselves.

SUMMARY

Environmental psychology studies the reciprocal relationship between the physical environment and human behavior. This includes the effects of the environment on behavior, and the effects of our behavior on the environment.

Personal space and territoriality are two aspects of spatial behavior. Personal space is a portable boundary between ourselves and others and has two functions: protection and communication. Its size varies with the situation. Inadequate personal space or inappropriate interpersonal positioning is aversive, as is the act of invading the personal space of others. Territoriality involves the staking out and defending of space against one's own species. While personal space is portable, territories are often characterized by specific boundaries. In animals, territory serves survival-related functions; among human beings, it affords control. Research evidence suggests that people engage in territorial behavior and have an advantage when in their own home territory. Also, territories that are well marked off are not likely to be vandalized.

It has been found that the observed environment does not necessarily correspond to objective physical conditions. Individual differences and situational conditions appear to combine with objective physical factors to determine environmental perception.

In the growing body of literature on the effects of environmental stressors (high density, heat, noise, pollution) on behavior, a few consistent findings have emerged. First, high levels of environmental stressors do not always have negative effects on behavior; it depends on the specific situation and on individual differences. Second, environmental stressors that are unpredictable or uncontrollable have a greater impact on behavior than those which can be predicted and controlled. Exposure to uncontrollable stimuli can have serious long-term effects.

Man-made environmental conditions can also have important behavioral consequences. Inadequately designed environments can have negative effects on behavior, while some architectural innovations can have quite beneficial effects.

Finally, recent social psychological research suggests some very useful strategies for modifying environmentally destructive behavior.

GLOSSARY

Behavioral-constraint model. An explanation of crowding effects in terms of reduced freedom of movement.

Bubble. Another way of designating personal space, the invisible boundary surrounding each individual, into which others may not trespass.

Cognitive map. An individual's mental image of a particular environmental setting.

Crowding. A stressful experience in which an individual feels restricted by high density.

Density. A physical state referring to the number of people in a given area.

Ecological model. An explanation of crowding effects in terms of scarcity of resources.

Environmental psychology. The area of social psychology which investigates the reciprocal relationship between physical surroundings and human behavior.

Intimate distance. In Hall's system, the appropriate interpersonal distance ($0-1\frac{1}{2}$ feet) for intimate contacts and physical sports.

Invasion of personal space. When another individual occupies an inappropriately close interpersonal distance.

Learned helplessness. Refers to feelings of helplessness stemming from exposure to situations in which individuals cannot control or influence their own outcomes. Such reactions lead to deficits in performance on many tasks and may contribute to strong feelings of depression.

Lost-letter technique. Research methodology in which stamped, addressed envelopes are apparently lost.

Personal distance. In Hall's system, the appropriate interpersonal distance ($1\frac{1}{2}-4$ feet) for contacts between close friends and acquaintances.

Personal space. The concept of an invisible boundary that surrounds each individual, into which others may not trespass.

Primary territory. In Altman's system, an area that is used regularly on a long-term basis as an essential part of an individual's (or group's) everyday activities.

Proxemics. The study of interpersonal distance.

Public distance. In Hall's system, the appropriate interpersonal distance (more than 12 feet) for formal contacts between an individual and the public.

Public territory. In Altman's system, an area that is occupied only temporarily and which is available to almost anyone.

Secondary territory. In Altman's system, an area which is used regularly by a specific group of people who have less complete control than in the case of primary territories.

Social density. When groups of different sizes occupy a space of constant size.

Social distance. In Hall's system, the appropriate interpersonal distance (4–12 feet) for impersonal and business-like contacts.

Sociofugal space. Spatial arrangement that discourages social interaction.

Sociopetal space. Spatial arrangement that encourages social interaction.

Spatial density. When a group of constant size occupies spaces of different sizes.

Stimulus-overload model. An explanation of crowding effects in terms of excessive arousal.

Territorial behavior. Various acts that serve to stake out and defend space against members of one's own species.

SUGGESTED READINGS FOR CHAPTER 13

Altman, I. *The environment and social behavior.* Monterey: Brooks-Cole, 1975. This text provides excellent coverage of work on privacy, personal space, territory, and crowding.

Freedman, J. *Crowding and behavior.* San Francisco: W. H. Freeman, 1975. A very readable book on the effects of crowding on human behavior. It focuses on the ability of man to withstand high density without aversive effects.

Ittelson, W. H., Proshansky, H. M., Rivlin, L. G., and Winkel, G. H. *An introduction to environmental psychology.* New York: Holt, Rinehart & Winston, 1974. A broad introductory text in environmental psychology, at an advanced undergraduate level. Covers such topics as environmental theory, environmental perception, crowding, territory, a developmental approach to environmental behavior, behavioral effects of the "built" environment, and research methods in environmental psychology.

Moos, R. H., and Insel, P. M., eds. *Issues in environmental psychology: Human milieus.* Palo Alto: National Press Books, 1974. A book of readings at advanced undergraduate level. Focuses on environmental research from a broad array of subareas.

Sommer, R. *Tight spaces: Hard architecture and how to humanize it.* Englewood Cliffs, N.J.: Prentice-Hall, 1974. This book deals with how to design architectural environments so as to satisfy human needs—very readable and a high interest level.

BIBLIOGRAPHY

Abel, G. G., Barlow, D. H., Blanchard, E. B., and Mavissakalian, M. Measurement of sexual arousal in male homosexuals: Effects of instructions and stimulus modality. *Archives of Sexual Behavior,* 1975, *4,* 623–629.

Abelson, H., Cohen, R., Heaton, E., and Suder, C. National survey of public attitudes toward and experience with erotic materials. In *Technical Report of the Commission on Obscenity and Pornography,* vol. 4. Washington, D.C.: U.S. Government Printing Office, 1971.

Abramson, P. R., and Mosher, D. L. Development of a measure of negative attitudes toward masturbation. *Journal of Consulting and Clinical Psychology,* 1975, *43,* 485–490.

Adams, G. R., and Huston, T. L. Social perception of middle-aged persons varying in physical attractiveness. *Developmental Psychology,* 1975, *11,* 657–658.

Adams, J. S. Inequity in social exchange. In *Advances in experimental social psychology,* vol. 2, edited by L. Berkowitz. New York: Academic Press, 1965.

Aderman, D., Brehm, S. S., and Katz, B. Empathic observation of an innocent victim: The just world revisited. *Journal of Personality and Social Psychology,* 1974, *29,* 342–347.

Adorno, T. W., Frenkel-Brunswik, E., Levinson, D. J., and Sanford, R. N. *The authoritarian personality.* New York: Harper, 1950.

Aiello, J. R., and Jones, S. E. Field study of the proxemic behavior of young school children in three subcultural groups. *Journal of Personality and Social Psychology,* 1971, *19,* 351–356.

Albert, S., and Dabbs, J. M., Jr. Physical distance and persuasion. *Journal of Personality and Social Psychology,* 1970, *15,* 265–270.

Alexander, C. N., and Sagatun, I. An attributional analysis of experimental norms. *Sociometry,* 1973, *36,* 127–142.

Allen, B. P. Social distance and admiration reactions of "unprejudiced" whites. *Journal of Personality,* 1975, *43,* 709–726.

Allen, B. P. Race and physical attractiveness as criteria for white subjects' dating choices. *Social Behavior and Personality,* 1976, *4,* 289–296.

Allen, V. L., and Levine, J. M. Consensus and conformity. *Journal of Experimental Social Psychology,* 1969, *5,* 389–399.

Allen, V. L., and Levine, J. M. Social support and conformity: The role of independent assessment of reality. *Journal of Experimental Social Psychology,* 1971, *7,* 48–58.

Allen, V. L., and Newtson, D. Development of conformity and independence. *Journal of Personality and Social Psychology,* 1972, *22,* 18–30.

Allgeier, A. R., and Byrne, D. Attraction toward the opposite sex as a determinant of physical proximity. *Journal of Social Psychology,* 1973, *90,* 213–219.

Allgeier, E. R. The influence of sex roles on heterosexual attitudes and behavior. Unpublished doctoral dissertation, Purdue University, 1976.

Allport, F. H. *Social psychology.* Boston: Houghton Mifflin, 1924.

Allport, G. W. *The nature of prejudice.* Cambridge, Mass.: Addison-Wesley, 1954.

Allport, G. W. The historical background of modern social psychology. In *The handbook of social psychology,* 2nd ed., edited by G. Lindzey and E. Aronson. Reading, Mass.: Addison-Wesley, 1968.

Altman, I. *The environment and social behavior.* Monterey, Calif.: Brooks-Cole, 1975.

Altman, I. Environmental psychology and social psychology. *Personality and Social Psychology Bulletin,* 1976, *2,* 96–113.

American Psychological Association. *Ethical principles in the conduct of research with human participants.* Washington, D.C.: American Psychological Association, 1973.

Amir, Y. Contact hypothesis in ethnic relations. *Psychological Bulletin,* 1969, *71,* 319–342.

Amoroso, D. M., Brown, M., Pruesse, M., Ware, E. E., and Pilkey, D. W. An investigation of behavioral, psychological, and physiological reactions to pornographic stimuli. In *Technical Report of the Commission on Obscenity and Pornography,* vol. 8. Washington, D.C.: U.S. Government Printing Office, 1971.

Anderson, N. H. Averaging versus adding as a stimulus combination rule in impression formation. *Journal of Experimental Psychology,* 1965, *70,* 394–400.

Anderson, N. H. Application of a linear-serial model to a personality-impression task using serial presentation. *Journal of Personality and Social Psychology,* 1968a, *10,* 354–362.

Anderson, N. H. Likableness ratings of 555 personality-trait words. *Journal of Personality and Social Psychology,* 1968b, *9,* 272–279.

Anderson, N. H. Cognitive algebra: Integration theory applied to social attribution. In *Advances in experimental social psychology,* vol. 7, edited by L. Berkowitz. New York: Academic Press, 1974.

Apsler, R. Effects of embarrassment on behavior toward others. *Journal of Personality and Social Psychology,* 1975, *32,* 145–153.

Argyle, M., and Dean, J. Eye-contact, distance, and affiliation. *Sociometry,* 1965, *28,* 289–304.

Arkin, R. M., and Duval, S. Focus of attention and causal attributions of actors and observers. *Journal of Experimental Social Psychology,* 1975, *11,* 427–438.

Aronfreed, J. *Conduct and conscience.* New York: Academic Press, 1968.

Aronson, E., and Linder, D. Gain and loss of esteem as determinants of interpersonal attractiveness. *Journal of Experimental Social Psychology,* 1965, *1,* 156–171.

Aronson, E., and Mills, J. The effect of severity of initiation on liking for a group. *Journal of Abnormal and Social Psychology,* 1959, *59,* 177–181.

Aronson, E., Turner, J. A., and Carlsmith, J. M. Communicator credibility and communication discrepancy as a determinant of opinion change. *Journal of Abnormal and Social Psychology,* 1963, *67,* 31–36.

Asch, S. E. Forming impressions of personality. *Journal of Abnormal and Social Psychology,* 1946, *41,* 258–290.

Asch, S. E. Effects of group pressure upon the modification and distortion of judgment. In *Groups, leadership, and men,* edited by H. Guetzkow. Pittsburgh: Carnegie, 1951.

Asch, S. E. Studies of independence and conformity: I. A minority of one against a unanimous majority. *Psychological Monographs,* 1956, *70,* 9 (Whole No. 416).

Asch, S. E. Forming impressions of personality. *Journal of Abnormal and Social Psychology,* 1963, *67,* 31–36.

Ashmore, R. D. Prejudice: causes and cures. In *Social Psychology,* by B. E. Collins. Reading, Mass.: Addison-Wesley, 1970.

Asimov, I. Colonizing the heavens. *Saturday Review,* 1975, *2* (20), 12–13, 15–17.

Astrachan, A. People are the most precious. *Saturday Review/World,* 1974, *2* (3), 10, 58–59.

Austin, W., and Walster, E. Participants' reactions to "equity with the world." *Journal of Experimental Social Psychology,* 1974, *10,* 528–548.

Austin, W., and Walster, E. Equity with the world: The trans-relational effects of equity and inequity. *Sociometry,* 1975, *38,* 474–496.

Aves, P., and Byrne, D. Evaluating adoptive parents: Attitude similarity and topic relevance. Unpublished manuscript, Purdue University, 1976.

Bandura, A. Influence of models' reinforcement contingencies on the acquisition of imitative responses. *Journal of Personality and Social Psychology,* 1965, *1,* 589–595.

Bandura, A. *Aggression: A social learning analysis.* Englewood Cliffs, N.J.: Prentice-Hall, 1973.

Bandura, A. Analysis of modeling processes. In *Modeling: conflicting theories,* edited by A. Bandura. New York: Lieber-Atherton, 1974.

Bandura, A., Blanchard, E. B., and Ritter, B. Relative efficacy of desensitization and modeling approaches for inducing behavioral, affective, and attitudinal changes. *Journal of Personality and Social Psychology,* 1969, *13,* 173–199.

Bandura, A., and Jeffery, R. W. Role of symbolic coding and rehearsal processes in observational learning. *Journal of Personality and Social Psychology,* 1973, *26,* 122–130.

Bandura, A., Jeffery, R. W., and Wright, C. L. Efficacy of participant modeling as a function of response induction aids. *Journal of Abnormal Psychology,* 1974, *83,* 56–64.

Bandura, A., and Menlove, F. L. Factors determining vicarious extinction of avoidance behavior through symbolic modeling. *Journal of Personality and Social Psychology,* 1968, *8,* 99–108.

Bandura, A., and Mischel, W. Modification of self-imposed delay of reward through exposure to live and symbolic models. *Journal of Personality and Social Psychology,* 1965, *2,* 698–705.

Bandura, A., and Rosenthal, T. L. Vicarious classical conditioning as a function of arousal level. *Journal of Personality and Social Psychology,* 1966, *3,* 54–62.

Bandura, R., Ross, D., and Ross, S. Imitation of film-mediated aggressive models. *Journal of Abnormal and Social Psychology,* 1963a, *66,* 3–11.

Bandura, A., Ross, D., and Ross, S. A. Vicarious reinforcement and imitative learning. *Journal of Abnormal and Social Psychology,* 1963b, *67,* 601–607.

Banks, W. C. The effects of perceived similarity upon the use of reward and punishment. *Journal of Experimental Social Psychology,* 1976, *12,* 131–138.

Banuazizi, A., and Movahedi, S. Interpersonal dynamics in a simulated prison: A methodological analysis. *American Psychologist,* 1975, *30,* 152–160.

Barclay, A. M. Urinary acid phosphatase secretion in sexually aroused males. *Journal of Experimental Research in Personality,* 1970, *4,* 233–238.

Barclay, A. M. Linking sexual and aggressive motives: Contributions of "irrelevant" arousals. *Journal of Personality,* 1971, *39,* 481–492.

Barefoot, J. C., Hoople, H., and McClay, D. Avoidance of an act which would violate personal space. *Psychonomic Science,* 1972, *28,* 205–206.

Baron, R. A. Attraction toward the model and model's competence as determinants of adult imitative behavior. *Journal of Personality and Social Psychology,* 1970a, *14,* 345–351.

Baron, R. A. Effects of magnitude of model's apparent pain on observer reaction time. *Psychonomic Science,* 1970b, *20,* 229–231.

Baron, R. A. Behavioral effects of interpersonal attraction: Compliance with requests from liked and disliked others. *Psychonomic Science,* 1971, *25,* 325–326.

Baron, R. A. Reducing the influence of an aggressive model: The restraining effects of peer censure. *Journal of Experimental Social Psychology,* 1972, *8,* 266–275.

Baron, R. A. Threatened retaliation from the victim as an inhibitor of physical aggression. *Journal of Research in Personality,* 1973, *7,* 103–115.

Baron, R. A. Aggression as a function of victim's pain cues, level of prior anger arousal, and exposure to an aggressive model. *Journal of Personality and Social Psychology,* 1974a, *29,* 117–124.

Baron, R. A. The aggression-inhibiting influence of heightened sexual arousal. *Journal of Personality and Social Psychology,* 1974b, *30,* 318–322.

Baron, R. A. Heightened sexual arousal and physical aggression. Paper presented at the meetings of the Midwestern Psychological Association, Chicago, 1976a.

Baron, R. A. The reduction of human aggression: A field study of the influence of incompatible reactions. *Journal of Applied Social Psychology,* 1976, *6,* 260–274.

Baron, R. A., and Ball, R. L. The aggression-inhibiting influence of nonhostile humor. *Journal of Experimental Social Psychology,* 1974, *10,* 23–33.

Baron, R. A., and Bell, P. A. Effects of heightened sexual arousal on physical aggression. *Proceedings of the American Psychological Association,* 81st annual convention, 1973, 171–172.

Baron, R. A., and Bell, P. A. Aggression and heat: Mediating effects of prior provocation and exposure to an aggressive model. *Journal of Personality and Social Psychology,* 1975, *31,* 825–832.

Baron, R. A., and Bell, P. A. Aggression and heat: The influence of ambient temperature, negative affect, and a cooling drink on physical aggression. *Journal of Personality and Social Psychology,* 1976, *33,* 245–255.

Baron, R. A., and Bell, P. A. Physical distance and helping: Some unexpected benefits of "crowding in" on others. *Journal of Applied Social Psychology,* 1976, *6,* 95–104.

Baron, R. A., and Kepner, C. R. Model's behavior and attraction toward the model as determinants of adult aggressive behavior. *Journal of Personality and Social Psychology,* 1970, *14,* 335–344.

Baron, R. M., Mandel, D. R., Adams, C. A., and Griffen, L. M. Effects of social density in university residential environments. Unpublished manuscript, University of Connecticut, 1975.

Baron, R. S., Dion, K. L., Baron, P. H., and Miller, N. Group consensus and cultural values as determinants of risk taking. *Journal of Personality and Social Psychology,* 1971, *20,* 446–455.

Baron, R. S., Monson, T. C., and Baron, P. H. Conformity pressure as a determinant of risk taking. *Journal of Personality and Social Psychology,* 1973, *28,* 406–413.

Baron, R. S., and Roper, G. Reaffirmation of social comparison views of choice shifts: Averaging and extremity effects in an autokinetic situation. *Journal of Personality and Social Psychology,* 1976, *33,* 521–530.

Bartell, G. D. *Group sex.* New York: New American Library, 1971.

Bass, B. M. *Leadership, psychology, and organizational behavior.* New York: Harper & Row, 1960.

Bass, B. M., and Bass, R. Concern for environment: Implications for industrial and organizational psychology. *American Psychologist,* 1976, *31,* 158–166.

Bates, J. E. The effects of a child's imitation versus nonimitation of adult's verbal and nonverbal positivity. *Journal of Personality and Social Psychology,* 1975, *31,* 840–851.

Batson, C. D. Attribution as a mediator of bias in helping. *Journal of Personality and Social Psychology,* 1975, *32,* 455–466.

Baum, A., and Koman, S. Differential response to anticipated crowding: Psychological effects of social and spatial density. Unpublished manuscript, Trinity College, 1975.

Baum, A., and Valins, S. Residential environments, group size and crowding. *Proceedings of the American Psychological Association,* 81st Annual Convention, 1973, 211–212.

Beach, F. A. It's all in your mind. *Psychology Today,* 1969, *3* (2), 33–35, 60.

Beach, F. A., and LeBouef, B. J. Coital behavior in dogs. I. Preferential mating in the bitch. *Animal Behavior,* 1967, *15,* 546–558.

Beach, F. A., Westbrook, W., and Clemens, L. G. Comparisons of the ejaculatory response in men and animals. *Psychosomatic Medicine,* 1966, *28,* 749–763.

Beale, F. Double Jeopardy: To be black and female. In *The black woman,* edited by T. Cade. New York: New American Library, 1970.

Becker, F. D. Study of spatial markers. *Journal of Personality and Social Psychology,* 1973, *26,* 439–445.

Beckhouse, L., Tanur, J., Weiler, J., and Weinstein, E. And some men have leadership thrust upon them. *Journal of Personality and Social Psychology,* 1975, *31,* 557–566.

Bell, P. A. Affective and cognitive factors in interpersonal attraction: Misery loves more than miserable company. Unpublished manuscript, Colorado State University, 1976.

Bell, P. A., and Baron, R. A. Aggression and heat: The mediating role of negative affect. *Journal of Applied Social Psychology,* 1976, *6,* 18–30.

Bell, P. A., and Byrne, D. Repression-sensitization. In *Dimensions of personality,* edited by H. London and J. E. Exner, Jr. New York: John Wiley & Sons, 1977.

Bem, D. J. *Beliefs, attitudes, and human affairs.* Belmont, Calif.: Brooks/Cole, 1970.

Bem, D. J. Self-perception theory. In *Advances*

in experimental social psychology, vol. 6, edited by L. Berkowitz. New York: Academic Press, 1972.

Bem, S. L. Psychology looks at sex-roles: Where have all the androgynous people gone? Paper presented at UCLA Symposium on Women, May 1972.

Bem, S. L. Sex-role adaptability: One consequence of psychological androgyny. *Journal of Personality and Social Psychology,* 1975, *31,* 634–643.

Bem, S. L, and Bem, D. J. Case study of a nonconscious ideology: Training the woman to know her place. In *Beliefs, attitudes and human affairs,* edited by D. Bem. Belmont, Calif.: Brooks/Cole, 1970.

Benson, J. S. and Kennelly, K. J. Learned helplessness: The result of uncontrollable reinforcements or uncontrollable aversive stimuli? *Journal of Personality and Social Psychology,* 1976, *34,* 138–145.

Benton, A. A. Some unexpected consequences of jeopardy. *Proceedings of the American Psychological Association,* 79th Annual Convention, 1971, *6,* 223–224.

Berdie, R. F. Playing the dozens. *Journal of Abnormal and Social Psychology,* 1947, *42,* 120–121.

Berger, S. M. Conditioning through vicarious instigation. *Psychological Review,* 1962, *69,* 450–466.

Bergmann, G. *Philosophy of science.* Madison: University of Wisconsin Press, 1966.

Berkowitz, L. The frustration-aggression hypothesis revisited. In *Roots of aggression,* edited by L. Berkowitz. New York: Atherton, 1969.

Berkowitz, L. The contagion of violence. In *Nebraska symposium on motivation,* edited by W. J. Arnold and M. M. Page. Lincoln: University of Nebraska Press, 1970.

Berkowitz, L. Social norms, feelings, and other factors affecting helping and altruism. In *Advances in experimental social psychology,* vol. 6, edited by L. Berkowitz. New York: Academic Press, 1972.

Berkowitz, L. Some determinants of impulsive aggression: Role of mediated associations with reinforcements for aggression. *Psychological Review,* 1974, *81,* 165–176.

Berkowitz, L., and Alioto, J. T. The meaning of an observed event as a determinant of its aggressive consequences. *Journal of Personality and Social Psychology,* 1973, *28,* 206–217.

Berkowitz, L., and LePage, A. Weapons as aggression-eliciting stimuli. *Journal of Personality and Social Psychology,* 1967, *7,* 202–207.

Berkowitz, L., Lepinski, J. P., and Angulo, E. J. Awareness of own anger level and subsequent aggression. *Journal of Personality and Social Psychology,* 1969, *11,* 293–300.

Berkowitz, L., and Turner, C. W. Perceived anger level, instigating agent, and aggression. In *Cognitive alteration of feeling states,* edited by H. London and R. E. Nisbett. Chicago: Aldine, 1974.

Berkowitz, W. R., Nebel, J. C., and Reitman, J. W. Height and interpersonal attraction: The 1969 mayoral election in New York City. Paper presented at the meeting of the American Psychological Association, Washington, D. C., September, 1971.

Bermant, G. Response latencies of female rats during sexual intercourse. *Science,* 1961, *133,* 1771–1773.

Berscheid, E. Opinion change and communicator-communicatee similarity and dissimilarity. *Journal of Personality and Social Psychology,* 1966, *4,* 670–680.

Berscheid, E. Theories of interpersonal attraction. In *International encyclopedia of neurology, psychiatry, psychoanalysis, and psychology,* edited by B. B. Wolman and L. R. Pomeroy. New York: Springer, 1976.

Berscheid, E., Boye, D., and Walster, E. Retaliation as a means of restoring equity. *Journal of Personality and Social Psychology,* 1968, *10,* 370–376.

Berscheid, E., Dion, K., Walster, E., and Walster, G. W. Physical attractiveness and dating choice: A test of the matching hypothesis. *Journal of Experimental Social Psychology,* 1971, *7,* 173–189.

Berscheid, E., and Walster, E. *Interpersonal attraction.* Reading, Mass.: Addison-Wesley, 1969.

Berscheid, E., and Walster, E. A little bit about love. In *Foundations of interpersonal attraction,* edited by T. L. Huston. New York: Academic Press, 1974a.

Berscheid, E., and Walster, E. Physical attractiveness. In *Advances in experimental social psychology,* vol. 7, edited by L. Berkowitz. New

York: Academic Press, 1974b.

Bickman, L. The effect of another bystander's ability to help on bystander's intervention in an emergency. *Journal of Experimental Social Psychology,* 1971, *7,* 367–379.

Bickman, L. Social influence and diffusion of responsibility in an emergency. *Journal of Experimental Social Psychology,* 1972, *8,* 438–445.

Bickman, L. Bystander intervention in a crime: The effect of a mass-media campaign. *Journal of Applied Social Psychology,* 1975, *5,* 296–302.

Bickman, L., and Green, S. K. Is revenge sweet? The effect of attitude toward a thief on crime reporting. *Criminal Justice and Behavior,* 1975, *2,* 101–112.

Bixenstine, V. E., Potash, H. M., and Wilson, K. V. Effects of level of cooperative choice by the other player on choices in a prisoner's dilemma game, Part I. *Journal of Abnormal and Social Psychology,* 1963, *66,* 308–313.

Black, T. E., and Higbee, K. L. Effects of power, threat, and sex on exploitation. *Journal of Personality and Social Psychology,* 1973, *27,* 382–388.

Blalock, H. M., Jr. *Toward a theory of minority-group relations.* New York: John Wiley & Sons, 1967.

Bleda, P. R. Smoking and interpersonal social behavior. *Journal of Applied Psychology,* 1977 (in press).

Bleda, P. R., and Bleda, S. E. Sex differences in personal space invasion at a shopping mall. Paper presented at the meeting of the American Psychological Association, Washington, D. C., September 1976.

Bogardus, E. S. Measuring social distance. *Journal of Applied Sociology,* 1925, *9,* 299–308.

Borden, R. J. Witnessed aggression: Influence of an observer's sex and values on aggressive responding. *Journal of Personality and Social Psychology,* 1975, *31,* 567–573.

Borden, R. J., Bowen, R., and Taylor, S. P. Shock setting behavior as a function of physical attack and extrinsic reward. *Perceptual and Motor Skills,* 1971, *33,* 563–568.

Borden, R. J., and Taylor, S. P. The social instigation and control of physical aggression. *Journal of Applied Social Psychology,* 1973, *3,* 354–361.

Borgatta, E. F., and Bales, R. F. Sociometric status patterns and characteristics of interaction. *Journal of Social Psychology,* 1956, *43,* 289–297.

Boring, E. G. *A history of experimental psychology.* New York: Appleton-Century-Crofts, 1950.

Bramel, D. A dissonance theory approach to defensive projection. *Journal of Abnormal and Social Psychology,* 1962, *64,* 121–129.

Braver, S. L., and Barnett, B. Effects of modeling on cooperation in a prisoner's dilemma game. *Journal of Personality and Social Psychology,* 1976, *33,* 161–169.

Breedlove, W., and Breedlove, J. *Swap clubs.* Los Angeles: Sherbourne, 1964.

Brehm, J. W. Post-decision changes in desirability of alternatives. *Journal of Abnormal and Social Psychology,* 1956, *52,* 384–389.

Brehm, J. W. *Responses to loss of freedom: A theory of psychological reactance.* Morristown, N.J.: General Learning Press, 1972.

Brehm, J. W., and Behar, L. B. Sexual arousal, defensiveness, and sex preference in affiliation. *Journal of Experimental Research in Personality,* 1966, *1,* 195–200.

Brehm, J. W., and Mann, M. Effect of importance of freedom and attraction to group members on influence produced by group pressure. *Journal of Personality and Social Psychology,* 1975, *31,* 816–824.

Brickman, P., Meyer, P., and Fredd, S. Effects of varying exposure to another person with familiar or unfamiliar thought processes. *Journal of Experimental Social Psychology,* 1975, *11,* 261–270.

Brickman, P., Ryan, K., and Wortman, C. B. Causal chains: Attribution of responsibility as a function of immediate and prior causes. *Journal of Personality and Social Psychology,* 1975, *32,* 1060–1067.

Brockner, J., and Swap, W. C. Effects of repeated exposure and attitudinal similarity on self-disclosure and interpersonal attraction. *Journal of Personality and Social Psychology,* 1976, *33,* 531–540.

Broll, L., Gross, A. E., and Piliavin, I. Effects of offered and requested help on help seeking and reactions to being helped. *Journal of Applied Social Psychology,* 1974, *4,* 244–258.

Broverman, I. K., Broverman, D. M., Clarkson, F. E., Rosenkrantz, P., and Vogel, S. R. Sex-role stereotypes and clinical judgments of mental health. *Journal of Consulting Psychology,* 1970, *34,* 1–7.

Broverman, I. K., Vogel, S. R., Broverman, D. M.,

Clarkson, F. E., and Rosenkrantz, P. S. Sex-role stereotypes: A current appraisal. *Journal of Social Issues*, 1972, *28*, 59–78.

Brown, B. R. The effects of need to maintain face on interpersonal bargaining. *Journal of Experimental Social Psychology*, 1968, *4*, 107–122.

Brown, B. R. Face-saving following experimentally induced embarrassment. *Journal of Experimental Social Psychology*, 1970, *6*, 255–271.

Brown, B. R., and Garland, H. The effects of incompetency, audience acquaintanceship, and anticipated evaluative feedback on face-saving behavior. *Journal of Experimental Social Psychology*, 1971, *7*, 490–502.

Brown, P., and Elliott, R. Control of aggression in a nursery school class. *Journal of Experimental Child Psychology*, 1965, *2*, 103–107.

Brown, R. Further comment on the risky shift. *American Psychologist*, 1974, *29*, 468–470.

Bryan, J. H., and London, P. Altruistic behavior by children. *Psychological Bulletin*, 1970, *73*, 200–211.

Bryan, J. H., Redfield, J., and Mader, S. Words and deeds about altruism and the subsequent reinforcement power of the model. *Child Development*, 1971, *42*, 1501–1508.

Bryan, J. H., and Test, M. A. Models and helping: Naturalistic studies in aiding behavior. *Journal of Personality and Social Psychology*, 1967, *6*, 400–407.

Bryan, J. H., and Walbek, N. H. Preaching and practicing generosity: Children's actions and reactions. *Child Development*, 1970, *41*, 329–353.

Bryant, N. J. Petitioning: Dress congruence versus belief congruence. *Journal of Applied Social Psychology*, 1975, *5*, 144–149.

Buck, R. Nonverbal communication of affect in children. *Journal of Personality and Social Psychology*, 1975, *31*, 644–653.

Buck, R., Miller, R. E., and Caul, W. F. Sex, personality, and physiological variables in the communication of emotion via facial expression. *Journal of Personality and Social Psychology*, 1974, *30*, 587–596.

Buckhout, R. Toward a two-child norm: Changing family planning attitudes. *American Psychologist*, 1972, *27*, 16–26.

Burnstein, E., Vinokur, A., and Pichevin, M. F. What do differences between own, admired, and attributed choices have to do with group induced shifts in choice? *Journal of Experimental Social Psychology*, 1974, *10*, 428–443.

Burnstein, E., and Worchel, P. Arbitrariness of frustration and its consequences for aggression in a social situation. *Journal of Personality*, 1962, *30*, 528–540.

Buss, A. H. *The psychology of aggression.* New York: John Wiley & Sons, 1961.

Buss, A. H. Physical aggression in relation to different frustrations. *Journal of Abnormal and Social Psychology*, 1963, *67*, 1–7.

Buss, A. H. Instrumentality of aggression, feedback, and frustration as determinants of physical aggression. *Journal of Personality and Social Psychology*, 1966, *3*, 153–162.

Buss, A. H. Aggression pays. In *The control of aggression and violence,* edited by J. L. Singer. New York: Academic Press, 1971.

Buss, A. H., Booker, A., and Buss, E. Firing a weapon and aggression. *Journal of Personality and Social Psychology*, 1972, *22*, 296–302.

Butz, R. A., and Hasazi, J. E. Developing verbal imitative behavior in a profoundly retarded girl. *Journal of Behavior Therapy and Experimental Psychiatry*, 1973, *4*, 389–393.

Byrne, D. The influence of propinquity and opportunities for interaction on classroom relationships. *Human Relations*, 1961, *14*, 63–69.

Byrne, D. *The attraction paradigm.* New York: Academic Press, 1971.

Byrne, D. *An introduction to personality: Research, theory, and applications.* Englewood Cliffs, N.J.: Prentice-Hall, 1974.

Byrne, D. Sexual imagery. In *Handbook of Sexology,* edited by J. Money and H. Musaph. Amsterdam: Excerpta Medica, 1977.

Byrne, D., Allgeier, A. R., Winslow, L., and Buckman, J. The situational facilitation of interpersonal attraction: A three-factor hypothesis. *Journal of Applied Social Psychology*, 1975, *5*, 1–15.

Byrne, D., Baskett, G. D., and Hodges, L. Behavioral indicators of interpersonal attraction. *Journal of Applied Social Psychology*, 1971, *1*, 137–149.

Byrne, D., Bond, M. H., and Diamond, M. J. Response to political candidates as a function of attitude similarity-dissimilarity. *Human Relations*, 1969, *22*, 251–262.

Byrne, D., and Buehler, J. A. A note on the influence of propinquity upon acquaintanceships. *Journal of Abnormal and Social Psychology,* 1955, *51,* 147–148.

Byrne, D., and Clore, G. L. A reinforcement model of evaluative responses. *Personality: An International Journal,* 1970, *1,* 103–128.

Byrne, D., Ervin, C. R., and Lamberth, J. Continuity between the experimental study of attraction and real-life computer dating. *Journal of Personality and Social Psychology,* 1970, *16,* 157–165.

Byrne, D., Fisher, J. D., Lamberth, J., and Mitchell, H. E. Evaluations of erotica: Facts or feelings? *Journal of Personality and Social Psychology,* 1974, *29,* 111–116.

Byrne, D., and Lamberth, J. The effect of erotic stimuli on sex arousal, evaluative responses, and subsequent behavior. In *Technical Report of the Commission on Obscenity and Pornography,* vol. 8. Washington, D.C.: U.S. Government Printing Office, 1971.

Byrne, D., and Nelson, D. Attraction as a linear function of proportion of positive reinforcements. *Journal of Personality and Social Psychology,* 1965, *1,* 659–663.

Byrne, D., Rasche, L., and Kelley, K. When "I like you" indicates disagreement: An experimental differentiation of information and affect. *Journal of Research in Personality,* 1974, *8,* 207–217.

Byrne, D., and Rhamey, R. Magnitude of positive and negative reinforcements as a determinant of attraction. *Journal of Personality and Social Psychology,* 1965, *2,* 884–889.

Byrne, D., and Wong, T. J. Racial prejudice, interpersonal attraction and assumed dissimilarity of attitudes. *Journal of Abnormal and Social Psychology,* 1962, *65,* 246–253.

Calder, B. J., Ross, M., and Inkso, C. A. Attitude change and attitude attribution: Effects of incentive, choice, and consequences. *Journal of Personality and Social Psychology,* 1973, *25,* 84–99.

Calder, B. J., and Staw, B. M. Self-perception of intrinsic and extrinsic motivation. *Journal of Personality and Social Psychology,* 1975, *31,* 599–605.

Calhoun, J. B. Population density and social pathology. *Scientific American,* 1962, *206* (3), 139–148.

Calhoun, J. B. The role of space in animal sociology. *Journal of Social Issues,* 1966, *22,* 46–58.

Calhoun, J. B. Space and the strategy of life. In *Environment and behavior: The use of space by animals and men,* edited by A. H. Esser. New York: Plenum, 1971.

Callahan, D. Ethics and population limitation. *Science,* 1972, *175,* 487–494.

Campbell, A. Subjective measures of well-being. *American Psychologist,* 1976, *31,* 117–124.

Campbell, D. T., Kruskal, W. H., and Wallace, W. P. Seating aggregation as an index of attitude. *Sociometry,* 1966, *29,* 1–15.

Cann, A., Sherman, S. J., and Elkes, R. Effects of initial request size and timing of a second request on compliance: The foot-in-the-door and the door-in-the-face. *Journal of Personality and Social Psychology,* 1975, *32,* 774–782.

Cannavale, F. J., Scarr, H. A., and Pepitone, A. Deindividuation in the small group: Further evidence. *Journal of Personality and Social Psychology,* 1970, *16,* 141–147.

Caplow, T., and Forman, R. Neighborhood interaction in a homogeneous community. *American Sociological Review,* 1950, *15,* 357–366.

Carlsmith, J. M., and Gross, A. E. Some effects of guilt on compliance. *Journal of Personality and Social Psychology,* 1969, *11,* 240–244.

Carver, C. S., and Glass, D. C. The coronary prone behavior pattern and interpersonal aggression. Unpublished manuscript, University of Texas, 1977.

Castore, C. H., and DeNinno, J. A. Investigations in the social comparison of attitudes. In *Theoretical and empirical perspectives in social comparison theory,* edited by J. Suls and R. Miller. Washington, D.C.: Hemisphere Press, 1976.

Castro, M. A. C. Reactions to receiving aid as a function of cost to donor and opportunity to aid. *Journal of Applied Social Psychology,* 1974, *4,* 194–209.

Cattell, R. B., Kawash, G. F., and DeYoung, G. E. Validation of objective measures of ergic tension: Response of the sex erg to visual stimulation. *Journal of Experimental Research in Personality,* 1972, *6,* 76–83.

Cautela, J. R. Covert conditioning of addictive behaviors. *Behavior modification with the individual patient: Proceedings of the third annual Brockton symposium on behavior therapy,* 1972, 3–24.

Centers, R. Evaluating the loved one: The motivational congruency factor. *Journal of Personal-*

ity, 1971, *39,* 303–318.

Chaikin, A. L., Sigler, E., and Derlega, V. J. Nonverbal mediators of teacher expectancy effects. *Journal of Personality and Social Psychology,* 1974, *30,* 144–149.

Chemers, M. M., Rice, R. W., Sundstrom, E., and Butler, W. M. Leader esteem for the least preferred co-worker score, training, and effectiveness: An experimental examination. *Journal of Personality and Social Psychology,* 1975, *31,* 401–409.

Chen, S. C. Social modification of the activity of ants in nest-building. *Physiological Zoology,* 1937. *10,* 420–436.

Cherry, F. The use of models to influence interest in gender-inconsistent behavior. Unpublished manuscript, Indiana University, 1975.

Cherry, F., and Byrne, D. Authoritarianism. In *Personality variables in social behavior,* edited by T. Blass. Hillsdale, N.J.: Erlbaum, 1976.

Cherry, F., Byrne, D., and Mitchell, H. E. Clogs in the bogus pipeline: Demand characteristics and social desirability *Journal of Research in Personality,* 1976, *10,* 69–75.

Cherry, F., and Deaux, K. Fear of success versus fear of gender-inconsistent behavior: A sex similarity. Paper presented at the meeting of the Midwestern Psychological Association, Chicago, May, 1975.

Chertkoff, J. M., and Baird, S. L. Applicability of the big lie technique and the last clear chance doctrine to bargaining. *Journal of Personality and Social Psychology,* 1971, *20,* 298–303.

Chertkoff, J. M., and Conley, M. Opening offer and frequency of concession as bargaining strategies. *Journal of Personality and Social Psychology,* 1967, *7,* 181–185.

Chevalier-Skolnikoff, S. Heterosexual copulatory patterns in stumptail macaques (*Macaca arctoides*) and in other macaque species. *Archives of Sexual Behavior,* 1975, *4,* 199–220.

Cheyne, J. A., and Efran, N. G. The effect of spatial and interpersonal variables on the invasion of group-controlled territories. *Sociometry,* 1972, *35,* 477–489.

Christie, R., and Geis, F. L., eds. *Studies in Machiavellianism.* New York: Academic Press, 1970a.

Christie, R., and Geis, F. L. The ten dollar game. In *Studies in Machiavellianism,* edited by R. Christie and F. L. Geis. New York: Academic

Press, 1970b.

Christie, R., Gergen, K. J., and Marlowe, D. The penny-dollar caper. In *Studies in Machiavellianism,* edited by R. Christie and F. L. Geis. New York: Academic Press, 1970.

Christy, P. R., Gelfand, D. M., and Hartmann, D. P. Effects of competition-induced frustration on two classes of modeled behavior. *Developmental Psychology,* 1971, *5,* 104–111.

Cialdini, R. B., Vincent, J. E., Lewis, S. K., Catalan, J., Wheeler, D., and Darby, B. L. Reciprocal concessions procedure for inducing compliance: The door-in-the-face technique. *Journal of Personality and Social Psychology,* 1975, *31,* 206–215.

Clark, K., and Clark, M. The development of consciousness of self and the emergence of racial identity in Negro preschool children. *Journal of Social Psychology,* 1939, *10,* 591–599.

Clark, K., and Clark, M. Racial identification and racial preference in Negro children. In *Readings in social psychology,* edited by T. M. Newcomb and E. L. Hartley. New York: Holt, 1947, pp. 169–178.

Clark, M. S., Gotay, C. C., and Mills, J. Acceptance of help as a function of similarity of the potential helper and opportunity to repay. *Journal of Applied Social Psychology,* 1974, *4,* 224–229.

Clark, R. D., III, and Word, L. E. Why don't bystanders help? Because of ambiguity? *Journal of Personality and Social Psychology,* 1972, *24,* 392–400.

Clark, R. N., Burgess, R. L., and Hendee, J. C. The development of anti-litter behavior in a forest campground. *Journal of Applied Behavior Analysis,* 1972, *5,* 1–5.

Clark, R. N., Hendee, J. C., and Burgess, R. L. The experimental control of littering. *Journal of Environmental Education,* 1972, *4,* 22–28.

Clemens, L. G. Effect of stimulus female variation on sexual performance of the male deermouse, *peromyscus manifulatus. Proceedings of the American Psychological Association,* 75th annual convention, 1967, 119–120.

Cline, V. B., Croft, R. G., and Courrier, S. Desensitization of children to television violence. *Journal of Personality and Social Psychology,* 1973, *27,* 360–365.

Clore, G. L. *Interpersonal attraction: An over-*

view. Morristown, N.J.: General Learning Press, 1975.

Clore, G. L., and Byrne, D. A reinforcement-affect model of attraction. In *Foundations of interpersonal attraction,* edited by T. L. Houston. New York: Academic Press, 1974.

Clore, G. L., and Jeffery, K. McM. Emotional role playing, attitude change, and attraction toward a disabled person. *Journal of Personality and Social Psychology,* 1972, *23,* 105–111.

Clore, G. L., Wiggins, N. H., and Itkin, S. Gain and loss in attraction: Attributions from nonverbal behavior. *Journal of Personality and Social Psychology,* 1975a, *31,* 706–712.

Clore, G. L., Wiggins, N. H., and Itkin, S. Judging attraction from nonverbal behavior: The gain phenomenon. *Journal of Consulting and Clinical Psychology,* 1975b, *43,* 491–497.

Coale, A. J. The history of human population. *Scientific American,* 1974, *231* (3), 40–51.

Cohen, A. R. Social norms, arbitrariness of frustration, and status of the agent of frustration in the frustration-aggression hypothesis. *Journal of Personality and Social Psychology,* 1955, *51,* 222–226.

Cohen, S., Glass, D. C., and Singer, J. E. Apartment noise, auditory discrimination, and reading ability in children. *Journal of Experimental Social Psychology,* 1973, *9,* 407–422.

Comer, J. P., and Poussaint, A. F. *Black child care: How to bring up a healthy black child in America.* New York: Simon & Schuster, 1975.

Comfort, A. *The joy of sex.* New York: Crown, 1972.

Commission on Obscenity and Pornography. *The report of the Commission on Obscenity and Pornography.* Washington, D.C.: U.S. Government Printing Office, 1970.

Connor, J. Olfactory control of aggressive and sexual behavior in the mouse (*Mus musclus L.*). *Psychonomic Science,* 1972, ·*27,* 1–3.

Conot, R. *Rivers of blood, years of darkness.* New York: Bantam, 1967.

Cook, S. W. Motives in a conceptual analysis of attitude-related behavior. *Nebraska Symposium on Motivation,* 1970, *18,* 179–231.

Cook, S. W. A comment on the ethical issues involved in West, Gunn, and Chernicky's "Ubiquitous Watergate: An Attributional Analysis." *Journal of Personality and Social Psychology,* 1975, *32,* 66–68.

Cooper, J. B. Emotional response to statements congruent with prejudicial attitudes. *Journal of Social Psychology,* 1969, *79,* 189–193.

Cooper, J., Zanna, M. P., and Goethals, G. R. Mistreatment of an esteemed other as a consequence affecting dissonance reduction. *Journal of Experimental Social Psychology,* 1974, *10,* 224–233.

Cosby, P. C. Effects of density, activity, and personality on environmental preferences. *Journal of Research in Personality,* 1973, *7,* 45–60.

Costanzo, P. R., and Shaw, M. E. Conformity as a function of age level. *Child Development,* 1966, *37,* 967–975.

Costrich, N., Feinstein, J., Kidder, L., Marecek, J., and Pascale, L. When stereotypes hurt: Three studies of penalties for sex-role reversals. *Journal of Experimental Social Psychology,* 1975, *11,* 520–530.

Cottrell, N. B. Social facilitation. In *Experimental social psychology,* edited by C. G. McClintock. New York: Holt, Rinehart, & Winston, 1972.

Cottrell, N. B., Rittle, R. H., and Wack, D. L. The presence of an audience and list type (competitional or noncompetitional) as joint determinants of performance in paired-associate learning. *Journal of Psychology,* 1967, *35,* 425–434.

Cottrell, N. B., Wack, D. L., Sekerak, G. J., and Rittle, R. H. Social facilitation of dominant reponses by the presence of an audience and the mere presence of others. *Journal of Personality and Social Psychology,* 1968, *9,* 245–250.

Craig, K. D. and Neidermayer, H. Autonomic correlates of pain thresholds influenced by social modeling. *Journal of Personality and Social Psychology,* 1974, *29,* 246–252.

Craig, K. D., and Weiss, S. M. Vicarious influences on pain threshold determinations. *Journal of Personality and Social Psychology,* 1971, *19,* 53–59.

Craig, K. D., and Weiss, S. M. Verbal reports of pain without noxious stimulation. *Perceptual and Motor Skills,* 1972, *34,* 943–948.

Crantz, G., and Schumacher, T. The built environment for the elderly. Paper presented at Conference on Human Response to Tall Buildings, American Institute of Architects, Chicago, July 7, 1975.

Crowne, D. P., and Marlowe, D. A new scale of

social desirability independent of psychopathology. *Journal of Consulting Psychology,* 1960, *24,* 349–354.

Crutchfield, R. A. Conformity and character. *American Psychologist,* 1955, *10,* 191–198.

Cundy, D. T. Partisanship and political attitude formation: A social learning model. Unpublished doctoral dissertation, University of Oregon, 1975.

Curran, J. P. Convergence toward a single sexual standard? *Social Behavior and Personality, 1975, 3,* 189–195.

Curran, J. P., and Lippold, S. The effects of physical attraction and attitude similarity on attraction in dating dyads. *Journal of Personality,* 1975, *43,* 528–539.

Cvetkovich, G., and Baumgardner, S. R. Attitude polarization: The relative influence of discussion group structure and reference group norms. *Journal of Personality and Social Psychology,* 1973, *26,* 159–165.

Dabbs, J. M., Jr., and Stokes, N. A., III. Beauty is power: The use of space on the sidewalk. *Sociometry,* 1975, *38,* 551–557.

Daher, D. M., and Banikiotes, P. G., Interpersonal attraction and rewarding aspects of disclosure content and level. *Journal of Personality and Social Psychology,* 1976, *33,* 492–496.

Daniels, R., and Kitano, H. H. L. *American racism.* Englewood Cliffs, N.J.: Prentice-Hall, 1970.

Darley, J. M., and Batson, C. D. "From Jerusalem to Jericho:" A study of situational and dispositional variables in helping behavior. *Journal of Personality and Social Psychology,* 1973, *27,* 100–108.

Darley, J. M., and Cooper, J. The "clean for Gene" phenomenon: The effect of students' appearance on political campaigning. *Journal of Applied Social Psychology,* 1972, *2,* 24–33.

Darley, J. M., and Latané, B. By stander intervention in emergencies: Diffusion of responsibility. *Journal of Personality and Social Psychology,* 1968, *8,* 377–383.

Darley, J. M., Moriarty, T., Darley, S., and Berscheid, E. Increased conformity to a fellow deviant as a function of prior deviation. *Journal of Experimental Social Psychology,* 1974, *10,* 211–223.

Darroch, R. K., and Steiner, I. D. Role playing: An alternative to laboratory research? *Journal of Personality,* 1970, *38,* 302–311.

Darwin, C. *The expression of emotions in man and animals.* London: Murray, 1872.

Dashiell, J. F. An experimental analysis of some group effects. *Journal of Abnormal and Social Psychology,* 1930, *25,* 190–199.

Davis, D., and Brock, T. C. Use of first person pronouns as a function of increased objective self-awareness and performance feedback. *Journal of Experimental Social Psychology,* 1975, *11,* 381–388.

Davis, J. H., Kerr, N. I., Sussman, M., and Rissman, A. K. Social decision schemes under risk. *Journal of Personality and Social Psychology,* 1974, *30,* 248–271.

Davis, K. E., and Braucht, G. N. Exposure to pornography, character, and sexual deviance: A retrospective survey. *Journal of Social Issues,* 1973, *29* (3), 183–196.

Davison, G. C., and Neale, J. M. *Abnormal psychology: An experimental clinical approach.* New York: John Wiley & Sons, 1974.

Davison, G. C., and Valins, S. Maintenance of self-attributed and drug-attributed behavior change. *Journal of Personality and Social Psychology,* 1969, *11,* 25–33.

Deaux, K. *The behavior of women and men.* Belmont, Calif.: Brooks/Cole, 1976a.

Deaux, K. Sex: A parameter in the attribution process. In *New directions in attribution research,* edited by J. Harvey, W. Ickes, and R. F. Kidd. Hillsdale, N.J.: Erlbaum, 1976b.

Deaux, K., and Emswiller, T. Explanations of successful performance on sex-linked tasks: What is skill for the male is luck for the female. *Journal of Personality and Social Psychology,* 1974, *29,* 80–85.

Deci, E. L. *Intrinsic motivation.* New York: Plenum, 1975.

DeFleur, M. L., and Westie, F. R. Verbal attitudes and overt acts: An experiment on the salience of attitudes. *American Sociological Review,* 1958, *23,* 667–673.

DeJong, W. Another look at Banuazizi and Movahedi's analysis of the Stanford prison experiment. *American Psychologist,* 1975, *30,* 1013–1015.

Demeny, P. The populations of underdeveloped countries. *Scientific American,* 1974, *231* (3), 148–159.

Denfeld, D., and Gordon, M. The sociology of mate swapping: Or the family that swings together clings together. *Journal of Sex Research,* 1970, *6,* 85–100.

Dengerink, H. A. Anxiety, aggression, and physiological arousal. *Journal of Experimental Research in Personality,* 1971, *5,* 223–232.

Dermer, M., and Thiel, D. L. When beauty may fail. *Journal of Personality and Social Psychology,* 1975, *31,* 1168–1176.

Deur, J. D., and Parke, R. D. Effects of inconsistent punishment on aggression in children. *Developmental Psychology,* 1970, *2,* 403–411.

Deutsch, M., and Collins, M. E. *Interracial housing.* Minneapolis: University of Minnesota Press, 1951.

Deutsch, M., and Gerard, H. B. A study of normative and informational social influences upon individual judgment. *Journal of Abnormal and Social Psychology,* 1955, *51,* 629–636.

Deutsch, M., and Krauss, R. M. The effect of threat upon interpersonal bargaining. *Journal of Abnormal and Social Psychology,* 1960, *61,* 181–189.

Dickens, C. *The old curiosity shop.* New York: Heritage Press, 1941 (reprint of 1841 edition).

Diener, E. Effects of prior destructive behavior, anonymity, and group presence on deindividuation and aggression. *Journal of Personality and Social Psychology,* 1976, *33,* 497–507.

Diener, E., Dineen, J., Endresen, K., Beaman, A. L., and Fraser, S. C. Effects of altered responsibility, cognitive set, and modeling on physical aggression and deindividuation. *Journal of Personality and Social Psychology,* 1975, *31,* 328–337.

Diener, E., Fraser, S. C., Beaman, A. L., and Kelem, R. T. Effects of deindividuation variables on stealing among Halloween trick-or-treaters. *Journal of Personality and Social Psychology,* 1976, *33,* 178–183.

Diener, E., Westford, K. L., Dineen, J., and Fraser, S. C. Beat the pacifist: The deindividuation effects of anonymity and group presence. *Proceedings of the American Psychological Association,* 81st Annual Convention, 1973, *8,* 221–222.

Dies, R. R., and Greenberg, B. Effects of physical contact in an encounter group context. *Journal of Consulting and Clinical Psychology,* 1976, *44,* 400–405.

Dillehay, R. C. On the irrelevance of the classical negative evidence concerning the effect of attitudes on behavior. *American Psychologist,* 1973, *28,* 887–891.

Dion, K. K., Berscheid, E., and Walster, E. What is beautiful is good. *Journal of Personality and Social Psychology,* 1972, *24,* 285–290.

Dion, K. K., and Dion, K. L. Self-esteem and romantic love. *Journal of Personality,* 1975, *43,* 39–57.

Dion, K. L., Baron, R. S., and Miller, N. Why do groups make riskier decisions than individuals? In *Advances in experimental social psychology,* vol. 5, edited by L. Berkowitz. New York: Academic Press, 1970.

Dion, K. L., and Dion, K. K. Correlates of romantic love. *Journal of Consulting and Clinical Psychology,* 1973, *41,* 51–56.

Doise, W. Intergroup relations and polarization of individual and collective judgments. *Journal of Personality and Social Psychology,* 1969, *12,* 136–143.

Dollard, J., Doob, L., Miller, N., Mowrer, O. H., and Sears, R. R. *Frustration and aggression.* New Haven: Yale University Press, 1939.

Donnerstein, E., Donnerstein, M., and Evans, R. Erotic stimuli and aggression: facilitation or inhibition. *Journal of Personality and Social Psychology,* 1975, *32,* 237–244.

Donnerstein, E., Donnerstein, M., Simons, S., and Ditrichs, R. Variables in interracial aggression: Anonymity, expected retaliation, and a riot. *Journal of Personality and Social Psychology,* 1972, *22,* 236–245.

Doob, A. N., and Wood, L. Catharsis and aggression: The effects of annoyance and retaliation on aggressive behavior. *Journal of Personality and Social Psychology,* 1972, *22,* 156–162.

Dorr, D., and Fey, S. Relative power of symbolic adult and peer models in the modification of children's moral choice behavior. *Journal of Personality and Social Psychology,* 1974, *29,* 335–341.

Doty, R. L., Ford, M., Preti, G., and Huggins, G. R. Changes in the intensity and pleasantness of human vaginal odors during the menstrual cycle. *Science,* 1975, *190,* 1316–1318.

Dovidio, J. F., and Morris, W. N. Effects of stress and commonality of fate on helping behavior. *Journal of Personality and Social Psychology,* 1975, *31,* 145–149.

Driscoll, R., Davis, K. E., and Lipetz, M. E.

Parental interference and romantic love: The Romeo and Juliet effect. *Journal of Personality and Social Psychology,* 1972, *24,* 1–10.

Dubos, R. *Man adapting.* New Haven: Yale University Press, 1965.

Duke, M. P., and Mullens, M. C. Preferred interpersonal distance as a function of locus of control orientation in chronic schizophrenics, non-schizophrenic patients, and normals. *Journal of Consulting and Clinical Psychology,* 1973, *41,* 230–234.

Duncan, S. Some signals and rules for taking speaking turns in conversation. *Journal of Personality and Social Psychology,* 1972, *23,* 283–292.

Duncan, S., and Niederehe, G. On signalling that it's your turn to speak. *Journal of Experimental Social Psychology,* 1974, *10,* 234–247.

Dunlap, K. Are there any instincts? *Journal of Abnormal Psychology,* 1919, *14,* 307–311.

Dutton, D. G., and Aron, A. P. Some evidence for heightened sexual attraction under conditions of high anxiety. *Journal of Personality and Social Psychology,* 1974, *30,* 510–517.

Dutton, D. G., and Lake, R. A. Threat of own prejudice and reverse discrimination in interracial situations. *Journal of Personality and Social Psychology,* 1973, *28,* 94–100.

Dutton, D. G., and Lennox, V. L. Effect of prior "token" compliance on subsequent interracial behavior. *Journal of Personality and Social Psychology,* 1974, *29,* 65–71.

Duval, S. Conformity on a visual task as a function of personal novelty on attitudinal dimensions and being reminded of the object status of self. *Journal of Experimental Social Psychology,* 1976, *12,* 87–98.

Duval, S., and Wicklund, R. A. *A theory of objective self awareness.* New York: Academic Press, 1972.

Duval, S., Wicklund, R. A., and Fine, R. Unpublished manuscript, cited in *A theory of objective self awareness,* by S. Duval and R. A. Wicklund. New York: Academic Press, 1972.

Eagly, A. H., and Telaak, K. Width of the latitude of acceptance as a determinant of attitude change. *Journal of Personality and Social Psychology,* 1972, *23,* 388–397.

Eaton, W. O., and Clore, G. L. Interracial imitation at a summer camp. *Journal of Personality and Social Psychology,* 1975, *32,* 1099–1105.

Ebbesen, E. B., and Bowers, R. J. Proportion of risky to conservative arguments in a group discussion and choice shift. *Journal of Personality and Social Psychology,* 1974, *29,* 316–327.

Ebbesen, E. B., Duncan, B., and Konečni, V. Effects of content of verbal aggression on future verbal aggression: A field experiment. *Journal of Experimental Social Psychology,* 1975, *11,* 192–204.

Eberts, E. H., and Lepper, M. R. Individual consistency in the proxemic behavior of preschool children. *Journal of Personality and Social Psychology,* 1975, *32,* 841–849.

Edney, J. J. Property, possession and permanence: A field study in human territoriality. *Journal of Applied Social Psychology,* 1972, *2,* 275–282.

Edney, J. J. Territoriality and control: A field experiment. *Journal of Personality and Social Psychology,* 1975, *31,* 1108–1115.

Edney, J. J., and Jordan-Edney, N. L. Territorial spacing on a beach. *Sociometry,* 1974, *37,* 92–104.

Efran, M. G. Visual interaction and interpersonal attraction. Unpublished doctoral dissertation, University of Texas, 1969.

Efran, M. G. The effect of physical appearance on the judgment of guilt, interpersonal attraction, and severity of recommended punishment in a simulated jury task. *Journal of Research in Personality,* 1974, *8,* 45–54.

Efran, M. G., and Cheyne, J. A. Shared space: The cooperative control of spatial areas by two interacting individuals. *Canadian Journal of Behavioural Science,* 1973, *5,* 201–210.

Efran, M. G., and Cheyne, J. A. Affective concomitants of the invasion of shared space: Behavioral, physiological, and verbal indicators. *Journal of Personality and Social Psychology,* 1974, *29,* 219–226.

Efran, M. G., and Patterson, E. W. J. Voters vote beautiful: The effect of physical appearance on a national election. *Canadian Journal of Behavioral Science,* 1974, *6,* 352–356.

Ehrlich, P. R., and Ehrlich, A. H. The population crisis. *Britannica Book of the Year.* Chicago: William Benton, 1971.

Eisenberger, R., Park, D. C., and Frank, M. Learned industriousness and social reinforcement. *Journal of Personality and Social Psychol-*

ogy, 1976, *33*, 227–232.

Eisinger, R., and Mills, J. Perception of the sincerity and competence of a communicator as a function of the extremity of his position. *Journal of Experimental Social Psychology*, 1968, *4*, 224–232.

Ekman, P., and Friesen, W. V. Detecting deception from the body or face. *Journal of Personality and Social Psychology*, 1974, *29*, 288–298.

Ekman, P., and Friesen, W. V. *Unmasking the face.* Englewood Cliffs, N.J.: Prentice-Hall, 1975.

Ekman, P., Friesen, W. V., and Ellsworth, P. *Emotion in the human face: Guidelines for research and an integration of findings.* New York: Pergamon Press, 1972.

Ellis, L. J., and Bentler, P. M. Traditional sex-determined role standards and sex stereotypes. *Journal of Personality and Social Psychology*, 1973, *25*, 28–34.

Ellsworth, P. C., and Carlsmith, J. M. Eye contact and gaze aversion in an aggressive encounter. *Journal of Personality and Social Psychology*, 1973, *28*, 280–292.

Ellsworth, P. C., Carlsmith, J. M., and Henson, A. Staring as a stimulus to flight in humans: A series of field studies. *Journal of Personality and Social Psychology*, 1972, *21*, 302–311.

Ellsworth, P. C., and Langer, E. J. Staring and approach: An interpretation of the stare as a nonspecific activator. *Journal of Personality and Social Psychology*, 1976, *33*, 117–122.

Ellsworth, P. C., and Ross, L. Intimacy in response to direct gaze. *Journal of Experimental Social Psychology*, 1975, *11*, 592–613.

Elms, A. C. The crisis of confidence in social psychology. *American Psychologist*, 1975, *30*, 967–976.

Elms, A., and Milgram, S. Personality characteristics associated with obedience and defiance toward authoritative command. *Journal of Experimental Research in Personality*, 1966, *1*, 282–289.

Emler, N. P., and Rushton, J. P. Cognitive-developmental factors in children's generosity. *British Journal of Social and Clinical Psychology*, 1974, *13*, 277–281.

Emswiller, T., Deaux, K., and Willits, J. E. Similarity, sex, and requests for small favors. *Journal of Applied Social Psychology*, 1971, *1*, 284–291.

Endler, N. S. The effects of verbal reinforcement on conformity and deviant behavior. *Journal of Social Psychology*, 1965, *66*, 147–154.

Endler, N. S. Conformity as a function of different reinforcement schedules. *Journal of Personality and Social Psychology*, 1966, *4*, 175–180.

Enzle, M. E., Hansen, R. D., and Lowe, C. A. Causal attribution in the mixed motive-game: Effects of facilitory and inhibitory environmental forces. *Journal of Personality and Social Psychology*, 1975a, *31*, 50–54.

Enzle, M. E., Hansen, R. D., and Lowe, C. A. Humanizing the mixed-motive paradigm: Methodological innovations from attribution theory. *Simulation and Games*, 1975b, *6*, 151–165.

Eron, L. D. Relationship of TV viewing habits and aggressive behavior in children. *Journal of Abnormal and Social Psychology*, 1963, *67*, 193–196.

Esser, A. H. Interactional hierarchy and power structure on a psychiatric ward. In *Behavior studies in psychiatry*, edited by S. J. Hutt and C. Hutt. New York: Oxford University Press, 1970.

Etaugh, C., and Rose, S. Adolescents' sex bias in the evaluation of performance. *Developmental Psychology*, 1975, *11*, 663–674.

Evans, G. W., and Howard, R. B. Personal space. *Psychological Bulletin*, 1973, *80*, 334–344.

Evans, R. I., Rozelle, R. M., Lasater, T. M., Dembroski, T. M., and Allen, B. P. Fear arousal, persuasion, and actual versus implied behavioral change: New perspective utilizing a real-life dental hygiene program. *Journal of Personality and Social Psychology*, 1970, *16*, 220–227.

Exline, R. V. Visual interaction. In *Nebraska symposium on motivation*, edited by W. J. Arnold and M. M. Page. Lincoln, Nebraska: University of Nebraska Press, 1971.

Eysenck, H. J. Obscenity—officially speaking. *Penthouse*, 1972, *3* (11), 95–102.

Fagot, B. I., and Patterson, G. R. An *in vivo* analysis of reinforcing contingencies for sex-role behaviors in the pre-school child. *Developmental Psychology*, 1969, *1*, 563–568.

Fast, J. *Body language.* New York: Pocket Books, 1970.

Feldman-Summers, S., and Kiesler, S. B. Those who are number two try harder: The effect of sex on attributions of causality. *Journal of Personality and Social Psychology*, 1974, *30*, 846–855.

Feleky, A. M. The expression of the emotions. *Psychological Review,* 1914, 21, 33–41.

Felipe, N. J., and Sommer, R. Invasions of personal space. *Social Problems,* 1966, *14,* 206–214.

Feshbach, S., and Singer, R. D. *Television and aggression.* San Francisco: Jossey-Bass, 1971.

Feshbach, S., Stiles, W. B., and Bitter, E. The reinforcing effect of witnessing aggression. *Journal of Experimental Research in Personality,* 1967, *2,* 133–139.

Festinger, L. A theory of social comparison processes. *Human Relations,* 1954, *7,* 117–140.

Festinger, L. *A theory of cognitive dissonance.* Evanston, Illinois: Row, Peterson, 1957.

Festinger, L., and Carlsmith, J. M. Cognitive consequences of forced compliance. *Journal of Abnormal and Social Psychology,* 1959, *58,* 203–210.

Festinger, L., Schachter, S., and Back, K. *Social pressures in informal groups: A study of a housing community.* New York: Harper, 1950.

Fiedler, F. E. *A theory of leadership effectiveness.* New York: McGraw-Hill, 1967.

Fiedler, F. E. Personality, motivational systems, and behavior of high and low LPC persons. *Human Relations,* 1972, *25,* 391–412.

Fiedler, F. E., and Chemers, M. H. *Leadership and effective management.* Glenview, Ill.: Scott, Foresman, 1974.

Filter, T. A., and Gross, A. E. Effects of public and private deviancy on compliance with a request. *Journal of Experimental Social Psychology,* 1975, *11,* 553–559.

Finger, F. W. Changes in sex practices and beliefs of male college students over 30 years. *Journal of Sex Research,* 1975, *11,* 304–317.

Fischer, E. H. Birth planning of youth: Concern about overpopulation and intention to limit family size. *American Psychologist,* 1972, *27,* 951–958.

Fishbein, M., and Azjen, I. *Belief, attitude, intention, and behavior: An introduction to theory and research.* Reading, Mass.: Addison-Wesley, 1975.

Fisher, J. D. Situation specific variables as determinants of perceived environmental aesthetic quality and perceived crowdedness. *Journal of Research in Personality,* 1974, *8,* 177–188.

Fisher, J. D., and Byrne, D. Too close for comfort: Sex differences in response to invasions of personal space. *Journal of Personality and Social Psychology,* 1975, *32,* 15–21.

Fisher, J. D., and Nadler, A. The effect of similarity between donor and recipient on recipient's reactions to aid. *Journal of Applied Social Psychology,* 1974, *4,* 230–243.

Fisher, J. D., and Nadler, A. Effect of donor resources on recipient self-esteem and self-help. *Journal of Experimental Social Psychology,* 1976, *12,* 139–150.

Fisher, J. D., Rytting, M., and Heslin, R. Hands touching hands: Affective and evaluative effects of an interpersonal touch. *Sociometry,* 1976, *39,* 416–421.

Fisher, S. *The female orgasm: Psychology, physiology, fantasy.* New York: Basic Books, 1972.

Fisher, W. A. Individual differences in behavioral responsiveness to erotica: Cognitive labeling, transfer of arousal, and disinhibition considerations. Unpublished master's thesis, Purdue University, 1976.

Fisher, W. A., and Byrne, D. Individual differences in socialization to sex as mediators of responses to an erotic film. Paper presented at the meeting of the Midwestern Psychological Association, Chicago, May 1976.

Freedman, J. L. Role playing: Psychology by consensus. *Journal of Personality and Social Psychology,* 1969, *13,* 107–114.

Freedman, J. L., and Fraser, S. C. Compliance without pressure: The foot-in-the-door technique. *Journal of Personality and Social Psychology,* 1966, *4,* 195–202.

Freedman, J. L., Heshka, S., and Levy, A. Population density and pathology: Is there a relationship? *Journal of Experimental Social Psychology,* 1975, *11,* 539–552.

Freedman, J. L., Klevansky, S., and Ehrlich, P. I. The effect of crowding on human task performance. *Journal of Applied Social Psychology,* 1971, *1,* 7–26.

Freedman, J. L., Levy, A. S., Buchanan, R. W., and Price, J. Crowding and human aggressiveness. *Journal of Experimental Social Psychology,* 1972, *8,* 528–548.

Freud, S. Some psychical consequences of the anatomical distinction between the sexes. *Standard edition of the complete psychological works of Sigmund Freud,* vol. 19, edited by J. Strachey. London: Hogarth Press, 1925 (reprint of 1961).

Freud, S. *New introductory lectures on psycho-*

analysis. New York: W. W. Norton, 1933.

Freund, K., Sedlacek, F., and Knob, K. A simple transducer for mechanical plethysmography of the male genital. *Journal of the Experimental Analysis of Behavior,* 1965, *8,* 169–170.

Frieze, I., and Weiner, B. Cue utilization and attributional judgments for success and failure. *Journal of Personality,* 1971, *39,* 591–605.

Frodi, A. The effect of exposure to weapons on aggressive behavior from a cross-cultural perspective. *International Journal of Psychology,* 1975, *10,* 283–292.

Frodi, A. Sexual arousal, situational restrictiveness, and aggressive behavior. *Journal of Research in Personality,* 1977, *11,* 48–58.

Fromkin, H. L. Reversal of the attitude similarity/attraction effect by uniqueness deprivation. Paper presented at the meeting of the Midwestern Psychological Association, Detroit, May 1971.

Fromkin, H. L. Feelings of interpersonal undistinctiveness: An unpleasant affective state. *Journal of Experimental Research in Personality,* 1972, *6,* 178–185.

Gaebelein, J. W. Third-party instigation of aggression: An experimental approach. *Journal of Personality and Social Psychology,* 1973, *27,* 389–395.

Gaertner, S. L. Nonreactive measures in racial attitude research: A focus on liberals. In *The Handbook toward the Elimination of Racism,* Society for the Psychological Study of Social Issues, 1976.

Galbraith, G. G., and Lieberman, H. Associative responses to double entendre words as a function of repression-sensitization and sexual stimulation. *Journal of Consulting and Clinical Psychology,* 1972, *39,* 322–327.

Galbraith, G. G., and Mosher, D. L. Associative sexual responses in relation to sexual arousal, guilt, and external approval contingencies. *Journal of Personality and Social Psychology,* 1968, *10,* 142–147.

Galizio, M., and Hendrick, C. Effect of musical accompaniment on attitude: The guitar as a prop for persuasion. *Journal of Applied Social Psychology,* 1972, *2,* 350–359.

Galle, O. R., Gove, W. R., and McPherson, J. M. Population density and pathology: What are the relationships for man? *Science,* 1972, *176,* 23–30.

Gallo, P., and Sheposh, J. Effects of incentive magnitude on cooperation in the prisoner's dilemma game: A reply to Gumpert, Deutsch, and Epstein. *Journal of Personality and Social Psychology,* 1971, *19,* 42–46.

Garcia, L. T. Evaluation and recall of evidence: Authoritarianism and the Patty Hearst case. Paper presented at the Psychonomic Society meeting, St. Louis, November 1976.

Garcia, L. T., and Griffitt, W. Impact of testimonial evidence as a function of witness characteristics. Unpublished manuscript, Kansas State University, 1976.

Garland, H., and Brown, B. R. Face-saving as affected by subjects' sex, audiences' sex, and audience expertise. *Sociometry,* 1972, *35,* 280–289.

Gates, M. G., and Allee, W. C. Conditioned behavior of isolated and grouped cockroaches on a simple maze. *Journal of Comparative Psychology,* 1933, *13,* 331–358.

Gebhard, P. H. Fetishism and sadomasochism. *Science and Psychoanalysis,* 1969, *15,* 71–80.

Geen, R. G. Effects of frustration, attack, and prior training in aggressiveness upon aggressive behavior. *Journal of Personality and Social Psychology,* 1968, *9,* 316–321.

Geen, R. G. Perceived suffering of the victim as an inhibitor of attack-induced aggression. *Journal of Social Psychology,* 1970, *81,* 209–215.

Geen, R. G., and Berkowitz, L. Some conditions facilitating the occurrence of aggression after the observation of violence. *Journal of Personality,* 1967, *35,* 666–676.

Geen, R. G., and O'Neal, E. C. Activation of cue-elicited aggression by general arousal. *Journal of Personality and Social Psychology,* 1969, *11,* 289–292.

Geen, R. G., and O'Neal, E. C., eds. *Perspectives on aggression.* New York: Academic Press, 1976.

Geen, R. G., and Pigg, R. Acquisition of an aggressive response and its generalization to verbal behavior. *Journal of Personality and Social Psychology,* 1970, *15,* 165–170.

Geen, R. G., and Stonner, D. Effects of aggressiveness habit strength on behavior in the presence of aggression-related stimuli. *Journal of Personality and Social Psychology,* 1971, *17,* 149–153.

Geen, R. G., and Stonner, D. Context effects in

observed violence. *Journal of Personality and Social Psychology,* 1972, *25,* 145–150.

Geen, R. G., Stonner, D., and Shope, G. L. The facilitation of aggression by aggression: Evidence against the catharsis hypothesis. *Journal of Personality and Social Psychology,* 1975, *31,* 721–726.

Geer, J. H. Direct measurement of genital responding. *American Psychologist,* 1975, *30,* 415–418.

Geer, J. H., and Fuhr, R. Cognitive factors in sexual arousal: The role of distraction. *Journal of Consulting and Clinical Psychology,* 1976, *44,* 238–243.

Geer, J. H., Morokoff, P., and Greenwood, P. Sexual arousal in women: The development of a measurement device for vaginal blood volume. *Archives of Sexual Behavior,* 1974, *3,* 559–564.

Geer, J. H., and Quartararo, J. D. Vaginal blood volume responses during masturbation and resultant orgasm. *Archives of Sexual Behavior,* 1976, *5,* 403–413.

Gelb, P. M. High-rise impact on city and neighborhood livability. Paper presented at Conference on Human Response to Tall Buildings, American Institute of Architects, Chicago, July 1975.

Gelfand, D. M., Hartmann, D. P., Walder, P., and Page, B. Who reports shoplifters? A field-experimental study. *Journal of Personality and Social Psychology,* 1973, *25,* 276–285.

Geller, D. M., Goodstein, L., Silver, M., and Sternberg, W. C. On being ignored: The effects of the violation of implicit rules of social interaction. *Sociometry,* 1974, *37,* 541–556.

Gentry, W. D. Effects of frustration, attack, and prior aggressive training on overt aggression and vascular processes. *Journal of Personality and Social Psychology,* 1970, *16,* 718–725.

Gerard, H. B., and Mathewson, G. C. The effects of severity of initiation on liking for a group: A replication. *Journal of Experimental Social Psychology,* 1966, *2,* 278–287.

Gerard, H. B., Wilhelmy, R. A., and Conolley, E. S. Conformity and group size. *Journal of Personality and Social Psychology,* 1968, *8,* 79–82.

Gergen, K. J. Social psychology as history. *Journal of Personality and Social Psychology,* 1973, *26,* 309–320.

Gergen, K. J., Ellsworth, P., Maslach, C., and Seipel, M. Obligation, donor resources, and reactions to aid in three nations. *Journal of Personality and Social Psychology,* 1975, *31,* 390–400.

Gergen, K. J., Morse, S. J., and Bode, K. A. Overpaid or overworked? Cognitive and behavioral reactions to inequitable rewards. *Journal of Applied Social Psychology,* 1974, *4,* 259–274.

Gergen, K. J., Morse, S. J., and Kristeller, J. The manner of giving: Cross-national continuities in reactions to aid. *Psychologia,* 1973, *16,* 121–131.

Gerst, M. S. Symbolic coding processes in observational learning. *Journal of Personality and Social Psychology,* 1971, *19,* 7–17.

Gewirtz, J. L., and Stingle, K. C. The learning of generalized imitation as the basis for identification. *Psychological Review,* 1968, *75,* 374–397.

Gibson, J. J. *The senses considered as perceptual systems.* Boston: Houghton Mifflin, 1966.

Giesen, M., and Hendrick, C. Effects of false positive and negative arousal feedback on persuasion. *Journal of Personality and Social Psychology,* 1974, *30,* 449–457.

Gilbert, G. M. Stereotype persistence and change among college students. *Journal of Abnormal and Social Psychology,* 1951, *46,* 245–254.

Gillig, P. M., and Greenwald, A. G. Is it time to lay the sleeper effect to rest? *Journal of Personality and Social Psychology,* 1974, *29,* 132–139.

Gilmore, T. M., and Minton, H. L. Internal versus external attribution of task performance as a function of locus of control, initial confidence, and success-failure outcome. *Journal of Personality,* 1974, *41,* 159–174.

Gintner, G., and Lindskold, S. Rate of participation and expertise as factors influencing leader choice. *Journal of Personality and Social Psychology,* 1975, *32,* 1085–1089.

Glass, D. C., Singer, J. E., and Friedman, L. N. Psychic cost of adaptation to an environmental stressor. *Journal of Personality and Social Psychology,* 1969, *12,* 200–210.

Goldberg, P. Are women prejudiced against women? *Trans-action,* 1968, *5,* 28–30.

Goldberg, P. Prejudice toward women: Some personality correlates. *International Journal of Group Tensions,* 1974, *4,* 53–63.

Goldberg, P., Gottesdiener, M., and Abramson, P. R. Another put-down of women? Perceived attractiveness as a function of support for the feminist movement. *Journal of Personality and Social Psychology,* 1975, *32,* 113–115.

Goldman, J. A., and Olczak, P. V. Psychosocial maturity and interpersonal attraction. *Journal of Research in Personality,* 1976, *10,* 146–154.

Goldring, P. Role of distance and posture in the evaluation of interactions. *Proceedings of the American Psychological Association,* 75th Annual Convention. 1967, *2,* 243–244.

Goldstein, M., and Davis, E. E. Race and belief: A further analysis of the social determinants of behavioral intentions. *Journal of Personality and Social Psychology,* 1972, *22,* 345–355.

Goldstein, M. J., Kant, H. S., and Hartman, J. J. *Pornography and sexual deviance.* Berkeley: University of California Press, 1974.

Good, K. J. Social facilitation: Effects of performance anticipation, evaluation, and response competition on free associations. *Journal of Personality and Social Psychology,* 1973, *28,* 270–275.

Good, L. R., and Good, K. C. Attitude similarity and evaluation of potential counselors. *Psychological Reports,* 1972, *31,* 963–966.

Goodman, M. E. *Race awareness in young children.* Cambridge, Mass.: Addison-Wesley, 1952.

Goranson, R. E. Media violence and aggressive behavior: A review of experimental research. In *Advances in experimental social psychology,* vol. 5, edited by L. Berkowitz. New York: Academic Press, 1970.

Goranson, R. E., and King, D. Rioting and daily temperature: Analysis of the U.S. riots in 1967. Unpublished manuscript, York University, Toronto, 1970.

Gordon, M., and Shankweiler, P. J. Different equals less: Female sexuality in recent marriage manuals. *Journal of Marriage and the Family,* 1971, *33,* 459–466.

Gorkin, L. The sensuous doctor: Response to sex-role logic problems. Unpublished manuscript, State University of New York at Stony Brook, 1972.

Gotestam, K. G., and Melin, L. Covert extinction of amphetamine addiction. *Behavior Therapy,* 1974, *5,* 90–92.

Gouaux, C. Induced affective states and interpersonal attraction. *Journal of Personality and Social Psychology,* 1971, *20,* 37–43.

Gouaux, C., Lamberth, J., and Friedrich, G. Affect and interpersonal attraction: A comparison of trait and state measures. *Journal of Personality and Social Psychology,* 1972, *24,* 53–58.

Graen, G. B., Orris, J. B., and Alvares, K. M. The contingency model of leadership effectiveness: Some experimental results. *Journal of Applied Psychology,* 1971, *55,* 205–210.

Greco, J. T. Carpeting versus resiliant flooring: A comparative study in a metropolitan hospital. *Hospitals,* 1965, *39,* 55–58.

Green, D. Dissonance and self-perception analysis of "forced compliance:" When two theories make competing predictions. *Journal of Personality and Social Psychology,* 1974, *29,* 819–828.

Greenwald, A. G. Does the Good Samaritan parable increase helping? A comment on Darley and Batson's no-effect conclusion. *Journal of Personality and Social Psychology,* 1975, *32,* 578–583.

Greenwell, J., and Dengerink, H. A. The role of perceived versus actual attack in human physical aggression. *Journal of Personality and Social Psychology,* 1973, *26,* 66–71.

Griffith, M., and Walker, C. E. Menstrual cycle phases and personality variables as related to response to erotic stimuli. *Archives of Sexual Behavior,* 1975, *4,* 599–603.

Griffitt, W. Environmental effects on interpersonal affective behavior: Ambient effective temperature and attraction. *Journal of Personality and Social Psychology,* 1970, *15,* 240–244.

Griffitt, W. Response to erotica and the projection of response to erotica in the opposite sex. *Journal of Experimental Research in Personality,* 1973, *6,* 330–338.

Griffitt, W. Attitude similarity and attraction. In *Foundations of interpersonal attraction,* edited by T. L. Huston. New York: Academic Press, 1974.

Griffitt, W. Sexual experience and sexual responsiveness: Sex differences. *Archives of Sexual Behavior,* 1975, *4,* 529–540.

Griffitt, W., and Jackson, T. The influence of ability and non-ability information on personnel selection decisions. *Psychological Reports,* 1970, *27,* 959–962.

Griffitt, W., and Jackson, T. Simulated jury decisions: The influence of jury-defendant attitude similarity-dissimilarity. *Social Behavior and Personality,* 1973, *1,* 1–7.

Griffitt, W., May, J., and Veitch, R. Sexual stimulation and interpersonal behavior: Heterosexual evaluative responses, visual behavior, and physical proximity. *Journal of Personality and Social Psychology,* 1974, *30,* 367–377.

Griffitt, W., Nelson, J., and Littlepage, G. Old age and response to agreement-disagreement. *Journal of Gerontology,* 1972, *27,* 269–274.

Griffitt, W., and Veitch, R. Hot and crowded: Influence of population density and temperature on interpersonal affective behavior. *Journal of Personality and Social Psychology,* 1971, *17,* 92–98.

Griffitt, W., and Veitch, R. Preacquaintance attitude similarity and attraction revisited: Ten days in a fall-out shelter. *Sociometry,* 1974, *37,* 163–173.

Gross, A. E., Kelley, H. H., Kruglanski, A. W., and Patch, M. E. Contingency of consequences and type of incentive in interdependent escape. *Journal of Experimental Social Psychology,* 1972, *8,* 360–377.

Gross, A. E., and Latané, J. G. Receiving help, reciprocation, and interpersonal attraction. *Journal of Applied Social Psychology,* 1974, *4,* 210–223.

Grusec, J. E. Demand characteristics of the modeling experiment: Altruism as a function of age and aggression. *Journal of Personality and Social Psychology,* 1972, *22,* 139–148.

Grusec, J., and Brinker, H. Reinforcement for imitation as a social learning determinant with implications for sex-role development. *Journal of Personality and Social Psychology,* 1972, *21,* 149–158.

Grush, J. E. Attitude formation and mere exposure phenomena: A nonartifactual explanation of empirical findings. *Journal of Personality and Social Psychology,* 1976, *33,* 281–290.

Grush, J. E., Clore, G. L., and Costin, F. Dissimilarity and attraction: When difference makes a difference. *Journal of Personality and Social Psychology,* 1975, *32,* 783–789.

Grush, J. E., and McKeogh, K. L. The finest representation that money can buy: Exposure effects in the 1972 congressional primaries. Paper presented at the meeting of the Midwestern Psychological Association, Chicago, May 1975.

Haan, N. Hypothetical and actual moral reasoning in a situation of civil disobedience. *Journal of Personality and Social Psychology,* 1975, *32,* 255–270.

Haase, R. S., and Pepper, D. T. Nonverbal components of empathic communication. *Journal of Counseling Psychology,* 1972, *19,* 417–424.

Haber, G. M. The impact of tall buildings on users and neighbors. Paper presented at Conference on Human Response to Tall Buildings, American Institute of Architects, Chicago, July 1975.

Hacker, H. M. Women as a minority group. *Social Forces,* 1951, *30,* 60–69.

Hacker, H. M. Women as a minority group: Twenty years later. *International Journal of Group Tensions,* 1974, *4,* 122–132.

Hagen, R., and Kahn, A. Discrimination against competent women. *Journal of Applied Social Psychology,* 1975, *5,* 362–376.

Hall, E. T. A system for the notation of proxemic behavior. *American Anthropologist,* 1963, *65,* 1003–1026.

Hall, E. T. *The hidden dimension.* New York: Doubleday, 1966.

Hall, W. S., Cross, W. E., and Freedle, R. Stages in the development of black awareness: An exploratory investigation. In *Black psychology,* edited by R. L. Jones. New York: Harper & Row, 1972.

Hamilton, D. L., and Fallot, R. D. Information salience as a weighting factor in impression formation. *Journal of Personality and Social Psychology,* 1974, *30,* 444–448.

Hamilton, D. L., and Zanna, M. P. Differential weighting of favorable and unfavorable attributes in impressions of personality. *Journal of Experimental Research in Personality,* 1972, *6,* 204–212.

Hamilton, P., and Copeman, A. The effect of alcohol and noise on components of a tracking and monitoring task. *British Journal of Psychology,* 1970, *61,* 149–156.

Hamm, N. H., Baum, M. R., and Nikels, K. W. Effects of race and exposure on judgments of interpersonal favorability. *Journal of Experimental Social Psychology,* 1975, *11,* 14–24.

Hamner, W. C. Effects of bargaining strategy and pressure to reach agreement in a stalemated negotiation. *Journal of Personality and Social Psychology,* 1974, *30,* 458–467.

Haney, C., Banks, W., and Zimbardo, P. Interpersonal dynamics in a simulated prison. *International Journal of Criminology and Penology,* 1973, *1,* 69–97.

Hanratty, M. A., O'Neal, E., and Sulzer, J. L. Effect of frustration upon imitation and aggression. *Journal of Personality and Social Psychology,* 1972, *21,* 30–34.

Harding, J., Proshansky, N., Kutner, B., and

Chein, I. Prejudice and ethnic relations. In *Handbook of social psychology,* vol. 5, edited by G. Lindzey and E. Aronson. Reading, Mass.: Addison-Wesley, 1969.

Hardy, R. C. Effect of leadership style on the performance of small classroom groups: A test of the contingency model. *Journal of Personality and Social Psychology,* 1971, *19,* 367–374.

Hariton, E. B., and Singer, J. L. Women's fantasies during sexual intercourse: Normative and theoretical implications. *Journal of Consulting and Clinical Psychology,* 1974, *42,* 313–322.

Harris. M. B. Mediators between frustration and aggression in a field experiment. *Journal of Experimental Social Psychology,* 1974, *10,* 561–571.

Harris, V. A., and Jellison, J. M. Fear-arousing communications, false physiological feedback, and the acceptance of recommendations. *Journal of Experimental Social Psychology,* 1971, *7,* 269–279.

Harrison, A. A. Response competition, frequency, exploratory behavior, and liking. *Journal of Personality and Social Psychology,* 1968, *9,* 363–368.

Harrison, A. A. Exposure and popularity. *Journal of Personality,* 1969, 359–377.

Harrison-Ross, P., and Wyden, B. *The black child: A parent's guide to raising happy and healthy children.* New York: Medallion, 1973.

Hartley, R. E., and Hardesty, F. P. Children's perceptions of sex roles in childhood. *Journal of Genetic Psychology,* 1964, *105,* 43–51.

Hartman, W. E., and Fithian, M. A. *Treatment of sexual dysfunction.* New York: Aronson, 1974.

Hartup, W. W. Peer interaction and social organization. In *Manual of child psychology,* edited by P. H. Mussen. New York: John Wiley & Sons, 1970.

Hartup, W. W., Moore, S., and Sager, G. Avoidance of inappropriate sex-typing by young children. *Journal of Consulting Psychology,* 1963, *27,* 467–473.

Hartup, W. W., and Zook, E. Z. Sex-role preferences in three- and four-year-old children. *Journal of Consulting Psychology,* 1960, *24,* 420–426.

Harvey, J. H., Harris, B., and Barnes, R. D. Actor-observer differences in the perceptions of responsibility and freedom. *Journal of Personality and Social Psychology,* 1975, *32,* 22–28.

Hastorf, A. H. The reinforcement of individual actions in a group situation. In *Research in behavior modification,* edited by L. Krasner and L. P. Ullman. New York: Holt, Rinehart, & Winston, 1965.

Hayes, S. C., Johnson, S. V., and Cone, J. D. The marked item technique: A practical procedure for litter control. Unpublished manuscript, West Virginia University, 1975.

Heberlein, T. A., and Black, J. S. Attitudinal specificity and the prediction of behavior in a field setting. *Journal of Personality and Social Psychology,* 1976, *33,* 474–479.

Heider, F. *The psychology of interpersonal relations.* New York: John Wiley and Sons, 1958.

Heilbroner, R. L. *An inquiry into the human prospect.* New York: Norton, 1974.

Heilman, M. E. Threats and promises: Reputational consequences and transfer of credibility. *Journal of Experimental Social Psychology,* 1974, *10,* 310–324.

Heilman, M. E., and Garner, K. A. Counteracting the boomerang: The effects of choice on compliance to threats and promises. *Journal of Personality and Social Psychology,* 1975, *31,* 911–917.

Heingartner, A., and Hall, J. V. Affective consequences in adults and children of repeated exposure to auditory stimuli. *Journal of Personality and Social Psychology,* 1974, *29,* 719–723.

Heller, J. F., Pallak, M. S., and Picek, J. M. The interactive effects of intent and threat on boomerang attitude change. *Journal of Personality and Social Psychology,* 1973, *26,* 273–279.

Henchy, T., and Glass, D. C. Evaluation apprehension and the social facilitation of dominant and subordinate responses. *Journal of Personality and Social Psychology,* 1968, *10,* 446–454.

Hendrick, C. *Perspectives on social psychology.* Hillsdale, N.J.: Lawrence Erlbaum, 1976.

Hendrick, C., Bixenstine, V. E., and Hawkins, G. Race versus belief similarity as determinants of attraction: A search for a fair test. *Journal of Personality and Social Psychology,* 1971, *17,* 250–258.

Hendrick, C., Giesen, M., and Borden, R. False physiological feedback and persuasion: Effect of fear arousal versus fear reduction. *Journal of Personality,* 1975, *43,* 196–214.

Hendrick, C., and Jones, R. A. *The nature of theory and research in social psychology.* New York: Academic Press, 1972.

Herrell, J. M. Sex differences in emotional responses to "erotic literature." *Journal of Consulting and Clinical Psychology,* 1975, *43,* 921.

Heshka, S., and Nelson, Y. Interpersonal speaking distance as a function of age, sex, and relationship. *Sociometry,* 1972, *35,* 491–498.

Higbee, K. L. Fifteen years of fear arousal: Research on threat appeals, 1953–1968. *Psychological Bulletin,* 1969, *72,* 426–444.

Hiroto, D. S., and Seligman, M. E. P. Generality of learned helplessness in man. *Journal of Personality and Social Psychology,* 1975, *31,* 311–327.

Hobart, C. W. Sexual permissiveness in young English and French Canadians. *Journal of Marriage and the Family,* 1972, *34,* 292–303.

Hochberg, J., and Galper, R. E. Attribution of intention as a function of physiognomy. *Memory and Cognition,* 1974, *2,* 39–42.

Hockey, G. R. J. The effect of loud noise in attention selectivity. *Quarterly Journal of Experimental Psychology,* 1970, *22,* 28–36.

Hodges, L. A., and Byrne, D. Verbal dogmatism as a potentiator of intolerance. *Journal of Personality and Social Psychology,* 1972, *21,* 312–317.

Hoffman, M. L. Altruistic behavior and the parent-child relationship. *Journal of Personality and Social Psychology,* 1975a, *31,* 937–943.

Hoffman, M. L. Sex differences in moral internalization and values. *Journal of Personality and Social Psychology,* 1975b, *32,* 720–729.

Hogan, R. Moral conduct and moral character: A psychological perspective. *Psychological Bulletin,* 1973, *79,* 217–232.

Hokanson, J. E. Psychophysiological evaluation of the catharsis hypothesis. In *The dynamics of aggression,* edited by E. I. Megargee and J. E. Hokanson. New York: Harper & Row, 1970.

Hokanson, J. E., and Burgess, M. The effects of three types of aggression on vascular processes. *Journal of Abnormal and Social Psychology,* 1962, *64,* 446–449.

Hokanson, J. E., Burgess, M., and Cohen, M. E. Effects of displaced aggression on systolic blood pressure. *Journal of Abnormal and Social Psychology,* 1963, *67,* 214–218.

Hollander, E. P. Independence, conformity and civil liberties: Some implications from social psychological research. *Journal of Social Issues,* 1975, *31,* 55–67.

Hollander, E. P., and Julian, J. W. Contemporary trends in the analysis of leadership processes. *Psychological Bulletin,* 1969, *71,* 387–397.

Hollander, E. P., and Julian, J. W. Studies in leader legitimacy, influence, and innovation. In *Advances in experimental social psychology,* vol. 5, edited by L. Berkowitz. New York: Academic Press, 1970.

Holmes, D. S., and Bennett, D. H. Experiments to answer questions raised by the use of deception in psychological research. *Journal of Personality and Social Psychology,* 1974, *29,* 358–367.

Holmes, J. G., Miller, D. T., and Lerner, M. J. Symbolic threat in helping situations: The "exchange fiction." Unpublished manuscript, University of Waterloo, 1974.

Holstein, C. M., Goldstein, J. W., and Bem, D. J. The importance of expressive behavior, involvement, sex, and need-approval in inducing liking. *Journal of Experimental Social Psychology,* 1971, *7,* 534–544.

Homans, G. C. *Social behavior: Its elementary forms.* New York: Harcourt, Brace, 1961.

Horner, M. S. Feminity and successful achievement: A basic inconsistency. In *Feminine personality and conflict,* edited by J. M. Bardwick et al. Belmont, Calif: Wadsworth, 1970.

Horner, M. S. Toward an understanding of achievement-related conflicts in women. *Journal of Social Issues,* 1972, *28,* 157–176.

Hornstein, H. A., Lakind, E., Frankel, G., and Manne, S. Effects of knowledge about remote social events on prosocial behavior, social conception, and mood. *Journal of Personality and Social Psychology,* 1975, *32,* 1038–1046.

Horowitz, M. J., Duff, D. F., and Stratton, L. O. Body-buffer zone. *Archives of General Psychiatry,* 1964, *11,* 651–656.

Hovland, C. I., Lumsdaine, A. A., and Sheffield, F. D. *Experiments on mass communication.* Princeton: Princeton University Press, 1949.

Hovland, C. I., and Weiss, W. The influence of source credibility on communication effectiveness. *Public Opinion Quarterly,* 1951, *15,* 635–650.

Howard, J. L., Reifler, C. B., and Liptzin, M. B. Effects of exposure to pornography. In *Technical report of the Commission on Obscenity and Pornography,* vol. 8, Washington, D.C.: U.S. Government Printing Office, 1971.

Howard, W., and Crana, W. D. Effects of sex, conversation, location, and size of observer group on bystander intervention in a high risk situation. *Sociometry,* 1974, *37,* 491–507.

Hoyt, M. F., Henley, M. D., and Collins, B. E. Studies in forced compliance: Confluence of choice and consequence on attitude change. *Journal of Personality and Social Psychology,* 1972, *23,* 204–210.

Hraba, J., and Grant, G. Black is beautiful: A reexamination of racial preference and identification. *Journal of Personality and Social Psychology,* 1970, *16,* 398–402.

Hunt, M. *Sexual behavior in the 1970s.* Chicago: Playboy, 1974.

Husband, R. W. Cooperative versus solitary problem solution. *Journal of Social Psychology,* 1940, *11,* 405–409.

Huston, T. L., ed. *Foundations of interpersonal attraction.* New York: Academic Press, 1974.

Huston, T. L., and Korte, C. The responsive bystander: Why he helps. In *Moral development and behavior: Theory, research, and social issues,* edited by T. Lickona. New York: Holt, Rinehart, & Winston, 1976.

Huxley, A. *Brave new world.* Avon, Conn.: Heritage Press, 1974 (reprint of 1932 edition).

Ickes, W. J., Wicklund, R. A., and Ferris, C. B. Objective self awareness and self esteem. *Journal of Experimental Social Psychology,* 1973, *9,* 202–219.

Innes, J. M., and Young, R. F. The effect of presence of an audience, evaluation apprehension and objective self-awareness on learning. *Journal of Experimental Social Psychology,* 1975, *11,* 35–42.

Insel, P. M., and Moos, R. H. Psychological environments: Expanding the scope of human ecology. *American Psychologist,* 1974, *29,* 179–188.

Insko, C. A., and Melson, W. H. Verbal reinforcement of attitude in laboratory and nonlaboratory contexts. *Journal of Personality,* 1969, *37,* 25–40.

Isen, A. M. Success, failure, attention, and reaction to others: The warm glow of success. *Journal of Personality and Social Psychology,* 1970, *15,* 294–301.

Isen, A. M., Horn, N., and Rosenhan, D. L. Effects of success and failure on children's generosity. *Journal of Personality and Social Psychology,* 1973, *27,* 239–247.

Isen, A. M., and Levin, P. F. The effect of feeling good on helping: Cookies and kindness. *Jour-nal of Personality and Social Psychology,* 1972, *21,* 384–388.

Izard, E. E., and Caplan, S. Sex differences in emotional responses to erotic literature. *Journal of Consulting and Clinical Psychology,* 1974, *42,* 468.

Izard, E. E. *The face of emotion.* New York: Appleton-Century-Crofts, 1976.

Izzett, R. R. Effects of self-praise and self-esteem on interpersonal attraction. *Representative Research in Social Psychology,* 1976, *7,* 1–5.

Jacobs, P. A., Brunton, M., and Melville, M. M. Aggressive behavior, mental subnormality, and the XYY male. *Nature,* 1965, *208,* 1351–1352.

Jaffe, Y., Malamuth, N., Feingold, J., and Feshbach, S. Sexual arousal and behavioral aggression. *Journal of Personality and Social Psychology,* 1974, *30,* 759–764.

Janis, I. L. *Victims of groupthink.* Boston: Houghton Mifflin, 1972.

Janis, I. L., Kaye, D., and Kirschner, P. Facilitating effects of 'eating while reading' on responsiveness to persuasive communications. *Journal of Personality and Social Psychology,* 1965, *1,* 181–186.

Jarvik, L. F., Klodin, V., and Matsuyama, S. S. Human aggression and the extra Y chromosome: Fact or fantasy? *American Psychologist,* 1973, *28,* 674–682.

Jazwinski, C. H., Nadler, A., and Lau, S. The consequences of social comparison: Being worse is bad, but so is being better. Unpublished manuscript, Purdue University, 1976.

Jeffers, H. P., and Levitan, D. *Sex in the executive suite.* Chicago: Playboy, 1972.

Jellison, J. M., and Davis, D. Relationships between perceived ability and attitude extremity. *Journal of Personality and Social Psychology,* 1973, *27,* 430–436.

Jones, C., and Aronson, E. Attribution of fault to a rape victim as a function of respectability of the victim. *Journal of Personality and Social Psychology,* 1973, *26,* 415–419.

Jones, E. E. *Ingratiation: A social psychological analysis.* New York: Appleton-Century-Crofts, 1964.

Jones, E. E. Conformity as a tactic of ingratiation. *Science,* 1965, *149,* 144–150.

Jones, E. E., Bell, L., and Aronson, E. The reciprocation of attraction from similar and dissimilar others. In *Experimental social psychol-*

ogy, edited by C. McClintock. New York: Holt, Rinehart, & Winston, 1972.

Jones, E. E., and Davis, K. E. From acts to dispositions: The attribution process in person perception. In *Advances in experimental social psychology,* vol. 2, edited by L. Berkowitz. New York: Academic Press, 1965.

Jones, E. E., Gergen, K. J., and Jones, R. G. Tactics of ingratiation among leaders and subordinates in a status hierarchy. *Psychological Monographs,* 1963, *77,* 3 (Whole No. 566).

Jones, E. E., and Nisbett, R. E. The actor and the observer: Divergent perceptions of the causes of behavior. In *Attribution: Perceiving the causes of behavior,* edited by E. E. Jones et al. Morristown, N.J.: General Learning Press, 1972.

Jones, E. E., and Sigall, H. The bogus pipeline: A new paradigm for measuring affect and attitude. *Psychological Bulletin,* 1971, *76,* 349–364.

Jones, E. E., Worchel, S., Goethals, G. T., and Grumet, J. F. Prior expectancy and behavioral extremity as determinants of attitude attribution. *Journal of Experimental Social Psychology,* 1971, *7,* 59–80.

Jones, J. M. *Prejudice and racism.* Reading, Mass.: Addison-Wesley, 1972.

Jones, R., and Cooper, J. Mediation of experimenter effects. *Journal of Personality and Social Psychology,* 1971, *20,* 70–74.

Jovanovic, U. J. The recording of physiological evidence of genital arousal in human males and females. *Archives of Sexual Behavior,* 1971, *1,* 309–320.

Kagan, J., Hosken, B., and Watson, S. The child's conceptualizations of the parents. *Child Development,* 1961, *32,* 625–636.

Kahn, A., Hottes, J., and Davis, W. L. Cooperation and optimal responding in the prisoner's dilemma game: Effects of sex and physical attractiveness. *Journal of Personality and Social Psychology,* 1971, *17,* 267–279.

Kalven, H. G., Jr., and Zeisel, H. *The American Jury.* Boston: Little, Brown, 1966.

Kangas, L. W. Integrated incentives for fertility control. *Science,* 1970, *169,* 1278–1283.

Kaplan, M. F. Dispositional effects and weight of information in impression formation. *Journal of Personality and Social Psychology,* 1971, *18,* 279–284.

Kaplan, M. F. The modifying effect of stimulus information on the consistency of individual differences in impression formation. *Journal of Experimental Research in Personality,* 1972, *6,* 213–219.

Kaplan, M. F. Information integration in social judgment: Interaction of judge and informational components. In *Human judgment and decision processes,* edited by M. Kaplan and S. Schwartz. New York: Academic Press, 1975.

Kaplan, M. F. Measurement and generality of response dispositions in person perception. *Journal of Personality,* 1976, *44,* 79–194.

Kaplan, R. Some psychological benefits of gardening. *Environment and Behavior,* 1973, *2,* 145–161.

Karaz, V., and Perlman, D. Attribution at the wire: Consistency and outcome finish strong. *Journal of Experimental Social Psychology,* 1975, *11,* 470–477.

Karlins, M., Coffman, T. L., and Walter, G. On the fading of social stereotypes: Studies in three generations of college students. *Journal of Personality and Social Psychology,* 1969, *13,* 1–16.

Katz, D., and Braly, K. W. Racial stereotypes of 100 college students. *Journal of Abnormal and Social Psychology,* 1933, *29,* 280–290.

Katz, I. Experimental studies of Negro-white relationships. In *Advances in experimental social psychology,* vol. 5, edited by L. Berkowitz. New York: Academic Press, 1970.

Katz, I., and Gurin, P., eds. *Race and the social sciences.* New York: Basic Books, 1969.

Keating, J. P., and Brock, T. C. Acceptance of persuasion and the inhibition of counterargumentation under various distraction tasks. *Journal of Experimental Social Psychology,* 1974, *10,* 301–309.

Kelley, H. H. Moral evaluation. *American Psychologist,* 1971, *26,* 293–300.

Kelley, H. H. Attribution in social interaction. In *Attribution: Perceiving the causes of behavior,* edited by E. E. Jones et al. Morristown, N.J.: General Learning Press, 1972.

Kelley, H. H. The processes of causal attribution. *American Psychologist,* 1973, *28,* 107–128.

Kelley, H. H., and Stahelski, A. J. Errors in perception of intentions in a mixed-motive game. *Journal of Experimental Social Psychology,* 1970, *6,* 379–400.

Kelley, K., and Byrne, D. Attraction and altruism: With a little help from my friends. *Journal of Research in Personality*, 1976, *10*, 59–68.

Kelman, H. C. Human use of human subjects: The problem of deception in social psychological experiments. *Psychological Bulletin*, 1967, *67*, 1–11.

Kennedy, J. F. *Profiles in courage.* New York: Harper, 1956.

Kerpelman, J. P., and Himmelfarb, S. Partial reinforcement effects in attitude acquisition and counterconditioning. *Journal of Personality and Social Psychology*, 1971, *19*, 301–305.

Kessler, J. J., and Wiener, Y. Self-consistency and inequity dissonance as factors in undercompensation. *Organizational Behavior and Human Performance*, 1972, *8*, 456–466.

Kiesler, C. A. Attraction to the group and conformity to group norms. *Journal of Personality*, 1963, *31*, 559–569.

Kiesler, C. A., and Kiesler, S. B. *Conformity.* Reading, Mass.: Addison-Wesley, 1969.

Kiesler, C. A., and Munson, P. A. Attitudes and opinions. In *Annual review of psychology,* vol. 26, edited by M. R. Rosenzweig and L. W. Porter. Palo Alto, Calif.: Annual Reviews, 1975.

Kilham, W., and Mann, L. Level of destructive obedience as a function of transmitter and executant roles in the Milgram obedience paradigm. *Journal of Personality and Social Psychology*, 1974, *29*, 696–702.

Kimbrell, D. L., and Blake, R. E. Motivational factors in the violation of a prohibition. *Journal of Abnormal and Social Psychology*, 1958, *56*, 132–133.

Kinsey, A., Pomeroy, W. B., and Martin, C. E. *Sexual behavior in the human male.* Philadelphia: Saunders, 1948.

Kinsey, A. C., Pomeroy, W. B., Martin, C. E., and Gebhard, P. H. *Sexual behavior in the human female.* Philadelphia: Saunders, 1953.

Kinzel, A. S. Body buffer zone in violent prisoners. *American Journal of Psychiatry*, 1970, *127*, 59–64.

Kitano, H. H. L. *Race relations.* Englewood Cliffs, N.J.: Prentice-Hall, 1974.

Klapper, J. T. The impact of viewing "aggression:" Studies and problems of extrapolation. In *Violence and the mass media,* edited by O. N. Larsen. New York: Harper & Row, 1968.

Kleck, R. E., Buck, P. L., Goller, W. C., London, R. S., Pfeiffer, J. R., and Vukcevic, D. P. Effect

of stigmatizing conditions on the use of personal space. *Psychological Reports*, 1968, *23*, 111–118.

Klein, D. C., Fencil-Morse, E., and Seligman, M. E. P. Learned helplessness, depression, and the attribution of failure. *Journal of Personality and Social Psychology*, 1976, *33*, 508–516.

Kleinke, C. L. *First impressions: The psychology of encountering others.* Englewood Cliffs, N.J.: Prentice-Hall, 1975.

Kleinke, C. L., Meeker, F. B., and LaFong, C. Effects of gaze, touch, and use of name on evaluation of "engaged" couples. *Journal of Research in Personality*, 1974, *7*, 368–373.

Kleinke, C. L., Staneski, R. A., and Berger, D. E. Evaluation of an interviewer as a function of interviewer gaze, reinforcement of subject gaze, and interviewer attractiveness. *Journal of Personality and Social Psychology*, 1975, *31*, 115–122.

Kleinke, C. L., Staneski, R. A., and Pipp, S. L. Effects of gaze, distance, and attractiveness on males' first impressions of females. *Representative Research in Social Psychology*, 1975, *6*, 7–12.

Knapp, M. L. *Nonverbal communication in human interaction.* New York: Holt, Rinehart, & Winston, 1972.

Knowles, E. S., Kreuser, B., Haas, S., Hyde, M., and Schuchart, G. E. Group size and the extension of social space boundaries. *Journal of Personality and Social Psychology*, 1976, *33*, 647–654.

Knott, P. D., and Drost, B. A. Effects of varying intensity of attack and fear arousal on the intensity of counter aggression. *Journal of Personality*, 1972, *40*, 27–37.

Knox, R. E., and Inkster, J. A. Postdecision dissonance at post time. *Journal of Personality and Social Psychology*, 1968, *8*, 319–323.

Knox, R. E., and Safford, R. K. Group caution at the race track. *Journal of Experimental Social Psychology*, 1976, *12*, 317–324.

Kogan, N., and Wallach, M. A. *Risk taking: A study in cognition and personality.* New York: Holt, Rinehart, & Winston, 1964.

Kohlberg, L. A. A cognitive developmental analysis of children's sex-role concepts and attitudes. In *The development of sex differences,* edited by E. E. Maccoby. Stanford: Stanford University Press, 1966.

Kohlberg, L. A cognitive-developmental approach to socialization. In *Handbook of sociali-*

zation, edited by D. Goslin. Chicago: Rand-McNally, 1969.

Komorita, S. S., and Brenner, A. R. Bargaining and concession making under bilateral monopoly. *Journal of Personality and Social Psychology,* 1968, *9,* 15–20.

Komorita, S. S., Sheposh, J. P., and Braver, L. S. Power, the use of power, and cooperative choice in a two-person game. *Journal of Personality and Social Psychology,* 1968, *8,* 134–142.

Konečni, V. J. Annoyance, type and duration of postannoyance activity, and aggression: The "cathartic" effect. *Journal of Experimental Psychology: General,* 1975a, *104,* 76–102.

Konečni, V. J. The mediation of aggressive behavior: Arousal level versus anger and cognitive labeling. *Journal of Personality and Social Psychology,* 1975b, *32,* 706–712.

Konečni, V. J., and Ebbesen, E. G. Disinhibition versus the cathartic effect: Artifact and substance. *Journal of Personality and Social Psychology,* 1976, *34,* 352–365.

Konečni, V. J., Libuser, L., Morton, H., and Ebbesen, E. B. Effects of a violation of personal space on escape and helping responses. *Journal of Experimental Social Psychology,* 1975, *11,* 288–299.

Korte, C., and Kerr, N. Response to altruistic opportunities in urban and nonurban settings. *Journal of Social Psychology,* 1975, *95,* 183–184.

Kovel, J. *White racism: A psychohistory.* New York: Pantheon, 1971.

Kraemer, H. C., Becker, H. B., Brodie, H. X. H., Doering, C. H., Moos, R. H., and Hamburg, D. A. Orgasmic frequency and plasma testosterone levels in normal human males. *Archives of Sexual Behavior,* 1976, *5,* 125–132.

Krames, L., Costanzo, D. J., and Carr, W. J. Responses of rats to odors from novel versus original sex partners. *Proceedings of the American Psychological Association,* 75th Annual Convention, 1967, 117–118.

Kravetz, D. F. Heart rate as a minimal cue for the occurrence of vicarious classical conditioning. *Journal of Personality and Social Psychology,* 1974, *29,* 125–131.

Krebs, D. L. Altruism—An examination of the concept and a review of the literature. *Psychological Bulletin,* 1970, *73,* 258–302.

Krebs, D. L. Empathy and altruism. *Journal of Personality and Social Psychology,* 1975, *32,* 1134–1146.

Krieger, W. The effects of visual aesthetics upon mood and problem solving efficiency. Unpublished master's thesis, Purdue University, 1972.

Krivonos, P. D., Byrne, D., and Friedrich, G. W. The effect of attitude similarity on task performance. *Journal of Applied Social Psychology,* 1976, *44,* 179–194.

Krout, M. An experimental attempt to produce unconscious manual symbolic movements. *Journal of General Psychology,* 1954, *51,* 93–120.

Kruglanski, A. W., Riter, A., Amitai, A., Margolin, B., Shabtai, L., and Zaksh, D. Can money enhance intrinsic motivation?: A test of the content-consequences hypothesis. *Journal of Personality and Social Psychology,* 1975, *31,* 479–486.

Kryter, K. D. *The effects of noise on man.* New York: Academic Press, 1970.

Kuhlman, D. M., and Marshello, A. F. J. Individual differences in game motivation as moderators of preprogrammed strategy effects in prisoner's dilemma. *Journal of Personality and Social Psychology,* 1975, *32,* 922–931.

Kuralt, C. Reporting the "little people." *Columbia Journalism Review,* 1972, *10,* 17–22

Kutner, S. J. Sex guilt and the sexual behavior sequence. *Journal of Sex Research,* 1971, *7,* 107–115.

Kutschinsky, B. The effect of pornography: A pilot experiment on perception, behavior, and attitudes, In *Technical report of the Commission on Obscenity and Pornography,* vol. 8. Washington, D.C.: U.S. Government Printing Office, 1971.

Kutschinsky, B. The effect of easy availability of pornography on the incidence of sex crimes: The Danish experience. *Journal of Social Issues,* 1973, *29* (3), 163–181.

Lamm, H., and Sauer, C. Discussion-induced shift toward higher demands in negotiation. *European Journal of Social Psychology,* 1974, *4,* 85–88.

Landy, D., and Mettee, D. Evaluation of an aggressor as a function of exposure to cartoon humor. *Journal of Personality and Social Psychology,* 1969, *12,* 66–71.

LaPiere, R. T. Attitudes and actions. *Social Forces,* 1934, *13,* 230–237.

Latané, B., and Dabbs, J. M., Jr. Sex, group size and helping in three cities. *Sociometry,* 1975,

38, 180–194.

Latané, B., and Darley, J. M. Group inhibition of bystander intervention in emergencies. *Journal of Personality and Social Psychology,* 1968, *10,* 215–221.

Latané, B., and Darley, J. M. *The unresponsive bystander: Why doesn't he help?* New York: Appleton-Century-Crofts, 1970.

Latané, B., and Glass, D. C. Social and nonsocial attraction in rats. *Journal of Personality and Social Psychology,* 1968, *9,* 142–146.

Latané, B., and Rodin, J. A lady in distress: Inhibiting effects of friends and strangers on bystander intervention. *Journal of Experimental Social Psychology,* 1969, *5,* 189–202.

Latta, R. M. There's method in our madness: Interpersonal attraction as a multidimensional construct. *Journal of Research in Personality,* 1976, *10,* 76–82.

Laughlin, P. R., and Jaccard, J. J. Social facilitation and observational learning of individuals and cooperative pairs. *Journal of Personality and Social Psychology,* 1975, *32,* 873–879.

Lavrakas, P. J. Female preferences for male physiques. Paper presented at the meeting of the Midwestern Psychological Association, Chicago, May 1975.

Law, O. T., and Gerbrandt, L. K. Sexual preference in female rats: I. Choices in tests with copulation. *Psychonomic Science,* 1967, *8,* 493–494.

Lazarus, R. S. *Psychological stress and the coping process.* New York: McGraw-Hill, 1966.

Lazarus, R. S., Speisman, J. C., and Mordkoff, A. M. Experimental analysis of a film used as a threatening stimulus. *Journal of Consulting Psychology,* 1964, *28,* 23–33.

Lazarus, R. S., Speisman, J. C., Mordkoff, A. M., and Davison, L. A. A laboratory study of psychological stress produced by a motion picture film. *Psychological Monographs,* 1962, *76* (Whole No. 553).

Leak, G. K. Effects of hostility arousal and aggressive humor on catharsis and humor preference. *Journal of Personality and Social Psychology,* 1974, *30,* 736–740.

Leary, R. W., and Moroney, R. J. The effects of home-cage environments in monkeys. *Journal of Comparative and Physiological Psychology,* 1962, *55,* 256–259.

Lee, R. The advantages of carpets in mental hospitals. *Mental Hospitals,* 1965, *16,* 324–325.

Lefkowitz, M. M., Eron, L. D., Walder, L. O., and Huesman, L. R. Television violence and child aggression: A followup study. In *Television and social behavior,* vol 3, edited by G. A. Comstock and E. A. Rubinstein. Rockville, Md.: National Institute of Mental Health, 1972.

Legant, P., and Mettee, D. R. Turning the other cheek versus getting even: Vengeance, equity, and attraction. *Journal of Personality and Social Psychology,* 1973, *25,* 243–253.

Leonard, R. L., Jr. Self-concept and attraction for similar and dissimilar others. *Journal of Personality and Social Psychology,* 1975, *31,* 926–929.

Lepper, M. R., and Greene, D. Turning play into work: Effects of adult surveillance and extrinsic rewards on children's intrinsic motivation. *Journal of Personality and Social Psychology,* 1975, *31,* 479–486.

Lepper, M. R., and Greene, D. On understanding "overjustification:" A reply to Reiss and Sushinsky. *Journal of Personality and Social Psychology,* 1976, *33,* 25–35.

Lepper, M. R., Greene, D., and Nisbett, R. E. Undermining children's intrinsic interest with extrinsic reward: A test of the "overjustification" hypothesis. *Journal of Personality and Social Psychology,* 1973, *28,* 129–137.

Lerner, M. J. The desire for justice and reactions to victims. In *Altruism and helping behavior,* edited by J. Macaulay and L. Berkowitz. New York: Academic Press, 1970.

Lerner, M. J. Social psychology of justice and interpersonal attraction. In *Foundations of interpersonal attraction,* edited by T. L. Huston. New York: Academic Press, 1974.

Lerner, M. J., and Agar, E. The consequences of perceived similarity: Attraction and rejection, approach and avoidance. *Journal of Experimental Research in Personality,* 1972, *6,* 69–75.

Lerner, M. J., Miller, D. T., and Holmes, J. G. Deserving versus justice: A contemporary dilemma. In *Advances in experimental social psychology,* vol. 12, edited by L. Berkowitz and E. Walster. New York: Academic Press, 1975.

Lerner, M. J., and Simmons, C. H. Observer's reaction to the "innocent victim:" Compassion or rejection? *Journal of Personality and Social Psychology,* 1966, *4,* 203–210.

Lerner, R. M., and Gellert, E. Body build identification, preference, and aversion in children. *Developmental Psychology,* 1969, *1,* 456–462.

Leventhal, G. S. The distribution of rewards and resources in groups and organizations. In *Advances in experimental social psychology,* edited by L. Berkowitz and E. Walster. New York: Academic Press, 1976a.

Leventhal, G. S. Fairness in social relationships. In *Contemporary topics in social psychology,* edited by J. Thibaut, J. T. Spence, and R. Carson. Morristown, N.J.: General Learning Press, 1976b.

Leventhal, G. S., Michaels, J. W., and Sanford, C. Inequity and interpersonal conflict: Reward allocation and secrecy about reward as methods of preventing conflict. *Journal of Personality and Social Psychology,* 1972, *23,* 88–102.

Leventhal, G. S., Weiss, T., and Long, G. Equity, reciprocity, and reallocating rewards in the dyad. *Journal of Personality and Social Psychology,* 1969, *13,* 300–305.

Leventhal, G. S., and Weiss, T. Status congruence, needs, and the response to inequity. *Journal of Personality and Social Psychology,* 1977, (in press).

Leventhal, G. S., and Weiss, T. Attribution of value, equity, and the prevention of waste in reward allocation. *Journal of Personality and Social Psychology,* 1973, *27,* 276–286.

Leventhal, H. Findings and theory in the study of fear communications. In *Advances in experimental social psychology,* vol. 5, edited by L. Berkowitz. New York: Academic Press, 1970.

Leventhal, H., Watts, J. C., and Pagano, F. Effects of fear and instructions on how to cope with danger. *Journal of Personality and Social Psychology,* 1967, *6,* 313–321.

Levin, I. *The Stepford wives.* New York: Random House, 1972.

Levin, P. F., and Isen, A. M. Further studies on the effect of feeling good on helping. *Sociometry,* 1975, *38,* 141–147.

Levinger, G. Little sand box and big quarry: Comments on Byrne's paradigmatic spade for research on interpersonal attraction. *Representative Research in Social Psychology,* 1972, *3,* 3–19.

Levinger, G. A three-level approach to attraction: Toward an understanding of pair relatedness. In *Foundations of interpersonal attraction,* edited by T. L. Huston. New York: Academic

Press, 1974.

Levinger, G., and Breedlove, J. Interpersonal attraction and agreement: A study of marriage partners. *Journal of Personality and Social Psychology,* 1966, *3,* 367–372.

Levinger, G., and Schneider, D. J. A test of the risk is a value hypothesis. *Journal of Personality and Social Psychology,* 1969, *11,* 165–169.

Levinger, G., and Snoek, J. D. *Attraction in relationship: A new look at interpersonal attraction.* Morristown, N.J.: General Learning Press, 1972.

Levitt, E. E., and Brady, J. P. Sexual preferences in young adult males and some correlates. *Journal of Clinical Psychology,* 1965, *21,* 347–354.

Lewin, K., Lippitt, R., and White, R. K. Patterns of aggressive behavior in experimentally created "social climates." *Journal of Social Psychology,* 1939, *10,* 271–299.

Lewis, C. A. People-plant interaction: A man environment relationship. Paper presented at the fifth annual convention of the Environmental Design Research Association, Milwaukee, May 1974.

Lewis, J., Baddeley, A. D., Bonham, K. G., and Lovett, D. Traffic pollution and mental efficiency. *Nature,* 1970, *225,* 96.

Ley, D., and Cybriwsky, R. The spatial ecology of stripped cars. *Environment and Behavior,* 1974, *6,* 53–68.

Leyens, J. P., Camino, L., Parke, R. D., and Berkowitz, L. Effects of movie violence on aggression in a field setting as a function of group dominance and cohesion. *Journal of Personality and Social Psychology,* 1975, *32,* 346–360.

Libby, R. W., and Nass, G. D. Parental views on teenage sexual behavior. *Journal of Sex Research,* 1971, *7,* 226–236.

Lickona, T. *Moral development and behavior: Theory, research, and social issues.* New York: Holt, Rinehart, and Winston, 1976.

Lieberson, S., and Silverman, A. R. The precipitants and underlying conditions of race riots. *American Sociological Review,* 1965, *30,* 887–898.

Liebert, R. M., and Baron, R. A. Some immediate effects of televised violence on children's behavior. *Developmental Psychology,* 1972, *6,* 469–475.

Linder, D. *Personal space.* Morristown, N.J.: General Learning Press, 1974.

Linder, D. E., Cooper, J., and Jones, E. E.

Decision freedom as a determinant of the role of incentive magnitude in attitude change. *Journal of Personality and Social Psychology,* 1967, *6,* 245–254.

Little, K. B. Cultural variations in social schemata. *Journal of Personality and Social Psychology,* 1968, *10,* 1–7.

Lohr, J. M., and Staats, A. W. Attitude conditioning in Sino-Tibetan languages. *Journal of Personality and Social Psychology,* 1973, *26,* 196–200.

Lombardo, J. P., Steigleder, M., and Feinberg, R. Internality-externality: The perception of negatively valued personality characteristics and interpersonal attraction. *Representative Research in Social Psychology,* 1975, *6,* 89–95.

London, J. *White fang.* Avon, Conn.: Heritage Press, 1973 (reprint of 1906 edition).

Lorenz, K. *On aggression.* New York: Harcourt, Brace, & World, 1966.

Lorenz, K. *Civilized man's eight deadly sins.* Harcourt, Brace, and Jovanovich, 1974.

Lott, A. J. The potential power of liking as a factor in social change. Paper presented at the meeting of the Southwestern Psychological Association, Austin, May, 1969.

Lott, A. J., and Lott, B. E. Group cohesiveness and individual learning. *Journal of Educational Psychology,* 1966, *57,* 61–73.

Lott, A. J., and Lott, B. E. The role of reward in the formation of positive interpersonal attitudes. In *Foundations of interpersonal attraction,* edited by T. L. Huston. New York: Academic Press, 1974.

Lott, B. S., and Sommer, R. Seating arrangements and status. *Journal of Personality and Social Psychology,* 1967, *7,* 90–95.

Luttage, W. G. The role of gonadal hormones in the sexual behavior of the rhesus monkey and human: A literature survey. *Archives of Sexual Behavior,* 1971, *1,* 61–88.

Lynch, K. *The image of the city.* Cambridge, Mass.: MIT Press, 1960.

Macaranas, E. A., and Savell, J. M. An experimental examination of two types of explanation for the prior-agreement/conformity relationship. *Representative Research in Social Psychology,* 1973, *4,* 75–84.

Maccoby, E. E., and Jacklin, C. N. *The psychology of sex differences.* Stanford: Stanford University Press, 1974.

Maccoby, E. E., and Wilson, W. C. Identification and observational learning from films. *Journal of Abnormal and Social Psychology,* 1957, *55,* 76–87.

Mallick, S. K., and McCandless, B. R. A study of catharsis of aggression. *Journal of Personality and Social Psychology,* 1966, *4,* 591–596.

Mann, J., Berkowitz, L., Sidman, J., Starr, S., and West, S. Satiation of the transient stimulating effect of erotic films. *Journal of Personality and Social Psychology,* 1974, *30, 729–735.*

Mann, R. D. A review of the relationships between personality and performance in small groups. *Psychological Bulletin,* 1959, *56,* 241–270.

Manning, S. A., and Taylor, D. A. Effects of viewed violence and aggression: Stimulation and catharsis. *Journal of Personality and Social Psychology,* 1975, *31,* 180–188.

Marsella, A. J., Escudero, M., and Gordon, P. The effects of dwelling density on mental disorders in Filipino men. *Journal of Health and Social Behavior,* 1970, *11,* 288–294.

Marshall, D. S., and Suggs, R. C. *Human sexual behavior.* Englewood Cliffs, N.J.: Prentice-Hall, 1971.

Martens, R. Palmar sweating and the presence of an audience. *Journal of Experimental Social Psychology,* 1969, *5,* 371–374.

Martens, R., and Landers, D. M. Evaluation potential as a determinant of coaction effects. *Journal of Experimental Social Psychology,* 1972, *8,* 347–359.

Martindale, D. A. Territorial dominance behavior in dyadic verbal interactions. *Proceedings of the American Psychological Association,* 79th Annual Convention, 1971, *6,* 305–306.

Maruyama, G., and Miller, N. Physical attractiveness and classroom acceptance. Social Science Research Institute Research Report 75–2. University of Southern California, Los Angeles, 1975.

Maslow, A. H., and Mintz, N. C. Effects of esthetic surroundings: I. Initial effects of three esthetic conditions upon perceiving "energy" and "well being" in faces. *Journal of Psychology,* 1956, *41,* 247–254.

Mason, W. A., and Lott, D. F. Ethology and comparative psychology. In *Annual review of psychology,* vol. 26, edited by M. R. Rosenzweig and L. W. Porter. Palo Alto, Calif.: Annual

Reviews, 1976.

Masor, H. N., Hornstein, H. A., and Tobin, T. A. Modeling, motivational interdependence, and helping. *Journal of Personality and Social Psychology,* 1973, *28,* 236–248.

Masters, W. H., and Johnson, V. E. *Human sexual response.* Boston: Little, Brown, 1966.

Masters, W. H., and Johnson, V. E. *The pleasure bond.* Boston: Little, Brown, 1974.

Mathews, K. E., and Cannon, L. K. Environmental noise level as a determinant of helping behavior. *Journal of Personality and Social Psychology,* 1975, *32,* 571–577.

Matlin, M. W., and Zajonc, R. B. Social facilitation of word associations. *Journal of Personality and Social Psychology,* 1968, *10,* 455–460.

McArthur, L. A. The how and what of why: Some determinants and consequences of causal attribution. *Journal of Personality and Social Psychology,* 1972, *22,* 171–193.

McCarthy, J. D., and Yancey, W. L. Uncle Tom and Mr. Charlie: Metaphysical pathos in the study of racism and personal disorganization. In *Race relations: Current perspectives,* edited by E. G. Epps. Cambridge, Mass.: Winthrop, 1973.

McCary, J. L. *Sexual myths and fallacies.* New York: Van Nostrand-Reinhold, 1971.

McCary, J. L. *Human sexuality.* New York: Van Nostrand-Reinhold, 1973.

McCauley, C., Kogan, N., and Teger, A. I. Order effects in answering risk dilemmas for self and others. *Journal of Personality and Social Psychology,* 1971, *20,* 423–424.

McCauley, C., Stitt, C. I., Woods, K., and Lipton, D. Group shift to caution at the race track. *Journal of Experimental Social Psychology,* 1973, *9,* 80–86.

McClelland, L. Interaction level and acquaintance as mediators of density effects. *Personality and Social Psychology Bulletin,* 1976, *2,* 175–178.

McClintock, C. G. Development of social motives in Anglo-American and Mexican-American children. *Journal of Personality and Social Psychology,* 1974, *29,* 348–354.

McClintock, C. G., Messick, D. M., Kuhlman, D. M., and Campos, F. T. Motivational basis of choice in three choice decomposed games. *Journal of Experimental Social Psychology,* 1973, *9,* 572–590.

McDougall, W. *Introduction to social psychology.* London: Methuen, 1908.

McFall, R. M., and Twentyman, C. T. Four experiments on the relative contributions of rehearsal, modeling, and coaching to assertion training. *Journal of Abnormal Psychology,* 1973, *81,* 199–218.

McGee, M. G., and Snyder, M. Attribution and behavior: Two field studies. *Journal of Personality and Social Psychology,* 1975, *32,* 185–190.

McGovern, L. P. Dispositional social anxiety and helping behavior under three conditions of threat. *Journal of Personality,* 1976, *44,* 84–97.

McGovern, L. P., Ditzian, J. L., and Taylor, S. P. The effect of one positive reinforcement on helping with cost. *Bulletin of the Psychonomic Society,* 1975a, *5,* 421–423.

McGovern, L. P., Ditzian, J. L., and Taylor, S. P. Sex and perceptions of dependency in a helping situation. *Bulletin of the Psychonomic Society,* 1975b, *5,* 336–338.

McGuire, W. J. Resistance to persuasion confirmed by active and passive prior refutation of the same and alternative counterarguments. *Journal of Abnormal and Social Psychology,* 1961, *63,* 326–332.

McGuire, W. J. The nature of attitudes and attitude change. In *Handbook of social psychology,* vol. 3, edited by G. Lindzey and E. Aronson. Reading, Mass.: Addison-Wesley, 1969.

McGuire, W. J. The Yin and Yang of progress in social psychology: Seven koan. *Journal of Personality and Social Psychology,* 1973, *26,* 446–456.

McGuire, W. J., and Papageorgis, D. The relative efficacy of various types of prior belief-defense in producing immunity against persuasion. *Journal of Abnormal and Social Psychology,* 1961, *62,* 327–337.

McKenna, R. H. Good Samaritanism in rural and urban settings: A nonreactive comparison of helping behavior of clergy and control subjects. *Representative Research in Social Psychology,* 1976, *7,* 58–65.

McMillen, D. L. Transgression, self-image, and compliant behavior. *Journal of Personality and Social Psychology,* 1971, *20,* 176–179.

McMillen, D. L., and Austin, J. B. Effect of positive feedback on compliance following transgression. *Psychonomic Science,* 1971, *24,* 59–61.

McNeel, S. P. Training cooperation in the prisoner's dilemma. *Journal of Experimental Social*

Psychology, 1973, *9,* 335–348.

McPeek, R. W., and Gross, A. E.   Evaluations of presidential campaign speakers as a function of similarity and expectancy disconfirmation. *Journal of Applied Social Psychology,* 1975, *5,* 75–85.

Mead, M.   *Sex and temperament in three primitive societies.*   New York: William Morrow, 1935.

Megargee, E. I.   Undercontrolled and overcontrolled personality types in extreme antisocial aggression. *Psychological Monographs,* 1966, *80* (Whole No. 611).

Megargee, E. I.   The role of inhibition in the assessment and understanding of violence.   In *The control of aggression and violence,* edited by J. L. Singer.   New York: Academic Press, 1971.

Mehrabian, A.   Inference of attitudes from the posture, orientation, and distance of a communicator. *Journal of Consulting and Clinical Psychology,* 1968a, *32,* 296–318.

Mehrabian, A.   Relationship of attitude to seated posture, orientation, and distance. *Journal of Personality and Social Psychology,* 1968b, *10,* 26–30.

Mehrabian, A.   Nonverbal communication.   In *Nebraska symposium on motivation,* edited by W. J. Arnold and M. M. Page.   Lincoln: University of Nebraska Press, 1971.

Meichenbaum, D. H.   Examination of model characteristics in reducing avoidance behavior. *Journal of Personality and Social Psychology,* 1971, *17,* 298–307.

Mendelsohn, M., Linden, J., Gruen, G., and Curran, J.   Heterosexual pairing and sibling configuration. *Journal of Individual Psychology,* 1974, *30,* 202–210.

Meyer, T. P.   The effects of sexually arousing and violent films on aggressive behavior. *Journal of Sex Research,* 1972, *8,* 324–333.

Michael, R. P., Keverne, E. B., and Bonsall, R. W.   Pheromones: Isolation of male sex attractants from a female primate. *Science,* 1971, *172,* 964–966.

Michener, H. A., and Burt, J. R.   Components of "authority" as determinants of compliance. *Journal of Personality and Social Psychology,* 1975, *31,* 606–614.

Michener, H. A., and Tausig, M.   Usurpation and perceived support as determinants of the endorsement accorded formal leaders. *Journal of Personality and Social Psychology,* 1971, *18,* 364–372.

Middlemist, R. D., Knowles, E. S., and Matter, C. F.   Personal space invasions in the lavatory: Suggestive evidence for arousal. *Journal of Personality and Social Psychology,* 1976, *33,* 541–6.

Midlarsky, E., and Bryan, J. H.   Affect expression and children's imitative altruism. *Journal of Research in Personality,* 1972, *6,* 195–203.

Milgram, S.   Behavioral study of obedience. *Journal of Abnormal and Social Psychology,* 1963, *67,* 371–378.

Milgram, S.   Group pressure and action against a person. *Journal of Abnormal and Social Psychology,* 1964, *69,* 137–143.

Milgram, S.   Liberating effects of group pressure. *Journal of Personality and Social Psychology,* 1965a, *1,* 127–134.

Milgram, S.   Some conditions of obedience and disobedience to authority. *Human Relations,* 1965b, *18,* 57–76.

Milgram, S.   The experience of living in cities. *Science,* 1970, *167,* 1461–1468.

Milgram, S.   *Obedience to authority.*   New York: Harper & Row, 1974.

Milgram, S., Bickman, L., and Berkowitz, L.   Note on the drawing power of crowds of different size. *Journal of Personality and Social Psychology,* 1969, *13,* 79–82.

Milgram, S., and Shotland, R. L.   *Television and antisocial behavior: Field experiments.*   New York: Academic Press, 1973.

Miller, A. G.   Role playing: An alternative to deception? A review of the evidence. *American Psychologist,* 1972, *27,* 623–636.

Miller, C., Byrne, D., and Fisher, J. D.   Preliminary scaling of 40 erotic slides for sexual arousal and disgust.   Unpublished manuscript, Purdue University, 1976.

Miller, C., Byrne, D., Fisher, W. A., and White, L.   Affective and attributional responses to communicating a sexual message.   Paper presented at the Psychonomic Society meeting, St. Louis, November 1976.

Miller, H., and Geller, D.   Structural balance in dyads. *Journal of Personality and Social Psychology,* 1972, *21,* 135–138.

Miller, N., and Maruyama, G.   Ordinal position

and peer popularity. *Journal of Personality and Social Psychology,* 1976, *33,* 123–131.

Miller, N. E. The frustration-aggression hypothesis. *Psychological Review,* 1941, *48,* 337–342.

Miller, N. E., and Dollard, J. *Social learning and imitation.* New Haven: Yale University Press, 1941.

Miller, R. E., Caul, W. F., and Mirsky, I. A. Communication of affects between feral and socially isolated monkeys. *Journal of Personality and Social Psychology,* 1967, *7,* 231–239.

Miller, R. E., Levine, J. M., and Mirsky, I. A. Effects of psychoactive drugs on nonverbal communication and group social behavior of monkeys. *Journal of Personality and Social Psychology,* 1973, *28,* 396–405.

Miller, R. L., Brickman, P., and Bolen, D. Attribution versus persuasion as a means for modifying behavior. *Journal of Personality and Social Psychology,* 1975, *31,* 430–441.

Mills, J., and Harvey, J. Opinion change as a function of when information about the communicator is received and whether he is attractive or expert. *Journal of Personality and Social Psychology,* 1972, *21,* 52–55.

Mintz, N. C. Effects of esthetic surroundings: II. Prolonged and repeated experience in a "beautiful" and an "ugly" room. *Journal of Psychology,* 1956, *41,* 459–466.

Mischel, H. W. Sex bias in the evaluation of professional achievements. *Journal of Educational Psychology,* 1974, *66,* 157–166.

Mischel, W. Preference for delayed reinforcement: An experimental study of a cultural observation. *Journal of Abnormal and Social Psychology,* 1958, *56,* 57–61.

Mischel, W. A social learning view of sex differences. In *The development of sex differences,* edited by E. E. Maccoby. Stanford: Stanford University Press, 1966.

Mischel, W. *Introduction to personality.* New York: Holt, Rinehart, & Winston, 1976.

Mischel, W., Ebbesen, E. B., and Zeiss, A. R. Cognitive and attentional mechanisms in delay of gratification. *Journal of Personality and Social Psychology,* 1972, *21,* 204–218.

Momboisse, R. M. *Riots, revolts, and insurrections.* Springfield, Ill.: Charles C Thomas, 1967.

Monahan, L., Kuhn, D., and Shaver, P. Intrapsychic versus cultural explanations of the fear of success motive. *Journal of Personality and Social Psychology,* 1974, *29,* 60–64.

Money, J., and Ehrhardt, A. A. *Man and woman: Boy and girl.* Baltimore: Johns Hopkins Press, 1972.

Moreland, R. L., and Zajonc, R. B. A strong test of exposure effects. *Journal of Experimental Social Psychology,* 1976, *12,* 170–179.

Morgan, C. P., and Aram, J. D. The preponderance of arguments in the risky shift phenomenon. *Journal of Experimental Social Psychology,* 1975, *11,* 25–34.

Moriarty, T. Crime, commitment, and the responsive bystander: Two field experiments. *Journal of Personality and Social Psychology,* 1975, *31,* 370–376.

Morin, S. F. Attitudes toward homosexuality and social distance. Paper presented at the meeting of the American Psychological Association, Chicago, September 1975.

Morris, W. N., and Miller, R. S. The effects of consensus-breaking and consensus-preempting partners on reduction of conformity. *Journal of Experimental Social Psychology,* 1975a, *11,* 215–223.

Morris, W. N., and Miller, R. S. Impressions of dissenters and conformers: An attributional analysis. *Sociometry,* 1975b, *38,* 327–339.

Morse, S., and Gergen, K. Material aid and social attraction. *Journal of Applied Social Psychology,* 1971, *1,* 150–162.

Moscovici, S., and Zavalloni, M. The group as a polarizer of attitudes. *Journal of Personality and Social Psychology,* 1969, *12,* 125–135.

Mosher, D. L. Measurement of guilt in females by self report inventories. *Journal of Consulting and Clinical Psychology,* 1968, *32,* 690–695.

Mosher, D. L. Sex callousness toward women. In *Technical report of the Commission on Obscenity and Pornography,* vol. 8. Washington, D.C.: U.S. Government Printing Office, 1971.

Mosher, D. L., and Abramson, P. R. Subjective sexual arousal to films of masturbation. *Journal of Consulting and Clinical Psychology,* 1977, (in press).

Mosher, D. L., and Cross, H. J. Sex guilt and premarital sexual experiences of college students. *Journal of Consulting and Clinical Psychology,* 1971, *36,* 27–32.

Moss, M. K., and Page, R. A. Reinforcement and helping behavior. *Journal of Applied Social Psychology,* 1972, *2,* 360–371.

Mueller, C., and Donnerstein, E. The effects of humor-induced arousal upon aggressive behavior. *Journal of Research in Personality,* 1976 (in press).

Murstein, B. I. A theory of marital choice and its applicability to marriage adjustment. In *Theories of attraction and love,* edited by B. I. Murstein. New York: Springer, 1971a.

Murstein, B. I., ed. *Theories of attraction and love.* New York: Springer, 1971b.

Murstein, B. I. Physical attractiveness and marital choice. *Journal of Personality and Social Psychology,* 1972, *22,* 8–12.

Murstein, B. I. *Love, sex, and marriage through the ages.* New York: Springer, 1974.

Myers, D. G. Social comparison processes in choice dilemma responding. *Journal of Psychology,* 1974, *86,* 287–292.

Myers, D. G. Discussion-induced attitude polarization. *Human Relations,* 1975, *28,* 699–714.

Myers, D. G., and Bishop, G. D. Discussion effects on racial attitudes. *Science,* 1970, *169,* 778–789.

Myers, D. G., and Bishop, G. D. Enhancement of dominant attitudes in group discussion. *Journal of Personality and Social Psychology,* 1971, *20,* 386–391.

Myers, D. G., and Kaplan, M. F. Group-induced polarization in simulated juries. *Personality and Social Psychology Bulletin,* 1976, *2,* 63–66.

Myers, D. G., and Lamm, H. The group polarization phenomenon. *Psychological Bulletin,* 1976a, *83,* 602–627.

Myers, D. G., and Lamm, H. The polarizing effect of group discussion. *American Scientist,* 1975, *63,* 297–303.

Myers, D. G., Wong, D. W., and Murdoch, P. H. Discussion arguments, information about others' responses and risky shift. *Psychonomic Science,* 1971, *24,* 81–83.

Mynatt, C., and Sherman, S. J. Responsibility attribution in groups and individuals: A direct test of the diffusion of responsibility hypothesis. *Journal of Personality and Social Psychology,* 1975, *32,* 1111–1118.

Myrdal, G. A parallel to the Negro problem. In *An American dilemma.* New York: Harper & Row, 1944.

Nadler, A., Fisher, J. D., and Streufert, S. The donor's dilemma: Recipient's reactions to aid from friend or foe. *Journal of Applied Social Psychology,* 1974, *4,* 275–285.

Nadler, A., Fisher, J. D., and Streufert, S. When helping hurts: Effects of donor-recipient similarity and recipient self-esteem on recipient reactions to aid. *Journal of Personality,* 1976, *44,* 392–409.

Nadler, A., Jazwinski, C., and Lau, S. The cold glow of success: Effects of the interpersonal success of a similar or a dissimilar other on the observer's self and other perceptions. Unpublished manuscript, Purdue University, 1976.

Nahemow, L., and Lawton, M. P. Similarity and propinquity in friendship formation. *Journal of Personality and Social Psychology,* 1975, *32,* 205–213.

Nawy, H. The San Francisco erotic marketplace. In *Technical report of the Commission on Obscenity and Pornography,* vol. 4. Washington, D. C.: U. S. Government Printing Office, 1971.

Nelson, D., and Meadow, B. L. Attitude similarity, interpersonal attraction, actual success, and the evaluative perception of that success. Paper presented at the meeting of the American Psychological Association, Washington, D. C., September 1971.

Nesbitt, P. D., and Steven, G. Personal space and stimulus intensity at a Southern California amusement park. *Sociometry,* 1974, *37,* 105–115.

Newcomb, T. M. *Personality and social change.* New York: Dryden, 1943.

Newcomb, T. M. *The acquaintance process.* New York: Holt, Rinehart, & Winston, 1961.

Newcomb, T. M. Dyadic balance as a source of clues about interpersonal attraction. In *Theories of attraction and love,* edited by B. I. Murstein. New York: Springer, 1971.

Newcomb, T. M., Koenig, K. E., Flacks, R., and Warwick, D. P. *Persistence and change: Bennington College and its students after twenty-five years.* New York: John Wiley & Sons, 1967.

Newman, O. *Defensible space.* New York: Macmillan, 1972.

Newman, S. Perceptions of building height: An approach to research and some preliminary findings. Paper presented at Conference on Human Response to Tall Buildings, American Institute of Architects, Chicago, July 1975.

Newtson, D. Dispositional inference from effects of actions: Effects chosen and effects forgone. *Journal of Experimental Social Psychology,* 1974, *10,* 489–496.

Nguyen, M. L., Heslin, R., and Nguyen, T. D. The meaning of touch: Sex and marital status differences. *Representative Research in Social Psychology,* 1976, *7,* 13–18.

Nguyen, T. D., Heslin, R., and Nguyen, M. L. The meaning of touch: Sex differences. *Journal of Communication,* 1975, *25* (3), 92–103.

Nillson, H. *The Point.* RCA Victor, 1971.

Nisbett, R. E., Caputo, C., Legant, P., and Marecek, J. Behavior as seen by the actor and as seen by the observer. *Journal of Personality and Social Psychology,* 1973, *27,* 154–164.

Nisbett, R. E., and Schachter, S. Cognitive manipulation of pain. *Journal of Experimental Social Psychology,* 1966, *2,* 227–236.

Norum, G. A., Russo, N. F., and Sommer, R. Seating patterns and group task. *Psychology in the Schools,* 1967, *4,* 276–280.

Nydegger, R. V. Information processing complexity and leadership status. *Journal of Experimental Social Psychology,* 1975, *11,* 317–328.

O'Connor, R. D. Modification of social withdrawal through symbolic modeling. *Journal of Applied Behavior Analysis,* 1969, *2,* 15–22.

O'Connor, R. D. Relative efficacy of modeling, shaping, and the combined procedures for modification of social withdrawal. *Journal of Abnormal Psychology,* 1972, *79,* 327–334.

O'Leary, M. R., and Dengerink, H. A. Aggression as a function of the intensity and pattern of attack. *Journal of Experimental Research in Personality,* 1973, *7,* 61–70.

O'Leary, V. H. Some attitudinal barriers to occupational aspirations in women. *Psychological Bulletin,* 1974, *81,* 809, 926.

O'Neill, G. C., and O'Neill, N. Patterns in group sexual activity. *Journal of Sex Research,* 1970, *6,* 101–112.

Orne, M. T. On the social psychology of the psychological experiment: With particular reference to demand characteristics and their implications. *American Psychologist,* 1962, *17,* 776–783.

Osgood, C. E. *An alternative to war or surrender.* Urbana: University of Illinois Press, 1962.

Osgood, C. E., Suci, G. J., and Tannenbaum, P. H. *The measurement of meaning.* Urbana: University of Illinois Press, 1957.

Osmond, H. Function as the basis of psychiatric ward design. *Mental Hospitals,* 1957, *8,* 23–30.

Ostrom, T. M. The bogus pipeline: a new *ignis fatuus? Psychological Bulletin,* 1973, *79,* 252–259.

Page, M. P., and Scheidt, R. J. The elusive weapons effect: Demand awareness, evaluation apprehension, and slightly sophisticated subjects. *Journal of Personality and Social Psychology,* 1971, *20,* 304–318.

Pallak, M. S., and Pittman, T. S. General motivational effects of dissonance arousal. *Journal of Personality and Social Psychology,* 1972, *21,* 349–358.

Parke, R. D., Berkowitz, L., Leyens, J. P., and Sebastian, R. The effects of repeated exposure to movie violence on aggressive behavior in juvenile delinquent boys: Field experimental studies. In *Advances in experimental social psychology,* vol. 8, edited by L. Berkowitz. New York: Academic Press, 1975.

Pastore, N. The role of arbitrariness in the frustration-aggression hypothesis. *Journal of Abnormal and Social Psychology,* 1952, *47,* 728–731.

Patterson, M. L. Factors affecting interpersonal spatial proximity. Paper presented at the annual meeting of the American Psychological Association, New Orleans, September 1974.

Patterson, M. L., Mullens, S., and Romano, J. Compensatory reactions to spatial intrusion. *Sociometry,* 1971, *34,* 114–121.

Paulus, P. B., Aunis, A. B., Seta, J. J., Schkade, J. K., and Matthews, R. W. Crowding does affect task performance. *Journal of Personality and Social Psychology,* 1976, *34,* 248–253.

Paulus, P. B., Cox, V., McCain, G., and Chandler, J. Some effects of crowding in prison environment. *Journal of Applied Social Psychology,* 1975, *5,* 86–91.

Paulus, P. B., and Murdoch, P. Anticipated evaluation and audience presence in the enhancement of dominant responses. *Journal of Experimental Social Psychology,* 1971, *7,* 280–291.

Pederson, D. M., and Shears, L. M. A review of personal space research in the framework of general system theory. *Psychological Bulletin,* 1973, *80,* 367–388.

Pellegrini, R. J., and Empey, J. Interpersonal spatial orientation in dyads. *Journal of Psychology,* 1970, *76,* 67–70.

Pessin, J. The comparative effects of social and mechanical stimulation on memorizing. *American Journal of Psychology,* 1933, *45,* 263–270.

Peterson, K., and Curran, J. P. Trait attribution as a function of hair length and correlates of subjects' preferences for hair style. *Journal of Psychology,* 1976, *93,* 331–339.

Peterson, C., Peterson, J., and McDonald, N. Factors affecting reward allocation by preschool children. Unpublished manuscript, Northern Illinois University, 1974.

Pettigrew, T. F. Racially separate or together? *Journal of Social Issues,* 1969, *25,* 43–69.

Phares, E. J., and Lamiell, J. T. Internal-external control, interpersonal judgments of others in need, and attribution of responsibility. *Journal of Personality,* 1975, *43,* 23–38.

Pheterson, G. I., Kiesler, S. B., and Goldberg, P. A. Evaluation of the performance of women as a function of their sex, achievement, and personal history. *Journal of Personality and Social Psychology,* 1971, *19,* 114–118.

Piaget, J. *The moral judgment of the child.* Glencoe, Ill.: Free Press, 1948 (first published 1932).

Picek, J. S., Sherman, S. J., and Shiffrin, R. M. Cognitive organization and coding of social structures. *Journal of Personality and Social Psychology,* 1975, *31,* 758–768.

Pierce, J. T., and Nuttall, R. L. Self-paced sexual behavior in the female rat. *Journal of Comparative and Physiological Psychology,* 1961, *54,* 310–313.

Piliavin, I. M., Piliavin, J. A., and Rodin, J. Costs, diffusion, and the stigmatized victim. *Journal of Personality and Social Psychology,* 1976, *32,* 429–438.

Piliavin, I. M., Rodin, J., and Piliavin, J. A. Good Samaritanism: An underground phenomenon? *Journal of Personality and Social Psychology,* 1969, *4,* 289–299.

Piliavin, J. A., and Piliavin, I. M. Effect of blood on reactions to a victim. *Journal of Personality and Social Psychology,* 1972, *23,* 353–361.

Piliavin, J. A., and Piliavin, I. M. The Good Samaritan: Why *does* he help? In *Positive forms of social behavior,* edited by L. Wispé. Harvard University Press, 1976.

Pilisuk, M., and Skolnick, P. Inducing trust: A test of the Osgood proposal. *Journal of Personality and Social Psychology,* 1968, *8,* 121–133.

Pliner, P., Hart, H., Kohl, J., and Saari, D. Compliance without pressure: Some further data on the foot-in-the-door technique. *Journal of Experimental Social Psychology,* 1974, *10,* 17–22.

Pocs, O., and Godow, A. G. The shock of recognizing parents as sexual beings. In *Exploring human sexuality,* edited by D. Byrne and L. A. Byrne. New York: Harper and Row, 1977.

Pollis, N. P., Montgomery, R. L., and Smith, T. G. Autokinetic paradigms: A reply to Alexander, Zucker, and Brody. *Sociometry,* 1975, *38,* 358–373.

Pomazal, R. J., and Clore, G. L. Helping on the highway: The effects of dependency and sex. *Journal of Applied Social Psychology,* 1973, *3,* 150–164.

Pomazal, R. J., and Jaccard, J. J. An informational approach to altruistic behavior. *Journal of Personality and Social Psychology,* 1976, *33,* 317–326.

Porter, J. *Black child, white child.* Cambridge: Harvard University Press, 1971.

Pressman, I., and Carol, A. Crime as a diseconomy of scale. Paper delivered at the convention of the Operations Research Society of America, 1969.

Price, K. O., Harburg, E., and Newcomb, T. Psychological balance in situations of negative interpersonal attitudes. *Journal of Personality and Social Psychology,* 1966, *3,* 265–270.

Price, W. H., and Whatmore, P. B. Behavior disorders and pattern of crime among XYY males identified at a maximum security hospital. *British Medical Journal,* 1967, *1,* 533–536.

Pritchard, R. D., Dunnette, H. D., and Jorgenson, D. O. Effects of perceptions of equity and inequity on worker performance and satisfaction. *Journal of Applied Psychology,* 1972, *56,* 75–94.

Proctor, E. B., Wagner, N. N., and Butler, J. C. The differentiation of male and female orgasm: An experimental study. In *Perspectives on human sexuality,* edited by N. N. Wagner. New York: Behavioral Publications, 1974.

Pruitt, D. G. Choice shifts in group discussion: An introductory review. *Journal of Personality and Social Psychology,* 1971a, *20,* 339–360.

Pruitt, D. G. Conclusions: Toward an understanding of choice shifts in group discussion. *Journal of Personality and Social Psychology*, 1971b, *20*, 495–510.

Pruitt, D. G. Indirect communication and the search for agreement in negotiation. *Journal of Applied Social Psychology*, 1971c, *1*, 205–239.

Pruitt, D. G., and Lewis, S. A. Development of integrative solutions in bilateral negotiation. *Journal of Personality and Social Psychology*, 1975, *31*, 621–633.

Raboch, J., and Starka, L. Coital activity of men and the levels of plasmatic testosterone. *Journal of Sex Research*, 1972, *8*, 219–224.

Rachman, S. Sexual fetishism: An experimental analogue. *Psychological Record*, 1966, *16*, 293–296.

Rainwater, L. Fear and the house-as-haven in the lower class. *Journal of the American Institute of Planners*, 1966, *32*, 23–31.

Rajecki, D. W., Kidd, R. F., and Ivins, B. Social facilitation in chickens: A different level of analysis. *Journal of Experimental Social Psychology*, 1976, *12*, 233–246.

Rajecki, D. W., Kidd, R. F., Wilder, D. A., and Jaeger, J. Social factors in the facilitation of feeding chickens: Effects of imitation, arousal, or disinhibition? *Journal of Personality and Social Psychology*, 1975, *32*, 510–518.

Rapaport, A. *Experimental games and their uses in psychology*. Morristown, N.J.: General Learning Press, 1973.

Rawls, J. R., Trego, R. E., McGaffey, C. N., and Rawls, D. J. Personal space as a predictor of performance under close working conditions. *Journal of Social Psychology*, 1972, *86*, 261–267.

Regan, D. T. Effects of a favor and liking on compliance. *Journal of Experimental Social Psychology*, 1971, *7*, 627–639.

Regan, D. T., and Cheng, J. B. Distraction and attitude change: A resolution. *Journal of Experimental Social Psychology*, 1973, *9*, 138–147.

Regula, R. C., and Julian, J. W. The impact of quality and frequency of task contribution on perceived ability. *Journal of Social Psychology*, 1973, *89*, 115–122.

Reiss, S., and Sushinsky, L. W. Overjustification, competing responses, and the acquisition of intrinsic interest. *Journal of Personality and Social Psychology*, 1975, *31*, 1116–1125.

Reiss, S., and Sushinsky, L. W. The competing responses hypothesis of decreased play effects: A reply to Lepper and Greene. *Journal of Personality and Social Psychology*, 1976, *33*, 233–244.

Rice, M. E., and Grusec, J. E. Saying and doing: Effects on observer performance. *Journal of Personality and Social Psychology*, 1975, *32*, 584–593.

Ring, K. Experimental social psychology: Some sober questions about some frivolous values. *Journal of Experimental Social Psychology*, 1967, *3*, 113–123.

Rogers, R. W., and Mewborn, R. Fear appeals and attitude change: Effects of a threat's noxiousness, probability of occurrence, and the efficacy of coping responses. *Journal of Personality and Social Psychology*, 1976, *34*, 54–61.

Rohe, W., and Patterson, A. H. The effects of varied levels of resources and density on behavior in a day care center. Paper presented at Environmental Design Research Association, Milwaukee, 1974.

Rokeach, M., ed. *The open and closed mind.* New York: Basic Books, 1960.

Rokeach, M. *Beliefs, attitudes, and values.* San Francisco: Jossey-Bass, 1968.

Rokeach, M., and Kliejunas, P. Behavior as a function of attitude-toward-object and attitude-toward-situation. *Journal of Personality and Social Psychology*, 1972, *22*, 194–201.

Rokeach, M., and Mezei, L. Race and shared belief as factors in social choice. *Science*, 1966, *151*, 167–172.

Rokeach, M., Smith, D. W., and Evans, R. I. Two kinds of prejudice or one? In *The open and closed mind,* edited by M. Rokeach. New York: Basic Books, 1960.

Rosenbaum, M. E., and Levin, I. P. Impression formation as a function of source credibility and order of presentation of contradictory information. *Journal of Personality and Social Psychology*, 1968, *10*, 167–174.

Rosenbaum, M. E., and Levin, I. P. Impression formation as a function of source credibility and the polarity of information. *Journal of Personality and Social Psychology*, 1969, *12*, 34–37.

Rosenbaum, M. E., and Tucker, I. F. The competence of the model and the learning of imitation and nonimitation. *Journal of Experimental Psychology*, 1962, *63*, 183–190.

Rosenberg, M. J. When dissonance fails: On

eliminating evaluation apprehension from attitude measurement. *Journal of Personality and Social Psychology,* 1965, *1,* 28–42.

Rosenfeld, H. M. Effect of an approval-seeking induction on interpersonal proximity. *Psychological Reports,* 1965, *17,* 120–122.

Rosenhan, D. L. On being sane in insane places. *Science,* 1973, *179,* 250–258.

Rosenhan, D. L., Underwood, B., and Moore, B. Affect moderates self-gratification and altruism. *Journal of Personality and Social Psychology,* 1974, *30,* 546–552.

Rosenman, M. F. Resistance to family planning centers in the black community. *JSAS Catalogue of Selected Documents in Psychology,* 1973, *82,* Ms. No. 410.

Rosenthal, R., and Jacobson, L. *Pygmalion in the classroom.* New York: Holt, Rinehart & Winston, 1968.

Rosenthal, T. L., Zimmerman, B. J., and Durning, K. Observationally induced changes in children's interrogative classes. *Journal of Personality and Social Psychology,* 1970, *16,* 681–688.

Rosnow, R. L., Goodstadt, B. E., Suls, J. M., and Gitter, A. G. More on the social psychology of the experiment: When compliance turns to self-defense. *Journal of Personality and Social Psychology,* 1973, *27,* 337–343.

Ross, A. S. Effect of increased responsibility on bystander intervention: The presence of children. *Journal of Personality and Social Psychology,* 1971, *19,* 306–310.

Ross, A. S., and Braband, J. Effect of increased responsibility on bystander intervention: II. The cue value of a blind person. *Journal of Personality and Social Psychology,* 1973, *25,* 254–258.

Ross, E. A. *Social psychology.* New York: Macmillan, 1908.

Ross, L., Bierbrauer, G., and Hoffman, S. The role of attribution processes in conformity and dissent: Revisiting the Asch situation. *American Psychologist,* 1976, *31,* 148–157.

Ross, L., Rodin, J., and Zimbardo, P. G. Toward an attribution therapy: The reduction of fear through induced cognitive-emotional misattribution. *Journal of Personality and Social Psychology,* 1969, *12,* 279–288.

Ross, M., Karniol, R., and Rothstein, M. Reward contingency and intrinsic motivation in children: A test of the delay of gratification hypothesis. *Journal of Personality and Social Psychology,* 1976, *33,* 442–447.

Ross, M., Layton, B., Erickson, B., and Schopler, J. Affect, facial regard, and reactions to crowding. *Journal of Personality and Social Psychology,* 1973, *28,* 69–76.

Roszak, B. The human condition. *Masculine/ Feminine,* edited by B. Roszak and T. Roszak. New York: Harper & Row, 1969.

Roth, S., and Kubal, L. Effects of noncontingent reinforcement on tasks of differing importance: Facilitation and learned helplessness. *Journal of Personality and Social Psychology,* 1975, *32,* 680–691.

Rotton, J., Barry, T., Frey, J., and Soler, E. Air pollution and interpersonal attraction. Unpublished manuscript, University of Dayton, 1976.

Rubin, Z. Measurement of romantic love. *Journal of Personality and Social Psychology,* 1970, *16,* 265–273.

Rubin, Z. *Liking and loving: An invitation to social psychology.* New York: Holt, Rinehart and Winston, 1973.

Rubin, Z. From liking to loving: Patterns of attraction in dating relationships. In *Foundations of interpersonal attraction,* edited by T. L. Huston. New York: Academic Press, 1974.

Rubin, Z., and Peplau, A. Belief in a just world and reactions to another's lot: A study of participants in the national draft lottery. *Journal of Social Issues,* 1973, *4,* 73–93.

Rubovits, P. C., and Maehr, M. L. Pygmalion black and white. *Journal of Personality and Social Psychology,* 1973, *25,* 210–218.

Rule, B. G., Dyck, R. J., and Nesdale, A. R. Arbitrariness of frustration: Inhibition or instigation effects on aggression. Unpublished manuscript, University of Alberta, 1976.

Rule, B. G., and Hewitt, L. S. Effects of thwarting on cardiac response and physical aggression. *Journal of Personality and Social Psychology,* 1971, *19,* 181–187.

Rule, B. G., and Leger, G. J. Pain cues and differing functions of aggression. *Canadian Journal of Behavioral Science,* 1976, *8,* 213–222.

Rule, B. G., and Nesdale, A. R. Emotional arousal and aggressive behavior. *Psychological Bulletin,* 1976a, *83,* 851–863.

Rule, B. G., and Nesdale, A. R. Environmental stressors, emotional arousal, and aggression.

In *Anxiety and stress,* vol. 3, edited by C. Spielberger and I. Sarason. New York: Hemisphere, 1976b.

Rule, B. G., and Nesdale, A. R. Moral judgments of aggressive behavior. In *Perspectives on aggression,* edited by R. G. Geen and E. C. O'Neal. New York: Academic Press, 1976c.

Rushton, J. P. Generosity in children: Immediate and long-term effects of modeling, preaching, and moral judgment. *Journal of Personality and Social Psychology,* 1975, *31,* 459–466.

Rushton, J. P. Socialization and the altruistic behaviour of children. *Psychological Bulletin,* 1976, *83,* 898–913.

Rushton, J. P., and Campbell, A. C. Altrusitic modeling and donating blood. Paper presented at the meeting of the Eastern Psychological Association, New York City, April 1976.

Rushton, J. P., and Wiener, J. Altruism and cognitive development in children. *British Journal of Social and Clinical Psychology,* 1975, *14,* 341–349.

Saarinen, T. F. *Perception of the environment.* Resource paper no. 5. Association of American Geographers, 1969.

Sachs, B. D., and Marsan, E. Male rats prefer sex to food after six days of food deprivation. *Psychonomic Science,* 1972, *28,* 47–49.

Saegert, S. C., and Jellison, J. M. Effects of initial level of response competition and frequency of exposure to liking and exploratory behavior. *Journal of Personality and Social Psychology,* 1970, *16,* 553–558.

Saegert, S. C., Swap, W., and Zajonc, R. B. Exposure, context, and interpersonal attraction. *Journal of Personality and Social Psychology,* 1973, *25,* 234–242.

Sakurai, M. M. Small group cohesiveness and detrimental conformity. *Sociometry,* 1975, *38,* 340–357.

Salili, F., Maehr, M. L., and Gillmore, G. Achievement and morality: A cross-cultural analysis of causal attribution and evaluation. *Journal of Personality and Social Psychology,* 1976, *33,* 327–337.

Sanders, C. L. Is Archie Bunker the real white America? *Ebony,* 1972, *27.* 186–192.

Sanders, G. S., and Baron, R. S. The motivating effects of distraction on task performance. *Journal of Personality and Social Psychology,* 1975,

32, 956–963.

Sarason, I. G., and Ganzer, V. J. Modeling: An approach to the rehabilitation of juvenile offenders. Final report to the Social and Rehabilitation Service of the Department of Health, Education, and Welfare. Washington, D.C., June 1971.

Satow, K. L. Social approval and helping. *Journal of Experimental Social Psychology,* 1975, *11,* 501–509.

Savell, J. M. Prior agreement and conformity: An extension of the generalization phenomenon. *Psychonomic Science,* 1971, *25,* 327–328.

Savitsky, J. C., Izard, C. E., Kotsch, W., and Christy, L. Aggressor's response to the victim's facial expression of emotion. *Journal of Research in Personality,* 1974, *7,* 346–357.

Schachter, S. Deviation, rejection, and communication. *Journal of Abnormal and Social Psychology,* 1951, *46,* 190–207.

Schachter, S. *The psychology of affiliation.* Stanford: Stanford University Press, 1959.

Schachter, S. The interaction of cognitive and physiological determinants of emotional state. In *Advances in experimental social psychology,* vol. 1, edited by L. Berkowitz. New York: Academic Press, 1964.

Schachter, S., and Singer, J. E. Cognitive, social, and physiological determinants of emotional state. *Psychological Review,* 1962, *69,* 379–399.

Scheier, M. F., Fenigstein, A., and Buss, A. H. Self-awareness and physical aggression. *Journal of Experimental Social Psychology,* 1974, *10,* 264–273.

Schein, E. H., Schneier, I., and Barker, C. H. *Coercive pressure.* New York: Norton, 1961.

Schell, R. E., and Silber, J. W. Sex-role discrimination among young school children. *Perceptual and Motor Skills,* 1968, *27,* 379–389.

Scherer, S. E. Proxemic behavior of primary school children as a function of their socioeconomic class and subculture. *Journal of Personality and Social Psychology,* 1974, *29,* 800–805.

Schettino, A. P., and Borden, R. J. Sex differences in response to naturalistic crowding: Affective reactions to group size and group density. *Personality and Social Psychology Bulletin,* 1976, *2,* 67–70.

Schiffenbauer, A., and Schiavo, R. S. Physical distance and attraction: An intensification effect. *Journal of Experimental Social Psychology,* 1976,

12, 274–282.

Schill, T., and Chapin, J. Sex guilt and males' preference for reading erotic magazines. *Journal of Consulting and Clinical Psychology*, 1972, *39*, 516.

Schlenker, B. R. Social psychology and science. *Journal of Personality and Social Psychology*, 1974, *29*, 1–15.

Schmidt, G. Male-female differences in sexual arousal and behavior during and after exposure to sexually explicit stimuli. *Archives of Sexual Behavior*, 1975, *4*, 353–364.

Schmidt, G., and Sigusch, V. Sex differences in responses to psychosexual stimulation by films and slides. *Journal of Sex Research*, 1970, *6*, 268–283.

Schmidt, G., and Sigusch, V. Changes in sexual behavior among young males and females between 1960–1970. *Archives of Sexual Behavior*, 1972, *2*, 27–45.

Schmidt, G., Sigusch, V., and Schäfer, S. Responses to reading erotic stories: Male-female differences. *Archives of Sexual Behavior*, 1973, *2*, 181–199.

Schmitt, D. R., and Marwell, G. Withdrawal and reward reallocation as responses to inequity. *Journal of Experimental Social Psychology*, 1972, *8*, 207–221.

Schoedel, J., Frederickson, W. A., and Knight, J. M. An extrapolation of the physical attractiveness and sex variables within the Byrne attraction paradigm. *Memory and Cognition*, 1975, *3*, 527–530.

Schofield, J. W. Effect of norms, public disclosure, and need for approval on volunteering behavior consistent with attitudes. *Journal of Personality and Social Psychology*, 1975, *31*, 1126–1133.

Schönemann, P., Byrne, D., and Bell, P. A. A statistical reinterpretation of an attraction model. Unpublished manuscript, Purdue University, 1976.

Schultz, D. P. The human subject in psychological research. *Psychological Bulletin*, 1969, *72*, 214–228.

Schultz, L. G. The wife assaulter. *Journal of Social Therapy*, 1960, *6*, 103–111.

Schwartz, S. Effects of sex guilt and sexual arousal on the retention of birth control information. *Journal of Consulting and Clincial Psychology*, 1973, *41*, 61–64.

Schwartz, S. H., and Clausen, G. T. Responsibility, norms, and helping in an emergency. *Journal of Personality and Social Psychology*, 1970, *16*, 299–310.

Scott, W. A., and Peterson, C. Adjustment, Pollyannaism, and attraction to close relationships. *Journal of Consulting and Clinical Psychology*, 1975, *43*, 872–880.

Segal, M. W. Alphabet and attraction: An unobtrusive measure of the effect of propinquity in a field setting. *Journal of Personality and Social Psychology*, 1974, *30*, 654–657.

Seligman, C., Bush, M., and Kirsch, K. Relationship between compliance in the foot-in-the-door paradigm and size of first request. *Journal of Personality and Social Psychology*, 1976, *33*, 517–520.

Seligman, M. E. P. Phobias and preparedness. *Behavior Therapy*, 1971, *2*, 307–320.

Seligman, M. E. P. *Helplessness*. San Francisco: Freeman, 1975.

Seligman, M. E. P., and Maier, S. Failure to escape traumatic shock. *Journal of Experimental Psychology*, 1967, *74*, 1–9.

Sensenig, J., and Brehm, J. W. Attitude change from implied threat to attitudinal freedom. *Journal of Personality and Social Psychology*, 1968, *8*, 324–330.

Shaffer, D. R., Rogel, M., and Hendrick, C. Intervention in the library: The effect of increased responsibility on bystanders' willingness to prevent a theft. *Journal of Applied Social Psychology*, 1975, *5*, 303–319.

Shaffer, D. R., and Wegley, C. Success orientation and sex-role congruence as determinants of the attractiveness of competent women. *Journal of Personality*, 1974, *42*, 586–600.

Shaver, K. G. *An introduction to attribution processes*. Cambridge, Mass.: Winthrop, 1975.

Shemberg, K. M., Leventhal, D. B., and Allman, L. Aggression machine performance and rated aggression. *Journal of Experimental Research in Personality*, 1968, *3*, 117–119.

Sherif, M. A study of some social factors in perception. *Archives of Psychology*, 1935, No. 187.

Sherif, M. An experimental approach to the study of attitudes. *Sociometry*, 1937, *1*, 90–98.

Sherif, M. *In common predicament: Social psychology of intergroup conflict and cooperation*. Boston: Houghton Mifflin, 1966.

Sherif, M., Harvey, O. J., White, B. J., Hood, W. R., and Sherif, C. W. *Intergroup conflict and cooperation: The robbers' cave experiment.* Norman: University of Oklahoma Press, 1961.

Sherrod, D. R. Crowding, perceived control, and behavioral aftereffects. *Journal of Applied Social Psychology,* 1974, *4,* 171–186.

Sherrod, D. R., and Downs, R. Environmental determinants of altruism: The effects of stimulus overload and perceived control on helping. *Journal of Experimental Social Psychology,* 1974, *10,* 468–479.

Shipley, T. W., and Veroff, J. A projective measure of need for affiliation. *Journal of Experimental Psychology,* 1952, *43,* 349–356.

Shomer, R. W., Davis, A., and Kelley, H. H. Threats and the development of coordination: Further studies of the Deutsch and Krauss trucking game. *Journal of Personality and Social Psychology,* 1966, *4,* 119–126.

Shope, D. F. *Interpersonal sexuality.* Philadelphia: Saunders, 1975.

Shure, G. H., Meeker, R. J., and Hansford, E. A. The effectiveness of pacifist strategies in bargaining games. *Journal of Conflict Resolution,* 1965, *9,* 106–117.

Siegal, A., and Siegal, S. Reference groups, membership groups, and attitude change. *Journal of Abnormal and Social Psychology,* 1957, *55,* 360–369.

Sigall, H., and Aronson, E. Liking for an evaluator as a function of her physical attractiveness and nature of the evaluations. *Journal of Experimental Social Psychology,* 1969, *5,* 93–100.

Sigall, H., Aronson, E., and Van Hoose, T. The cooperative subject: Myth or reality? *Journal of Experimental Social Psychology,* 1970, *6,* 1–10.

Sigall, H., and Ostrove, N. Beautiful but dangerous: Effects of offender attractiveness and nature of the crime on juridic judgment. *Journal of Personality and Social Psychology,* 1975, *31,* 410–414.

Sigusch, V., Schmidt, G., Reinfeld, A., and Wiedemann-Sutor, I. Psychosexual stimulation: Sex differences. *Journal of Sex Research,* 1970, *6,* 10–24.

Silverman, B. I. Consequences, racial discrimination, and the principle of belief congruence. *Journal of Personality and Social Psychology,* 1974, *29,* 497–508.

Simpson, C., and Yinger, J. M. Racial and cultural minorities: An analysis of prejudice and discrimination. New York: Harper & Row, 1965.

Simpson, R. L. *Theories of social exchange.* Morristown, N.J.: General Learning Press, 1972.

Singer, J. L., ed. *The control of aggression and violence.* New York: Academic Press, 1971.

Sintchak, G. H., and Geer, J. H. A vaginal plethysmograph system. *Psychophysiology,* 1976 (in press).

Sistrunk, F., and McDavid, J. W. Sex variable in conforming behavior. *Journal of Personality and Social Psychology,* 1971, *17,* 200–207.

Skinner, B. F. *Beyond freedom and dignity.* New York: Knopf, 1971.

Skolnick, P., and Heslin, R. Approval dependence and reactions to bad arguments and low credibility sources. *Journal of Experimental Research in Personality,* 1971a, *5,* 199–207.

Skolnick, P., and Heslin, R. Quality versus difficulty: Alternative interpretations of the relationship between self-esteem and persuasibility. *Journal of Personality,* 1971b, *39,* 242–251.

Smith, G. F., and Dorfman, D. D. The effect of stimulus uncertainty on the relationship between frequency of exposure and liking. *Journal of Personality and Social Psychology,* 1975, *31,* 150–155.

Smith, R. E. Social anxiety as a moderator variable in the attitude similarity-attraction relationship. Paper presented at the meeting of the Western Psychological Association, Los Angeles, April 1970.

Smith, R. E., Meadow, B. L., and Sisk, T. K. Attitude similarity, interpersonal attraction, and evaluative social perception. *Psychonomic Science,* 1970, *18,* 226–227.

Smith, W. P., and Anderson, A. J. Threats, communication, and bargaining. *Journal of Personality and Social Psychology,* 1975, *32,* 76–82.

Snyder, M., and Cunningham, M. R. To comply or not comply: Testing the self-perception explanation of the "foot-in-the-door" phenomenon. *Journal of Personality and Social Psychology,* 1975, *31,* 64–67.

Snyder, M., and Ebbesen, E. B. Dissonance awareness: A test of dissonance theory versus self-perception theory. *Journal of Experimental Social Psychology,* 1972, *8,* 502–517.

Snyder, M., Grether, J., and Keller, K. Staring and compliance: A field experiment on hitchhiking. *Journal of Applied Social Psychology,* 1974,

4, 165–170.

Solomon, L. The influence of some types of power relationships and game strategies upon the development of interpersonal trust. *Journal of Abnormal and Social Psychology,* 1960, *71,* 223–230.

Sommer, R. Studies in personal space. *Sociometry,* 1959, *22,* 247–260.

Sommer, R. Further studies of small group ecology. *Sociometry,* 1965, *28,* 337–348.

Sommer, R. Man's proximate environment. *Journal of Social Issues,* 1966, *22,* 59–70.

Sommer, R. Intimacy ratings in five countries. *International Journal of Psychology,* 1968, *3,* 109–114.

Sommer, R. *Personal space.* Englewood Cliffs, N.J.: Prentice-Hall, 1969.

Sommer, R. *Tight spaces: Hard architecture and how to humanize it.* Englewood Cliffs, N.J.: Prentice-Hall, 1974.

Sommer, R., and Becker, F. D. Territorial defense and the good neighbor. *Journal of Personality and Social Psychology,* 1969, *11,* 85–92.

Sommer, R., and Gilliland, G. W. Design for friendship. *Canadian Architect,* 1961, *6,* 59–61.

Sommer, R., and Ross, H. Social interaction on a geriatric ward. *International Journal of Social Psychiatry,* 1958, *4,* 128–133.

Sonnenfeld, J. Variable values in space and landscape. Unpublished manuscript, University of Delaware, 1964.

Sorrentino, R. M., and Boutillier, R. G. The effect of quantity and quality of verbal interaction on ratings of leadership ability. *Journal of Experimental Social Psychology,* 1975, *11,* 403–411.

Spanier, G. B. Sexualization and premarital sexual behavior. *Family Coordinator,* 1975, *24,* 33–41.

Spence, J. T. The Thematic Apperception Test and attitudes toward achievement in women: A new look at the motive to avoid success and a new method of measurement. *Journal of Consulting and Clinical Psychology,* 1974, *42,* 427–437.

Spence, J. T., and Helmreich, R. The attitudes toward women scale: An objective instrument to measure attitudes toward the rights and roles of women in contemporary society. *Journal Supplement Abstract Service,* 1972a, *2,* 66.

Spence, J. T., and Helmreich, R. Who likes competent women? Competence, sex-role congruence of interests, and subjects' attitudes toward women as determinants of interpersonal attraction. *Journal of Applied Social Psychology,* 1972b, *2,* 197–213.

Spence, J. T., Helmreich, R., and Stapp, J. Likability, sex-role congruence of interest, and competence: It all depends on how you ask. *Journal of Applied Social Psychology,* 1975, *5,* 93–109.

Staats, A. W., and Staats, C. K. Attitudes established by classical conditioning. *Journal of Abnormal and Social Psychology,* 1958, *57,* 37–40.

Stainbrook, E. Architects not only design hospitals: They also design patient behavior. *Modern Hospital,* 1966, *106,* 100.

Stang, D. J. Conformity, ability, and self-esteem. *Representative Research in Social Psychology,* 1972, *3,* 97–103.

Stang, D. J. Effects of "mere exposure" on learning and affect. *Journal of Personality and Social Psychology,* 1975, *31,* 7–12.

Stass, J. W., and Willis, F. N. Eye-contact, pupil dilation, and personal preference. *Psychonomic Science,* 1967, *7,* 375–376.

Staub, E. A child in distress: The influence of age and number of witnesses on children's attempts to help. *Journal of Personality and Social Psychology,* 1970, *14,* 130–140.

Staub, E. Helping a person in distress: The influence of implicit and explicit "rules" of conduct on children and adults. *Journal of Personality and Social Psychology,* 1971, *17,* 137–144.

Staub, E. Helping a distressed person: Social, personality, and stimulus determinants. In *Advances in experimental social psychology,* vol. 7, edited by L. Berkowitz. New York: Academic Press, 1974.

Staub, E. *The development of prosocial behavior in children.* Morristown, N. J.: General Learning Press, 1975a.

Staub, E. To rear a prosocial child: Reasoning, learning by doing, and learning by teaching others. In *Moral development: Current theory and research,* edited by D. J. DePalma and J. M. Foley. Hillsdale, N.J.: Lawrence Erlbaum, 1975b.

Steele, C. M. Name-calling and compliance. *Journal of Personality and Social Psychology,* 1975, *31,* 361–369.

Stein, A. H., and Bailey, M. M. The socialization of achievement orientation in females. *Psychological Bulletin*, 1973, *80*, 345–366.

Stein, D. D., Hardyck, J. A., and Smith, M. B. Race and belief: An open and shut case. *Journal of Personality and Social Psychology*, 1965, *1*, 281–290.

Stein, G. M. Children's reactions to innocent victims. *Child Development*, 1973, *44*, 805–810.

Stein, R. T. Identifying emergent leaders from verbal and nonverbal communications. *Journal of Personality and Social Psychology*, 1975, *32*, 125–135.

Steiner, I. D. Whatever happened to the group in social psychology? *Journal of Experimental Social Psychology*, 1974, *10*, 94–108.

Stephan, W., Berscheid, E., and Walster, E. Sexual arousal and heterosexual perception. *Journal of Personality and Social Psychology*, 1971, *20*, 93–101.

Sternglanz, S. H., and Serbin, L. A. Sex-role stereotyping in children's television programs. *Developmental Psychology*, 1974, *10*, 710–715.

Stokols, D. On the distinction between density and crowding: Some implications for future research. *Psychological Review*, 1972, *79*, 275–278.

Stokols, D. The experience of crowding in primary and secondary environments. Unpublished manuscript, University of California at Irvine, 1975.

Stokols, D., Rall, M., Pinner, B., and Schopler, J. Physical, social, and personal determinants of the perception of crowding. *Environment and Behavior*, 1973, *5*, 87–117.

Stokols, D., and Schopler, J. Reactions to victims under conditions of situational detachment: The effects of responsibility, severity, and expected future interaction. *Journal of Personality and Social Psychology*, 1973, *25*, 199–209.

Storms, M. D. Videotape and the attribution process: Reversing actors' and observers' points of view. *Journal of Personality and Social Psychology*, 1973, *27*, 165–175.

Stratton, L. O., Tekippe, D. J., and Flick, G. L. Personal space and self-concept. *Sociometry*, 1973, *36*, 424–429.

Stumphauzer, J. S. Modification of delay choices in institutionalized youthful offenders through social reinforcement. *Psychonomic Science*, 1970, *18*, 222–223.

Stumphauzer, J. S. Increased delay of gratification in young prison inmates through imitation of high-delay peer models. *Journal of Personality and Social Psychology*, 1972, *21*, 10–17.

Suedfeld, P., Bochner, S., and Matas, C. Petitioner's attire and petition signing by peace demonstrators: A field experiment. *Journal of Applied Social Psychology*, 1971, *1*, 278–283.

Suedfeld, P., Epstein, Y. M., Buchanan, E., and Landon, P. B. Effects of set on the "effects of mere exposure." *Journal of Personality and Social Psychology*, 1971, *17*, 121–123.

Suls, J. M., and Gutkin, D. C. Children's reaction to an actor as a function of expectations and of the consequences received. *Journal of Personality*, 1976, *44*, 149–162.

Sung, Y. H. Effects of attitude similarity and favorableness of information on Bayesian decision making in a realistic task. *Journal of Applied Psychology*, 1975, *60*, 616–620.

Suttles, G. D. *The social order of the slum.* Chicago: University of Chicago Press, 1968.

Swart, C., and Berkowitz, L. Effects of a stimulus associated with a victim's pain on later aggression. *Journal of Personality and Social Psychology*, 1976, *33*, 623–631.

Swingle, P. G. Exploitative behavior in nonzero-sum games. *Journal of Personality and Social Psychology*, 1970a, *16*, 121–132.

Swingle, P. G., ed. *The structure of conflict.* New York: Academic Press, 1970b.

Swingle, P. G., and Santi, A. Communication in nonzero-sum games. *Journal of Personality and Social Psychology*, 1972, *23*, 54–63.

Tannenbaum, P. H., and Zillmann, D. Emotional arousal in the facilitation of aggression through communication. In *Advances in experimental social psychology*, vol. 8, edited by L. Berkowitz. New York: Academic Press, 1975.

Tavris, C. Who likes women's liberation—and why! The case of the unliberated liberals. *Journal of Social Issues*, 1973, *29*, 175–198.

Taylor, D. Should we integrate organizations? In *Integrating the organization*, edited by H. Fromkin and J. Sherwood. New York: Free Press, 1974.

Taylor, G. R. *Sex in history.* New York: Ballantine, 1954.

Taylor, S. E., and Fiske, S. T. Point of view and

perceptions of causality. *Journal of Personality and Social Psychology,* 1975, *32,* 439–445.

Taylor, S. E., and Koivumaki, J. H. The perception of self and others: Acquaintanceship, affect, and actor-observer differences. *Journal of Personality and Social Psychology,* 1976, *33,* 403–408.

Taylor, S. P., and Gammon, C. B. Effects of type and dose of alcohol on human physical aggression. *Journal of Personality and Social Psychology,* 1975, *32,* 169–175.

Taylor, S. P., Gammon, C. B., and Capasso, D. R. Aggression as a function of the interaction of alcohol and threat. *Journal of Personality and Social Psychology,* 1976, *34,* 938–941.

Taylor, S. P., and Pisano, R. Physical aggression as a function of frustration and physical attack. *Journal of Social Psychology,* 1971, *84,* 261–267.

Taylor, S. P., Vardaris, R. M., Rawitch, A. B., Gammon, C. B., Cranston, J. W., and Lubetkin, A. I. The effects of alcohol and delta-9-tetrahydrocannabinol on human physical aggression. *Aggressive Behavior,* 1976, *2,* 153–162.

Taynor, J., and Deaux, K. When women are more deserving than men: Equity, attribution, and perceived sex differences. *Journal of Personality and Social Psychology,* 1973, *28,* 360–367.

Thayer, S., and Saarni, C. Demand characteristics are everywhere (anyway): A comment on the Stanford prison experiment. *American Psychologist,* 1975, *30,* 1015–1016.

Thelen, M. H., Dollinger, S. J., and Roberts, M. C. On being imitated: Its effects on attraction and reciprocal imitation. *Journal of Personality and Social Psychology,* 1975, *31,* 467–472.

Thelen, M. H., and Kirkland, K. D. On status and being imitated: Effects on reciprocal imitation and attraction. *Journal of Personality and Social Psychology,* 1976, *33,* 691–697.

Thibaut, J. W., and Kelley, H. H. *The social psychology of groups.* New York: John Wiley & Sons, 1959.

Thurstone, L. L., and Chave, E. J. *The measurement of attitude.* Chicago: University of Illinois Press, 1929.

Tilker, H. A. Socially responsible behavior as a function of observer responsibility and victim feedback. *Journal of Personality and Social Psychology,* 1970, *14,* 95–100.

Toch, H. *Violent men.* Chicago: Aldine, 1969.

Tognacci, L. N., and Cook, S. W. Conditioned autonomic responses as bidirectional indicators of racial attitude. *Journal of Personality and Social Psychology,* 1975, *31,* 137–144.

Touhey, J. C. Effects of additional men on prestige and desirability of occupations typically performed by women. *Journal of Applied Social Psychology,* 1974a, *4,* 330–335.

Touhey, J. C. Effects of additional women professionals on ratings of occupational prestige and desirability. *Journal of Personality and Social Psychology,* 1974b, *29,* 86–89.

Travis, L. E. The effect of a small audience upon eye-hand coordination. *Journal of Abnormal and Social Psychology,* 1925, *20,* 142–146.

Triandis, H. C. A note on Rokeach's theory of prejudice. *Journal of Abnormal and Social Psychology,* 1961, *62,* 184–186.

Triandis, H. C., and Davis, E. E. Race and belief as shared determinants of behavioral intentions. *Journal of Personality and Social Psychology,* 1965, *2,* 715–725.

Triandis, H. C., Loh, W. D., and Levin, L. A. Race, status, quality of spoken English, and opinion about civil rights as determinants of interpersonal attitudes. *Journal of Personality and Social Psychology,* 1966, *3,* 468–472.

Triplett, N. The dynamogenic factors in pace-making and competition. *American Journal of Psychology,* 1897, *9,* 507–533.

Turner, C. W., Layton, J. F., and Simons, L. S. Naturalistic studies of aggressive behavior: Aggressive stimuli, victim visibility, and horn honking. *Journal of Personality and Social Psychology,* 1975, *31,* 1098–1107.

Turner, C. W., and Simons, L. S. Effects of subject sophistication and evaluation apprehension on aggressive responses to weapons. *Journal of Personality and Social Psychology,* 1974, *30,* 341–348.

Udry, J. R. *The social context of marriage.* Philadelphia: Lippincott, 1971.

Udry, J. R., and Morris, N. M. Distribution of coitus in the menstrual cycle. *Nature,* 1968, *220,* 593–596.

Ueda, T., and Taniguchi, K. Self-concept and affiliation tendency. *Bulletin,* Nara University of Education, 1974, *23,* 169–177.

Ulrich, R. E., Johnston, M., Richardson, J., and

Wolff, P. The operant conditioning of fighting behavior in rats. *Psychological Record,* 1963, *13,* 465–470.

Valins, S. Cognitive effects of false heart-rate feedback. *Journal of Personality and Social Psychology,* 1966, *4,* 400–408.

Valins, S., and Baum, A. Residential group size, social interaction and crowding. *Environment and Behavior,* 1973, *5,* 421–440.

Van Hoof, J. A. R. A. M. The facial displays of the catarrhine monkey and apes. In *Primate ethology,* edited by D. Morris. Chicago: Aldine, 1967.

Vance, E. B., and Wagner, N. N. Written descriptions of orgasm: A study of sex differences. *Archives of Sexual Behavior,* 1976, *5,* 87–98.

Veitch, R., and Griffitt, W. Good news, bad news: Affective and interpersonal effects. *Journal of Applied Social Psychology,* 1976, *6,* 69–75.

Venn, J. R., and Short, J. G. Vicarious classical conditioning of emotional responses in nursery-school children. *Journal of Personality and Social Psychology,* 1973, *28,* 249–255.

Vidmar, N. Group-induced shifts in simulated jury decision. Paper presented at the meetings of the Midwestern Psychological Association, Cleveland, May 1972.

Vidmar, N. Effects of group discussion on category width judgments. *Journal of Personality and Social Psychology,* 1974, *29,* 187–195.

Vidmar, N., and Rokeach, M. Archie Bunker's bigotry: A study in selective perception and exposure. *Journal of Communication,* 1974, *24,* 36–47.

Vinokur, A., and Burnstein, E. Effects of partially shared persuasive arguments on group-induced shifts: A group problem-solving approach. *Journal of Personality and Social Psychology,* 1974, *29,* 305–315.

Vogel, S. R., Broverman, I. K., Broverman, D. M., Clarkson, F. E., and Rosenkrantz, P. S. Maternal employment and perception of sex-roles among college students. *Developmental Psychology,* 1970, *3,* 384–391.

Wagner, C., and Wheeler, L. Model, need, and cost effects in helping behavior. *Journal of Personality and Social Psychology,* 1969, *12,* 111–116.

Wahrman, R., and Pugh, M. D. Sex, nonconformity and influence. *Sociometry,* 1974, *37,* 137–147.

Walker, T. G., and Main, E. C. Choice-shifts in political decision making: Federal judges and civil liberties cases. *Journal of Applied Social Psychology,* 1973, *2,* 39–48.

Wall, G. Public response to air pollution in South Yorkshire, England. *Environment and Behavior,* 1973, *5,* 219–248.

Wallace, D. H. Obscenity and contemporary community standards: A survey. *Journal of Social Issues,* 1973, *29,* 53–68.

Wallace, D. H., and Wehmer, G. Evaluation of visual erotica by sexual liberals and conservatives. *Journal of Sex Research,* 1972, *8,* 147–153.

Wallace, J., and Sadalla, E. Behavioral consequences of transgression: I. The effects of social recognition. *Journal of Experimental Research in Personality,* 1966, *1,* 187–194.

Wallach, M. A., and Wing, C. W. Is risk a value? *Journal of Personality and Social Psychology,* 1968, *9,* 101–106.

Walster, E. Assignment of responsibility for an accident, *Journal of Personality and Social Psychology,* 1966, *3,* 73–79.

Walster, E., Aronson, E., and Abrahams, D. On increasing the persuasiveness of a low prestige communicator. *Journal of Experimental Social Psychology,* 1966, *2,* 325–342.

Walster, E., Aronson, V., Abrahams, D., and Rottman, L. Importance of physical attractiveness in dating behavior. *Journal of Personality and Social Psychology,* 1966, *4,* 508–516.

Walster, E., Berscheid, E., and Walster, G. W. New directions in equity research. *Journal of Personality and Social Psychology,* 1973, *35,* 151–176.

Walster, E., and Festinger, L. The effectiveness of "overheard" persuasive communications. *Journal of Abnormal and Social Psychology,* 1962, *65,* 395–402.

Walster, E., and Piliavin, J. A. Equity and the innocent bystander. *Journal of Social Issues,* 1972, *28,* 165–189.

Walster, E., Walster, G., Piliavin, J., and Schmidt, L. "Playing hard-to-get:" Understanding an elusive phenomenon. *Journal of Personality and Social Psychology,* 1973, *26,* 113–121.

Walters, R. H. Implications of laboratory studies of aggression for the control and regulation of violence. *Annals of the American Academy of*

Political and Social Science, 1966, *364,* 60–72.

Walters, R. H., Leat, M., and Mezei, L. Inhibition and disinhibition of responses through empathetic learning. *Canadian Journal of Psychology,* 1963, *17,* 235–243.

Watson, O. M., and Graves, T. D. Quantitative research in proxemic behavior. *American Anthropologist,* 1966, *68,* 971–985.

Watson, R. I. Investigation into deindividuation using a cross-cultural survey technique. *Journal of Personality and Social Psychology,* 1973, *25,* 342–345.

Weick, K. E., and Gilfillan, D. P. Fate of arbitrary traditions in a laboratory microculture. *Journal of Personality and Social Psychology,* 1971, *17,* 179–191.

Weiner, M. J., and Wright, F. E. Effects of undergoing arbitrary discrimination upon subsequent attitudes toward a minority group. *Journal of Applied Social Psychology,* 1973, *3,* 94–102.

Weiss, R. F., Buchanan, W., Alstatt, L., and Lombardo, J. P. Altruism is rewarding. *Science,* 1971, *171,* 1262–1263.

Weisstein, N. Psychology constructs the female. In *Roles women play,* edited by M. H. Garskof. Belmont, Calif.: Brooks/Cole, 1971.

Weitzman, L. J., Eifler, D., Hokada, E., and Ross, C. Sex role socialization in picture books for preschool children. *American Journal of Sociology,* 1972, *77,* 1125–1150.

Wellens, A. R., and Thistlewaite, D. L. Comparison of three theories of cognitive balance. *Journal of Personality and Social Psychology,* 1971, *20,* 82–92.

West, S. G., and Brown, T. J. Physical attractiveness, the severity of the emergency and helping: A field experiment and interpersonal simulation. *Journal of Experimental Social Psychology,* 1975, *11,* 531–538.

West, S. G., Gunn, S. P., and Chernicky, P. Ubiquitous Watergate: An attributional analysis. *Journal of Personality and Social Psychology,* 1975, *32,* 55–56.

West, S. G., Whitney, G., and Schnedler, R. Helping a motorist in distress: The effects of sex, race, and neighborhood. *Journal of Personality and Social Psychology,* 1975, *31,* 691–698.

Wheeler, L. Toward a theory of behavioral contagion. *Psychological Review,* 1966, *73,* 179–192.

Wheeler, L. *Interpersonal influence,* 2nd ed. Boston: Allyn and Bacon, 1978.

Wheeler, L., and Caggiula, A. R. The contagion of aggression. *Journal of Experimental Social Psychology,* 1966, *2,* 1–10.

White, G. M. Immediate and deferred effects of model observation and guided and unguided rehearsal on donating and stealing. *Journal of Personality and Social Psychology,* 1972, *21,* 139–148.

Whyte, W. W., Jr. *The organization man.* New York: Simon and Schuster, 1956.

Wichman, H. Effects of isolation and communication on cooperation in a two-person game. *Journal of Personality and Social Psychology,* 1970, 16, 114–120.

Wicker, A. W. An examination of the "other variables" explanation of attitude-behavior inconsistency. *Journal of Personality and Social Psychology,* 1971, *19,* 18–30.

Wicklund, R. A. Objective self awareness. In *Advances in experimental social psychology,* vol. 8, edited by L. Berkowitz. New York: Academic Press, 1975.

Wicklund, R. A., and Duval, S. Opinion change and performance facilitation as a result of objective self awareness. *Journal of Experimental Social Psychology,* 1971, *7,* 319–342.

Wiesenthal, D. L., Endler, N. S., Coward, T. R., and Edwards. J. Reversibility of relative competence as a determinant of conformity across different perceptual tasks. *Representative Research in Social Psychology,* 1976, *7,* 35–43.

Wiggins, J. S., Wiggins, N., and Conger, J. C. Correlates of heterosexual somatic preference. *Journal of Personality and Social Psychology,* 1968, *10,* 82–90.

Wilkins, J. L., Scharff, W. H., and Schlottmann, R. S. Personality type, reports of violence, and aggressive behavior. *Journal of Personality and Social Psychology,* 1974, *30,* 243–247.

Williams, J. E., Bennett, S. M., and Best, D. L. Awareness and expression of sex stereotypes in young children. *Developmental Psychology,* 1975, *11,* 635–642.

Willis, F. N. Initial speaking distance as a function of the speakers' relationship. *Psychonomic Science,* 1966, *5,* 221–222.

Willis, R. H., and Willis, Y. A. Role playing versus deception: An experimental comparison. *Journal of Personality and Social Psychology,*

1970, *16*, 472–477.

Wilson, L., and Rogers, R. W. The fire this time: Effects of race of target, insult, and potential retaliation on black aggression, *Journal of Personality and Social Psychology*, 1975, *32*, 857–864.

Wilson, W., and Nakajo, H. Preference for photographs as a function of frequency of presentation. *Psychonomic Science*, 1965, *3*, 577–578.

Wilson, W. C., and Abelson, H. I. Experience with and attitudes toward explicit sexual materials. *Journal of Social Issues*, 1973, *29* (3), 19–39.

Wispé, L., ed. *Positive forms of social behavior.* Cambridge: Harvard University Press, 1976.

Wolf, D. Effects of a live-modeled sex-inappropriate play behavior in a naturalistic setting. *Developmental Psychology*, 1973, *9*, 120–123.

Wolfe, B. M., and Baron, R. A. Laboratory aggression related to aggression in naturalistic social situations: Effects of an aggressive model on the behavior of college students and prisoner observers. *Psychonomic Science*, 1971, *24*, 193–194.

Wolosin, R. J. Cognitive similarity and group laughter. *Journal of Personality and Social Psychology*, 1975, *32*, 503–509.

Wolosin, R. J., Sherman, S. J., and Cann, A. Predictions of own and other's conformity. *Journal of Personality*, 1975, *43*, 357–378.

Woodmansee, J. J. The pupil response as a measure of social attitude. In *Attitude measurement*, edited by G. Summers. New York: Rand-McNally, 1970.

Woodworth, R. S. *Experimental psychology.* New York: Holt, 1938.

Worchel, S. The effect of three types of arbitrary thwarting on the instigation to aggression. *Journal of Personality*, 1974, *42*, 301–318.

Worchel, S., and Brand, J. Role of responsibility and violated expectancy in the arousal of dissonance. *Journal of Personality and Social Psychology*, 1972, *22*, 87–97.

Worchel, S., and Brehm, J. W. Direct and implied social restoration of freedom. *Journal of Personality and Social Psychology*, 1971, *18*, 294–304.

Wright, P. H. A model and a technique for studies of friendship. *Journal of Experimental Social Psychology*, 1969, *5*, 295–309.

Wright, P. H., and Crawford, A. C. Agreement and friendship: A close look and some second thoughts. *Representative Research in Social Psychology*, 1971, *2*, 52–69.

Wrightsman, L. S., Jr. Effects of waiting with others on changes in level of felt anxiety. *Journal of Abnormal and Social Psychology*, 1960, *61*, 216–222.

Wrightsman, L. S., Jr. Wallace supporters and adherence to "law and order." *Journal of Personality and Social Psychology*, 1966, *4*, 328–332.

Yakimovich, D., and Saltz, E. Helping behavior: The cry for help. *Psychonomic Science*, 1971, *23*, 427–428.

Yarrow, M. R., and Scott, P. M. Imitation of nurturant and nonnurturant models. *Journal of Personality and Social Psychology*, 1972, *23*, 259–270.

Yukl, G. Effects of the opponent's initial offer, concession magnitude, and concession frequency on bargaining behavior. *Journal of Personality and Social Psychology*, 1974a, *30*, 323–335.

Yukl, G. The effects of situational variables and opponent concessions on a bargainer's perception, aspirations, and concessions. *Journal of Personality and Social Psychology*, 1974b, *29*, 227–236.

Zajonc, R. B. Social facilitation. *Science*, 1965, *149*, 269–274.

Zajonc, R. B. Attitudinal effects of mere exposure. *Journal of Personality and Social Psychology Monograph Supplement*, 1968, *9*, 1–27.

Zajonc, R. B., Heingartner, A., and Herman, E. M. Social enhancement and impairment of performance in the cockroach. *Journal of Personality and Social Psychology*, 1969, *13*, 83–92.

Zajonc, R. B., and Rajecki, D. W. Exposure and affect: A field experiment. *Psychonomic Science*, 1969, *17*, 216–217.

Zajonc, R. B., and Sales, S. M. Social facilitation of dominant and subordinate responses. *Journal of Experimental Social Psychology*, 1966, *2*, 160–168.

Zajonc, R. B., Shaver, P., Tavris, C., and Kreveld, D. V. Exposure, satiation, and stimulus discriminability. *Journal of Personality and Social Psychology*, 1972, *21*, 270–280.

Zanna, M. P., Klossen, E., and Darley, J. M. How television news viewers deal with facts that contradict their beliefs: A consistency and attribution analysis. *Journal of Applied Social Psychology,* 1976, *11,* 159–176.

Zanna, M. P., and Cooper, J. Dissonance and the pill: An attribution approach to studying the arousal properties of dissonance. *Journal of Personality and Social Psychology,* 1974, *29,* 703–709.

Zanna, M. P., Kiesler, C. A., and Pilkonis, P. A. Positive and negative attitudinal affect established by classical conditioning. *Journal of Personality and Social Psychology,* 1970, *14,* 321–328.

Zdep, S. M., and Oakes, W. F. Reinforcement of leadership behavior in group discussion. *Journal of Experimental Social Psychology,* 1967, *3,* 310–320.

Zellner, M. Self-esteem, reception, and influenceability. *Journal of Personality and Social Psychology,* 1970, *15,* 87–93.

Zillmann, D. Excitation transfer in communication-mediated aggressive behavior. *Journal of Experimental Social Psychology,* 1971, *7,* 419–434.

Zillmann, D., and Bryant, J. Effect of residual excitation on the emotional response to provocation and delayed aggressive behavior. *Journal of Personality and Social Psychology,* 1974, *30,* 782–791.

Zillmann, D., and Cantor, J. R. Effects of timing of information about mitigating circumstances on emotional responses to provocation and retaliatory behavior. *Journal of Experimental Social Psychology,* 1976, *12,* 38–55.

Zillmann, D., Johnson, R. C., and Day, K. D. Attribution of apparent arousal and proficiency of recovery from sympathetic activation affecting excitation transfer to aggressive behavior. *Journal of Experimental Social Psychology,* 1974, *10,* 503–515.

Zillmann, D., Katcher, A. H., and Milavsky, B. Excitation transfer from physical exercise to subsequent aggressive behavior. *Journal of Experimental Social Psychology,* 1972, *8,* 247–259.

Zimbardo, P. G. The human choice: Individuation, reason, and order versus deindividuation, impulse, and chaos. In *Nebraska symposium on motivation, 1969,* edited by W. J. Arnold and D. Levine. Lincoln: University of Nebraska Press, 1970.

Zimbardo, P. G. On the ethics of intervention in human psychological research: With special reference to the Stanford prison experiment. *Cognition,* 1974, *2,* 243–256.

Zimbardo, P. G., Haney, C., Banks, W. C., and Jaffe, D. A Pirandellian prison: The mind is a formidable jailer. *New York Times Magazine,* April 8, 1973, pp. 38–60.

Zuckerman, M. Belief in a just world and altruistic behavior. *Journal of Personality and Social Psychology,* 1975, *31,* 972–976.

Zuckerman, M., and Wheeler, L. To dispel fantasies about the fantasy-based measure of fear of success. *Psychological Bulletin,* 1975, *82,* 932–946.

NAME INDEX

Abel, G. G., 474
Abelson, H., 483
Abelson, H. I., 492
Abrahams, D., 71, 114
Abramson, P. R., 465, 491
Adams, G. R., 215
Adams, J. S., 544
Aderman, D., 549
Adorno, T. W., 11, 166
Agar, E., 209
Aiello, J. R., 610
Albert, S., 614
Allee, W. C., 561
Alexander, C. N., 136
Alioto, J. T., 320, 441
Allen, B. P., 102, 157, 162
Allen, V. L., 260, 270, 273
Allgeier, A. R., 238
Allman, L., 413
Allport, F. H., 9–11
Allport, G. W., 7, 156
Altman, I., 607–608, 621
Alvares, K. M., 600
American Psychological Association, 32
Amir, Y., 174
Amoroso, D. M., 499
Anderson, A. J., 523–524
Anderson, N. H., 81, 83
Angulo, E. J., 76
Apsler, R., 285
Aram, J. D., 575
Argyle, M., 615
Aristotle, 7
Arkin, R. M., 64, 66
Aronfreed, J., 397
Aronson, E., 33, 69, 71, 102, 114, 117, 136, 218, 230
Asch, S. E., 86, 257–259, 266–267, 298
Ashmore, R. D., 154, 170, 174, 176
Austin, J. B., 284
Austin, W., 546

Aves, P., 239
Azjen, I., 95, 144, 146

Back, K., 218–219, 264
Baird, S. L., 534
Bales, R. F., 594
Ball, R. L., 446
Bandura, A., 306, 308, 311, 314–315, 318, 320–321, 330, 339, 342–343, 406, 411, 414–415, 424, 438, 549
Banikiotes, P. G., 230
Banks, W., 589
Banks, W. C., 239
Banuazizi, A., 590
Barclay, A. M., 479, 490
Barefoot, J. C., 618
Barker, C. H., 278
Barnes, R. D., 64
Baron, P. H., 575
Baron, R. A., 23–24, 26, 276, 306, 317, 320, 333, 361, 413, 423, 426–427, 439, 444, 446, 642
Baron, R. M., 632
Baron, R. S., 569, 574–575, 580
Bartell, G. D., 478
Baskett, G. D., 238
Bass, B. M., 591, 638
Bass, R., 638
Bates, J. E., 309
Batson, C. D., 365, 385
Baum, A., 632, 634
Baum, M. R., 127
Baumgardner, S. R., 573
Beach, F. A., 461, 477–478
Beale, F., 177
Becker, F. D., 623
Beckhouse, L., 592–593
Behar, L. B., 499
Bell, L., 102
Bell, P. A., 208, 223, 317, 426, 482, 642
Bem, D. J., 76–78, 143, 181, 214

Bem, S. L., 156, 181, 190
Bennett, D. H., 30–31
Bennett, S. M., 188
Benson, J. S., 636
Benton, A. A., 529
Berdie, R. F., 419
Berger, D. E., 53, 214
Berger, S. M., 338–339, 446
Bergmann, G., 6
Berkowitz, L., 34, 76, 312, 320, 410–411, 417, 428–429, 441, 446, 543
Berkowitz, W. R., 214
Bermant, G., 485
Berscheid, E., 115, 199, 200, 212, 214–215, 231, 234, 499, 544, 546, 549
Best, D. L., 188
Bickman, L., 312, 372, 374–375, 386, 634
Bierbrauer, G., 266
Bishop, G. D., 571, 573, 580
Bitter, E., 446
Bixenstine, V. E., 162
Black, J. S., 144, 146
Black, T. E., 519
Blake, R. E., 308
Blanchard, B., 342–343
Bleda, P. R., 618
Bleda, S. E., 618
Bochner, S., 236
Bode, K. A., 395
Bolen, D., 651
Bond, M. H., 236
Bonsall, R. W., 458
Booker, A., 34, 429
Borden, R., 121
Borden, R. J., 414, 419, 632
Borgatta, E. F., 594
Boring, E. G., 8
Boutillier, R. G., 594–595
Bowen, R., 419
Bowers, R. J., 575
Boye, D., 549

Elkes, R., 283
Elliott, R., 437
Ellsworth, P. C., 45–46, 53–54, 240, 377
Elms, A., 293
Elms, A. C., 11
Emler, N. P., 357
Empey, J., 610
Emswiller, T., 184, 276
Endler, N. S., 260
Enzle, M. E., 518, 526
Eron, L. D., 18–20, 23–24
Ervin, C. R., 226, 238
Escudero, M., 631
Esser, A. H., 623
Etaugh, C., 180
Evans, G. W., 620
Evans, R., 426–427
Evans, R. I., 118, 162
Exline, R. V., 52
Eysenck, H. J., 497

Fagot, B. I., 186
Fallot, R. D., 86
Fast, J., 55–56
Feinberg, R., 228
Feldman-Summers, S., 184
Feleky, A. M., 46
Felipe, N. J., 615
Fencil-Morse, E., 637
Fenigstein, A., 83
Ferris, C. B., 83
Feshbach, S., 323, 446
Festinger, L., 12–13, 114–115, 133,
    138–139, 141, 143, 218–220, 264–265,
    299, 476
Fey, S., 315
Fiedler, F. E., 596–598, 600
Filter, T. A., 286
Fine, R., 83
Finger, F. W., 485
Fishbein, M., 95, 144, 146
Fisher, J. D., 395–397, 472, 610, 616
Fisher, S., 627
Fisher, S., 468
Fisher, W. A., 472, 500
Fiske, S. T., 66, 68
Fithian, M. A., 463
Flick, G. L., 612
Forman, R., 219
Fraser, S. C., 278
Fredd, S., 221
Frederickson, W. A., 214
Freedman, J. L., 30, 278, 631–634
Freud, S., 355, 357, 359, 399, 408–410
Freund, K., 493
Friedman, L. N., 635
Friedrich, G., 212
Friedrich, G. W., 240
Friesen, W. V., 45–46, 51–52, 56
Frieze, I., 63
Frodi, A., 426, 429
Froman, R., 352
Fromkin, H. L., 210
Fuhr, R., 494

Gaebelein, J. W., 414
Gaertner, S. L., 166
Galbraith, G. G., 480, 482

Galizio, M., 123
Galle, O. R., 631
Gallo, P., 513
Galper, R. E., 212
Gammon, C. B., 430
Ganzer, V. J., 347
Garcia, L. T., 239
Garland, H., 538
Garner, K. A., 275
Gates, M. G., 561
Gebhard, P. H., 460
Geen, R. G., 320, 333, 411, 417, 421, 424,
    432, 442, 446, 637
Geer, J. H., 494, 496
Geis, F. L., 531
Gelb, P. M., 645
Gelfand, D. M., 374–375, 424
Geller, C., 202
Geller, D. M., 217
Gellert, E., 214
Gentry, W. D., 417
Gerard, H. B., 136, 258, 260
Gerbrandt, L. K., 477
Gergen, K. J., 6, 262, 395, 531
Gerst, M. S., 315
Gewirtz, J. L., 306
Giesen, M., 120–121
Gilbert, G. M., 160
Gilfillan, D. P., 257
Gillig, P. M., 116
Gilliland, G. W., 646
Gillmore, G., 356
Gilmore, T. M., 63
Glass, D. C., 245, 432, 565, 635–636
Godow, A. G., 470
Goethals, G. R., 139
Goldberg, P., 177, 181
Goldman, J. A., 212
Goldring, P., 610
Goldstein, J. W., 214
Goldstein, M., 163
Goldstein, M. J., 497
Good, K. J., 239
Good, K. J., 569
Good, L. R., 239
Goodman, M. E., 168
Goranson, R. E., 441, 639
Gordon, M., 478, 482
Gordon, P., 631
Gorkin, L., 177
Gotay, C. C., 397
Gotestam, K. G., 347
Gouaux, C., 212, 222
Graen, G. B., 600
Grant, G., 168
Graves, T. D., 611
Greco, J. T., 647
Green, D., 143
Green, S. K., 375
Greenberg, B., 610
Greene, D., 77–80
Greenwald, A. G., 116, 389
Greenwell, J., 420
Greenwood, P., 496
Grether, J., 393
Griffith, M., 457
Griffitt, W., 202, 209–210, 223–224, 236,
    239, 475, 500, 632, 639

Gross, A. E., 237, 280, 286, 333, 396
Grove, W. R., 631
Grusec, J., 187
Grusec, J. E., 318, 325
Grush, J. E., 221, 228
Gunn, S. P., 29
Gutkin, D. C., 354

Haase, R. S., 610
Haber, G. M., 645
Hacker, H. M., 177
Hagen, R., 181
Hall, E. T., 611, 613–615, 619
Hall, J. V., 127
Hamilton, D. L., 86
Hamilton, P., 635
Hamm, N. H., 127
Hamner, W. C., 536
Haney, C., 589
Hanratty, M. A., 318
Hansen, R. D., 518, 526
Harburg, E., 202
Hardesty, F. P., 186
Harding, J., 167–168
Hardy, R. C., 598
Hardyck, J. A., 163
Hariton, E. B., 477
Harris, B., 64
Harris, M. B., 25, 418
Harris, V. A., 120
Harrison, A. A., 128, 221
Harrison-Ross, P., 172
Hartley, R. E., 186
Hartman, J. J., 497
Hartman, W. E., 463
Hartmann, D., 424
Hartup, W. W., 186, 273
Harvey, J., 114–115
Harvey, J. H., 64
Hasazi, J. E., 347
Hastorf, A. H., 592
Hawkins, G., 162
Hayes, S. C., 649
Heberlein, T. A., 114, 146
Heider, F., 58, 200
Heilman, M. E., 275
Heingartner, A., 127, 566
Heller, J. F., 129
Helmreich, R., 181
Henchy, T., 565
Hendee, J. C., 649
Hendrick, C., 15, 95, 120–121, 162, 379
Henley, M. D., 139
Henson, A., 53
Herman, E. M., 566
Herrell, J. M., 489
Heshka, S., 609, 631
Heslin, R., 122–123, 610
Hewitt, L. S., 421
Higbee, K. L., 117, 519
Himmelfarb, S., 109
Hiroto, D. S., 636
Hobart, C. W., 498
Hobson, L. Z., 170
Hochberg, J., 212
Hockey, G. R. J., 635
Hodges, L., 238
Hodges, L. A., 243

Loh, W. E., 162
Lohr, J. M., 106
Lombardo, J. P., 228
London, J., 198
London, P., 380
Long, G., 545
Lorenz, K., 409–410
Lott, A. J., 202, 241
Lott, B. E., 202, 241
Lott, B. S., 610
Lott, D. F., 9, 410
Lowe, C. A., 518, 526
Lumsdaine, A. A., 116
Luttage, W. G., 461
Lynch, K., 626–627

Macaranas, E. A., 265
Maccoby, E. E., 180
Mader, S., 111, 325
Maehr, M. L., 173–174, 356
Main, E. C., 573
Mallick, S. K., 442
Mann, J., 499
Mann, L., 293–294
Mann, M., 264
Mann, R. D., 591
Manning, S. A., 320
Marlowe, D., 389, 531
Marsan, E., 464
Marsella, A. J., 631
Marshall, D. S., 489
Marshello, A. F. J., 518, 525–526
Martens, R., 563, 565
Martindale, D. A., 623
Maruyama, G., 214–215, 229
Marwell, G., 546
Maslow, A. H., 645
Masters, W. H., 456, 468, 483–484, 496
Mason, W. A., 9, 410
Masor, H. N., 324
Matas, C., 236
Mathews, K. E., 637
Mathewson, G. C., 136
Matlin, M. W., 563
Matsuyama, S. S., 438
Matter, C. F., 620
May, J., 500
McArthur, L. A., 63
McCandless, B. R., 442
McCarthy, J. D., 168
McCary, J. L., 459
McCauley, C., 570, 575
McClay, D., 618
McClelland, L., 632
McClintock, C. G., 526
McDavid, J. W., 273
McDonald, N., 544
McDougall, W., 8–9
McFall, R. M., 347
McGee, M. G., 25
McGovern, L. P., 361, 388, 393
McGuire, W. J., 14, 17, 122–123, 130
McKenna, R. H., 375
McKeough, K. L., 221
McMillen, D. L., 284
McNeel, S. P., 525–526
McPeek, R. W., 237
McPherson, J. M., 631

Mead, M., 488
Meadow, B. L., 239, 241
Meeker, F. B., 53
Megargee, E. I., 433–434
Mehrabian, A., 52, 55, 238, 610
Meichenbaum, D. H., 342–343
Melin, L., 347
Melson, W. H., 109
Melville, M. M., 438
Mendelsohn, M., 229
Menlove, F. L., 342
Mettee, D., 446–447
Mettee, D. R., 549
Mewborn, R., 118
Meyer, P., 221
Meyer, T. P., 426
Mezei, L., 163, 308, 329
Michael, R. P., 458
Michaels, J. W., 544
Michener, H. A., 295, 596
Middlemist, R. D., 620
Midlarsky, E., 333
Milavsky, B., 424
Milgram, S., 29, 289, 293–294, 296, 298–299, 312, 323, 378, 412–413
Mill, J. S., 7
Miller, A. G., 30
Miller, C., 472
Miller, D. T., 69, 391–392
Miller, H., 202
Miller, N., 214–215, 229, 569, 574
Miller, N. E., 306, 417
Miller, R. E., 48, 51, 336
Miller, R. L., 651
Miller, R. S., 268, 270
Mills, J., 70, 114–115, 136, 397
Minton, H. L., 63
Mintz, N. C., 645
Mirsky, I. A., 336
Mischel, H. W., 181
Mischel, W., 166, 187, 200, 330, 332, 344
Mitchell, H. E., 102
Momboisse, R. M., 423
Money, J., 489
Monson, T. C., 575
Montgomery, 256
Moore, B., 382
Moore, S., 186
Moos, R. H., 648
Mordkoff, A. M., 336
Moreland, R. L., 221
Morgan, C. P., 575
Moriarty, T., 25, 378–379
Morin, S. F., 620
Morokoff, P., 496
Moroney, R. J., 623
Morris, N. M., 457
Morris, W. N., 268, 270, 384
Morse, S. J., 395
Moscovici, S., 571
Mosher, D. L., 232, 465, 467–468, 477, 480, 491
Moss, M. K., 360–361
Movahedi, S., 590
Mueller, C., 446
Mullens, M. C., 615
Mullens, S., 615
Munson, P. A., 95, 134

Murdoch, P., 565
Murdoch, P. H., 575
Murstein, B. I., 214, 225
Myers, D. G., 569, 571, 573, 575, 580
Mynatt, C., 366

Nadler, A., 210, 240, 395–397
Nahemow, L., 219
Nakajo, H., 221
Nass, G. D., 465
Nawy, H., 483
Neale, J. M., 338
Nebel, J. C., 214
Neidermeyer, H., 334
Nelson, D., 207, 241
Nelson, J., 209
Nelson, Y., 609
Nesbitt, P. D., 608
Nesdale, A. R., 407, 418, 432
Newcomb, T. M., 200–202, 247, 264
Newman, O., 647
Newman, S., 645
Newtson, D., 59, 273
Nguyen, M. L., 610
Nguyen, T. D., 610
Niederehe, G., 57
Nietzsche, F., 7
Nikels, K. W., 127
Nisbett, R. E., 64–65, 75, 77
Norum, G. A., 611
Nuttall, R. L., 477, 485
Nydegger, R. V., 592

O'Connor, R. D., 345
Oakes, W. F., 592
Olczak, P. V., 212
O'Leary, M. R., 419
O'Leary, V. H., 177, 180
O'Neal, E., 318
O'Neal, E. C., 424, 432, 637
O'Neill, G. C., 478
O'Neill, N., 478
Orne, M. T., 34
Orris, J. B., 600
Osgood, C., 536
Osgood, C. E., 100
Osmond, H., 646
Ostrom, T. M., 102
Ostrove, N., 215

Pagano, F., 118
Page, M. P., 34, 429
Page, R. A., 360–361
Pallak, M. S., 129, 133, 143
Papageorgis, D., 130
Parke, R. D., 321, 437
Pastore, N., 417
Patterson, A. H., 634
Patterson, E. W. J., 236
Patterson, G. R., 186
Patterson, M. L., 612, 615
Paulus, P. B., 565, 632, 634
Pedersen, D. M., 609
Pellegrini, R. J., 610
Pepitone, A., 586
Peplau, A., 391
Pepper, D. T., 610
Perlman, D., 63

Stass, J. W., 53
Staub, E., 353, 356, 380, 399
Staw, B. M., 78, 80
Steele, C. M., 285
Steigleder, M., 228
Stein, D. D., 163
Stein, G. M., 547
Stein, R. T., 594
Steiner, I. D., 12, 30
Stephan, W., 499
Sternglanz, S. H., 188–189, 315
Steven, G., 608
Stiles, W. B., 446
Stingle, K. C., 306
Stokes, N. A., III, 619
Stokols, D., 547, 630, 633
Stoner, J., 569
Stonner, D., 320, 411, 442
Storms, M. D., 64, 66, 68
Stratton, L. O., 612
Streufert, S., 396
Stumphauzer, J. S., 330
Suci, G. J., 100
Suedfeld, P., 127, 221, 236
Suggs, R. C., 489
Suls, J. M., 354
Sulzer, J. L., 318
Sung, Y. H., 239
Sushinsky, L. W., 78, 80
Suttles, G. D., 623
Swap, W., 221
Swart, C., 446
Swingle, P. G., 519–521

Taniguchi, K., 227
Tannenbaum, P. H., 100, 320, 424
Tausig, M., 596
Tavris, C., 180
Taylor, D., 175
Taylor, D. A., 320
Taylor, G. R., 464
Taylor, S. E., 64, 66, 68
Taylor, S. P., 361, 393, 414, 417, 419, 430–431
Teger, A. I., 575
Tekippl, D. J., 612
Telaak, K., 117
Test, M. A., 313, 323
Thayer, S., 590
Thelen, M. H., 309
Thibaut, J. W., 510
Thiel, D. L., 215
Thistlewaite, D. L., 202
Thurstone, L. L., 97–98
Tilker, H. A., 378
Tobin, T. A., 324
Toch, H., 434–436
Tognacci, L. N., 104
Touhey, J. C., 178
Travis, L. E., 561

Triandis, H. C., 162
Triplett, N., 560
Tucker, I. F., 306
Turner, C. W., 428–429, 444
Turner, J. A., 71, 114, 117
Twentyman, C. T., 347

Udry, J. R., 231, 457
Ueda, T., 227
Ulrich, R. E., 411
Underwood, B., 382

Valins, S., 75–76
Vance, E. B., 483
Van Hoof, J. A. R. A. M., 53
Veitch, R., 210, 223–224, 500, 632
Venn, J. R., 339
Veroff, J., 227
Vidmar, N., 170, 573
Vinokur, A., 578–579

Wack, D. L., 563
Wagner, C., 324
Wagner, N. N., 483
Wahrman, R., 256
Walbek, N. H., 325
Walker, C. E., 457
Walker, T. G., 573
Wall, G., 647
Wallace, D. H., 465, 492
Wallace, T., 282
Wallace, W. P., 610
Wallach, M. A., 574
Walster, E., 69, 71, 114–115, 200, 212, 213, 215, 230, 231, 234, 384, 499, 544, 546, 549
Walster, G. W., 544, 546
Walters, G., 160
Walters, R. H., 308, 329, 437
Watson, O. M., 611
Watson, R. I., 583, 586
Watts, J. C., 118
Wegley, C., 181
Wehmer, G., 465
Weick, K. E., 257
Weiner, B., 63
Weiner, M. J., 172–173
Weiss, R. F., 361–362
Weiss, S. M., 334
Weiss, T., 543, 545
Weiss, W., 114
Weisstein, N., 155
Weitzman, L. J., 189
Wellens, A. R., 202
West, S. G., 29, 392–393
Westbrook, W., 477
Whatmore, P. B., 438
Wheeler, L., 185, 311, 324, 423
White, G. M., 325
White, L., 472

White, R. K., 11
White, W. W., Jr., 219
Whitney, G., 392
Wichman, H., 521
Wicker, A. W., 144
Wicklund, R. A., 82–83
Wiener, J., 357
Wiener, Y., 544
Wiesenthal, D. L., 261
Wiggins, J. S., 214
Wiggins, N., 214
Wiggins, N. H., 55, 230
Wilhelmy, R. A., 260
Wilkins, J. L., 320, 432
Williams, J. E., 188
Willis, F. N., 53, 610, 612
Willis, R. H., 30
Willis, Y. A., 30
Willits, J. E., 276
Wilson, L., 421, 440
Wilson, W., 221
Wilson, W. C., 492
Wing, C. W., 574
Wolf, D., 190
Wolfe, B. M., 413
Wolosin, R. J., 241, 265
Wong, D. W., 575
Wood, L., 442
Woodmansee, J. J., 101
Woodworth, R. S., 45
Worchel, S., 129, 141, 418
Word, L. E., 32, 375, 377
Wortman, C. B., 69
Wright, C. L., 342–343
Wright, F. E., 172–173
Wright, P. H., 210, 225
Wrightsman, L. S., Jr., 144, 245
Wyden, B., 172

Yakimovich, D., 377
Yarrow, M. R., 306
Yancey, W. L., 168
Young, R. F., 565
Yukl, G., 529, 534–535

Zajonc, R. B., 127, 220–221, 561–563, 565–566, 568
Zanna, M. P., 71, 86, 106, 133, 139
Zavalloni, M., 571
Zdep, S. M., 592
Zeisel, H., 573
Zeiss, A. R., 330
Zellner, M., 123
Zillmann, D., 320, 417–418, 424–426
Zimbardo, P. G., 32, 76, 581, 583–584, 586, 589–590
Zimmerman, B. J., 313
Zook, E. Z., 186
Zuckerman, M., 185, 391

SUBJECT INDEX

Acceptance, private, 258
Acid phosphatase, 479
Acquaintance process, 224–233
Active aggression, 406
Actor-observer difference in attribution, 63–68
Adding model of impression formation, 81–85
Aesthetics, and behavior, 645
Affect:
  and compliance, 277
  and interpersonal attraction, 221–224
  and personal space, 611
  and prosocial behavior, 381–384
  and temperature, 639–643
Affection, in erotic stories, 489
Affiliation, and attraction, 227
Age, and conformity, 273
Aggression, 404–449
  and catharsis, 440–443
  contagion of, 422–424
  and crowding, 431, 632, 634
  definition of, 405–408
  drive theories of, 410
  effects of drugs on, 430–431
  effects of sexual arousal on, 426–427
  and frustration, 415–419
  and heat, 431, 637–639
  and heightened arousal, 424–428
  instinct theory, 408–410
  measurement of, 412–413
  and noise, 637–639
  and obedience, 431
  prevention and control of, 436–448
  situational determinants of, 414–432
  social learning theory of, 410–414
  theoretical perspectives on, 408–414
  various forms of, 406
  working definition of, 405–408
Aggression machine, 412–413
Aggressive cues, 428–430

Aggressive drive, 410
Aggressive intent, 407, 419–420
Aggressive models, 422–424, 439
  effects of, 317–323
Air pollution, and behavior, 642–644
Alcohol, effects upon aggression, 430–431
Altruism, 350–401
  theories of, 353–365
Ambiguity:
  effect on altruism, 375–377, 380–381
  reduction of 398–399
Ambivalence, sexual, 467
Androgyny, 190–191
Anonymity, and deindividuation, 583–585
Aphrodisiac, 477
Approval, need for, and prosocial
  behavior, 388–389
Arousal:
  effects of on aggression, 424–428
  in response to invasion of personal
    space, 620–621
Asch conformity paradigm, 257–274
Attack, effects on aggression, 419–421
Attention, role of in observational
  learning, 314
Attentiveness, and noise, 637
Attitude change, 111–141
  and attitude-discrepant behavior,
    131–132, 136–141
  and boomerang effects, 129–130
  communication, characteristics of and,
    116–122
  communicator, characteristics of, and
    113–116
  distraction and, 124
  emotional appeals and, 117–122
  forced compliance, and, 136–141
  frequency of exposure and, 126–127
  inoculation and, 130–131
  mood, role of in, 123–124
  resistance to, 128–131

  self-esteem and, 122–123
Attitude, definition of, 95
Attitude-discrepant behavior, 131–132,
  136–141
  and attitude change, 131–132, 136–141
Attitude formation, 105–111
  role of classical conditioning in, 105–106
  role of instrumental conditioning in,
    106–109
  role of observational learning in,
    109–111
Attitude questionnaire, 96–101
Attitude similarity:
  and attraction, 206–212, 216–217
  and environmental perception, 627
Attitudes, 93–147
  behavioral measures of, 101
  formation of, 105–111
  and group polarization, 571–573
  measurement of, 96–101
  physiological measures of, 101, 104
  self-report measures of, 96–101
Attitudes and behavior, relationship
  between, 141–146
Attraction, 197–249
  and compliance, 276–277
  and conformity, 263–265
  consequents of, 233–242
  and crowding, 632
  definition of, 199
  development of, 224–233
  interpersonal determinants of, 206–218
  and interpersonal distance, 609–610
  and prosocial behavior, 395–397
  in real world, 209–212
  situational determinants of, 218–224
  and temperature, 639–640
  theoretical approaches to, 199–206
  ways to increase, 242–246
Attractiveness, physical:
  and evaluations, 218–219

Defiance of authority, 295–298
Deindividuation, 581–586
  role of anonymity in, 583–585
Delay of gratification, effects of social
  models on, 330–332
Demand characteristics, 33–35
Density of population, 630–634
  and helping behavior, 633–634
Dependent variable, 21
Depression, and learned helplessness,
  637
Derogating innocent victims, 547–549
  and tolerance of social injustice,
  547–548
Destructive obedience, 412–413, 431
Development
  cognitive, 356–358
  stages of moral, 356–358
Diffusion of responsibility, 366
  and deindividuation, 583
Direct aggression, 406
Disconfirmed expectancies, and
  cognitive dissonance, 135–136
Discrimination, 156, 170–176
  definition of, 156
  reduction of, 170–176
Discriminatory practices against women,
  180–181
Dissonance, 131–140
  and disconfirmed expectancies, 135–136
  effects of following decisions, 134–135
  role of in decisions, 134–135
  and interpersonal attraction, 200
Dissonance versus self-perception
  controversy, 143
Distance, interpersonal, 608–619
  determinants of, 609–610
  inappropriate, 613–619
  personality determinants, 612
  racial and cultural determinants,
  611–612
  similarity and, 610–611
  type of interaction and, 611
Distraction, effects of upon attitude
  change, 124–126
Distributive justice, 541
Dogmatism, and interpersonal
  attraction, 243
Dominance-submissiveness, in
  intercourse, 490
Door-in-the-face technique, 282–283
Drive theories of aggression, 409
Drugs, effects of on aggression, 430–431

Ecological model of crowding, 630–631
Education, and interpersonal attraction,
  241–242
Effects of being imitated, 309
Egocentrism, 356
Embarrassment, and compliance, 282–286
Emotion, and interpersonal attraction,
  221–224
Emotional appeals, and attitude change,
  117–122
Emotional expression, individual
  differences in, 48–50
Emotions, recognition of in others, 45–52

Emotions, social communication of,
  333, 336–337
Empathy, 445–446, 549
  and derogation of innocent victims, 549
  and interpersonal attraction, 245–246
  and reduction of aggression, 445–446
Environment, 604–656
  changing, 647–653
  effects on behavior, 624–647
  spatial behavior, 608–624
Environmental change, 647–653
Environmental perception, 625–629
Environmental psychology, defined, 607
Environmental quality, perception of, 627
Equality, in social exchange, 543–544
Equilibrium, and interpersonal space, 615
Equity, 541–549
  across relationships, 546
  in social exchange, 541–549
  tactics for restoring, 544–549
Equity theory:
  and compliance, 275–277
  and prosocial behavior, 395–397
  "Equity with the world," 546
Erection, 493–496
Erotic stimulation, effects of, 492–501
Erotic stimuli, 468–469, 472–477
  arousing aspects of, 469, 472–474
  explanation of arousal property, 474–475
  popularity, explanation of, 475–477
  scaling of, 473–474
Eroticaphile, 500–501
Eroticaphobe, 500–501
Ethics:
  of obedience research, 288
  of research on prosocial behavior,
  388–389
  of social research, 28–32
Evaluation:
  and interpersonal attraction, 216–218
  and physical attractiveness, 218–219
Evaluation apprehension, and social
  facilitation, 565–568
Experimental method of research, 21–24
Exploitation of cooperative others,
  reasons for, 517–518
Exploitation, sexual, 489–490
Exposure, repeated, and interpersonal
  attraction, 220–221
Externalizers, 50
Extramarital sex, 483
Eye-contact, 52
"Eye of the Storm," 172–173

"Face," 538–539
  loss of, 538–539
  in social exchange, 538–539
Face-to-face invasion of personal space,
  616–618
Face-to-face seating and attraction, 239,
  243
Facial deceit, 51–52
Facial expressions, 45–52
  recognition of, 45–52
  universal recognition of, 47–49
  universality of, 46–47
Fairness, 540–549

in social exchange, 540–549
tactics for restoring, 544–549
Falsifying emotional expression, 52
Familiarity, 220–221, 377–380, 478–479,
  493–494, 627
  and environmental perception, 627
  and interpersonal attraction, 220–221
  and prosocial behavior, 377–380
  and response to erotica, 478–479,
  493–494
Fantasy, and sexual arousal, 461–462,
  494–496
Fear:
  of success, 186–187
  vicarious extinction of, 341–344
Fear appeals, 117–122
  and attitude change, 117–122
  drive-reduction explanation for
  effectiveness of, 120–122
Fellatio, 472–474
Fetish, 461
Field research, 24–28
  advantages of, 25
  disadvantages of, 25
  in social psychology, 24–28
Fighting instinct, 409
Flight behavior, in response to invasion
  of personal space, 615
Followers, 586–600
Foot-in-the-door technique, 278–280
  self-perception and, 278–280
Forced compliance, 136–141
  factors mediating effects of, 139–141
Frequency of exposure, 126–127
Friendship, 228–233
Frigidity, 468
Frustration, 415–419
  arbitrariness of, 418
  effects of on aggression, 415–419
Frustration-aggression hypothesis,
  415–418
Furniture design and arrangement,
  behavioral effects of, 646–647

Gain-loss theory, 230
Gaze, and interpersonal attraction, 240
Geographic location:
  and helping behavior, 375, 393–394
  and reporting illegal acts, 374–375
Gestures, 54, 55
Graduated reciprocation in tension
  reduction, 536
"Great man/women" theory of
  leadership, 587, 590–592
Group, definition of, 558
Group polarization, 569–580
  and attitudes, 571–573
  and court decisions, 573
  explanations for, 574–580
  generality of, 571–573
  implications of, 580–581
  and persuasive arguments, 575, 578–580
Group pressure, 257–274
  and obedience, 294
Groups, 554–600
  decisions in, 569–580
  and patterns of influence within,
  586–600

as releasers of antisocial actions, 581–586
Guilt:
and compliance, 280–284
and conscience, 355–356

Hair length, and interpersonal attraction, 215–216
Harmony, ways to increase, 242–246
Heat:
behavioral effects of, 639–643
effects on aggression, 431, 637–639
Helping behavior, 350–401
effects of social models on, 323–327
and noise, 637
Helplessness, learned, 636–637
Heredity, and aggression, 438–439
High-LPC leaders, 597–600
High-rise buildings, and behavior, 644–645
Home, and territorial behavior, 623–624
Home-court advantage, 623–624
Homosexual fears, and personal space, 620–621
Hormones, sexual, 457
House plants, behavioral effects of, 645–646
Humor, and reduction of aggression, 446–447
Hypotheses, in social research, 16

Illegal acts, bystander response to, 373–375
Imagination, and sexual arousal, 461–462, 494–496
Imbalance, 201–202
Imitation, 306–308, 309
Impression formation, 80–87
Inappropriate personal space, 612–619
Incentive factors, role of in observational learning, 315
Incompatible responses, as technique for reducing aggression, 444–448
Independence, value of, 267–268
Independent variable, 21
Indirect aggression, 406
Individual differences:
effects of erotica, 500–501
and personal space, 609–610
in prosocial behavior, 388–394
in sexual behavior, 480–492
Individualists, 526
Industriousness, learned, 637
Inequity, in social exchange, 542–549
Information-processing, and air pollution, 644
Informational social influence, 258–259
Informed consent, in social research, 30–32
Ingratiation, and conformity, 261–263
Inhibitions, 432–434
and aggression, 432–434
excessive, and aggression, 432–434
Initial dispositions, role of in impression formation, 86–87
Initial offer, effects upon bargaining, 529, 532–534
Inoculation, 130–131

and attitude change, 130–131
and resistance to persuasion, 130–131
Inside density, 631
Instinct theory of aggression, 408–410
Instrumental conditioning, role of in attitude formation, 106–109
Integration theory, and interpersonal attraction, 200
Integrative solutions, and conflict resolution, 537–538
Intent, aggressive, 407, 419–420
Interaction theory, and interpersonal attraction, 224–233
Intergroup contact, and reduction of prejudice, 174–176
Intergroup dynamics as basis for prejudice, 164
Internal regulation of behavior, effects of social models on, 327–332
Internalizers, 50
Interpersonal behavior, and sex arousal, 499–500
Interpersonal Judgment Scale, 207–208
Intimate distance, 613–615
Intrinsic motivation, 77–80
competing response interpretation of, 78–80
overjustification interpretation of, 77–80
Invasions of personal space, 615–619
effects on invader, 618–619, 624–625
physiological effects, 620–621

Just world, belief in, and prosocial behavior, 391–392

Kelley's theory of causal attribution, 61–63

Labeling others, effects of, 72
Laboratory studies of hurting, 320–321
Laughter, and reduction of aggression, 446–447
Leader effectiveness, contingency model of, 596–600
Leaders, 586–600
high-LPC, 597–600
low-LPC, 597–600
recognition of, 594–596
Leadership, 586–600
"great man/woman" theory of, 587, 590–592
modern perspective on, 592–596
situations view of, 592
transactional view of, 596
Learned helplessness, 636–637
Learned industriousness, 637
Learning, and sexual behavior, 460–463
Likert scales, 98–99
Linear relationship, attitudes and attraction, 207–209
Littering, ways of preventing, 649–653
Locus of control:
and love, 231
and prosocial behavior, 391
Love, 228–233
controversy about research, 234–235
effects of, 231–232

in erotic stories, 489
passion versus mutual respect, 231–233
scale, 232
theory of, 231

Mach scale, 531
Machiavellianism, 530–531
Man-made environments, behavioral effects of, 644–647
Mapping environmental perceptions, 626–629
Marihuana, effects on aggression, 430–431
Marked item technique, 649
Marriage, 232–233
Mass media, 170–171, 188–189
and prejudice, 170–171
and sex-role stereotyping, 188–189
Masturbation, 466
response to depictions of, 490–492
Matching hypothesis, 214
Mate swapping, 478
Maturity, moral, 356–358
Mediators, 538
Menstrual cycle, 457
"Mere exposure" effect, 127–128
Minority group, definition of, 154–155
Model's verbal preaching, effects of, 325–327
Modeling, 303–349
theoretical framework for, 306–315
as treatment for behavior disorders, 341–347
Modulating, of emotional expression, 51–52
Mood:
and interpersonal attraction, 221–224
and prosocial behavior, 381–384
role of in attitude change, 123–124
Morale, and furniture arrangement, 646–647
Motivation, and learned helplessness, 636–637
Motoric reproduction, role of in observational learning, 315
Multiple orgasm, 484
Multiple requests, and compliance, 277–280, 282–283
Mutuality, 228–233

Nature, therapeutic effects, 646
Need for affiliation, 227
Negative correlation, 18
Negotiation, 528–540
Nervousness, and crowding, 632
Noise:
and aggression, 637–639
and auditory discrimination, 635
behavioral effects, 634–638
definition of, 634–635
and helping behavior, 637
pollution, 635
and reading ability, 635
steady versus unpredictable, 635–637
Nonbalance, 201–202
Nonverbal communication, 45–56
Nonverbal cues, 57
and regulation of conversation, 57
as regulators of social interaction, 57

Normative social influence, 258–259
Norms, social, 251–252, 255–257
  definition of, 252
  transmission of, 257
Novelty, 477–479, 493–494
  in erotica, 478–479, 493–494
  in sexual partners, 477–478

Obedience, 286–298
  definition of, 254
  resistance to, 295–298
Objective self-awareness, 82–83
  and conformity, 261
Observational learning, 313–317
  role of in attitude formation, 109–111
  role of in prejudice, 168
  role of in socialization, 315–317
Odor, behavioral effects, 644
One- versus two-sided arguments, 116
Open-mindedness, and interpersonal
  attraction, 243
Oral sex, 472–474
Orders, effects of on aggression, 431
Orgasm, 483–484
  experience of, 483–484
  multiple, 484
  types of, 483
Orgasm phase, 460, 463, 468
  emotional level, 468
  learning level, 463
  reproduction level, 460
Outside density, 631
Overcontrolled aggressors, 433–434
Overload, effects on prosocial behavior,
  380
Overpopulation, 652–653
Overstimulation, and noise, 637

Pain, effects of social models on, 334–335
Pain-tolerant model, 334–335
Parental sex, offspring's perceptions of,
  470–472
Passionate love, 231
Passive aggression, 406
Penile plethysmograph, 493–496
Performance:
  and air pollution, 642–644
  effect of interpersonal attraction,
    242
  and population density, 634
Person perception, 40–90
Personal distance, 613–615
Personal evaluation:
  and interpersonal attraction, 216–218
  and physical attractiveness, 218–219
Personal responsibility, role of in
  forced compliance, 139–141
Personal space, 609–619
  determinants of size of, 609–610
  inappropriate, 613–615
  invasions of, 615–619
  personality determinants of, 612
  racial and cultural determinants of,
    611–612
  similarity and, 610–611
  type of interaction and, 611
Personality, 432–436, 480–482, 524–528, 612
  and aggression, 432–436

and cooperation, 524–528
and personal space, 612
and sexual behavior, 480–482
Personality structure, role of in
  prejudice, 165–166
Person-Other-Object (P-O-X), 200–202
Persuasibility, 122
Persuasion, and behavioral change,
  651–652
Persuasive arguments, and group
  polarization, 575, 578–580
Persuasive communications, 112–131
  comprehension of, 122
  reception of, 122
  role of in attitude change, 112–131
Petition signing, and attraction, 236–237
Pheromones, 458
Physical aggression, measurement of,
  412–413
Physical attack, effects of on aggression,
  419–420
Physical attractiveness, 162, 212–219,
  236–237
  and dating choice, 162
  and evaluations, 218–219
  explanation of its effect, 214–215
  and interpersonal attraction, 212–216
  and political decisions, 236–237
Physical proximity, and attraction,
  238–243
Physical reality, 265
Physiological response, 620–621, 644
  to air pollution, 644
  to invasions of personal space, 620–621
Physiological response, to sexual arousal,
  485, 488, 493–496
  measurement of, males, 493–496
  measurement of, females, 496
Plants, behavioral effects of, 645–646
Playing hard-to-get, 230
Political choice, and attraction, 236–237
Pollution, and behavior, 642–644
Popularity, and birth order, 229
Population control, 652–653
Population density, 630–634
  animal studies, 630
  definition of, 630
Pornography, 467, 479, 492–501
  effects of, 479, 492–501
  labeling, 467
Positive correlation, 18
Postconventional level, 358
Postdecision dissonance, 134–135
Power, and spatial invasions, 619
Preconventional level, 357
Predictability of noise, effects of on
  behavior, 635–637
Prejudice, 155–186
  against women, 178–186
  attempts to eliminate, 170–176
  contrasting patterns of, 166–167
  definition of, 155–156
  measurement of, 159–161
  origins of, 163–170
  reduction of, 170–176
  theoretical approaches to, 163–170
Prejudice and discrimination, 151–194
  relationship between, 158–159

Prejudice and discrimination against
  women, means for counteracting,
  190–191
Premarital sex, 483
Presence of others, effects of, 560–569
Primacy effects, in impression
  formation, 86
Primary territory, 621–622
Prisoner's dilemma, 514–516
  validity of as measure of cooperation,
  516
Propinquity, 218–221
  explanation of effect, 220–221
  and interpersonal attraction, 218–221
Proportion of similar attitudes, and
  attraction, 208
Prosocial behavior, 350–401
  characteristics of helper and person
    helped, 387–397
  conditions affecting, 365–381
  definition of, 354
  guidance systems, 354–358
  increasing, 397–399
  internal factors, 381–387
  reward value, 360–362
  situational determinants, 359–365
  theories of, 353–365
Proxemics, 613
Proximity, and willingness to harm
  victim, 293–294
Psychological reactance, 128–130
Psychopathology, and personal space,
  612
Psychotherapy, and personal space,
  614–615
Public distance, 613–615
Public territory, 622
Punishment, as deterrent to aggression,
  436–440

Qualifying, of emotional expression, 51
Quality of life, 647–649

Race, 162, 611–612
  and personal space, 611–612
  role of in dating choice, 162
Race versus beliefs controversy, 161–163
  resolution of, 162–163
Rape, as erotic theme, 490
Rate of participation, and leadership,
  594–596
Reactance, 128–130
  and conformity, 264
  and love, 232
Reactions to cooperation from others, 513,
  516, 517–518
Reading ability, and noise, 635
Recipients, characteristics of and
  attitude change, 122–123
Reciprocity, role of:
  in compliance, 275–277
  in cooperation, 513
Reference group, 264
Refractory period, 477
Refutational defense, 130
Regulation of sexual behavior, 464–465
Reinforcement, 202–206, 214–215, 260–261,
  360–362, 649–650